A TALE OF MICHAEL COLLINS AND WINSTON CHURCHILL

Stepping Stone to a Free Ireland

Volume Two: Treaty

JOHN DEANE

For Jack and Peg

for their love and support

For Heidi Stoeckley and Rev. James Orthmann, OCSO

for their advice and enthusiasm

For Richard Salmon

for his mentoring

For Tim Pat Coogan

for his inspiration and encouragement

Contents

List of Illustrations

Front Cover:

Michael Collins and Arthur Griffith arriving at Longford Cathedral for the wedding of General Seán MacEoin and Alice Cooney, 22 June 1922. Image courtesy of the National Library of Ireland.

Irish Treaty Conference - Winston Churchill - Downing Street, London. PA Images / Alamy Stock Photo

Back Cover:

The last page of the Anglo-Irish Treaty, signed 6 December 1921. Signatories David Lloyd George, Austen Chamberlain, Birkenhead, Winston S. Churchill, L. Worthington-Evans, Hammar Greenwood, Gordon Hewart, Arthur Griffith, Michael Collins, Robert Barton, Eamonn Duggan, George Gavan Duffy. Smith Archive / Alamy Stock Photo.

Map:

Ireland in June 1922. Courtesy Axiom Maps Limited, The Map Archive

Ireland in June 1922

- Anti-Treaty (Republican)
- Pro-Treaty (Free State)
- Disputed territory
- Towns including both Free State and republican troops

Northern Ireland

Coleraine
Derry
ANTRIM
DERRY
Larne
DONEGAL
Donegal
Pettigo
TYRONE
Belfast
FERMANAGH
Armagh
DOWN
Downpatrick
Sligo
Enniskillen
ARMAGH
Clones
Newry
Collooney
SLIGO
MONAGHAN
Carrickmacross
Dundalk
MAYO
LEITRIM
CAVAN
LOUTH
Boyle
Castlebar
ROSCOMMON
LONGFORD
Drogheda
Connacht
Ballinalee
Granard
MEATH
Roscommon
WESTMEATH
GALWAY
Athlone
DUBLIN
Galway
Leinster
Dublin
OFFALY
KILDARE
LAOIS
WICKLOW
CLARE
Nenagh
Kilkenny
CARLOW
Limerick
Thurles
KILKENNY
WEXFORD
TIPPERARY
Listowel
LIMERICK
Tipperary
Enniscorthy
Tralee
Waterford
Wexford
Munster
WATERFORD
KERRY
CORK
Béal na mBláth
Cork
Bandon
Bantry
Clonakilty
Woodfield

0   20 km
0   20 miles

SEVENTY-THREE

Welcome, Mr. Collins

LLOYD GEORGE EXTENDED HIS HAND, "WELCOME, MR. COLLINS. So, we meet at last, welcome. And Mr. Griffith, welcome back. It's a pleasure to see you once again." Then he added, politely but with considerably less warmth, "Mr. O'Brien, always a pleasure."

"Mr. Prime Minister."

Michael introduced two colleagues who were visiting Downing Street for the first time, Eamonn Duggan and Gavan Duffy.

Continuing to welcome each arrival by shaking hands, Lloyd George assured them, "The pleasure is all mine. Excellent! Now, gentlemen, please join my associates at the table."

Art O'Brien whispered something to Thomas Jones, excused himself, and went to wait in the entrance hall.

Lloyd George proceeded to escort the Irish delegates to their places at the table and introduced them to their British counterparts as he stood beneath the portrait of Sir Robert Walpole, England's first Prime Minister. "Now, Mr. Duffy," he began, "we have set aside a place for you opposite Mr. Gordon Hewart, our Attorney General. Mr. Barton, who accompanied Mr. de Valera here earlier this year, and with whom I had a nice visit recently up in Gairloch, welcome back. Your seat will be across from the Secretary of State for the Colonies, Mr. Winston Churchill."

Barton looked blankly at Churchill, then past him and up at the portrait of Walpole, and then back at Churchill, who just smiled back, apparently slightly amused.

Lloyd George, meanwhile, continued with the introductions, "Mr. Collins, if you would be so kind as to take this seat facing Lord Birkenhead, the Lord Chancellor. Unfortunately, Austen Chamberlain, the Lord Privy Seal and Leader of the House of Commons, is not well today but should recover in time for our next session, when he will be seated next to Lord Birkenhead. Mr. Griffith, you and I will take our places at the centre of the table, so this chair is reserved for you." He smiled pleasantly as Griffith took his place opposite him at the table. "Now, Mr. Duggan, oh, excellent, you've found your place opposite the Secretary of State for War, Sir Laming Worthington-Evans, and seated next to him is the Chief Secretary for Ireland, with whom I am sure you are all acquainted, Sir Hamar Greenwood. Finally, the delegation secretaries will join us in the chairs directly behind. Assisting us will be Mr. Lionel Curtis, and I believe you all now know Mr. Thomas Jones." He looked over to the Irish secretaries and smiled expectantly.

Griffith seized the opportunity, "Thank you, Prime Minister. I think you'll remember Mr. Erskine Childers from our last visit."

"Yes, quite," Lloyd George replied somewhat tersely.

"And also assisting us will be Mr. John Chartres."[1]

"Mr. Chartres," Lloyd George replied with a slight nod and then said with great enthusiasm, "So, gentlemen, a hearty welcome to you all."

With this affable display of politesse, Lloyd George deftly avoided the two awkward aspects of protocol that had worried both sides. While everyone took their places across the wide table, the need to shake hands was obviated, as was the presentation of credentials. Whether Lloyd George had suspected something untoward might be lurking in those letters of introduction is a moot point, but de Valera's backhanded attempt at forcing an early recognition of the Republic was neatly and silently circumvented. Fortunately, in the debates that followed later in Parliament, no one thought to mention the issue of whether the Irish credentials had been presented or accepted. The Dáil would be another story. Affable though the Prime Minister might have been, the atmosphere in the room was merely civil and even somewhat stiff as these sworn enemies faced each other across the table for the first time. The Irish delegates felt awkward and looked a bit ill at ease standing in that famous history-laden room where the destiny of many nations around the globe had been decided, but, with the exception of Lloyd George, no one from either delegation displayed any emotion, neither antagonism nor amiability, not wishing to show their hands, literally or figuratively.

"Now, gentlemen, if you will all be seated," Lloyd George said, remaining standing. When everyone had taken their seats, he began in a friendly yet grave tone, "As I am sure we all realise, we all bear a tremendous responsibility as members of this conference. People on both sides of the Irish Sea have entrusted us with their hopes for peace. Yet within this awesome responsibility lies a golden opportunity to put an end to the tragic story of misunderstanding and war between our two countries. In the past when England was in the mood for peace, Ireland was not, and when Ireland had been in the mood for peace, England was not. I believe that today, at long last, both our countries are eager for peace, and if peace were made now, it would be a peace between the two peoples and not between oligarchies as in the past. However, my colleagues and I are bound by certain limitations, as no doubt, Mr. Griffith, you and your colleagues are as well. These limitations have been imposed upon us by public opinion, but within these limitations it is our duty to seek every possible path to peace. The Government has gone too far already, and certain details are being fastened upon which, if pressed, would make peace increasingly difficult. As to the precise procedure to be followed to achieve our mutual goals, I am entirely in the hands of Mr. Griffith."

With that, Lloyd George sat down with another slight bow of his head to Griffith while inviting him to speak, "Perhaps you would like to address the conference, Mr. Griffith?"

Griffith nodded in appreciation and said, "Thank you, Prime Minister. We, too, see the golden opportunity inherent in the tremendous responsibility with which we have been entrusted, yet, as you rightly surmise, we have our limitations as well." He spoke in such a soft voice that he was barely audible to some delegates, who had to lean forward to make out what he was saying. However, having just graciously agreed with the Prime Minister, and his mild tone notwithstanding, he delivered a stinging, though politely worded barb, "We feel that from the days of Pitt onwards, it has been the policy of this country to keep Ireland in a subordinate position. It is possible that there is a new England and a new attitude in the people over here towards Ireland. As to procedure, we are in your house and will follow your suggestions."[2]

Lloyd George shot a glance at Churchill, who smiled briefly with a nod as if to express a benign forbearance if not surprise at not only the brevity of Griffith's response, but its mild belligerence as well.

"Then, Mr. Griffith," Lloyd George suggested, "may we have your comments on the proposals already offered, as outlined in our letter of invitation to these talks?"

Rather than opening the conference with a debate on the more contentious issues of allegiance to the Crown and the position of Ulster, Griffith chose to confront a still volatile, though potentially less fractious subject. "Though the nature of your letter inviting us here was taken in Dublin as a promising overture to fruitful discussions for peace, it nevertheless contained several conditions on defence that could be construed as qualifying all the powers reserved to Ireland in the rest of the letter. England would attain political dominance of Ireland plus military powers."[3]

Exhibiting an early display of his showmanship, Lloyd George expressed horror at this, and he said in a tone of shock, "This is a most amazing statement. What do we take away? We wish no military domination over Ireland any more than we wish it over Canada. If you refer to our needs for a guarantee to the use of Irish ports, you surely must realise that the coast of Ireland is essential to us, largely for the defence against submarines. Without the use of these facilities being guaranteed in times of war, our people might starve.[4] You ought not to put us in the position of having to break a treaty with you in order to defend ourselves."[5]

Childers brought up an unfortunate precedent. "England already has a long history of breaking treaties with Ireland, such as the Treaty of Limerick, to name one. When the Irish Catholics were defeated at the Battle of the Boyne, they were guaranteed religious tolerance and property rights if they swore an oath of allegiance to the English King and Queen, William and Mary, only to see these protections abrogated in less than two years."[6]

Some seated at the English side of the table blanched at this remark but, true to form, concealed any discomfort, though the Prime Minister had an intriguing answer for this complaint. "You have never made a treaty with the *people* of this country before. As I mentioned earlier, treaties in the past have been with oligarchies ruling this country."[7]

Wishing to head off a disagreeable turn, Griffith here intervened. "We are all of one mind that if we can agree on the general issues, we can certainly reach consensus on these matters of defence."

Churchill then spoke for the first time. "That would be splendid. If I may, on the matter of defence, I would like to draw your attention to an analogous arrangement Britain enjoys with the dominion of South Africa regarding the use of the naval base at Simonstown, not far from Cape Town. I have recently been in touch with our good friend, General Smuts, to update this agreement to the mutual satisfaction of both countries."

This time Barton had a contrary view to offer. "That may be so, but as a dominion, South Africa need not join in a British war."

Lord Birkenhead's opening sally was made in support of his friend, Winston. In a withering, condescending tone, he checked Barton by answering, "*That* is not conceded."[8]

After this terse riposte, there wasn't much to add to the subject, so Lloyd George moved the topic to trade, more specifically, free trade, of which he was a staunch defender. As was Churchill, whose principal reason for "crossing the aisle" years earlier to join Lloyd George and the Liberals was the Conservative Party's abandonment of its free-trade principles.

"There have been some previous discussions regarding tariffs, which can only harm relations between our two countries. A tariff war would only serve to destroy the peace we are here to achieve."

Griffith interrupted, "A tariff war never entered our heads."

"No? Ireland would suffer the most if it came to one," Lloyd George responded. "After all, England is Ireland's only market for food-stuffs, for example, whereas England could obtain them from other countries. So why not forgo tariffs altogether?"

Birkenhead tried to reassure the Irish, "Nothing is intended to prevent the economic development of Ireland."

Barton countered once again, saying, "If we are dependent on you, as you say, then why do you fear a tariff war with us?"

Lloyd George responded coolly, "There is a temptation on both sides. I want peace."

Barton was unrelenting, "We want to be self-sufficient. Our independence in the past was always restricted by you."

Churchill interjected, "We are offering you the most terrific guarantee that Ireland can have. The market secure to you quite independently of all the fluctuations of our political parties."

Collins tried to calm things down, "We have already given you assurances of free trade in de Valera's letter of August tenth."

The Prime Minister answered forcefully, "I don't want general assurances. I want it in the Treaty."[9] He then backed off a little, smiled, and said, "However, it seems we agree in general, and it's just the details that will need to be worked out." There seemed to be no objections to this assessment as gentlemen on either side of the table nodded in agreement. He had surmised that the initial atmosphere of tension in the room had dissipated somewhat and decided to pause the proceedings on this positive note.

Lloyd George glanced at the window and noted, "Well, gentlemen, it's turned into a lovely day outside. Shall we adjourn for lunch and meet again at, say, four o'clock?" More nods of agreement. "Very well, then. Thank you, everyone."

BARTON SAT BETWEEN COLLINS AND GRIFFITH IN THE CAR RETURNING to Hans Place for lunch. He and Childers seemed inclined to continue the morning debates on the ride back.

From the front seat, Childers complained, "Lloyd George can talk all he wants about oligarchies of the past, but the fact remains that he can't be trusted. None of the British can."

Collins was annoyed at this early condemnation of the proceedings. "Well, if that's the case, Erskine, maybe we should just pack up and go home now."

"No need to get in a snit, Michael."

Griffith looked across the seat to Michael, sighed, and turned to look out the window.

Barton, too, seemed unwilling to concede a point as well. "I can't see South Africa following England into any and every entanglement she finds herself in."

Michael was about to answer but decided against it.

After pausing a moment, Barton said quietly, "I don't mind admitting it, but I was rather nervous standing there at that table, looking at Churchill and Lloyd George beneath Robert Walpole's portrait. I imagined it was right there that the English had met and outmanoeuvred or intimidated their opponents in countless struggles similar to ours.[10] It was fairly daunting."

This honest admission softened Michael's feelings for the moment, and he attempted to encourage him by saying, "It's a new experience for us all. Not long ago we were soldiers; now we're diplomats. We all have to adapt."

They soon pulled up in front of the house in Hans Place and, huddled together, barged through the throng of press. After everyone made it inside, Michael tugged slightly at Griffith's sleeve. "Well, Arthur, what do you think?"

Griffith looked him in the eye and said softly, "Frankly, I think it went well, but, Barton's frank admission aside, we might have made a better impression without the impolitic remarks from him and some of our other members."

"My thoughts, exactly. Lloyd George seems to have developed an instant dislike for Erskine, and Barton rubbed everyone else wrong. There's no controlling them, though."

"Let's see. We may not have to." He smiled and said, "Things might just work themselves out on their own. Let's have a good meal before we return."

Tuesday, 11 October 1921, London, Second Session

When everyone had returned to their seats at the conference table, Lloyd George looked at the clock on the mantelpiece and noted in a pleasant manner, "Four o'clock it is. Let's begin." He looked around the table amiably and then addressed Griffith. "There are understandably some differences in opinion as to the interpretation of the conditions for these talks. Before we go too far afield, perhaps, Mr. Griffith, the Irish delegation would like to propose amendments to our original letter?"

Griffith agreed, "Excellent idea, Prime Minister. We would like to submit a re-drafting of the issues."[11]

"Fine. Might we have these after the weekend?"

"Yes, I think we can manage that. Thank you." Still hoping to keep the discussions on the less controversial issues, Griffith kept in a similar vein. "The clause regarding Irish debt is a bit vague."

Lloyd George responded, "Ah, yes. The Irish war debt."

Collins spoke up, "The way we see it, it's not so much of what Ireland owes England, but rather, what England owes Ireland after centuries of unjust taxation."

Greenwood began rapping the table with his knuckles in protest. However, Birkenhead just smiled, amused at the temerity of Michael's postulation, which did indeed shock others on the entire British team. Someone gasped, "I say," but Lloyd George intervened calmly, "Yet, Mr. Collins, the Irish representatives to Parliament voted in favour of the war at the outset."

Griffith defended Michael's remark by adding, "Those representatives may have voted for the war, but they were not truly representative of the Irish people."

Not wanting to argue the finer points of Irish representation in Parliament before the Great War, Lloyd George instead said, "I propose we form a joint sub-committee to discuss finances between the two countries. What we want to get is something fair between the two countries, not a Jew bargain."

This time it was Arthur who blanched at this uncivil remark, but as the English had done during the morning session, he masked any disquiet. If Michael was shocked at this slur, he also realised that Lloyd George's proposal recognised the possibility that the Irish claim for relief from war debt might bear some merit. He pressed the point further, "As long as this committee can conduct any investigations without prejudice."

Ignoring any reproachful implications of the word *prejudice*, the Prime Minister agreed. "Yes, of course. It will examine financial relations in general. Ireland will be like a partner pulling out of a business firm, so an equitable accounting of mutual assets and liabilities would be appropriate."[12]

Here at least was an analogy that appealed to Michael's book-keeping background. "Then we accept your proposal. Thank you."

Griffith then brought up another issue. "Prime Minister, this morning's discussion touched on our concerns regarding Ireland's foreign relations and ability to remain neutral in the event of a war England might find herself in again."

Lloyd George answered, "In the recent war with Germany, South

Africa offered troops to the effort on a purely voluntary basis, though neutrality was not allowed. So it would be with Ireland. We would not be in a position to compel you to put in all your resources and send in your manhood."

"But what of a guarantee to that effect?"

"Your rights would be written into the Treaty. You would join us with absolute guarantees of freedom, with full recognition of nationhood, and as a member of our fraternity of free nations. At the Imperial Conference we just held with our Dominion partners, Canada, for example, sat at this table and discussed on equal terms our policy with the United States, Japan, and Egypt, and this is what we now offer you. But to allow Ireland to remain neutral would be to repudiate the King's sovereignty."

"We cannot enter freely if it is not a free choice," Griffith answered. "Personally, I think your position would be much stronger in time of war if Ireland were neutral."

Michael added, "The previous Conservative leader, Bonar Law, said that the Dominions could vote themselves out of the British Empire."

Lloyd George replied, "Yes, but all that means is we might not undertake military operations against the Dominions which did so."

Churchill pointed out, "What would probably happen in such a case is civil war in the Dominion, as was the case in South Africa."

Michael was unconvinced. "Still, you are asking more from us than from them in this naval business."

Lloyd George was politely dismissive of this notion. "No, I think not."[13] He noticed the deflating effect this had on Michael, so he added cheerfully, "But I think it would be useful if we also had a subcommittee to go into naval and air defence."

This satisfied Michael, as had the proposal for a Finance subcommittee, though he imagined he would have a growing workload. "We would like that very much."

Turning to Churchill, Lloyd George asked him, "Winston, perhaps with your experience at the Admiralty, you would like to chair this committee?"

Smiling at Lloyd George and then Michael, Churchill replied happily, "I'd be delighted. I would probably like to have Admiral Beatty sit in to advise us on submarine warfare."

Lloyd George was equally pleased. "Well, then that's decided. You could convene next week, I should think."

Churchill asked Michael, "Mr. Collins?"

"Delighted," was his simple response, though he was anything but, imagining what it would be like having to deal directly with Churchill. He nodded to Churchill and then asked Lloyd George, "If I may, there is another matter I would like to raise today."

"Yes, Mr. Collins, please go ahead," the Prime Minister answered.

"It regards the status and treatment of prisoners. We would have thought that conditions might improve since the Truce, but there have been several serious reports of abuse. May I suggest the formation of a joint visiting committee?"

Lloyd George seemed concerned. "This Truce is not a treaty, so the handling of prisoners has not been addressed as, say, for example, it was with the Germans at the end of the war. However, this is beside the point if there have been, as you may have been informed, any instances of abuse. We are most anxious to do our best in the matter of treatment.[14] To that end, I suggest we refer the matter to a Committee on the Observance of the Truce and do so without delay. General Macready is in London. Would you be available to meet with him and the appropriate members of this conference tomorrow?"

"Yes, thank you, Prime Minister." Michael turned to Eamonn Duggan. "Mr. Duggan, as you and Mr. Barton negotiated the terms of the Truce with General Macready in the first place,[15] I think it only fitting you both should also serve on this proposed committee."

Duggan nodded, saying, "Yes, it would be a pleasure, and I'm sure Mr. Barton would concur."

"Yes, of course," Barton replied.

Lloyd George smiled approvingly and proposed members for the British. "Besides General Macready, I would suggest the Secretary of State for War and the Chief Secretary for Ireland join this committee, if they are so inclined."

Sir Laming Worthington-Evans and Sir Hamar Greenwood both assented.[16]

"Well, that's settled for time being. We have covered a lot of ground this first day. I commend you all, gentlemen. Shall we meet the day after tomorrow? Noon, say? Fine. Until then."

"LUCKY YOU, MICHAEL. YOU GET TO LOCK HORNS OVER SUBMARINES and naval facilities with the former Lord of the Admiralty." Griffith smiled at Michael as they left the conference and walked briskly along Downing Street. Liam and Ned, ever vigilant, studied the crowd as they approached their waiting cars.

Michael sighed, "That could be a slow death by discourse, from all that's said of him."

Arthur advised him, "Churchill may be a lot of bully and bluster, but you may find that you actually get along with him. Sometimes your worst enemies can be your best friends."

"Really? I don't know quite whether he would be a crafty enemy in friendship. Just ask the Conservatives. They don't trust him, and neither do I." Michael laughed a little, "Having said that, we might get some real work done in these sub-committees, even with Winston."[17]

"As I said earlier, things might work themselves out. I appreciate your willingness to take on so much work right from the outset. You get to make a case for reparations on the Finance committee, and then tomorrow…" Arthur tilted his head with a smile.

Michael chuckled as he said, "I have a face-to-face with Greenwood! He must be seething! And Macready, too! After years of gummin' to see me shot, the P.M. has him sit down and discuss Home Rule with me."

"Ironic, isn't it? As for Lloyd George, he is certainly a suave and astute man, and though we have the more difficult issues to face, I think, on the whole, we scored today. I get the impression that the English are anxious for peace.[18] I'll write to de Valera this evening and inform him."

As they approached the cars and the surrounding crowd, Michael lowered the brim of his hat, still wishing to shield his face from any camera lens. They got in the car and drove back to Hans Place.

"Arthur, I'll drop you off and continue on. I think I need an early night."

"Certainly, Mick. So do I. Good night."

After Arthur exited the car, Ned leaned over with an arm straddling the front seat and asked, "So, straight to Cadogan?"

"Straight to Cadogan."

Liam put the car into gear and drove off.

When they arrived, the three of them went into the kitchen, and Michael plopped down in a chair.

"Oh, Mr. Collins," Peggy asked, "can I get you something?"

"That would be grand, Peggy. Just something light, maybe just a couple of *oiges*."

"How's that?" Peggy asked, perplexed.

"What?" Michael replied with a yawn. "Oh, excuse me, scrambled, please."

Peggy stood motionless, thinking. "So… you'd like some scrambled eggs?"

Now Michael looked perplexed. "Yes, scrambled oiges, please."

Pleased that she had deciphered Michael's personal variant of a Cork accent without embarrassment, she smiled and asked Liam and Ned, "You lads?"

"Yes, Peggy. Same for me," Ned replied.

"Yes, ma'am, scrambled oiges will do nicely," Liam said with a smirk. "Thank you."[19]

"Won't take a minute," Peggy said cheerfully as she walked by Liam and bopped him on his head with her spatula.

Michael narrowed his eyes at Liam, who just looked back and shrugged his shoulders.

A short while later Michael finished his supper and bid Ned and Liam a good night. "I was thinking I'd turn in early."

Ned checked the kitchen clock and remarked, "Yes, it *is* an early night for you, Mick. You're usually up till one in the morning."

"Yes, well," and he walked upstairs but paused at Emmet Dalton's room and knocked softly. Getting no answer, he walked in and looked around for a moment until he spied something that brought a smile to his face.

"Ah! Just the thing."

The frame of the bed rested on hinged legs, and he knelt and bent back both legs at the foot of the bed so that it sloped down at what surely promised to be an extremely uncomfortable angle.

"Is my work never done? Tsk! Tsk!" He rubbed his hands and went upstairs to his own bedroom on the top floor. First, he checked Ned's bedroom, which was next to his, but the door was locked. "Ah, well. Another night," he thought to himself, went into his room, and sat down at a small desk to write a letter to Kitty.

SEVENTY-FOUR

Inventions o' the Divil

THURSDAY, 13 OCTOBER 1921, LONDON, THIRD SESSION

"MICHAEL, HAVE YOU SEEN YESTERDAY'S PAPERS? THERE'S A LOVELY photograph of you," Alice Lyons said coyly.

"What? Let me see that damn thing," Michael demanded. He and Alice were having coffee in the Hans Place dining room before he and the rest of the delegation left for Downing Street.

Alice pushed the paper across the table and then walked around to read it over his shoulder. "Still camera shy, aren't we? With your hat over your face, you can hardly make out it's you."

Michael grinned, "At least you can make out the tie Kitty gave me."[1]

"So, that's what all the fussing over that tie was about. All you have to do now is convince her that's you in the picture."

"Hold on," Michael said, reading further, "*The Irish team was accompanied by four young typists as good-looking as most Dublin girls.*"[2] He looked at Alice with a scowl, "You girls been flirting with these reporters?"

"They had better not!" May Duggan exclaimed. "I won't hear of it!"

Alice defended herself and the other young women, "We did nothing of the kind, I can assure you."

Liam Tobin looked over Michael's shoulder, too, and then read a little from the story, "*Upon emerging from the house in Hans Place, Collins boasted of having sneaked into London undetected.*"

Michael protested, "Damn that eejit! I never said any such thing. Newspapermen are the inventions o'the divil."[3]

Arthur Griffith emerged from the kitchen and joined the rest of the team having a laugh at Michael's expense. "Yet, you're usually pretty good at getting them to help when it suits your needs." Arthur then turned to a more serious matter. "I'm more concerned about this article about a Republican court being convened in Dublin. Not that the British aren't guilty of similar breaches. We have some ammunition for argument but don't need to be giving them any."

Michael scanned through the newspaper article. "Reports like this can leave us out on a limb."

Griffith sighed, "Yes, and before we go over to Downing Street, gentlemen, I suggest we keep the day's talks again on trade and defence. Let's not get bogged down over Ulster just yet."

The sound of the front door opening and closing was heard, and Tom Cullen joined the breakfast gathering, still wearing his coat and a smile from ear to ear.

Michael taunted him, "Tom, you've got a grin on your puss like the Cheshire Cat. What's the story?"

Tom explained, "You'll love this! I went out to a local newsstand for the morning papers, and there was a poster in nine-inch letters screaming, *Mick and Mac*." He tossed a paper on the table and said, "Look at the *Freeman's* headline."

Michael turned the paper around and read it, "*Michael Collins and General Macready Face to Face*." He chuckled and said, "I'll bet his mates are giving him a good ribbing over that."

Arthur put his coffee down and exclaimed, "There's so much going on, Mick, that I almost forgot to ask. How did your meeting with Macready and the Committee on the Observance of the Truce go?"

"Fairly business-like, I should say. Eamonn and Bob were in top form, as was General Macready."

"How did you find him?" Arthur asked.

"Surprisingly straightforward. Barton had a list of complaints, and he said he'd address each one of them and get back to us quickly. Macready seems to be a man of his word, a man we can do business with."

"That's good. I'm sure he felt the same about you."[4]

"Mick and Mac. You were right, Tom. I love it!"

A WHILE LATER THEY WERE USHERED INTO THE CONFERENCE ROOM AT Downing Street. Once everyone had taken their places, the previously absent member of the British team was introduced. Lloyd George, as usual, began in his affable manner, "Welcome back, everyone. I am pleased the House Leader, Mr. Austen Chamberlain, is with us at last, and we look forward to his contributions. Now then, my colleagues and I were just going over a report from yesterday's meeting of the Observance of the Truce Committee, and I am heartened at the progress made in so many areas of common agreement. However..." He opened a large leather-bound folder on the table before him and produced a newspaper. "There is this item in last evening's *Star*, and I am afraid it gives one pause." Griffith and Collins would have liked to have said to each other, "I knew it!" but remained stoically silent.

Lloyd George continued, "Let's see, yes, apparently, a gentleman claiming to be a judge at a Republican court stated, 'I now declare this Court open in the name of the Irish Republic.' My, my, a declared Republic once again. Now, I hope my Irish friends at this table realise that this simply will not do."

Chamberlain spoke for the first time, "And there is another matter. Given the high level of Parliamentary criticism which this conference has been enduring, it is quite impossible to allow the Irish Republican Army to drill in open defiance of the Truce, and especially with photographers and motion picture cameramen in attendance."[5]

This could have proved embarrassing to the Irish team, but Griffith drew from the "ammunition" he mentioned to Michael over breakfast. "On the other hand, English forces have commandeered the Victoria Hotel in Sligo and the Courthouse where the city's municipal offices were situated, all this without notice to the Liaison Officer."

The Prime Minister turned to Worthington-Evans, "Is this true?"

Put on the spot, all he could say was, "I suppose the troops were probably going into billets for the winter."

Collins laughed at this, "Winter billets already? With this lovely autumn weather we've been enjoying? I think not. This is an obvious case of manoeuvring for strategic advantage."

Duggan added, "Throwing elected representatives out on the street is the worst way of procuring accommodations."

Lloyd George decided to tone down the rhetoric by simply saying,

"I think we should defer to General Macready on these matters and then take them up again in the Truce Committee."[6]

Having neatly dodged a bullet, Griffith was relieved when the discussion turned to a productive debate on trade, as he had hoped it would. After the meeting came to a close, Lloyd George walked Griffith to the door, saying as they walked along, "As I said earlier, I am encouraged at the considerable progress we are making on the issues. I look forward to your ideas on the question of Ulster, and then, of course, there's the matter of the Crown."

Griffith smiled back but avoided the substance of the Prime Minister's suggestion, "Yes, well, we do seem to be taking strides in the right direction. Until tomorrow then?"

Griffith nodded to Collins and Barton to hurry them along. When they got outside and headed for their cars, he told them, "We squeaked out of a bind over that damn fool Republican Court, and Mick and Bob, you both made some fine points on trade."

"We had to," Michael answered. "Without freedom of trade, we don't have fiscal autonomy. I sent one of the lads to New York to discuss finance, and he says without fiscal autonomy, the new state would be unable to borrow from American banks. By the way, he met up with Harry Boland, who apparently is preparing people there for the resumption of hostilities in Ireland."[7]

Arthur looked worried at that prospect, saying, "It hasn't come to that yet. However, the P.M. just now prodded me a bit about Ulster. We may be able to stall them again at tomorrow's meeting, but if we don't have clear instructions on Ulster by Monday morning, the initiative will pass to the British, and we'll have to fight them on ground of their own choosing."[8]

They paused before they got in their car, and Michael answered cryptically, "There'll be no fighting on the ground here. Nor in the air."

Perplexed, Arthur asked, "Come again?"

"Why don't I let Emmet Dalton explain over a cuppa at Cadogan Gardens? The clever bugger has quite a plan."

"Whatever you say. I'm intrigued."

As HE AND ARTHUR SETTLED INTO CHAIRS AT THE CADOGAN KITCHEN table next to Emmet, Michael said, "Thanks for the tea, Eddie. Now, be off with yourself."

"Righto, Mick. I'll just be in the…"

"Thank you, Eddie."

Ned Broy followed Eddie out of the kitchen, walked through the adjoining rooms, came back, and nodded.

Michael took a sip of tea and said, "Go ahead, Emmet. Tell Arthur about your travel plans."

"Ah, yes," Emmet replied, realising the reason for this little get-together. "Arthur, General Headquarters have been gravely concerned about Mick's safety here in London. If the negotiations were to break down and anything happened to him, the entire Army position would be jeopardised. I suggested to Mick that we purchase an aeroplane here in London and have it standing in readiness to fly him out of here if there is a break. It would have to be a small one, with perhaps seating for only one other passenger, and that would be you."

"Good Lord!" Arthur exclaimed. "Is that really necessary?"

"G.H.Q. think so. They've authorised the purchase."

"Do we even have anyone capable of flying an aeroplane?"

"Oh, yes. We have a couple of Volunteers who served in the Royal Air Force during the Great War. Jack McSweeney collaborated with me on the attempt to free Seán MacEoin, and Charlie Russell has extensive experiencing flying in France, the United States, and Canada. Our cover story will be that Charlie is buying the aircraft for the Canadian forestry department."

Michael added, "Emmet will have them keep the aircraft ready at Croydon airfield. We could leave here and be in the air in less than an hour."[9]

"Well, I'll be damned," Arthur exclaimed. "Now I understand all the secrecy. Of course, I've never been in an aeroplane, but if I ever do have the opportunity, I hope it won't be under such dire circumstances." His hand trembled slightly as he sipped his tea. "Good Lord!"

SEVENTY-FIVE

A Show of Force

FRIDAY, 14 OCTOBER 1921, LONDON, FOURTH SESSION

"GOOD MORNING, THOMPSON. GOT YOUR GUN?"

Detective Sergeant Thompson grinned, patted his jacket and answered cheerfully, "Right here, sir, at the ready."

"Good, good, let's be off, then."

They got in the car, drove from Sussex Square, and headed to Whitehall for that morning's meeting of the conference on Ireland. Even with Treaty talks on in London, Thompson's duties for protecting Winston were not in the least diminished, and for safety's sake, he still accompanied him in the back seat of the car. That morning Winston busied himself with some notes on naval defence that he wanted to discuss with the Prime Minister, so Thompson remained respectfully quiet. After a while, Winston patted his notes together and put them away in his valise.

"There, that does it. It'll be a good day," Winston said cheerily.

"I take it things are going well," Thompson commented.

"It would appear so, though the real brass knuckle discussions lay ahead of us."

"Hmm," Thompson mused, "I'd like to use a set of brass knuckles on this fellow Collins."

Winston laughed, "With or without the knuckledusters, you might be in for a tough match. He looks to be a pretty rough character."

"It's passing strange. The most wanted man in Europe, sitting down to talk peace with you and the Prime Minister, after evading the police all these years."

"That's the pride of Scotland Yard in you, Thompson, and I don't begrudge you it one bit. Point of fact, many members in Parliament have voiced the same concerns."

"Well, we all have our jobs to do, I suppose. From the P.M. down to Number 10's kindly maid, Betty."

Winston looked over at his bodyguard and said, "That we do," admiring this simple bit of philosophy. "And here we are."

They had reached Downing Street and walked together over to Number 10. "I'll just wait outside, sir," Thompson said as Winston went inside.

Winston tipped his hat to two men standing by the door as he and Thompson approached. After Churchill went in, one of them asked Thompson in an obvious Irish brogue, "Ye couldn't spare us a light, could ye?"

Thompson checked his pockets, pulled out a box of matches, and struck one for the man, who cupped his hands over his cigarette and looked up to Thompson as he held the lit match.

"Cheers, mate. Liam's the name."

"Cheers. Walter."

"Say hello to my mate, Tom."

"Hello, Tom."

"G' morning."

As Churchill walked along the hall to the conference room, he encountered the maid, Betty. "Good morning, Betty, and greetings from a friend of yours, Detective Sergeant Thompson, who sends his regards."

"Oh, how kind. Thank you, Mr. Churchill. Another big day today?"

"Yes, and I think they'll all be big days for some time." He then joined the rest of the delegates at the conference table, and at eleven o'clock, Lloyd George convened the meeting.

"Good morning, gentlemen. I trust that the Truce Committee is still making progress. We would like very much to have some satisfactory answers to present to Parliament."

Collins answered, "We have made our recommendations to Dublin on the issues of the courts and drilling and await their reply. Meanwhile, Mr. Childers has prepared a copy of the formulas proposed for your reading."[1]

"Thank you, Mr. Collins," Lloyd George replied. "So, Mr. Griffith, could you explain your proposals for Ulster?"

"I'd be happy to," Griffith responded, though his expression hardly conveyed any sense of delight. "Prime Minister, your letter inviting us to this conference expressed the hope for a harmonious cooperation amongst all Irishmen in achieving unity, but a concern as well that there would be the temptation to resort to force, and with force, bloodshed and violence, to achieve that unity. You will recall Mr. de Valera's reply that while we do not contemplate the use of force, neither would we tolerate division of our country." He paused a moment and then said softly, "This is one of the great obstacles we have to deal with. If the British Government stands aside and does not throw its force behind Ulster, we will come to an agreement, but as long as they feel the British Government behind them, there is *non possumus*.[2] We can do nothing."

He then launched into an exhaustive delineation of the demographics of the nine counties comprising Ulster, six of which were represented in the Parliament of Northern Ireland established the previous year. He gave detailed summaries of their populations and how they broke down Protestant versus Catholic, and how these areas of mixed loyalties would make a nightmare of partition.

Austen Chamberlain followed Griffith's arguments closely but grew increasingly impatient. Seeing as he shared the anti-Home Rule sentiments of his father, the famous politician, Joseph Chamberlain, a kindred spirit of Churchill's father, Randolph, it was remarkable that he was a member of this conference at all. He was well known as an astute parliamentarian who consistently exhibited the best of manners, but he lacked human warmth, and even Lord Birkenhead found him aloof and reserved.[3] After enduring Griffith's analysis of county-by-county religious percentiles, he could not restrain himself from interrupting. He removed his monocle from his eye and said very deferentially, "Excuse me, Mr. Griffith, this is all very interesting, but I'm afraid I do not quite understand what exactly it is all leading up to."[4]

Griffith stormed ahead confidently for someone who had entered this meeting lacking full and proper instructions from Dublin and hoping to avoid such scrutiny. "We contend that partition is unnatural. It boils down to this: In two of the counties of Ulster, Tyrone and Fermanagh, there are Catholic majorities. Partition cuts them off and envelops large, disaffected parts of its population."

"What would you propose?"

"What does the British Government propose?" Griffith asked back. "Whatever the Twenty-Six Counties of the South get, the North gets the same. Is this not backing them up?"[5]

Chamberlain posed a logical follow-up question. "So, do you object to the same powers being given to the North as to the South?"

"Your proposal would do more. It would increase the powers of Northern Ireland *pari passu*, on an equal footing, with the powers given to the Southern Parliament. We are not willing to allow them a Parliament equal to the Southern Parliament but would grant them local government powers."

Lloyd George followed this up by musing with a wry smile, "Here's an interesting hypothetical. Leaving aside the question of boundaries for the moment, suppose the South has all the requisite powers, and whatever powers not conferred on Ulster were to remain with the British Government. That would involve a customs barrier between the Northern and Southern areas. Is that practicable?"

More than interesting, this question was a trap. If Griffith were to answer "Yes," to a customs barrier, the spectre of long queues at every border crossing would spring to mind. In contrast, if he said "No" to a customs barrier, the British could construe this as an excuse in the event of partition to deny the right to impose tariffs and, by logical extension, deny fiscal autonomy for Southern Ireland, which was paramount to Michael. Undaunted, Griffith sidestepped this trap by stating simply, "It would be practicable, but we do not want it."

Collins elaborated, "It would be lovely for us, but not for them."

Griffith agreed, explaining, "The trade of the six counties is enormous with the South. They would not stand for a trade war."

Lloyd George backed away somewhat, saying, "We do not want to set up two states against each other. Without free trade between the North and South, it is all too easy to imagine delays, confusion, and strife all along the borders."

Now it was Griffith's turn for a wry smile. "Here's another interesting hypothetical," he said with a bow of his head to Lloyd George. "Supposing five or six socialist counties of England decided to withdraw from a Tory Government they disliked or five or six Tory counties from a Socialist Government they disliked."

Lloyd George enjoyed this parry, which stirred some old memories. "When I began my political career, you could hardly find a soul in South East Wales with sympathy for Welsh aspirations of national identity, but today Cardiff is home to several Welsh national institutions. Most residents of Cardiff and its neighbouring city, Newport, are as different in race from the rest of the inhabitants of Wales as the Protestants of Ulster are from the Catholics."[6]

"And there are two ways of annoying the ordinary working-class Orangeman of Ulster," Griffith mused. "One is to speak respectfully of the Pope, and the other is to call him an Englishman."

Everyone laughed at this quip, and Lloyd George added, "Yes, they are a pugnacious people with a touch of the Scots about them and, like them, are a very stubborn race."

Griffith countered, not losing the opportunity to make a point despite all this mirth, "As long as they have your force behind them."

"But only to the extent that we cannot allow a civil war to take place at our doors which would embroil our own people."

"Catholics and Protestants could live in harmony if support were withdrawn for those stirring people up with the bogey of the Pope and the Battle of the Boyne."[7]

Lloyd George saw it was time to outline a new line of thought. "From the days of Gladstone, Ulster has been the stumbling block. Mr. Churchill and I were with him on Home Rule, but Ulster was arming and would fight. We were powerless. They said to us, 'Let us remain with you,' and we answered, 'Out you go, or we fight you.' Yet we could not have done it. I am glad that Mr. de Valera has come to the same conclusion that force is not a weapon you can use. It would break in your hands. You do not want to begin your new life with a civil war that would leave you with desolation in its train. We, therefore, propose to come out of Ireland. We begin with no force, only persuasion, without pressure from us. We are prepared to make that clear to you. Now, as to the areas. We do not want to interfere in any effort you make to induce the North to come in. British opinion would rather they come in. We are *not* anxious to divide Ireland."

Duffy replied, "That would be useful if you had not created a partition Parliament in the North."

Lloyd George answered back, "The alternative would have been a

Boundary Commission which would have looked at the demographics of religion and would have divided the country accordingly and inalterably. That aside, we now promise to stand aside, and you will have not only our neutrality but our benevolent neutrality."

Collins had a response. "There would have been an alternative to your Boundary Commission, that is, local option by plebiscite. This is a case that can be settled by Irishmen. If we are not going to coerce the Protestants of Antrim, a county in the North East where they hold a solid majority, they must not be allowed to coerce the others."

The Prime Minister raised some eyebrows with his response, "This would be perfectly fair if you could apply it all around." A surprise to his colleagues, this simple statement opened the door to the possibility of the Irish settling the question of Ulster on their own through the vote and possibly increasing the South beyond Twenty-Six Counties. Unfortunately, this opportunity was squandered later in the talks when the issue of the Crown was to be raised.

Michael then brought up one of the themes from his September speech in Armagh to bait Austen Chamberlain by asking accusatorially, "Why did you hand out two Parliaments that no one wanted?"

His answer was simple, "So that Ireland could settle her own destinies and unite if she chose to do so."

This retort made Michael's outburst seem gratuitous, but his tone brightened as he said, "There is a great difference between this conference's attempts at settlement and those that have gone before. At the present moment, there is a general desire to settle. This is the first time practically all parties wish a settlement."

Chamberlain had a parting thought on Michael's buoyant statement. "That is our hope, but I beg of you, do not press it too far." He looked directly at Michael as he spoke, or as directly as he could through the monocle that magnified his weak right eye. Michael shifted in his seat uncomfortably, slightly unnerved by the cycloptic effect, but returned the gaze as steadfastly as he could as Chamberlain explained further, "You are not aware of the risks we are taking with our whole political future. We are bound to it as a coalition, but do not believe that it is plain sailing."

After this sobering admission, the meeting broke up. On the way out, Michael noticed a pair of rifles on stands in the hallway. "What is the meaning of this provocative display?" he asked in mock anger.

When Lloyd George followed into the hall and heard all the laughter, he asked, "What was that?"

Michael stood by the rifles and demanded, "So you think you can intimidate us with this show of force?"

Lloyd George laughed and picked up one of the rifles, "I can assure you it is not loaded. This model is the very first American rifle made for the Great War under a contract I placed when I was Minister of Munitions." As he brandished the rifle with its gleaming bayonet, he explained further, "It's a Lee-Enfield, made with that new rustless steel."

Michael commented, "Very impressive, but careful with that bayonet. You should call in a photographer from the *Morning Post* and get a picture of me sitting in a chair holding it."

Lloyd George burst out laughing, "Good Lord, no, I think not. The Press would throw themselves in a state of delirium with *that*." As he carefully put the rifle back on its stand, he said, still laughing, "And I daresay it might instil in some members of Cabinet a slight sense of unease. Till Monday, gentlemen."[8]

SEVENTY-SIX

Mo Chuisle Mo Chroí

SUNDAY, 16 OCTOBER 1921, LONDON

UP EARLY AS USUAL, MICHAEL READIED HIMSELF FOR SUNDAY MASS. The night before, he had picked up the day's mail left for him on the entrance hall table and sifted through the small pile on his way up to his bedroom. There was nothing from Kitty, but a graceful, rolling Catholic school script stood out on one of the envelopes, and this one was special. He recognised his sister Helena's elegant handwriting, the product of a childhood spent under the tutelage of the nuns and perfected in the years since she had taken the sacred vows herself. Standing before the dresser mirror, he glanced down at the envelope purposely left unopened until that morning. He looked at himself in the mirror, straightened his tie, one of the gifts from Kitty, combed his hair, and sat down on the edge of the bed. He reached for the envelope and letter opener on the dresser, unsealed the envelope, and read its contents.

Micheal, Mo Chuisle Mo Chroí,
  (Irish for Michael, pulse of my heart.)
  God bless you on this special day, your 31st birthday, and may he also bless your efforts on behalf of us all. Bring Peace home to Ireland.
  Slán agus beannacht leat,
  (Goodbye and blessings on you)
  Lena

Michael reread the simple note, folded it away in its envelope, and put it in the breast pocket of his jacket.[1] He took out a handkerchief, blew his nose, and went downstairs, where he found Eddie and Peggy McIntyre bustling about the kitchen table.

"Coffee, Mick?" Eddie asked.

"No, thanks. I'm heading over to Mass."

"Eight o'clock at Brompton Oratory?" Eddie asked.

Michael narrowed his eyes at Eddie and said coldly, "Yes, why?"

Eddie smiled cheerfully and answered, "Oh, just wanted to know if you'd like breakfast later here."

"No, I was thinking I'd take it at Hans Place, if it's all the same."

"Oh, that's fine, then. In that case, I'll head over there to lend a hand." Eddie felt he was being closely examined by Michael and awkwardly walked over to the window to escape his gaze. He peered out through the drapes and remarked, "Cloudy day. Might rain."

"It's a fine day," Michael answered back. "I'll see you later."

"Right, then, Mick. See you later."

Peggy had been listening silently to this odd exchange, and when Michael shut the door behind him, she asked Eddie, "Now, what was that all about?"

"Er, nothing, really, Miss Mack. I'll explain later."

Michael walked up Cadogan Place and headed toward Brompton Road. After a couple of minutes, he looked over his shoulder, feeling somewhat ill at ease. He paused, knelt to tie his shoelaces, then abruptly rose, doubled back, and found someone trying to hide behind a large tree.

"Out with yer hands up, man, or I'll plug you right here and now," he threatened, drawing a pistol from his jacket.

"You wouldn't shoot a man on your way to Mass, now would ye?" a familiar voice asked. Ned Broy stepped forward with a huge grin on his face.

"Damn it, man, what are ye about?"

"Just following you."

"I can see that, ye bleedin' eejit."

"Then, to be more precise, just looking after you, Mick."

"The Director of Intelligence can look after himself, thank you very much."

"Oh, can he, then? And how intelligent is it for you to be

wandering about London on your own? I need to know where you are at all times."

"Like hell! Where I go is none of your business. I'll be fine."

"Is that so? And if you went missing and were captured, or worse, could I say it was no business of mine? Now sure, if nobody else accompanies you to Mass, I will, and to do anything less would be gross negligence on my part."[2]

Michael glowered at his old friend a moment and then laughed out loud, admitting, "Well, come to think of it, you would have hell to pay. First of all, from Eddie. He put you on to me, didn't he?"

"In a manner of speaking."

"Come on, let's go. I can't stay angry. Not today, of all days."

Ned didn't understand this comment, but just let it pass.

Michael took Communion at Mass and stopped to light two candles on the way out.

"I know the first one is for Kitty, but what of the other?" Ned asked, smiling.

"My sister, the nun."

"Oh, Helena, or rather, Sister Mary Celestine? How is she? Have you heard from her lately?"

"Just yesterday. And she's still the same Lena to me. Sends me her blessings," was all he said.

Hans Place was a much shorter walk from the church than Cadogan Gardens, and they set off to join the rest of their delegation there for breakfast. Walking along Brompton Road brought back some memories for Michael, and he suddenly picked up the pace. "Come on, Ned, there's something I'd like to see. It's just a little out of the way."

A couple of streets later, in the heart of Knightsbridge, they reached the gleaming façade of Harrods, with its windows filled with luxury items many people could only dream of bringing home with them. Michael wistfully admired the showcases, but not out of envy. "You know, Ned, many fine Irishmen worked here when I lived in London."[3]

UPON THEIR RETURN TO HANS PLACE, EDDIE DUCKED INTO THE kitchen as soon as he saw the look of reproach in Michael's eyes, but

Michael followed after him. Eddie fussed with the coffee pot on the stove with his back to Michael.

"Eddie?"

"Yes, Mick?"

"Fancy a stuff in the kisser for yourself?"

"Not today, thank you."

"Hmm. Eddie?"

"Yes, Mick?"

"I'll have a drop of tea."

Eddie turned around and smiled, "You got it, Mick."

When everyone had finished breakfast, Eddie announced, "So, today is a special day, isn't it, Mick?"

Michael looked embarrassed but said nothing in reply. May Duggan did, though, "Yes, it is. There's a special Mass being celebrated on behalf of the Treaty Conference at Corpus Christi Church in Maiden Lane this morning. I hope everyone can attend."

Michael felt a slight pang of regret mixed with relief. He would have liked it if someone had remembered his birthday, but at the same time would have been embarrassed at any fuss. He shrugged and said cheerfully, "I don't know about the rest of these Philistines, but I wouldn't miss it."

"Ah, sure, Mick, we'll go; Ay, I'll be going; Me, too," came a chorus of protestations.

"Mrs. Duggan," one of the maids asked timidly, "may we go, too?"

"Certainly, dear. It's our first Sunday together here, and since everyone will be going to Mass anyway, we should celebrate a bit, wouldn't you think, Mary?"

"Absolutely," she answered. "We should ask Peggy to organise all the staff over by her. That is if we have enough cars, Michael."

"Ay, should do. If not, we can make up the difference with cabs. Eddie…"

"I'll call the Military House now."

"The what?" Mary asked, a bit shocked.

"That's what the staff here are calling the Cadogan house, seeing as that's where most of the guns are."

"Oh dear," May responded. "And what do they call us?"

Arthur's private secretary, Kathleen MacKenna, answered, "We're the Politicians' House, since all of the delegates, save Mick, are here." She looked timidly over at Arthur as he cleared his throat.

"Well, then, I suppose that's all right," May replied uncertainly.

Smiling weakly, Arthur wiped his glasses and said, "I'm not sure I approve."

Michael laughed it off, "It sounds like two branches of government, but a little friendly rivalry won't hurt. But I agree, having everyone celebrate Mass together on our first Sunday here will get us off on the right foot." [4]

So, after breakfast, there was a festive atmosphere when the sizable entourage of the two houses converged at the church in Covenant Gardens. No sooner had they arrived when Tom Cullen cried out, "For fuck's sake, Mick, look! It's Dave Neligan!" [5]

Dave was standing at the top of the steps at the church entrance. He stared right at Michael and walked into the vestibule of the church.

Tom asked, "Should I approach him?"

"Too risky for us," Michael answered. "Too risky for him."

Liam had an idea, "Some of our London Brotherhood lads are here. I'll send a couple over to make contact."

Liam walked up behind two young men and greeted them, "Morning, fellas."

"Jaysus, Liam!"

"Hush up; I've got something for you. Up the steps." Talking in a low tone as they walked toward the vestibule, he instructed them, "There's a tall fellow named Dave in there. Tell him Mick says hello."

The two men nodded wordlessly, entered the vestibule, and found Dave waiting for them. They walked up to him, and one of them murmured, "Mick says hello."

"Hello, back. He's being watched here. So, you watch me. When you see me holding my hat behind my back as I talk to someone, that's an agent." He looked around and then reached into the breast pocket of his jacket and took out an envelope. "I thought I could count on you boys showing up here today. See that Mick gets this."

Dave passed the envelope over, waited a minute, entered the nave of the church, spotted Michael and the others, walked along the side aisle under the Stations of the Cross, and approached two other men looking for a place in the pews, garnering ill looks as they did so. Women's heads were covered with veils or hats in the church proper, and all the men had tossed their hats on the benches. All except one, whose partner hissed, "Lose the titfer in the Lord's house, you silly twat!"

As any Londoner would have known, titfer, tit for tat, rhymes with and means hat, so the would-be undercover worshipper quickly removed the offending article with a sheepish grin.

Dave pulled up in the pew beside these two men, held his hat behind his back, leaned over and whispered, "Blending right in, I see."

"Oh, hello, Dave. What's the good word?"

"The Gospel according to Saint Matthew."

"Come again?"

Dave shook his head and said, "Never mind. See that big bloke over there? That's Mick Collins."

"You don't say! Thanks, Dave. We're on it."

The two men, British agents, separated, and each of them squeezed in at either end of the pew a couple of rows behind Michael, who may have seemed unaware of all this attention, but none of this activity escaped the notice of Liam and Tom.

After reading the Gospel, the priest officiating the Mass gave a very conciliatory sermon of hope for the success of the Treaty talks. During Communion, the pews emptied as the congregants entered the centre aisle and joined the queue to the altar. Michael had received the Eucharist at the earlier Mass, so he remained in his seat but turned around nonchalantly, seemingly to admire the church. He spotted Dave standing at the back of the church. They stared at each other momentarily, but neither made any sign of recognition, and Michael turned to face the altar again. He leaned over to Liam and whispered, "Good old Dave. I knew we'd see him sooner than later."

Tom heard this and said, "Yes, but what about your shadows?"

"Those two gacks? You'd think they'd leave us be for Mass. Just outrageous!"

Liam agreed, saying, "What mischief do they think we're going to get ourselves up to in a church?"

Tom kept the same tone, "Yes, isn't this some kind of sacrilege? You know, asylum in a church or something like that?"

Michael grinned and said, "I'm glad I have two such fine Catholic lads on either side of me to keep me safe. You're absolutely right, Tom, my boy, and I intend to relay your objection to the Prime Minister when I see him tomorrow."

Tom seemed pleased that his remarks would make it to the conference table. "I'd love to be a fly on the wall for that!"

Leaving the church after Mass, they saw Dave at the curbside. He saw them, too, but did not acknowledge them in any way but just turned away and walked down the street. The local Brotherhood agent came back bearing the envelope Dave had given him and passed it to Michael.

"Cheers, mate," Michael said as he accepted the delivery. "As I said, good old Dave," Michael exclaimed and then turned to Tom. "Keep tabs on him, Tom. He'll know you're following him, but don't let anyone else see what you're up to. I'll leave it to you and Liam to work out how to contact him from here on."

Just then, a photographer came along and snapped his picture.

Michael just sighed, "So much for the elusive Michael Collins!"

Liam said with deadpan humour, "Well, looking on the bright side, if it makes the papers, at least he got a good shot of another one of Kitty's ties."

"Now, let's see what we have here from Secret Agent Neligan." He scanned the document, whistled, and said, "British G.H.Q. in Ireland is up to no good. Arthur and I can make good use of this at tomorrow's meeting. My, my." Michael then took out his watch and said, "Good, there's still time to make it to Islington."

"Islington?"

"Ay, come on, Liam. Let's pay Pat Harte a visit in Pentonville Prison. I want to see if he's getting proper care. Tom Hales is recovering from torture at the hands of Major Percival, but Pat is not doing so well."

Liam said quietly, "Friends who have visited say he's in an awful mental state."

"It's sad. He refused food initially, so they had to force-feed him. Lately he's been complaining that people could read his thoughts." Michael sighed heavily, "We'll have to brace ourselves for the worst. This won't be easy. Still…"

"A mate's a mate. Too bad Tom Hales is still being held so far away in Dartmoor Prison."

"Ay, no amnesty for him. Let's get over to see Pat while we can."[6]

SEVENTY-SEVEN

The Case of the Poison Letter

MONDAY, 17 OCTOBER 1921, LONDON, FIFTH SESSION

THAT MONDAY MORNING NED BROY NOTICED THE MAILMAN WALKING up the path at Cadogan Place and opened the door to greet him. "Good morning; I'll take whatever you have."

"Very good, sir." He searched his bag and handed over some envelopes. "I hope all's well; that is, I wish you all good luck."

"Well, thank you. Good day to you, sir."

Ned stepped back into the parlour and sorted the envelopes but stopped when he came across one for Michael that lacked a return address. "Oh, no!" he muttered to himself.

Peggy McIntyre happened to walk by and asked, "What is it, Mr. Broy?"

"I'm afraid this might be another of those abusive, threatening letters we've been getting."

"Oh, dear!"

Ned slit open the envelope with a knife and unfolded the letter to reveal a piece of cloth, which he picked up to examine. "That's odd," he mumbled and then read the note aloud as Peggy leaned over his shoulder to get a closer look. "*The enclosed cloth is saturated with disease germs that I hope will kill Collins and everyone near him.*"

Peggy took a sniff, but before she could say anything, Ned shouted, "Oh, shite! I've touched it already! Damn!" and with that, he ran into the kitchen.

"But Mr. Broy!" she called after him. Peggy mumbled to herself, "Smelled like rotten eggs to me," but Ned was already standing over the sink, burning the letter and its contents. Peggy was fast on his heels and pulled up alongside him, saying, "Well, there's a right mess that will need cleaning up. Just look at my sink!"

Michael heard all the commotion and came into the kitchen and asked, "What's all the fuss?"

Ned was still excited and hyperventilating as he explained, "It was a poison letter. I mean, actually a *real* poison letter, hoping it would kill you."

Michael glanced at Peggy, who calmly took a deep breath and shook her head, and then he lit into Ned. "Damn it, man! You're supposed to be my Private Secretary. All letters received by a good secretary should be properly recorded, filed, and indexed. Can you please explain to me what precedent you have for destroying official correspondence?" Then in a true display of just how angry he was, he put his hands on his hips, his chin out, and leaned into Ned's face. "Poison, ye say, man? Where's the evidence? How can I justify a request to the Dáil for a chemical analyst to be added to the Delegation?"

Ned stammered, "I, I…"

"Well?" Michael waited a moment and then, hands still on his hips, turned toward Peggy and asked, "Rotten *oiges*, did I hear you say?"

Peggy bit the inside of her cheeks and then answered, completely deadpan, "Two weeks old if a day."

Michael turned back to Ned, glaring at him for a moment longer. He tilted his head to one side and queried, "And not the poison letter deduced by Mr. Sherlock Broy, consulting detective?" Now Michael bit his cheeks until he could no longer contain himself. He exploded in laughter and laughed so hard that he had to sit down on a chair. He took a napkin from the kitchen table and wiped his eyes. Peggy giggled, and finally, Ned started to shake with laughter, too.

"Poison letter!" Michael cried. He sat there trying to catch his breath for a minute until he looked up at Ned and blurted again, "Rotten *oiges*! Ahhh!" and convulsed in laughter again.[1]

ALL THE DELEGATES ARRIVED FOR THE FIFTH SESSION OF THE conference late that Monday afternoon. Lloyd George approached

Arthur Griffith in the hallway leading into the Cabinet Room and asked pleasantly, "Enjoy the weekend? I hope you were able to enjoy the respite from our work here."

"Yes, thank you," Arthur answered. "There was a very nice church service on our behalf at a church in Maiden Lane. Perhaps you had news of it?"

Lloyd George just smiled and said, "I hope you have had a constructive word from Dublin."

"Oh, yes, we have. I'd be happy to share it with you."

So, when the meeting began, Griffith spoke first at the invitation of the Prime Minister. "I am pleased to report that our colleagues in Dublin have endorsed the recommendations of the Truce Committee, and hopefully any issues on courts and drilling and things of that nature will no longer be of any further concern to us here." He delivered this message pleasantly enough but then continued in a matter-of-fact tone, "However, we have obtained a copy of a secret document issued by one of your officers in G.H.Q. that is being circulated to the military and divisional commanders. It is written with the political aim of stirring up the blood of the soldiers and police to fill them with the idea that fighting is inevitable. In addition, it says that in the event of the Truce breaking down, you should use your Intelligence Service to arrest our leaders."[2]

There was dead silence at the table, but Griffith continued, "Now, I do not believe for a moment that you are aware of circulars of this character, and we have not come here intending to break off negotiations, but clearly, we must protest."

To ensure that the seriousness of the issue was driven home, Collins added, "Even if this has occurred without your knowledge, this memo is in accordance with many other documents which have come into our possession since the Truce. It is the temper of the Truce that is lacking. This is bound to lead to a miskeeping of the Truce."

Worthington-Evans tried to excuse the breach half-heartedly, "For the moment, I don't know for sure that this memo was issued."

Collins was incensed at this contradiction of their complaint, and just to make sure that everyone at the table realised the strength of his intelligence service, he countered, "Well, *we* know. You cannot issue these documents without *my* knowledge."[3]

Lloyd George seemed to all appearances to be aghast at the existence of such a memo. "We must get this examined by General

Macready. We shall be able to let you have a reply by tomorrow. I assure you he is loyal to the spirit of the Truce. Yet it is true there are men on both sides who are ready to break the Truce. I warned you that there was a growing sentiment, in a powerful section of Mr. Chamberlain's party particularly, who view with grave disfavour our attempts to produce a settlement. We have serious evidence here of it today. But we shall face it. We are sincere and determined in our resolve to make peace. If there is a failure, the responsibility will not be ours."

Griffith listened quietly up to this point, and this remark about responsibility for a break in the Truce irked him, but he held his tongue for the moment. Lloyd George concluded his comments by saying, "But do not blind your eyes to the growing resistance in this country."

Then Griffith said simply and dispassionately, "To have officials working against the Government is treachery." This was a condemnation of the acts committed, not necessarily of the British officials at the table, which allowed for some breathing room.

However, unable to leave well enough alone, Worthington-Evans worsened the situation by claiming, "This document is advice to be taken if the Truce breaks down. There is nothing here which is an incitement to break the Truce."

That was just the sort of British finessing of the truth that always angered the Irish, and Michael answered accordingly, "You had me shadowed at Mass at Maiden Lane yesterday. Was that in the spirit of the Truce?"

Lloyd George answered, "Mr. Collins, we have, of course, had to contemplate what to do in the event of a break, not as an act of menace but as an act of prudence. That is not treachery to the peace."

Tempers on both sides simmered near a boil, but for the moment, nothing was said. Lloyd George turned to Churchill and said, "We are rather at a point like when Mr. Boland and Mr. McGrath visited me at Gairloch and had to be sent home empty-handed."

Griffith tried to bring things back from such a point, saying, "Prime Minister, we are not accusing you of treachery."

Silence. After a long pause, Michael said, "Well, if you are going to have me followed, I hope your man was a Catholic, as I don't wish to be accused of conversion as well as subversion!"[4]

Laughter broke out on both sides of the table, with Winston shaking in his seat while Chamberlain wiped his monocle with his handkerchief.

However, the jovial mood was broken when Duggan spoke, bringing up another document, "Instructions have also been circulated to note the movement of all our men back home. This, too, is a direct breach of the Truce."

Birkenhead was unconvinced and put Duggan down, "Have you seen the document? It depends on the document."

This patronising remark sparked Michael's quick return to anger. "One of your officers has been circulating photos of me."

Griffith supported Michael by saying, "These are all indications of the temper of the Truce."

As the Prime Minister said, one of the men at the table who stood to lose the most in these negotiations was the Conservative Party leader, Austen Chamberlain. The Liberal-Conservative coalition government laboured under enormous pressures that threatened to pull it asunder along with the careers of everyone in it. Chamberlain said plaintively, "Gentlemen, we appreciate your concerns regarding the spirit of the Truce, but we do, in fact, still have a Truce. Perhaps we could move on to the more substantive issues. My position gets more difficult day by day, and my authority less and less within my party. Let us not waste precious time."

So, they stepped back from the precipice and turned to the issue of Ulster. Once again, Griffith took up the subject of the relative proportions of Protestants and Catholics throughout the area, but this time he illustrated his points by passing around coloured maps showing the disposition of the two constituencies.

After another dose of statistics, Lloyd George asked, "Yes, but what is your proposition about Ulster?"

Proposals on Ulster had been sent from Dublin, but not with instructions on how to implement them, so Griffith forged ahead on his own. He answered, "If you stand aside, we will give them a fair proposal: Let them vote to come to us or stay with Northern Ireland." Much discussion followed on how to conduct elections and reconcile the results with the wishes of the minorities, but no clear decision was reached.

At one point, an exasperated Lloyd George said, "We do not care in the slightest degree where Irishmen put Tyrone and Fermanagh." This cavalier statement regarding these two predominantly Catholic counties of Ulster was a potentially enormous concession regarding two counties with a clear majority of Catholics. Still, it was neither a promise nor a guarantee. He warned, "But it is no use making peace with you if we are going to have civil war in Ulster."

Michael was quick to add, "But you will have civil war because nearly half the area of Ulster will come into the Southern Parliament."

One of the British delegates asked, "And what of the fifty thousand Protestants in Dublin?"

"I have yet to meet the Dublin Protestant," Griffith answered, "who wants to come into a Northern Parliament."

Growing impatient, but exuding equanimity, Lloyd George said, "Clearly, we shall not settle this matter today, but if we are to reach a settlement, we cannot leave this in doubt." He then rose and said, "So, let us adjourn for a few days to gather our thoughts on these issues. Until this Friday, then? Oh, and tomorrow, I believe the Naval and Air Defence Committee meets at the Colonial Office?"

Churchill affirmed this as he rose, "Yes, sir." Turning to face Collins, he asked, "Tomorrow morning at eleven?"

"That will be fine," Michael answered.

When the Irish delegates had left the room, Thomas Jones conferred with Lloyd George, who remarked in a very depressed state, "They are intransigent on Ulster. This is going to wreck settlement."[5]

Churchill finished packing up his valise and then joined them and asked, "So what do we think of our Irish guests so far?"

Though Lloyd George was frustrated with the slow pace, he brightened at Winston's question. "Arthur Griffith is a fine man and an honest man, but he never commits to anything. He is a clever man as well, but I have my doubts as to whether he is capable of making a definitive decision."

"Yes," Winston agreed, "he has the air of a tired scholar and presents that unusual figure, a silent Irishman."[6] He smiled and said, "I find Collins to be quite the engaging fellow, though."

"Yes," Jones remarked, "He and Lord Birkenhead seem to share a mutually competitive fascination with each other."

Churchill smiled at this, "It's the athlete in both of them."

Lloyd George said, "Perhaps that's it. He certainly is a handsome young Irishman. None could mistake his nationality, Irish through and through, in every respect a contrast to his taciturn neighbour, Griffith. Vivacious, buoyant, highly strung, gay and impulsive, but passing readily to grimness and back again to gaiety. A young man full of fascination and charm—but also of dangerous fire."[7]

Birkenhead said off-handedly, "At any rate, they're all a sight better than that ambassador of theirs, Art O'Brien. Thankfully, we've been spared any dealings with him."

Lloyd George's response explained the reserved welcome he had afforded O'Brien the day the talks started. "That swine. Ambassador, my Celtic arse. A little man neglected. Nothing is so pitiable as a small man trying to handle big things."[8]

SEVENTY-EIGHT

The Point Is

THE FOLLOWING MORNING, MICHAEL WENT OVER TO HANS PLACE TO pick up the delegation secretary, Erskine Childers, for the naval defence meeting with Churchill. In the car with him were Ned Broy and Emmet Dalton.[1]

"By the way, Emmet," Michael commented, "I got a letter from Kitty this morning, and she asked after you."[2]

Emmet, so pleased to be accepted into the inner circle of the one man he held in the highest esteem, blushed and said, "That's good of her. Please send her my best."

"Will do. That'll be enough pleasantries for now; we're here to pick up Erskine. You go in and get him, will you, Emmet? Ned and I will wait here."

"Sure, Mick, back in a minute."

Watching Emmett go up to the house, Ned remarked, "That was something running into Dave Neligan at Mass on Sunday, wasn't it?"

"Arrah, but he's a wily one, he is," Michael answered. "They don't seem to be using him to his full potential, though. I expected him to have a more strategic assignment for the Secret Service in these negotiations, which, of course, would have been to our benefit, so frankly, I'm a little disappointed."

"We may see more of him now, but only in a limited capacity. I'll warrant there's a bit of a turf war going on here. British agents on British soil, no Irishmen need apply."

"Speaking of a turf war, have a sconce at those two," Michael commented, pointing to the front door. Ned turned and looked that way, where he could see Griffith lecturing Childers. Michael laughed, "If Arthur had his way, Erskine would be sent packing today. Arthur does not like him one bit."

"Doesn't like," Ned replied, "doesn't trust."

"You're one to talk, then, aren't you, Detective Broy?" Michael asked sarcastically but good-naturedly. "You must have a few English noses bent out of shape with the fine company you're keeping over here."

Ned laughed. "Maybe, but I'm looking forward to saying hello to General Macready. I haven't crossed paths with him yet. I'm sure he'll derive some satisfaction in seeing his suspicions about me confirmed."

"On the other hand, Arthur has always harboured his suspicions about Erskine."

"Ay, the effete Englishman."

Erskine Childers was an unusual figure in the Irish cause for a Republic. Born into a distinguished English family, he was six years of age when his father died, and he was sent to live with his cousin Robert Barton's family in County Wicklow. Like most young Anglo-Irishmen of his background and social bearing, Childers was a staunch supporter of the British Empire, yet he gradually had a change of heart and joined his Irish cousin, Robert, in the struggle for Home Rule. Childers was also the author of a hugely popular espionage novel, *The Riddle of the Sands*, in which a skilled sailor helps uncover a German plot to invade England. Whereas Roger Casement's gunrunning escapade failed back in 1914, Childers, unlike his novel's protagonists, ironically put his own sailing skills to use not in service of but against England and successfully sailed his yacht, the *Asgard*, into Howth harbour bearing German armaments that were later used in the Easter Rising.[3] Still, he just rubbed Arthur the wrong way, and Arthur never trusted him.

"He *is* a stuffed shirt; I'll give you that," Michael commented, "but he has some promising ideas for this naval conference. Last night he and I spent a good part of the evening putting together a working memo that we'll present to Churchill today." As Childers and Dalton approached the car, Michael opened the car door. "Morning, Erskine. Have that report finished?"

"Yes, Michael. Good morning, Ned."

"Good morning, Erskine," Ned answered with a wink to Michael.

Childers and Dalton got in the car, and they all headed for the meeting of the Committee on Naval and Air Defence at the Colonial Office. Once in Whitehall, they arrived at the enormous neoclassical building that stretched between Downing and King Charles Streets from Whitehall to St. James's Park. The park end of the street housed the Foreign and India Offices, while the Home and Colonial Offices lay before them at the Whitehall end.

Michael whistled. "Nice gaff. We should consider something like this in Dublin—say, for the Ministry of Defence. That would keep Cathal happy."

Ned laughed. "I would hope so. A little rich for my tastes, though. I'll stay here with the car. Good luck."

Inside the Colonial Office, Churchill's Private Secretary, Eddie Marsh, had been expecting them and showed them the way. Churchill welcomed them all warmly, but in adhering to the protocol adopted among the delegates at Downing Street, still did not offer his hand. An officer in full naval dress stood slightly to the rear.

"Welcome, Mr. Collins, Mr. Childers." He smiled at Emmet.

Michael did the honours, "Mr. Churchill, I don't believe you have met our liaison officer, Emmet Dalton. I hope you don't mind if he sits in on our meeting."

"No, not at all," he said with a mischievous smile. "Mr. Dalton, I understand you served as an officer in the British Army during the War."

"That's right, sir," Emmet replied. "The Dublin Fusiliers."

"Extraordinary." Churchill then revealed much more knowledge of Emmet's exploits than his original greeting had let on. "And His Majesty gave you the Military Cross for subduing and capturing a much larger force at Ginchy during the Battle of the Somme." He looked him over and said, "Tell me, how old were you at the time?"

"Twenty-four, sir."

"All of twenty-four! Well done, sir. Allow me to introduce you to Admiral Beatty. He will be assisting me in a similar capacity. Look, Admiral. It's Ginchy!" This was a well-known nickname for Emmet, and word of his exploits had probably reached Whitehall.[4]

Beatty bowed slightly, "Gentlemen." Turning to Emmet, he smiled and asked in a friendly tone, "Not beset by divided loyalties, I presume?"

"Not at all, sir. I fought for Ireland with the British and fought for Ireland against them."[5]

"I see." Slightly bemused, he looked at Winston.

"I like an honest answer from an honest man." Winston acknowledged his secretary, "And you all have met Mr. Marsh." Churchill waved everyone to seats at a small table across from his desk. "So, gentlemen, where shall we begin?"

Michael nodded to Childers, who produced the memo he and Michael had worked on and handed it to Churchill. "We took the liberty of outlining a few points regarding coastal defence."[6]

"Well, thank you. Admiral, perhaps you and I should withdraw to review this? You don't mind, do you? Please excuse us for a moment."

Michael answered, "Please do."

When they had finished studying the new proposals, Churchill and Beatty returned to their seats, and Churchill placed the document over a map on the table before them, beaming a smile. "Gentlemen, this able memorandum will shorten the task of this committee." Hearing this brought a slight smile to Childers' face, but Churchill continued, "In fact, it will bring it to an end. It amounts to a reasoned, measured, uncompromising refusal to meet us on any point. It advances the theory to which we could not become a party—that Ireland is a foreign Ireland. The right to build an Irish navy is claimed. I regard this as a mortal blow."[7]

Childers' smile vanished, and all colour drained from his face. Michael, though, was unfazed and answered in a friendly enough tone, "We would have hoped you would see it in the light of the need for mutual security."

"With an Irish navy on our doorstep? And what possible harm do you find in allowing us access to Irish ports?"

Childers said in his deferential manner, "You would have Ireland, an island with a maritime frontier, denied responsibility for her own naval defence. It is a denial of Ireland's existence as a nation."[8]

Churchill rejected this, saying, "I refuse to admit to that. We are here to establish Ireland as a nation, as a member of the Commonwealth."

Michael decided to sidestep the issue of the Commonwealth for the time being. Not wanting to end the meeting before it had hardly begun, he sought a middle ground. "I suggest we begin with an examination of the map. Let's see where our mutual interests lie."

However, Childers only exacerbated the issue. "Excellent idea, Michael. Now, gentlemen, I mean to demonstrate that Ireland is not only no source of danger to England, but from the military standpoint, is virtually useless."

Churchill suppressed a smile and stared in wonder at Beatty, who nodded and pursed his lips as if to say, "Do tell."

Childers proceeded to do just that. "Take the matter of Irish bases for English submarine chasers. From the viewpoint of naval expediency, Plymouth, over here," he explained patiently, pointing it out on the map on the southwest coast of England, "is a far better base than any port on the Irish coast."

Restraining a lifetime of naval strategy and earned wisdom, Beatty humoured him, "You really think so?"

Oblivious to any irony, he went on, "Oh, yes, admiral. For instance," he paused and tapped on the map before them, "supposing Ireland was not there at all…"

Upon hearing this, Beatty indulged himself by interrupting with the obvious, "Ah, but Ireland *is* there…"

Churchill, who already harboured a palpable distaste for Childers, clearly was not amused with his pedantry and interjected, "And how many times have we wished she were not!"[9]

Michael smiled at this remark, but Churchill, not one who took well to being preached to, began pointing out various strategically essential points along the English and Irish coasts. He gave a thorough disposition on nautical distances, sailing times, and the tactical requirements of submarine warfare, occasionally deferring to Beatty for confirmation.

After a spell of this lecturing, Michael scribbled a note and passed it to Emmett, "Have you any answer to these points?"

Emmett read the note, looked at Michael, shrugged his shoulders and shook his head.

Churchill went on, "In the event of another war, without the use of critical ports on the south coast of your home, County Cork, British support ships would have to sail hundreds of miles further out to sea to protect the defenceless merchant shipping we depend upon."

Beatty elaborated, "Our naval facilities at Queenstown and Bere-haven are essential to protecting the Western Approaches."

Michael tapped his fingers on the table and looked over at Emmett.

Churchill continued with an explanation of cruising distances and submersion capabilities of German submarines and other minutiae. Unable to restrain himself any further, Michael finally stood up, slammed his fist on the table, and shouted, "For Christ's sake, come to the point!"[10]

The room went deathly silent. Eddie Marsh put his pen down with his mouth agape, and Admiral Beatty looked up to the ceiling. Childers twittered slightly; Dalton gulped. Dumbstruck, Churchill stared at Michael, a look of disbelief evolving into a scowl. Michael's jaw protruded as he leaned forward with both hands supporting all his weight on the table. Churchill's eyes narrowed, as did Michael's. Suddenly Michael exploded with a fit of his signature high-pitched yelp of a laugh and pounded his fist again on the table. He could not stop laughing and beguiled by Michael's infectious laugh, Churchill's stocky frame began to tremble with laughter, too, and soon everyone fell into convulsions along with the two antagonists.

"*The point is*, Mr. Collins," he said, echoing Michael's outburst, "is that we beg to differ with you."

"Well, the feeling is mutual, so at least we have *something* in common," Michael responded with a grin. "This memorandum is a technical document and, taken in conjunction with your own technical requirements, perhaps an agreed policy can be established. I think we could proceed on that basis."

Churchill was quite impressed not only with Michael's sense of humour but also his common-sense practicality and felt encouraged. "Yes, I think we can, Mr. Collins. However, I would ask you to consider these issues touched on here today in the light of your relationship within the Empire."

This was hardly a subject that would be definitively settled by a naval defence sub-committee, but it was discussed at length. Ultimately, nothing had been resolved when the meeting broke up, but a barrier had been broken, and a new prospect for frank, open negotiations seemed possible to Churchill. When Michael and his companions left, Eddie Marsh walked with them back down the hall. Clearing his throat, he began cautiously, "Mr. Collins, if you don't mind, I'd like to interject a personal observation."

"Oh," Michael replied, "what would that be, Mr. Marsh?"

"Please, Eddie will do nicely."

"Fine. Mick will do for me. So, Eddie, you were about to say…"

"Yes, well, when Winston first asked me to work for him, I had thought him the most brilliant person I had ever come across, but he struck me as rather truculent and overbearing. I asked a lady friend who knew him well for advice. She said the first time you meet Winston, you see all his faults, and the rest of your life you spend in discovering his virtues."[11]

Michael stopped and laughed, "Thank you for that, Eddie. I'll bear that in mind, though I don't imagine he and I will have the pleasure of each other's company for the rest of our lives."

"You never know. So long, Mick, and best of luck."

When Marsh returned to the office, Churchill and Beatty were assessing the merits of the meeting.

"My lord, Winston," Beatty mused, "I thought you would jump clear over that table to get at that young upstart's throat."

"Don't think I didn't consider it and could have done, I'll have you know." Churchill smiled broadly. "Isn't that right, Eddie?"

"I agree with the admiral. I thought that Collins was in for the surprise of his life."

Churchill went on, "That young upstart may not enjoy the same advantages of education as his elder colleague, Arthur Griffith, but he is possessed of remarkable elemental qualities and a mother wit. I'll tell you this; I would rather talk business with someone with his unbridled spirit than some over-educated snob any day of the week."

Beatty agreed, "Yes, it was refreshing to hear someone speak with such candour."

"Yet," Churchill said as he walked back to the table and looked down at the map of Britain and Ireland. "And yet, we mustn't lose sight of the fact that that young man is the leader of what until so recently we all declaimed as the terror gang. That young man," he repeated, gathering his thoughts, "has stood far nearer to the terrible incidents of this conflict than either Mr. Griffith or Mr. de Valera, for that matter. His prestige and influence with the extreme parties in Ireland are for that reason far higher, and the difficulties in his own heart and with those associates are far greater."[12]

SEVENTY-NINE

An Act of Impertinence

MICHAEL ROSE, WASHED, SHAVED, DRESSED, AND THEN WENT ABOUT THE latest addition to his morning ritual. He walked across the hall, banged on Ned's door, and shouted, "Come on! Ye about to while away day in bed, or what?"

He walked down a flight to Emmet's room and provided a similar wake-up service, banging on the door and singing out, "Emmet! Emmet, dear! Rise and shine!"

When Ned and Emmet joined him in the kitchen, Michael had already finished his coffee and toast.

"Eggs, anyone?" Peggy asked.

Michael answered for them all, "Oh, there's no time for that now. I can't be going to Mass without a bodyguard, now, can I?"

"Can a man at least drink his coffee in peace?" Emmet asked. He looked imploringly to Peggy.

"Anything the matter, Emmet?" Michael asked with apparent concern. "You're looking a bit peaked this morning. Sleep all right?"

"I've been having some trouble with my bed. Sometimes when I go to my room at night, the legs of the bedframe have collapsed. Last night I didn't notice anything askew, but I must have turned over in my sleep at some point, and the whole bed collapsed to the floor."

Michael appeared infuriated. "That's terrible! Tell Joe McGrath about it. He should lodge a complaint with the rental agency. We can't have an insomniac for a liaison officer."

Peggy poured Emmet a cup and gave Michael a withering glare.

Michael smiled sweetly at her. "Now, which of you will accompany me to Mass this fine morning? Emmet?"

"I think I'll pass, if it's all the same."

"Suit yourself. Ned?"

Ned took the coffee cup right out of Emmet's hand, took a swig, and said, "Sure, let's go."

As they left the room, Peggy raised her voice slightly and said, "Now, Emmet, dear boy. How about a nice Irish breakfast of eggs, sausages, and some fried tomatoes and potatoes?"

As Michael and Ned went out the front door, they could hear Peggy practically yelling, "We can't have you going peckish as well as sleepless." They fell about laughing and set out for Brompton Oratory.

"That was worth every bit of effort that went into it," Michael said. "But it does nothing to allay a fresh new problem we have on our hands. We need to get the morning paper right after Mass, Ned."

"Worried about that telegram to the Pope?"

Michael didn't answer so much as think aloud, "You know, Pope Benedict meant well enough writing to King George, extending his blessings on the negotiations. In all fairness to the King, all he said in return was, 'I, too, pray for a new era of peace for my people.' *My people.* Sure, it's an implied, condescending denial of an Irish nation, but the King isn't negotiating this Treaty, so who gives a damn who or what he prays for?"

"Apparently, the Long Fellow does."

"But, Christ Almighty, Dev went too far."

"It's another case of the old schoolteacher giving a lecture, except this time he deems to lecture the Pope on politics. It's just *not* done. He should have just ignored the entire incident."

"Ay, pontificating is the Pope's job, not Dev's."

De Valera had sent a telegram to the Pope that was released to the Press the day before. It read, *The people of Ireland are confident that the ambiguities in the reply sent in the name of King George will not mislead you into believing that the troubles are in Ireland, or that the people of Ireland owe allegiance to the British King. The independence of Ireland has been formally proclaimed. The trouble is between England and Ireland, and its source that the rulers of Britain have endeavoured to impose their will on Ireland.*[1]

They arrived at the church and went inside. After Mass, Ned waited for Michael on the church's steps as Michael lit his daily candle for Kitty. When he emerged from the church into the open air, Michael spotted a scrappy young boy hawking the morning papers on the pavement, and he hurried down the steps with Ned close behind to get a copy of *The Times*.

He picked up the paper and pressed a coin into the lad's hand.

"Say, aren't you that Mick Collins?" the boy asked in wide-eyed amazement.

"No, I am not, you little scoundrel." Michael scanned the paper and then suddenly shouted, "Wreckers?"

"What's that, Mick?" Ned asked.

"Look at this headline! *Wreckers!*" he bellowed back. "Well, this just sets us up beautifully for today's conference. We're the ones fucking wrecked, Ned."

"Can I see that?" Ned took the newspaper from Michael, stood there, and read it aloud. "*Mr. de Valera has sent a telegram to the Pope which, we imagine, will fill His Holiness with dismay, as it will certainly arouse indignation among the people of this country and of the British Dominions. Towards the Pope himself, it is an act of impertinence; and towards the King, whose solicitude for the Irish people needs no proof, it is unmannerly to the point of churlishness.* So, the Chief managed to kill two birds with one stone. One telegram, he insults the Pope and the King. Not bad for a day's work. But was all this really necessary, Mick? What do we gain?"

"Very little that I can see," Michael answered, "except a cool reception at today's conference."

The "little scoundrel" who had been standing listening to all this was unconvinced. "See, now, you can't fool me. You are so Collins."

Michael grabbed the paper from Ned, rolled it up and hit the boy over the head with it. "What do ye want, an autograph?"

The boy rubbed his head but grinned and said, "That would be nice. Do you have a pen on you?"

Michael was in a bad mood now but could not continue to extend it to the blameless boy, so he just said, "Keep yer yammer shut about it. You'll see me here again." He unrolled the paper and read more as he and Ned walked away. "*We are fully aware, as our Parliamentary Correspondent points out today, that irreconcilable forces in this country are working deliberately to wreck the Irish Conference.*"[2] He looked at Ned and said, "Apparently, there are some forces in Dublin doing the same. Let's head over to the Politicians' House. I'll need to discuss this with Arthur."

"Then there's the matter of Erskine Childers," Ned said, reminding him of a conversation they had earlier.

"Yes, that will have to be addressed, too. Thanks for reminding me, Ned."

Upon arriving, Michael went straight up to Griffith's room to talk things over. He knocked on his door, went in and threw the newspaper down on Arthur's dresser. Arthur greeted him, "Good morning, Mick. I know. I saw it, too. *Wreckers!* How will we wiggle out of this one? It's hard enough as it is arguing with Lloyd George over Ulster."

"Try keeping Winston Churchill and the British Navy at bay, no pun intended."

"What in blue hell was Dev thinking? This puts us in a horrible position."

Michael was fuming but said evenly, "Dev was thinking of Dev and of what makes him appear omniscient and omnipotent from afar. If he wants to make outrageous pronouncements like this, let him climb down from his mountaintop, come over here and pronounce to his heart's content, and then explain himself to Lloyd George."

He then put a finger to his lips, went over to the door, opened it, looked up and down the hallway, closed the door again and motioned Arthur over to a couple of chairs by the window.

"Arthur, the other day Alice Lyons told me about a packet of letters Erskine wanted Seán MacBride to take with him on his next trip back to Dublin. She was sharp enough to notice a handwritten one to Dev amongst the others."

"I see," Arthur said thoughtfully. "I have been keeping Dev informed on a daily basis with official reports that my secretary, Lily Brennan, prepares for me."[3]

"I've been doing the same when necessary—Alice types mine. I've kept Seán busy with endless round-trip errands back to Dublin. It seems Erskine is taking advantage of Seán's travels and conducting a private back channel of communication with Dev."

"As you know, Mick, I never liked Erskine, never trusted that *Englishman*," he said with sarcastic emphasis, "and certainly did not want him here with us, attached to the delegation. If he's going behind my back to undermine these talks, I'll give him a good thrashing."

Michael chortled at the thought. "And I know you could do it, too."

And he could have, for Arthur may have looked like a mild-mannered professor, but he was tough as nails. "But maybe we can cut him out somehow."

"Yes, we'll see about that. You know, Dev refused to send an assistant I requested but instead tried to get me to send someone back home to Dublin. I refused! I can't have my staff whittled down. I need more help, not less!"

"Well, in that case, you can have Austin Stack. Dev tried to foist him on me."[4] Austin Stack was the Minister of Home Affairs and had accompanied de Valera to London back in July. He could usually be relied upon to vote with de Valera and Brugha on just about anything, though he was one of those who spoke out against the proposals de Valera had brought back. He was known to be grossly inefficient, to such an extent that he was a real danger to the safety of the Volunteers.

"Stack is a dud, and he hates your guts, Mick. Talk about 'wrecking' the talks. Cathal Brugha aside, I can think of no one who could be more disruptive than Austin."[5]

"Perhaps that was the intention." Michael sighed and said, "And to think I named a favourite Blue of mine after him."

"Come again?"

"I named a Blue Terrier after him."

Incredulous, Arthur asked, "You have a *dog*? You named him *Austin*?"

Michael laughed while patting Arthur on the knee and explained, "Sure, I have a dog, but not by that name. When Stack was held at Lewes Prison after the Easter Rising, his number was 224. We were fast friends back then, so I named one of my terriers Convict 224."

"Charming name," Arthur replied drily.

"As is the dog. Sadly, I don't have a place of my own to keep him, so he stays with a friend of mine in town, and I see him when I visit there. He competed at the inaugural meeting of the Dublin Irish Blue Terrier Club in October last year. It was quite an affair. A fellow founding member of the club was there, Sir James MacMahon."

"The Under-Secretary for Ireland was there?" Arthur said incredulously. "Did he see you?"

"Ah, to be sure. It was all very civilized. Mutual respect among admirers of the Blue Terrier, you know."[6]

"What a lark!"

"Ay, but we have Lloyd George, the Pope, and the King to deal with now. What will we say?"

"Try a prayer. Let's get going."

"WELL, HERE WE ALL ARE ONCE AGAIN, GENTLEMEN. GOOD MORNING." Remembering it was exactly noon, Lloyd George corrected himself, "Excuse me, good afternoon." His tone was not as friendly as usual, just merely civil. He asked politely, "I wonder, Mr. Collins, have you any preliminary questions which you would be anxious to raise before we proceed with business?"[7]

Michael was not anxious to raise any complaints at the moment. Sensing Michael was ill at ease, Eamonn Duggan spoke up, "Your military has not entirely evacuated the office in Sligo we spoke of the other day, and they have been harassing the local people with demands for permits of some sort."[8]

Lloyd George looked to the Secretary of War, Worthington-Evans, who assumed responsibility for investigating the matter. "I'll look into it, Mr. Duggan."

Forgoing any further pleasantries, Lloyd George launched into the expected tirade, prefaced by some accusations unforeseen by the Irish. "I am sorry I have to raise two or three questions of the gravest character. I will first deal with an unmistakable proof that whilst the Truce is on in Ireland, advantage is being taken of it to accumulate destructive stores for the purpose of manufacturing bombs and arming your forces."[9]

Collins sat immobile in his seat, wondering to himself, "What the hell?"

Lloyd George went on, "We have been informed that the German police in Hamburg have seized a shipment of weapons destined for Ireland. Closer to home in Wales, arrests have been made in connection with a bomb-making operation in Neath and a store of weapons seized in Cardiff."[10]

Griffith and Collins were caught unawares by these revelations, which in both cases were part of the usual ongoing search for weapons by the I.R.A. that continued without Michael's direct involvement while he was engrossed in the Treaty negotiations in London. Nevertheless, they were infuriated by this embarrassing turn of events but could not show it there at the table. Instead, they each silently scrambled to come up with an adequate response.

Lloyd George then continued with his tirade. "The next matter of which we have to complain is the publication of Mr. de Valera's telegram to His Holiness the Pope. It is challenging, defiant, and, I must say, ill-conditioned in its attitude to the King. It will make our task almost impossible.[11] These attempts at arms smuggling will be responsible for creating a serious uprising of feeling in Parliament, but this telegram is the gravest incident."[12]

However grave the British considered these developments to be, Griffith replied quite dispassionately, "First, with regard to the question of the Truce, and the importation of war-like material which you complain of, my conception is that the Truce does not mean that your military forces should prepare during the period of the Truce, and that we should not. We have done nothing since the Truce which was not being done before the Truce."[13] The logic to this was so deceptively self-evident that it caught the British off-balance since it skirted the fact that the Truce's purpose was to halt what had been occurring before it went into effect.

While they mulled this over, Collins spun another web of twisted logic. "As far as this business in Cardiff goes, the fault lies with the British police force, who took advantage of a condition which did not exist prior to the Truce."

Utterly at a loss as to how this could possibly be true, Lloyd George asked, "In what way?"

"Because our people took less precautions!"[14]

Perhaps because this observation was so preposterous, the flabbergasted British had nothing to offer in response, but Michael wasn't done yet. "And regarding this ship in Hamburg, I refuse to believe it was destined for Ireland. You made similar accusations of a plot back in 1918 involving guns and German submarines. Unfortunately, there was no truth in that."[15]

With all the British thunder dissipated by these bewildering obfuscations, Griffith ploughed ahead, feeling compelled to defend something he personally believed to be ill-advised. "With regard to President de Valera's message, I must demur to the view that it was defiant and insulting. Mr. de Valera only stated public facts. King George's letter refers to troubles in Ireland. The trouble is not a trouble in Ireland, but it is one between Ireland and Great Britain."[16]

Having, with Michael's help, just demolished all the major British debating points of the day, Griffith offered an olive branch. "So far, we have begun by seeing how far we could find points of agreement. If we could reduce our points of disagreement to a small number, we could probably find a means of getting over the main difficulty. Therefore, it is our intention to hand in our written proposals this Monday."[17]

This invitation to continue in a positive vein successfully side-tracked the Prime Minister from his opening parry. Somewhat disoriented for the first time in the discussions, he attempted to recover, "This situation cannot be prolonged. We must know where we are on the main issues on which settlement depends. A formidable document has been put in by Mr. Collins that challenges our whole position with regard to naval defence."[18]

Michael still was in no mood to back down. "I think it safeguards your security."[19]

"Mr. Churchill," Lloyd George responded, "perhaps as Chairman of the Sub-Committee on naval and Air Defence, you would care to respond?"

"Yes, I think I would." Churchill was, in fact, a junior member of the British negotiating team and, as such, had remained remarkably reserved in his participation, but now seized the moment with true Churchillian zeal. "The document in question is of marked ability, but it amounts to a reasoned rejection of every one of our points and to a claim of neutrality for Ireland. We cannot be sure that the Irish would have the power to keep an effective neutrality. We could not guarantee the confluence of trade in an area where submarines were lurking unless we had Queenstown and other Irish ports at our disposal. When our Committee met, I pointed out how the battleship *Audacious* was lost to German mines laid in the Irish Channel in the last war. Our destroyers would have to go out to meet the enemy with a radius of operation reduced by one hundred miles. We have the support of all our naval experts in the view we take. I also pointed out that the concept of neutrality raised a fundamental issue beyond the purview of the Committee, and I informed Mr. Collins that in my view no British Government could entertain it."

Michael now had some experience with Churchill's rhetoric but ignored most of his points and harked back to his own. "Mr. Churchill, do you not agree that if neutrality were a greater safeguard to you than anything else, it would be a greater value to you than your proposals?"

Churchill certainly could be long-winded if not thorough in formulating an argument, but he could also be as tersely dismissive as his friend Birkenhead. Churchill replied, "I do not accept that."

A lengthy discussion ensued regarding the need to protect British ships and shipping, whether a neutral Ireland would be able to provide that security, and even whether Ireland could always be relied upon to be friendly to British needs. Finally, Chamberlain brought the discussion to the question Churchill had touched upon, the constitutional basis of neutrality. "But neutrality means that you would be outside the Empire?"

Gavan Duffy joined in with a somewhat legalistic argument. "Not necessarily. Whatever final status is here agreed upon for Ireland need not be influenced by a neutrality independent of status."

Griffith tried to pick up the pieces. "In his discussions with Mr. de Valera last July, General Smuts championed the concept of Dominion status for Ireland. Dominion status is not our claim, but your offer falls short of it in every way. It is not a question of building a navy, but of denying us the right to build if we wanted to."

Lloyd George saw no problem in this. "We began with each Dominion in this way. We ask you to go through the same process as the Dominions. The memory of the recent war will pass away, but you must allow a few years to pass. We cannot take risks for forty million people."[20]

This was a clever way of informing the Irish that British politics required these restraints to be part of any agreement, but if the Irish would only agree to them now, they would be lifted with the passing of time. Future events would bear this out, but this was expecting a lot of trust on the part of the Irish that day.

Michael's perspective was somewhat different. "In other words, just trust in the better nature of the British people and their government, wait a few years, and all our wishes will come true. Well, is it really that simple?"

At this point, Lloyd George frowned and asked, "If you don't mind, I would like to propose a short adjournment so I might confer with my colleagues."

They retired to Frances Stevenson's office, and Lloyd closed the door behind him. He smiled at Frances and then addressed his colleagues, "Gentlemen, this will not do. After ten days, we have not achieved much progress on the fundamental issues."

Churchill agreed, "I am afraid I must concur. The Truce is at risk."

"And I agree with Winston," Birkenhead said. "I am sure all my colleagues were appalled at Mr. Griffith's notion that the Truce would allow the illegal importation of arms. Simply absurd!"

Churchill shook his head, saying, "And Mr. Collins ascribing blame for the Cardiff affair to the police. The audacity!"

Sir Hamar Greenwood was bellicose as usual, "If it's war they want, we can let them have it."

"Yes, general," Chamberlain sighed, "though we're hardly there yet."

"So where are we, then?" Lloyd George asked but answered himself, "We must have definitive answers on the Crown, the Empire, and defence no later than, say…"

Thomas Jones reminded him, "Mr. Griffith mentioned he would have in hand a document setting forth the Irish counter-proposals by Monday."

"Then let them have until then."

Lloyd George opened the door and ushered everyone back to the Cabinet Room. Before leaving, he gave a wink to Frances, smiled, and joined the others. When everyone had settled in again, he began in a firm but friendly tone, "I understand Mr. Griffith will send us a document with the counter-proposals of the Irish Representatives. I hope we can have them before our next meeting. It is essential that they contain the clear and definite attitude of the Irish Delegation on three points, namely: *One*, allegiance to the Crown; *Two*, the question of whether Ireland is prepared to come freely of her own accord within the fraternity of nations known as the British Empire; *Three*, Whether Ireland is prepared to accept in principle our claim that we must have the necessary facilities to ensure the security of our shores from attack by sea."

He continued, "With regard to Mr. Griffith's claim regarding the accumulation of material for attacks in this country as well as in Ireland, not only on our forces, but on our citizens—I cannot accept that. I regard it as completely outside the Truce and a breach of the Truce, and we will take the necessary action to deal with it. We want to act in the spirit of conciliation. However, nothing is to be gained at the moment by further discussion. Our proposals represent a greater advance than anything ever made before in the whole history of British statesmanship, but we have met with no concession from the Irish side."[21]

———————

"I KNEW THAT DAMN TELEGRAM WOULD MEAN TROUBLE, BUT THIS SHITE about Hamburg and Wales blindsided me." Michael was seething with anger as he discussed the meeting with Arthur on the way back to Hans Place. "I'm going to get to the bottom of this. I sense the hand of Cathal Brugha in this bomb-making business. Just the sort of hare-brained scheme he'd try to pull off."

Arthur seemed surprised Michael would be unaware of such operations and brought up the related matter Lloyd George had raised. "This Hamburg business seems particularly alarming and high-risk. You knew nothing of this?"

"No, not specifically. Gavan Duffy could be behind it, cashing in on his time in Berlin as our ambassador." They soon arrived at Hans Place. "Let's go in and ask."

When they went inside, they found Duffy, Barton, Childers, and MacBride sitting at the kitchen table playing bridge, which they often did to pass the time.[22] Erskine checked his cards and said, "I think Gavan is holding a trick."

Michael stormed over to Duffy and angrily declared, "Up his sleeve, probably. I'll show you a trick or two, Gavan. What's all this about a fucking shipment of arms that's been held up in Germany? Why didn't you tell me about this? I knew nothing about it, but Lloyd George sure as hell did."

Duffy protested, "What shipment? I know nothing about any arms shipment!"

Seán answered, "Gavan's telling the truth, Mick, but I know quite a bit about it since I've continued my Dublin G.H.Q. work buying and importing arms. A load of arms that was supposed to be brought over on our steamer, the *Santa Maria*, has been left sitting on a dock in Hamburg."

"Well, it sure went arseways, didn't it?" Michael exclaimed.

"I can look into it personally, Mick. I have some contacts of my own over there."

"All right, see if you can salvage this mess. You had better leave right away."

As Seán went upstairs to prepare to leave, Arthur asked, "Michael, may I have a word?" They stepped over to the other side of the room. "Seán's just a lad, Mick. Are you sure he's up to it?"

"Ah, sure he is. He was one of our 'littlers,' but he's seventeen now and has experience far beyond his years. Also, he's as bright as they come. He grew up in France, speaks French fluently, and some German, too, I think. If anyone can sort this out, it'll be him."[23]

"I wish Dev were here to sort out his own messes. That damn telegram, and now this looming showdown on Monday. We still have no clear instructions."

"No, we don't. Sometimes I don't know whether we're being instructed by Dublin or confused. The latter, I would say."[24]

Arthur sighed, "That's a sad thought."

Michael paused a moment. "You're right about Dev sorting out his messes. I'll cross over tonight and try to get him to come over here."

There was a sound of the front door opening and closing and Emmet Dalton appeared at the entrance to the kitchen. "Hello, everyone," he said, grinning from ear to ear.

"You look well pleased," Michael snapped. "What the deuce have you been up to?"

"This and that. Could I have a word, Mick?" Emmet replied.

Michael got up to leave and said, "Come along. You can have your word on the way to Euston. I have to take the damn boat train to Dublin again."

Once they were outside Emmet asked, "Wouldn't you rather fly?"

Michael stopped, his jaw went slack, and he whispered, "You mean you got it already?"

Emmet smiled and said, "I've just come from Croydon airfield. Signed, sealed, delivered. It's a beauty. Rolls Royce engine; seats four; and can even be fitted to take off and land on water."[25]

"You can forget about any water landings. Can you see Arthur and me swimming ashore?" He laughed and slapped Emmet on the back, "Well done, lad. Well done!"

EIGHTY

Unrequited Love

SATURDAY, 22 OCTOBER 1921, DUBLIN

"No, MICHAEL, AS I SAID FROM THE OUTSET, WE CANNOT HAVE THE President in the heat of discussion seen as compromising on principle."[1]

"Ah, right, Dev, that's my portfolio."

Michael had taken the overnight train and ferry to Dublin and after checking on things at his office in the Gresham Hotel that morning, went to see de Valera at Mansion House.

De Valera ignored the sarcasm and said plainly, "If you adhere to your instructions, you will acquit yourself well and to the satisfaction of everyone here in Dublin. You have been quite successful in achieving that so far."

"Thanks, but Arthur and I have held them off on the relatively minor points, like observance of the Truce, trade, and finance. Granted, we have some room for compromise on a larger issue like defence, which they take very seriously, but that's as far as it goes. They are expecting a full draft from us this Monday. We need your authority to carry the day when it comes to the Crown and the Empire, not to mention Ulster."

"Once you explain our concept of 'External Association' to them, which we find to our surprise has not yet been presented, you should find the path of argument on Ulster more easily ascertained."

Michael thought to himself that for the leader of a Republic, de

Valera lapsed a little too easily into the royal 'we,' even if he meant it to convey the will of the Dáil and all the people they represented. Without dwelling on the thought, he continued his argument, "But it's a formal written proposal they'll be expecting, not more argument. They want to know once and for all where we stand."

"Then tell them. You have your instructions," de Valera said in a benevolent enough tone.

Despite his difficulty pinning him down to accept what seemed to Michael the most sensible course to take, or perhaps because of it, Michael smiled as something Andy Cope had told him came to mind. De Valera noticed and, his curiosity aroused, asked, "What is it, Michael?"

"Oh, nothing, just something I was told Lloyd George said about you." Michael shook his head, laughed, and said good-naturedly, "He said negotiating with you is like picking up mercury with a fork!" He laughed again. "What do you think of that?"

Because Michael had relayed this potentially insulting remark seemingly without guile but with such good humour de Valera answered, "Well, then, he should have used a spoon."[2]

Michael roared with laughter. "See, Dev, my point exactly. You're the best choice to cross swords with these devils. They'll listen to you."

"They will listen to *you*, and have done. I'm sorry, Michael, it's out of the question." He ended the subject by changing it. "How is Kitty? There are rumours of an imminent announcement."

"None that I know of." They had been seeing so much of each other that most people thought they were engaged or were about to be. Michael deflected all such questions out of respect for Harry Boland, to whom, even at this late date, Kitty still had not given a definitive answer to Harry's marriage proposal.

Michael almost brought up the subject of the Treaty negotiations again when de Valera asked, "Is she in town from Granard?"

Michael gave up arguing by saying, "Yes, we're having dinner and might go to a dance after. Care to join us?"

"No, thank you. Sinéad and I are eating in tonight."

"Saturday night? When was the last time you took her for a spin on the dance floor? You don't want to lose your happy feet, you know."

De Valera laughed, "Some other time."

Michael took his leave and found Tom Cullen in the hallway outside.

"Let's go, Tom."

"How did it go, Mick?"

"Great! Couldn't have gone better. He's going to London Monday, meets with the British all on his own Tuesday, signs the Treaty on Wednesday; we have an independence parade here a day or two later."

"So… it didn't go well at all, then, did it?"

"Not really."

"Sorry, Mick."

They reached the car waiting in front of Mansion House, and Michael opened the door but then pounded his fist on the car's roof in a flash of anger.

"Shite!" he muttered through clenched teeth. They both stood there for a moment, still and silent. Tom was afraid to say anything, but then Michael let it go. He stuck his head in the car and told the driver, "Don't mind me, Pat."

"Not to worry, Mick," he replied. Pat McCrea, the man who steered the Peerless into Mountjoy prison in the attempt to rescue Seán MacEoin, frequently drove for Michael.

"What's to worry about?" Michael decided to turn from bitter irony to outright teasing, knowing that with the weekend home from London, Tom would be grateful for a visit with his bride. "At least I have my trusted bosom friend and bodyguard, young Tom here, to protect me from harm and keep me company the rest of the weekend." He put an arm around his shoulder and pretended to weep, "You know, Tom, if it weren't for bosom friends such as yourself…" His voice faded into a sob.

"Well, sure, Mick." The humour was starting to sink in. "I'll just call Delia and tell her maybe next trip back."

They both laughed and wrestled a little bit before getting into the car, and then they headed over to the Gresham Hotel. They went inside and bounded up the stairs to the office to find Liam Tobin sitting at a desk, reviewing some mail.

"How did it go, Mick?" Liam looked up and asked.

"Hardly worth all the effort coming home, except for those of us with pretty young brides waiting breathlessly to welcome us back," he said with a wink in Tom's direction.

"Oh, give over," came the defensive reply.

"Speaking of the fairer sex, Mick, Kitty called while you were out,"

Liam said. "She said to tell you she'll arrive on the six o'clock train from Longford."

Tom coughed loudly for effect.

Michael laughed, "All right, Tom, off with you now. I'll be taking the ferry tomorrow night. Why don't you stay on another day and, if you could, just look in on Kitty at the Gresham after I leave?"

"Sure, Mick. No problem."

Pat drove Michael over to Amiens Street Station to meet Kitty. Michael waited outside the gate for the train to arrive, pacing back and forth in anticipation of seeing Kitty for the first time since he left for the negotiations in London. When her train pulled into the station and Kitty alighted, she craned her neck until she caught sight of Michael and then waved and ran over to him and into his arms.

"Oh, Michael, it's so good to see you again. It's seemed like ages with you away." He held her close with her head against his chest, and then Kitty exclaimed, "Oh, you have on the striped tie I gave you."

"Did you see it and the other one you gave me in the newspaper photos?"

"Yes, I did. It was like you were sending a secret little signal."

"Yes, our secret code. Come on," Michael said, "the car is over here. You remember Pat?"

"Of course, I do. Hello, Pat."

"Miss Kiernan," he politely answered as he opened the door for her. Pat McCrea may have had excellent manners, but he was more than a mere chauffeur. Besides being a highly skilled driver, he was also a member of the Squad and had dispatched several British agents to an early grave.[3]

"We'll keep your bags in the boot for now, but I'd like to introduce you to some friends you haven't met yet over at Conlon's," he beamed.

"Bill and Mary Conlon? I'd love to meet them!" she said as they all got in the car.

Michael explained, "Mary is still in London, but you'll meet her if you come over there." Then he suggested cheerfully, "If you like, perhaps we could go dancing later?"

"Maybe," she said doubtfully.

"Say, you wrote the other day that you went dancing with some boy in Granard. What's the matter? Did he wear you down and put you off dancing?"

"Oh, he was just a boy, seventeen if he was a day."

"I know. I'm not jealous; just asking." He patted her hand to assure her and then shouted to Pat up front, "What are you waiting for, man? Let's go!"

Cheerfully replying, "Sure, Mick," Pat put the car in gear.

Kitty continued her story, "Well, speaking of that night, there was a grey-haired R.I.C. inspector there who also asked me to dance. He started telling me how he had been in love with my mother and how I reminded him of her. Funny story, isn't it?"[4]

"A sad sort of story, actually," Michael said softly. "The poor aul boy had probably carried that secret within his breast his whole life, and he unburdens himself on the dance floor. He sees a glint of an old flame in a daughter's eye and finally confesses to an unrequited love. No, it's not funny; it's really quite tragic." Michael smiled at Kitty, then looked out the window and said, "He'd probably waited his whole life to tell his story. Maybe he has found peace in having done so at last— poor old bugger. I'm glad he didn't get popped before the Truce. I just hope we all find that kind of peace soon." He looked back at her and said, "I feel so responsible for so much, for so many. Partly, that's why I came back to see the Chief."

Kitty's eyes welled with tears. "I'm sorry, Michael. I know you're under such stress. And here I am prattling on in my letters about dances and dresses and what I had for dinner."

"No, Kit. That's all I want to hear about. Just life. Day-to-day life. Even if we can't trust that our letters don't go unread by British agents."

"I feel so ashamed. You write to me almost every day while you have so much work to do negotiating with Lloyd George, Churchill, and the rest of them, and I sometimes can't find time away from the family shop."

Michael laughed, "Well, at least you admit I am busy. Between going to Mass every morning to light a candle for you, butting heads with Winston, and writing you every day while keeping a full staff of secretaries busy, I hope you realise there's little time for anything else."

Kitty looked at him guiltily and whispered, "I know. I wrote asking you if you had met any nice girls or kissed anybody."[5]

"Silly Kit." He reached over and squeezed her hand.

The car had arrived at Conlon's. "Come on, here we are. Join us, Pat?" Michael asked as they got out.

"Ah sure, Mick, I'll just deal with the car first. See you in a flash, Miss Kiernan."

When they went inside, Billy bellowed out, "Michael, my boy!" With that, a roar of welcome resounded throughout the pub, and people gathered around to shake Michael's hand or pat him on the back. In the past, in deference to Michael's safety, people had remained more circumspect in his presence, but since the Truce, the relaxed atmosphere made for a more open friendliness.

"Hello, Billy. Missing the wife?"

Billy scratched his head for a second and answered, "By God, Michael, I surely do!" Billy turned to Kitty and said, "Now I can take one look into this pretty young woman's eyes, and I know just who she is."

"Well, Billy, I'm sure you're right," Michael admitted. "This is Kitty Kiernan. Kitty, Billy Conlon."

"Well, come along, come along. We'll fix you two up with a fine dinner. Follow me." He turned, looked over his shoulder and said, "Maureen's working tonight. She'll be so glad to see you."

"Oh," said Kitty, "I've been looking forward to meeting her."

Michael beamed with pride as they walked into the pub's back room to make their way upstairs. When Maureen saw him, she came rushing over, but seeing the other woman with him, her usual shyness returned. "Michael, it's so good to see you again." She smiled at him with her head slightly bowed and then extended her hand to Kitty, saying, "You must be Miss Kiernan. *Fáilte.* We've all been looking forward to meeting you."

Kitty felt genuinely welcomed and gave Maureen a kiss saying, "And I have been looking forward to meeting you and all Michael's friends here. I know you all have taken such good care of him."

"Well, everyone, upstairs," Billy said. "I'm buying dinner for these two, something special. What do you say, Maureen?"

"With pleasure."

As they walked up the stairs to the family dining room, Nelly appeared and started jumping up and down with glee. When Michael reached the landing, she leapt into his arms. "Uncle Mick, you're back!" she shouted with joy. After a big hug from Michael and a curtsy to Kitty, Nelly walked them over to their table. "I'll be back in a minute to set your table."

When they were alone waiting for their meal, Kitty said, "The

Conlons are all just as you described them. Lovely people." She paused a moment and then ventured a question, "Are you sure about us? Are you sure what we have will last a lifetime?"

"Kitty, when you ask me these things, in your letters, or like now, in person, I have to wonder, is it you? Are you trying to get out of it? Because I don't want to get out of it."[6]

"No. Michael, it's just that with all the temptation…"

Kitty stopped short as Billy appeared with a bottle of wine. "Here's a little something to go along with the meal." He sat down on a chair facing his two guests. "Mick, it's great to see you. Christ, it's been ages since I've been to London. How's my wife, Mary, doing? Things running smoothly?"

"Like a Swiss watch," he answered with a smile for Kitty.

Billy smiled proudly. "Any time for fun while you're winning us nationhood?" he asked as he started to work on the bottle's cork.

"Yes, Billy. We were just talking about that. Kitty's sister and her new husband were over, and we took in a West End show. I've been around to see my sister, Hannie, and all's well with her. So, it's not all work. I don't know how, but occasionally I do get a chance to catch my breath."

Billy poured out two glasses and rose from his chair, saying, "That's grand." As Maureen came in with plates of food, Billy asked her, "Honey, aren't you and your friends going out dancing tonight?" Before she could answer, he turned to Kitty and asked, "Maybe you two would like to join her?"

"Good idea, Billy. We were thinking about doing just that. Thanks for the wine."

After Billy had poured the wine, Michael smiled and asked Kitty, "What do you say?"

"Oh, not tonight, Michael." She cast her eyes down. "I haven't been feeling all that well."

Maureen put the plates down and said, "Well, if you change your mind, it would be wonderful if you could join us."

After she left the room, Michael asked Kitty, slightly alarmed, "Nothing serious?"

"No, no, but someone mentioned a Dr. Farnan. I thought I might look him up while I'm in town."

"You won't need to. He's a friend of mine. I'll set you up with him."[7]

"Really? That's wonderful, Michael. He is very sought after among the society women in town."

He looked at her with great concern but closed the subject for the time being with one of his favourite pronouncements, "Well, that's that. This looks like the beginning of a great meal."

After their meal, Billy joined them for after-dinner drinks, and so did Pat McCrea, who had remained at the bar with Billy to allow Michael and Kitty some time alone. When it started getting late, they said their goodbyes, and since dancing was not an option that evening, they headed back to the Gresham Hotel. Michael walked Kitty to her room, awkwardly pausing as she opened the door with her room key and turned to face him.

"It was a lovely evening, Michael."

"That it was. So, good night, Kit. My room is upstairs. See you in the morning."

"Good night, Michael."

He turned and walked away but heard her whisper after him, "Michael."

As he turned, she walked across the hall and kissed him on the lips gently, slowly, tenderly. He put his arms around her and held her tightly against him until she pushed away gently and said, "G' night now. Thank you for everything."[8]

EIGHTY-ONE

Some Idea of a President

SUNDAY, 23 OCTOBER 1921, DUBLIN TO GREYSTONES

After Sunday morning Mass, Michael spent the rest of the day preparing for his trip back to England, but by late afternoon he had finished all his work in his Gresham Hotel office and was ready to go. Michael paused at the landing as he and Pat McCrea walked down the stairs to the lobby. "Pat, I'll run over and get Kitty while you get the car."

When Kitty opened her door, Michael grinned and announced proudly, "I've got a special treat for you, Kit. Sunday dinner by the seaside. We can be in Greystones in half an hour."[1]

"That sounds lovely, Michael."

So, they got in the car and headed south to the shore. A little while later they arrived in Greystones and had dinner at the Grand Hotel restaurant with a view of the Irish Sea.

"It's as lovely here as it sounded, Michael."

"Isn't it? I came here almost every week when Dev was in America to check in on his family." He looked around. "Not a bad spot to get away to, eh?"

After their meal, Pat excused himself to ostensibly tend to something in the car while Michael and Kitty had a romantic stroll along the shore.

"Why don't you join me over in London, Kit?"

"Oh, I don't know, Michael, you'll be so busy, I'll just get in the way, and, besides, I have so much to tend to in Granard, getting things back into shape."

"Well, think about it. It would be great to have you over, and no bother, but a boon. May Duggan is keen to have you over, too."

After walking along for a while, Michael checked the time. "Well, Kit, let's get back to the car. I have to meet Liam at the ferry, but after Pat drops me there, he'll take you straight back to the Gresham Hotel. Tom Cullen will look in on you there."

"In that case, Michael, let's say our goodbyes now while we're relatively alone."

They kissed gently and then, holding hands, walked out front to the car.

"All right, Pat, you can get yer noggin' out of the bonnet, like you even know what's in there, and get me over to Dunleary."

MONDAY, 24 OCTOBER 1921, HOLYHEAD AND LONDON

ABOUT THREE HOURS LATER, JUST PAST MIDNIGHT, THE FERRY PULLED into its berth in the port of Holyhead on the Isle of Anglesey in North Wales. There was no rush to make the connecting train to London, but no time to waste. Michael nudged Liam Tobin, who had joined him at Dunleary for the crossing.

"Let's go, Liam," Michael said as he got up and stretched, "That's the Irish Mail across the way."

They gathered their things, disembarked the ferry, and walked along the pier past the clock tower to the train terminus next door. Small lorries with armed guards pulled wagons of the mail from Dublin and loaded it into the mail carriage of the renowned train for delivery that morning in London. Michael and Liam walked down the platform alongside the emerald green and amber coaches with "Irish Mail" emblazoned in gold letters on the sides. Michael checked his ticket, "This is us, Liam. Hop on."

They walked down the aisle to the reserved semi-private sleeper compartment they had booked and slid the door open. Liam whistled, "Pretty posh. I could get used to this."

"Like I keep telling you, stick with me, son; I'll show you the world."

Liam smiled at this and replied, "That reminds me. After Dave Neligan sent us word on contacting him in London, Joe Dolan and I have been meeting him most nights.[2] He's not entirely sure what he's supposed to be doing there. Dave meets daily with an English agent who seems a nice enough fella but never has any further instructions. He just shows him the sights around town, and they go out for meals. He even offered to arrange 'feminine companionship' for Dave, as he put it. You know Dave, straight as an arrow, of course, he turned that part of the tour down!"[3]

Michael laughed, "Straight as an arrow, and wise as an owl not to step into a compromising situation. Keep in touch with him. Maybe something will come of it."

After stowing their bags, they settled in for the night ride back to Euston Station.

"I'm all fagged out, Liam. Don't wake me when we get there. I'll want to have a lie-in for a couple of hours, but don't let me sleep past seven-thirty."[4]

"Sounds fine to me. Good night."

As usual, the train arrived at Euston on time at five-fifty in the morning, but the two men slept in. As a courtesy to overnight passengers in that less hurried era, occupants of the sleeper coaches who required a couple more hours of sleep were left undisturbed. When seven-thirty came around, Michael was already writing a letter to Kitty. After sealing and stamping it, he took a pillow and threw it at Liam's head.

"I'm up, I'm up," Liam protested as he bolted upright and tried to focus his eyes. "What time is it anyhow?"

"Time to get the hell off this train before they send it back to Wales. Up with you."

They made their way back to Cadogan Gardens, where Michael got cleaned up, shaved, put on a fresh set of clothes, and then headed to Hans Place to discuss the day's business with Arthur.

"So, HE WOULDN'T BUDGE, WOULD HE?" ARTHUR ASKED OVER A morning cup of coffee upstairs in his room.

"No, it's just as he told someone before we left. 'We must have scapegoats.'[5] And unfortunately, you and I fit the bill. Point of fact, he wanted to know why we had not brought up 'External Association' yet."

Arthur sighed, "I was afraid that would be the case. So, in lieu of any practical help from Dublin, I've been going over our Treaty draft while you were away and was up quite late last night working on it. A copy for the British will be ready later today, just in time for the meeting."

"Let us have a look," Michael said. Arthur went to a table for the latest draft and handed it to him. Michael perused it for a moment and then read aloud, "We propose that Ireland shall be recognised as a Neutral State, that the British shall recognise Ireland's freedom and integrity..." He stopped there, struck by an idea. "Why not change it from 'Neutral State' to 'Free State?' That would solidify my argument that an Ireland freely choosing to assist England in times of difficulty would be a better friend than one compelled to do so as a subservient colony."[6]

"Or remain neutral if she were to so choose. I go along with that. I'll make the change. We can extol the beauties of External Association as best as we can, but I'll be damned if I'm going to draw silly little circles to get the point across."

"I know, I know," Michael commiserated with him. "Listen, Arthur, one of the reasons we haven't been able to get around to hammering out our proposals, apart from waiting for instructions from Dublin, is that we waste so much damn time in the conferences. If Duffy were less enamoured of the sound of his own voice, we'd do better.[7] Barton does all he can to be obstructive, and Childers is more stubborn than any Irishman I've ever known."

"Yes, and he's English."

"As you are wont to point out."

They both laughed at this, but Michael continued, "I've been thinking, maybe you and I could suggest to Lloyd George smaller gatherings in which we could work more efficiently."

"Not a bad idea. He'd probably like to get rid of some of the blowhards on his team, too."

"Probably, but I'll wager we never free ourselves of Churchill and his bombastic ex-officer jingo."[8]

Arthur laughed, "No, but how should we broach the subject?"

Michael gleamed with a smile. "Duggan's earlier work as liaison officer kept him in regular contact with Andy Cope. I'll have him ask Andy to put in a word with the P.M."[9]

"It's worth a try." Arthur got up from the table and put his hand out to steady himself.

"Ye all right, Arthur?"

"Yes, Michael, I'm all right." He said heavily. "I'm just so tired. I didn't think it would be such a strain. That's why I'm so grateful for all you've taken on. The Finance Committee, Defence, Trade, Truce Observance. It's quite a load on top of the plenary sessions."

"It's nothing, but smaller meetings should be more effective. Just you take care, Arthur. I couldn't do what you're doing."

"Thank you, Mick, but we both know you could." He smiled and said, "But don't worry about me. I'll be fine. Let's have a word with Duggan and then try to get this document polished up and sent to Lloyd George in time for this evening's conference."

"THANK YOU, EVERYONE, FOR ASSEMBLING HERE IN COMMONS ON SUCH short notice," Lloyd George said, welcoming the British team to the emergency meeting he had called to a House of Commons conference room.[10] "I know today's conference is not scheduled to resume until five this evening, but we finally, at long last, received the Irish proposals, and I knew you would all like to review them in advance." He turned to Thomas Jones and gave him a nod.

"Yes, sir," Jones said as he rose to speak. "Due to the late arrival of the document, we do not have copies to circulate, but the Prime Minister and I have taken the liberty of taking note of some key points, and with your indulgence, I will read some of these." There was a series of grunts around the table, so he proceeded. "First, and quite notably, there is this: *If Irish national aspirations are to be reconciled with the British Community of Nations, British statesmanship must keep the fact constantly before its mind, that Ireland is no colony or Dependency but an ancient and spirited Nation.*"

This opening elicited another grunt from Hamar Greenwood. "I don't think I care for the tone of *that.*"

"Nor do I," agreed Churchill. "Might we suspect from its condescending tone that its author has some experience addressing schoolboys?"

Though much of the language was probably Griffith's, everyone around the table appreciated the less-than-oblique reference to de Valera. This inauspicious start to the Irish document left them all mirthless.

Jones nodded to Churchill and went on. "The document refers to Ireland as a Free State," reading the phrase inserted by Collins, "and, let me see, yes, this: *On the one hand, Ireland will consent to adhere for all purposes of common agreed concern to the,* ahem, *the League of Sovereign States associated and known as the British Commonwealth of Nations...*"

"Now there's a mouthful," interjected Greenwood. "Personally, I would prefer simply, *British Empire.*"

"Yes, Sir Hamar, quite so," Jones said politely. "It continues: *On the other, Ireland calls upon Great Britain to renounce all claims to authority over Ireland and Irish affairs.*"[11]

"Rather sweeping denial of the Empire," Worthington-Evans commented.

Churchill was of a different mind but began by agreeing, "This is quite a singular document in that it could not fail to give offence. Yet, despite its haughty, didactic tone, at least it omits any reference to a Republic. Though it is quite unsatisfactory in its present form, it is not a sufficient cause for coercion."[12]

Lloyd George weighed in, "I quite agree with Winston. I think we should do well to press them on the three main points we demanded answers on last week. There has been an interesting development. Griffin and Collins have inquired whether they might speak privately with Mr. Chamberlain and me today. I would welcome the opportunity to speak freely without that gadfly Childers fluttering about."

Most of the men at the table murmured approval and for a moment talked among themselves. Lloyd George leaned over toward Chamberlain and whispered, "And I wouldn't miss the sabre-rattling Greenwood and W-E, either. Frankly, I was about to suggest it myself!"

Chamberlain peered through his monocle over the Prime Minister's shoulder to make sure this had not been heard and then said quietly, "Nor would I, and so was I."

Lloyd George smiled and said, "Good, good."

Chamberlain continued, "I must say, Winston has remained surprisingly restrained in his somewhat junior role."

"Yes, he has, hasn't he?" Lloyd George whispered. "Winston's true value in these proceedings will most probably be realised when they are at their end. Mark my words."

Chamberlain nodded and smiled at Churchill as he turned to join in their conversation. Lloyd George asked him, "So I take it you approve, Winston?"

"Of smaller meetings? Definitely. I find all the other Irish delegates overshadowed by the two leaders." He thought for a moment, "However, I do find Duggan to be a sober, resolute man."[13]

"Yes, and it was Duggan who approached Andy Cope with the proposal. Your powers of perception remain intact, Winston."

"And humbly at your service," he replied, grinning broadly.

"Winston," Lloyd George continued in a soft tone, "I just want you to know that when the time comes, I shall most probably be required to draw upon those powers even further. Whatever transpires at these deliberations, we will need to win the support of Parliament and the British people. Your wit and eloquence will undoubtedly be much needed to carry the day."

Winston's blushed at this frank appraisal, and for once, he found himself at a loss for words, except to mumble, "Yes, sir."

The Prime Minister then addressed everyone in the room. "So, gentlemen, shall we repair to Downing Street? This evening's meeting may very well prove to be pivotal."

MONDAY, 24 OCTOBER 1921, LONDON, SEVENTH SESSION

WHEN THE IRISH DELEGATION ARRIVED AT FIVE O'CLOCK, THEY ALL took their seats, but there was a delay of half an hour before Lloyd George joined them.

"Sorry to keep you waiting, gentlemen, but we just had a visit from the Prince of Wales, who stopped by to say goodbye before his tour of India."[14]

"You don't say? Then no apology required," Michael said with a slight smile.

"Thank you, Mr. Collins," the Prime Minister said and then got right down to business, addressing all the Irish delegates. "Gentlemen, we have received your document but too late for effective consultation with my colleagues. But it is clear we have arrived at a critical stage of the deliberations, and I will accordingly treat this document as you treated ours, Mr. Griffith, and put to you some questions upon it."[15]

"Very well, Prime Minister," he answered.

"Let me see, where is…" Lloyd George scanned over the first couple of pages. "Yes, I have it. *Ireland will consent to adhere for all purposes of agreed common concern.* Does that mean all other conditions being satisfactory, you are prepared to come in freely and voluntarily within the British Empire?"

"Yes," Griffith answered cagily, "we are prepared to be associated."

"Come within in the sense of New Zealand and Canada?" Lloyd George asked.

Hedging again, Griffith replied, "That is not quite our idea of association."

"No? What distinction do you draw then between association and coming inside the Empire?"

"We would accept the Crown as the bond of association."

"Meaning you would adhere as allies?"

"Something more. Permanent allies, not temporary."

That sounded nice, but Lloyd George pressed the issue, "But not as members of the same Empire?"

Arthur replied, "Not as members except that we would be represented on your Imperial council. We would take its decisions on all these matters."

"Now as to 'agreed common concern.' What do you mean by that?"

"War and peace, trade, all the large issues. It is a matter of drafting."

"To put it bluntly, will you be British subjects or foreigners? You must be either one or the other."

"We would share a common, reciprocal citizenship. We would be Irish subjects. We would be British subjects. We would assume that Irishmen in England and Englishmen in Ireland would have the same rights. The position would be the same as at the present. In other words, it would be *status quo*."

"Well," Lloyd George sighed, "I believe we would all like to improve on the *status quo*, but this concept of shared citizenship surely must be unique in international law."

He glanced over to the Lord Chancellor, Birkenhead, who saw an opening for a series of chess-like moves and began, saying, "Not entirely. More than once, either Mr. Griffith or Mr. Collins has dealt with the state of things which would result in time of war. The word 'neutrality' has been used a great deal. You say that a friendly neutrality would be better, but our naval experts advise us that in order to safeguard ourselves, we must have the permitted use of your harbours, but if you are neutral, you cannot give it us. If we require their use, no country would recognise that neutrality." He then summarised, saying, "Would not the essence of common citizenship be that all who enjoy it are at peace or at war together? It is not compatible with neutrality in any form."[16]

There was little to answer this logic, and Griffith had to defer to Birkenhead's expertise. "On a point of international law, I cannot say. You are an authority. In principle, we make no objection to taking those safeguards which are necessary to your security." Finally, with that statement, he had conceded to the British position on naval defence and did so again by repeating, "We agree in principle."

So, Birkenhead sought confirmation of his victory on the point by asking, "In principle, you would agree to afford these facilities? That would entitle other nations with whom we were at war to make you an enemy."

However, Michael tried to have another stab at neutrality by suggesting, "There would be a compensating point. A country refusing to recognise Ireland's neutrality would make Ireland an enemy."

Birkenhead looked Michael square in the eye and delivered the *coup de grace* on neutrality, "If you are prepared to render un-neutral services, is it not a mistake to pin yourselves therefore to a meaningless trophy which angers our people?"

Michael had no answer to this, but Griffith covered for his silence by responding as if they were already in agreement, "If principles are agreed upon, we can get to details and adjust them."

Lloyd George took this as an opportune juncture to consult with his team. "Thank you, Mr. Griffith. I am sorry, but if you would pardon the interruption, I would like to again confer with my colleagues in private. Please excuse us."

When they had gathered together in Miss Stevenson's office as they had the last session, Lloyd George asked his colleagues, "Well, gentlemen, where do we stand?"

Chamberlain looked doubtful, "They contemplate a situation where they would not automatically be at war."

Birkenhead felt his last point had been made effectively enough. "They will give way on that."

Chamberlain did not disagree but voiced another concern, "They seem to avoid allegiance to the Crown."

Lloyd George pointed out, "It might be more useful to explore the ground of agreement reached. Mr. Griffith's answers today do, however, mark a new advance over previous discussions." There was general agreement on this, and he continued, "First of all, they are not to be aliens. Rather, there is to be common and interchangeable citizenship. Secondly, they agree to partake in Imperial conferences on common defence of the coasts, and as a corollary to that, they finally agree to open their ports to us. This is a great advance. True, they did not accept the Crown, preferring the head of their government to be chosen by them."

Birkenhead stressed this last item of dispute. "Some of their answers have shaken me. We must raise the issue of the Crown and make it plain that we cannot possibly have agreement without that."

Churchill said caustically, "They have some idea of a president."

Birkenhead shook his head and said wistfully, "All these men fought for the Crown in the old days."

Churchill echoed this sentiment, noting, "That may be so, but let us not forget who taught them republicanism. The curse of Cromwell lies upon us all still."[17]

Lloyd George smiled upon hearing this old Irish curse that referred to Cromwell's murderous campaign of terror against the Irish in 1649 and responded, "Let us hope their descendants will think of us more kindly than they now do Oliver Cromwell. I think now might be a suitable time for Mr. Chamberlain and me to have our little conclave with their two principals."

Thomas Jones then returned to the Cabinet Room to make the arrangements with his opposite secretary, Erskine Childers. "Excuse me, Mr. Childers. The Prime Minister and Mr. Chamberlain would like to have a private chat with Mr. Griffith and Mr. Collins. If you don't mind, allow me to introduce you and your fellow delegates to the Parliamentary Secretary, Sir Philip Sassoon, who will keep you comfortable in his office while you wait."

Before Childers had a chance to react, Sir Philip entered the

Cabinet room and greeted everyone cheerily. "Good day, gentlemen. Just follow me, if you will," and everyone obligingly did so.

Childers looked inquiringly at Griffith, who nodded, "It's all right, Erskine. Eamonn will explain." Though Eamonn Duggan had initiated this meeting with the help of Andy Cope, as they all filed into Sir Philip's office, he only told his colleagues, as Jones had just re-iterated, that the Prime Minister wanted to meet privately with Griffith and Collins. Duggan just failed to mention that the idea originated with the Irish, Michael Collins in particular, and not the British. Childers, obviously kept in the dark on the circumstances, accepted the situation at face value, as did all the others, not having any real reason to object.

After everyone had left, Griffith and Collins were able to share a moment alone in the Cabinet Room. Arthur said in a low tone, "Michael, I hope you did not think I was contradicting you on your notion of neutrality."

Michael laughed and said, "Not at all. Obviously, this naval business is of such importance to them, so I just wanted them to think we'd be giving up a lot in exchange. Whatever happens years down the road is another story," he said with a wink.

"Very good. Oh, they are coming now."

Lloyd George and Chamberlain re-entered the Cabinet Room and sat down opposite Michael and Griffith, and the Prime Minister began by saying, "Thank you for meeting us on these circumstances. I think we can all agree that we can conduct business more efficiently this way, without so many, shall we say, dissonant voices heard around the table."

No one said anything in response, which was as good as agreeing, so he went on, "Now, Mr. Griffith, where do you stand on the Crown?"

"As representatives of a Republic, we cannot fully accept the Crown, but if we come to an agreement on all other points, I could recommend some form of association."

Furthering this suggestion, Michael asked, "What would this involve?"

Lloyd George answered simply, "The Oath of Allegiance."

Michael tried to finesse the point. "That's a pretty big pill. Cannot we have an oath to the constitution?"

Chamberlain needed more to assuage his critics. "Something less ethereal is required."

Arthur, for the longest time not opposed to *some* sort of association with the Crown, was sometimes accused of being a Royalist. Now he was willing to make concessions on this issue for the sake of preserving a united Ireland. Accordingly, he suggested, "The only way to reconcile Ireland to the Crown is to secure Irish unity. This does not mean a denial of autonomy for Ulster, but Ulster and Ireland cannot be equal."

Michael was of a like mind and said, "Let's formulate proposals and see where we're agreed."

Lloyd George smiled at this and said, "Excellent suggestion, Mr. Collins. I think we've made considerable progress here today. I believe our mutual purposes would be best served by proceeding on this more informal basis for the time being."

Griffith nodded in agreement but was balanced in his response, "Yes, but any perceived progress must be measured against the likelihood of approval by the Dáil. We will naturally keep our colleagues in Dublin apprised of all our proceedings."

"Naturally. As you may have heard, my colleagues in Parliament have been keeping me apprised of their take on our proceedings, and in their infinite wisdom they have awarded my Cabinet and me that unique example of the workings of English parliamentary democracy, a vote of censure."

"Ah, yes, Prime Minister, we are aware of that unfortunate development. Our best wishes are with you."

"I appreciate that, Mr. Griffith. Then you must realise how important it is that I have something of substance to report before the censure vote a week from today."

"We all are under pressure of one sort or another, I'm afraid."

"Well, the sooner we can get this business down on paper in workable language, the better off we all shall be."

"Agreed. Until tomorrow, Mr. Chamberlain, Prime Minister."

When they left the Cabinet Room, Thomas Jones, who had been sitting alone outside, rose and greeted them by saying, "Very good, gentlemen. I'll advise the waiting parties that you have finished. He first went to Frances Stevenson's office, where the British representatives were waiting, knocked, and went in, "Excuse me, Frances, gentlemen, the Prime Minister is free now." He then went to Philip Sassoon's office, where Duggan and the other Irish delegates were waiting, "Excuse me, everyone. Mr. Griffith and Mr. Collins will be leaving shortly."

As the two delegations emerged from their sequestration, they met in the hallway, composing a slightly awkward gathering, but Sir Philip lightened the moment by saying, "Hello, Frances. I hope you've enjoyed your little party as much as I have mine."

All the delegates were mildly amused at this light banter but still somewhat stiffly said goodbye to each other. Once outside, Griffith took Collins by the arm. "Michael, I believe this was, indeed, a decisive meeting. I must hurry back and write a report for Dev in time to make the evening Irish Mail."

Michael nodded in agreement, "Normally, I'd send Seán MacBride, but he's not back yet from Hamburg. I'll send one of the lads over. This way, Dev will have it tomorrow morning."

"And we can have an answer no later than the day after." He said softly, "I think I might not mention the private nature of today's talk. Not just yet," he said with a wink.

"Understood." Michael paused for a moment before they reached the car. "By the way, Arthur, I'm hoping for a rather important delivery from Dublin already."

"Oh?"

"I've been pressing Kitty to come over. Even May Duggan has joined in the effort to convince her. Kit's never been to London, and I think she's a bit skittish about the prospect. If she does come over, I'm hoping with this new routine of smaller conferences, we might have a little more breathing room."

"I wouldn't count on that, but it would be splendid if she could come." He smiled, thinking, and then said, "This may be another pivotal moment, Michael. This shows commitment, from her as well as you. Splendid!"

"Well, thanks," Michael answered a little sheepishly.

As soon as he arrived back at the Cadogan Gardens house, Michael sent Liam to Hans Place to pick up the report Arthur was preparing for de Valera, and from there, he headed to Euston Station for the overnight mail train. After Liam left, Michael, Ned and Emmet had a quiet dinner together. Eventually, Emmet yawned and said, "I'm turning in early. Good night."

"Sleeping better lately?" Michael asked.

"Oh, yes, I am. Thank you for asking."

After a while, Ned said, "Well, that's me. 'Night, Mick."

"I'm staying up for a while. Good night."

However, Michael heard Ned crying out a moment later, "What the hell, Emmet?"

Michael bolted upstairs to find Emmet lying on his bed, reading a book, with the bed tilted at a thirty-degree angle. "Yes, Emmet, what the hell are you doing?"

"Well, Mick, I figured you would come in to bend the legs later on, so to save you the bother, I did it myself." He then leaned forward, reached behind his back, picked up a pillow, and threw it at Michael.[18]

Michael screamed out, "Arghh!" and flung himself at Emmet, and with that, the bed collapsed on the floor with a loud bang. Emmet got up, stood on a rickety chair, and was about to pounce on Michael when the chair gave way under his weight and shattered. Ned grabbed another pillow and proceeded to smother Michael with it, but he broke free and wrestled Ned to the floor and issued the ultimate threat, "Give us a bit of ear!"

"Fuck, Mick! Not the ears!" Ned screamed as Michael attempted to bite him on the ear, but Michael tore into a pillow instead, shredding it and sending feathers flying around the room. At that point, Peggy McIntyre appeared in the doorway to find Michael with the pillow still between his teeth and feathers gracing everyone's shoulders or gently floating to the floor. The three men stood there motionless, staring at Peggy, unsure what form or degree of chastisement was about to befall them.

Peggy stared back, blinked, and said, "Goodnight, boys. Breakfast at seven, as usual." She walked back downstairs smiling, saying softly to herself, "Mary Conlon was right. It eases his mind, bless his soul."

EIGHTY-TWO

If War is the Alternative

WEDNESDAY, 26 OCTOBER 1921, LONDON

MICHAEL AND TOM CULLEN WERE UP EVEN EARLIER THAN USUAL, AND this time not for Mass. They were at the platform entrance at Euston Station, waiting for Kitty's train to arrive from Holyhead. It was nearly five-fifty, and though Kitty would be coming on the same train Michael had taken a few days earlier, she would not be sleeping in as Michael had. Pacing back and forth, Michael continually checked his watch, too anxious to sit and read an early edition newspaper.

"By the way, Tom, thanks for looking in on Kitty at the Gresham Sunday night after Pat dropped me off at Dunleary. Wonderful evening entirely."[1]

"Don't mention it, Mick. Delia and I made a lovely day of it, too."

"What? I don't need to hear about it!"

Tom blushed and blurted, "No, I meant we…"

"Relax, I'm pulling your leg. Arrah, I tease you a lot, Tom, but you've done well there. Delia's a fine girl, and no mistake."

"Thanks, Mick," he mumbled bashfully, barely regaining his composure. "Say, I think that's Kitty's train arriving now."

A few minutes later, as excited as she was, Kitty embraced Michael briefly but, given her shyness, just gave him a peck on the cheek. Still, after weeks and months of courtship, they were breaking new ground that morning.

"Oh, Michael, this is so special, seeing you here." She saw Tom standing off to the side and beckoned him to her. "Come, give us a kiss, young Tom."

"That's all right," Michael protested. "He's had more than enough of that last weekend. Let him save his strength to save me. He is my bodyguard, you know."

"Nonsense," she said and planted a kiss on Tom's cheek, causing him to assume a bright shade of crimson. She turned to Michael again and sighed, "I feel like such a big girl now, meeting my beau in another country."

"I know what you mean. We've had our little trysts before, but meeting on foreign soil seems so, so…"

"Illicit?" Tom offered, earning himself a slap on the ear.

"No, ye muck savage! 'Adult' is the word I was looking for."

"Oh, ay, adult. Sorry, Miss Kitty, I didn't mean anything by it."

They all laughed and headed for a taxi, Michael having let any driver from the house have a lie-in that morning. He pointed out landmarks on the way through the London streets, starting with the great arch at the front of the station.

Kitty remarked, "Oh, of course, I recognise this from all the newspaper photos of Mr. de Valera and then Mr. Griffith arriving to such crowds." They passed Marble Arch at Oxford Street and went down along Hyde Park, then through Knightsbridge on their way to Cadogan Gardens. "It's all so lovely. I had no idea. It's just so lovely."

"I've booked you a room at the Cadogan Hotel.[2] It's a posh hotel on Sloane Street that Oscar Wilde used to stay at, not far from where the lads and I are staying. We'll get you settled in there soon enough, but first, Mary Conlon will have my head if I don't bring you around right away. When she heard you were coming, she made a special trip from the other house to see you."

"Oh, Michael, I can't wait to meet her. Will Peggy McIntyre be there, too?"

"Ay, and they're just as anxious to meet you. They make a formidable pair, the two of them, and you're going to just love them, as they will you."

MARY DROPPED WHAT SHE WAS DOING IN THE KITCHEN AT CADOGAN Square when she heard the front door open and close, wiped her hands on her apron, and told Peggy, "Oh, that'll be Michael with Kitty."

"Oh, my, oh, yes!"

Michael proudly introduced Kitty and then watched with delight as the two women fawned over her.

"Oh, now, is she not the prettiest?"

"We've been so excited to meet you!"

"How was your journey? Not too tired?"

"Come on; we'll fix you a nice cuppa."

"Oh, what a lovely jacket you've on."

Michael followed them all into the kitchen, where Mary announced, "Eddie, say hello to Kitty Kiernan."

Kitty went over and gave Eddie a peck on the cheek, explaining, "We know each other from the Gresham, don't we, Eddie?"

"Heh-heh, hello, Miss Kitty," he responded with uncharacteristic reserve.

Mary nodded and introduced the two secretarial sisters, "This is Alice Lyon, and this is her sister, Ellie."

After more niceties, Peggy instructed Kitty, "Now you just sit yourself down, dear."

Mary added, "Yes, dear, you must be famished. Eddie, just don't stand there. Set her a plate."

Oh, Mary," Kitty said, "Your husband Billy treated us to a wonderful dinner at your place, and your daughters are so charming."

"Well, they didn't get that from their father," Mary countered. "How are you getting on with your hotel restoration in Granard?"

Michael stood there a few moments, superfluous to the little gathering, and cleared his throat, "Ahem! Ladies, if you don't mind?"

"Yes, what is it?"

"I have to get over to the Hans Place house for a meeting."

"Yes, Michael, you run along. We have so much to talk about."

"Whatever you say, Mary. Eddie, if they ever stop talking, take Kitty to her hotel."

"Will do, Mick."

"Kit, if you're free tonight, we'll have a night out, shall we? I mean, if you're not otherwise engaged."

"Pardon? Oh, yes, that would be lovely."

"THE MEETING AT DOWNING STREET A COUPLE OF DAYS AGO WAS gruelling, but I believe we made our case on Ulster fairly plain," Griffith said to all the delegates gathered in the Hans Place dining room. With no planned conference of any kind with the British that day, Arthur was anticipating an answer from de Valera on his report regarding the discussion with Lloyd George on association with the Crown in exchange for guarantees on Ulster.

Seán MacBride came downstairs, smartly dressed as always, but still looking a bit rough from his recent German adventure.

"It's the Hero of Hamburg!" Michael greeted him. "You look like shite, though."

May Duggan suggested, "Perhaps you could do with a cup of coffee?"

"Yes, I could. Cheers, May," he said, accepting a cup.

Arthur shook hands with him and commented, "You take after your boss, don't you, son?"

"Sir?" Seán asked.

"You always dress the part of the young gentlemen."

"Oh, that." Seán shrugged his shoulders. "As Mick says, dress the part, and no one seeks you out."

Michael laughed, "That's right. And you did a superb job for us in Hamburg, sorting out that mess about the arms shipment."

"Yes, Seán," Arthur agreed. "How did you manage that?"

"Well, on a tip from a friend," Seán started to explain, "I went straight to the Hamburg harbourmaster, who turned out to be the same man who helped us run guns back in 1916, so I laid my cards on the table. I told him we had a steamer, the *Santa Maria*, arriving soon and that somewhere on the docks we had a load of guns stored in cases that, unfortunately, the British Secret Service had gotten wind of and would be searching for in the morning. Being no friends of the British, he and the German police looked the other way, and we removed the guns and loaded them onto another ship, leaving empty dummy cases on the dock."

"Good Lord, that's remarkable," Arthur exclaimed. "I'm sorry; go on."

Seán continued, "Then in the middle of the night, the *Santa Maria* pulled up along the other ship, the guns were transferred over, and the *Santa Maria* took off under a full head of steam for Ireland."[3]

"Well, son," Arthur beamed at him, "you did well at a critical time for us. When Lloyd George confronted us with this mess, we were nearly at a loss for words. Which reminds me, I hope we hear back from Dev soon."

He didn't have to wait any longer, for Liam Tobin arrived, just back from Dublin. "Hello. You must be waiting for this," he deadpanned and handed an envelope to Michael.

Michael tore it open, saying as he unfolded the letter, "Let's see what the Chief has to say..." His voice trailed off, and he looked around the table, his face revealing his disappointment.

"Dammit, Mick, what does it say? Read it to us, Mick," came the demands.

"All right, all right, keep your shirts on, but, well, get a load of this." He began to read, "*What is this reference to recognition of the Crown as head of the association? We are all here at one that there can be no question of our asking the Irish people to enter into an arrangement which would make them subject to the Crown, or demand from them allegiance to the King. If war is the alternative,*" he paused here, his face getting redder, "*If war is the alternative, we can only face it, and I think the sooner the other side is made to recognise it, the better.*"

Everyone at the table groaned in disappointment at the tone of this letter, but Arthur was furious. He pounded the table with his fist and shouted, "Damn it, that does it! If the Cabinet does not leave our hands free, I'm going home!"

Michael was even angrier. "There are those in Dublin, Cathal Brugha in particular, who are scheming to lead me into a trap. They would like nothing better than to put me in the wrong. They want me to do their dirty work for them. Well, damn it all, I won't have it! Those Dublinites can come over here and do it themselves."

Eamonn Duggan was next to speak, "I'm afraid I have to agree with Michael and Arthur. This is despicable behaviour. They know damn well some sort of compromise is called for, but they don't dare to admit it."

Even Erskine Childers had to agree. "We must protest. We have come so very far but can go no further with this interference in our powers."

"Well, let's put that in writing," Arthur said, still seething.

May Duggan took the initiative and said, "I'll go and fetch Kathleen." She returned a moment later with Kathleen MacKenna, who took a place at the end of the table while May stood behind her.

Arthur smiled faintly but said in a disheartened voice, "Kathleen, be a dear and take this down."

"Yes, sir." Kathleen flipped open her shorthand notebook, and Arthur began, "*The responsibility, if this interference breaks the very slight possibility there is of settlement, will not and must not rest on the Plenipotentiaries. The instructions they received admittedly laid down the necessity of reference back to Dublin before decisions on major issues but imposed no limits on the fullest freedom of discussion.*"

Everyone discussed the issue of recognition of the Crown and came up with this wording, which Kathleen then read back to them, "*Obviously, any form of association necessitates discussion of recognition in some form or another of the head of the association.*"

"Good," Arthur said. "Now, take this down. *We would very much like the President to come to London if it were possible to do so privately, but we otherwise counsel him not to come unless sent an urgent message.*"[4] He then looked around the table and said, "I think this is something we can agree on unanimously. Will everyone sign this?"

To everyone's surprise, Michael said most vociferously, "Not unless you leave out that bollocks about asking him to come here only if he can do so privately, without fanfare. There's no way he can arrive on the scene without stirring up the world Press, and this gives him a tailor-made excuse for opting out and thereby shirking what should be *his* responsibility. Sorry, Arthur, but I won't sign that. I'll go home first."

In an unusual display of unanimity with Michael, Duffy then said, "If Michael won't sign it, neither will I. I don't want it to look like everyone except Michael is ready to recognise the Crown."

Barton realised the implication of Duffy's statement and agreed, "I won't sign it either, then."

Arthur was losing his patience with everyone but concentrated his efforts on Michael. "Listen, Mick, if you want to register a protest, don't do it by returning home, which would ruin everything. You know better than any of us that there's little chance of Dev coming over here, anyway. Just sign the damn letter and be done with it."[5]

Kathleen finished typing the letter and handed it to Arthur, who looked it over, turned it around and gave it to Michael. Arthur even took his pen out and offered it to Michael with a smile.

"Oh, for fuck's sake, all right." He looked over to May, who had been quietly absorbing the entire discussion, "Excuse me, May."

May said in all seriousness, "Quite understandable, Mick, given the circumstances."

Michael smiled at her and took Arthur's pen. He examined it a moment, turning it around in his fingers, saying, "Nice pen, Arthur," and signed the letter. "There, that's that. Come on, Duffy, Barton, sign the damn thing." And so it was done.

EIGHTY-THREE

A Letter of Assurances

SATURDAY, 29 OCTOBER 1921, LONDON

WITH NO IMMEDIATE APPOINTMENTS AT DOWNING STREET, MICHAEL managed to find some time here and there to take Kitty around town. With half of the British Cabinet out of town for the weekend, Michael thought Saturday would be a safe bet for a night out with Kitty and her sister Helen, who was in London on honeymoon with her husband, Paul McGovern. It would also be an excellent opportunity to introduce his sister Hannie to everyone.

Before that, he planned to take Kitty for some sightseeing and was getting ready that morning, standing before his mirror shaving, when he heard the doorbell ring and the front door slam.

"Hell, who could that be so early?" he mumbled, irritated at any possible interruption of his arrangements.

"I'll get it!" he heard Emmet call out from downstairs.

Michael poked his head into the stairwell and heard Emmet say, "Oh, good morning, Joe. What brings you here?"

Michael shrugged and went about his business.

Joe McGrath, who was in charge of keeping tabs on the household expenses, had come over from Hans Place and was rather upset. "Emmet, I got the bill for that furniture repair, and, I have to say, it beggars one's imagination how to pass this off as 'wear and tear,' as you would have me do. Look at this," he said, handing over the invoice.

Emmet whistled and exclaimed, "My, my! Bed frame, spring mattress, chair, bedside lamp." He looked up, "Was there a broken lamp?"

Joe tapped the table impatiently, "Yes, there was. Damn it, Emmet. This is over fifty quid! I can't just shell out some Petty Cash for an amount like this."

Ned came along and said, "Fifty quid? What cost fifty quid?" He picked up the invoice and said, "You're right, Joe. This is far too serious a matter to slip through Petty Cash. You need to show this to the Minister of Finance."

"Oh, don't I know it, and do I ever dread doing so? Is Mick around?"

"What's all this?" Michael angrily demanded as he entered the room. "Give me that!"

He scanned the document and exclaimed, "This is terrible! We're here to decide the future of Ireland, and we have this sort of carousing going on? Well, it stops right here, right now. Anyone engaging in horseplay in future will have to be sent back to Dublin immediately." He took out his fountain pen, signed the invoice, and handed it back to Joe. "Terrible! Don't ever let me see a bill like this again, Joe."

Joe stammered, "But, Mick, I, I, er, yes, Mick. Say hello to Kitty for me."

Michael finally cracked a smile and said, "You can do so yourself later, Joe. We'll see you at the Politicians' House later."[1]

"READY, KIT, HELEN?" MICHAEL ASKED AS HE CAME DOWN THE STAIRS at Cadogan Gardens and entered the parlour. After a day of sight-seeing and a short rest at her hotel, Kitty sat on a sofa talking with Mary Conlon and Helen.

"My, don't you look handsome!" Helen called out.

"I suppose I do," Michael said matter-of-factly.

Kathleen MacKenna, who had popped over from Hans Place, covered her mouth to stifle a laugh.

Michael squinted at her but looked around and asked, "Say, where's Peggy?"

"Having dinner with May at the other house," Mary answered.

"Ah, then we'll see her over there. Good night, Mary. Don't wait up for us."

Mary stood up, put her hands on her hips, and exclaimed, "Oh, not to worry; I'm going with ye!"

"Ah, Jaysus, Mary; forgive me, of course, you are. Get your coat. The lads will escort you, won't you, fellas?"

"At your service!"Ned Broy and Liam Tobin responded as they reached for their jackets.

"That's better," Mary said, holding back a laugh.

Then she smiled and shook her head as Michael turned back to Kitty and Helen and offered each of them an arm. "Shall we, ladies?"

They each stood up, and Michael escorted them to the door. "You don't mind, do you, Paul?" he asked the groom with a big grin. This was slightly more than a rhetorical question, for when Michael first met the beautiful Kiernan sisters, he was initially attracted to Helen. After it became evident that Paul McGovern would be the successful suitor, Michael found his affections transferred to Kitty, even though she was already being wooed by Harry Boland.

Paul considered these bygone caprices a thing of the past and good-naturedly acquiesced, "Not at all. Do the honours, Mick."

"Fine, then let's go, everyone. I have to see Arthur in Hans Place, so I arranged for Hannie to join us there." They all stepped out into the cool fall evening air.

"Beautiful evening. Shall we walk?" Helen asked. "It's only a few streets."

"That would be lovely," Kitty answered without hesitation.

Michael seemed concerned and asked Kitty, "Are you sure? Are you feeling up to it after the full day we've already had?" He had not forgotten that Kitty had inquired about Dr. Farnan and did not want her to exert herself.

"Oh, yes, Michael, I'll be fine." She then whispered in his ear, "I saw Dr. Farnan in Dublin. All is well." She took hold of Michael's arm, Helen took the other, and the three of them walked down the street together. Paul and Kathleen followed behind, along with Ned and Liam on either side of Mary.

Kathleen looked over her shoulder to Ned and asked, "Did you ever see a man so proud in the company of two such lovely girls?"

"I've seen peacocks with more humility," he grinned back.

"You can see he's very much in love with Kitty," Kathleen sighed as she took Paul's arm.[2]

Paul was confident that his bride Helen felt the same for him and nodded in agreement.

Walking between the two men on their usual bodyguard duty, Mary now sighed, "And London is such a romantic city."

Ned and Liam leaned forward, glared at each other and shrugged their shoulders without saying a word.

They soon crossed the road at Pont Street and went into Hans Place. Joe McGrath happened to be outside leaning on one of Rolls Royces, relaxing with a cigarette.

"Howaya, Mick. Oh, hello, Kitty. So nice to see you here. Hello, everyone."

Michael slapped Joe on the back and smiled, "Hello, Joe. Everything all right?"

"Ah, sure, all is grand, Mick."

Once inside, Michael found his sister Hannie chatting with Peggy McIntyre, who was paying her visit with May Duggan. He took Kitty by the hand and marched her across the room. Hannie looked up to see them coming, but Michael cut her off before she could say anything, "Now Hannie, I hope you're not filling dear Miss McIntyre's head with old stories of our salad days in London."

"Yes, Michael, I have been doing just that, telling her all about your scandalous behaviour at the bank," Hannie shot back while beaming at Kitty.

"Ah, g'way with that. Hannie, please allow me to introduce you to Miss Kitty Kiernan. Kitty, this is my much, much older sister, Hannie."

Hannie grimaced at Michael but took Kitty's hand and held it firmly, "This is a pleasure, my dear Kitty. I've heard so much about you from letters from home, not that my little brother takes the time to write."

"Oh, here we go, then," Michael said with a grimace of his own.

Hannie ignored this and continued, "But Kitty, you are even lovelier than I imagined. I'm so glad we could finally meet."

"Hannie is right, Miss Kiernan," Peggy said. "Your reputation precedes you."

Mary Conlon agreed, adding, "It's been lovely having you here."

Kitty blushed but answered happily, "Oh, thank you so much. I've been so looking forward to seeing everyone here."

May Duggan gave her a hug, "Yes, Kitty, my dear girl, Mary is right. These last few days together have been wonderful. All my letters were not in vain."

Hannie's eyes suddenly filled with tears, and she said, "Oh, look at me. What am I crying for? I suppose I'm so glad to see my little Mick so happy. I think it reminds me how much I miss the family back home. Have you heard from Lena, Michael?" She explained to Kitty, "Our sister Helena is now Sister Mary Celestine. As kids we always called her Lena."

Michael shifted uncomfortably on his feet and said, "Well, yes. I haven't seen her since she left home and joined the convent twenty years ago, but I got a note from her a couple of weeks back."[3]

Hannie had a sudden realisation and wiped the tears from her eyes, "Oh, Mick, I missed your birthday! I'm sorry. Here, give us a kiss."

Michael accepted the kiss but was embarrassed by the fuss until Arthur Griffith and Eamonn Duggan came downstairs and greeted Kitty warmly.

"Excuse me, everyone," Michael said with some relief, "I have to talk to Arthur and Eamonn." They walked into the next room to go over de Valera's reply to the delegation's ultimatum.

"I have de Valera's letter upstairs," Arthur began, "but the first thing he said was, *There can be no question of tying the hands of the plenipotentiaries.* Then he goes on to say a Cabinet decision cannot be made except by the Cabinet as a whole."[4]

"True enough," Michael said, "but what about the Dáil? Don't they have the final word?"

"Precisely, Michael." He just shook his head. "At least he's backed off somewhat from his stubborn posturing."

One of the servant girls came up to Duggan and politely interrupted, "Excuse me, Mr. Duggan, there's a call for you. A Mister Cope."

As Duggan left to take the call, Michael asked, "Andy Cope? What could he want at this hour?"

A few minutes later, Duggan returned to the room, "Excuse me, everyone. I have to go meet Andy and Thomas Jones somewhere in Whitehall."

Michael walked him to the door and asked, "You'll be wanting a car. I'll get Joe McGrath to take you."

"Thanks, Mick."

Michael leaned out the front door and called out. "Joe! Up for a short trip?"

"Sure, Mick!"

A minute later, Michael walked outside with Duggan as Joe started one of the cars.

"Good luck, then. See you later." He waved to Joe, who waved back with a happy, if not relieved, look on his face.

Michael closed the car door and rejoined the others inside when Hannie met him at the front door, clutching her handbag.

"Michael, I wanted to give you these letters that arrived for you."

"Oh, what have you got there?"

She opened her handbag and gave him a couple of envelopes addressed to him in a woman's handwriting. "They're from Lady Lavery, the wife of Sir John, the famous painter."

"Really? She's quite sympathetic to the Republican cause, they say. Then again, her family *is* from Galway."[5]

"And a stunning society beauty, they say as well. Kitty seems a sensitive type, so I thought you might prefer, I mean, that she…"

Michael chuckled, "Whatever you're trying to say, you're absolutely right. Thanks, Hannie. But let's see what the grand lady has to say for herself." He opened one of the letters, skimmed through it and laughed. "Well, well. Her husband wants to do a series of portraits of all the delegates. Arthur and even Dev sat for him when they were here in July. Now she is inviting me over for a sitting. Hmm, we'll see about that."[6] He took his sister by the arm and said, "Come on, let's show this crowd a good time."

Set in a row of houses fronting the River Thames and Victoria Embankment on one side and Whitehall on the other, Number 2 Whitehall Gardens served as the home for the Cabinet and the Imperial Defence Committee. Thomas Jones and Andy Cope thought it might provide a more discreet rendezvous point with Duggan than Downing Street, just a short walk away. A clerk escorted him to a grand room on the second floor, where the Welshman and the Englishman were waiting for him at a large round table in front of an ornately carved statuary marble mantelpiece with a trumeau mirror. Above, a stunning glass chandelier hung from a ceiling adorned with a painted floral wreath. Walking across the room, Duggan glanced at the wall panels decorated in nineteenth-century French style with oil paintings of pastoral scenes. It was a grand display of empire, but he was not intimidated, only curious about the reason for the invitation.[7]

"Welcome, Mr. Duggan," Jones stood up and greeted him, "I'm so glad you could come over on such short notice and on what must be, to some extent, a day of rest."

"No, not to worry. Hello, Andy. Good to see you again."

They then got down to business.

"Mr. Duggan," Jones began, "I'm afraid your reply to our latest document rather dances around the issues."

"I'm sorry?" Duggan replied, not stating but asking.

"Well, in face-to-face discussions, we seem to concur on many of the topics of discussion, but when it comes to getting them down on paper, you seem rather hesitant. I'm afraid Mr. Chamberlain fears you are just playing with us, as he put it."

"I think that may be due to our fear of being caught offering more than we need or are authorised to, for that matter."

Jones shook his head slightly and said, "If our documents are written and read in that spirit, I am afraid there is little prospect for progress. Might we not draw up something together? Perhaps Mr. Griffith could sit down with Mr. Gordon Hewart, the Attorney General, and hammer things out."

"I could certainly ask."

"Good. I have a further, more immediate suggestion. As you know, the Prime Minister is facing a vote of censure on Monday, and he has truly little to show the House for all our efforts to date. However, suppose he were to have a private letter of assurances from Mr. Griffith acknowledging, as has been discussed, allegiance to the Crown, common citizenship, and Imperial Defence. In that case, he could address Parliament with greater confidence."

Duggan said warily, "If such a letter were to be given, there would have to be equally binding assurances that it would not be published. The political damage could be devastating to our delegation."

"Of course."

"I will pass along your suggestions," Duggan replied, adding in a carefully considered tone, "but I think a private meeting with the P.M. and Mr. Griffith and Michael Collins would prove helpful."

Jones said with satisfaction, "Oh, I heartily agree. Very good, then.

I will inquire about making arrangements for tomorrow evening on the P.M.'s return from Chequers."[8]

Duggan got up to leave. "In that case, I'll have a word later this evening with Mr. Griffith and Mr. Collins. Thank you, gentlemen."

EIGHTY-FOUR

A Good Price

F.E. SMITH PATTED HIS LIPS WITH HIS NAPKIN AND LEANED FORWARD TO address his hostess, "Mrs. Churchill, that was a remarkably delicious dinner. We are all in your debt."

"Yes, Clementine," Lloyd George agreed, "simply wonderful."

"Thank you, Lord Birkenhead, Prime Minister, but the debt is owed to our cook. I had little to do with it," Clementine answered.[1]

"Nevertheless," F.E. replied, "the art lies in the presentation, and no princely table has a lovelier hostess presiding."

"I may be prejudiced, but I must agree," Winston joined in.

Clementine rose from the table, professing disdain for all the compliments, as she lapsed into the familiar, "F.E., if you and your friends think you can charm your way into an 'artistic' dessert, you're absolutely correct. Let me see how the kitchen is coming along."

"Please ask Detective Sergeant Thompson if he has gotten his fill," Lloyd George said. "We don't want Scotland Yard's finest getting peck-ish. Not with the leader of the 'murder gang' dropping by."

"Really, Prime Minister, talk like that at the dinner table!" Clementine protested but then smiled sweetly, "but, not to worry, I've already made sure the good sergeant is well looked after."

As Clementine went to look in on the kitchen, Winston smiled after her and then remarked, "She is so desirous of peace and does her best to restrain me."

"Bless her soul on both accounts," F.E. replied.

Winston chuckled at this and said, "She may want to work on Thompson in that regard. He's not too happy about having Michael Collins in the house tonight. He brooks little sympathy for him."

F.E. noted, "I rate the sergeant to be more balanced in his views than my unrelenting Unionist associates in the Conservative party, the Die-Hards. The Prime Minister deals with them tomorrow in Parliament, and I shall have to make peace behind the scenes at the Conservative Party conference in Liverpool in two weeks."

Lloyd George felt a sudden wave of anger and said, "In that regard, I may be more fortunate. I am not going to talk to these worms, but to the country."[2]

"The Die-Hards begrudge us for talking with the Irish, yet it begs explanation as to how a treaty can be negotiated without doing so," Winston said.

"True," F.E. agreed, "but I hope tonight's meeting finds the Irish more talkative on our three demands on allegiance, the Empire, and defence. Without that, the P.M. and I have no rebuttal to our critics."

The phone in the parlour rang, and Clementine's maid Bessie entered shortly. "Phone call for the Prime Minister," she announced with a slight bow of her head.

"I'll take it there and keep my old friend Thompson company. Excuse me, everyone."

Lloyd George went into the parlour and found Thompson finishing his meal with his plate balanced on his knees. Usually, he would have taken his meal in the kitchen, but with the Irish delegates on their way, he was leaving nothing to chance and had chosen a spot between the front door and the dining room. When he saw the Prime Minister, he started to get up, but Lloyd George waved him back down, "Don't let me disturb you, Thompson. Very good to see you," he added in recognition of the two years Thompson had served as his bodyguard during and after the Great War. "Please, do sit down. Delicious dinner tonight."

"Yes, sir. Thank you. Good to see you again, too, sir," Thompson replied.[3]

"Always a pleasure, detective sergeant. Excuse me." He took the telephone receiver from Bessie, saying, "Thank you, my dear," and spoke into the set, "Hello?"

"Good evening, sir. Jones here. I hope I'm not disturbing dinner."

"Not at all, T.J., just finishing. Everything all right? Please tell me the Irish are still coming."

"Oh, yes. They will be there at 10 p.m." Then for the sake of privacy, he continued in Welsh, saying, "However, if I may, I think I should suggest a private talk between you and Mr. Griffith before a general discussion with everyone there."

"Oh?"

"Yes. I believe both Mr. Collins and Mr. Griffith harbour a great deal of distrust for Mr. Churchill and Lord Birkenhead, and accordingly, Mr. Griffith would prefer to meet alone with you first."[4]

Lloyd George smiled at Thompson and, out of politeness to him, answered discreetly in English, "Yes, well, I'm glad you told me. Excellent suggestion. Anything else, T.J.?"

"No, I think that covers it."

"Then it's settled. Thank you, Thomas. Goodbye."

After coffee and dessert had been served, Winston took out his pocket watch. He was about to announce the time when the doorbell rang. "Ah, then. Our guests have arrived on time. This should be an interesting evening. Let's retire to the parlour."

On their way into the parlour, Lloyd George took Churchill by the elbow and said softly, "Winston, I wonder if you wouldn't mind if I had a private word with Griffith before we all meet. Perhaps you and F.E. could entertain Collins for a while in your study."

"Entertain him? Shall I sing him a few songs?"

"Whatever you think best. I trust your judgment."

As they gathered in the parlour, Thompson stood up and went to the entrance to observe the arriving Irish. He checked the gun in his jacket and nodded to the parlourmaid to open the door.

OUTSIDE ON THE TOP STEP TO CHURCHILL'S SUSSEX SQUARE HOME, Michael Collins looked around at all the Secret Service agents milling about.[5] Tom Cullen and Liam Tobin were leaning against their car parked at the pavement and gestured to Michael, who nodded back and said only half-jokingly, "Arthur, there's enough firepower out here for a small war."

Arthur turned around and said, "Maybe so, but the big guns are waiting inside. Either way, I'm not fussed."

"Nor I, but imagine this, Arthur. Here we are, a couple of alumni of the British prison system at Winston Bloody Churchill's doorstep for a late evening chat."

"Arthur sighed, "Yes, strange how life takes you from one improbable happenstance to the next."

The door opened, and the parlourmaid looked out warily.

Arthur reassured her, "Good evening, my dear. Arthur Griffith and Michael Collins to see Mr. Churchill."

"Yes, sir."

They took off their hats, stepped inside, and found Thompson facing them with a blank stare. Michael could sense the loathing held in restraint, but in that blank stare saw something of his own sentiments and sensed an odd kinship. No one was in any mood for shaking hands, and protocol still forbade it, but Michael disarmed Thompson, figuratively at least, by returning the cold stare with a friendly enough nod and a smile. "Howaya, mate?"

They stood there a moment, facing each other face to face, and Thompson could not help but crack a smile. "Good evening. Right this way, gentlemen."

Winston and Clementine observed this exchange from across the room, and Winston whispered to his wife, "Thank God Thompson let him pass unmolested. We could have been at war in the morning."

"Winston, shush!"

They stepped forward to greet their guests, and Winston greeted them warmly, "Good evening, gentlemen. Allow me to introduce my wife, Clementine. Dear, this is Arthur Griffith, and this is Michael Collins."

"Good evening, gentlemen. I have been very much looking forward to making your acquaintance and welcoming you into our home." She offered her hand, not restrained by political protocol herself, if not, in fact, disdainful of it.

Holding his hat over his heart with his left hand, Arthur extended his right hand and took Clementine's with a deep bow. "It is an honour to meet you, ma'am. Thank you for inviting us into your home."

Michael followed suit, saying, "*Rath Dé ort*," and then translated the venerable Irish expression for her, "The grace of God be with you."

She smiled her thanks and replied, "And also with you." She turned to her husband, "Winston, take good care of our guests. I'll be inside if you need me."

"Yes, dear, but just a moment, please." Winston said to Michael, "Mr. Collins, if I may, perhaps you would like to join Lord Birkenhead and me in the study? I believe the Prime Minister wanted to have a little chat first with Mr. Griffith."

Michael looked over to Arthur, who nodded reassuringly that he would be fine with this arrangement. Michael shrugged his shoulders in assent, and then Churchill replied, "Fine, now Clementine, could you please show the Prime Minister and Mr. Griffith to the upstairs sitting room?"

"Yes, of course, dear. I'll look in on the children, too."

So, Michael and Birkenhead followed Churchill into his study while Clementine showed Lloyd George and Griffith the way upstairs. "If you need anything, gentlemen, just give a call, and the maid will assist you. There's a bottle of sherry on the small table. Please help yourselves."

"Thank you, Clementine," Lloyd George answered. "We just might."

Arthur bowed, "Thank you, Mrs. Churchill."

Once they were alone, Lloyd George smiled, looked around and said, "Now, where is that sherry? Ah, here we are. Shall we, Mr. Griffith?"

"No, thank you."

"Are you sure? I do think I will."

Arthur relaxed a little and said as he stepped forward, "Very well, then."

As he poured out two glasses, Lloyd George began his argument for the evening with a compliment, "I am glad you have agreed to meet this evening, Mr. Griffith. I perceive you to be a man of your word, and as such, I have been anxious to hear from you in private your true feelings and assessment of our negotiations, free from the extraneous pressures of all the other delegates, some of whom seem to hold differing opinions as to how to proceed."

"Thank you, but all our delegates have the same goal."

"Do they? I wonder if they realise the precarious position our Government finds itself in. All is teetering on the brink over Ireland, and the Government may fall tomorrow. The premise of my speech in Parliament will be peace or war with Ireland. Even if we prevail tomorrow, in two weeks' time, we face a comparable situation at the Conservative Party conference in Liverpool. Now, Mr. Griffith, I was under the impression that you and I had reached some accord, but your written statements have ignored the core issues upon which we must stand. If you can promise me tonight that you can give me your personal assurances on the three main points, the Crown, the Empire, and defence, I will have the strength of conviction, both yours and mine, to go down to smite the Die-Hards in Commons tomorrow and defeat this motion of censure."

"In return for assurances on Ulster? We must have that in return."

"Mr. Griffith, if I get your assurances on those three points, we would fight on the Ulster matter to secure essential unity. I could carry a Six-County Northern Parliament subordinate to an All-Ireland Parliament in Dublin."

"And you think Ulster's Prime Minister, Sir James Craig, would acquiesce to this?"

'I would prevail upon him to do just that. He could keep his Belfast Parliament as long as it recognised the supremacy of the one in Dublin."

"We hear in Ireland that Craig has boasted that he could not care a fig for whatever arrangement we arrive at, that, as he reportedly put it, he was prepared to 'sit on Ulster like a rock.'" Arthur put his glass down, leaned forward and asked, "If this were so, what remedy would you seek?"

Lloyd George walked over to the table, picked up the decanter of sherry and was about to pour himself another glass, but then sighed and put the decanter back down. He walked back to Arthur, stood before him, and said solemnly, "We would try to carry a plan for a new boundary. If I do not survive this vote of censure tomorrow, I will not be around to seek any such remedy. That is why I need your word on these assurances to strengthen my position."[6]

Arthur answered warily, "Again, it comes down to the specific language."

Lloyd George smiled, "In anticipation of that, our venerable Mr. Jones has begun working up a possible draft.[7] As you know, he has put considerable effort into accommodating both sides in his behind-the-scenes discussions."

"Yes, he is an honourable man and well respected by everyone on our side. I'll consider any suggestions he has to offer in accord with what we have discussed."

The Prime Minister said nothing, but looked back in expectation.

Arthur looked Lloyd George in the eye. After a long pause, he said, "Very well, then. I give you my word."

Lloyd George returned his gaze and said solemnly, "You have given me your word. You now have mine."

They stood there a moment in silence until Arthur said, "I think I'll have another sherry, if you don't mind."

"Yes, I think I shall join you."

They had barely sipped their sherries when there was the sound of an angry, raised voice from downstairs. Arthur frowned, "Oh dear, that sounds like Mick. Perhaps we should join them downstairs?"

"Yes, perhaps we should. He's a rather stormy young man, isn't he? Quite an open, honest demeanour, in that he's apparently never afraid to let you know how he feels."

"It's one of his more endearing qualities and springs from a seemingly inexhaustible source of energy and wit."

"Before we join them, allow me to thank you, Mr. Griffith. You have made my task tomorrow somewhat more palatable."

"Yes, as you have made mine."

They went to the door, opened it, and heard peals of laughter from the study downstairs. "Evidently, it was just a passing storm," Lloyd George commented. "But let's go and see."

While Griffith and Lloyd George were upstairs, the conversation down in the study had started amicably enough. When Clementine mentioned that she would look in on the children, Michael recalled that he had read in the papers that Marigold had died a couple of months earlier. He knew that the pain would have been fresh and wondered if he should say anything, but as a guest in Winston's home, he felt it would be appropriate to say something. He was about to do so when Winston picked up a bottle in an offer for a drink.

"No, thank you, sir, but please go ahead."

"No? Perhaps a little later." He put the decanter back on its serving tray, causing F.E. to frown in disappointment.

Michael cleared his throat and said softly, "Mrs. Churchill is very kind. I heard of your recent loss. I am deeply sorry for both of you."[8]

Winston murmured, "Thank you, Mr. Collins. Clemmie will be touched as am I to hear you say so. Our daughter was just shy of three years of age, and the loss makes us treasure the other children all the more, but still, the heart aches." He looked to F.E. for support. "And this followed the passing of my mother. It has been a difficult year so far."

As Winston spoke, F.E. scrutinized Michael with a piercing gaze, impressed by his solicitous demeanour. He then consoled his friend, saying, "Yes, Winston, you have had much to endure as of late. It has been a difficult time for many families. Even more reason to endeavour to achieve a lasting peace between our two peoples."

Michael seized on this statement, saying, "That is the crux of the matter for all Irishmen. Ireland *is* a nation. Every Irishman feels this in his heart. This is not a theory. It *is* there."

Rather than arguing the point of nationhood, F.E. brought up a related matter. "In conference the other day Mr. Griffith spoke of a common, reciprocal citizenship. With such an arrangement, where would the King come in?"

"Oh!" Michael exclaimed with a dismissive wave of his arm, "we'll find room for the King."[9]

F.E. said in a deadpan monotone, "Oh, how very generous of you. I'm sure His Majesty will be much relieved to hear of your good intentions."

On hearing this banter, Winston regained his stride, laughed a little and said, "I think we might need something a little more reassuring to pass along to the King, not to mention the British public at large, but all in good time, I hope." He then brought up the current situation looming the next day. "Much depends on tomorrow's vote, and much of that depends on what we can all agree to this evening. If this Government falls, Bonar Law will most likely succeed as Prime Minister."

Birkenhead explained, "As you know, he has long opposed Home Rule, and Ulster would welcome him."

"And Ulster will fight," Michael quipped.

Churchill defended himself, saying, "I had to face down that cry from one of my constituents at a speech I gave in Dundee before the war when Lloyd George and I were trying to push through the Home Rule Bill. I informed the gentleman that that is a slogan from which every street bully with a brickbat and every crazy fanatic fumbling with a pistol may draw inspiration."[10]

Michael laughed and said, "I had not heard of that. No disrespect, but what would your father have said if he had?"

"I'd rather not venture a guess, but a few months later, despite numerous death threats, I travelled to Belfast to deliver a speech in defence of Home Rule."

Birkenhead added, "And Clemmie accompanied him, brave woman."

"Yes, she thought her presence might damper tempers, but the local citizenry would have none of it. Along the way, four infantry battalions, thirty-five hundred troops, guarded our route from Belfast Station to our hotel. Even this was not enough to shield us from attacks on our car, and the mood was so ugly we had to change venues from Ulster Hall to a park in a Catholic neighbourhood in the pouring rain."

Michael nodded and said, "Yes, I remember reading about this."

"Then perhaps you can forgive me for quoting again from one of my own speeches, but that day I told the crowd that the reverence which I feel for my father's memory, and the care with which I have studied his public life, make me quite content to leave others to judge how far there is continuity or discontinuity between his work and any I have tried to do. I finished telling them if Ulster would fight for the honour of Ireland, for reconciliation of races and forgiveness of ancient wrongs, for the consolidation of the Empire, then indeed Ulster will fight, and Ulster will be right."

"What was the reaction?" Michael asked, not entirely convinced.

"Very good, in fact, but then that was in a Catholic area. However, on our return to port at Larne, we were pelted with rotten fish as we mounted the gangplank to our ship."[11]

"I'll say this. It took nerve to go there."

"I read your speech in Armagh. Rather brave on your part, I thought."

Birkenhead then said, "Getting back to Bonar Law. A few months earlier, he resigned from the Coalition due to health reasons, and his position as Conservative leader is now held by Chamberlain. However, Law has lately recovered enough to begin manoeuvring behind the scenes toward a possible attempt to unseat Lloyd George himself."

Winston concluded, saying, "If that were to occur, it would fairly well guarantee renewed war in Ireland."

Michael took this as a veiled threat and responded, "If so, it would be a war you would never finish fighting."

F.E. intervened, "Come now, Mr. Collins, you cannot wish for that. You surely could not want to resume a life on the run in your own country, living under the constant threat of capture or worse."

"No," Michael answered and turned to Winston, "but there was a time not so long ago when you must have wanted it pretty badly." Suddenly, Michael shouted angrily, "You hunted me day and night! You put a price on my head!"

Winston remained calm and said with a twinkle in his eye, "Did we? Wait a minute. You are not the only one." He went over to the wall, took down a framed "Wanted" poster issued by the Boers after Winston's escape from prison, and handed it to Michael.

As Michael looked the poster over, F.E. leaned over his shoulder and read it out loud, "*Winston Churchill, Escaped Prisoner, Wanted Dead or Alive. £25 reward.*"

Winston began rocking on his heels and said, "At any rate, Mr. Collins, your head fetched a good price—£5,000. Look at me—£25, dead or alive. How would you like that?"[12]

In a flash, Michael's anger dissolved into wit. "Don't feel bad. Prices have gone up since your day, Mr. Churchill."[13]

Winston veritably exploded in laughter, but Michael wasn't finished. "Even so, that was a lot of money back then."

F.E. struggled to contain himself, but not Michael. His head shot back, and he let out one of his high-pitched yelps, and finally F.E. succumbed. The three were still laughing when Lloyd George and Arthur joined them.

"Everything all right in here?" Lloyd George asked. "We're not at war again, are we?"

"Very nearly diverted, I should say," F.E. said.

"We may have done the same upstairs," Lloyd George answered.

"In that case," Winston said, "perhaps we might all do well with a drink." He went to a cabinet and withdrew a bottle of some very special, very old brandy.

"I don't know, Mr. Churchill," Arthur said hesitantly. "I'm afraid we already helped ourselves to your sherry."

"Splendid," he answered, "but a sip of this, and you'll forget the sherry. Mr. Collins, I insist." Winston poured out small glasses for everyone and proposed a toast. "To peace and reconciliation."

"I can drink to that," Michael rejoined, "for surely it would be a discredit to us all if after coming together in conference we did not manage to agree."[14]

As there was no arguing with Winston's toast or Michael's rejoinder, everyone repeated, "To peace and reconciliation," and took a sip.

"Mr. Churchill," Arthur said, savouring his brandy, "this may be quite simply the best cognac I have ever tasted."

"Naturally," Birkenhead said dryly. "Winston is a man of simple tastes. He is always prepared to put up with the best of everything."[15]

EIGHTY-FIVE

To Negotiate With Murderers

MONDAY, 31 OCTOBER 1921, LONDON

THE PUBLIC GALLERY IN THE HOUSE OF COMMONS WAS PACKED FOR the Irish policy debate and the ensuing vote of censure. Downstairs the benches were filled with boisterous M.P.s shouting at each other from across the aisle as Colonel Gretton, the Conservative member who had raised the resolution for censure, accused Lloyd George of perfidy.

"The Prime Minister has spoken often of the 'murder gang' in Ireland. It is with the representatives of that gang that the Government are now negotiating."

Upstairs three Irish spectators, Tom Cullen, Alice Lyons, and May Duggan, were utterly captivated. Looking across the open space to the side gallery, Tom recognised someone. "Look, Alice, there's Lord Fitz-Alan, the Lord Lieutenant of Ireland."[1]

Unsurprisingly, members of the Opposition shouted their support of Gretton, *"Hear, hear!"*

Encouraged, the Tory continued, *"The country has never before suffered such humiliation."*

Tom raised his voice, declaring, "I'll wager FitzAlan has no argument with that."

"Probably not. The Archbishop of Canterbury is over there, too," Alice said. "I wonder how he would vote if he could."

Equally predictably, government backbenchers howled their disapproval.

"Order, order." The Speaker of the House banged his gavel repeatedly. *"We must have order."*

"It was good of Thomas Jones to get us tickets," May commented.

"Well, *someone* from our delegation should be here," Alice replied as she took out a small notebook.

"Mick should've been the one to come. You know how he likes a bit of theatre," Tom replied. "Mr. Duggan, too."

"I think they'd have got their money's worth," May replied.

Tom grinned, "I thought these tickets were gratis."

"Oh, shush! The Prime Minister is about to speak."

Lloyd George rose to answer, approached the table separating the Government from the Opposition, and placed his portfolio on his side's dispatch box, one of the two from which all frontbenchers traditionally spoke.

"We have been charged with going against our pledge not to negotiate with murderers. I would like to remind the right honourable member that not one of the members of the Irish delegation has been legally convicted of murder."[2]

Another member rose to ask accusatorily, *"What about Michael Collins?"*

The Irish observers just looked at one another in amazement. Lloyd George responded.

"He has not been convicted, and under British law every man until he is convicted of a crime is regarded as innocent. This is one of the elementary principles of English law, and I am rather surprised to hear this question raised in this House."

"He's splitting hairs on that one," Tom whispered to Alice. "But Mick would be so pleased to hear the P.M. rise to defend him in Commons."

Lloyd George continued. *"It might be necessary to make an appeal to the country to make sacrifices to stamp out disorder in Ireland. If it has to be done, and the people of this country are convinced it must be done, it can be done, and it will be done."*[3] There was a roar of cheers at this defiant stance, but he qualified his bluster as he continued. *"Before you do that you must convince the people of this country that there is no alternative. You must convince the Empire, and we must convince ourselves. Before that the Government must be given the chance to negotiate, inasmuch as the fate of the Empire is concerned, to bring an end to an age-long feud. However, I feel compelled to warn this body that this island, a country which raised six or seven millions of men to fight for the liberties of Europe, is still quite equal to defending its own safety and maintaining its own honour."*

"They raised six or seven million soldiers? That's twice the population of all of Ireland! I wonder if he realises the Volunteers never numbered more than four thousand."[4]

"Tom, be quiet!"

"It is a ridiculous notion that the Government should come to the House of Commons during the progress of negotiations to obtain consent to detailed proposals. No pact can be entered into without the ultimate consent of Parliament. I am not asking the House of Commons to face anything which someone at this box might not ask it to face, perhaps in a few days."

Alice looked at Tom and whispered, "You realise by 'someone at this box' he means there could be a new Prime Minister in a few days."

"Yes, he is sticking his neck out."

"We are fighting for the security of the Empire, for the honour of Britain, for freedom and right, and we have done everything in our power to secure peace. If concessions can be made which will bring an honourable peace which will strengthen the Empire, then we will hazard all on the possibility of achieving that peace."

His entire speech lasted about an hour, after which he summed up his defence against censure.

"The decision tonight may be a fateful one in the history of the Empire. It may be—who knows?—that it may be written in the annals of this Parliament that on this day the House of Commons equipped the Government, whose life depends upon its will, with a new authority to enter upon a peace which brought an accession of strength to this great Empire by bringing to its side a gifted and a gallant people, who for centuries have been at feud, by removing from the path of Empire the peril that always beset it in the hour of our deepest perplexity, and by adding that chaplet to the renown which this Empire has won throughout the world as the one Empire that has found the wisdom and the way of transfusing freedom into power."

The chamber exploded into a roar of cheers, and there was little doubt about how the voting would go. The Speaker of the House called out, "Division! Clear the lobbies!" The division bells rang throughout Parliament and the surrounding area, signalling to any M.P.s who may have slipped out for a pint in a local pub that they had eight minutes to rush back to the House—not that anyone needed such inducement on such a crucial vote that night. The division proceeded as the members passed out of the chamber into either the "Ayes" or the "Noes" lobby. The tellers counted the M.P.s as they left the respective lobbies, and the tally showed the censure was soundly defeated by an overwhelming majority of ten to one.

Alice, May, and Tom left, much relieved, and headed to Hans

Place, where Michael and Arthur were waiting. In the cab back, Alice looked over the shorthand notes she had scribbled down of some of the essential points in the speech. "You know, Tom, 'transfusing freedom into power' sounded pretty earnest to my ear."

"Ay, mine, as well. What was strange was hearing Mick accused by name of murder and witnessing the Prime Minister rising to defend him. I never thought I'd see that. Wait until Mick hears of it."

"Yes," May agreed. "It was quite a performance."

THEY WERE ALL FEELING OPTIMISTIC, IF NOT ELATED. IT WAS QUITE late, after eleven in the evening, when they arrived back at Hans Place, but everyone was waiting for them in the dining room for news on the vote of censure. When they came through the front door, Liam Tobin exclaimed, "They're back!"

Michael squeezed Kitty's hand, sprang to his feet, and asked anxiously, "So, how did it go?"

"Well, there's good news, and there's bad news," Tom said teasingly.

"Come on, man, spit it out! What happened?" Michael shot back anxiously.

Kitty came over and squeezed his arm, "Michael, there's no need for that. Let him speak."

"Yes, Mick," May added, "you should be well pleased."

"Well, then, Tom? Go on," Michael said.

Tom started to explain, "The good news is that you won't be meeting Bonar Law anytime soon. Lloyd George crushed the Die-Hards by almost four hundred votes."

Michael grinned and said, "I'm so happy for him. And the bad news?"

Tom said sardonically, "Apparently, in the eyes of some M.P.s, you are a wanted murderer." He halted as he saw Kitty's face blanch and Michael's eyes squint narrowly at him.

"What the blazes is that supposed to mean?" Michael demanded.

"One of the Die-Hards dragged out the old complaint about having to negotiate with the 'murder gang' and mentioned you in particular, but Lloyd George came to your defence, proclaiming innocence until being found guilty." He realised that his attempt at humour was falling flat but tried to smooth things over. "It was pretty amazing seeing the Prime Minister defending you so eloquently from the box in the House of Commons, citing traditions of English law. As Alice and I said to each other, it was quite a show."

After listening quietly, Emmet Dalton turned to Kitty, "Don't pay any mind, Kit. It's all just bluster."

May held her hand and said, "Emmet's right. It was just a bit of political theatre."

"Thank you, yes, I'm sure you're both right," she replied unconvincingly.

For a change in mood, May then enquired after Kitty's sister, "How is Maud? I certainly hope I'll be able to see her again by Christmas. Come to think of it, so would Gearoid O'Sullivan, from what I gather."

Michael interrupted to come to the defence of his friend, referring to him by his nickname, "I think George can speak for himself."

Kitty smiled, saying, "She's fine, and I think she's hoping to see you and George by then, too." These polite pleasantries were a thinly-veiled attempt to conceal a budding romance.

Alice also thought it best to steer the conversation away from any mention of Michael at the debate. "I took some notes for you, for the delegation, that is," she said, looking around the room. "I'll tell you all about it, but it's been a long evening, and I could use a bite to eat."

May, Alice, and Tom were served plates of leftovers from dinner and took turns explaining how events had unfolded that evening.

Arthur surmised that the next day could prove busy. "Mick, I think we had better plan on visiting Downing Street privately again in the morning. And you still have a meeting with the Truce Committee in the afternoon, don't you?"

"That I do. And Kitty leaves for Dublin tomorrow. Oh, and speak of the devil. Kitty, I've asked George to meet you at Dunleary."[5]

Kitty replied, "Oh, thank you. That will be lovely."

"So then, I think we'll call it a night."

Everyone expressed their dismay on learning that Kitty would be leaving them, and she shook hands with or kissed just about everyone in the room. "Thank you, everyone. It was such great fun being here with all of you. Thank you, all, for being so nice when you were all so busy. I'll never forget it."

Tom had sensed the disquiet in Kitty's reaction to his story earlier and said apologetically, "Kitty, I hope I didn't upset you with that talk about Mick in Parliament."

"No, not at all," she answered sweetly. "It sounds like it was an exciting evening."

Michael appreciated Tom's concern and clapped him on the back. "Thanks, Tom, and you, too, Alice. You did a fine job this evening. Shall we all go back to Cadogan Gardens together? Let's go, Kit. We could walk unless you'd prefer to take a car."

"No, some fresh air and another evening walk would be nice. Good night, May, everyone."

Realising this would be Michael and Kitty's last night together in London, Liam and Emmet led the way at some distance while Tom and Alice trailed behind.

They strolled through the dark in silence until Michael said softly, "You know, we need to start thinking of a date."

Kitty smiled and said, "To announce our engagement? Oh, that would be nice."

"Let's talk it over at Christmas after all this business has settled down."

"I'd like that, Michael."

A few quiet moments later Michael asked, "Are you sure Tom didn't upset you, Kit?" He put his arm around her and explained, "People are always going to talk about me that way."

"Well, it was a bit of a shock. I mean, calling you a murderer in the House of Commons! I have to be honest; I don't like it one bit," she admitted with tears in her eyes. "I don't see how you just take it in stride. Doesn't it upset you?"

"I can't let every little thing said or written about me get to me. It would just wear me down," he explained. "Don't let it get to you. All that matters is how we feel about each other, not what the outside world says of us, right?"

"I suppose so," Kitty sighed.

This tentative reply sparked a swift response from Michael. "What do you mean, you suppose?"

"I don't know, Michael. I sometimes wonder if we can ever sustain what we have under such pressure. One day you're accused from the floor of the House of Commons of being a murderer; the next day, you meet with the Prime Minister. When I'm home in Granard minding the store, you'll still be here with a busy social life in glamorous London. I wonder if we can keep it together like this."

Michael looked behind them to make sure everyone was still out of earshot. "Not that line again! What are you trying to say?"

Kitty looked at him in alarm and answered, "Don't be vexed with me if I say even now that you are free to think it over and think differently if you wish."[6]

"Blast, woman! Did I ever say so?" Michael exclaimed, losing his patience.

"No need to curse," she cried and took out a handkerchief to wipe away her tears. They walked along in silence again until they reached Cadogan Gardens. Everyone gathered in front of the house to say goodbye to Kitty before going inside. Michael then walked her to her hotel with Tom and Liam following them as discreetly as possible.

When they reached the Cadogan Hotel, Michael followed her to the hotel desk, where she asked for the key to her room.

"I'm sorry, Kit," Michael said gently. "You know how difficult my task here is, and you know me, I always visit my nastiness on my best friends.[7] I'm sorry."

"I'm sorry, too, Michael." She got up on her toes and kissed him good night, her eyes welling with tears. "See me off in the morning?"

"Sure. Till the morning." He stood there a moment in silence before adding, "Unless…"

Sometime later, outside by the hotel entrance, Tom looked up and down Sloane Street, checked his watch, and said, "Er, Liam, maybe we can call it a night?"

Liam concurred, "No, here comes Mick. He's looking spry, isn't he?"

EIGHTY-SIX

All the Ends Thou Aim'st At

TUESDAY, 1 NOVEMBER 1921, LONDON

THOMAS JONES HEARD VOICES IN THE HALL OUTSIDE THE CABINET room, so he poked his head into Frances Stevenson's office to tell her, "It sounds like the Truce Committee is finished for the day, Miss Stevenson. I'll prepare the room for the Cabinet meeting."

"Oh, yes, it's nearly five. I'll remind the Prime Minister."

"By the way, Frances, is Mr. Duggan still about?"

"I believe he just stepped outside."

"Oh, good, thank you."

Jones went into the hall where Sir Hamar Greenwood and Sir Nevil Macready were making their way out. He joined them, saying, "Well, gentlemen, I hope all goes well."

Macready looked over Jones' shoulder to see if he could get a glimpse of Frances and answered, "Yes, things are progressing quite well."

They all reached the front door, and Macready and Greenwood donned their hats.

"Good night, Mr. Jones."

"Yes, good night, T.J."

"Good evening, gentlemen."

Macready and Greenwood stepped outside, where Eamonn Duggan was chatting and having a cigarette with Ned Broy. Though he had heard that Broy was attached to the Irish delegation, Macready was nonetheless startled to run into him.

Broy smiled and said, "Good evening, general."

Nonplussed, Macready answered gruffly, "Broy, heard you were here." He paused for an awkward moment before simply saying, "Good night."

Broy stifled a laugh but said to Duggan as they watched the two generals walk down the lane, "I suppose he just misses me too much to say."

"Yes, Ned. That must be it." They both laughed heartily.

Jones, who had been quietly observing this reunion at the door, cleared his throat. "Excuse me, Mr. Duggan, might I have a word?"

"Certainly; what is it?"

Jones glanced at Broy.

"That's all right, Mr. Jones. This is Ned Broy, one of our most trusted agents."

Ned stepped forward and shook hands with Jones, saying as he did, "As well as one of General Macready's."[1]

Jones smiled uncertainly at Ned and said slowly, "I see." He reached into his breast pocket, produced an envelope, and asked, "In that case, could you relay this letter to Mr. Griffith for me?" He handed it over, adding, "Please tell him that I hope he finds it of some use. Pleasure meeting you, Mr. Broy."

"The pleasure was all mine."

After Jones went back inside, Ned looked around and asked, "Where's Mick?"

"Still in there somewhere. He should be out soon."

When Jones returned to the Cabinet room, he was surprised to find Michael lingering at a glass-enclosed bookcase by the entrance to the room. Michael looked up and just smiled a hello.

"Mr. Collins. I didn't realise you were still here."

As he approached, he noticed Michael was more subdued than usual, perhaps even sombre, so he thought a little historical background on the room might offer an agreeable distraction. "These cases hold books written by or about past Prime Ministers."

Michael stooped down to get a closer look. "Hmm. *Cromwell's Letters and Speeches*. Does the current P.M. feel the need to refer to this one from time to time?"[2]

Jones laughed and said, "I should think not, unless he needed a reference on how *not* to deal with the Irish."

Michael replied ruefully, "No, on second thought, he seems quite capable of dealing with Irishmen without having to refer to a manual."

Jones expressed some concern at Michael's tone. "You seem a trifle disconsolate, if you'll pardon my saying so, Mr. Collins."

Michael turned from the bookcase and answered, "I wouldn't go so far as to say that, but I came away somewhat disappointed and, well, flat, from this morning's meeting with the P.M. I thought that after our meeting at Churchill's home and then last night's vote, there would be more momentum, perhaps more of a sign of commitment to our requirements on Ulster, especially when we have done our share to meet you midstream on most of the essential issues."

"Personally, I think I can assure you that the Prime Minister *is* committed to what are now common goals. The key now is how the North will respond, and he will do all in his power to convince Craig to accept your agreements. However, Mr. Collins, I have every reason to believe that if his hopes and expectations fall short, the P. M. would rather resign than start a war of re-conquest in Ireland."[3]

"Really? He would go that far? Resignation would not be an option for me. I would have no choice but to fight. Regardless of Mr. Lloyd George's intentions or those of whoever might succeed him, for us it would be like facing Cromwell all over again." Michael tapped the bookcase and said, "This reminds me of a line from Shakespeare regarding Oliver's much earlier distant relation, Thomas: *Cromwell, I charge thee, fling away ambition.*"

"*By that sin fell the angels*," Jones answered. "Cardinal Wolsey in *Henry VIII.*"

"Yes, lines I learned when I was a lad of, oh, let's see, I was all of seventeen taking classes at King's College."[4] He rubbed the back of his head, sighed, and said, "I have no ambition for war."

"No, none of us wants renewed war. Surely there's some solace to be had in that." Jones looked at the clock over the mantelpiece.

Michael realised that the Cabinet Secretary had chores to address other than keeping him company and said, "I'm sorry, I'm sure you have things to do this evening."

"That's all right. By the way, I think you realise why the letter of assurances from Mr. Griffith is so important. I just asked Mr. Duggan to pass along a letter to Mr. Griffith with some thoughts on the subject."

"Oh? I'll make sure he gets it. Well, it was nice talking to you."

"It was my pleasure, Mr. Collins." He hesitated, thinking a moment, and then asked, "You reminded me of something. Do you mind waiting a minute?"

"No, not at all."

Soon Jones returned with a large book, holding a place in it with his forefinger. He opened it and said, "As I was saying, you reminded me of something. It's from the same speech by Cardinal Wolsey:

> *Be just, and fear not:*
> *Let all the ends thou aim'st at be thy country's,*
> *Thy God's, and truth's; then if thou fall'st,*
> *O Cromwell,*
> *Thou fall'st a blessed martyr!"*

Michael smiled, "Yes, good advice for Thomas that Oliver should have heeded, sound advice for us all, but don't worry about me. I don't intend to be anybody's damn martyr."[5]

Jones laughed and replied, "Glad to hear it. Well, it's been a hectic week already. Please try to get some rest, and give my regards to Mr. Griffith."

"Thank you; I will. Good night."

Once outside on Downing Street, Michael found his fellow Truce Committee member Eamonn Duggan waiting with Ned Broy. "Everything all right, Mick?" Duggan asked.

"Yes, sure, Eamonn. Thanks for waiting. Barton left already?"

"About ten minutes ago."

Ned said matter-of-factly, "My old boss General Macready is just after leaving with Hamar Greenwood."

Duggan smiled and said, "Yes, Ned and Neville had a very touching reunion."

"Did they? Sorry I missed that."

Ned rubbed his eye and said, "Yes, I'll admit it brought a tear."

Michael replied, "Dear, dear. We had better get back. I have to talk to Arthur about that damn letter of assurances."

Duggan pulled Jones' letter from his pocket. "A little guidance on that, perhaps, from Mr. Jones."

"Yes, he mentioned it. Better him than Cromwell."

"Cromwell?"

"Oh, it's nothing. I'll bet there will be a real punch-up when the others hear of this letter."

WHEN THEY RETURNED TO HANS PLACE, NED WENT STRAIGHT TO THE kitchen, from which Arthur emerged, anxious to talk with Michael. Duggan put a finger to his lips and nodded to the dining room, which was empty at the time, and the three of them retired there.

"How was the Truce Committee meeting?" Arthur asked.

"Not bad. No better or worse than our meeting with the P.M. this morning," Michael said in a desultory tone. Realizing how he must have sounded, he tried to be more upbeat as he continued, "I had a nice chat with Jones, though. He's all right."

Duggan whispered, "Speaking of Mr. Jones, he gave me this for you to look over," and handed Arthur the envelope.

"Thank you, Eamonn," Arthur said as he started to open the envelope, but he paused and looked at Michael. "You seem down, Michael, and I know the stresses you are under, but these things will take their own time." He tapped the envelope with his fingers and was tempted to open it but instead asked, "Something else bothering you?"

"No, it's nothing. Well, except..." He stopped short, glanced at Duggan, but then went on, "The thing is, Kitty and I had a bit of a row last night, though we made up in the end."

"She's a great girl but a sensitive girl, so you'll have to learn to go easy with her. I'm sure she's both proud of you and fearful for you. I saw her face when Tom Cullen mentioned you being called a murderer by that gack in Parliament. It has to be hard on her to hear you spoken of in that way, not to mention the possibility of reprisals against your person." He paused and smiled, saying, "Still, have you not noticed Tom tends to put his foot in it from time to time?"

"Ay, you've noticed that, too, have you? With the constant risk of some nutter taking a poke at me, I hardly ever go anywhere in this town without one of the boys." He amended this by saying, "Not that Ned or the rest of them would let me."

"That's certainly sensible enough. Now, let's see what Mr. Jones has to say." He opened the envelope and showed its contents to Michael and Duggan. Jones had handwritten at the head of the letter, *Draft of private letter of assurance which I suggested to Mr. Duggan that Arthur Griffith might give to the Prime Minister. T.J.*[6] Arthur then pulled an envelope from his jacket. "I've been working on my version. Let's sit down and go through this together."

After the three men talked it over, Arthur said, "Now, Mick, Eamonn, it's essential that this be seen as my letter, and mine alone. If it ever came out that this was based on a draft suggested by an Englishman or, as it happens, a Welshman, there would be hell to pay, and everything would fall apart. I don't want any accusations thrown at either of you, especially you, Mick, from the likes of Cathal back home."

Michael protested, "I agree with it; I'm not afraid to put my name to it."

"No, you are going to be around a lot longer than I, and you won't need the political baggage this sort of document carries." He sighed, "As for me, it doesn't really matter."

Michael was now concerned for Arthur, considering the implications of this last remark, but found himself at a loss for words.

"So, Mick, I'll carry the argument tonight. Knowing I have your support will be enough, as you will have mine when the time comes. Same goes for you, Eamonn."

Mary Conlon entered the dining room bearing a stack of dinner plates, followed by Ned Broy and Liam Tobin gingerly carrying trays of glasses. "Just put those down on the sideboard. Thank you. Sorry to interrupt, gentlemen," Mary announced as she started setting the table, "but I'm going to have to throw you fellows out. We've got a big dinner on tonight, earlier than usual, in case you've forgotten."

"Really?" Michael asked and continued facetiously, "We were just getting ready to go out to grab a bite at the local chipper."

"Fine. *You* won't be missed, now, shoo!" Mary said with a twinkle in her eye but then paused, sighed, and remarked, "Isn't it romantic? Young Kevin O'Higgins and his bride over here for their honeymoon."

"There seems to be a surfeit of young love wafting about lately," Arthur deadpanned.

"Yes," Mary nodded. "Billy and I spent our honeymoon here, as well. Oh, it was so lovely…" She paused, still holding half a stack of plates, as the men just stared back in wonderment.

Michael interrupted the reverie, saying wistfully, "And Billy being such a strapping, handsome lad back in the day."

Ned nudged Liam and murmured, "Not to mention what a romantic city London is."

Eamonn stifled a laugh as Mary slammed the remaining plates down on the table and barked, "G'wan with ye, then. Stop lounging around when there's work here to be done." She turned and stormed off back into the kitchen.

BEFORE DINNER, ROBERT BARTON WAS TALKING WITH ARTHUR IN THE parlour. "By the way, Bob, I'd like to discuss with you and the rest of the team a letter the Prime Minister has requested from me."

"Oh, really? What would that entail?"

Gavan Duffy and Erskine Childers were nearby and joined them, and Duffy asked, "What's this about, Arthur?"

Suddenly feeling cornered, Arthur tried to deflect questions for the time being, "Nothing. It can wait until after dinner."

Duffy, however, pushed, saying calmly, "If you have it on you, could I just have a glance?"

"Well, all right," Arthur relented, reached into his pocket, and handed the letter over.

As the lawyer for what had openly developed into the opposing side loyal to de Valera, Duffy responded with indignation, "This letter undermines everything we have stated in previous memoranda and ignores all instructions from Dublin."

Michael saw the group talking, and judging from Duffy's reaction, knew trouble was brewing and came over just as Arthur protested, "It does nothing of the kind."

"Whatever it is, it can wait, fellows," Michael said, attempting to intervene in the looming argument. "Let's not spoil the evening. Come along; here are the bride and groom."

"Oh, very well."

A sumptuous dinner attended by all the residents of Cadogan Gardens and those there in Hans Place followed, but, unfortunately, conversation among the delegates was subdued and strained, though the women made up for it, chatting amiably. Kevin O'Higgins noticed the stilted atmosphere but smiled across the table at his wife, who was seated between Mary Conlon and May Duggan, talking merrily with them. Before dessert was served, Michael stood and, clinking his glass with a spoon, proposed a toast. "Here's a toast to the eminent *Teachta* for Dublin, Mr. Kevin O'Higgins, and his lovely bride, Brigid:

> *May you be poor in misfortune,*
> *Rich in blessings,*
> *Slow to make enemies,*
> *Quick to make friends,*

At this point, everyone at the table joined in, finally, with enthusiastic unison.

> *But rich or poor, quick or slow,*
> *May you know nothing but*
> *Happiness from this day forward."*

Brigid was beaming with joy, and Kevin rose to thank everyone. "Brigid and I are so happy and so honoured to be here with you all tonight. We never expected to be feted like this. Thank you, from the bottom of our hearts. And may God look over you and guide you in all you do. God bless Ireland!"

"God bless Ireland!"

Michael checked his watch and nodded as Joe McGrath came in from outside. "Joe, is their car ready?"

"Ay, their carriage awaits."

"Fine. Now, that's enough blessings for now. If you're going to make your West End show, you'd better get a move on and hop into Joe's Rolls Royce."

Brigid went over to Michael and kissed him on the cheek. "Thank you so much for the dinner, Mick, and, good heavens, box seats at the show! My head is spinning."

After receiving another kiss, Michael blushed and said, "Now, now, save that for your groom. On with you, now. Enjoy the show!"[7]

After they left, the room fell silent except for some awkward small talk. After a short spell, Michael stood and said, "We need a few minutes to discuss a new development. Let's adjourn to the parlour."

Soon the expected argument resumed.

Duffy repeated his complaint. "This letter undermines everything we have stated in previous memoranda and ignores all instructions from Dublin."

Childers agreed, "It caves in to the British on the Empire and allegiance to the Crown."

Griffith repeated his earlier protest, "It does nothing of the kind."

Duffy disagreed, "It most certainly does. You speak of, how did you put it?" he asked. He motioned for the letter, which he took from Arthur and proceeded to quote from, *"free partnership of Ireland with the British Commonwealth, the formula to be arrived at later,* which sounds to my ear suspiciously more like a dominion than the Republic that we are all sworn to uphold. Furthermore, you go much further on the Crown than any of us have discussed to this point, and you say, what was it, *recognition of the Crown,* the formula," he repeated mockingly, *"to be arrived at in a similar discussion at a later stage."*[8] He tossed the letter indignantly down onto the table. "What do you want, Arthur, a president or a king?"

Griffith was incensed. "If you mean to impugn my loyalty to a free Ireland, you are treading on dangerous ground. Wake up, Gavan. This letter is as close as we'll ever get the British to buy into the Chief's idea of External Association."

However, Barton maintained, "Arthur, this letter goes further than either we or the Cabinet at home have been prepared to go."[9]

Duffy argued, taking it one step further than he should have, "You have no right, no authority to speak on behalf of us all, but this letter is worse than that. It is a personal letter from you to the Prime Minister of England, as if you possessed the sole authority to conduct these negotiations. It is an affront to the entire team, not to mention our colleagues in Dublin, and undermines the legitimacy of the delegates besides yourself."

Arthur had heard enough. He slammed his fist on the table. Just then, from inside the kitchen came the sound of a plate shattering on the floor. Arthur turned his head toward the kitchen, paused and then rose and leaned across the table, shouting, "Damn you, Duffy, and your legalistic pettifogging piffle. I *am* the leader of this delegation, and *if* the Prime Minister wants to have a private talk with me the night before he faces a vote of censure and possible removal from office, I'll damn well do so if I think it will advance our case. And *if* I think it appropriate to put into writing something I have given him my word on, I'll damn well do that, too. If I had been unwilling to give him my private assurances, our next meeting at Downing Street would have been not with Lloyd George but with Bonar Law. No, I take that back, there would have been no meeting at all, and we'd be back in Dublin empty-handed by the end of the week, bracing ourselves for war. Now, *if* you have any problem accepting this fact, you can damn well clear out and get the next boat to Dublin. And when you do, you can tell our *colleagues*," he said sarcastically, "that I am operating with the full authority as the chief plenipotentiary here. If they don't like any of the practical steps I take to achieve a settlement, when the time comes, they can vote it down in the Dáil." He then turned his wrath on Childers and said through clenched teeth, "As secretary to this delegation, *Mister* Childers, please try to restrain yourself from offering your interpretation of the events you are here merely to record. If I require your opinion, I will ask for it. And if I hear of any secret communications between you and Dublin, you had better watch your back, for I'll break it and your prissy, feckin' neck."

Michael and Duggan remained stonily silent through all these exchanges. Arthur then slammed his fist again on the table. "Do I make myself clear, everyone? If you're looking for another war, you can damn well vote for one in the Dáil, but don't expect me to partake in it. Good night."[10]

He stormed out of the room but did not go directly upstairs. He walked over to the kitchen and poked his head in, and found Mary nursing a cup of tea at the table. She looked up nervously.

Arthur tried to soothe her nerves, "Sorry for all the commotion, Mrs. Conlon. Have a good night."

"Yes, sir, and thank you," she responded somewhat coolly. "And a good night to you."

EIGHTY-SEVEN

British Pharmacopoeia

WEDNESDAY, 2 NOVEMBER 1921, LONDON

DESPITE THE PREVIOUS NIGHT'S FRACTIOUS ENDING, ARTHUR GRIFFITH slept soundly and rose early the next morning in Hans Place. There was a knock at his bedroom door, and he walked over and opened it a crack to find Michael standing in the hallway with a cup of coffee in hand.

"G' morning, Arthur."

"Howaya, Mick?" came the cheery reply. "What brings you here so early?"

"Oh, just thought I'd let Alice Lyons try the morning coffee over here. She and Eddie walked over with me."

Arthur crooked his head to one side.

"Don't worry; Tom came with us, too."

"Good. And what else?"

"What else? Well, we all thought you might need some protection of your own after that late-night brawl." Michael looked down at the floor of the doorway. "What's that you have there?" Michael asked, pointing to an envelope.

"Hello, what's this?" Arthur stooped down and picked up the letter. "Well, my, my. It's a note from Duffy."

"What does our *colleague* Gavan have to say for himself, then?" Michael asked, echoing Arthur's sarcasm from the night before.

Arthur stood there a moment reading the one-page letter and then sighed, "Perhaps I was a bit too hard on the man last night." He handed the letter to Michael.

"Hmm, let me see."

Arthur took Michael by the elbow and said, "Maybe this can all be sorted out over some of that coffee. Let's go downstairs."

Eddie was standing by the stove, nervously observing Mary as she darted about the kitchen. She did not pause when she saw Michael and Arthur, but she said rather less warmly than usual, "Good morning to you. I'll be with you in a moment."

Gavan Duffy and Eamonn Duggan were already seated at the kitchen table, nursing their cups in stony silence while Alice was at the cupboard, helping May Duggan put some dishes away. May looked over her shoulder, shook her head, and sighed.

Arthur was the first to try to break the ice, "Morning, Gavan."

"Arthur," came a cautious reply.

"Listen, Gavan, about last night."

"Sorry, Arthur. I hope my letter explains how I feel."

"Yes, well, it's a good start. Let's talk it over a bit."

Mary emitted an audible sigh of relief, smiled, and put a plate of hot toast down on the table. "Oh, that's better. I don't mind telling you I don't like to hear you all shouting and yelling at each other. And I don't abide by that kind of language. No, I surely do not."

May sighed again, this time with a smile on her face.

"Yes, Mrs. Conlon," Arthur answered respectfully. "I do apologize. We do tend to get all caught up in the moment." He turned to Duffy as Michael sat down at the table with them. "Let's see what we have here." He started re-reading Duffy's letter.

Duffy spoke as Arthur was reading. "Well, for one thing, if that letter you promised Lloyd George gets out, we'll all be held responsible. So, we should all have some say about what goes into it and try to agree as best we can."

"I understand. Where should we begin?"

"Take the Crown," Duffy began. "Instead of agreeing to *recognition of the Crown, the formula to be arrived at in a similar discussion at a later stage,* why not change it to *a* recognition? That little indefinite article makes it less definite, would you not agree?"

"Yes, I can go along with that," Arthur replied. "What do you think, Michael?"

"Ay, Gavan makes a good point there." Michael looked over to Alice. "You'll want to get your notepad. It looks like we have some work for you."

Just then, Erskine Childers and Robert Barton joined them, so now the entire delegation had gathered there in the kitchen. Feeling much encouraged, Duffy welcomed them in, saying, "Good morning, gentlemen. Arthur and I were just continuing our discussion from last night. Have a seat." Childers looked uncertainly at Arthur, who smiled thinly at him, but any remaining tension was broken as Eddie picked up the coffee pot from the stove and cheerily announced, "This'll get the day off on the right foot."

As Alice joined them at the kitchen table, Duffy continued. "Well, as I was about to say, in a similar vein, rather than *the formula to be arrived at a later stage,* which is quite open-ended and could lead to all sorts of mayhem, why not try to define it somewhat now? I thought something like *recognition of the Crown as head of the proposed Association of Free States* would be appropriate. Since you mentioned Dev's concept of External Association last night, why not insert it here with this language?"[1]

Michael looked over to Duggan, "You're the lawyer, Eamonn. Sound good to you?"

"Yes, at this point, they would probably be glad to hear us even mention the Crown."

Everyone laughed at this, but Eddie, who was still standing at the edge of the table brandishing the pot of coffee, chimed in, "Excuse me, Mr. Duffy, but I think you left out your indefinite article. Didn't you mean to say, *a recognition of the Crown?*"

Alice stopped writing on her pad and mumbled, "Oh, dear!"

Everyone else fell silent, turned around, and stared at Eddie. They all held their breath, except for Michael, who got up, walked around to where Eddie was standing, and calmly said, "Eddie, put the coffee pot down."

"Why's that, Mick?"

"Just put the pot down."

"I think I'd rather not, if it's all the same, Mick."

"And why would that be, Eddie?"

Eddie shifted his weight from one foot to the other, looked up to the ceiling as if in deep contemplation, and then smiled and said, nodding his head like a student who thinks he has the answer to a question in an oral quiz, "Because you'll box my ears?"

Everyone burst out laughing, Michael included, who squeezed Eddie's cheek and said, "Stop acting the maggot and just pour the coffee, with that gob of yours screwed shut!"

In this lighter atmosphere, Barton felt encouraged to say something. "Arthur, if you are going to write to the Prime Minister, it's best that you do so on behalf of all of us. We need to show a united front, with full engagement of the entire delegation."

Arthur answered, "Yes, Gavan said just that right before you came in. Ay, that's what is needed, a show of unity."

That may have sounded reassuring enough, but in truth, Michael and Duggan were not prepared to abandon the sub-committee arrangement that had been working so well with the British since they had embarked on this tack. However, Michael answered simply, "Absolutely right, Gavan. We wouldn't have it any other way."

"No, of course not," Arthur agreed.

Michael checked his watch. "Well, Birkenhead is expecting Arthur and me at his chambers in Lords this morning to go over this letter. Alice, as soon as you can get it typed up, we had better get going."

"Right away, Mick."

Arthur said to them all gathered there, "Whatever finagling over this letter they pull on us, I won't sign it until we have all seen it and had a chance to discuss it."

Smiles around the table indicated satisfaction at this assurance, so Michael and Arthur soon left for Westminster.

12.00 NOON, WEDNESDAY, 2 NOVEMBER 1921, HOUSE OF LORDS

"RIGHT THIS WAY, GENTLEMAN. IF YOU'LL BE SO KIND AS TO follow me."

Michael and Arthur followed the elderly Doorkeeper, walking down the wood-panelled corridors of the House of Lords.[2] Doorkeepers ran messages for the Peers and were generally responsible for maintaining order and security in the Chamber. Michael whispered as they passed a long row of portraits of Peers of the Realm, "Jaysus, Arthur. And Bob Barton thought the Cabinet Room was impressive. He'd shit his cacks if he could see these digs."

"Yes, Downing Street is imposing. This is majestic."

"Downright intimidating, you mean," Michael added, and then quipped, "But I'll warrant that's the point."

The Doorkeeper may not have actually heard this banter but was used to the general reaction and turned and smiled politely over his shoulder. A moment later they arrived at Birkenhead's chambers.

"Mr. Griffith and Mr. Collins to see the Lord Chancellor," the Doorkeeper announced to the secretary at the desk in the anteroom.

They were immediately brought into Birkenhead's inner office, and he stood up to welcome his guests. "Please have a seat, gentlemen. I'm glad you could come. Tea? No? Well, let's get down to business. Do you have your letter with you?"

"Yes, I have it right here," Arthur answered, handing the letter across the desk.

Birkenhead sat back in his chair and read it over. "Excellent, Mr. Griffith. Now, if I might make a suggestion or two."

"I rather thought you might," Arthur answered with a smile.

"And I rather thought you might think I would, as well," he said, smiling first at Arthur and then at Michael. "At the threat of possibly being tediously repetitive, may I remind you that our position as a coalition government is a bit tenuous? Having successfully survived a vote of censure, we still must face a similar scenario at the Conservative Party conference coming soon in Liverpool. If the Conservatives were to withdraw support from the Coalition, it would collapse. The P.M.'s mention of your assurances might not hold up under Tory scrutiny if we don't have something more concrete in hand. And then, of course, there's Sir James Craig to convince. Your letter is fine, as far as it goes. Now, as for a suggestion. Where you mention *a free partnership with the British Commonwealth*, might we not substitute *within* for *with*? It would be more direct and to the point."

Arthur now smiled, "Yes, it would be more to the British point of view. However, *a free partnership within the British Commonwealth* would mean partnership with the Dominions as a Dominion, that is, as members of the British Empire, rather than a free state associated with it."

"I'm afraid anything less would not come up to scratch in Liverpool," Birkenhead replied. "To begin with, the Die-Hards in my party want nothing to do with Home Rule. They could only accept it if it were within the context of Dominion status. Why not leave semantics aside, take what is being offered now, and see if it does not suffice in the long run?"

Michael interjected, "Lawyers make a handsome living off semantics. We wouldn't dare ask you to forgo that."

"Excellent point, Mr. Collins, but you might find yourselves quite content being a free state within the Commonwealth."

"That is not what we have sworn oaths to fight for," Michael answered. "Men die for principles, not semantics, and too many have done so already."

"Yes, I dare say besides being responsible for the deaths of many of my compatriots, you bear responsibility for the lives and deaths of many of your own. I'm sure that cannot be an easy burden to bear."

"Yes, and it's a burden that would lie heavy on any man, but living under the thumb of England is more burdensome still. Possibly even more so for the Catholics in Ulster. What of them? Any concessions we grant on the Crown and the Commonwealth are contingent on the basic unity of all Ireland."

"Yes, that is understood. However, as regards Ulster, Mr. Griffith," Birkenhead said, turning to Arthur, "you have stated your case rather bluntly. *On no account could I recommend any association with the Crown or the Commonwealth if the unity of Ireland were denied in word or fact.*"[3]

"Yes," Arthur stated, "that's correct."

"Well, isn't that rather like putting the cart before the horse? We have not yet arrived at a formula for form or fact. Until we define the nature of the association, could you not think of some language not so judgmental?"

Arthur thought for a moment, then answered slowly, "Well, let's see, we could borrow a phrase from the Prime Minister and say agreement was *conditional on the recognition of the essential unity of Ireland.*"

"Excellent!" Birkenhead responded. As he scribbled this change into the margin of the letter, he asked jestingly, "Are you sure you have not studied law yourself? *Essential unity* fits the bill very nicely. Now, as regards the Crown, I wonder if you might submit to someone perhaps more persuasive than myself?"

"Your reputation as a lawyer would seem to contradict that possibility," Arthur answered.

"Unless you mean either the King or the old Welsh Wizard," Michael asked.

Birkenhead laughed, "Rather the latter, I should think, Mr. Collins. You both have made a very favourable impression on the Prime Minister."

Arthur replied, "He can be very persuasive, but we have our principles to adhere to."

Birkenhead laughed, "Then be on your guard. Lloyd George could charm a bird off a bough.[4] Could I at least persuade you to discuss this further with him this evening, say around 6.45?"

Arthur smiled as he asked, "Around 6.45? That sounds rather precise. Are we to be flattered into believing that you anticipated failure to convince us this afternoon and already lined up the troops for this evening?"

"The possibility had occurred to me."

Michael asked, "Will Mr. Churchill be there?"

"No, my good friend Winston will not be there."

"I see," Michael replied, perhaps exhibiting some sense of relief.

Birkenhead took notice and pressed him on the matter, "You find Winston difficult?"

"Difficult?" Michael thought out loud. "No, very thorough, perhaps a touch argumentative or possibly overbearing."

"A touch, you say? Possibly?" Birkenhead laughed heartily. "That's generous of you. Listen, and take a word of advice, if you don't mind it being offered. Winston will fight you tooth and nail for everything he believes in, but as great an adversary he may be, he's as formidable an advocate with unmatchable powers of persuasion. Are you familiar with the incident in Amritsar, India, involving General Dyer a couple of years ago?"

"The Amritsar massacre where hundreds of unarmed Sikhs were slaughtered? I certainly do. What of it?"

"Winston backed a Government Commission and Army Council decision and insisted that Dyer be relieved of his command, which infuriated the Conservative majority in the House, who felt Dyer had acted to protect British life and uphold British imperial authority. The tide was running strongly against the Government for not supporting him, especially after the arch-Conservative Sir Edward Carson spoke."

An ironic grin passed over Michael's face as he recalled that Birkenhead's nickname, Galloper Smith, was coined for his former support of Carson.

F.E. smiled back, "Yes, *that* Edward Carson."

Michael answered, not in anger, but in a tone of incredulity, "I don't know how someone like you could have aligned himself with such an odious man after what he did to Oscar Wilde."

A quarter-century earlier, Carson was the barrister whose cruel cross-examination of Oscar Wilde in the Marquess of Queensberry's criminal libel suit led to the Irish poet and playwright's bankruptcy and imprisonment.

F.E. delivered a pithy retort, "I evolved. He devolved."

Arthur noted, "So, the man who eviscerated Oscar Wilde defended a murderer who butchered harmless Indians."

"Yes, and he nearly succeeded in having those heinous actions vindicated by Parliament. It seemed that if a vote were held then and there, the Government would have been rebuked, with serious political consequences. That's when Winston rose to speak. He asserted, *there should be a prohibition against a policy of frightfulness,* as he put it, *in which the inflicting of great slaughter or massacre upon a particular crowd of people, with the intention of terrorizing not merely the rest of the crowd, but the whole district or the whole country. We cannot admit this doctrine in any form. Frightfulness is not a remedy known to the British pharmacopoeia.*"

"Unless those people are Irish. What about British actions on Bloody Sunday?"

F.E. sat upright. "I strongly advise against ever including Bloody Sunday in debate points anywhere in the environs of Westminster. Let he who is without sin…"

"Go on, then."

"Thank you. I remember Winston's words quite well. He continued, *We have to make it absolutely clear, some way or other, that this is not the British way of doing business. Our reign in India or anywhere else has never stood on the basis of physical force alone, and it would be fatal to the British Empire if we were to try to base ourselves only upon it.* It was perhaps one of the greatest speeches ever delivered in Parliament, and it turned the House completely around. The time may come, and I hope it will, that you will be the beneficiary of that quality of rhetoric."[5]

Michael thought quietly for a moment and then smiled at this admission of goodwill, "Thank you. We'll certainly take that endorsement under advisement."

"Good. To answer your earlier question, Mr. Chamberlain and I will attend this evening's meeting, as we have quite a bit at stake in this matter."

Arthur answered, "In any case, we'd be delighted. Until around 6.45 this evening, then."

"Give or take, thank you."

Michael smiled wryly, "Give and take. That's what negotiations are all about, aren't they?"

"You give one hope with that remark, Mr. Collins. Oh, if it's all the same, I'll hold onto your letter for now and have an updated copy typed for this evening's meeting. Until then."

6.45 P.M., WEDNESDAY, 2 NOVEMBER 1921, 10 DOWNING STREET

WHEN MICHAEL AND ARTHUR WERE USHERED INTO THE CABINET Room that evening by Thomas Jones, they found Birkenhead and Chamberlain huddled together around Lloyd George with a fresh copy of Arthur's letter before them on the table. The Prime Minister looked up, smiled, and waved his guests over, "Come in, come in. Welcome back. I've been looking forward to this evening's meeting, and I am sure we can get the matter of this letter settled in short order. Please, take a seat."

"Thank you," and "Good evening," they answered.

"Now, we can discuss some of the naval issues in a moment, but it seems Mr. Collins is getting along famously with the Colonial Secretary and that the naval issues are well on their way to be resolved."

"Yes, Mr. Churchill is rather persistent, certainly very thorough," Michael said cautiously.

Birkenhead turned to his colleagues and said, "I do think Mr. Collins is trying to say Winston can be domineering and long-winded." He then turned to Michael and said with mock indignation, "As I warned him earlier today, I won't have my friend spoken of in such insulting terms, especially not in this hallowed office."

All was said with a great dose of irony, but still, the three men on the British side of the table waited to see what Michael's reaction to this challenge would be, but there was no need for concern.

Michael's head went back with a laugh, and he said cheerfully, "Hah! As much as Mr. Churchill and I enjoy our little get-togethers, I'd hate to prolong this conference any longer than necessary."

This amused everyone at the table. "Well said and amen," Chamberlain said dryly, with about as much irony as he could muster.

"In that case," Lloyd George said, "let's get right to it. The wording in Mr. Griffith's letter regarding the Crown seems fine, but Lord Birkenhead informs me of a certain hesitation to clearly define Ireland's association with the Empire. We would prefer if you were to say *a free partnership within the British Commonwealth*." [6]

Arthur replied, "As I told the Lord Chancellor earlier today, *with the British Commonwealth* would better describe our concept of the relationship of the free state of Ireland to the Empire."

"Then, in that case, might I offer a slight variant on your phrasing? Why not say *a free partnership with the other states associated within the British Commonwealth*?" Lloyd George asked with a shrug of his shoulders and an inquisitive smile.

"Well," Arthur said after a moment and then repeated the phrase, "*a free partnership with the other states associated within the British Commonwealth.*" He turned to Michael and asked, "How does that sound to your ears, Mick?"

"Hmm, well," Michael turned to the others and asked, "Do you mind if Mr. Griffith and I confer privately for a moment?"

"No, that would be fine," Lloyd George answered. "Would you like to use my secretary's office?"

"No, that won't be necessary," Michael replied. "We'll just join Mr. Cromwell for a moment over by the door."

As Michael and Arthur rose from the table and walked away, Birkenhead and Chamberlain looked at them and then at each other with puzzled expressions, but Lloyd George smiled and explained to them, "Curse or not, Oliver is in the bookcase."

Standing by the bookcase, Arthur spoke in a low tone of voice, "*Partnership with the other states associated within the British Commonwealth* can be taken to define our relationship to the other states, that is, from outside the Commonwealth. On the other hand…"

"On the other hand," Michael continued for him, "it places Ireland squarely back within the Commonwealth, and for them, that means the Empire. It is somewhat ambiguous, but maybe not for them, or Dublin, for that matter."

"Nevertheless, we can probably go no further than this," Arthur said resignedly. "As I see it, it doesn't alter the essence of the formula."

"Keep *with the British Commonwealth*; we go back home empty-handed. Accept *within*; we keep on talking. This isn't the final Treaty."

"No, Mick, but what we decide now is the basis for it."

"Sorry, I disagree, Arthur. That was decided when de Valera was here back in July. I've said it before. We're doing his dirty work for him now."

Arthur's eyes wandered down to the bookcase. "Faith, you weren't kidding! Cromwell *is* here, all right."

"Well, God fuck the old bastard. Let's get back to the table."

Arthur said as he returned to the table, "We will accept your phrasing on his matter, again provided we include recognition of the unity of Ireland."

The meeting continued for another two hours until everyone was fundamentally satisfied with the final agreed-upon wording, including the stipulation on Ulster. Lloyd George rose from the table and announced, "I think it is time we have this prepared in a somewhat more legible fashion for our Irish friends." He turned the draft around for all to see the muss of scribbles and cross-outs and explained, "This surely would not do. I'll have Miss Stevenson type up a fresh copy. I won't be a moment."

A short while later, Frances entered the room and placed the freshly typed draft of the letter on the table before Lloyd George. "There you are, sir," she said and left quickly with a furtive glance at Arthur and Michael as she left the room.

Lloyd George glanced briefly at the sheet of paper and then handed it across the table. Michael and Arthur began reading the document together. Halfway through it, Arthur said, "Oh, I'm afraid there's a slight mistake."

Michael agreed, saying, "Yes, I see it. It reads simply, *Ireland should consent to recognition of the Crown.* Apparently, your secretary omitted the article *a*."

Lloyd George said in an even tone, "Oh, did she?"

Michael smiled as he took his fine ink pen from his breast pocket, "Oh, that's all right, Prime Minister. I'll just write it back in myself: *consent to 'a' recognition of the Crown.* There, that should do it. We wouldn't want to offend the delicate sensibilities of our associate, Edward, would we, Arthur?"

"Edward?" Birkenhead asked.

"A member of our team back at the house," Michael explained. "He's a real stickler on grammar."

"I see."

Michael put his pen back into his pocket. "There, that's that."

EIGHTY-EIGHT

Not Budge One Inch

MONDAY, 7 NOVEMBER 1921

6.30 P.M., 10 DOWNING STREET

SIR JAMES CRAIG STORMED OUT OF THE CABINET ROOM, BRUSHING past Thomas Jones. Pausing at the door to put on his hat and coat, he looked back at Jones. A sinister smile came over his face as he turned and went outside. Jones shook his head and entered the Cabinet Room, where Lloyd George greeted him with a tirade.

"Damn the Die-Hards, damn the Unionists, and above all else, damn James Craig to everlasting hell!"

"Prime Minister, I take it Sir James remains unyielding." Jones had summarized the situation perfectly.

Lloyd George paced furiously from the Cabinet Room table to the window and back again, shouting out, "Craig will not budge one inch! He has his six counties and couldn't care less what we negotiate on the other twenty-six. He's betting on the Tory conference to back him up. The Treaty negotiations would collapse in a couple of days, and we'd be done for. I want you to see Griffith and Collins as soon as possible and prepare them for it. I will not be a party to coercing the South. I shall be forced to keep my word and resign my office by week's end. There is too much anti-Irish feeling in this country."[1]

Jones thought for a moment but held his tongue until Lloyd George stopped pacing and looked at him. "Sir," Jones ventured, "surely your own personal power is great enough to dominate the situation. Now is the time to appeal to the people for their support against the Unionists, not to resign."

Lloyd George walked to the window, thought for a full minute in silence, and then pulled the lace curtain aside and stared out. "There is just one possible way out," he said slowly.

Jones smiled to himself with relief as well as satisfaction for having suspected correctly that the Prime Minister would, of course, have some plausible way out of his promise to resign. "Yes, sir? What would that be?"

"Go ahead and make plans to see Griffith and Collins, not here, of course. Someplace neutral, discreet."

"Perhaps a hotel room?"

"Yes, that would do. I want you to find out if they will support me on this. Namely, that the Twenty-Six Counties should take their own Dominion Parliament and have a Boundary Commission to decide which districts in Ulster remain with the North, and which with the South. Ulster should have her present powers plus representation in the Imperial Parliament and share the same burdens of taxation which we bear. I might be able to put this through if Sinn Féin will accept it. Don't let on that it was my idea; put it out as your own, but find out, T.J."[2]

"Very good, sir." He paused and then commented with a smile, "If I remember correctly, Sir James Craig had a similar suggestion a couple of years ago."[3]

Lloyd George smiled in return, "Let's not reveal the proposal's pedigree and spoil any positive effect it may have on our Irish friends. Besides, Craig is against the idea now."

"Yes, sir. I'll be on my way, then."

EIGHTY-NINE

Once a Bookkeeper

TUESDAY, 8 NOVEMBER 1921, GROSVENOR HOTEL, LONDON

"DAMN THAT BASTARD, CRAIG!" MICHAEL WAS INFURIATED BY THE news just given to him by Thomas Jones.

"There seems to be quite a lot of that sentiment about these days," Jones responded somewhat cryptically.

"What? Well, good, there should be!"

"Yes, unfortunately, Sir James is standing pat. Quite obdurate."

"Obdurate? Bloody fuckin' obnoxious!" Michael looked over at Arthur, who remained silent, apparently deep in thought. Michael paced back and forth across the floor of the room they had reserved at the Grosvenor Hotel for this meeting. "I just got back from another Dublin trip, only to face this!"[1]

"I truly am deeply sorry to have to relate this news to you and Mr. Griffith," Jones continued. "And to make matters worse, Craig has the backing of Bonar Law, who could form a new government, assured of the large majority the Unionists enjoy in the House of Commons. Things are looking rather bleak over at Downing Street, I'm afraid. The Prime Minister has reiterated his intention to resign if things do not turn around somehow. Birkenhead and Chamberlain would both probably go into retirement."

Michael continued to pace the floor in a fury, but Arthur sat there calmly and said dispassionately, "The Prime Minister needs to stand up to Craig. This rejection has all the appearance of a colossal piece of bluff, and the P.M. needs to call them out on it."

"Rest assured, he will fight for all he's worth, but he has to prepare for possible failure. He has already discussed it with his wife, his secretaries, and even the King himself."[2]

Arthur sighed, "After we have come this far. It would be such a sad waste."

Michael ceased his pacing about and stood before Griffith and Jones silently for a moment before saying softly, "This means renewed war. What a waste, indeed."

They all stood there a moment in silence when Jones said, "Unless…"

The other two men looked at him expectantly.

"Unless this. Suppose the Twenty-Six Counties of the South were to be given all the new powers now offered, and Ulster was restricted to its existing powers and had to submit to a Boundary Commission to define her area. Such a commission would set boundaries based on population, religion, local preference, and so on. How would that strike you?"[3]

Michael was quick to answer, "Not at all well. We discussed this earlier. It sacrifices unity entirely."

Arthur appeared at first to agree but tempered his remarks, "Yes, absolute unity would be sacrificed, but in theory, we could gain most of Tyrone and Fermanagh, as well as a good part of Armagh, Londonderry, Down, given their predominately Catholic areas. We may now want to consider this while we sit and see how it is received."

Michael, now not so quick to dismiss the proposal out of hand, asked, "Do you think Lloyd George would approve?"

Visibly encouraged, Jones replied in a positive tone, "Yes, I think he very well might. Let me ask, and report back to you tomorrow, say here again at the same time?"

Arthur answered for them both, "That will do nicely. Godspeed."

As soon as Jones left, Arthur went to a writing table in the room, took out some stationery, and sat down to write.

"Sending a report to Dev?" Michael asked.

"Yes, things will be moving very quickly this week. We will want to keep him informed. The British Government is up against Ulster, and for the moment, we need to stand aside and see what happens. Craig will most likely refuse this offer, but then he'll be seen as even more obstructionist."

"I see your point." Michael sat on the edge of the desk and began swinging his feet and whistling a tune. Arthur looked up for a moment, thought of saying something, but put his mind back to his report.

Suddenly Michael blurted out, "You know, coming across Wales on the early train this morning, Lough Owel never looked so beautiful. The rising sun shone brilliantly on the lake and transformed it into a glimmering silver.[4] Just beautiful!"

Arthur sighed, put down his pen, and smiled up at Michael.

"Oh, sorry, Arthur, I've broken your train of thought."

"I take it you had a nice weekend back in Ireland."

"Oh, I did."

"In Granard, to be precise about it?"

"Yes," Michael answered with a blush. "Kit sends her love."

"So, I surmise you've managed to smooth things over."

"Just about."

"That's grand, Michael. Now, if you'll allow me."

"Oh right, sorry. Arthur, when you're done, there's so much going on at once. Maybe we should step back for a moment and compile a list of the issues and all our options. You know, a sort of balance sheet."[5]

"That's a splendid idea, Michael, but first, let me get this letter to Dev off right away while everything is still fresh in my mind. I wonder…" He stopped short and asked, "Do we even have enough time to get a response before tomorrow's meeting with Jones?"

"No," Michael answered. He slapped his thigh and said, "But Seán MacBride should be back tomorrow morning, hopefully with a response from Dev on your other letters."

After Arthur finished his letter, Michael made a phone call to arrange to send it by another courier to Dublin.

"Now for that balance sheet," Michael said, taking out a fresh sheet of paper. He sat at the desk and began to write, speaking his words as he did so: "*What will be the outcome if the present talks break down? 1, Declaration of war by the British. 2, We have, mistakenly, put all our cards on the table; we have laid ourselves open to the British.*" Michael paused from writing and said, "When the Truce was declared, I told Batt O'Connor, 'We'll be like rabbits coming out of their hole.' We couldn't possibly be more exposed than we are now."

"True, but there's no going back now. Go on."

Michael went on, *"3, Continuation of talks because world opinion is with us."*

Arthur said, "Put this down: *No declaration of war by the British. Point number 3 here is the most likely."*

"All right, then, and I hope you're right," Michael said. "How about this: *How best to reconcile our ideas with the fixed ideas at present held by certain members of the Cabinet? I will not agree to anything which threatens to plunge the people of Ireland into a war—not without their authority. Still less do I agree to being dictated to by those not embroiled in these negotiations."*

Arthur answered, *"It is not so much a question of who dictating to whom. It is a question of powers invested in us as representatives of our country. Sooner or later, a decision will have to be made."*

Michael responded, "Exactly. What are our powers? Are we to commit our country one way or the other, yet without the power to do so?"

"Put it down, Michael."

"Oh, right, sorry. You know, I'm enjoying this. It's sort of like a Socratic dialogue." He repeated the lines as he wrote and then stated, again writing as he did, *"The advantages of Dominion status to us, as a stepping stone to complete independence are immeasurable."*

"I agree wholeheartedly," Arthur said, "but I am glad in our discussions with the British that you never let on you felt that way. Oh, don't put that down."

"No, I wasn't about to." Michael grinned, "Pity I don't have any ledger paper for this little project."

Arthur chuckled and quipped, "Being in London brings back fond memories of tallying rows of numbers at a Davenport desk like Bob Cratchit?"

"I can't help myself. Old habits die hard."

"Well, Mick, there's another old saying."

Michael offered, "Once a bookkeeper, always a bookkeeper?"

Arthur laughed and said, "No, all good things must come to an end. Come to think of it, bad things, as well. Dominion status, the Oath, all this drivel about with or within the Commonwealth, I'm sure that in a few years' time it will be like water under the bridge."

"Exactly. With stepping stones across the water. Which reminds me of Churchill and all his concerns over ports for his navy. As you say, all that can change in a few years' time. Why go to war over it now?"

"Why, indeed? Let's continue. By the way, let's put our initials before each statement. You can put this down:

A.G.: How far can we trust the signatures of the British delegation in this matter? Once signed we are committed. But are they?"

Michael responded, *"M.C.: No, we are not committed—not until both the Dáil and Westminster ratify whatever agreement is made."*

They continued in this vein, *"A.G.: Ratification by the Dáil means what precisely? That a certain amount of power is still in the hands of those we know will be against anything which treats of Empire status.*

M.C.: I agree in part with the above. Supposing, however, we were to go back to Dublin tomorrow with a document which gave us a Republic. Would such a document find favour with everyone? I doubt it.

A.G.: So do I. But sooner or later a decision will have to be made, and we shall have to make it—whatever our position and authority."[6]

Michael replaced the cap on his fountain pen, put it in his jacket breast pocket, and smiled at Arthur.

Arthur said it for him, "There, that's that. Now, how did you mend the mess you made of your courtship of Miss Kiernan?"[7]

NINETY

Nine Points of Roguery

THURSDAY, 10 NOVEMBER 1921, LONDON

MICHAEL WALKED THROUGH THE LONDON EVENING FOG WITH HIS collar pulled up and a scarf wrapped around his neck. He turned into Hans Place and walked up to the Politicians' House, where Eddie greeted him at the door.

"Evening, Mick. Venturing out alone today?"

"I was worried about you, not finding you at the other house. Walked all the way from Cadogan all by myself."

"Oooh, living dangerously, are we?" Eddie asked, then spotted Liam Tobin and Joe Dolan smoking cigarettes at the edge of the grass. "What about that lot over there?"

"See, now, Eddie, that's how good those two are—I never noticed them."

Tom Cullen appeared from the shadows and brushed past them, saying on his way in, "Hello, Eddie. What's the craic?"

Michael gave Eddie a tug on his ear and said, "If you're going to be my bodyguard, you could learn something of the undercover arts from *that lot*."[1]

"All right, all right, point taken. So, howaya?"

"Not bad, but chilly. The mornings here look promising, but the days let you down.[2] Howandever, could ye wet the tea for us? Oh, and you wouldn't know if our private postman has arrived yet?"

"Yes, the kettle's on already, and no, Seán's not back yet."

"Shite. Well, just the cuppa."

"Coming right up," Eddie said before disappearing into the kitchen.

Michael greeted the others there, "Hello, Arthur, Eamonn." Michael was slightly startled to see Barton, Duffy, and Childers playing cards at a small table set up in the middle of the parlour.

"Ye at playing bridge again, are ye? Who's the fourth hand?"

All three of them replied mournfully, "Eddie."

"Ye coddin' me! It must be a challenge, playing with a handicap like that."

"It's been interesting," Barton admitted.

Michael poked his head into the dining room, where Joe McGrath was seated at the table, sifting through a pile of bills. "Are we keeping within our budget, Joe? You'll not have to rob a bank, will ye?"

Joe smiled and said, "The local banks are safe."

Just then, the front door sprang open, and Seán MacBride, accompanied by another man, came in tired but smiling, "Hello, everyone. You all know Seán O'Hegarty, the commander of the Cork No. 1 Brigade."

"Hello, Seán, Hello Seán," came greetings from around the room, to everyone's amusement, possibly with the exception of the new Seán.

Barton added, "Yes, welcome, Mr. O'Hegarty, welcome."

"That's Commanding Officer O'Hegarty, if you don't mind," he replied with a scowl.

Everyone's eyes went wide at this officious retort, but Barton answered politely, "My apologies. I stand corrected, commander. Welcome."

MacBride turned his gaze to the bridge table, looked slightly puzzled, and asked Erskine, "Who's holding my spot?"

Childers nodded in the direction of the kitchen.

"Not Eddie?"

"The very one," Barton answered.

"Oh, dear."

"Oh, yes," Childers replied.

"At least there's no mistaking who the dummy is," Barton added, employing a term from the card game.

Arthur then asked MacBride, "So, Seán, you have a letter on you?"

"Oh, yes, special delivery," Seán MacBride said, brandishing an envelope as he walked over to Arthur.

"Thank God!" Barton exclaimed. "We've been waiting for that."

"The first of two, in fact," MacBride replied.

"Thank you, Seán," Arthur said, taking the letter from him. "Two special deliveries? Where's the other?"

"Should be along any minute."

Mary Conlon came over and asked, "What's all the fuss? Oh, Seán, you're back. Saints alive, you must be famished. Let me get you a plate. Oh, now, who's your friend?"

Everyone in the room responded in unison, "*Commanding Officer O'Hegarty!*"

"I'll get two plates."

"Thanks, Mary," MacBride replied.

Arthur patted him on the back. "Come into the dining room. Sit yourself down and relax."

Sitting beside him, Arthur commented, "I have not heard from Dev in over a week. Let's see what he thinks about Lloyd George's plan. Have a seat, Eamonn," he added as everyone else joined them at or around the dining table.

As Arthur opened the letter and began to read, Michael stood behind him and matter-of-factly said as Eddie returned with his tea, "Oh, Eddie, I should mention that your name came up in conversation with the Prime Minister one day last week."

Eddie's eyes opened wide. "It *did?*"

"Yes, he was rather impressed with your attention to detail regarding the wording of that letter we were working on."

"He *was?*"

"Very. Wasn't he, Arthur?"

Arthur continued to read for a moment but then paused, looked up at Eddie and said, "Oh, yes, very impressed indeed. And what with the Treaty and the Republic in the balance. You've made quite an impression, young man."

"I, I'll see to a fresh pot."

"That would be lovely, Eddie. Thank you. I'm sure our two Seáns could each do with a cuppa." Arthur smiled and said, "Dev seems rather impressed with our work, too, for a change. He speaks quite favourably of this new plan on Ulster."

"That *is* good for a change," Michael said, relieved. "His last letter was a disaster. What does he say this time?"

"Let's see, here it is." Arthur read out loud, "*I have always been of the opinion that the break in the negotiations, if there should be one, should come on Ulster provided that Ulster not go out with the cry, 'Attachment to the Empire and loyalty to the Throne!' Provided, which was always the difficulty, that the fundamental national claim was not prejudiced. There can be no doubt whatever that the delegation has managed to do this admirably."*

Michael whistled and said, "Such exalted praise from the Chief. We are riding high these days, are we not? This calls for a drink."

Returning to the room and reacting to Michael's tone, Eddie asked, "You mean a *drink* drink?"

"Ay, I do. Leave the tea and break out the Jameson's, Eddie." Turning back to Arthur, he asked, "What else does he say?"

"He goes on: *Opinion among the Cabinet in Dublin was unanimous that if a break came, Ulster would be condemned by the public opinion of England, Ireland, and the world.*"

"All good."

"Ay, Mick," Arthur replied. "There's more, though: *I think, as far as the Crown-Empire connection is concerned, we should not budge a single inch from the point to which the negotiations have led us.*"[3]

"Ah, yes," Michael exclaimed. "The soaring rhetoric crashes back to earth. He's not here; we are. Was it not said that Craig himself would not budge an inch? Maybe he and Dev should just fight a duel to settle everything. Neither one of them is interested in actually negotiating. I suppose I should go see him again in Dublin tomorrow."

"Still," Duggan interjected, "the overall tone is positive and encouraging."

"Yes, it certainly is," Arthur agreed.

"I do believe Mr. Jameson concurs," Michael chimed in. "Let's all raise a glass to this *admirable delegation*, down to the last man, by whom I mean you, Eddie. Pour your good self one as well."

"If you say so, Mick."

Mary Conlon was helping clear the dining room table and offered a word of caution, "Careful, boys. Michael, you know there's only so much that stomach of yours can bear."

"Yes, Mrs. Conlon. I'll be careful," and with a wink, added, "we'll be careful."

"All the same, let's put away the rented china. Girls," she called to the kitchen, "come give me a hand in here." As she started stacking the dishes, the front bell rang. Mary looked at a clock on the cupboard and shook her head, "Eight o'clock! What kind of vagabond shows up unannounced at such an hour? I'll see to this myself, by God," she exclaimed as she stormed over to the front door. She swung the door open and gave out a scream.

Everyone came running, Liam, Tom, and Joe Dolan with guns drawn.

"What in blue hell?" Michael exclaimed.

Mary glanced at Michael and repeated, "Yes, Billy, what the hell?"

"I, er, well, that is…" Billy Conlon attempted to explain, standing there holding a suitcase.

"Mummy, Mummy! We're here!" Nelly cried as she ran up to the door.

Maureen waved from the pavement as Tim Kelly paid a taxi driver.

The three bodyguards holstered their weapons as Mary stood there motionless with her hands on her hips. Everyone went deadly silent for what seemed an eternity before she burst into tears and cried out, "Oh, my darlings, come in, get yourselves in from this damp London weather."

"Mummy, we missed you so much; we had to come to visit you!" Nelly explained.

Relieved, everyone called out their welcomes, some going out to help Tim with the suitcases, everyone ushering the second special delivery of the evening inside.

Seán MacBride explained, "We bumped into each other at Euston."

Tim said sheepishly, "We hadn't realised we were on the same boat and train. Heh-heh!"

Mary wiped the tears from her eyes, regained her stride, and questioned Billy, "And just who is taking care of the pub?"

"Christy O'Shea and Toby Kelly," Billy answered, "and they're doing just grand. They send their regards."

"Toby? Is he even old enough to be in a pub? Is that even legal?" Mary asked.

Maureen offered her father some support. "Toby works out of sight, behind the scenes, but he's practically running the pub, maintaining the kegs, ordering supplies. Amazing. He takes after his big brother," she added, squeezing Tim on the arm.

"Heh-heh," Tim repeated with his usual eloquence.

Mary seemed unconvinced, so Michael tried to console her, "I'm sure everything is fine, Mary. Come on in, everyone." He bent down to give Nelly a hug, "Hello, my little angel," and then stood up and said, "Someone call over to Cadogan Gardens. Let's get Peggy and everyone else over here right away."

"I'll make the call," Eddie offered excitedly. "One more special delivery is in order."

Michael looked over at Childers and asked with mock seriousness, "Erskine, as delegation secretary, can you please inform us what tomorrow's schedule holds for us?"

"No meetings. A free day."

"That settles it. Tonight, we celebrate."

Billy sighed in relief, "Thanks, Michael. We won't be imposing on you. Miss Kitty stopped by when she passed through Dublin on her way home, and she recommended the Cadogan Hotel, so we'll be staying there."

"That's grand. How long are you here for?"

"We go back Sunday."

"Pity I leave for Dublin tomorrow night, so we won't have much time together."[4]

"Ah, well. Still, it's good to see you." Billy then turned to Mary and said, "It's been donkey's years since we were here, luv. It could be our second honeymoon, this time with the kids."

Mary gave him a soft slap on the chest, "You big softy, get over here," and finally gave him a hug and a kiss.

A short while later Peggy McIntyre and the secretaries Alice and Ellie Lyons arrived, accompanied by Ned Broy and Emmet Dalton, the latter carrying a violin case.

"That looks lethal, Emmet," Michael quipped. "You think you'll fool anyone with that?"

"Only if I keep it shut. Here you go, Eddie."

Maureen went over to Peggy and whispered, "Here's a little gift from Christy," and gave her a small, gift-wrapped box.

"Oh, my, why, well, thank you. Oh, dear, I think I, well, come sit with me over here, and we'll open it together." She took Maureen by the hand, and they sat down on the couch. Peggy carefully removed the gift wrapping, folding it neatly before slowly opening the box. She just stared inside it for a moment, her eyes filling with tears, then lifted a silver and gold Saint Christopher medal on a chain, admiring it as she wiped her tears away.

"The patron saint of travellers," Maureen mentioned.

"Yes, I know," Peggy said softly.

"Christy said he should have gotten this for you before you left."

"No, this is perfect. Thank you, my dear. Will you please help me put it on?" After Maureen closed the clasp, Peggy pressed the medal against her breast, "Thank you. Let's join the others now."

As they stood up, Michael walked over and said softly, "I'm sorry to intrude, but I couldn't help but notice you two having what looked like a very tender moment. All is well, I trust?"

Peggy seemed eager to respond. "Oh, yes, Mr. Collins. I don't wish to make a fuss, but look at what Christy sent me," she said as she showed him the medal.

Michael bent down to look and said, "Well, that *is* nice, asking his namesake Saint Christopher to watch over you while you're so far from home. Good ole Christy."

Peggy put the medal inside her blouse and said, "Yes, he's a good old soul, is he not? Thank you. Let's join the others now."

After all the new arrivals were properly fed, everyone sat around the dining room table or spilt out into the parlour and told stories of their adventures in London or back home in Dublin. Drinks flowed freely, and Michael grabbed Eddie by the arm as he passed by with a bottle of Jameson.

"This time, I really do mean refills, Eddie. Remember that night, Tim?"

"Oh, God, yes."

"So, what're you waiting for, Eddie?" Michael demanded after he downed the drink Eddie poured for him. "Crack open that case and give us something to move our feet to."

"Yes, sir!"

"Come along, everyone. Let's go into the parlour and see if we can't break up that game of bridge."

People started shouting, "*Ceilidh, ceilidh!*" as they converged on the parlour.

Peggy took a pair of spoons from the dining table, walked over to the bridge players, and asked, "Excuse me, Mr. Childers, could I borrow your chair?" She dragged the chair to the middle of the room, sat down, and looked over at Eddie, "So what are we playing, Eddie?"

Eddie stood beside her, replying, "Just a sec," and quickly tuned up.

Michael went over to Maureen and said, "Peggy Mack seems

rather sprightly tonight." He gave Maureen a knowing look and a wink. Maureen laughed and squeezed his arm.

Eddie called out, "*Nine Points of Roguery*," Peggy nodded in satisfaction, he stomped his foot three times, and they tore into the lively, fast reel as she kept the beat with a blur of hands and spoons against her thigh.

"Go, Peggy, go!"

To everyone's amazement, Tim Kelly walked up alongside Eddie, nodded to him, counted a couple of beats, and proceeded to give an extraordinary display of step-dancing as everyone in the room clapped along.

"Jaypers," Michael cried out, "will you look at him! Who knew? Liam, you already walk with your hands at your sides; get over there and give it a lash!"

Liam shook his head and hands furiously in refusal and moved to the back of the crowd, but as the next verse rolled around, Tim stepped forward and raised his arms, beckoning him to join in.

"Liam! Liam!" the crowd shouted and pushed him forward until he stood there before Tim, utterly humiliated. Tim took him by the wrist and spun him around so their feet were parallel to give him his first lesson in step-dancing. Liam bowed to Peggy and then stared down at Tim's feet with a fierce, single-minded concentration.

Ned quipped, "Careful! I've seen that look of intensity before— right before he pulls a trigger."

Michael agreed, "Oh, this will be deadly, all right."

Liam tried valiantly to imitate Tim's blazing feet, failing miserably, but broke out in a huge smile as Tim clapped him on the back and encouraged him, "That's it. Fabulous! Now try this!"

Again, Liam studied Tim's example and, buoyed by his praise and the roomful of cheers, flailed about joyfully to everyone's ecstasy. As the next verse rolled around, Eddie winked at Peggy, and they both stopped playing, Tim kept the rhythm going with his shoes on the hardwood floor for a few bars, Peggy took a solo for a few more, and Liam had a go, cavorting at a shade less than strict tempo, and they all went into the final chorus with a wild spell of improvisation from Eddie. Now they were all dancing and playing together furiously, the whole room shaking with people stamping their feet and clapping. Eddie raised his fiddle over his chin to bring the reel to a dramatic finish, and on the last beat of the last bar, his bow sawed across the strings with a long staccato flourish, and the four performers stood together and bowed to an explosion of applause.

"Jaysus," Michael exclaimed through tears of laughter, "That was something fierce, Liam! And you, Peggy, I had no idea!" he called out. Then shaking his head, still laughing, he exclaimed, "Will the wonders of Tim Kelly never cease? What else is the lad capable of?"

Maureen said slyly, "There's a lot he can do you that would surprise you."

"I don't think I like the sound of that," Billy protested.

"Oh, Daddy, whatever do you think I meant?"

Michael poked Billy in the belly and scolded him, "Have some respect, ye big lout."

"And a little faith," Mary added.

Chastened, Billy walked over to Eddie and whispered in his ear. Eddie smiled, nodded, and announced, "And now, Ladies and Gentlemen, if I may, a special request." He waited until the room went quiet and started to play the stately early eighteenth-century waltz, "Planxty Irwin," by the famous Irish composer, Turlough O'Carolan.

Billy walked back to Mary, bowed before her, took her by the hand, and explained in a hoarse whisper to Michael, "This was our wedding dance," then proceeded to lead Mary in graceful, sweeping spins around the floor. After the first go-around, everyone else joined the dance until Eddie called out, "Last verse!" and everyone stopped to watch Billy and Mary again. By the time Eddie finished the tune, most of the people in the room were in tears, and as Billy bowed again, everyone gave them a round of applause.

In a quick change of mood and pace, Eddie pulled his bow sharply across the strings three times while simultaneously stamping his right foot, ripping into another fast reel and calling out, *"Drowsy Maggie!"* which was anything but. Everyone in the room, even the tiresome bridge players, partnered up and danced with abandon. Billy and Mary, Eamonn and May, Michael and Peggy, Tim and Maureen, bodyguards and secretaries, delegates, drivers, maids, and cooks, and even Arthur and little Nelly all went at it feverishly, constantly changing partners until half a dozen verses later, predictably, Michael and Billy were swinging each other around the middle of the floor until they finally collapsed along with Eddie, who fell to his knees to end his performance. Everyone cheered again, but they were all gasping for air and in need of drink.

The bridge players, too, refilled their drinks but sat down again at their little table to resume their game. Michael, who by this time had refreshed his drink more frequently than usual, wobbled over to them, holding a handful of peanuts. Someone at the card table mentioned something about a trick, inspiring Michael to respond, "Oh, I know a trick or two, as well. Can you do this?"

He held a nut in his outstretched left hand, hit the crook of his arm with the opposite hand, and set the nut sailing in the air into his mouth.

"Very amusing, Michael," Erskine responded drily.

"Dextrous, even," Barton added.

Michael cocked his head to one side and answered, "Then, in that case," and started pelting all the card players with nuts.

Seán MacBride folded his cards and said, "I think that's quite enough for me. I could do with a proper pint. Anyone care to join me?"

Erskine stood up and said, "Yes, this is no way for grown men to behave. Gavan, Bob, are you coming?"

Gavan shrugged his shoulders while Barton gingerly reached into his glass, pulled out an errant peanut and sent it back on its way to Michael's neck. After MacBride and Childers left and slammed the front door behind them, an apple went crashing into it. "Good Christ! What's with them?" more than a couple of revellers asked. A moment later someone sent an orange whizzing past Michael's ear and into Tom Cullen's lap as he sat on a couch. Tom responded with some couch pillows, and the missile-firing escalated from there until the room was a cloud of projectiles. Mary Conlon stood by the fireplace patiently waiting for the furore to subside, and explained to May Duggan with considerable sang-froid, "It's a long time since I've seen Michael with more than his fair share of liquor, but, ah, the stress they're all under, where's the harm? It eases their minds, poor lads."

"Oh, my, if you say so, Mary," May said uncertainly.

However, when someone helped themselves to lumps of coal from the scuttle by the fireplace, Peggy McIntyre, who had joined the other two matrons, took her spoons and drummed them on the thief's head. She then took up the fireplace shovel and tongs and started banging on the shovel until everyone stood where they were, brandishing various types of food and household weapons. "That will be quite enough."

"Peggy is right," Mary agreed. "Now, girls, gather up all these glasses and plates, and take everything into the kitchen and start washing up."

At this point, Peggy's years of stewardship at St. Mary's came to the fore. "As for you lads, hear me now: When we finish the cleaning up in the kitchen, I expect to find this room as neat as the day we arrived. Do I make myself clear?"

Mumbles of, "Yes, Peggy," and "Yes, Miss Mack," indicated she had made her point clearly enough.

"Very well," she said defiantly but added, breaking into a smile, "'twere great *craic* though, eh?"

"A little too much, if you ask me," the new arrival from Cork, Seán O'Hegarty, said from the side of his mouth on his way out. "Wait until Liam Lynch and Richard Mulcahy hear of this."

Robert Barton overheard this snide remark and said to Michael, "Did you hear that, Michael? I can't remember ever meeting such a snob."

Michael laughed and told him, "I'm none too worried. Commander Lynch of the 1st Southern Division has more important things to deal with. Dick Mulcahy was right. Commanding Officer O'Hegarty is a snarly gob."[5]

Joe McGrath came over and said, "Excuse me, Mick. The Conlons will want a ride to their hotel, so I'll do the honours."

"That's grand, Joe. Thanks."

Joe stepped closer and lowered his voice, saying, "Mick, about those local banks."

Michael burst into laughter, "Don't worry, Joe, if there's any damage, I'll reimburse Petty Cash."

THE NEXT MORNING NELLY CARRIED A BREAKFAST TRAY CAREFULLY from the kitchen into the parlour where Michael was fast asleep on the couch. The bridge table was now next to the couch, and she placed the tray down and began to sing softly, "*Some like a girl who's slender in the waist...*"

Michael stirred from his dreams, yawned, and said grumpily, "What's that? Who's that singing that bawdy old ditty? It's not our Nelly, is it? She's supposed to be with her dad at that fancy hotel. Her mother, too, I would have thought."

Nelly giggled and said, "You and Dad need to learn a new dance routine. Momma said I could stay here with Miss McIntyre so I could bring you your favourite breakfast."

"Curds and whey, just what the doctor ordered."

"And black coffee. I'll be back with more when you need it."

"Just like old times. You're too good to me. I'll miss having you all here with me."

NINETY-ONE

Not Queer Your Pitch

SATURDAY, 12 NOVEMBER 1921

11.30 A.M., 10 DOWNING STREET

WORTHINGTON-EVANS SPOKE DELIBERATELY, "PRIME MINISTER, IN light of Sir James Craig's refusal to even consider an all-Ireland Parliament, may I prevail upon our Liberal Cabinet members to allow my Conservative colleagues and myself a short private chat?"

Lloyd George rose and said, "By all means, take all the time you need. This is disappointing news from Craig, but not out of character. Come gentlemen, let's retire to Miss Stevenson's office and let Lord Birkenhead and Mr. Chamberlain put their heads together with the Secretary of State for War."[1]

"Oh, don't let us put you out."

"Not at all. You're entitled to your privacy."

On the way to the secretary's office, Churchill asked Lloyd George, "Actually, Prime Minister, I was wondering if you and I might have a little chat, too."

"Certainly, Winston." They stepped into an empty office. "Yes, now, Winston, what is it?"

Churchill got directly to the point, "It's this business about resigning. However lofty your motives may be for keeping true to your word with the Irish delegation regarding Ulster, I greatly fear the consequences of such tactics."

Lloyd George murmured, "Tactics?" but then just tilted his head with a slight smile as if to say, "Go on," which Winston would have done anyway.

"If this were to occur, Mr. Bonar Law would be invited to form a government, and why should he not do so? And what would be the result? A very great public disaster might easily ensue with a reactionary Conservative government at the helm, and all hope for a settlement in Ireland would be lost."

"I know, all of this weighs heavily on me, and I only brought up the possibility of resigning the other day in the face of Craig's latest refusals."

"I shudder to think of the outcome. Most men sink into insignificance when they quit office. Very insignificant men acquire weight when they obtain it.[2] Why give Bonar Law this undeserved fillip?"

"To be shared with James Craig."

Churchill nodded in agreement, "Precisely. It is our duty to carry forward the policy about Ireland in which we believe, until we are defeated in the House of Commons, and thus honourably relieved from our duty to the Crown. Consider this, then, if you will. Why not give the South the status of an Irish State, with an All-Ireland Parliament, a position in the Imperial Conference and the League of Nations? Ulster could have no grievance if she preferred to stand out."[3]

"But the South would."

Churchill shrugged his shoulders, "That's where the Boundary Commission would come into play."

"Ah, I see," Lloyd George replied, not letting on that this possible circumvention of his promise to resign had already occurred to him. "Yes, thank you, Winston. I think I might put this to Griffith privately."

"Perhaps at Sir Philip's house. Discreet location, equally discreet host."

"Excellent idea."

LATER THAT AFTERNOON ARTHUR GRIFFITH WAS WALKING BRISKLY through Belgravia toward Green Park with his much younger escort panting as he did his best to keep up.

"A little fresh air will do us both some good, eh, Tom?"

"If you say so, Arthur," Tom Cullen answered breathlessly.

They had left Hans Place a few minutes earlier and were en route to meet Lloyd George at Sir Philip Sassoon's London mansion at 25 Park Lane. Soon they reached the imposing mansion across the road from the park.

"Shall I wait out here, Arthur?"

"As you like. I don't think I will be very long."

A few moments later Arthur was shown into the drawing room where Sassoon and his sister were chatting with Lloyd George. "Good afternoon, Mr. Griffith," Sir Philip greeted him. "It's an honour to welcome you into my home. Allow me to introduce my sister, Sybil."

After the introductions and pleasantries, Arthur and the Prime Minister were left alone to discuss business. A soft evening light filtered through the window, mingling with the soft glow from the chandelier suspended from the high ceiling, casting a mixture of coloured light upon what appeared to be family portraits on either side of a large fireplace. Upon the mantelpiece above, Chinese vases framed a large mirror that reflected the soft light into the room. Arthur looked around, duly impressed, though he did his best not to show it.

The two men stood there as Lloyd George explained, "As you are aware, from Mr. Jones' visit this morning, Sir James Craig has refused our latest offer. Perhaps this would be a good point to review the progress of our negotiations with him." He paused, smiled and said, "Or lack thereof. Not surprisingly, our offer of an all-Ireland Parliament fell on deaf ears, even though Belfast would retain its own Parliament with full powers and would not in substance be subordinate to Dublin. The alternative could have been two separate Parliaments with Ulster retaining representation at Westminster. However, this latter arrangement would require an equal share of taxation with England. This was met with equal disdain. The looming presence of Mr. Bonar Law no doubt has stiffened Craig's resolve. Today, however, brings a new wrinkle to his intransigence."

Intrigued, Arthur asked, "Oh?"

Lloyd George motioned him toward the waning light by the window. "I have something to show you, Mr. Griffith. The actual fruits of our deliberations with Sir James Craig."[4] As Arthur began to skim through Craig's letter to the British Cabinet, Lloyd George continued his explanation, "Craig now says he would accept a Parliament equal to status to that being offered to the South as acceptable, even if it meant having to forgo representation at Westminster. This he sees as a lesser evil than being included in an all-Ireland Parliament provided Ulster would pay none except voluntary contributions in taxation to England!"[5]

Arthur immediately saw the implication, "So, rather than partake in an All-Ireland Parliament, he would accept demotion to Dominion status in exchange for lower taxes." He replied disparagingly, "So, the cloven hoof of Ulster's sordidness has shown itself."[6]

Lloyd George chuckled, "Personally, I find this mendacity shocking. Forsaking principle and union with Britain for Dominion status by merely weighing a six-bob tax as against three bob."

Arthur shook his head, "Astonishing. Perhaps once the Free State is set up, we might entice Sir James to join us with an even lower rate of tax."

Lloyd George laughed and said, "I must tell you, everyone in my Cabinet was simply astounded by this proposal. Even Bonar Law is said to be a bit knocked out by it."[7]

"Is that so?"

"Well, of course, this is totally out of line. Here is how we intend to reply. We will refuse their Dominion proposal but offer to create an All-Ireland Parliament, from which Ulster would have the right to vote itself out within twelve months. But if it did, the Boundary Commission would be set up to delimit the area, and the part of Ulster that remained after the Commission had acted would be subject to equal financial burdens with England. I would be prepared to play the Boundary Commission as an absolutely last card if I could feel secure that Sinn Féin would take it."

"Do you think Craig would accept this Boundary Commission?"

"If I were to ask him today, definitely not. After the Liverpool conference, at which we hope to prevail against the Die-Hards once again, probably still not. However, at that point, I would summon Parliament and proceed to set up the all-Ireland Parliament and the Boundary Commission as we see fit."

Arthur thought for a moment and then nodded, saying, "This all sounds fine to me, but this must be seen as your proposal, not ours."[8]

"Yes, of course. But when we're in the thick of it next Thursday in Liverpool fighting the Die-Hards, we will be lost if you were to cut the ground away from us by repudiating the proposal."

Arthur shook his head slightly, "You can rest assured we will not do that. I cannot guarantee its acceptance since my colleagues, with the exception of Mr. Collins and Mr. Duggan, know nothing of our recent communications yet. But I can guarantee that I would not queer your pitch by repudiating the proposal."

"Well, then, thank you. I thought I could depend upon you for as much." He then said off-handedly, "Just to be sure, I think I will explain our discussion with Mr. Jones and have him draw up a memo. Just to be clear on the salient points."

While Lloyd George was speaking, Arthur went over Craig's letter again, but stopped and looked up. "Excuse me, a memo, you say?" Arthur murmured. "Oh, yes, very well."

"Well, thank you, once again. This is most encouraging. I am sure we will persevere once and for all over the Die-Hards." He looked at his watch and said, "Well, I'll say our goodbyes to Sir Philip. I hope to get away for the rest of the weekend."

They shook hands, and Arthur wished him a pleasant time. He left and found Tom Cullen waiting just outside.

"How did it go, Arthur?"

"What? Oh, fine." He pulled his coat around his neck, "Though, I am a bit tired. Let's hail a cab, shall we?"

NINETY-TWO

What Memo Is This

SUNDAY, 13 NOVEMBER 1921, LONDON

7 p.m., HANS PLACE

THOMAS JONES LEANED FORWARD FROM THE CAR'S BACK SEAT TO TELL the driver, "I don't expect to be very long. At least, I should hope not to be."

"Not to worry, sir. The meter's all yours."

Jones walked up to the door at 22 Hans Place and rang the bell.[1] Things at Cadogan Gardens were quiet that weekend with Michael once again back in Dublin, so Eddie had gone over to Hans Place to lend a hand there. Eddie was passing by the hall, so he answered the door. "What can I do for you, mate?"

"Thomas Jones to see Mr. Griffith. Is he available?"

Eddie immediately recognised the name from the many conversations he had overheard regarding the ongoing talks. He straightened his posture, put his shoulders back, and suddenly assumed an uncharacteristically formal demeanour. "Very good, sir. Right this way, if you will. We were all just about to sit for dinner," which was not entirely true, as Eddie would have been serving, not sitting.

"Oh dear, I don't mean to disrupt your dinner, sir."

"Not at all, Mr. Jones. If you'll just have a seat in the drawing room this way, I'll inform Mr. Griffith of your arrival."

A few moments later Eddie reappeared with Arthur, who looked a little tired but smiled a welcome for his visitor. "Good evening, Mr. Jones. To what do we owe the pleasure?"

Jones smiled and said, "I have the memo for you." He looked hesitantly at Eddie and continued in an enquiring tone, "The memo from the Prime Minister?"

Arthur was aware of the reason for Eddie's lingering presence but said, "That's all right, Edward. I think Mr. Jones would like to speak privately, but I will call you if I need you."

"Very good. I'll just be in the dining room, Arthur."

Resisting the urge to give him a good clout right then and there for his familiar attitude in the presence of someone attached to the British team, Arthur merely said, rather coldly, "Very well, then. I'll see you as soon as we're done here. You can count on it."

Blissfully unaware of any irony, Eddie smiled and said, "Nice to meet you, Mr. Jones," and walked back to join the others at dinner. Liam Tobin was observing this all from the hallway, and when Eddie returned, he just shook his head.

Jones was pleasantly solicitous, though, and asked, "Another member of your team, Mr. Griffith?"

"Oh, yes, quite indispensable, in his way. I may have mentioned him before. Our grammatical scholar."

"Yes, I remember. Perhaps you would have preferred him to look this over with you? Mr. Chamberlain performed a similar service for me."

"No, that won't be necessary." Arthur then asked, "Now, what memo is this you referred to?"

As Jones produced an envelope from his briefcase, he explained, "The memo about your conversation with the Prime Minister at Sir Philip Sassoon's Park Lane home."

"Oh yes, of course."

As Arthur opened the envelope and took out the typed memo, Jones asked, "I hope I have not come at an inopportune time."

"No, not at all. Dinner will be served shortly, but it's no bother." He briefly skimmed the document and then read a couple of passages out loud. "*If Ulster did not see her way to accept immediately the principle of a Parliament of all Ireland,* hmm, yes." He skimmed down the page, "*necessary to revise the boundary of Northern Ireland,* yes, that's right, *Boundary Commission,* and *conform as closely as possible to the wishes of the population.*"[2]

He handed the memo back to Jones, saying, "Yes, it's fine. That's the gist of my conversation with the Prime Minister."

"Very good, then. I won't keep you any longer; I have a taxi waiting outside. Please give my regards to your colleagues."

"Oh, I certainly shall."

"Oh, one more thing, the Cabinet should be able to offer a Treaty draft in a few days' time."

"Excellent. We'll be looking forward to it. Good night, Mr. Jones. Thank you for stopping by."

Arthur returned to the dining room where the others had begun the evening meal and took his seat. Eddie came along with a plate for him. "I kept this warm for you on the kitchen stove. Corned beef and cabbage."

Arthur glanced at Liam and replied with the slightest hint of sarcasm, "Why, thank you, *Edward*."

Liam responded, "Yes, Edward, how do you ever find the time with all you have on *your* plate?"

Some at the table looked over with puzzled expressions.

Robert Barton asked, "What did Mr. Jones want, Arthur?"

"Oh, he just wanted to review a couple of points regarding the Die-Hard conference this week in Liverpool. Nothing much, though he did mention that they will be submitting a draft Treaty very soon." He smiled at everyone and said matter-of-factly, "He made an interesting comparison between Austen Chamberlain and our Eddie here."

"He did?" Eddie asked incredulously as he put Arthur's plate down before him.

"Yes, Mick will be very amused. And I know exactly how he would have responded had he been here." With that, Arthur dug his heel in hard down on Eddie's foot.

NINETY-THREE

Roast Beef in Old England

WEDNESDAY, 16 NOVEMBER 1921, LONDON

AROUND LUNCHTIME, AN ASSOCIATE OF THOMAS JONES ARRIVED AT Hans Place and was met at the door by Erskine Childers.[1]

"Mr. Childers, I have two copies of the first British Treaty draft from the Deputy Cabinet Secretary."

"Oh, excellent," he responded. "Please give my regards to Mr. Jones."

As Childers, Michael, Arthur, and the other delegates poured over the draft, the mood was cautiously optimistic.

"The language on Ulster strikes me as fairly vague, but even still..." Michael said encouragingly.

"This Boundary Commission, I don't know..." Childers wondered aloud, but in a carefully muted tone so as not to start an immediate argument.

Surprisingly, Arthur announced, "I think we should send it immediately to Dublin, recommending non-acceptance in its present form but also asking for any refinements." He looked over at Seán MacBride, "Sorry, Seán, looks like another round-trip home for you."

"That's all right. Part of the job, isn't it?"

"There's a good man, Seán."

Michael added, "I only arrived back from Dublin yesterday, but I should probably return this weekend to follow up."

Arthur looked around the table, "Overall, I think it's a decent start.

Let's celebrate tonight, shall we?" Seeing Mary Conlon go by in the hall, he called to her, "Oh, Mary?"

She turned and entered the dining room, folded her arms and asked with a wry smile, "I heard you. How many will there be?"

"Everyone," Arthur answered.

"It'll be grand, don't you worry. Right Eddie?" she asked, dragging him by the ear into the room. "Eavesdropping again, eh?"

With a nervous glance at Arthur and Michael, he said defensively, "Just in case someone needed to ask my opinion. I have some ideas for the evening's menu."

Satisfied, Michael replied, "Then we'll leave you and Mary to it. I have to go, but I'll be back in time for dinner, say…"

"Seven o'clock?" Mary suggested.

———

GALES OF LAUGHTER FILLED THE DRAWING ROOM AT NUMBER 5, Cromwell Place, where the society painter Sir John Lavery and his famously beautiful wife, Hazel, were entertaining F.E. Smith at afternoon tea, or rather, he was entertaining them.

"So, I sez to me cabbie, right, guv'ner, quick as you like to the Adelphi Hotel. There's an old mate that what owes me a favour I'm anxious to collect on." It was Lord Birkenhead, assuming a broad Lancashire accent.

Another guest, Elizabeth, Lady Fingall, tittered with laughter, prompting Sir John to ask, addressing her by her nickname, "What do you say, Daisy? Would the Lord Chancellor have passed for a Lancashire lad?"

F.E. took a long draw on his big cigar, blew a cloud of smoke above his head, and waited for her response. "Oh, very convincing, John," Lady Fingall replied, "though I would never presume to refer to Lord Birkenhead as a lad. But very convincing, though F.E. has the advantage of having been raised in Liverpool, if I am not mistaken."

"Right, ye be, m'lady, right as rain," F.E. answered, momentarily continuing his pantomime. "But therein lay the fun of it. I needed to travel incognito to see Salvidge in Liverpool to avoid causing too much of a stir. He may be the local party boss and an old friend and patron from my early days, but it would not have done him or myself any good if it became common knowledge that I was there to put any pressure on him in handling the Conservative conference. So, I thought I might as well have a little fun while I was at it."

Lady Lavery smiled and said, "It's hard to believe you went unrecognised. Especially since you stand a head above most other men."

"Perhaps, but height is not nearly noticed as readily as beauty, for which reason I was able to pass unnoticed while you could never escape the wonder of people everywhere you go." He paused and resumed his Liverpool accent, "But even a big fella like me? No one looked twice!"

Hazel Lavery may have been uncommonly beautiful, but she held herself with equanimity and accepted such compliments gracefully. "Why, F.E., you are not one to sell yourself short, not in any sense of the word."

"*Touché*, my dear."

"Funny you should refer to yourself as a big fellow, though. Isn't that what they call this man Michael Collins from the Irish delegation?" Sir John asked.

"Yes, I believe it is, and a big fellow he is. Would you and Hazel like to meet him?"

"Hazel has invited him over here more than once, haven't you, dear?" Sir John said in answer.

"Yes, and my entreaties have fallen on deaf ears, I'm afraid," she sighed. "When one is so concerned about an issue of such importance, one does wish to become involved, to do their utmost to bring some positive influence to the matter. You all know my interest in the negotiations between the Irish and the British Cabinets." Hazel was indeed very sympathetic to the Irish cause, and as a famous hostess to London's political elite, she was uniquely placed to bring the two sides together, at least socially.

"Hazel managed to overcome Arthur Griffith's objections, and he came over for a sitting when he was here with de Valera back in July," Sir John mentioned, "but no sign of Mr. Collins yet."[2]

"Perhaps I could encourage him," F.E. responded. "We get along all right."

"Do you, really?" Hazel answered back. "How do you find him?"

"Well, he's quite simple, really. Very straightforward fellow. Brash, unsophisticated, apparently uneducated, but outspoken, nonetheless. To put it short, I quite like him."

Countess Fingall laughed and asked, "Why on earth do you say so after such a dreary description of him?"

"The truth is, Daisy," F.E. answered, "we seem to have quite a bit in common. He's a fast thinker, albeit a somewhat erratic one, but he speaks his mind unreservedly with a most disarming candour, and above all, it's obvious how much he loves his country and is willing to fight for it."

"And in the last of these qualities, I'm sure you'll find the strongest bond," Sir John responded. "So, F.E., returning to Liverpool, how did your meeting with Salvidge go?"

F.E. laughed out loud, "I could have saved myself all the intrigue, not to mention the bother of tearing across the country."

"Oh, dear," Hazel exclaimed. "It didn't go well?"

"Quite the opposite. I left my trusty cabbie at the entrance to the Adelphi, promising to return within half an hour, pulled my collar up and my hat down, and stormed into the hotel. When I met Salvidge in the appointed hotel room, I wasted no time getting to the point. I told him, 'Give me twenty minutes. Don't interrupt me. Don't argue. Don't raise any point till I have finished.'"

Sir John rubbed his hands together, "This is delicious, F.E. How did a political power broker like the 'King of Liverpool' take being spoken to in that manner?"

F.E. smiled and said, "I had quite the rapt audience, or so it seemed, so I plunged ahead and gave him a full reckoning of our deliberations with Hazel's would-be friend, the Big Fellow, and his elder colleague, Arthur Griffith."

"Oh, he's a sweetheart. How did you find him?" Daisy asked.

"Winston has described him as a tired scholar, which is apt enough, but Griffith is a force to be reckoned with, especially for someone his age, shrewd when the much younger Collins is bombastic, reserved when the other is boisterous. Rather reminds one of the fable of the turtle and the hare, but in this case, they both might wind up at the finish line together. Quite a formidable duo. The others, of course, are just there to fill the chairs."

Lady Fingall shook her head, asking, "That's a bit hard, isn't it?"

He paused and then corrected himself, "Actually, yes, it is. I should make an exception for this chap, Eamonn Duggan, one of their lawyers. Though I could make mincemeat of him in court, I don't mind admitting…"

"I'm sure you don't," Sir John interjected.

F.E. bowed his head in thanks and continued, "But Duggan is an earnest, decent fellow. Those of us on the British side of the table can brook no truck with the rest of the lot."

"F.E., we were in Liverpool."

"Ah, yes, John, I digress. I was going to say the Irish team seems to be split right down the middle, but I refrained from burdening my old friend Salvidge with this observation. No need to muddy the waters when I'm trying to make a case in favour of our deliberations."

"I'm sure you didn't," Sir John commented wryly. "Muddying the waters of a case is certainly not something for which you are known. How did Salvidge react? Did he rule in favour of your case?"

"Well, I explained how our deliberations on all the key issues, Ulster, the Crown, defence, had brought us very close to a settlement with our Emerald Isle compeers. Speaking of whom, I assured him that they were the type of men who, if they once pledged their word to an agreement, would keep it even with their lives."[3]

"You feel that strongly about them?" Hazel asked.

"Yes, and that applies to the lot of them. But I digress once again. I had one more point to make. I told him that the British formula only required the impetus of a successful vote at the Liverpool conference to carry it on to fruition. I then asked him if he would help obtain that vote or would he ruin what was undoubtedly the last chance to reconcile the nationalist aspirations of Ireland with loyalty to the Throne and Empire. Finally, I reminded him that the alternative was war more bloody and more terrible than anything known previously between the two peoples."[4]

"Good Lord, what could he possibly have said to all that?" Sir John asked.

"He gave me his answer by simply throwing the *Morning Post* on the table before us. For some reason, I failed to see the papers that morning, but there it was in black and white: *Salvidge urges conference to back treaty negotiations with Irish.*" He laughed heartily, "I could have saved myself all the bother and stayed home. Still, it was good to see my old friend and express my gratitude for his support in person."

"So, it turned out all right, after all?" Hazel asked.

"Well, the final upshot…"

Just then, the doorbell rang, and Sir John looked at the clock on the mantelpiece. "Who could that be?"

Annoyed at having his story interrupted, F.E. drawled, "Who, indeed?"

A young maid entered the room and announced, "Mr. Michael Collins here to see Lady Lavery. Shall I show him in?"

"Remarkable!" Daisy exclaimed.

"My word!" Sir John agreed.

Hazel, however, rose from the table, quite pleased as well as excited, but placed a hand on F.E.'s shoulder and said calmly, "Perhaps you can save the end of your story for Mr. Collins, F.E.?" She finally answered the maid, "Yes, my dear, do show Mr. Collins in." She explained to her guests, "We weren't exactly expecting him, but rather hoped he would come, sometime, that is. We just didn't think it would be today."

Hazel followed the maid but paused in the hall, waving her hand to the maid to continue to the front door. With a glance back at her mistress, who nodded with approval, the maid opened the door, apologising with polite deference for the delay, "So sorry to keep you waiting, Mr. Collins. Please, do come in. Lord and Lady Lavery are entertaining inside."

It had taken Michael nearly a month to finally respond to Hazel's invitations, and while he had been waiting outside, his lingering doubts about coming only increased. As he ran his fingers along the brim of his hat, he said uncertainly, "I hope I am not intruding. I'm probably disturbing the Laverys and their guests. Perhaps I should come back another day."

Hazel had been standing to the side of the entrance to the foyer listening, and when she heard the hesitation in Michael's voice, she gathered the train of her gown and with a grand flourish, glided to the doorway to greet him, "Not at all, Mr. Collins. We'd be delighted to have you join us. Tea and scones are just being served. You could not possibly have chosen a more opportune time to arrive."

So Michael stepped forward and entered as Hazel approached with her hand extended. They met just under the chandelier in the centre of the foyer, and as he took her hand, he looked into her lovely face, softly and entrancingly illuminated by the twinkling light from above. He stood there for perhaps a moment longer than decorum would have allowed, momentarily spellbound by the vision of beauty and sophistication before him. Hazel was certainly used to the effect she invariably had on men; however, this time she could not dismiss it so readily, for she was experiencing a similar reaction herself.

Regaining his senses, Michael said with a broad smile, "Well, then, in that case, I'd be delighted."

"Wonderful, come in, then, and make yourself comfortable."

As Michael followed her in, he took off his coat and carefully folded it over his arm. Hazel put her hand on his arm, saying, "Let me take your coat for you, Mr. Collins."

"That's all right," he said, somewhat embarrassed, and continued *sotto voce*, "You see, there's a gun in the pocket."[5]

"Really? Oh, how thrilling, though I trust you'll not need it today. Your friend Lord Birkenhead is here."

Before Michael could react to this information, he was led into a drawing room like none he had ever been in before. The walls were covered in a gold crepe-like cloth that glinted in the late afternoon light that also fell upon multi-hued butterfly specimens on the mantelpiece. There was a casual, almost bohemian feel to the room, bizarre but comfortable.[6]

Sir John got up to welcome him in. "Mr. Collins, how good of you to come. John Lavery. Pleased to meet you."

As they shook hands, Michael glanced around the room and saw Birkenhead smiling through a cloud of cigar smoke. Michael nodded to him but then returned his attention to Sir John, "The pleasure is all mine. Especially since I've just shown up on your doorstep unexpected and unannounced."

"Nonsense, Mr. Collins. There's no statute of limitations on invitations for such distinguished guests in this house."

"Thank you, but please, you can call me Michael. In fact, I prefer 'Mick' among friends."

"Then, Mick, allow me to introduce Elizabeth, Lady Fingall."

Michael bowed and addressed her as Lady Fingall, but she protested, "Oh, please, Mick, I prefer 'Daisy' among friends."

Then F.E. rose from the table as Sir John said, "And of course, you know Lord Birkenhead. He has been extolling your qualities to us all this afternoon."

"Has he, really? Good afternoon, Lord Birkenhead."

"And to you, Mick, but please, do call me 'F.E.' All my friends seem to insist upon doing so."

Hazel was pleased with the pleasantries and began, "Mick, er, no," she corrected herself and continued in a velvety purring tone, "I think I prefer Michael." She teased her new guest, "I was beginning to despair if you would ever come. What took you so long? We're practically neighbours, with you and your team ensconced in Kensington."

Michael was a little embarrassed at being admonished but shook it off, saying, "Maybe that's just it, your address, that is, here in Cromwell Place. It seems there's no escaping Cromwell, the old bugger." He chuckled but then turned slightly pale, "Oh, excuse me, I tend to, er…"

Sir John kept things light by saying, "Quite all right, Mick, and perfectly understandable, especially from your point of view. Ancient history aside, as I was saying, F.E. has been extolling your virtues. But, please, have a seat."

Michael smiled as he sat and commented, "Maybe he doesn't know me well enough yet to expand upon my faults."

F.E. voiced an objection, "That didn't prevent me from saying some less than complimentary things about some of your compatriots. My only complaint, Mick, is that you interrupted a good story. If you can keep this to yourself, and I trust that you can and will, I was just telling our gracious hosts about a secret mission I just carried out, partly on your behalf."

"Really? And what would that have been?"

F.E. merely smiled benignly.

Michael responded immediately, "My lips are sealed. Forgive me for interrupting. Please go on."

"Good. You are forgiven and thank you. I really should not give you the particulars, but suffice to say that yesterday's papers predicted that a positive outcome in Liverpool can be expected, in large part due to the intervention of my old friend Stanley Salvidge. However, the *Morning Post* saw fit to describe this turn of events as 'Salvidging Ulster,' a rather clever if unfortunate play on words."[7]

"That *is* rather unkind," Sir John commented.

"Quite," F.E. agreed. "Nevertheless, Mick, you can rest assured that my affirmations of your goodwill and character will echo through the halls of tomorrow's Die-Hards conference."

"Is that so?" Michael asked. "My, my, flattery where least expected."

"And in F.E.'s case," Sir John replied with a chuckle, "rarely given. How did you put it?"

"That Mick is the type of man who, once he pledged his word to an agreement, would keep it even with his life."

Michael smiled and said, "In the hope I can live up to such high praise, let me tell you a story about my father. He was a very stern but highly respected man in Clonakilty, our little village in Cork. Once a local shopkeeper got it in his head that Dad had stiffed him on a bill, though he assured the man he was mistaken. Nevertheless, as it played out, Dad allowed the issue to go all the way to court, and it wasn't until he stood before the local magistrate that he finally produced the paid receipt. Now, this shopkeeper had known Dad all his life. What does this little story tell you about my father?"

F.E. smiled and answered, "That Dad's word should have been evidence enough.[8] Point taken, Mick." He then leaned forward and said, "And the corollary to this little parable is, we are meant to presume, 'Like father, like son?'"

Michael laughed and said, "Well, let me just say my father's reputation for honesty is equalled by yours for deductive reasoning."

Everyone was pleased with the turn the discussion had taken, and F.E. continued in the same vein by adding, "The Prime Minister and I have both come to the same conclusion regarding you and Mr. Griffith. For this reason and with our expected success in Liverpool, we have today submitted a draft of the Treaty to our Irish friends."[9]

Michael acknowledged this fact, "Yes, Arthur and I and the rest of our team have begun going over it, but I think I'll leave it at that for now. I'm sure you'll all understand."

Suddenly F.E.'s head shot up, and he turned to Hazel with a look of surprise and cleared his throat dramatically before lifting the tablecloth and looking down.

"Whatever is the matter, F.E.?" Hazel exclaimed as she, too, looked down at the floor. "Oh, come here, sweetie," she exclaimed as she reached down and picked up her little Pekingese.

"Oh, I *am* sorry, Hazel," F.E. said facetiously. "I thought you were making advances."

Michael quickly rose and stood over F.E., demanding in an angry voice, "D'ye mean to insult her?"

Hazel stopped petting her little dog a moment to reach over and take Michael by the hand, "Lord Birkenhead was only joking, Michael."

His pique unassuaged, Michael retorted, "I don't understand such jokes."[10]

Hazel held her dog up and gently scolded him, "See what mischief you've caused, you bad little boy?" Still trying to calm Michael's nerves, she added, "Poor thing, he's actually getting on in age and hasn't been well lately."

Out of courtesy to his hostess, Birkenhead explained, "Mr. Collins, Lord and Lady Lavery are only too used to my biting tongue, which I am afraid I may be known to use more liberally than I ought, but I despair to think I could have upset you. Please excuse me."

"Well, then," Michael mumbled. "Perhaps I overreacted."

"Nonsense. A gentleman can never overreact when defending the honour of a lady."

Sir John thought it best to alter the conversation, "Yes, Mr. Collins, er, Mick, all of us here are all too accustomed to F.E.'s brand of humour. Now, change of subject, I plan on doing a series of portraits of all the delegates from both teams. I hope your appearance here today can be taken as a sign that you have agreed to sit for yours."

"Well, yes, it is," Michael answered, glad for the chance to speak more amiably, "though I'm not sure I'd make a suitable change of subject."

F.E. assumed a puzzled expression and interrupted, "I say, was that a pun?"

Michael laughed, "A poor one, I'll admit. Sir John, I'm sorry it took me so long to get around to your invitation to sit for you. I haven't found myself with very much free time since we've been over here. Would it take awfully long?"

"I assure you, I work rather quickly, though it does entail a bit more patience on your part than a photographic sitting. Still, it shouldn't be too painful."

"Well, that's fine. But that reminds me, the *Tatler* has just asked me to do a sitting for a photograph. I don't know what all the fuss is all about."[11]

"The price of fame, my dear boy," F.E. drawled. "You'll be much in demand, I'm sure."

"For a man in my position, fame comes at too dear a cost and is not worth any price."

Hazel replied, "That may have been the case before the Truce, but now that you are here representing your country, the people of England want to know more about the people with whom their government is negotiating. You are at the very heart of a *cause célèbre*."

Michael remained silent, but Sir John said encouragingly, "Then,

Mick, if you would accompany me to the studio, perhaps we could begin?"

Michael hesitated, asking, "Hmm, you want to start right now?" He glanced around uncertainly.

F.E. took that as his cue. "Well, Mick, you don't need me to upset your sitting. I need to get back to Whitehall anyway. I'm sure we'll see each other there soon, eh? Have a good day, everyone. Daisy, always a pleasure. And thank you, Hazel, John."

"So, Mick, come with me. Excuse us, ladies," Sir John said, motioning to Michael.

Meanwhile, Hazel walked Birkenhead to the door and apologised, saying, "I hope my little peke hasn't damaged Anglo-Irish relations, F.E."

F.E. answered in his Lancashire lad accent, "Not in the slightest, m'lady, all's well. The fact is, I like him now all the more. As John said, a fighting spirit after myself. Good evening, Hazel."

Michael followed Sir John upstairs to his painting studio, which had its own other-worldly feel. Twilight streamed in from a glass roof onto hand-painted gold leaf Chinese screens scattered about the room. Michael looked around admiringly.

"At this time of day the roof windows offer a soft, natural light ideal for portraiture," Lavery explained as he slid one of the screens to the side, revealing some canvasses on easels. "Oh, let me show you; here are some paintings I did of your friends."

"Oh, it's Arthur. Very good, very nice. I see what you mean about the light; very flattering. Oh, and look, here's Gavan Duffy. My, doesn't he look distinguished?"

"Yes, well, thank you."

"Distinguished windbag, I might add."

"Be that as it may, have a seat, Mick."

"All right, but I can't stay for long. Sorry, but I do have to get back to discuss that Treaty draft we received earlier."

"We'll just start with a preliminary sketch today. I assure you, I work rather quickly."

Lavery gestured to a chair in the middle of the room, but as it was facing away from the door, Michael hesitated at first, then swung it around, asking, "Would this be all right?"[12]

Sir John walked around to observe the light on Michael's face and then nodded, "Yes, if you'll be more comfortable there, that will be fine." He then threw a dark backcloth over the screen a few feet behind Michael.

"You see, I never sit with my back to a door. Nothing personal, just force of habit." Michael shifted uneasily in the chair, trying different poses to get comfortable.

"That's quite all right. If you could just sit still for a while."

"Hmm, well, that's another thing I rarely do, but I'll give it a go."

―――――

WHEN MICHAEL RETURNED TO HANS PLACE, HE FOUND EDDIE conspiring with Alice and Ellie Lyons, who had run off copies of the evening menu on the publicity staff's mimeograph machine at Cadogan Gardens. Eddie was delighted, "They look great on these cards, ladies. Well done!"

Over a colour illustration of an elegantly dressed woman emerging from a *trompe-l'œil* frame was the scripted writing, "*Irish Republican Delegates Reception, London, Nov 16 1921.*"

"What're ye playin' at there?" Michael demanded. "Wasting the girls' time, are ye?"

"Never you mind, not in the slightest, and wait until dinner, sir!" Eddie answered back saucily.

Soon after, when everyone was seated, Eddie came along and passed out the menus with pencils, explaining as he went around the table, "*Ce soir, madams et messieurs*, we will commence with a choice of soup, *Publicity, a clear broth*, or *Peace, thick.*"

Puzzled looks were followed by mild chuckles.

"Please circle your menu choices, and kindly affix your signatures at the bottom." He then announced, "The fish this evening is a filet of *Hans Plaice*," emphasizing the French word for fish, substituted for "Place."

A few groans at the play on words were followed by a question. "Eddie, why does it say *Cadogan Steaks* under fish?"

Tom Cullen answered for him, "Because the men at *Cadogan* only eat meat."

"Ah, well. Stands to reason."

Eddie continued, "For entrées, we are offering a choice of *Economic Cutlets…*"

"I'll have that with an extra helping of the *Reparation Gravy*," Bob Barton chimed in.

"I thought as Economic advisor you might, sir. Just circle it on your menu and sign at the bottom, please."

"Eddie, the other entrée, *Minced Ulster*, what's that like?" Eamonn Duggan asked.

"I don't recommend it, sir. Even with the *North East Sauce*, it's quite tough." Everyone roared with laughter as he explained further, "You may find it indigestible."

"Maybe to Sir James Craig, it is," Michael shot back, "but I'll have it anyway. Someone has to try it."

"Mick is right; we simply must try to swallow Ulster."

"Oooh," came more groans mixed with laughter.

"For the main course, we have a joint of beef. In fact," Eddie cleared his voice and began to belt out the rousing tune from the famous song dating back to the eighteenth century…

"Oh! The Roast Beef of Old England, and old English Roast Beef!"

He raised his arms to conduct, calling on, "Everyone, we'll have…" and everyone joined in the refrain,

"The Roast Beef of Old England, and old English Roast Beef!" [13]

Amidst a festive table full of laughter, Eddie nodded and said, "Excellent choice, one and all."

"But what about the sides?" Liam asked. "It says here a *Side of Potatoes, Delegates Solution*, or a *Formula of Beans, No Solution*."

"*Précisément, monsieur*," Eddie replied with a prepared answer. "Beans are off, potatoes only. After all, we're all Irish here, are we not?"

"That's right, Eddie. Let the English have their beans. We'll stick to our purdies."

"Very good, sir. Not that we want to risk falling into a stereotype, favouring potatoes."

"And for afters, Eddie?" Arthur asked. "What is the *Compote de Fruits* like?"

"Oh, very sweet, indeed. A delectable mixture of *Gerty, Ellie, Alice, Kathleen, and Lily*. It does come with a mandatory cheese dish, *Chaperon Duggan*."

All the women, whether secretaries or maids, either giggled or blushed, but May Duggan said sternly, "No substitutions allowed, and mind who or what you describe as delectable. It's fruit with the accompanying cheese, or nothing at all."

"Yes, Mrs. Duggan. Yes, May. We wouldn't dream of it," came a despondent chorus of answers from the men around the table.

"Finally, we finish with un *Café* and, for the very brave, *Mícheál's Mixture.*"

"What's in it?"

"No one knows. It's an Intelligence team secret."

"Oh, God, I don't know if I can eat anything now. My belly hurts too much from laughing."[14]

NINETY-FOUR

Are They In or Are They Out

TUESDAY, 22 NOVEMBER 1921, LONDON

AFTER ANOTHER TRIP TO DUBLIN FOR A MEETING WITH DE VALERA, Michael returned to London and was back for morning Mass the following day.[1] Ned Broy watched Liam Tobin as he walked slowly back down the side aisle of the Brompton Oratory. Ned noticed that Liam's wan, doleful demeanour was still evident even in the sanctuary of the church as he glided along stealthily, his arms barely moving, nearly lifeless at his side. He eased his body into the pew next to Ned and sat, silently staring at the front of the church.

Ned leaned over and whispered, "Liam, whatever joys you derived from your stint at step-dancing have clearly worn off. You should give it another whirl."

Liam sat quietly for a moment as if he were considering this friendly suggestion, but then announced dispassionately, "Hazel Lavery is up there again with Mick."

Ned looked up to the side chapel and commented in a somewhat derisive tone, "She joined him the morning he left for Dublin, and there she is again, his first morning back. What do you make of that, Liam?"

Liam turned to Ned with an ashen expression, stared at him for a moment and then looked straight ahead again, "Oh, nothing."

Ned commented, "Beautiful woman, though."

"Very beautiful. If you like older women."

Ned stifled a laugh and answered, "Well, she does have a good ten years on Mick." He then asked in a more serious tone, "Still, would you say this is going to become a regular thing?"

"Say nothin' to no one about nothin,' and keep sayin' it."

"Well said." Ned thought for a moment and then added, with some worry and concern in his voice, "Well, I hope there's nothing in it to concern Miss Kiernan."

Liam turned to Ned again and said calmly, "So should Lady Lavery, if you ask my opinion." He returned his gaze to the chapel at the front of the church, watching as Michael lit a candle. "But as I said, I make nothing of it."

The two men then just sat silently, observing the couple at the chapel and keeping a watchful eye on any of the parishioners who headed that way.

Michael lit another candle and knelt again. Hazel waited a minute and then asked, "I know the first one was for your fiancée, but who is that one for, if you don't mind my asking?"

Michael made the sign of the cross and stood up, offering a hand to Hazel. "It's for Arthur Griffith. I worry about him. He looks increasingly worn out, so I try to ease his burden as best I can. More and more responsibility rests with me, and what responsibility it is."[2] He smiled weakly and said, "But let's keep that between ourselves." He then looked down the aisle to Ned and Liam and said, "I better be going. The boys are anxious to get me to a big meeting in Hans Place."

"Michael, will you be able to join John and me for dinner tonight?" Perhaps as a way of distinguishing herself from Michael's other friends, since the day they met, Hazel continued to call him Michael, never Mick.[3] "John is anxious to show you the painting. It certainly is a handsome portrait."

Michael smiled, "Not tonight, I should think, but soon. I promise. Want to come and say hello to the boys?"

Hazel pouted and said, "I rather think your friend Liam disapproves of me."

"Liam? Not a chance."

"Oh, a woman knows these things."

"Fiddle-faddle, come, let's go."

A little while later, after polite hellos and goodbyes, the three men were on their way over to Hans Place.

"How was your meeting in Dublin with the Chief, Mick?" Ned asked.

"An inch forward. Dev gave me a rough outline for a counter-proposal to the British draft of the Treaty. Not what the British want to hear, I'm afraid, but a shade closer. That's what we have to discuss today."

Liam had a pressing matter to discuss, "Look, Mick, we have some news concerning the head of police in Ulster, Colonel Wickham."

"Oh?"

Ned explained, "Yes, he's encouraging senior officers under his command to enrol illegal Loyalist para-military bands into the Ulster Specials. All this with the purpose of preparing the North for a fight in the event the Treaty negotiations break down."

Michael asked, "Yes, the A Specials full-timers, the B Specials part-timers, the C Specials reserves, and I suppose the D to Z Specials before they're done with it all. But who's behind this?"

"Sir Henry Wilson is. Along with someone on the British team you're dealing with, Worthington-Evans. But Wilson is the driving force behind it."[4]

Michael replied prophetically, "That old bastard Wilson will get his just desserts, all in good time. But for now, this is crucial information to bring to the table at Downing Street." He thought for a moment and then said, "But first, we have to hammer out a response to the British draft." They turned the corner at Hans Place, and Michael sighed, "Time to face our adversaries, by which, unfortunately, I mean our fellow delegates."

After three long hours of exhaustive wrangling, the first formal Irish draft had been patched together, incorporating to some degree the latest input from Dublin, and it was decided to take a short break before reviewing the morning's work. Some men stood up to stretch their legs or peek into the kitchen for something to nibble on. Michael sat on the edge of the dining room table, swinging his legs as he chatted with Arthur.

Erskine Childers sat at the other end of the table, leaned over to Barton, and whispered, "This is a far cry from where we started and from what I stayed up half the night writing out."

Barton consoled him, "You did a commendable job, Erskine, but there was no getting around the fact that some people in this delegation have abrogated their sworn oaths. I'm sorry to have stolen your credit of authorship, but there seemed no other way to get our ideas accepted."

"Yes, well, little good it did us. This document is an abomination."

Given the outright animosity between Childers and Griffith, when the entire team met that morning, the Treaty proposals crafted by Childers were presented as the work of Barton.[5] More hours of debating and making amendments followed, resulting in a draft reflecting significant changes in some key parts, not all to Childers' liking.

Michael noticed Barton and Childers whispering to each other at the other end of the table. He hopped off the table, took his seat, and asked Arthur, "What do you think those two are up to now, Arthur?"

"Oh, bother them. It's getting close to noon, and I'd like to get this to the P.M. Let's go over the main points one more time." Arthur cleared his throat and announced to all the delegates, "All right, gentlemen, shall we continue? Without going through the entire document still again, let's just review the key issues." He paused, looked down at Childers, who was still whispering something to Barton, and waited until he had his attention. "Thank you, Erskine. Now, if I may," and he began to read from the freshly typed paper, "*The following proposals are put forward upon the assumption that the essential unity of Ireland is maintained.* I trust we all can agree on that. The first paragraph reads thusly, *Legislative and Executive authority in Ireland shall be derived exclusively from the Elected Representatives of the Irish people.*"

Barton interrupted, "Arthur, I think by now we are all familiar with this aspect of the document. May we go to the paragraph on the Crown?"

"Very well. *Ireland agrees to be associated with*—not *within*, as requested —*with the British Commonwealth for purposes of common concern and, in respect of those purposes, to recognise the Crown as the symbol and accepted head of the Association.*"[6]

After reviewing the clauses on Ulster, trade, finance and defence, Arthur handed the document to Michael, who went into the kitchen to find Ned Broy. "Here you go, Ned. Get this over to Downing Street."

"Sure thing, Mick."

Rejoining Arthur in the dining room, Michael said, "Well, I wonder how it will be received in Downing Street."

Childers answered sarcastically, "I wonder how it will be received in Dublin. Ireland's full claim is for a Republic, unfettered by any obligation or restriction whatever. That document is full of concessions from our stated position and instructions."[7]

Griffith was furious. "Childers, you have been nothing if not obstructionist throughout all these deliberations. While the rest of us have been trying to arrive at some sort of acceptable agreement with the British, you have been doing your utmost to prevent one."

Childers stood up and said through clenched teeth, "If you feel that way, put it in writing."

Realising he had gone too far and that the lawyerly demand for such a document would not only not play well back in Dublin but also destroy any chance for unanimity among the delegates, Arthur yielded. "I'm sorry, Erskine. I withdraw that remark." [8]

"Very well, then," Childers replied and sat back down.

Arthur sat there quietly a moment, waiting for all the ripe tempers to abate somewhat. Michael leaned over and whispered, "Isn't this grand? And the Brits haven't even had a chance to weigh in with their opinion."

"They will soon enough," Arthur whispered back. Then in a clear voice, he addressed everyone at the table. "Perhaps this document is not perfect. Perhaps it is not all that all of us wanted. But it is the fruit of our best efforts as a team, so let's save our arguing for the British."

THE PRIME MINISTER TOSSED THE IRISH PROPOSALS ON THE TABLE, threw his arms in the air, and shouted at Thomas Jones, "This is of no use! They are back to their independent state again. The clause about the navy won't do. There's nothing to safeguard Ulster, either!"[9]

Birkenhead, who was off to the side listening to this tirade, quietly walked over to the table, picked up the document, and began perusing it. In a hopeful tone, he started, "Excuse me, Prime Minister, but there *is* some mention here about safeguards. It reads…"

"I know what it says, damn it, and it won't do."

Seeing the state Lloyd George was in, F.E. thought it best not to take the point any further at that particular moment and gave Chamberlain a warning look as he entered the room.

"Prime Minister," Chamberlain said cautiously, "I take it the Irish have fallen short of the mark?"

"Show him, F.E."

Chamberlain took the document from F.E. and looked it over while Lloyd George fulminated.

"These Sinn Féiners have filled me with despair," the Prime Minister exclaimed. "Ministers in His Majesty's government are busy men. We have spent weeks and weeks on this matter and apparently have made no progress whatsoever." Here he turned to Jones, raising his voice even higher as if almost as if Jones were the cause of his distress. "Are they in the Empire, or are they out? Are we to control naval defence, or are we not?"

Jones remained respectfully silent, but F.E. and Chamberlain murmured their support.

Lloyd George paused from his rant and exclaimed. "By the way, Generals Tudor and Greenwood both report that they knew nothing of this damn circular that Wickham concocted. What a damn foolish complication."

On hearing this, Jones murmured, "Pity Henry Wilson has not gone for a voyage around the world," indicating the likely source of authorization for the circular.[10]

In his rage, Lloyd George missed this remark, but paused, stood with his hands on his hips, and leaned forward, declaring, "If the Irish are not coming into the Empire, then we will make them."

After a moment of silence, Chamberlain turned to Jones and said in a disheartened tone, "Thomas, please convey to the Sinn Féiners that I feel quite let down. I would not have gone to Liverpool and made the speech I did had I known this was the sort of document they were going to put in." By all accounts, Chamberlain had given the speech of his life at the Liverpool conference extolling the virtues of the Treaty negotiations.

Lloyd George nodded in agreement, "Yes, Austen, I quite understand." He turned to Jones and said, "Now, Thomas, go over there right now and tell them they can all pack up and go home!"

THE IRISH DELEGATES DID NOT HAVE TO WAIT LONG FOR A REACTION TO their proposals. Within the hour, Thomas Jones was knocking on the door at Hans Place. When he came inside, he exhibited extreme distress, which was unusual for him.

"You do realise, Mr. Griffith, the P.M. is in total despair and is prepared to break off negotiations? The general feeling is that we are all where we started six weeks ago, and all the discussions are being treated as if they had never taken place."

Arthur's cryptic answer was simply, "I see."

Jones went on, "Your document does not accept the Crown and the Empire; it omits what has been agreed to on the trade and defence issues and still does not offer guarantees for Ulster. I implore you, please, withdraw your document and in its stead offer a more conciliatory statement."

"I'm sorry," Arthur answered softly, "I cannot do that."

Lowering his voice so no one else would hear, Jones asked, "What of your personal letter of assurance? This document deviates item by item from what has been agreed to."

"No, it does not, and I stand by that letter. We offer a method of Association with the Crown and Empire entirely within the spirit of our discussions. On the naval issues, there are some contradictory positions put forth by the Admiralty that need to be defined more precisely before we give our assent. As far as trade goes, I personally believe in free trade, but there are protectionists in our Cabinet who feel your document reduces Ireland to a position of economic subordination, so there are issues that must be worked on further. Regarding Ulster, we are certainly willing to guarantee her safeguards but only ask that they be named to avoid any misunderstanding in the future."

Jones calmed down slightly but still felt ill at ease. "Well, perhaps the P.M. misunderstood your stance on Ulster. After all our discussions on the subject, can you not use *within* the Commonwealth as opposed to *with* and drop the word *associated*?"

Arthur sighed and said, "The problem is that we hesitate to put into black and white in advance all to which we might be willing to agree. That would be tantamount to giving Lloyd George a blank cheque that would be cashed by James Craig, who would then know what limits we would be willing to go to, and then he would stand pat, remaining unchanged and unyielding. Over and over again in the past, Irish negotiators have been let down in this way by British statesmen, and the result has always been the same."

"I'll admit the truth in that, but surely you can see how things are different this time and how close we are to mutual agreement."

At this point, Michael arrived, and Jones repeated Lloyd George's message to the Irish delegation and gave him a quick summary of the discussion he had been having with Arthur.

Michael listened intently, and when Jones repeated his remark that things would be different this time, he asked, chin jutting forward, "And what of Colonel Wickham? He has been whipping up Loyalist fervour in anticipation of war against the Catholics in Ulster."

"I have to admit there's truth in that, as well," Jones replied. "I feel certain the Cabinet was unaware of this latest breach in the chain of command and can assure you the P.M. was furious about the matter. Wickham's orders will be rescinded."

"Humph!"

"Please, I don't want to be the intermediary who breaks off these negotiations, especially since Mr. Griffith has given me some explanations of your document that would go a long way to mollify our objections to it."

Arthur and Michael just looked at him in silence without offering any response.

Jones then picked up his hat and said with great disconsolation, "I implore you, think about what I have said. Don't let all fall to nought at this late stage. Please consider taking back your letter."

He put on his coat, and they walked him to the door. "Good day, gentlemen."[11]

"Good day."

Michael closed the door behind Jones and turned back to Arthur, "Well?"

Arthur answered, "My, that was all a bit much, wasn't it? I have no intention of breaking off."

"No, of course not. Call him back?"

"Later will be fine, I should think."

"Well, that's that."

LATER THAT EVENING MICHAEL ALIGHTED FROM A CAB IN FRONT OF THE Royal Court Theatre on Sloane Square. Emblazoned on the illuminated marquee was the name of the current production, George Bernard Shaw's latest, *Heartbreak House*.[12] Since it was late in the evening, the long first act was nearing its end. Michael did not have a ticket, but when he encountered an usher smoking a cigarette in the lobby, he went up to him and explained, "I'm just here to meet a couple of friends. Mind if I just slip in, mate?"

"No, just be quiet about it, though."

"The second act is a short one, isn't it?"

"Yes, thankfully. I'm about done in."

"Cheers," Michael replied and slipped the usher a coin. The usher put a finger to his lips, opened the door to the rear orchestra seats a crack, peered in, and then whispered, "In you go, matey. You can stand here in the back."

Michael did just that and then began looking around the theatre for his sister Hannie, who was there with Eamonn and May Duggan, but he could not spot them, so he just took in the play. He leaned against the back wall, twirling the ends of a relatively new moustache as he squinted at the stage.

From the stage, a male character was explaining defensively, *"I began making love to her automatically. What am I to do? I can't fall in love, and I can't hurt a woman's feelings by telling her so when she falls in love with me. And as women are always falling in love with my moustache..."*

"Uh, oh," Michael said to himself as he folded his arms and looked around self-consciously. *"... I get landed in all sorts of tedious and terrifying flirtations in which I'm not a bit in earnest."*

"Shite, I'll bet Hannie will have something to say about *that*."

A few minutes later the expected intermission arrived, and Michael craned his neck to see if he could spot his sister and friends. He still could not find them, so he followed the crowd into the lobby to continue his search there.

"Why, Michael, what a surprise!" he heard a familiar voice call from behind.

He turned to see Andy Cope. "Andy, fancy seeing you here." He noticed that Cope was still wearing his hat and coat. "You're a bit late for the play, aren't you?"

"Not really. I only came to seek out Eamonn Duggan. I heard he would be here, and I was hoping to have a few words with him. Have you seen him?"

"No, but I only just arrived, with the same intention." Michael looked around and then shrugged his shoulders, "Well, maybe they're all still at their seats. Let me stand you a drink."

"Lovely."

As they waited in line at the theatre bar, Michael said, "So, Andy, as I'm sure you heard, Arthur and I had a lively chat with Thomas Jones today. It would seem the P.M. had his nose put well out of joint by our memorandum."

"Yes, there have been rumours to that effect." He smiled but then said quite seriously, "Things are very near the breaking point."

"Ah, g'wan with ye. Hang on a moment," Michael said as the barman awaited his order. "Jameson?" he asked Cope.

"Lovely again."

Turning back to the barman, he placed his order, "Make that two of 'em, mate."

Michael handed Cope his tumbler, "I had sworn this stuff off, but I need it these days." As they walked away, he continued his train of thought, "Listen, Andy, like we told Jones earlier today, we are not going to hand Craig a blank cheque. We need to get his reaction to the draft and then negotiate accordingly."

A bell rang out, announcing the second act of the play.

"Come on, Andy. Let's polish off these drinks and catch the rest of the show. Afterwards, we can both look for Eamonn and then have a chat."

"Good. In fact, I have a message for both of you from the P.M."

———

THE SHOW ENDED, AND THIS TIME MICHAEL HAD BETTER LUCK FINDING his sister and the Duggans. Or so he thought. When Hannie spotted Michael, she ran up to him and threw her arms around his neck, swooning as she cried, *"And women are always falling in love with my moustache."*

Michael looked over to Cope. "When I heard that line, I knew I was in for it."

Hannie laughed and said, "You? What about Kitty? She's the one that has to endure that scrub brush under your nose." She looked to the Duggans for support, but they just laughed.

"That's enough of that," Michael protested. "We're here on business."

"Oh, sorry," Hannie replied in a very serious tone, poking fun.

"Actually," Cope replied, "there is something I would like to discuss with the gentlemen, if I could impose upon the ladies for a moment."

Relieved to be extricated from his sister's teasing, Michael bowed slightly to May but just squinted at Hannie and said, "You don't mind, do you?"

Michael and Duggan walked over to the side with Cope, who got right to the point of his mission that evening. "The Prime Minister is very anxious to know how far you are willing to go to meet on middle ground."

"Relax, Andy," Michael answered. "I called Jones a while ago and suggested that Arthur and I meet Lloyd George and Birkenhead tomorrow to iron out our differences on the document."

"Yes, I know, and that's fine. Michael, allow me to pass along a word of advice from Jones, if I may. In order to prevent a complete collapse, please be prepared to give categorical assurances on fundamentals like allegiance and the navy."[13]

"Yes, yes, something will be forthcoming after we all put our heads together on it. It's better we discuss it in person."

Duggan agreed, adding, "Putting it in writing before discussion, as was suggested earlier, makes it sound like an ultimatum. What we all want is something mutually acceptable, isn't it?"

"Yes, of course," Cope had to concur.

Michael laughed and said, "Well, good, then. Listen, speaking of an ultimatum, I have a very formidable monsignor back in Dublin who gave his personal secretary leave to join us here in London. I say formidable because he'll have my head if I don't have her home in time for Christmas. How good do you think are the chances of my keeping my head where it is?"

Cope answered, "Well, if it were up to those here in London, you could close a deal by this month's end, but then we have to factor in our friends in Dublin, don't we?"

Michael groaned, "Argh! And I was just beginning to enjoy our little chat. Good night, Andy. Tell the P.M. we'll see him tomorrow and likely go to Dublin soon after."

NINETY-FIVE

L'Armée Nouveau

MICHAEL AND NED BROY EMERGED FROM BROMPTON ORATORY, AND Michael walked over to his brash young friend, the impudent newsboy.

"Hiya, Mick! It's *The Times*, right? Same as all my other high-class clients."

Michael shook his head and grinned, "*The Times* it is, boyo."

Michael pulled his coat collar tightly around his neck, tucked the newspaper under his arm, and he and Ned headed back to the house in Cadogan Gardens. They went straight into the kitchen, and Michael tossed the paper on the table and went to the stove to warm his hands. Liam Tobin was sitting at the kitchen table, sipping from a cup of coffee. He picked up the newspaper and browsed through it.

The faithfully ever-cheery Eddie welcomed the new arrivals, "Hi, Mick, Ned. I just brewed that coffee."

"Thanks, Eddie, I'll help myself," Michael replied. "Ned?" he asked, waving the pot.

"Ay, thanks."

Liam put the paper down and murmured, "Oh, no."

Michael sat down and asked, "What ails ye, Liam?" When Liam handed him the paper, Michael repeated, "Oh, no."

Liam agreed, "Yes, I'm afraid this confirms some unwelcome news I just got. You didn't see this?"

Ned came over and read the headline out loud, "*Raid on Windsor Barracks. Machine Guns and Rifles Stolen.*" He skimmed the short article, "*Monday night, Victoria Barracks, Windsor.*"

Michael sighed, "Well, how's that for a kick in the bollocks? This looks like the work of some of our boys."

Liam answered, "I'm afraid so. I received word it was Ned Lynch, three other local lads, and an Irish Guard named Roche. The sordid details will probably hit tomorrow's papers."

Michael was furious. He slammed his fist on the table, "Those skitter arses! I saw Lynch that very morning and told him to stay the hell out of trouble!"

Ned was surprised at the development, "You didn't know about the raid?"

"No, I tried to warn them off any such foolishness. Cathal Brugha's behind all this, I'll wager."

Ned offered his help, saying, "I'll look into it, Mick."

Michael was still seething, "That's not all. Arthur told me Dev is proposing to decommission all the officers in the I.R.A. and offer them commissions in a 'New Army,' provided they and their men take an oath of loyalty to the Dáil. He plans to shuffle the top positions in G.H.Q. and hold the ceremony this Friday, the twenty-fifth."

"Top positions which, coincidentally," Liam added in a questioning tone, "would be filled by his men?"

"Ay, that's the gist of it, Dev playing the cute hoor again."

Ned replied, "And everyone would take an oath to the Dáil, of which Dev is now President."

Liam summarized, "And an oath to the Dáil is an oath to Dev."

"Spot on, Liam."

"That old sleveen is looking to take over the entire Army."

Michael responded, "Well, I know how to take care of *that*. We call a meeting of the General Headquarters Staff of the 'Old Army'— which reminds me of Napoleon's Old Guard—early Friday morning."

"*Vive la* Dev," Ned said with a smirk.

"Maybe, maybe not. Let the old boys who have been around for a while talk it over and decide

if they want to join Dev's *armée nouveau*.[1] Christ, with me just after returning from Dublin, here I am on my way back again. Emmet has to go to Dublin tomorrow on some liaison business. I'll send Tom with him to make discreet inquiries to the Brotherhood. Something should come of our meeting with Lloyd George today, and Birkenhead tomorrow, so all the more reason enough for me to return."

NINETY-SIX

Curse All Secret Societies

FRIDAY, 25 NOVEMBER 1921, DUBLIN

As promised to Andy Cope Tuesday evening at the theatre, Michael and Arthur had their meeting with Lloyd George the following day. Surprisingly, not much was made of the item in the papers about the raid on Windsor Barracks, but neither was much progress made in the discussions. However, everyone had walked back from the brink and were at least talking again. The day after that, Thursday, accompanied by John Chartres for support on constitutional law, they met Birkenhead in his chambers in Westminster. As a sop to the intransigent camp of dissenters on the Irish team, Gavan Duffy and Erskine Childers came along, though thankfully, Childers got sidelined in the private secretary's room by Lionel Curtis. Duffy was long-winded as usual, and F.E. had a lively engagement with Chartres, but Michael and Arthur were the ones who garnered some considerable concessions. As Michael had predicted, this further warranted another overnight train and boat trip back to Dublin.[1]

After arriving in Dublin with Arthur Griffith and Robert Barton Friday morning, Michael took leave of his colleagues and headed to the Wicklow Hotel just off Grafton Street for a meeting with friends in the Irish Republican Brotherhood, Batt O'Connor among them. Michael had written Richard Mulcahy, the Chief of Staff of the I.R.A., to ask him to pull together this meeting with some senior members of General Headquarters, or G.H.Q. Eoin O'Duffy and Ginger O'Connell, who had accompanied Michael Collins to London as military advisors, were also present.[2] Their appointments to the London mission had irked de Valera, who would have preferred to send men of his choosing. He would have been granted his wishes if Michael had gone through the proper channel, that being the Minister of Defence, Cathal Brugha, who was also incensed by this slight.

Everyone had gathered around a couple of small lunch tables at the hotel and listened intently as Michael gave his synopsis of the latest developments in the treaty negotiations.

"So, Mick, what will this Oath entail?" Batt O'Connor asked.

"Ah, the expected palaver about allegiance to the King, if the Brits have it their way, or allegiance to the nations known as the Associated States commonly referred to as the British Commonwealth, or some such tongue-twisting if Dev has his. The thing is, there has to be some sort of oath, or no deal, but rather, renewed war."

"Which isn't much of a deal," Batt added.

"No, it isn't, not with the present state of affairs in the Army," Richard Mulcahy agreed.

Michael continued, "The precise wording has not been settled on by either side. That's one of the reasons we've returned from London. It's one of many issues that have to be sorted out here, no doubt *ad infinitum* and *ad nauseum*."

"And then there's this business about restructuring G.H.Q.," Mulcahy mused. "Well, don't worry, Mick. When we see Dev about his 'New Army,' I'll wager that our discussion will be short, sweet, and to the point."

"Well, thanks, boys, I thought it might." Michael got up to leave. "Not that I meant to influence your decision one way or the other."

"Oh, no, Mick," O'Duffy answered wryly as he stood up to shake Michael's hand. "Perish the thought."

Michael said grimly. "As for this Windsor Barracks burglary, I assured everyone I knew nothing of Ned Lynch's bungled arms raid. God, I could throttle the man! Dick, did you find out if Cathal had a hand in this?"

Mulcahy answered, "I did, and his hands are clean on this one. It seems Ned and the others were on a boozer and cooked up the scheme on the spot."

"What the hell were they thinking?" Michael responded. "The papers say Lynch and his cohorts had been under surveillance since they got here. They may have given their minders the slip long enough to get out to Windsor, but it didn't take the police long to find their stash at that house in Shepherd's Bush." Michael laughed, "I may not have been aware of what these lads of ours were up to, but it seems Macready, Tudor, and Greenwood were all in the dark about Colonel Wickham."

"True," O'Connell replied, "but it seems Sir Henry Wilson was the real culprit."

Batt spread out a newspaper he had with him and said, "Well, at least there's some good news today. It says here Craig has withdrawn Wickham's circular."[3]

"Lloyd George must have been livid," Mulcahy commented.

Michael stood up and said, "Well, now you have it. Now you know where we stand with the negotiations in London. Faith, we could be mere days away from a settlement there, and just when we need to show a united front..." He threw his arms up in the air in disgust. "All I can say is the Long Fellow picked a fine time to stir the pot with all this conniving and subterfuge with Cathal over G.H.Q. Boys, wish me luck in the negotiations, and by that, I mean the negotiations back here at home."

Mulcahy laughed, writing in the air with his fingers as usual while he spoke. "Well, if things go badly, not to worry. Dev wants to have his New Army signing-in ceremony right after meeting with you and Arthur. We'll all be there at Mansion House, waiting in the hall to be ushered in after you. Just blow a bugle or something if it gets nasty."

Michael smiled back and took stock of his friend. Richard Mulcahy was a handsome man with finely sculpted features and piercing eyes who always seemed capable of maintaining a graceful repose but equally capable of springing into action to devastating effect. In short, he was definitely a type of soldier after his own heart, and Michael appreciated having him by his side, and he said so in so many words, "I knew I could count on you to treat all this in your usual fashion.[4] Thanks, Dick. I'll probably see you later." Then he slapped Batt on the back and said, "Come along, Batt, catch me up on things here."

"Ah, well, I do have some news for you, Mick." Batt looked around and said confidentially, "It involves our friend Convict 224."

Slightly alarmed, Michael asked, "Is he all right?"

"Oh, I'd say so. He evidently had a highly successful encounter with a fetching Irish Blue Terrier bitch, and you have a litter of little puppies as proof."

Michael's eyes widened, and he slapped his thigh, "That's my boy!"

"Christy has Crumpet watching over them in her stable, but everyone is clambering for a puppy. Christy told them they'd have to wait for you to have the pick of the lot."

"Powerful news, Batt, and just in time for the dog show tomorrow. Let's pay Christy, Crumpet, and the proud papa a visit."

ARTHUR WAS GROWING WEARY OF THE EXTENDED MEETING THAT afternoon at Mansion House but nevertheless smiled at Kathleen O'Connell, de Valera's secretary, and asked, "May we hear that one more time, Kathleen?"

"Certainly, sir." Glancing first at de Valera, she read back from her notes, "*Ireland should recognise the British Crown for the purposes of the Association, as symbol and accepted head of the combination of Associated States.*"[5]

Austin Stack beamed happily, "Yes, I think this represents a substantial compromise on our part. Wouldn't you agree, Arthur?"

Arthur blinked and turned for support to Michael, who smiled weakly and replied, "Yes, we thought you might like that, Austin. Erskine Childers came up with the phrasing."

As Cathal Brugha nodded his approval, he said, "Yes, not bad. It represents a fair interpretation of the concept of External Association."

"Thank you, Cathal," Arthur replied. "I told Lord Birkenhead that for external affairs, such as peace, war and defence, Ireland would accept this form of association, while for internal affairs, she would retain the Republic. He found no fault with this view, so I took this argument a step further and told him he may prefer to translate *Saorstát Éireann* as 'Free State' instead of 'Republic.'"

Remembering the embarrassing situation he had with Lloyd George regarding translating the word *Saorstát* the day he met him, de Valera just listened quietly.

Arthur continued, "Birkenhead accepted this and replied that the title, 'Free State,' can go into the Treaty." He looked around at the members of the Cabinet. "This is a significant advance on their previous position."

This improvement was favourably received, even by Austin Stack and Cathal Brugha. Then Michael said, "I might add that when Birkenhead tried to stress Dominion status on the lines with Canada, Erskine argued very forcefully how that analogy would not be acceptable to us, but this will be discussed further when we return."

De Valera was pleased with these developments and rose to end the meeting. "Very well, gentlemen. Good luck upon your return to London. I now have to attend a ceremony for our officers in the Army, who have been waiting patiently outside."

Arthur and Michael rose from their seats and left the room. On their way out, they saw Richard Mulcahy waiting and talking with the men who had met with Michael earlier in the day. Mulcahy came over, smiled, and said, "I didn't hear any bugle calls. I assume all went well. How is His Excellency?"

"Ah, you'll find him in the rarest of moods, quite well pleased," Michael answered. "You should have a grand time of it with him. Let me know how it goes."

"Will do, Mick," Mulcahy answered. "Arthur," he said with a slight bow and went into de Valera's office.

Arthur and Michael walked through the hall and then lingered on the steps outside. "Well, Michael, what did you make of it?"

"On the surface, it seemed to go well, but in terms of getting useful instructions, not all that different from my last trip here."

"No, apparently not." Arthur sighed, "I hope you noticed, I managed to get the words external and association into a single sentence back in there, but it's remarkable how many different ways Dev and friends can labour to express the concept and how many different ways Lloyd George can say no. This is my first trip home since we started, and I'm not sure if I will return to London any more enlightened than before I left. Still, we inch ahead. I'm heading straight to the ferry back. Coming?"[6]

"No, I have lots of big plans for the weekend," he said, beaming happily. "Convict has done his manly best, and I have a puppy to choose."

"Finally, some purely good news. Just don't spoil it with an awkward name."

"Point taken, especially if I decide to enter him in the Dublin Blue Terrier Club dog show tomorrow. Then hopefully, on Sunday, I'll be able to get to Granard. I may ask Pat McCrea to drive me up.[7] I'll try to come up with as many ways I can of saying the right thing to Kitty."

"Good man. Then see you back in London?"

"See you there."

Back inside Mansion House, the cheery mood was about to take a sudden turn. De Valera was seated at his desk, explaining his plans for the composition of the New Army to Richard Mulcahy and his staff. "As you know, today is the anniversary of the founding of the Volunteers back in 1913. We thought this would be a fitting occasion to re-commission the Army. Now, you could retain Eoin O'Duffy here as your Deputy Chief of Staff, provided Austin Stack would be Cathal Brugha's ghost Deputy Chief on the Staff."[8]

Mulcahy stared back silently for a moment as if mulling this proposal over. Then he gave a jaundiced stare at Brugha, who was seated off to the side near de Valera, and replied coolly, "I'm satisfied with the Deputy Chief I have, and one is enough." He then smiled at de Valera, turned to his companions there and asked, "Well, what do you think, boys?"

Ginger O'Connell spoke up first, "With all due respect to the President," he said with a slight bow of his head to de Valera, eliciting from him an uncertain smile. "We on the current staff consider ourselves to be a band of brothers, and we see no reason to make any unnecessary changes."

This rebuke drained all colour from de Valera's face, but then Eoin O'Duffy pushed the point further, "The insinuation that you find it necessary to have a 'ghost' Deputy Chief looking over my shoulder is an affront to my abilities and integrity. I find these proposals personally insulting."

Cathal Brugha stood there aghast, and de Valera's face turned red with anger. He stood up, forcefully pushing his chair away from his desk and shouted in near hysteria, "Ye may mutiny if ye like, but Ireland will give me another army. Now consider yourselves dismissed!"[9]

Mulcahy answered coolly and calmly, "Yes, sir!" He barked out, "Gentlemen!" Then he, O'Duffy and O'Connell stood at attention, saluted, turned sharply, and walked brusquely out together.

De Valera breathed heavily through his nostrils and hissed through his teeth, "That Collins!"

Brugha whispered into his ear, "He and his feckin' Brotherhood are at the heart of this. They got to them first."

"Curse all secret societies," de Valera fumed with rage, echoing a similar condemnation by the Catholic Church, which throughout the ages had forbidden membership in secret societies that demanded oaths of allegiance, considering them a challenge to Church doctrine and authority.[10] This dictate was now something to which de Valera wholeheartedly subscribed. The "heresy" committed here by the Irish Republican Brotherhood, of which he was still nominally a member, was to question de Valera's supreme authority, and the risk of excommunication from his good graces was quite real.

Nevertheless, outside on the Mansion House steps, Mulcahy commented nonchalantly to his friends as he pointed with a thumb back over his shoulder, "Well, I thought that went rather well."

"Splendid!"

"Yes, lovely."

"Anyone fancy a pint?"

"Let's go find Mick. I have a feeling he'll be buying."

NINETY-SEVEN

No Harm Done

"PAT, YOU SHOULD'VE SEEN THE LITTLE TYKE. ALL THE GIRLS WERE fallin' over themselves to give him a pogue."

"Ay, we all know what that's like," Pat McCrea shot back as their car crossed into County Longford. "So, what did you name him?"

Michael laughed and explained, "Well, after Arthur berated me over the naming of his dad, Convict 224, I played it safe with something all the world would love."

"Oh, and what would that be?"

Michael started to sing his answer, "*Oh, Danny Boy…*"

"Danny Boy? That's lovely."

They both started to sing together, "*Oh, Danny Boy, the pipes, the pipes are calling…*"

They carried on like this as they drove through the streets of Granard until they reached the Greville Arms. As Pat slowed down to take a look, he and Michael sang more softly, finishing their duet, "*And I shall sleep in peace until you come to me.*"

"Doesn't look like they'll be taking reservations anytime soon, Mick."

"No, not much progress."

Pat turned the next corner into New Road, and he and Michael got out together.[1]

"Come on, Pat. Kitty will be expecting us for lunch."

"Well, now, the thing is, as you said yourself, we don't have a lot of time. I'll just stay down here and putter with the engine. Let you two have a bit of a visit on your own, as it were." He looked at his watch. "Oh, now, look at the time already."

Michael looked at him suspiciously, shrugged and said, "Suit yourself."

About half an hour later, when they were finishing up their cups of tea, Kitty exclaimed, "Danny Boy sounds like a real sweetheart. You must be so proud."

"Wait until you see the papers. The *Freeman's Journal* photographer assured me they'd run his picture with the by-line, 'Dublin Irish Blue Terrier Club. First Prize in the Puppy Class.' Proud? Ay, and pleased as Punch."

"Michael, are you sure Pat wouldn't want to come in and join us?" Kitty asked a little while later as she got up from the table to take a look outside. Pat was busying himself with the car across the road.

"I don't think so. He seemed anxious today." Michael walked over to join her, peered through the curtains, and shook his head. "Look at him with his noggin' in the bonnet, still trying to make out like he knows what's in it."

"Oh, dear, don't say that. After Pat's gone to such trouble to take you here to see me."

"Arrah, don't worry about him. The country air is doing us both some good," he snapped back, somewhat irritated, though more from exhaustion than anything Kitty said. He slumped down into a cushioned chair by the window.

"Humph!" Kitty teased. "Not that either of you will be getting that much of it. You've only just arrived, and you say you have to be going back soon?" She walked past him, stopped and turned, running a hand down her matching jacket and skirt.

Seemingly oblivious to this gesture, Michael answered curtly, "I said I'm sorry about the weekend, Kit." He realised his tone was sharper than he wished and lowered his voice. "We didn't have much time together, and I'm probably not at my best, anyway."

Kitty looked at him with genuine concern written in her eyes. "I just worry that you're pushing yourself too hard, darling."

"Ah, not to worry. You know what I always say, 'It's better to wear out than rust out.'[2] I'll be fine." He had a twinge of pain in his stomach and grimaced slightly.

"See, Michael, you really should have something proper to eat before you drive all the way back to Dublin," Kitty admonished him. "Can you not stay for supper?"

"Sorry, but there are more things to attend to early in the morning." He walked to the front door and called out to Pat, who had just closed the bonnet and was leaning on the side of the car. "About ready? We'll grab something on the way, won't we, Paddy?"

"Whatever you say, Mick."

"Everything with you is always in such great haste, as you are wont to say," Kitty complained, quoting a phrase Michael often used to sign off his letters to her. "You didn't even notice my new suit."

"Ay, but I did, and you look lovely in it."

"Then why didn't you say so?"

Michael turned again and looked outside at Pat, who looked down at his watch. "Why didn't I," Michael started with some irritation in his voice but stopped himself short. "You're right, but you know I am not demonstrative…"

"Except when you're angry," she corrected him.

"Yes, except when I sometimes show my temper. But I hate demonstrations of feeling in front of people, which to my mind just seems insincere. It may be an unpleasant, unappealing thing to admit to, but that's me. But what it really means is that I'm on the side of those who do things, not on the side of those who say things."

"And that's that,"[3] Kitty responded a little sarcastically.

"You could say so," he agreed. "Kit, I would never forgive myself if I made your life unhappy. Little wrongs I may have done people never cease coming back to my mind, but especially anything I've done to you. You may not see that side of me, but it *is* there."[4]

The tears welled in Kitty's eyes, and her voice softened as she sobbed, "Oh, Mick, I'm sorry to ask so much of you when you have so much pressing in on you as it is."

He held her by the shoulders but glanced across the street to Pat, who just turned away, taking out a rag to wipe a spot on the car. Michael whispered, "That's all right, Kit. Give us a smile, now. Got to go."

She smiled, stepped out onto the porch, and stood arms at her side as Michael walked over to the car.

"Shall we get going?" Pat asked uncertainly.

"Sure, Pat, but what's the big hurry?"

"Hurry? Oh, nothing. Let's go."

Michael got in the car, and Pat took off suddenly with a roar of the car's engine, the force of the acceleration pushing Michael back into his seat. "No hurry, eh?"

They both managed a farewell wave to Kitty, who waved back, watching them as they drove off.

As he sped down the road, Pat said, "Now, I hate to tear you away from your sweetheart, but you know, beat the traffic, and we'll get you back to Dublin."

Michael squinted narrowly over at his driver and suggested, "And you quick as a rabbit back to meet a sweetheart of your own, I'd judge by the speedometer."

"Something like that, you could say."

"Well, your sweetheart, poor unfortunate soul, whoever she may be, will just have to wait. Slow down." As they careened around a corner, Michael shouted back, "For Christ's sake, at least wait until we get on the open road."

After an hour or so, Michael began grasping his stomach in pain. "Ay, it's my stomach again, Paddy." He looked ahead and saw a small roadside restaurant. "Pull in here, Pat. I could do with a warm glass of milk."

"You sure, Mick? We'll be back in Dublin before you know it." He looked over to Michael, who was just staring back at him coldly. "Then again, what's the rush?"

"My sentiments exactly." He patted his stomach. "Kitty was right about travelling on an empty stomach."

"Ay, women usually are," Pat murmured back.

A short while after their rest stop, they were back on the road, and half an hour later, they pulled up to the Gresham Hotel in Dublin. Michael was easing himself out of the car when Pat leaned across the seat, saying, "Well, if that's it for now, Mick, I'll be going, then."

"Mother of Christ! Pat, can I get out of the car first?"

"Oh, sure, sorry about that." But a second later he was off in a cloud of dust.

MICHAEL WENT INSIDE AND USED THE HOTEL'S COURTESY PHONE TO call Emmet Dalton in the office upstairs.

Tom Cullen answered, "Hello?"

"Tom, it's me."

"Oh, you're back from Granard already?"

"No, I popped over to New York. Put Emmet on. This call's costing a fortune."

"We must have a good connection; it sounds like you're calling from the lobby. Here's Emmet."

"Hiya, Mick."

"Emmet, come down and join us for a bite. Bring Tom, if he likes."

"Will do. Hang on." Emmet covered the telephone mouthpiece for a moment, and then informed Michael, "Tom says he has an important phone call to make. He'll join us later."

"I understand completely. His wife would give him hell if he didn't call on a trip home. Hurry down."

Emmet and Michael met at the entrance to the hotel dining room, where they were warmly greeted by Mr. Donahue. "Mr. Collins, Mr. Dalton, how very good to see you again. I hope all fares well with your work in London."

"We're getting there, Mr. Donahue," Michael responded.

"And how is Master Eddie? I hope he is comporting himself properly."

"Ay, more than that, he's made some useful contributions to the negotiations."

"This is Eddie we are talking about, are we not?"

"You must miss him terribly."

"I, er, we manage. I'll be back in a moment to take your orders."

As they viewed their menus, Michael asked, "So, what's the story, Emmet? Any incidents recently?"

"Nothing, Mick. The British haven't done a single thing in violation of the Truce. Not the army, the police, not even the Tans or Auxis. Nothing. Of course, I cannot say the same for our fellows."

Suddenly Toby Kelly came bursting into the dining room.

"Toby, you little hooligan! Howaya, lad?" Michael asked cheerfully.

"Why then, not too good, Mick. I've got some terrible news!" he answered breathlessly. "Pat McCrea's been banged up!"

"What?"

"What for?" Emmet asked.

"Reckless driving, it seems," he answered.

Michael and Emmet just stared at each other with their mouths agape.

"They're holding him in the College Street Police Station."

A big grin spread across Michael's face, and then he erupted in laughter. "Well, at least it's him that's banged up, and not the car."

As Toby saw Emmet laughing along with Michael, he finally saw the humour in the situation and asked, only half kidding, "Ye going to bust him out, Mick?"

"Bust him out?!" Michael asked, still laughing. "Well, I think we'd better go assess the situation. After all, this is the man who bravely drove Emmet right into Mountjoy Jail to bust out Seán MacEoin."

"That's right, and we nearly made it out with him," Emmet concurred. "It's the least we could do for Pat."

On their way out, Mr. Donahue approached with a look of concern.

"Not to worry," Michael assured him. "We'll be back soon."

A SHORT WHILE LATER MICHAEL AND DALTON WERE AT THE COLLEGE Street police station, discussing the situation with the sergeant on duty. Michael occasionally looked over to Pat, who was standing in his cell, grasping the bars with clenched hands, with a hopeful but forlorn look on his face. Each time their eyes met, Michael just shook his head disconsolately. Michael and Emmet crossed the station floor over to Pat but paused for a moment and whispered to each other. Michael motioned Pat to join them at the corner of the cell, away from the other cellmates.

"So, what's the story, Mick? Can you not get me out?"

"Well, we could use dynamite, but we might kill you in the bargain."

"Dynamite? So help me fuckin' Christ! I was only speeding!"

"Furious driving, according to the sergeant," Emmet answered gravely. "You may be looking at some serious time here, Pat."

Michael nodded in agreement, saying, "Better give me the home address of that sweetheart of yours, Paddy. We'll see that she's well looked after, won't we, Emmet?"

"Goes without saying. We do that for all our men."

"Go on outta that!" Pat cried out. "Mick, get me the hell out of here!"

"Sorry, Pat, but at this delicate stage in the Treaty negotiations, we can't be too careful, you know." Michael looked to Emmet and said, "Well, we better be going. We have to get back to London, don't we? Be sure to write to me, Pat, that is, if they'll let you, and let me know how you're getting on. I promise to write back, when I can. *Slán leat.*"

Keeping with the gravity of the situation, Emmett enjoined him, "Take care of yourself now, Pat," adding solemnly with a nod toward the other prisoners, "and mind your back."

Pat glanced wide-eyed at the men on the other end of the cell, sitting with arms folded, staring back, bored and jaded. "For the love of Christ, Mick, do something!" Pat pleaded. "Emmett, you poxy little bastard, don't just leave me here!"

On their way out, they paused at the sergeant's desk. "Excuse me again, sergeant," Michael asked politely.

"Yes, what is it, Mick?" he asked with a pleasant smile.

"How long were you thinking you'd need to hold him?"

"Oh, I think we'll let him go in another hour or so. After all, no harm done."

"Thank you, sergeant. Good day."[5]

NINETY-EIGHT

As Stubble In Our Hands

MONDAY, 28 NOVEMBER 1921, CHEQUERS, BUCKINGHAMSHIRE

SITTING WITH HIS MATES ON THE DECK OF THE EVENING FERRY TO London, Michael took the day's issue of the *Freeman's Journal* from his briefcase to look at it again. He folded the front page and once again proudly read the heading over the photograph of Danny Boy.

Brandishing the paper, he asked, "Did you see this, fellas?"

Tom read the caption, "*Michael Collins Owns a Dog.*" [1]

"You must be fierce proud of the lad, Mick," Emmet said, smiling broadly.

Michael smiled broadly but then, wishing to remain anonymous, put a forefinger to his lips, quietly folded the paper, and put it away.

WHILE MICHAEL WAS AT SEA EXULTING IN DANNY BOY'S accomplishments, Arthur Griffith and Eamonn Duggan were en route to Buckinghamshire for their first visit to the Prime Minister's country residence, Chequers. Lloyd George, anxious to learn the results of the weekend consultations in Dublin, had asked Thomas Jones to invite the Irish delegates down for the night.

Jones arrived a little before eight o'clock and was greeted by Frances Stevenson and Sir Philip Sassoon. After exchanging pleasantries, Frances said gaily, "Come along, T.J. He's up in the Long Room."

They all went up the stairs to the historic chamber that housed a considerable collection of works of art and relics relating to Oliver Cromwell. There was a large fireplace in the middle of the room, and there Lloyd George was stretched out with his feet up on a couch, reading some dusty old tome.

"Oh, T.J., welcome. When are our Irish friends coming? They *are* coming, I trust."

"Yes, sir." Jones then informed the Prime Minister, "Mr. Tim Healy was going to join them but had a change of mind.[2] His input might have been useful. As for the others, they are coming, but I'm afraid they have declined your invitation to spend the night. In fact, they will forgo dinner here as well. It seems they have a strict rule not to fraternize with their opponents, er, excuse me, opposite numbers on the British delegation."

"Well, that's damn silly of them," Lloyd George said dismissively.

"Yes, sir." Jones was now standing before the mantelpiece beneath the great sword of Cromwell. Framed below it was a reproduction of a letter written by Cromwell after a famous battle. Jones glanced at the letter, which quoted a line from the Book of Isaiah: *The Lord made them as stubble in our hands.*[3] Looking back to Lloyd George, he surmised, "Perhaps they have their reasons."

"Well, damn silly. Anyway, I'm anxious to hear what developed on their trip to Dublin."

"As it happens, sir, they sent me a written report for you. I took the liberty of showing it to Mr. Chamberlain before taking the train here, so I also have a letter from him that states his views on the matter."

"Well done, Thomas. May I?"

Jones took the letters from his briefcase and handed them to Lloyd George, who read them out loud, the Irish letter first.

After reading the letter, he clutched it while dropping his hand onto the couch, saying, "This means war."[4]

"Can it wait until after dinner?" Birkenhead asked as he swept into the room. "Have I missed something important?"

"Judge for yourself," Lloyd George responded, handing him the Irish letter.

"Hmm, let's see. *That Ireland should recognise the British Crown for the purposes of association, as symbol and accepted head of the combination of Associated States.* Rather inelegantly put, I'd say."

"Can you imagine having to explain that to the King? 'Yes, Your Majesty, we do have a Treaty with your Irish subjects, but from now on, you shall be referred to as the symbol and accepted head of the combination of associated states.'"

Birkenhead smiled at this but said encouragingly, "Methinks this is not the Irishmen's last word, Prime Minister."

"It had better not be. Let's eat."

AFTER DINNER EVERYONE RETURNED TO THE LONG ROOM IN anticipation of the pending meeting. All were enjoying coffee or tea when a servant entered and announced, "The Irish delegates have arrived, Prime Minister. Will we be serving them anything in here?"

"Oh, Lord, no," Lloyd George said in a severe tone.

"Sir?"

Thomas Jones intervened, "That's all right, just show them in."

Lloyd George turned to F.E. and explained, "Apparently, fraternizing with the enemy is off."

"Really?" F.E. answered. "That's not been my experience with them, at least not with Collins."

"Has it not? Well, he seems to be the most pragmatic of the lot. Unfortunately, we're told he hasn't returned yet from Dublin."

"No? Pity."

Moments later Arthur Griffith and Eamonn Duggan were shown in, and after the usual civil exchanges, omitting handshakes, Lloyd George remarked, "As the Lord Chancellor was saying, it's a shame Mr. Collins could not be here for this meeting."

"Yes, Prime Minister," Arthur responded. Assuming Lloyd George and Birkenhead were not avid readers of the *Freeman's Journal*, he explained, "He had some urgent affairs to attend to in Dublin."

"I see. Well, please have a seat."

Lloyd George wasted no time expressing his displeasure with the Irish proposals. "This document is impossible. Any British Government that attempted to propose to the British people the abrogation of the Crown would be smashed to atoms."

Arthur showed little reaction and just responded calmly, "We have no authority to deal on any other basis than the exclusion of the Crown from purely Irish affairs."

Lloyd George responded, "Yet if you were to look to Canada, you'd find little evidence of Crown involvement in her affairs."

Arthur answered immediately, "The Crown in Canada is merely a symbol, but in Ireland it would be a reality." He argued further, "In Ireland the Crown would not function. We Irish require a symbolism acceptable to us."[5]

Birkenhead replied, "Yes, Mr. Chartres made that argument when he, you, and Mr. Collins visited my chambers last week. As I pointed out, we British have our own symbolism."

On hearing this, Lloyd George remained silent, but leaned forward, placed his elbows on his knees, spread the fingers of both hands far apart, then tapped his opposing fingertips together, all the while deep in thought, though staring right at Arthur. "Very well, then," he said at last, "I find myself at a complete loss for words to assuage your apprehensions on the Crown, so I will leave it up to you. You can insert in the Treaty any phrase you like which would ensure that the position of the Crown in Ireland should be no more in practice than it is in Canada or in any other Dominion."[6]

A wave of emotion swept over Arthur as he realised that all his objections regarding the Crown, and perhaps those of Erskine Childers, not to mention de Valera, were just knocked down by this offer.

He remained placidly silent, though, as F.E. reminded them, "Yes, and as I have already indicated, you may refer to yourselves as the Irish Free State."

Lloyd George affirmed this, "You would have the same national status as the Dominion of Canada and be known as the Irish Free State. I trust that this meets your needs?"[7]

Duggan cleared his throat and added a lawyerly point, "Well, this sheds new light on the subject. However, for our side, there remains the difficulty of the wording of the Oath of Allegiance."

F.E. waved his hand dismissively, "As it does for us. But we will try to modify it if that would help you."[8]

Arthur and Duggan looked at each other and nodded. Arthur then responded, "Yes, that certainly would." He looked at his watch and then again at Duggan, "My, it's nearly midnight. Perhaps we have already kept you up longer than we should have. Thank you, Prime Minister."

After they left, Lloyd George turned to Thomas Jones and said, "*Gwell.*"

F.E. looked inquisitively at Jones, who obliged by saying, "Better."[9]

NINETY-NINE

The Land Fit for Heroes

THURSDAY, 1 DECEMBER 1921, LONDON

TWO DAYS OF INTENSE DISCUSSIONS AMONG THE MEMBERS OF THE British delegation followed as they laboured to produce what they hoped to be a final draft of the Treaty that the Irish could then submit to their own Cabinet in Dublin. A little after six in the evening, Arthur Griffith visited the Prime Minister in Downing Street to ensure that some of his objections were addressed, but after a short while, he left to enable the British to discuss matters on their own. At nine-thirty, he returned to meet Lloyd George again, this time with Michael in support.

On the drive over, Tom Cullen pointed out a familiar London scene. "Look at that poor bloke over there."

A discharged army officer stood at a street corner behind a four-wheeled barrel organ with his combat decorations pinned to the front of the cart. As he cranked out a tune with one hand, he lifted his bowler hat at passers-by, soliciting donations.

Liam replied, "Dave Neligan and I were talking about these poor bastards. You see them all over town hawking toys or matches to scrape by. I suppose their pensions weren't so generous, or just plain ran out. Pitiable."

"So, this is the 'land fit for heroes' that Lloyd George promised," Michael added, quoting the Prime Minister's wartime slogan. "No wonder so many of them signed up for the Auxis and Tans. You might temper any pity you feel for that poor bastard cranking a barrel organ with the fact that he could just as easily be wielding a barrel gun in Ireland."[1]

They pulled up to the barricade at the end of Downing Street and were soon allowed to pass through.

Inside No. 10, members of the British team were finishing up their preparatory conference. Chamberlain was discussing the obduracy of the Irish on the Oath with Gordon Hewart, the Attorney General, while Robert Horne, the Chancellor of the Exchequer, went over some figures in his notes. Lloyd George seemed cheerful and relaxed, and Churchill took notice of this, commenting to Thomas Jones, "The P.M. seems quite at ease amid all this hubbub."

"Yes, Mr. Churchill. In fact, last night while other members were parsing the language for the draft, we took a break and watched a film called *The Inside of the Cup*, based on a novel by your American namesake."

"Indeed? Mr. Winston Churchill, the famous American author."

"No relation, I presume, though I hear you two have met."

"Yes, charming fellow. We met some twenty years ago when I was in America. After a thorough deliberation of our mutual lineages, we could discover no common ancestors, but, interestingly, we both served in our respective armed forces, and we do both write."

"Indeed, you do, quite admirably," Jones complimented him, which was rare, for he was usually rather critical of Churchill. "Though sharing the same name must sometimes lead to some confusion."

"Thank you, T.J. And so it has. We keep in touch from time to time. In one of my letters, I told him that I would forthwith sign my name Winston S. Churchill to avoid any further jumble."

"Excellent. Oh, but what is his middle initial?"

"Not a problem. He wrote back that he doesn't have one."

"My, my. Anything else in common?"

"Well, we both dabble with the brush, and..." At this point, the tell-tale rocking on his heels began, but he whispered so only Jones could hear him, "I told him when we met that I fully intended to be Prime Minister one day, and I encouraged him to enter politics. I said wouldn't it be a lark if I were Prime Minister at the same time he was President of the United States."

Jones could not contain himself at this, and the usually diffident secretary laughed loudly, to the surprised amusement of the other men present. "Well, has he entered the political arena?"

"As a matter of fact, yes. Two years later he was elected to the New Hampshire state legislature, and later twice ran for governor, lost, and there it ended."

"My, my," Jones repeated. "Quite a story."[2]

There was some commotion at the front door, prompting Churchill to ask, "Perhaps that would be our Irish guests?"

Jones responded, "Right, sir. I'll see them in right away."

A short while later they were all engrossed in a familiar discussion, that of the British Navy's control of Ireland's shores. Michael and Arthur had prepared their argument on the subject before the meeting, and apparently, they were soon to find out, so had the British.

Michael made his point, "Even though we might not choose to build a navy of our own, and gentlemen," and here he said as an aside, half-laughing, "speaking quite honestly, even if we could afford to," which brought wry smiles to the faces of the British, "we still maintain that we reserve the right to do so."

Churchill began to countermand this as usual by saying, "Yet we maintain that the coastal defence of Ireland is to be undertaken exclusively by His Majesty's Imperial forces," but at this point, he paused and looked to Lloyd George with a slight smile.

The Prime Minister continued, "Until an arrangement has been made between the British and Irish Governments whereby the Irish Free State undertakes her own coastal defence."

While Michael and Arthur silently took in this considerable compromise, Churchill explained further, "This matter could be reviewed at a joint conference some ten years or so later."

Greatly relieved at having won this concession, Michael nevertheless commented, "Ten years is a long time to wait just to discuss the matter."

Churchill laughed and said, "Well, we can see about that. The important thing is the essence of the thing, not the length of time."[3]

"Except that one could say *time* is of the essence," Michael responded slyly.

"True enough, Mr. Collins," Lloyd George said agreeably enough, though he turned to look over his shoulder at the clock on the mantlepiece behind him. With a mischievous grin, he altered the meaning of

Michael's quip by declaring, "My, look at the time. Might we move on?"

Michael shook his head, smiling, and relented, "Very well."

More deliberations on fiscal autonomy for the Free State and ethnic and financial safeguards for Ulster followed, and it was agreed that further discussion would be needed to resolve these differences.

"Mr. Griffith, we hope to have a draft of our agreement delivered to you later this evening," Lloyd George explained, "but perhaps Mr. Collins could meet with the Chancellor of the Exchequer and his advisors tomorrow morning to tidy up some loose ends. I could join in if necessary."

"That would be fine," Michael responded with a nod to Horne and felt confident that it would be, though he would find that more friction within his own team would ensue.

Arthur brought up a point he wanted to be resolved, "Prime Minister, regarding pensions for members of the police forces..."

With the prospective change in government in Ireland, some fair compensation was due to the various public servants, but Michael started to warn them, "If that were to include the Auxis and Tans..."

Lloyd George interrupted him, "Yes, we would omit members of the Auxiliary Police Force or those who had joined the R.I.C. in the last two years from that responsibility."

Michael simply nodded in agreement. Empathy for down-and-out ex-army men on the streets of London was one thing, but rewarding vicious reprobates in his homeland was another. He looked to Arthur to see if there was anything else.

"Well, gentlemen," Lloyd George said as he rose, "if my colleagues and I put ourselves to it, we should have the draft of the Treaty to you in a couple of hours."

"Very good, sir," Arthur answered. "In that case, I will take it with me to Dublin tomorrow morning."

IN THE CAR ON THE WAY BACK, ARTHUR LEANED BACK AND SIGHED, "We've come a long way, Michael. We're so close, so close, yet..."

"Yet there are the others to contend with, both here and in Dublin."

"Yes, that's it. I am sorry you have to stay still another day. I will advise Dev to hold a Cabinet meeting Saturday morning, but you probably won't see yourself free to leave for Dublin until the night before." He looked at Michael and continued, "Not to mention the fact that you'll be going head to head with Robert Horne, the current Chancellor of the Exchequer, Austen Chamberlain, a former one, and an expert from the Treasury who could probably befuddle your run of the mill economist. Oh, and maybe the P.M., too."[4]

"Arrah, a former bank bookkeeper should have no problems sorting out that lot."

EVEN THOUGH IT WAS ONE O'CLOCK IN THE MORNING, ERSKINE Childers was nearly shouting, declaiming his abhorrence of the Treaty draft that had just been delivered to Hans Place. "The Oath is impossible to accept, this Boundary Commission untenable, and these financial provisions will be our undoing. To think that the fate of Ireland is being settled hugger-mugger by men totally out of their depth…"

"Hold your tongue, you interloper," Griffith shouted back.

"What is that supposed to imply?" Childers shot back. "I have my credentials." He paused and sneered, "*And*, I deserve mine. Unlike some on this team, I, for one, lack sympathy for many of the British claims."[5]

"Do you mean to doubt our loyalties?" Michael demanded. "Take that back."

Griffith looked at his watch and stood up, "I've had enough of this. It's two in the morning, and I need to be on the train to Holyhead in six hours. Good night."[6]

To Go For a Drink Is One Thing

Despite having endured a long, gruelling day, Michael was in a positive frame of mind as he boarded the 8.45 evening train at Euston Station for Holyhead. Even his two desultory companions, Erskine Childers and Gavan Duffy, the members of the team he found the most disagreeable, could not dampen his spirits. He had gone two rounds earlier that day with the Chancellor of the Exchequer, first with Childers in attendance and then, for the sake of not infuriating the P.M at the second meeting, without, and had gotten what he considered the best deal on some of the outstanding financial issues. Overall, he felt what had been negotiated in London so far was the best anyone could have done, and he was satisfied that it was enough to build on for the future. And besides, at least he had Tom Cullen, always good for a laugh, along on bodyguard duty to keep him company.[1]

Gavan and Childers stopped by. "Care to join us for a drink in the dining car, Mick?" Gavan asked him.

"Ah, that would be lovely, but I'm feeling a bit rough. I think I'll relax here for a bit. You two go ahead." *Please*, he thought to himself but then offered a bit of a sop to Childers. "Say, Erskine, I appreciate your input on that tax issue with Ulster. I wasn't able to resolve the matter in my later meeting with the P.M., but, well, maybe next time around."

Erskine was surprised at this rare compliment from Michael and acknowledged it politely, "Thank you, Michael. I'm glad I was able to help move things along."

They left him in peace without bothering to ask Tom to join them, knowing he would not leave Michael's side. Michael smiled at Tom and said, "Thank God! To go for a drink is one thing. To be driven to it is another!"[2] He took out a letter received that day from Kitty that he had not had a chance to read through properly. It was hardly the panacea to his aches and pains he could have hoped for, as it was filled with self-doubts and recriminations and an admission that she had just had a glass of wine before sitting down to write.

"Silly, Kit, she knows she can't drink," Michael murmured.

"What's that, Mick?"

"Oh. Nothing." Then he came to a line that upset him. *But do please forgive me if I doubt you sometimes.* "Uh, oh!" *Perhaps it is that I'm selfish and expect too much attention. I never get tired of you, but it keeps coming up that you are tired of me and there's the trouble.*[3] "Christ Almighty, Tom, let's go and join our brethren for that drink!"

AT ABOUT TEN-THIRTY THAT EVENING, WHILE MICHAEL WAS STILL travelling across England by train, Arthur Griffith arrived winded and tired at a house on Kenilworth Square, a quiet residential neighbourhood in Dublin set around a village green. De Valera was staying at this house, but if Arthur expected any appreciation for having made this late-night courtesy call, he was soon to be disappointed.

"Welcome, Arthur, welcome. How was your journey?"

"A bit tiring, but I'm none the worse for it," Arthur responded as cheerfully as he could.

"Oh, I know. I drove here all the way from Clare just to meet you. Yes, the roads were quite treacherous, very slippery."

"Oh, were they?" Arthur was already getting a trifle annoyed.

"Well, that's all right. I insisted on doing all the driving myself, and I don't mind admitting I am exhausted, quite done in. But I'll need the practice in case hostilities recommence."

Arthur, eleven years de Valera's senior, had been arguing with Erskine Childers until two that very morning and had just undergone nearly twelve hours of gruelling travel after almost two months of intense negotiations. Nonplussed by this outrageous display of self-pitying narcissism, he restrained the true temper welling up inside, replying tersely, "I feel confident that will not be necessary."[4]

"Hmm, that depends. You have the British draft with you?"

"That's why I'm here, Dev," he said, opening his briefcase and handing the document over.

De Valera walked over to a table lamp to read it over. It wasn't long before he let it drop to his side and exclaimed, "We could never accept these proposals. The Oath is an abomination! Swearing allegiance to the King! How could you possibly think this was acceptable?"

Angered but still possessing a modicum of patience and restraint, Arthur explained, "The Oath is first to the Irish Free State and then to the King only as the head of the Associated States."

"Irishmen should not be making any oaths to any king, full stop. Where is the concept of External Association in any of this?"

"Now, Dev, you led me to believe that if a break were to come, it would not be over any damn oath. Look at the language on the relationship with the Crown. It says the Crown in Ireland would be no more in practice than it is in Canada."

"We sent you over there to get us a Republic, not a dominion!" de Valera exclaimed.

"Then what the hell does Free State mean, if not a Republic? If we nitpick over the Crown and this damn Oath, we can forget about keeping Ulster. The British people won't have it, the Orangemen won't, and neither will we. What is more important? Some meaningless oath or the unity of Ireland?"

"They are all important. So much so that it is all or nothing."

"Then take your pick, Dev. Either one means war."

"So be it."

It went on like this for another two hours, and they both realised they were getting nowhere. Finally, de Valera said, "Arthur, we're not going to settle this tonight, and I am too tired to argue any further. Let's leave it until tomorrow's Cabinet meeting, shall we?"

Arthur looked at his watch. "You mean today's? It's nearly one in the morning. I'll see you at the meeting. Good night."

ABOUT THE SAME TIME ARTHUR LEFT DE VALERA THAT NIGHT, MICHAEL and his companions boarded the mailboat at Holyhead and sleepily made their way to their compartments. Michael found some respite from a cold as he slept in his berth across from Tom Cullen, while Childers and Duffy shared another room. At three-thirty in the morning, they had barely cleared the harbour when there were screams, the sound of steel raking against steel, and then silence, followed by more screams. Michael had just dozed off but woke up and shook Tom, "What the hell was that?"

"Let's go and look."

They met Childers and Duffy in the hallway, and they all went to the ship's railing and were horrified to see that the ferry had run over a fishing trawler in the icy cold dark. A few minutes later someone yelled out, "We have three men dead here. Lord, help us! We have men injured here, too!"

Michael groaned, "Ah, that's a tragedy, but you know what this means? We'll have to return to port."

"Back to Holyhead?" Tom asked incredulously.

"It's only right," Michael sighed, "but it's going to be another long day."

As indeed it was. The ship was delayed a couple of hours in Holyhead and arrived late at Dunleary at ten-fifteen in the morning.[5]

"This is just grand," Michael sighed as the boat finally pulled into its berth in Dunleary. "We have three-quarters of an hour to make it to the Mansion House. Hopefully, Pat McCrea will be meeting us. If anyone can get us there in time, it'll be him."

When the delegates walked down the gangway from the ship onto the pier, they found Pat waiting for them. Michael walked up to him and slapped him on the back, saying, "God, it's good to see you, man."

"Hello, Mick. G'mornin' everyone," Pat answered somewhat stiffly. "I heard about the delay. Car's over there."

Tom got in the back with Childers and Duffy while Michael joined Pat next to the driver's seat. "Quick as you like, now, Pat. We don't want to be late."

Tom could not resist teasing Pat a little, "Yes, Pat, but nothing, you know, reckless."

"No," Pat answered, "we wouldn't all want to wind up sitting in the bridewell for no good reason, now, would we?" The memory of his little stint in the police station still rankled.

Michael burst out laughing, "Now, Paddy, you're the best, so just do your best. Let's get a move on."

You Can Get Another Five To Go Over

SATURDAY, 3 DECEMBER 1921, DUBLIN

Upon arriving at Mansion House, Pat McCrea parked the car in the entrance yard, and Michael got out immediately, bounded up the steps, and rushed inside with Tom Cullen close behind. Suddenly, Michael stopped in his tracks, and Tom nearly knocked into someone leaving the building.

"Jaysus, Tom, watch where you're going. Wait here; I'll be right back."

Michael ducked into a side office, winking at a young secretary as he explained, "Just have to call a friend." He placed the call with the switchboard operator and then spoke into the receiver, "Hello, Christy? Yes, it's me. Listen, I'm just about to go into the meeting at Mansion House, but I have a present from London for you and the boys. I'll leave it with Pat McCrea and Tom Cullen." He paused to listen and then continued, "Yes, right now."

He put down the receiver and said, "Thanks, luv," and met Tom back outside. He reached into his breast pocket and said, "Christy O'Shea is on his way now. Give this to him when he gets here. It's a copy of the Treaty. I want him and the lads in the I.R.B. to go over it. Have him meet me back here by lunchtime."[1]

Michael noticed Joe O'Reilly waiting patiently for him off to the side. "Howaya, Joe."

"I'm grand, Mick, but I thought you'd like to know that I hear Cathal's wife, Caitlín, is pretty sick."

"Is it serious? Cathal would never let *me* know."

"Couldn't say, but perhaps Cathal might be more on edge because of it."

"All right, come here to me, Joe, here's what I'd like you to do," he said as he took Joe off to the side and spoke quietly to him.

"Ok, Mick, I'll take care of it right away."

Entering the large drawing room at the Mansion House, Michael looked around for Arthur, who found him first. "Michael, thank God you've made it. We heard about the ferry collision. Terrible thing, just terrible." Arthur looked at him more closely and remarked, "Saints, but you look even worse than I feel. Ye all right?"

"Didn't sleep a wink, but I'll be fine, don't worry about me. Did you have a chance to talk with the Chief yet?"

"Yes, I did, and you would have been none too pleased with what transpired."

"And which will be continued presently, I daresay."

As soon it was. Before long, de Valera addressed the Cabinet, crying out as he waved the Treaty draft, "Gentlemen, this is totally unacceptable. Though I concede the delegation have done their utmost, they should show the British they are prepared to face the consequences, war or no war."[2] Shouts and angry protests ensued as members from both sides of the issue voiced their displeasure with each other. De Valera stoked the flames even higher by declaring, "I can possibly understand Mr. Griffith abandoning independence for national unity, but he is getting neither this nor that."[3]

It already looked to be a chaotic meeting. Men were shouting and arguing across the room and would carry on like this for another seven hours. Michael shook his head, muttering, "Oh, Christ!"

Before long, Cathal Brugha asked in a demanding tone, "And just who is responsible for this sub-conference arrangement? This was never authorised here in Dublin."

In a rare defence of Michael and Arthur, Gavan Duffy, realising the duplicity implied by this question, told him, "But, Cathal, I told you about this weeks ago."

Ignoring this, Brugha asked again, "Why is it that only Mr. Griffith and Mr. Collins attended these private meetings? Whose idea was this?"

Michael and Arthur kept stonily silent, but Barton responded. "The British, Cathal," he looked around the table. "We all knew that."

"Well, then, in that case," he responded, sneering at Michael, "they selected their men."[4]

Michael narrowed his eyes and just stared back coldly, but Arthur bolted out of his chair and went around the table to confront Brugha, "I demand you withdraw that insidious allegation."

"I will yea!" Brugha said as he rose in defiance.

Standing toe to toe with him, Arthur countered, "Then I insist that it be recorded in the minutes." He looked over to the table where the acting Cabinet Secretary was seated. "Colm, are you getting this down, man?"

"Uh, I, er, just a minute…" Colm responded lamely, as he was not actually recording much of anything.

Rather than let his remark be recorded for posterity, Brugha relented, "All right, all right, Arthur, I withdraw my statement."

Michael had been silently brooding through this exchange, but now he stood up and shouted, "If you are not satisfied with us, you can get another five to go over," and with that, he slumped back into his chair.

"That's all right, Mick," Robert Barton responded, joining Duffy in his defence of Michael and Arthur. "Mr. Collins and Mr. Griffith went to these meetings with the delegation's full knowledge and consent, and I refuse to have the private proceedings of the delegates discussed in this scurrilous manner."[5]

Eamonn Duggan concurred, "Besides, the proceedings of these sub-conferences were reported afterwards to the full delegation."

Finally backed into a corner with Griffith still confronting him, Brugha relented, "Fine. I said I withdraw my last statement."

"Very well, then," Arthur snorted as he returned to his seat.

ALTHOUGH TEMPERS WERE RUNNING VERY HOT, A SLIGHT RESPITE WAS soon granted when the meeting adjourned for lunch. Michael immediately left the room and walked outside to find Christy O'Shea, Tim Kelly, and Tom Cullen waiting for him.

"Mick, you look terrible."

Michael took out his handkerchief, blew his nose, and answered impatiently, "Thanks, Christy. So I've been told. Good to see you, though. I thought we might have lost you to the joys of tending bar."

"No, but, I'll admit, it was great craic while it lasted."

Michael then feigned a punch to Tim's belly and asked cheerfully, "Howaya, Timmy? You back to taking good care of everyone at Conlon's?"

"Heh-heh, everyone's fine. They miss you, though." He hung his head down and mumbled, "Me, too."

"Well, Tim, if all goes well, I'll be coming back again soon to stay. That reminds me, Christy, how is my Danny Boy?"

"Grand, Crumpet is doting over him, but I think he misses you, too."

"Poor fella, but I have an idea to keep him happy, and I may have homes for the others. I'll tell you about that sometime soon. So, now that all the lads have read the Treaty, what's the consensus? Faith, I could use some good news."

"Well," Christy started, "it's fine as far as it goes, but there's certainly room for improvement, starting with the Oath."

"That's not final yet, but the way things are going back in there, it will have to wait till we're back in London."

"Perhaps this will help. The boys in the Brotherhood put their heads together and came up with this." He handed Michael a piece of paper. As Michael looked it over, Christy explained, "None of us is anxious to subscribe to some oath, but everyone realises the position you've been put in. The general consensus is that what we have here is more palatable than what is currently on offer."

Michael looked it over and then began reading it out loud. "*I do solemnly swear to bear true faith and allegiance to the Constitution of the Irish Free State as by law established, and that I will be faithful to His Majesty King George in acknowledgement of the Association of Ireland in a common citizenship with Great Britain and the group of nations known as the British Commonwealth.*"[6] Michael mulled it over, then said, nodding his head, "This will do fine. A good piece of writing, this."

Christy smiled and said, "Like I said, the boys put their heads together on this, but it was Timmy here who put words to paper."

Michael looked at Tim in amazement. "Tim? By all the saints, Tim, if you didn't go to school, you met the scholars!"

Tim shrugged his shoulders and responded, "Heh-heh! Oh, I did go, but I wasn't much at schooling, though the nuns used to say, if nothing else, I was fairly good at writing." He looked at the ground and mumbled, "I guess it sort of stuck with me. I just listened to all the fellas and put down the gist of it." Looking back at Michael, he asked, "So, you like it?"

"Timmy, no one is ever to say that... I mean, if I ever hear anyone call you..." he hesitated to finish.

"'Dim Tim?' That's just schoolyard stuff. Even my army mates called me that. Didn't bother me."

"Timothy Kelly, you are an inexhaustible source of amazement. Now, Christy, what else?"

"Defence, for one thing, governing Ulster for another."[7]

"I agree, and none of that is final yet, either. So, the bulk of it passes muster?"

"Mick, we've got you covered. Go back and give 'em hell."

"Where? Here or in London?"

Christy laughed, "Both, I suppose."

"Will do."

"Say, Mick, if you don't mind my asking," Christy started slowly.

"Ask anything you like, Christy."

"How is, er, I mean, do you think you'll bring it all home by Christmas?"

"Yes, I do, Christy, and she's fine. Peggy Mack is fine, and a boon to us all. By the way, that was a lovely gift you sent her."

"Oh, well, I..."

"Not to worry, that's just between you and me. And Maureen, come to think of it. Now I have to get back in there."

"Thanks, Mick." Christy smiled sheepishly. "Good luck to you."

"So long, Mick," Tim added.

Michael watched Christy and Tim walk down the steps, and then he turned to Tom and said, "The way things are going, we'll probably have to go straight to the ferry from here. I have to go back inside now, but..." He hesitated as he noticed Pat McCrea leaning against his car, chatting with Christy. "Wait a minute, Tom. Christy has just given me an idea for an early Christmas present. I need to have a word with Pat."

Pat stood up straight when Michael approached. "What, leavin' already?"

"No, Paddy. You are."

"Now what the hell have I done?"

"Haven't done, you mean. You need an upgrade in your wheels. There's a Rolls Royce waiting for you in London. Meet us there tomorrow, but for now, after we're done here, you can drive us all to the ferry."

With that, Michael bounded back up the steps to join the meeting about to reconvene.

Pat shook his head and said to Christy with a smile, "See, that's Mick Collins for you. A box to the ear or some stupid joke one day, the grace of Saint Francis the next."[8]

INSIDE MANSION HOUSE, THE ADJOURNMENT HAD DONE LITTLE TO assuage the acrimony or quell tempers.

De Valera made a passing attempt to calm things down. "The Oath is totally unacceptable in its present form, but with modifications, could be honourably accepted."

"Amended, how?" Childers asked amid more loud, acrimonious banter.

"To recognise the King of Associated States."

Barton leaned over to Austin Stack and asked, "What was that? Associated States?"

"Association," Stack answered back.

Thinking the question was directed to himself, Colm looked down at his notes and called over, "To recognise the King of Great Britain as Head of the Associated States."

"That's different, isn't it?" Barton asked no one in particular.

"Splitting hairs is what it is," Michael responded, breaking the sullen silence he had slipped into. He rose to argue logically and eloquently, "Not accepting the Treaty would be a gamble, as England could arrange a war in Ireland within a week. I am confident that essential unity on Ulster can still be preserved and that further concessions from the British are forthcoming on trade and defence. As regards the Oath, personally, I would not agree to it as is, but I am sure the British are open to some modification. At any rate, the Oath would not come into effect for twelve months, so is it not worth taking these twelve months and see how the whole thing works?"[9]

Eamonn Duggan had a slightly different view. "I agree with Mick that we should take this Treaty and see where we stand a year later, but I do not think any more concessions can be obtained at present."

Arthur then rose to explain his position further. "I do not like this document, but I do not think it dishonourable. It practically gives us a Republic."

"Practically, but not actually!" someone complained.

Arthur responded to this charge, saying, "The first allegiance is to Ireland, to the Irish Free State. If this document is rejected, the people of Ireland are entitled to know what the alternative will be. The country would not fight on the question of allegiance, and there would be a split. The British would break off negotiations over the Crown, and there would be war. Overall, I would not recommend the Government to accept, but I think the plenipotentiaries should sign and leave it to the President and the Dáil to reject."[10]

Brugha stood up and said in a patronising tone, "Arthur, I'd like to ask you just one thing."

Arthur said wearily, "Yes, Cathal. What is it?"

"Don't you realise that if you sign this thing, you will split Ireland top from bottom?"

Raising his voice, not in anger, but so he could be heard over the commotion this question engendered, he acknowledged, "I suppose that's so. I'll tell you what I'll do. I'll not sign that document," he paused and then continued emphatically, "but I'll bring it back and submit it to the Dáil and, if necessary, to the people."

"Very well, then."

"However, I will not take the responsibility for breaking off the Treaty over the Crown. When as many concessions as possible are conceded, I will go before the Dáil. The Dáil is the body to decide for or against war."[11]

De Valera then rose and said, "I have made my opinion on this document quite clear, as has the head of the delegation, Mr. Griffith. Mr. Collins and Mr. Duggan seem to be in favour, perhaps with some amendments. Now let's ask the other plenipotentiaries for their views. Mr. Barton?"

Robert Barton rose and said passionately, "This Treaty does not give even Dominion status or offer any guarantee against partition. England's last word has not been reached. I disagree with those who claim the British would declare war on the question of allegiance."

Michael leaned over to Arthur and whispered, "He doesn't know Churchill."

Barton summarised by stating plainly, "Therefore, I am against acceptance."

As Barton sat down and looked over to Duffy, Arthur whispered back to Michael, "And he doesn't know Lloyd George or Birkenhead. The Die-Hards would rise again in revolt if the British Cabinet did not go to war over our rejection of the Treaty."

Gavan Duffy rose and spoke quite unequivocally, "I am against acceptance. I believe our proposals, with some slight reservations on defence and other matters, could be obtained if insisted upon. The Dáil should reject this Treaty and propose amendments to the British."

"Now that we have the views of the plenipotentiaries, perhaps the delegation secretary and some of the Cabinet members would like to express their view. Mr. Childers?"

Erskine Childers rose and said, "The proposed Treaty would give no national status and renders neutrality impossible."

Cathal Brugha said only, "I am in general agreement with the President. I am opposed to acceptance."

Michael said sarcastically, "Now, why am I not surprised?"

Austin Stack rose and said only, "Opposed," and sat back down with a sneer at Michael.

De Valera then rose and spoke again, "Thank you, gentlemen. Though there are significant differences within the Cabinet as well as within the delegation, I still believe that our differences can be reconciled and that an acceptable settlement can be secured. I feel if the British are made to realise that Ireland would rather face war than accept partition or inclusion in the Empire, they might be induced to withdraw those demands."[12]

As Michael heard these words, he dropped his head to his chest in dismay. The futility of all his efforts over the last few weeks in London bore down heavily on him, but he remained sitting silent, speechless.

At this point, Duggan said to Arthur and Michael, "I don't understand. The three of us are leaning toward signing, and we constitute a majority among the five delegates. If Dev wants his way, why doesn't he throw his weight in, come with us back to London, and state his case to the British? He's the only one who could possibly sway them to his view of things, but still he holds back."

"I'll tell you why," Arthur answered.

Duggan interrupted him, "I think we all know the answer. Dev won't come because he knows he can't get what he wants from them."

Arthur agreed with this assessment, "Yes, and he knew this after he met Lloyd George back in July."

"Michael," Duggan whispered, leaning across Arthur, "I believe you said before that he would have his scapegoats."

Michael remained silent as de Valera went on, "It has been suggested that the President accompany the delegation to London, but if this were to happen, the British might surmise division among the delegates, which of course, we cannot allow. In any event, with Mr. Griffith's assurance that he will bring a new draft back to Dublin for approval, there is no need for the President to do anything but remain here."

Duggan, Michael, and Arthur, just looked at one another blankly, and then Duggan rose and addressed everyone, "Gentlemen, the time has come for us to return to London."

As the meeting began to break up, Childers went to de Valera and said, "Dev, could I have a word?"

They stepped off to the side, and Childers then put his question to de Valera. "Does scrapping the Oath mean scrapping the first three clauses in the Treaty dealing with Dominion status?"

"Yes."[13]

"Thank you."

Meanwhile, as Arthur gathered his things, Michael asked him, "So, after seven hours of rancour, where do we stand? Do we accept or reject?"

Sighing as he clasped his briefcase closed, Arthur shrugged his shoulders and said simply, "Eamonn is right; it's getting late. Erskine is taking the Dublin ferry with Barton and Duffy. The three of us should give ourselves a respite from all this, that is, from *them*, and take the Dunleary boat."

"Good idea, but we had better hurry. It leaves soon," Michael said.

Once outside, they saw Tom and Pat standing astride the car. Eamonn Duggan joined Arthur and Michael in the rear seat as the other two sat up front.

"I'm fagged out," Michael admitted as he slumped back. "All right, Pat, let's be off to Dunleary."

Looking in his rearview mirror as he pulled away from the pavement, Pat asked them, "I gather it did not go so well."

Michael sat up, leaned forward, and rested his arms on the edge of the seat in front to answer, "Paddy, I've been there all day, and I can't get them to say yes or no, whether we should sign or not."

In a discouraged tone of voice, Arthur said, "They expect us to go to war not on the dismemberment of the country, but on the wording of the Oath."

Tom asked rhetorically, "Then what was the point of coming back home anyway?"

Michael sat back in his seat and, as he gazed out the car window, said dejectedly, "I don't know, Tom. I've said it before. I don't know whether we are being instructed or confused from here in Dublin."[14]

MEANWHILE, AFTER DISCUSSING THE DAY'S EVENTS WITH DE VALERA, Cathal Brugha was about to leave Mansion House when someone ran up and told him there was a call for him. When he stepped into the office, the receptionist handed him the phone.

"Hello? Yes, Caitlín, dear, it's me. What is it? Are you feeling any better? He did what? Really? Ah, isn't that grand? That's lovely! Ay, *mo chuisle*, I'll be home as soon as possible."

He put the phone down, and with tears welling up in his eyes, he remarked to the receptionist, "Mick is so kind, he thinks of everyone."[15]

ONE HUNDRED TWO

Back From This Precipice

SUNDAY, 4 DECEMBER 1921, LONDON

"Oh, Mr. Collins," Margaret McIntyre exclaimed as she entered the kitchen, a bit startled, "I thought you had joined the others for a meeting in Hans Place."

"What? Oh, no, Peggy," Michael answered as he devoured the food from his plate. "I had enough mindless aggravation in Dublin. I thought I'd stay in and indulge myself with some nice sausages and beans left over from breakfast."

"Well, these past few days, you were probably on trains and boats more than terra firma, so no wonder you're feeling a bit done in."

He looked down at his plate and smiled, remembering Eddie's pronouncement on the first day of negotiations about the benefits of an Irish breakfast, "I must say, though, I have a mouth on me for some Clonakilty black and white pudding." He looked up and cried, "Saints protect us! Does that make this an English breakfast?"

Peggy laughed and said, "You just got back, and you sound homesick already, and I'm sorry to say, but you *are* looking a bit peaky."

"No, I'm feeling in great form. I've managed to shake my cold, but it's such a dismal, grey day." He looked out the kitchen window and sighed, "I suppose I should appreciate the quiet, but London is just so unpleasant, so drearily dull on a Sunday morning. I just wrote as much to Kitty."[1]

"Besides homesick, maybe you're feeling a little lovesick, too?"

Peggy inquired gently. "Oh dear, that reminds me, a letter from Miss Kiernan arrived yesterday. I have it right here." She sifted through a few letters she had left on the kitchen table and handed the letter to Michael. "Sorry, I should have left it for you on your table upstairs."

"That's fine, dear. Hmm, let's see," Michael said as he opened the letter.

"Oh, I should allow you your privacy."

"No, Peg, let's have a cup of tea together. I could do with some company but not those louts over at the Politicians' House, Arthur and Eamonn excepted, of course." He read through the letter and shook his head when he got to the lines that read, *Then London came. I should not have come. It gave rise to such talk,* and further along, *If we were ever to part, it would be easier for us both, especially for me, to do it soon, because later it would be bitter for me. Now don't think by this I want a row or want you to end it.*

"Neither do I," Michael murmured to himself. Peggy was about to ask what he meant but saw that he was deep in thought and continued to busy herself at the cooker. Michael smiled to himself when he read, *We will, won't we, be real lovers? Say we will.*[2] He finished reading the last few lines, folded the letter, put it back into its envelope, and smiled at Peggy as she sat down across from him and poured them some tea. "Thanks, Peg."

"I hope it hasn't inconvenienced you getting your letter so late."

"Not in the slightest. It could not have come at a better time."

"Miss Kiernan is a fine young lady, if it's not too presumptuous of me to say so, Mr. Collins."

"No, there's nothing presumptuous about kindness or honesty, Peggy. Thank you."

Eddie appeared just then, but as he did, the phone on the private line with Hans Place rang, and he walked backwards a couple of steps to answer it. He returned to forward motion a moment later and announced, "Mick, it's Arthur for you."

Michael checked his watch and remarked, "We have a meeting in Downing Street at five o'clock, but there's plenty of time yet." He went to the phone in the hall, "Hello, Arthur."

"Michael, you had better get over here. Our own Die-Hards have been working up their version for a Treaty draft and insist on presenting it at today's meeting."

"For the love of God, would those blithering eejits ever just bugger off?"

"Actually, I have asked them to, Michael, but it might sound more convincing coming from you. Can you come over?"

"Only for you, Arthur. Only for you. I'm on my way."[3] Liam and Tom appeared in the kitchen, and Michael told them, "Trouble brewing at the Politicians' House. God, give me strength. Let's go."

---

3 P.M., SUNDAY, 4 DECEMBER 1921, LONDON

WHEN MICHAEL WALKED INTO THE DINING ROOM AT HANS PLACE, Arthur looked up and just shook his head as Erskine Childers sat at the end of the table with Barton and Duffy. Although Robert Barton and Michael were on opposite sides on practically every issue literally on the table, they were still long-time comrades and remained friends through it all. Accordingly, Barton spoke enthusiastically when he saw him enter the room, "How was your trip back, Mick?"

Before answering, Michael acknowledged the others, including Duggan, standing beside Arthur. "Hello, Eamonn, Gavan, Erskine." Then he answered Barton, "Same as usual, Bob," adding with a curious tilt of his head, "and yours?"

"We ran into Andy Cope and Tim Healy on the ferry."

Arthur asked, "Did you, then? What did they have to say for themselves?"

"Healy seemed anxious to have a private talk, so we left Cope and went for a cuppa."

Michael looked relieved, "That's good. Andy is on our side, but not as much as he's on theirs. Anything you confide in him would make it to the Prime Minister's ear, but Tim has always had my best interests at heart. What did he have to say?"

"Healy and I had a long talk, and he was aghast at the prospect of war again but seemed strongly in favour of the terms on offer so far. He urged us to build on that."

Arthur replied, "That's encouraging."

Barton seemed optimistic. "Yes, with that in mind, Mick, Arthur, come look. We've done a fairly good job of implementing the amendments recommended by the Cabinet back in Dublin."

"Do tell," Michael replied in a soft tone, nonetheless heavy with irony.

As Barton handed over some papers, he went on, "Healy said he was hoping to meet with Lloyd George when we got into London and relay pretty much the same message to him."[4]

Michael and Arthur quickly skimmed through the papers scrawled with notes, cross-outs, and corrections before turning back to read them more closely. Across the top sheet was written, *Amendments by the Irish Representatives to the proposed Articles of Agreement.* Michael mumbled as he read, apparently expressing approval, "No free trade, unlimited tariffs allowed, just what I have been advocating for. Defence, let's see, full control of our coasts in five years—I'm all for that. Oh, and as for Ulster, essential unity, et cetera." Barton and Duffy smiled at each other, but Childers sat there sulking, prepared for a sarcastic rebuff at the conclusion. "No mention of Dominion status," Michael went on, his voice now rising in smouldering anger, "a meandering garble of an Oath, so to hell with the Crown, but at least we do have External feckin' Association!" He threw the papers back onto the table. "Congratulations! It's a grand bit of work you've done. Now, if you'll excuse me, I'm going back to Cadogan Gardens to change my shirt. I think I'll skip Downing Street, go to the West End, and pick up a ticket for a show tonight. It'll probably be my last chance before we go to war!"

Arthur concurred, saying, "Michael is right. We've presented these proposals in one form or another time and time again, and each time we have been flatly turned down by the British. Apart from your work on trade and defence, these amendments are a waste of time."

"How can you say that?" Childers asked with venom in his voice. "These are the instructions of the President and the Cabinet."

"Are they?" Arthur said in answer. "I left Dublin with little more than confusion."

Duggan sided with Michael and Arthur. "We refuse to put forward this useless document. It's for those who want a break in the negotiations to do. You can go to Downing Street on your own. I think I can speak for Michael and Arthur when I say we will have nothing to do with it."

Duffy spluttered out, "Well, then, fine. That's just what we'll do. Come on, Robert, let's go."

The two of them got up to leave, and Childers rose from the table to join them.

"Where the hell do you think you're going, Mr. *Secretary?*" Arthur asked with disdain.

"Well, if you won't go…" Childers protested.

"Oh, set yourself down." Arthur got up. "I can't allow that pair of poltroons go over there on their own." He turned to Michael, "Will you join us then?"

Michael, however, was adamant, "I'll have no part in this fools' errand. I wasn't joking. I'm heading back to Cadogan Gardens." With that, he put on his hat and coat and left.

Once outside, Liam walked over and commented, "That was quick."

"But not painless," Michael quipped. "Tom, take Arthur and those eejits to Downing Street. Liam, let's walk back. I've had enough."

---

5 P.M., SUNDAY, 4 DECEMBER 1921, DOWNING STREET

WHILE ARTHUR ENDURED AN UNCOMFORTABLY QUIET RIDE TO Whitehall with Barton and Duffy, Lloyd George was conferring with Birkenhead, Chamberlain, and Horne. "You know that old Irish parliamentarian, Tim Healy, was just here, and he made the most remarkable admission. His exact words were, 'Collins is the only sensible man amongst us.'[5] Coming from a man with his breadth of knowledge and experience, both in Parliament and among the Sinn Féiners, we may do well to take him at his word and cleave to Collins."

Chamberlain agreed, "I agree. He and Griffith are the standouts."

The truncated Irish team soon arrived, and Thomas Jones showed them into the Cabinet room where Lloyd George greeted them politely as always but asked apprehensively, "And Mr. Collins, will he not be joining us?"

"He is ill-disposed this evening, Prime Minister."

With a knowing glance to Birkenhead, who raised an eyebrow in acknowledgement, he answered simply, "I see. Well, please be seated, gentlemen." He began the meeting with an admission of guilt, "Mr. Griffith, I owe you an apology. I misunderstood you when we were last discussing the Southern Unionists. I now understand they will be catered for in the Lower Chamber by Proportional Representation, in the Upper Chamber by a formula yet to be determined."

"Yes, that is correct. Now, if I may, Prime Minister, I would like to submit for your approval some amendments our delegation has proposed for the agreement." Then to the amazement of his fellow delegates, Arthur proceeded to argue with great fervour and all his will for the same amendments he had dismissed out of hand less than an hour earlier. However, knowing the trouble embodied in these new amendments on the Oath and the Crown, he launched his opening argument on Ulster. "The proposals on Ulster came from your side rather than ours, and we cannot take any responsibility for them."

"Perhaps not," Lloyd George answered, "but we did have your tacit approval for them, did we not?"

He was referring to his conversation with Arthur at Sassoon's Park Lane House, during which Arthur had agreed to accept the British proposals on Ulster that provided for either an All-Ireland Parliament or the setting up of the Boundary Commission. No one in the Irish delegation but Arthur was aware of his promise to Lloyd George just before the Liverpool conference not to "queer his pitch" and break on Ulster. Still, everyone knew about the letter of assurances regarding the Oath and the Crown that they had all discussed. Accordingly, when Arthur answered in the affirmative, neither Barton nor Duffy took particular notice. "Yes, but my support was contingent upon the essential unity of Ireland. Therefore, it only seems fair to us that Sir James Craig should submit a written statement saying he accepts the essential unity of North and South. We must know his intentions before we agree to sign. After all, his refusal would lead to partition."

"There is little to be gained from this request," Birkenhead replied. "Craig would never submit such a letter, for *he* has no intention of accepting our proposals. However, we stand fully behind our commitment to drive this agreement through Parliament and force the Northern Counties to submit to the Boundary Commission, through which you stand to make substantial gains in the Catholic areas. Your own Mr. Collins has admitted that the remaining areas would be induced to join the rest out of economic necessity."

After some discussion with Barton on trade, Lloyd George asked for a brief adjournment to discuss the Irish positions with his team. When they returned a few minutes later, he announced, "The amendments you have submitted today are a complete reversal of what we discussed only last week. We have offered Ireland a chance to become a willing member of the Empire like other nations, such as the Boers of South Africa, who had fought alongside British soldiers in the recent war with equal gallantry. However, these new amendments constitute a refusal to enter the Empire and accept the common bond of the Crown. They are nothing but the same proposals that have already been discussed and rejected. We are not averse to some modification to the Oath, but the document presented here is a refusal of the fundamental conditions. Or so it seems to us. Would you care to enlighten us?"

Although Arthur was embarrassed by these obvious criticisms, delegates on both sides of the table would have been hard-pressed to see it. Instead, he forged ahead gamely, pointing out, "Surely, though, Prime Minister, the mention of the King in our new variation of the Oath shows our good intentions in meeting your requirements."

Barton offered an olive branch of his own. "What we want, and I am sure what we all here need, is a peace based on goodwill, and this is what Ireland is offering."

Duffy tried to reinforce this by saying, "In fact, our proposals provide the necessary connection to all of your essential requirements."

Arthur glanced at Duffy with a look that could be described as asking, "*What on earth is that supposed to mean?*" but said instead, "You are asking us to give up our best ground without a guarantee that Craig will accept the essential unity of the Irish nation. We have nothing tangible in hand. How can Ireland trust the faith of the British government?"

Much to his surprise, Lloyd George had an answer to this very question. "I'll tell you how," he began. "If you sign this Treaty, we will immediately call Parliament together and pass the ratifying act before Christmas."

Lloyd George leaned back in his chair as Birkenhead assured them, "We would hand over Dublin Castle and withdraw our troops from the country."

Arthur was impressed by the tantalizing prospect of peace by Christmas but did not waver from his arguments. "That certainly is something all of us here would find most agreeable, but we would find achieving that desired result difficult if it means sacrificing the points raised in our amendments. We still find the language in your proposals troubling on defence, trade, and dominion status."

Birkenhead said with some impatience, "What is the difficulty about coming into the Empire with a standing like that of Canada?"

Gavan Duffy felt he could explain the matter to the Lord Chancellor and began to while Arthur listened with his breath held, "We should be as closely associated with you in all large matters as the Dominions." Sensing an impending equivocation, Birkenhead looked down his nose at Duffy but allowed him to speak uninterrupted. Duffy continued, "And in the matter of defence, still more so; but our difficulty is coming into the Empire."

For a split second, he sat there quite well pleased with himself, but Arthur was aghast at this statement, and Duffy's self-satisfaction evaporated at the end of that fleeting moment.

Austen Chamberlain jumped up from his chair and exclaimed, "That ends it!" Birkenhead, Horne, and Lloyd George also sprang to their feet.[6] The Prime Minister said dispassionately, "I shall inform Sir James Craig that these negotiations have broken down. Good evening, gentlemen. Mr. Jones will see you out."

————————

THE RIDE IN THE CAR BACK TO HANS PLACE BEGAN AS SULLENLY AS THE ride from there two hours earlier.

After a few minutes had passed, barely controlling his rage, Arthur began to speak slowly and deliberately, "I trust it did not pass anyone's attention that the Prime Minister just raised the prospect of summoning Parliament to pass and ratify the Treaty before Christmas."

Silence.

"Following ratification, the Lord Chancellor averred, the British would hand over Dublin Castle and withdraw their troops from Ireland."

No one dared utter a syllable.

"Perhaps the one clear mandate given to us at Saturday's Cabinet meeting in Dublin was that if a break were to come, it would be on Ulster."

Barton cleared his throat and ventured to praise Arthur, saying, "And a grand fight it was you put up on Ulster. Your arguments were unanswerable, Arthur."

Ignoring the compliment, Arthur continued, "It was not to be on defence, it would not be on the Oath," he alliterated in a rising crescendo, "and it would not be on Dominion status and the fucking Empire!" He turned to Duffy and screamed at him, "You gammy toe-rag! You ignorant bastard son of a poxsy whore and a monkey-buggered jackass! We'll be at war by week's end because of your bollix-ing, you diabolical feckin' gobshite!"[7]

Leaning into a turn as he drove, Tom Cullen muttered, "Well, it's a good thing Mary Conlon's not within earshot of all *that*."

BACK AT DOWNING STREET, LLOYD GEORGE WAS EQUALLY UPSET BUT had a more nuanced method to deal with his anger. "T.J.," he said to his Cabinet Secretary as he entered his office, "I must report to the King tomorrow morning at ten. If we cannot right this train wreck of a debacle, I shall have to inform His Majesty that we are at an impasse. No, worse still, that the negotiations have broken down entirely."

"I understand, sir. Whatever can we do?"

He mulled this over and concluded, "Griffith may be the leader of their delegation, but as we know, Collins is the one they will follow."

"And the path to Collins is through Griffith."

"Yes, and therein lies one possible way out of this deadlock."

"If I remember correctly, we had a similar discussion when we proposed the Boundary Commission to Mr. Griffith."

"Oh?" he responded innocently. "Yes, I suppose we did. Thomas, you have a good rapport with them both, but perhaps once again, you could approach Griffith first."

"I could suggest an eleventh-hour meeting between you and Collins before you meet with the King."

"Yes, as long as it happens sufficiently before 10.0 a.m." The Prime Minister assumed a mischievous smile and surprised Jones by saying, "*There is a path which no fowl knoweth and which the eye of the vulture hath not seen.*"

"Sir?"

"From the Book of Job. Yes, you could suggest an idea like that, but it might be more effective if you put it in such a way that it occurs to Arthur that its genesis was his own fertile imagination."

"I understand, sir," Jones responded. "I'm on my way."[8]

10 P.M., 4 DECEMBER 1921, LONDON

"SORRY, ARTHUR, I REFUSE TO HAVE ANYTHING TO DO WITH THAT muddle. If Jones is there, let him try sorting it out."

Michael hung up the private line at Cadogan Gardens and went into the kitchen. He found Pat McCrea nursing a cup of tea at the kitchen table while Liam and Tom leaned against the counter.

"There's the man," Michael said in greeting Pat, who had arrived in London earlier that evening. "Enjoy your journey? Settling in?"

"It was grand, and yes, no complaints."

"C'mon, Pat, I fancy a bit of air."

"Shall we join you, Mick?" Tom asked.

"No, thanks. I just need to clear my head. I'll see you later."

They went outside, where a Rolls Royce Silver Ghost was parked in front of the building.

Pat stopped and stared at it, saying, "Ah, I suppose this will do." As he eased himself into the driver's seat, he ran a hand along the soft leather seats and the smooth, polished wooden dashboard.

"So, Paddy," Michael asked as he sat next to him, "you gonna drive it or make love to it?"

"Now, the British may be oppressive, imperialist tyrants, but you have to hand it to them; they do know how to build a fine motorcar."

"Ay, and I was always fond of my old Raleigh bicycle.[9] Now, will ye ever drive the fuckin' thing?"

"I should think of a nice name for her," Pat mumbled, still in awe. He roused himself and asked, "Sure, where to, Mick?"

"The Laverys' house in Cromwell Road."

"Very good." Pat had heard about Michael's visits to John and Hazel Lavery from Ned and Liam and knew better than to say much about it. He started the engine but could not help himself, saying, "Ooh, I like the sound of that." He paused and turned to Michael. "Say, Mick?"

"What?"

"Would ye ever show us the way to Cromwell Road?"

"Oh, for the love of Christ!"

Watching from the doorstep and anticipating such a scenario, Tom Cullen laughed, walked to the car, and got in the back. "I'll show you the way, Pat."

"Oh, that would be grand, Tom."

After driving in silence broken only by occasional directions, Pat at last ventured a question, "So, Mick, things are all a muddle, you'd say?"

"You could say so." Michael clearly was not in the mood for any further conversation.

When they arrived a few minutes later, Michael got out, leaned down and said through the window, "Fellas, someone here will give me a ride back, so don't wait for me. I'll be all right."

"Whatever you say, Mick." Pat said as Tom joined him up front. "I was thinking I'd call her Betsy."

"What? Who?" Michael asked impatiently.

Pat just drummed his fingers on the steering wheel. Michael chortled, "Whatever you say, Pat."

After they drove off, Michael was welcomed in by Hazel. "Oh, Michael, my dear, John and I were just talking about you. Things are awfully bad, aren't they?"

"That they are." He looked around the room and saw that Sir John had placed Michael's portrait on an easel in the lounge. He walked toward it and asked uncertainly, "May I?"

"Of course, that's why I placed it there. I like to live with my paintings a bit when they're finished. I hope you like it."

Michael stood before it, staring at it in silence.

After a few awkward moments, Sir John glanced at Hazel and then asked, "Michael?"

Michael stirred himself and exclaimed, "Sorry, yes, I was just lost in thought there for a minute. It's quite good. It's a singular thing, seeing yourself in paint on a canvas. I, I just don't know..." he trailed off in a doubtful tone.

"Yes, Michael?" Lady Lavery asked. "What is it?"

"I'm not sure about the moustache."

Sir John laughed out loud, "No problem. I was thinking of doing another version. I could leave you clean-shaven."[10] Not getting a response, Sir John became concerned for Michael, whose mood seemed to be darkening. "So, Mick, how bad is it?"

Michael answered despondently, "It looks like it's all over."

"Yes, so I heard," Hazel replied.

"Did you, now? Where did you hear that?"

"From Winston's Private Secretary, Eddie Marsh."

"Really, what did he have to say?" Michael asked.

"That Winston says what you have now is the Cabinet's final offer."

John Lavery concurred, "Yes, Michael, if the negotiations break down, it appears the next step is war."

Michael paced about the room, clearly agitated. "War, war, war. If we don't accept, it's war with England. If we do, it could lead to war with the North, if not civil war at home."

Sir John asked, "Then, what would it take to avert war? Surely you have something of worth to take away from your discussions so far."

Michael sighed, "Some things. Concessions on trade, defence, recognition of a Free State, and to a lesser extent, some begrudging compromises on the Oath and allegiance to the Crown."

"Then what is lacking?" Hazel asked.

Michael answered, "A united Ireland. Craig won't budge, and we don't have solid enough assurances on redrawing the boundary with Ulster."

The three of them talked like this for quite a while, going over the pros and cons of the negotiations, and then Hazel said, "Michael, I know you haven't got all you came over here to get, but surely, you've made great strides. Why don't you just take what you can now and get the rest later?"

Sir John agreed, "Yes, you're a very practical-minded individual, Mick. I'm sure with the passing of time, you will obtain what you need."

Michael calmed down a little and thought for a moment. "That's not far from what I said to Arthur. We can use what we have been offered as a stepping stone to what we really need." He looked at his watch. "Well, forgive me. It's nearly midnight. I'll leave you now. Thank you for listening."

Sir John answered, "Not at all, Mick. You're always welcome here." He meant it, too. Although he was well aware of his wife's flirtatious manner with Michael, he realised it was just part of her personality and thought nothing of it. He was used to the mesmerising influence she had on most men and had long ago accepted it as part of his complicated relationship with his beguiling wife.

Accordingly, he saw no harm when Hazel asked, "Oh, why don't you let me drive you back?"

"Well, that would be fine. I told my driver not to wait for me. Good night, Sir John."

They got into Hazel's Rolls Royce and made the short drive back to Cadogan Gardens.

Before Michael got out, Hazel held his hand and asked, "Shall I see you in the morning at church?"

Michael smiled, "Yes, that will be a good way to start the day, a day that may prove to be a momentous one. Good night, Hazel."

Hazel leaned over and kissed Michael on the cheek. Michael looked over to the house and noticed movement at the front window curtain. "Yes, well, thanks again. See you in the morning."[11]

12.0 A.M., 5 DECEMBER 1921, LONDON

WHEN THOMAS JONES RANG THE DOORBELL AT 22 HANS PLACE AT midnight, it was his second trip there that night. Although his first attempt to revive the moribund negotiations three hours earlier failed, he returned to press his case once more.

"Why am I not surprised to see you again?" Arthur asked after he answered the door himself. "Everyone else in the house is fast asleep, but come in, Thomas, come in. I'm at my wit's end, I say, the end of my tether."

"I rather think we all are, sir. Even Winston will admit to that now."

"To think we have come this far, so close, and to have to go home empty-handed. It's a failing from which I shall never recover. Nor will Ireland."

Jones was deeply impressed by the depths of Arthur's despair and said in consolation, "The Prime Minister shares in your disappointment, sir."

Arthur looked at him and said, "I am sure he does. Michael and I have come to believe in his desire for peace. We realise his efforts have been taken at great political risk to himself and his Cabinet. Unfortunately, our colleagues in Dublin do not see it that way." He said with a pitiful expression in his eyes, "They think we have sold them out."

Jones waited a moment and asked, "Is there anything we can do yet?"

Arthur thought momentarily and then continued along the same line, "They think we have surrendered much. They accuse us of capitulating on the Crown, of abandoning their damn External Association, and then ask us, 'What have you secured in return?' Thomas, can you not get some sort of conditional recognition of Irish national unity from Craig in return for our acceptance of the Empire? Can he not write a personal letter to the Prime Minister, as I did, pledging unity if we accept the Commonwealth? If you could do this, I think we could push the rest of it through Dublin in a week."

"What of the others on your team?"

"Barton and Duffy have their quibbles on trade and such. These minor differences can be resolved."

"And what of the gunmen in Ireland, if you'll forgive the expression?"

"Mick still commands their loyalty and respect. Ninety per cent of them will follow his lead."

"And what about Mick?"

"Like me, he so desperately wants peace. Will Lloyd George help us attain it? If it is war, the people will obey the Dail, but we want peace and believe the Prime Minister does, too. Would he see Michael and have a heart-to-heart talk with him?"

"Why, yes, I am sure he would, if Mick could come to Downing Street at 9.15 a.m. before the Prime Minister visits the King within an hour later."

"All right, Thomas. I'll speak to Michael to fix it up."

"Oh, thank you, Arthur, thank you. Good night."

After Jones left, Arthur went to the hall and picked up the private telephone to Cadogan Gardens, where it rang immediately.

A sleepy-sounding voice answered immediately. "Hello?"

"Eddie, it's Arthur. I know it's late, but…"

"That's all right. I thought you might call again for Mick. He's in such a state. Let me get him for you."

Michael came to the phone and said, "Hello, Arthur. Ye all right?"

"Well, yes, but I just had Thomas Jones here with me again."

"Persistent fella, isn't he? I don't know what else I can say unless he has something new to bring to the table."

"I understand, Mick, but bear with me. If we go one step further down the path we currently find ourselves on, there will be no turning back. I fear in my heart that it will mean war, war more terrible than anything visited on us in all our history. Now, I am not saying that by acting as your conscience dictates, you are in any way responsible.

However, you are uniquely positioned to bring us back from this precipice."

"But has anything changed in the last three hours? What's the point?"

"Jones thinks that if you were to meet with Lloyd George tomorrow morning before he goes to the palace to tell the King the talks have broken off, he might be able to put it to Craig to show some sign of life and say something constructive. Would you reconsider along those lines?"

"Maybe, if it means we can finally get some sleep without Jones haranguing us through the wee hours. Let's talk again in the morning."

Arthur chuckled and said, "It *is* the morning, Mick."

"I'll sleep on it."

"Pleasant dreams. Now get some rest."[12]

Moral Courage So Rare

MONDAY, 5 DECEMBER 1921, LONDON

"*ITE, MISSA EST.*" OR "GO, THE MASS IS ENDED," THE PRIEST SAID TO the congregation at the Brompton Oratory.

"*Deo Gratias*," Michael and Hazel responded. Hazel gathered her long opera cloak about her and swept down the aisle beside Michael.

"Michael, I'm so glad you decided to go see Lloyd George. Let me drive you to Downing Street. My car is just at the side of the church," she said as they entered the vestibule.

"No, thank you, Pat is going to take me. He and Tom are waiting at the gate. I wouldn't want to put you out."

"Well, then, best of luck, dear. Remember what we discussed last night. Take what you can get now, and I'm sure the rest will follow later."

This hint of a lecture irked Michael ever so slightly, and he was about to say something in answer but changed his mind and simply said, "Thanks for meeting me this morning. Give my best to Sir John."[1]

9.30 A.M., MONDAY, 5 DECEMBER 1921, LONDON

· · ·

A SHORT WHILE LATER, THOMAS JONES BROUGHT MICHAEL INTO THE Cabinet room for his meeting with Lloyd George. "Ah, Mr. Collins, how very good of you to come. How have we come so far only to falter when we are so close to our goal? After all our deliberations, we are facing a point of final divergence. As soon as we are finished here, I must meet the King to inform him that as a result of our discussions last night, our conference has broken down, and then at noon, I shall have to make a similar announcement to our entire Cabinet."

"Yes, well, we would hate to upset His Majesty. Let's see if we can't offer him better news than that."

Lloyd George smiled at this but said, "That would be fine, but ultimately for the King and his Cabinet, it all comes down to the question of whether you will be within or without the Empire. As of last night, it appeared the latter was your final word."

"I wasn't here last night," Michael said. "If I were, perhaps I wouldn't be here this morning." Before Lloyd George could comment on this admission, Michael continued, "But now that I am here, I would like to express my opinion on some elements in your document."

"Please, I was rather hoping you would," Lloyd George said in an encouraging tone.

"The main problem is Ulster. I know Mr. Griffith pressed you on this issue, but it is vitally important to us that we have word from Sir James Craig stating his position."

"This came up in our discussion last night. It was noted, Mr. Collins, that even you had pointed out on a previous occasion that if Craig refuses, the results of the Boundary Commission would so drastically diminish the North's territories that it would be forced economically to join with the South. What difference does it make what Craig's position is? Either way, the results would be in your favour."

"Maybe so, but with all the recent violence against Catholics in his area, I am very anxious to secure a definite reply from him, one way or the other. In fact, I would be as agreeable to a reply rejecting as accepting. If he accepts, grand, we can sit down with him and talk it out. If he rejects, we should save Tyrone and Fermanagh, parts of Derry, Armagh, and Down through the Boundary Commission."

Lloyd George responded, "If you'd be content with an answer, any answer, then the matter could be put to him."[2]

Michael paused to contemplate this apparent concession and then brought up his next point. "Thank you. Now, I think the Oath needs some modification, and I brought along a slightly altered version for your approval." He handed over an envelope containing the Oath prepared by his friends in the I.R.B., not one of the versions approved at the Dublin Cabinet meeting.

Lloyd George looked it over and smiled, saying, "Yes, I think I'll ask the Lord Chancellor for his legal opinion. In point of fact, this is not dissimilar to some ideas on the Oath that Mr. Churchill has suggested. This might prove to be acceptable, but only if taken in the context of a Dominion within the Empire."

"Commonwealth."

"We can work with you on the wording of that status."

Michael nodded in agreement and bought up his next point. "Yes, well, another matter I'd like to bring up pertains to defence. It's your insistence that the coastal defences be undertaken exclusively by the British Navy, which implies that we can take no measures for raising even a coastal defence force."

"There can be no question of Irish submarines," Lloyd George replied.

"*Submarines?*" Michael cried in exasperation. "Do you really think we are going to build a fleet of submarines? What we resent is the assertion that we can build *nothing* for our defence."

"Such as the occasional dreadnaught?" Lloyd George asked with a smile.

"Irish fishermen take their trade very seriously," Michael shot back with a grin. "Practically speaking, though, you must realise we are only talking about a modest defensive force."

"Then tell them mention might be made of Irishmen protecting the Irish fisheries and that a conference in ten years' time will review the overall coastal defence strategy."

"As I said before, ten years is an awfully long time to wait just to bring the matter up again, but let's move on for now. The clause calling for free trade could be harmful to a small, young country trying to protect emerging industries."

Lloyd George responded, "If there were complete freedom on one side, there should also be complete freedom on the other. That is, Britain should be as free as Ireland to impose tariffs on the other's goods. However, we said at the outset that there could be great danger in a tariff war. Still, I will make notes of your objections, and hopefully, they can all be resolved if," he paused and then continued with a cagey, expectant look on his face, "if we resume our talks."

Michael just stared back.

Lloyd George smiled and asked, "Say, at two o'clock today?"

Michael nodded his head, smiled, and then looked over Lloyd George's shoulder to a map on the wall. Lloyd George turned to see what he was looking at and then rose, inviting Michael over to his side of the table with a wave of his hand. "Let me show you something." When Michael stood beside him and looked at the map of the world, Lloyd George put his arm around Michael's shoulder and said, "I believe this is the same map your Mr. de Valera admired when he was here."

"Oh, did he, then?" Michael said. "Well, he is an educated man of the world."

"You're a capable man, Mr. Collins, supposing you help us?[3] You know, Queen Victoria always looked forward to visits from her Prime Minister, Benjamin Disraeli, whenever he came with his maps to explain the goings-on in the Empire."

"Did she, then? However, if I'm not mistaken, she was no admirer of Gladstone or his advocacy of Home Rule."

Lloyd George chuckled, "No, perhaps not, and perhaps I am belabouring the analogy here, but the point is, ah!" he exclaimed as he picked up a wooden pointer from a small table beneath the map. "The point is," he repeated as he began tapping various points on the map, "You would not be in such bad company. Canada, Singapore, South Africa, Australia, and Victoria's favourite, India." He then purposely lapsed into the familiar and said, "Michael." He placed his hand once again on his shoulder and said, "Mick, if you could accept the clauses on the Empire and could convince your colleagues here to do so as well, I would be in a position to hold up any British action, whether Parliamentarian or, god forbid, military until you have had the opportunity, if you so desire, to submit the matter to the Dáil and the Irish people. What do you say?"

Michael thought this over for a moment but then surprised Lloyd George by asking, "Did you really say that negotiating with Éamon de Valera was like, how did you put it?"

"Like chasing a merry-go-round?"

Michael chuckled, "Now, that one I had not heard!" He shook his head again and said, "Unless I send word to the contrary, we'll see you at two o'clock. Enjoy your audience with His Majesty."

As soon as Michael left, Lloyd George went into Miss Stevenson's office, excitedly calling his not-so-secret lover by her pet name, "Pussy, my dear, I think we are very close. Send a telegram to General Macready asking him to come back from Dublin at once. Neville will need first-hand knowledge of these events as they unfold."

"Yes, of course, David."

10.15 A.M., MONDAY, 5 DECEMBER 1921, LONDON

WHEN MICHAEL STEPPED OUTSIDE, HE STARTED WALKING BACK DOWN the narrow lane of Downing Street toward his waiting car. There he saw the now familiar figure of Sir Philip Sassoon approaching, accompanied by a short, slender, fair-haired man. When they met mid-passage, Sassoon greeted him, "Oh, Mr. Collins, we were just talking about you."

Michael looked into the piercing blue eyes of Sassoon's companion and returned his engaging smile as Sassoon explained, "Allow me to introduce you to my good friend, Ned, otherwise known as T.E. Lawrence."[4]

Before Michael could give any consideration to protocol, Lawrence extended his hand, "My dear, Mr. Collins, this is indeed a great honour and pleasure. I have been following news of your exploits here in London with the most avid anticipation."

Something in his suave but friendly, assertive manner immediately disarmed Michael. He took the offered hand and shook it firmly, saying, "Colonel Lawrence, the whole world has been following your exploits for some time."

"Yours as well, my friend, yours as well. How are you faring with the famous Welsh wizard?"

"Oh dear," Sassoon interjected with an affected nervous titter, "I think I had better let you two Irishmen get acquainted. I believe the Welsh gentleman might be expecting me." With a slight bow, he departed and went into Number 10.

"Philip is a dear man," Lawrence said with a wink.

"He certainly has treated us like gentlemen. He's all right in my book," Michael said with a shrug. "But to answer your question, we've been holding our own with the Welsh gentleman. Just."

"Even that is saying a lot," Lawrence said encouragingly.

"Whether it's enough, I just don't know, Colonel."

"Oh, please, all my friends call me Ned."

"Mick will do for me," he answered with a grin.

"I understand you've been entertained by my friend Winston, as well. Enjoying your time with him?"

Michael laughed and said, "Ah, well, I might not put it quite that way, but he is, shall we say, compelling?"

"Well said, that he is, to an overwhelming degree." Then turning serious, Lawrence said softly, "The papers say things have reached a standstill. Apparently, the time has come to decide."

Michael looked around before replying, "Yes, it would seem that today is the day. It's a terrible responsibility, choosing between war with England or disappointment and discontent, if not worse, with the more strident Republicans back home."

"You mean civil war?"

Michael just looked back with a slight tilt of his head, not contradicting this.

Lawrence continued, "Then you find yourself leaning toward accepting what is being offered if I read you correctly?"

"Yes, I think that is so. I *want* to trust Lloyd George, Winston, and the rest of them, but I fear what will come of it."

"Then, Mick, you must have confidence in yourself to choose wisely. I have had my own disappointments with these men in high places, bitter disappointments, but we must choose what we feel in our hearts is right for ourselves. I sense that you are a man that can do that. Rather easily, I should imagine."

"Thank you," Michael said, nodding his head slightly.

"I'll tell you what, if things go badly, look me up. I'd love nothing better than to take one of your flying columns into righteous battle. Not a word of this to Winston, though, eh?"

"All right, Ned. You're on. Thanks again. Pleasure meeting you."

"The pleasure has been all mine. Until we meet again, Mick, best of luck."

Late Morning, Monday, 5 December 1921, London

After arriving back in Hans Place, Michael and Arthur soon found themselves arguing with one of the more strident Republicans Michael had spoken of with Colonel Lawrence. If the Treaty were to be accepted, it would doubtless have to be signed by the entire Irish delegation. However, the impending and possibly final conference with the British was still to be held on the sub-conference level, which usually meant for the Irish side, just Arthur and Michael. To have a fair representation of the Dublin Republican element, Arthur insisted that Robert Barton, perhaps the staunchest Republican on the team, should accompany them to this crucial meeting.

"I won't go," Barton protested. "By all accounts, the British won't budge on the Empire, so what's the point of showing up at another meeting and letting them deny us the Republic again?"

Arthur answered patiently, "The point was made back in Dublin, Bob, as I reminded our illustrious legal expert last night, that if there were to be a break, it would come over Ulster, not on the Oath or Empire."

Michael added, "Thanks to Gavan, we were nearly sent packing over Empire. That's not to say turning the focus back to Ulster will be easy. When I saw Lloyd George this morning, he kept preaching about the Empire. He brought it up no less than three times. I tell you, Bob, forgoing the Empire is a non-starter with the Brits."

Growing exercised on the issue, Arthur cut in to continue his original thought. "That's right, Mick. But if there's any hope of bringing the argument back around to where it rightly belongs, on Ulster and the unity of our nation, it's your moral obligation, Bob, to be there to make your contribution."

Outnumbered and outmanoeuvred, Barton finally relented, "I won't have it said that I didn't hold up my end of the argument. I'll go with ye."

---

3 p.m., Monday, 5 December 1921, London

. . .

ARTHUR, MICHAEL, AND BARTON RODE OVER TO WHITEHALL IN morose silence. Pat McCrea drove with Tom Cullen up front, occasionally glancing in the rear-view mirror or across the seat at Tom. They remained silent throughout the trip, both uneasy with the stilted atmosphere in the car.

The car pulled up at a crossing where a London bobby was directing traffic, and Michael rolled down his window to look up at the sky. As he peered up, he noticed a white dove perched in a tree and remarked, "Will you look at that, boys—a white dove! I wonder where she flew in from."

Pat leaned forward to peer out the windscreen, asking, "Where's that, Mick? Oh, I see. Lovely."

As the bobby signalled them to pull out, Michael rolled up his window, saying, "I received news from Nancy that my brother Johnny was just released from prison.[5] Free as a bird, at long last."

Tom turned around in his seat, "That's grand, Mick. How is he? Is his hand all mended?"

"No, he'll never be quite the same, and sadly, he has no one now. Still, he's alive and, for the most part, well."

"Amen to that," Pat replied. "And how is Nancy? That's your cousin, Nancy O'Brien, right?"

"Ay, that's her—well, second cousin, that is. She's fine but very concerned for Johnny's well-being." He paused, mulling over vague memories of things Nancy had said in the past. "I suspect deep waters there," he said cryptically with a smile. "Maybe Johnny is not quite without anyone."

Encouraged by the shift in the mood inside the car, Barton did his best to ease the tension between him and Michael. "Well, Mick, at least one way or the other, we're sure to be home in time for Christmas, eh?"

Michael appreciated this effort on Barton's part to act like the friends they had been and hoped to remain, patted him on the knee, and said, "You know, Bob, you're right. And that will relieve me of a terrible burden to Monsignor McManus at St. Mary's."

Arthur smiled at this, but Barton looked baffled. "How's that, then?"

"He made me promise to bring both peace and Peggy McIntyre back home before Christmas." He chuckled and said, "And then there's Christy O'Shea."

"Christy?" Barton asked.

"Oh, it's nothing," Michael said with a wink to Arthur. "Well, my friends, here we are."

They got out of their car and were quickly joined by Liam Tobin and Emmet Dalton, who had been following them in a car just behind. The extra security was deemed necessary in the heightened atmosphere of the past few days, and they were met by a phalanx of Scotland Yard men outside Number 10. Michael noticed a familiar face near the front door. "Howaya, mate?" he gave his customary greeting.

Detective Sergeant Thompson nodded in greeting politely, not exactly effusively, but with a wry grin. By this time, Liam Tobin and Tom Cullen had seen him on several occasions, and all these bodyguards had developed a mutual respect, restrained but polite.

"Howaya, Walter."

"Liam, Tom."

Austen Chamberlain turned around in his seat and looked at the map of the Empire on the Cabinet Room wall. Whether he was studying it intently or just staring at it blankly, he remained motionless for some time in this position before slowly turning around back to the table. He took a handkerchief from his pocket, removed his monocle, and sighed as he polished it. Replacing it before his eye, he acknowledged a glance from Lloyd George with a slight smile. Birkenhead and Churchill, both uncharacteristically subdued up to this point, witnessed this exchange. Churchill, never at a loss for words, filled the void. "After these two months of futilities and rigmarole, however weary and anxious we might find ourselves at this final hour, the Irish delegates themselves must have some sense of desperation, knowing well that death stands at their elbows."[6]

F.E. responded, "That may be construed somehow to be a guarantor of success, Winston, but I think I would prefer reason rather than desperation rule the day."

"Yes, of course," he agreed.

"Any desperation on their part," Lloyd George said, "might be evidence that the division of opinion manifested among the Irish Representatives also exists within the Irish Cabinet. Much of what was agreed to here seems to have been rejected in Dublin. Look at the counter-proposals they brought back with them. They quibbled over everything but the issue of Ulster."[7]

F.E. concurred, saying, "My general impression is that Collins is most concerned with the North."

"Which leads one to surmise," Churchill responded, "that if we can resolve the outstanding issues on Ulster, Collins, as the strongest among them, will lead the others to agreement."

Lloyd George agreed and said, "Which is why I intend to press them at Ulster first and foremost."

Thomas Jones appeared at the door and announced, "Prime Minister, gentlemen, they have arrived."

When the three Irish delegates entered the room, their appreciation of the grim situation awaiting them was matched by the subdued atmosphere among their British counterparts. However, in a show of resolve, Lloyd George wasted no time with niceties and got right to the crux of the matter, at least from the British point of view. "Gentlemen," he began, looking around at the small group of men on both sides of the table. "As we all know, the Ulster Parliament meets tomorrow, and I think I have made it abundantly clear that I have given Sir James Craig my word that he should know the outcome of our deliberations here before that session opens. Therefore, for the last time, I must ask where you stand on Ulster." He opened a folder on the table before him, took out his copy of the Treaty agreement, turned it around, placed it on the table facing the Irishmen, and pressed his right forefinger down upon it. "Can you deny that the Ulster proposals given to you last week and now in the document before you are exactly those to which Mr. Griffith agreed with his undertaking not to let us down?"[8]

Realising the predicament that his personal assurances to the Prime Minister had put him into, Arthur nonetheless did his best to extricate himself. "I stand by my undertaking to you, Prime Minister, and I, myself, am satisfied for the most part with the proposals as put forth in this document. However, I cannot be expected to agree to the opening articles on the Oath and Empire until I know whether Sir James will accept the Treaty."

Chamberlain had a swift response to this and said in great earnest. "Mr. Griffith, without the expressed undertaking which you have just reaffirmed, Lord Birkenhead and I would never have risked our political careers at the Liverpool conference by proclaiming our confidence in your fidelity to this pledge not to let us down."

Still not realising the extent to which Arthur's assurances had been given, Michael broke in, protesting angrily, "Every proposal put forward from our side has been conditional on the essential unity of Ireland being secured. We are entitled to know Craig's stance."

Lloyd George made a great show of temper, taking sheets of notes from his folder and shaking them in the air, crying, "You are deliberately trying to bring about a break on Ulster because your Cabinet in Dublin has refused to come inside the Empire. We have our sources, too, Mr. Collins."

This shrewd dig, compliments of Andy Cope, had its effect, but Arthur, resilient as ever, responded immediately. "Simply asking for a reply from Craig is not unreasonable, nor is it letting you down."[9]

"Oh, but it is," Lloyd George argued. "Sir James can only give one of two replies. He can either accept a Parliament subordinate to Dublin or refuse it. In the latter case, we would proceed with the Boundary Commission, whether he likes it or not." Growing exasperated, he said accusingly, "Mr. Griffith, you have previously admitted to being amenable to either outcome. You can have no other complaint."

There was a brief moment of silence. Having allowed the dramatic impact of his last comments to be absorbed, Lloyd George then said in a more conciliatory tone, "Perhaps we could adjourn for a short while. I would like to confer with my colleagues."

As the four British delegates rose to leave the room, Birkenhead nodded slightly to Michael and pulled an envelope from his breast pocket just far enough for Michael to see what it was. Birkenhead then nodded again and joined his fellow delegates outside.

Michael whispered to Arthur, "I think we may have a good shot at getting an acceptable Oath, if I read Birkenhead correctly."[10]

―――――――

WHEN THE MEETING RECONVENED, LLOYD GEORGE ASKED solicitously, "Perhaps we can return shortly to the issues pertaining to the North, but in the interim, Mr. Griffith, are there any other points you would like to raise?"

Relieved at the change in atmosphere and glad to have the opportunity to proceed to something that might prove less contentious, if even marginally less so, Arthur responded, "Yes, some alterations to the Oath have been offered, and I wonder if we could discuss those now."

At this, Birkenhead spoke up for the first time that day and produced the envelope he had revealed to Michael moments earlier. "I have here the excellent document Mr. Collins provided the Prime Minister with on the Oath. I hope you don't mind, but I have made one or two minor amendments I hope you will find acceptable."

This revised document remained close to the Oath suggested to Michael in Dublin by the I.R.B. Birkenhead handed the paper over to Michael, who looked it over, nodding his approval. "Yes, it now reads *adherence to and membership of the group of nations forming…*"

As Arthur and Barton leaned in to look at the paper, Birkenhead continued along with Michael, saying, "*forming the British Commonwealth of Nations*, which I understand you prefer to *British Empire*. This drops that awkward phrase *to recognise the King of Great Britain as Head of the Associated States.* The less said of the word *association* or its modifier, *associated*, the better off we all are. It carries for us, well, a rather unpleasant association."

Michael smiled slightly at this and said, "I see."

Barton realised that this was the death knell to "External Association," but not wanting to repeat the error made the day before by Gavan Duffy, registered his misgivings by only saying, "I would like to discuss this rephrasing of our relationship to the British Commonwealth."

Michael interrupted him from taking his doubts any further for the time being by saying, "That's all right for now. We can discuss it privately among ourselves later."

Barton felt unjustly chastised but, fearing to say anything to replicate Duffy's disastrous performance, just nodded to Michael.

"In that case," Lloyd George said, relieved not to be drawn into another lengthy discussion of the Oath, "In our meeting earlier this morning, Mr. Collins offered some suggestions regarding coastal defence. I have relayed these to Mr. Churchill, who I believe has a point or two to raise on the subject."

Michael gritted his teeth before enduring another round with Churchill, for he envisioned a lengthy, circular debate, which soon ensued. As belligerent as Winston had been in dealing with the "gunmen" on Irish soil, he was equally obstinate in refusing them any semblance of an actual Irish navy in those nearby seas. This was one of Lloyd George's main reasons for including the former Lord of the Admiralty in the treaty negotiations, and Winston took to his mandate with his usual energy by beginning, "If Ireland were permitted any navy, it would be impossible to get the Treaty through Parliament. The English people would believe that the Irish were going to build ships which, in a state of war, might be used against them. The possibility of Irish submarine and Irish mine-layers ready and eager to attack British food ships would be argued from every angle."[11]

Michael repeated his argument made to Lloyd George earlier. "Some protection of Irish fisheries is required. The British Navy is not entitled to the exclusive defence of our shores. We have the moral obligation to take up this responsibility, as do all maritime nations."

"No," Winston was adamant. "No Irish dreadnaughts so close to our ports and shipping lanes can be allowed. Out of the question."

Michael just sighed at the mention of the word "dreadnaughts" again.

Barton felt confident enough not to be contradicted in saying, "But surely, Ireland must be allowed to build *something*."

Here Chamberlain attempted to find a suitable middle ground. "It could be stipulated that the exclusive undertaking of Irish coastal defence by His Majesty's Forces was not to prevent the construction or maintenance of such vessels as are necessary for the protection of the Revenue and the Fisheries."[12]

Michael mulled this over and looked to Barton, who nodded back approval. "That will do," Michael responded, "provided the situation is reviewed at a later date."

Winston, however, snorted back, "Not only do I oppose any provision that Ireland should have a *real* navy of her own now, but given the opportunity, I will oppose it five years from now."

Michael stared at Winston, realising he had just opened the door for *some* sort of Irish naval presence and even allowed that the Irish might argue the issue not in ten years hence, but only five. Therefore, for the moment, he decided not to press Churchill for specifics on these matters and moved on to another subject. "If I may," Michael began, "I would like to revisit the issue of free trade. Prime Minister, you allowed at our meeting this morning that as regards trade and tariffs, if there were complete freedom on one side, there should also be complete freedom on the other. Do you stand by your word on this?"

Slightly piqued at having this mere supposition being presented as an agreed concession, he shot back, "I still hold that a tariff war is in neither side's best interests."

"Oh, I agree with you completely. So, in principle, you accept Ireland's right to impose whatever tariffs are deemed necessary?"

Realising that this right to impose tariffs carried with it the implication of complete freedom, Lloyd George responded, "I ought to confer with my colleagues on this and some other matters. If you'll excuse us, gentlemen."

LEFT ALONE FOR A SPELL IN THE CABINET ROOM, THE IRISH DELEGATES were again granted a respite to gather their thoughts.

"Oh dear, I hope I haven't rustled any Welsh feathers," Michael said sardonically.

"On trade? No, Michael," Arthur assured him. "You were honest and to the point."

Barton shook his head and said quite plaintively, "I can now sympathize with you, Mick, for having to suffer through all those meetings with Churchill. Good God, he can be an overbearing windbag!"

Arthur's view was simple. "Maybe so, but we can all see why he's here. If we can come to an agreement with a British team of which he is a member, all the better to sway the British public to accept whatever is agreed to here." He looked to Michael, "Besides, it hasn't all been overbearing rhetoric, has it?"

Michael smiled, "No, we've had our lighter moments. He's just fighting hard for what he believes, as are we. I can't fault the man for that. They already allowed that the time might come where we undertake our coastal defence on our own, so I think a compromise of some sort is coming."

"That fight is now coming to a head," Barton replied. "Where do we stand, Arthur?"

Before he could answer, the door to the hall opened, and Birkenhead came in through the door and walked swiftly over to his place at the table. "Sorry to interrupt, gentlemen. I need some notes I made on some of these amendments."

When Birkenhead had left with his papers, Barton repeated, "Where do we stand, Arthur? I still think we should hold out for word from Craig. What's the rush?"

Arthur thought for a moment and sighed, "I see your point. What difference would another day make? If they demand an immediate answer, we could refuse to sign, pending an answer from Craig."

Michael and Barton nodded in agreement and then continued to discuss some of the finer points they should bring up when the meeting resumed.

"WHERE IS THAT DAMN PAPER?"[13]

"Sir?" Thomas Jones asked the Prime Minister, who was now seeking a paper he needed.

"You know, that damn note you showed Griffith after I met him at Philip's home that night." Lloyd George was rummaging through all the pockets of a jacket he had hanging on a coat rack in his office.

"Let me help you look, sir," Frances said as she got up from her desk, pressing wrinkles in her blouse as she rose. "Did you check your extra pair of trousers?"

Birkenhead was sitting on the edge of Miss Stevenson's desk and looked over his shoulder to catch Churchill's attention. Winston began rocking on his heels and just looked away. Austen Chamberlain coughed politely, "Yes, well, check the extra pair of trousers, by all means."

Winston and Birkenhead stared in amused disbelief at the unusual bit of drollery from the Conservative Leader of Commons.

"I can't have Mick Collins accusing *me* of going back on *my* word," Lloyd George said with a great show of indignation. He then smiled at his colleagues as he patted down the clothes he was wearing again and said, "Then again, trade, tariffs, and such pale in comparison to the major points. Now, if I could only find that damn memo, that would certainly turn the tables on that old goat Griffith. But, please, let us continue. Where do we stand? F.E.?"

"Yes, well, you surmise correctly," Birkenhead answered. "They seem willing to compromise on much, but if there is a break, they seem anxious to ensure it comes on Ulster and no other issue."

Distracted by a sudden thought, Lloyd George exclaimed, "It must be upstairs. Come, Thomas, at once!"

"Shall I help?" Frances asked innocently enough.

Lloyd George answered hesitantly, "Er, no, that shouldn't be necessary, Frances." He turned to Birkenhead, Chamberlain and Churchill and said, "This should not take much longer. Why don't you three rejoin our guests and sort out some other details? Winston, I'm sure they would love to hear more about submarine warfare."

"Yes, sir," Winston answered with a wink for Birkenhead.

Lloyd George raced upstairs with Thomas Jones in fast pursuit.

Birkenhead gave Winston a pointed look and followed it with a quip, quoting Shakespeare as well as a more contemporary writer, "Apparently, the game is afoot."

Once upstairs in his private bedroom, Lloyd George checked every jacket and pair of trousers he could find. As he did, perhaps to alleviate his tension, he wondered out loud, "Why on earth did they bring that pipsqueak of a man Barton with them? I would not make him a Private Secretary to an Under-Secretary."

Over the Prime Minister's bed, Jones noticed a framed text from the Book of Job woven in silk threads that read, "*There is a path which no fowl knoweth and which the eye of the vulture hath not seen.*" Smiling to himself at this, Jones answered, "Perhaps they had failed to cure him of his protectionist views on trade and brought him along to be faithfully dealt with by you."[14]

"Hmm. Not unlikely." Lloyd George stopped suddenly. "Damn, I know where it is! Come, Thomas."

They rushed back downstairs and into the Prime Minister's office.

"Did you find it, sir?" Frances asked as Lloyd George rushed past her.

Too excited and agitated to answer, he ignored the question as he flung open a closet and dug into another pair of trousers. "Eureka!"

"You've found it?" Thomas and Frances asked in unison.

"Now I've got them!" Grinning from ear to ear, he added, "Frances, be a dear, and get me a pair of envelopes."

5.45 p.m., Monday, 5 December 1921, London

BACK INSIDE THE CABINET ROOM, CHURCHILL WAS NOW SLIGHTLY more amenable to compromise. "The clause on defence must remain as is but could be amended by this proviso, that five years from the signing of the Treaty, a conference of the British and Irish Governments will be held *with a view to the undertaking of a* share *in her own coastal defence.*"

Michael looked to Barton and said quietly, "A share of something is better than nothing, and five years is better than ten." Barton nodded his approval, and then Michael agreed, "That's better. We can live with that."

Michael expressed another concern over another stipulation insisted upon by Churchill. "The annex to the Treaty refers to Admiralty property and rights at various naval facilities. If at some time in the future these docks were to be handed over to Ireland, would the British government demand compensation?"

Birkenhead, superbly nonchalant as ever in his exposition of constitutional niceties, explained, "If the docks were handed over to the Crown representative in Ireland, the Crown could not demand payment from the Crown."[15]

This riposte elicited wry smiles around the table, but Michael pressed further, "And this Crown Representative…"

Birkenhead anticipated Michael's question, "Would be appointed in like manner as the Governor-General of Canada. The Government of the Irish Free State would be consulted to ensure a selection acceptable to the Irish Government before any recommendation is made to His Majesty."

Little else was made of the Crown Representative's inclusion in the Treaty, but it met with heated challenges when the Treaty was debated in the Dáil.

Just then, Lloyd George entered through the door holding an envelope and asked, "So, how are we progressing?"

Winston answered for everyone, "Quite well, Prime Minister. I believe we have manoeuvred our way around the naval obstacles."

"Good, fine, then," Lloyd George said calmly before delivering his broadside. "Mr. Griffith, earlier this evening you stated that it was not unreasonable to ask for a reply from Craig before giving us your answer."

"I did," Arthur answered coolly but suspected some trap as he looked at the open envelope from which a letter was partially visible.

"Then allow me to remind you, Mr. Griffith," he replied, brandishing the envelope before him, "that Mr. Jones showed you this memo after our meeting at Sir Philip Sassoon's house on November thirteenth and that you agreed to its contents."

"I did," Arthur repeated, even more icily.

Barton was utterly at a loss. He whispered to Michael, "What is this letter? I only know of the one from the night before the vote of censure."

Michael was just as mystified but could only growl back, "I don't know what the hell it is."

Hearing this, Lloyd George now swung around to face Michael. "Do you mean to tell me, Mr. Collins, that you never learnt of this document from Mr. Griffith?"[16]

Michael remained outwardly calm but inwardly was fraught with doubt, anger, and confusion. Under the circumstances, he surmised the best answer he could give would be none at all, but even his silence could be taken to be revealing to the British. Barton was flummoxed and sat there in stony silence as well.

Lloyd George removed the memo from the envelope and handed it to Chamberlain, who glanced at it and then at Lloyd George, who nodded in return. Chamberlain understood, leaned across the table, placed the memo before Michael, and said simply, "Gentlemen."

So now, for the first time, Michael and Barton learned of the further assurance Arthur had made to Lloyd George, and Arthur read it aloud in its entirety for the first time as the other two Irish delegates looked down and read along in silence.

"*If Ulster did not see her way to accept immediately the principle of a Parliament of all Ireland, she would continue to exercise through her own Parliament all her present rights; she would continue to be represented in the British Parliament, and she would continue to be subject to British taxation in so far as already modified by the Act of 1920. In this case, however, it would be necessary to revise the boundary of Northern Ireland. This might be done by a Boundary Commission which would be directed to adjust the line both by inclusion and exclusion so as to make the boundary conform as closely possible to the wishes of the population.*"[17]

None of this would have been startling to either Collins or Barton, as the setting up of a Boundary Commission had been discussed at great length. However, they were not aware it had been put into the form of a written pledge, one which Griffith had only given a cursory look before giving his assent to it. Lacking in the memo was any mention of its acceptance being contingent on any reply from Craig. Accordingly, when the three Irish delegates had finished reading the memo, they just looked back at Lloyd George in silence. Arthur began to tap his fingers slowly on the table. Seizing on their silence as an opportunity to deliver the decisive parry, Lloyd George said, "Mr. Griffith, I must remind you that you had undertaken that if we consented to such a provision for Ulster as we are offering to you now that you would not let us down." He could have said more, perhaps demanding an explicit answer, but he knew Arthur well enough at this point to know that his sense of honour would not need further prodding.

As indeed, it did not, nor did his sense of outrage, which welled up inside at having his given word impugned. His voice trembling with anger, Arthur looked straight at the Prime Minister and defended his integrity, saying, "I have never let a man down in my whole life, and I never will."

There was nothing to say in response to such an explicit declaration of both character and intent. Besides, the possibility of the Irish winning any further concession on Ulster had just been vanquished. Perhaps to sweeten the deal, if not soften the blow, Lloyd George turned to another subject that, given what he had in mind, might advance final acceptance by the Irish. "Gentlemen," he began, "as you know, among the members of our delegation, I, myself, am perhaps the most avid proponent of free trade, but I am not going to allow personal feelings to stand in the way of a successful conclusion to these discussions."

Lloyd George may well have been, as he claimed, the most avid proponent of free trade in the Cabinet. Still, as Churchill sat there, he may have begged to differ, since adherence to the principles of free trade was a significant factor in his leaving the Conservatives to join Lloyd George and the Liberals years ago. Nonetheless, Churchill remained silent, not wishing to interrupt.

"Accordingly," Lloyd George continued, "after discussing the matter with Mr. Collins this morning, I am prepared to agree that besides conceding to his points on defence, there should be freedom on both sides to impose any tariffs either country liked."[18]

This appealed to all three of the Irish delegates there, certainly to Michael but especially to Barton, the staunch Republican economist, who read into it the freedom to conduct international affairs in an unfettered fashion as an independent nation. This concession was not to come, though, without a price, which Barton was about to learn when he asked, "What provisions do you attach to this, sir?"

"This considerable concession is not satisfactory to our interests but is offered as a last sacrifice on the condition that you agree to voluntary membership in the British Commonwealth of Nations and affix your signatures to the other Articles of Agreement."[19]

That may have sounded tempting but meant capitulation on several subjects that would be difficult to persuade Cabinet members in Dublin to accept. Arthur made a desperate attempt to forestall a decision. "Prime Minister, if we could refer back to our colleagues in Dublin, we could have an answer for you within the week."

Lloyd George's answer was swift and to the point. "Gentlemen, on our side, we can concede no more and debate no further. The Irish delegates must settle now. You must sign the agreement for a Treaty or else quit. In that case, both sides would be free to resume whatever warfare they could wage against each other."

There was a deathly silence following these words. The three Irishmen sat there and stared at the Prime Minister. Chamberlain, Birkenhead, and Churchill stared back at the Irishmen, awaiting their response. At that moment, it was impossible to discern whether the outcome would be agreement or war. Of the four members of the British team present, perhaps none had a higher sense of drama nor possessed a more emotional temperament than Winston. To his mind, the Irishmen gulped down the ultimatum phlegmatically. When Arthur finally began to speak, Winston noticed the softness in his voice and modesty of manner that Winston would later record for prosperity.[20]

Arthur glanced at a clock on the mantelpiece and noted that it was already past six in the evening.[21] He then said quite simply and evenly, "I will give the answer of the Irish Delegation at nine tonight. But, Prime Minister, I personally will sign this agreement and recommend it to my countrymen."

After the slightest of pauses, during which each of the delegates on both sides of the table realised that after two months of debate, a momentous turning point had been reached, Lloyd George asked calmly but firmly, "Do I understand, Mr. Griffith, that though everyone else refuses, you will nevertheless agree to sign?"

"Yes, that is so, Prime Minister."[22] Then, almost to distract attention from the magnitude of this statement but also to shield his colleagues from possible future upbraiding, he added, "However, my colleagues are in a different position from myself. They were not parties to my promise not to let you down, and it is not fair to demand acceptance from them before Craig replies."

Lloyd George would have nothing of this further prevarication but countered it with a compliment of sorts. "I have always taken it that you spoke for the whole Delegation and that all of them were plenipotentiaries. It is now a matter of war or peace, and each of them must now make up his own mind. Every delegate must sign the document and undertake to recommend it, or there can be no agreement. We as a body have hazarded our political future. You must do likewise and take the same risk." He then reached into his jacket pocket and produced two envelopes and, holding them in either hand, declared, "I have to communicate with Sir James Craig tonight. The Ulster Parliament is to meet tomorrow, and I promised him that he should know the result of our conference before the Session opens. Here are the alternative letters I have prepared, one enclosing Articles of Agreement reached by His Majesty's Government and yourselves, and the other saying that the Sinn Féin representatives refuse to come into the Empire. If I send this letter, it is war, and war within three days. Which letter am I to send? Whichever letter you choose travels by special train to Holyhead, and by destroyer to Belfast. The train is waiting with steam up at Euston. Our messenger is ready. If he is to reach Sir James in time, we must know your answer by ten o'clock tonight.[23] You can have until then, but no longer, to decide whether you will give peace or war to your country."

Everyone was taken aback by this theatrical flourish, particularly Winston, who, reminded of his own description of Lloyd George as "never a greater artist than in the first moments of a fateful interview," noted that this performance in the final act was pure genius. Michael, Arthur, and Barton absorbed this ultimatum in dead silence and just stared back blankly at Lloyd George.

Knowing full well that the one man who needed the most persuading was Barton, Lloyd George then directed all his energies at him. "Mr. Barton, those who are not ready for peace must take the full responsibility for the war that would immediately follow refusal to sign the Articles of Agreement. I cannot impress upon you enough how essential it is that the signature of every member of your Delegation is necessary to avoid war."

Barton could find nothing to say in answer at that moment, so Arthur responded for him, "Prime Minister, we will acquiesce to your request and shall return with our answer by 10 p.m."

"Very well, then," Lloyd George answered.

Michael had been sitting there quietly, but the issue of the response from the North was troubling him. "Prime Minister, there is one further point I'd like to raise regarding Ulster."

"Yes, Mr. Collins?"

"Under the existing draft of the Treaty, Craig need not make his choice between an all-Ireland Parliament and a Boundary Commission for twelve months. This long period of transition could provoke uncertainty in the Free State and danger to the minority in the North. There is no reason we could not have his final answer within a month."

Lloyd George looked to his three colleagues, and no one raised any objections. "Very well, then, Mr. Collins. One month it is. Until ten o'clock then."

"Thank you."

Everyone then rose from the table to leave except Michael. He continued to sit there for a few moments, then finally got up slowly as if a great weight was bearing down on him. He stood there bracing himself with both arms at the edge of the table and his head slung down between his shoulders. Arthur peered at him with concern, never having seen Michael look quite so miserable. The British delegates chatted quietly among themselves, but they took notice of Michael's hesitation, and all eyes followed his unusually subdued departure.

After he had left the room, something stirred in Chamberlain and in a flash of imagination, he approached Arthur and in a near breach of protocol gently took hold of his elbow and said, "Excuse me, Mr. Griffith, but if you don't mind waiting a moment, I have something for you."

"Oh?" Arthur said, taken by surprise.

The other British delegates noticed this with some amusement and, their curiosity aroused, followed Chamberlain to a small room down the hall that he sometimes used as an office when spending extended lengths of time at Downing Street. Arthur wandered down to the end of the hall, pausing to gaze at some portraits near the staircase. Chamberlain emerged from his room, rifling through the yellowed pages of a slender old book. He paused, exclaimed softly, "Ah!" and then saved his place in the book with its ribbon marker. Acknowledging his curious colleagues, he announced, "I'll just be a moment. Why not wait here, and we can discuss the evening's events?" With that, he went to rejoin Arthur.

Winston murmured to Birkenhead, "My Lord, I've never seen Austen so animated."

"Nor I. He's positively delirious."

Arthur waited patiently and patted Michael on the back when he finally emerged from the Cabinet Room and passed on his way to the exit. "I'll be right with you, Mick."

Michael mumbled, "I'll be outside with the lads, then."

Chamberlain came up to Arthur and explained, "After all these weeks together here in Whitehall, I thought you might like to have a little memento of your time here. I don't know if you've had a chance to stroll through St. James's Park, but here is a delightful little comedy named after it."

"Why, that's very thoughtful of you. Very thoughtful, indeed," Arthur said softly. He opened the small book and murmured, "*St. James's Park, by P.Q.*" He looked up to Chamberlain and noted, "My, from 1733. This must be quite a rare edition. Are you sure you can part with something so valuable?"

As Arthur skimmed the pages, Chamberlain assured him, "Oh, it's probably only worth a couple of quid. Think nothing of it."

Arthur came to the ribbon in the middle of the book and read aloud a couplet from the end of the play's second act.

> *How swift to fly when Mischief leads the way!*
> *While to do Virtuous Actions we do delay.*

Chamberlain smiled at this and said, "Mr. Griffith, no one will ever accuse you of that. God be with you."[24]

Arthur was deeply moved by this extraordinary display of empathy and support. He said softly, echoing the response from Catholic Mass, "And also with you."

When Arthur left, Chamberlain walked slowly back to the small room where the other British delegates waited. While his comrades watched in silence, he took the monocle from his eye and polished it once again before replacing it, blew his nose softly into his handkerchief before folding it back into his pocket, and said quietly, "A braver man than Arthur Griffith I have never met."[25]

"Yes, remarkable man," Birkenhead agreed.

"As is Michael Collins," Winston added. "When he rose from the table, he looked as though he was going to shoot someone, preferably himself." No one laughed at this observation, for it was not far from the truth. Winston told his associates in all seriousness, "I have never seen so much pain and suffering in restraint."[26]

Lloyd George wondered to them all, "Do any of us suppose that anyone besides Mr. Griffith will sign?"

Birkenhead said cautiously, "It will be a great thing if, as Chairman of their Delegation, he stands by these proposals."

"Oh, I think he demonstrated well enough that at the very least, he will do that," Lloyd George said with confidence. "But what of the others?"

Winston answered, "We shall have to wait and see if he is able to convince the others to follow his example."

Lloyd George said ruefully, "The others might hold out for an answer from Ulster on Irish Unity first."

F.E. seemed to harbour some pessimism. "I have to speak in Birmingham tomorrow, and in anticipation of a breakdown, I have prepared a speech along the old Anti-Home Rule lines demanding suppression of the gunmen."[27]

Taking the hard line, as usual, Winston replied, "If we have no answer by 10 p.m., we shall leave them in no doubt as to what we are doing."[28]

---

7 P.M., MONDAY, 5 DECEMBER 1921, LONDON

ROBERT BARTON HAD AN UNCOMFORTABLE RIDE BACK TO HANS PLACE, sitting between Michael and Arthur, each of whom stared out their windows, deep in their thoughts, exhausted from the stress of the lengthy session with the British. Barton was more nervous than exhausted as he sensed his grasp of the situation slipping away. It was well past sunset now, and as they drove through the dark London streets, he made a weak effort to see things in a positive light. "Well, Mick, we did well with them securing free trade. Oh, aye, fiscal autonomy, now there's something."

"Hmm-hmm," was all the affirmation he got from Michael.

A moment later, Barton offered another bit of optimism. "Coastal defence, well, you made ground with old Churchill there."

Arthur listened silently, not responding. Michael continued to stare out at the passing cars and streetlights but managed to grunt, "Yes, I suppose."

"Well, I'd wager if we hold out on the Crown, we'll get our way."

At this, Michael turned and answered, "Are ye daft, man? Bob, it's over."

"What are you saying, Mick?"

Tom Cullen pulled the car up at a street corner. He and Liam Tobin both turned around from their front seats. Michael's general quietude of the past few days had mystified everyone, but it was borne not of an ill temper but a grim determination that comes with having come to a momentous decision. He now revealed this as he answered Barton, but did so staring at Tom and Liam. "What I'm saying, Bob, is that I'm signing the damn thing. And that's that."

"What? How can you, Mick? You, of all people!"

Arthur snarled at Barton, "What do you mean to imply by that? I'm signing it, as well."

Barton was incredulous and proceeded to go over many of the day's arguments again, but Michael shut his ears to his complaints.

"Robert," Arthur said, regaining his composure as the car pulled away, "let's discuss it as a group when we get back to Hans Place."

In a few minutes the car arrived in front of Number 22, and Arthur and Barton got out. Michael, however, stayed put. "I've had enough. You lot work it out. Let's go, Tom. Take me back to our house."

Hearing this, Arthur returned to the car to talk with Michael through the rear window. "Ye all right, Mick?"

"Tired, just fed up. I can't bear any more of this."

Then lowering his voice, Arthur asked, "So, what do you make of this business about sending a destroyer steaming up to Craig? Do you believe it?"

Looking past Arthur to see that Barton had gone into the house, he replied, "Oh, it's true enough. He told us last week he intended to provide Craig with a final draft of the Treaty. He knows you're willing to sign, and he suspects I will, so I think the brunt of this ultimatum was directed at the others, especially Bob. The P.M. is fed up, too, and he just wants it over and done with."[29]

Arthur nodded, adding, "Tonight." He stood up straight as if to leave, but another thought struck him. "You know, everyone back home will hear of this ultimatum. I wish he had not given it, whether he meant it or not. People will say we capitulated."

"Let them. You and I know we were willing to sign on the merits, destroyer or no destroyer, threat or no threat. Just more Welsh wizardry, but I'll say this: If we don't all sign, there will be war, sooner or later. Sooner, most likely. There's no bluff there."[30]

"I agree. Get some rest. Until later."

As Arthur turned and went into the house, Pat McCrea and Emmet Dalton drove up alongside Michael's car, and everyone rolled down their windows to talk. Seeing Michael sulking in the back seat, Pat called out, "What's the story, Mick?"

Tom answered for him, "Mick's mind is made up. I'm taking him back to the Military House while the rest of them make up theirs."

"In that case, eyes and ears, Tom."

"You sound like Mrs. Conlon," Tom quipped at hearing Mary Conlon's pet admonition from Pat's lips.

Emmet commented, "Even so, there's something in the air tonight."

Tom agreed, "That there is. Look around, all these men in the shadows, as if they know something's up."

Emmet asked, "What say our friends inside?"

Michael peered over at the Politicians' House. He explained, "They all know my mind on it. Let them wag their tongues all they want. I need some quiet."

"All right, Mick. I'll go with you."

As Emmet joined Mick in the back seat, Pat called over from the other car, "This is going to be a long night."

"Long and contentious," Tom agreed.

They were both right. After they parted, Pat parked his car up the street and walked back to the house. When he got inside, he heard shouting from one of the rooms upstairs. Pat paused at the bottom of the stairs to listen, shook his head, and went into the kitchen in search of something to eat.

There he found Mary Conlon and May Duggan nursing cups of tea at the kitchen table. "You must be famished," Mary surmised. "Sit yourself down. There's plenty of stew. I'll fix you a plate."

"Thank you, Mrs. Conlon," Pat answered. There was the sound of a door slamming. "They're at sixes and sevens already, aren't they?"

There was the sound of feet stamping down the stairs and then Barton calling from the upstairs landing, "Come back, please, Arthur. Let me explain."

"All right, then. But we don't have all night, you know," the people in the kitchen heard Arthur call back.

"Oh, I don't like this one bit," Mary said, shaking her head, "no, I tell you I don't."

"Not tonight, of all nights," May agreed. "Go on, son, eat up. It looks to be a long one."

"Indeed," Pat concurred.

A couple of helpings of stew later, the atmosphere upstairs seemed unchanged, with more loud arguing and shouting. Finally, Arthur returned down the stairs and into the kitchen, where Alice Lyons had joined the others. Arthur seemed relieved to find her there. "Alice, be an angel, call the other house, and persuade Mick to get over here. He'll come if you ask. I'm desperate here. Tell Mick I'm not making any headway with those blockheads upstairs." He noticed the worried expression on May's face and quickly amended his statement, "Your husband, Eamonn, excepted, of course, May."

ON THE RIDE BACK TO CADOGAN GARDENS, MICHAEL SAID, "EMMET, have our Canadian forestry pilot Charlie Russell on standby to take flight from Croydon."

"Faith! Is it that dire?" Emmet asked in astonishment.

"Lloyd George is beating the war drums. I think it's all a load of palaver, but you never know. Arthur and the rest would retain diplomatic immunity if there were a break, but I could have my pavement moniker of 'murderer' reinstated at a moment's notice. Make sure that the aeroplane has a full tank."[31]

"Christ!" Tom exclaimed from the driver's seat. "I should do the same."

As they pulled up to the house, Liam looked around and said, "For now, Tom, I think we should heed Mrs. Conlon's advice and stay with the car. I get the uneasy feeling we shouldn't leave it unwatched. You never know."

Michael rushed inside, went straight into the kitchen, and plopped down, exhausted, into a chair. "Any chance of a cuppa?" he pleaded.

Soon Eddie and Peggy McIntyre were keeping him company as he nursed a cup of tea. Even before his tea had a chance to grow cold, the private line rang.

"Hello?" came Kathleen MacKenna's voice in the hall.

"You sure I can't get you anything else, Mick?" Eddie asked.

"No, Eddie, I'm off food tonight—I don't think my stomach could take it, but you can pour out some more tea."

After taking Alice's call, Kathleen joined everyone in the kitchen. "Mick," she began as she came in, "Alice says there's so much shouting and arguing going on in Arthur's room, he came down to ask for you."

"They're still at it?" Michael asked.

"Yes, they're all at loggerheads," Kathleen answered. "Mick, I think Arthur really needs you over there. Alice is worried about him. She says she can hear the strain in his voice. Can't you go over there?"[32]

"All right. You don't have to boil your cabbage twice. I just needed a break. Get Ned to bring you to Hans Place and tell them I'll be there soon." He took out his pocket watch and exclaimed, "It's almost ten o'clock already, and the Brits will be expecting us."

---

10 P.M., MONDAY, 5 DECEMBER 1921, LONDON

AS NED AND KATHLEEN STEPPED OUT INTO THE EVENING MIST AND FOG enveloping Cadogan Gardens, dark shapes moved about in the shadows. Phantom whispers from unseen figures followed them on their way to the car. When they reached the edge of the grass, four men suddenly appeared, blocking their path. One of the men shone an electric torch over their bodies, especially scrutinising Ned, holding the light on his face and then passing it over his entire body from head to toe and back again.

"Nasty night, eh, boys?" Ned asked coolly, hoping to disarm the interlopers.

They just grunted, and the man with the torch waved them along as he and the others slinked back into the shadows. When they were safely in the car, Kathleen asked, "Who were those characters, Ned?"

"Just some blokes from Scotland Yard and maybe the Secret Service. I've seen a couple of them before over in Whitehall. They're all right, and they certainly are not going to make any moves, although that depends."

"Depends on what?" Kathleen asked.

"On whether the Treaty is signed tonight. If not, all bets are off. Anything could happen."[33]

When they turned the corner into Hans Place, Ned said, "Here you go, Kathleen."

"Aren't you coming in?"

Ned looked around, "No, I'll wait out here in the car for Mick, but I had better walk you to the door first. Too many characters in the shadows."

"Thanks, Ned. I'll feel safer walking the last fifty feet with you."

As Michael prepared to leave Cadogan Gardens, Eddie asked, "Can I come, Mick?"

Michael turned to Tom and Liam and asked, "What do you say? An extra bodyguard?"

"Sure, Mick."

"Get your coat, Eddie. You can guard Hans Place."

Peggy stood up, walked over to Michael, took him by the hand, and looked at him, tears welling in her eyes. "You take care of yourself, Mr. Collins."

Michael squeezed her hand, smiled, and left.

Soon they pulled up in their car in front of the Hans Place house. Liam whispered, "Tom, it's the same story here. The grounds are crawling with Scotland Yard and Secret Service agents. They can probably hear every word coming from inside."

"I wonder if Dave Neligan is here," Michael said, only half-kidding.

Liam told them, "I'll keep Ned company out here in his car."

"Good idea, Liam. You can watch these watchers. Come on, Tom, Eddie, let's go inside."

When they stormed past the figures outside and entered the house, everyone could hear all the arguing carrying on unabated upstairs. Michael had not bothered to put on his Mackintosh on the trip over, and it dangled loosely over his attaché case as he nervously paced back and forth in the dining room. He stopped with a grimace when he heard someone upstairs shouting. "What the hell are they on about? Oh, sorry, May, I didn't see you there."

"That's all right, Mick," May assured him as she and Mary came in with a pot of coffee and a tray of snacks. "Care for any?"

"No, I've had enough already."

"How about a sherry, then, Mick?" Tom asked.

"What? Oh, yes, thanks. Just a short one." He walked over to the staircase and beckoned Eddie, "Go upstairs and see what's keeping them." Finding a chair at the foot of the stairs, Michael collapsed onto it and waited for the others to come down. His enormous well of strength and energy, which had sustained him day after day, week after week, was finally depleted. Though still grasping his briefcase, with the tail of his coat and its belt dangling across the floor, he finally allowed himself to succumb to a release from the day's woes and fell deeply asleep.

"Poor Big Fellow!" Kathleen exclaimed when she entered the room and saw him there. "Look at him!"[34]

A few minutes later the other delegates finally came downstairs.

"It's about time!" Michael exclaimed as he stood up, re-invigorated. "Have you finally decided?"

Barton answered this question with one of his own. "Mick, I still don't see how after all you've done, you can give up the fight for the Republic by signing."

"Give up the fight?" Michael snorted. "So, Bob, you want to go back home and continue fighting? Do you have any idea how few men we have left?"

"I just thought…"

Michael cut him short, "I'm not talking about these so-called Trucileers. I mean real fighting men, active Volunteers."

"There must be…"

"You can be forgiven for not knowing, what with all the time you spent in prison. But we never had more than three or four thousand men, and it's far less than that now. Do you want to send them out to be slaughtered?"

Shocked and faltering, Barton tried to respond, "I, I…" but Arthur added to his turmoil by upbraiding him, "Bob, you will be hanged from a lamppost in Dublin if your refusal to sign causes a new war in Ireland."

Barton was visibly shaken and looked to Gavan Duffy for support, but Duffy had nothing to say, no solace to offer.

"Listen, Bob," Arthur went on, "I'll say it once again. Our instructions from Dublin were if we were to break on anything, it was to be on the question of Ulster, not on the Crown, and not on an oath to the Crown."

"What of our oaths of allegiance to a Republic? I cannot trifle with that oath."

Arthur assumed a more sympathetic tone, "I agree with you, Bob, and I ask no man to defy his conscience. Let's not break over their Oath, but try to get them to give us assurances on Ulster. If we fail, we have no choice but to refer back to the Dáil and damn any ultimatums."[35]

Suddenly Eamonn Duggan broke down in tears and cried out, "I recall so many deaths. I'll never forget that morning in Mountjoy when I saw the hangman who was to hang our young lads there." [36]

Barton then turned to his cousin Erskine Childers and said in a plaintive tone, "Erskine, could I please have a word in private?"

"Of course, Bob," Childers responded with a disdainful glance at Michael. "Let's retire to the kitchen." When they entered the kitchen, Childers looked down his nose at Eddie and said, "If you'll excuse us?"

"As you like."

When they were alone, Barton asked, "I don't know, Erskine, risking another war, like they say. What do you think?"

Childers answered coolly, "It's a matter of principle."

"Uh-huh," he said uncertainly.

Childers thought for a moment and replied, "You know, Bob, I feel Molly is with us here."

Barton was quite close to Childers' American wife, Molly, and had served as best man at their wedding, but this reference to her had an unintended effect. Barton responded sarcastically, "Well, I suppose I must sign."[37]

"What?" Childers asked in shock. "How can you say that?"

"Here I am, being put on the spot to decide whether we go to war with England, and you think it matters one tittle what your Yankee wife thinks about it?" He stormed out of the kitchen and rejoined the others. "I'm signing, and that's that," he said, looking at Michael.

Everyone turned to Duffy. "Well, Gavan," Arthur asked, "how about you?"

Childers rejoined the others in time to hear Duffy answer, "Yes, I'll sign." Childers stopped mid-stride and held his hand to his forehead.

Michael once again looked at his pocket watch. "It's getting late, too late. We were supposed to be there at ten o'clock, and it's past eleven already. We had better get over there before they let loose those dogs outside."

Duffy surprised everyone by saying, "Mick, why don't you and Arthur go over there and work out the final details? Tell them I'll sign, but I think I'll stay here."

Arthur took a deep breath and said, "Are you sure, Gavan?"

Duggan, still distraught, spoke up, "He's right, Arthur. You two go. I have no more to add. Tell them I'll sign, as well."

Michael looked over at Childers. "As Gavan says, we still have some things to settle, so the delegation secretary should come along, Erskine. We'll ask you in if we need you. Let's go. Time to shake the dust off our shoes."

---

11 P.M., MONDAY, 5 DECEMBER 1921, LONDON

"MY GOODNESS, BUT THIS HAS BEEN A DAY OF UNRELIEVED STRAIN."

"Yes, Austen, it has," Lloyd George agreed. The four core members of the British Delegation, Lloyd George, Chamberlain, Birkenhead, and Churchill, had been sitting in the Cabinet Room since ten o'clock.

Winston looked at the mantelpiece clock. "They are over an hour late now. I now wonder, as did the Prime Minister, if anyone besides Mr. Griffith will sign, and what validity would his solitary signature express?"[38]

Lloyd George offered his opinion, "I think Michael Collins will sign, provided he has as much moral courage as he has physical courage."

"Mark Twain," Winston interjected. Then responding to Lloyd George's quizzical expression, he explained, "He wrote that it is curious that physical courage should be so common in the world, and moral courage so rare."[39]

"Thank you, Winston. But moral courage is a much higher quality than physical courage, and it is a quality that brave men often lack.[40] Still, if he signs, as I think he will, hopefully, the rest will follow his example."

"I hope you are right." Just then, Winston remembered something.

"I understand Hamar Greenwood bet H.A.L. Fisher a good top hat we get a satisfactory agreement. The weather might turn nasty any day now. I'd hate to see Hamar go without his new hat."

This jest helped ease the tension in the room as everyone enjoyed a good laugh. Then Thomas Jones entered the room and announced, "Mr. Griffith, Mr. Collins, and Mr. Barton have arrived, gentlemen."

"What of the others?" Chamberlain whispered.

As Jones ushered them into the Cabinet Room, the Irishmen all wore the most severe expressions. As Winston was to remark later, they remained superficially calm and quiet, which masked the inward turmoil felt. After everyone had taken his seat, there was a short, silent pause. Then Arthur Griffith said softly but clearly, "Prime Minister, the Delegation is willing to sign the agreements, but there are a few points of drafting which perhaps it would be convenient if I mentioned at once."[41]

With this short statement, elegant in its simplicity but sweeping in its ramifications, the tensions in the room were supplanted by mutual attention to minor details, as well as the understated relief that the real prize, peace, was at last imminent. Michael was far from elated, but he took advantage of the changed atmosphere to suggest some changes beneficial to the Irish. "I would like to draw your attention to the clause that allows for a local military force. If we were to drop the word local, it would mean a great deal to many people."

Birkenhead said simply, "Accepted. Anything else?"

Some points were raised about finance and trade and were dealt with expeditiously. Birkenhead then looked to Michael with a raised eyebrow as if to ask again if there was anything else.

Michael responded with another question, "How will the new Parliament for Southern Ireland be summoned?"

"Ah, good point," Birkenhead complimented him. "The new Parliament, the Dáil, would be summoned by the Provisional Government of Ireland, to which the British Government would transfer the necessary powers. Quite easily done, actually."

Almost two hours after they had begun, it seemed to Lloyd George that all the outstanding issues had been raised and summarily dealt with, so he stood up to speak. "Mr. Griffith, I would now like to ask if all these changes are accepted by the British Government, will the Irish representatives sign as a Delegation and recommend the agreement with their united strength to the Dáil?"

Arthur glanced at Michael and Barton, rose and faced Lloyd George across the table, and said softly, "In the name of all the Irish plenipotentiaries, the answer is yes, we will."

"Then," Lloyd George replied, "we accept."

---

1 A.M., TUESDAY, 6 DECEMBER 1921, LONDON

As Lloyd George went to the door to summon Thomas Jones, he noticed Erskine Childers pacing back and forth down the hall. He whispered to Jones, "We're nearly done, I should think."

Jones, taken by surprise by the Prime Minister, enquired, "Yes, sir?"

Lloyd George smiled. "Ask Miss Stevenson to come in here. We have a Treaty that needs to be typed up and signed."

"Oh, excellent, sir. Yes, I'll send her in presently."

"Oh, and send in some brandy."

"Yes, sir."

Seeing Childers approach with an anxious expression, Lloyd George wished to avoid him entirely, so he quickly ducked back into the Cabinet Room, where the atmosphere was unlike any the delegates had yet had the opportunity to experience. There was much cordial conversation, humour, and sharing of anecdotes when a servant appeared with a tray of brandy and poured glasses for all.

Swept up in emotion, Winston expressed his feeling for the moment by raising his glass and declaring, "Gentlemen, we have become allies and associates in a common cause—the cause of the Irish Treaty and of peace between two races and two islands."[42]

"Hear, hear."

Before Birkenhead took a sip, he announced, "No one has been looking forward to this moment more than I. On the advice of my spiteful, sadistic doctor, I gave up drink earlier this year on a bet with a good friend of Mr. Churchill and myself." With an aside, he explained, "Lord Beaverbrook, Winston," then continued, "I bet him a thousand pounds I would not have a drink before Christmas." He took a swig from his glass, relishing the taste, "Ah..." and concluded, "I insist this Treaty is worth that thousand pounds."[43]

After about half an hour, Thomas Jones reappeared with the

freshly typed documents, one for each team of delegates. It was ten after two in the morning. The casual banter ceased, and the room went silent. Lloyd George placed the two copies of the Treaty on the table and announced, "Gentlemen, the time is come." As head of the British delegation, he signed first and then passed the two documents around the table.

Arthur Griffith was the first to sign for the Irish, signing his name in Irish, then again in English, enclosed in parentheses. He slid the papers over to Michael, who took out his best gold pen from his jacket pocket, took a deep breath, and affixed his signature solely in Irish, *Micheál Ó Coileáin*. He then passed the documents to Robert Barton, who followed suit.

Birkenhead, always one with *un bon mot* at the ready, signed the documents when they reached him, looked over at Michael and said, "I may have signed my political death warrant tonight."

This time Michael had the last word. He turned to Birkenhead, paused a moment and replied, "That may be so." He looked down at the copies of the Treaty and said wearily, "But I may have signed my actual death warrant." He rose from the table, as did Arthur and Barton.

The four British ministers rose as well and, on a strong impulse, walked around to join their counterparts on the other side of the table and, for the first time after two months of negotiations, instinctively, warmly shook hands. After a few moments of congratulations and well wishes, the meeting was at an end, and the Irishmen filed out of the Cabinet Room. They found a distraught Erskine Childers still pacing about the hall. On seeing his colleagues, he halted, his arms fell to his side, and his head dropped to his chest.[44]

Lloyd George appeared in the hallway carrying the Treaty with him just in time to witness this display of despair, but it would not affect his buoyant mood. Frances, who had come out of her office to join him, met him there, and he handed her the Treaty with a wink, whispering, "Pussy, be sure to lock this one up someplace safe."

When the three delegates met Childers in the hallway, Barton nodded grimly to him, and they all made their way toward the door onto Downing Street. Michael was about to step outside when he met General Macready on his way in, having just arrived after being summoned from Dublin, and blithely informed him, "It's done. I hope you will be satisfied with the arrangement we have come to."

Macready smiled back, telling him, "That depends on your ability to use your automatic effectively on a hundred or two of the extremists, which, as you will be untrammelled by the Press or Whitehall, I have no doubt you will be able to accomplish."

Michael laughingly replied, "Sir, something of the sort might be necessary, but let's hope not. I suppose the Whitehall Press are on the other side of this door waiting for one last go at us."

"Indeed, they are. Good luck and congratulations, Mr. Collins. I look forward to seeing you in Dublin."

"Thank you. Likewise."[45]

Macready left them and continued on his way inside. Before opening the door, Arthur said, "Gentlemen, given the enormity of what has transpired this evening, I think we should avoid any interaction with the Press for now. We can issue a statement tomorrow."

They all nodded sombrely.

The three plenipotentiaries and Childers emerged from Number 10 more exhausted than exhilarated, their grave expressions commensurate with the realisation that their two-month ordeal was over and a new era in their nation's history had just been ushered in. The reporters waiting outside sensed the solemnity of the occasion and, for once, ventured their questions with polite restraint.

"Mick, do you have anything to say?"

"Not a word."

"Are you coming back?"

"I don't know," he said, entering the car. As he closed the door, he looked at the men poised with their notepads to record his response and repeated, "I don't know."[46]

ONE HUNDRED FOUR

Peace to This Land of Ours

6 DECEMBER 1921

3 A.M., LIMERICK

IN THE DAYS LEADING UP TO THE SIGNING OF THE TREATY, DE VALERA was travelling around the country, giving speeches and visiting the Army, accompanied by the Minister of Defence, Cathal Brugha. The rage over Richard Mulcahy's alleged mutiny and his own threat to get himself "another army" seemed to have faded enough for de Valera to invite the Army Chief of Staff to join the tour.

Rather than embracing widespread hopes for peace held by most of the populace, de Valera's speeches seemed designed to prepare his listeners for a renewed struggle, keeping with his cabinet resolution to resist the British, "war or no war." The entourage, including an honour guard of thirty-two Volunteers, wound up at the large, well-appointed Limerick home of James O'Mara, who had given up a successful business to work for de Valera in America on the National Loan.[1]

After dinner, everyone sat around the fireside for hours, discussing the negotiations and wondering where things stood in London.

"Do you think an agreement will be reached soon?"

"Maybe it already has."

At this, de Valera's back went up, but he maintained a stony silence.

"If so, when will we find out?"

"Sure, but it won't be long now."

"Ay, I grant so."

"Do you, now? I think it'll be a while."

Irritated with the inane conversation, de Valera muttered, "Saints, preserve us," stood up and walked across the room to stare blankly into the fireplace.

It was the early hours of the morning when the phone rang, and the room went silent.

O'Mara looked at his watch and said to his daughter, "At this hour, it has to be important. Patricia, go see who it is."

She went over to the telephone and answered, listened for a moment, then held the phone out, "Dick, it's for you."

Mulcahy got up and walked over, and took the phone. "Yes, hello, George." He covered the mouthpiece with his hand and explained to those in the room, "Gearoid O'Sullivan," then spoke into the telephone again, "Really? You don't say!" He pointed in the air, punctuating his words, "Oh, that's grand, truly grand. I'll get him now." He held the phone out, "Chief, you should take this call. Big news out of London."

De Valera replied stiffly, "The call was for you. I don't need to speak to him."

Mulcahy paused a moment, turning his hand around mid-air as if to frame his question, "But they've reached an agreement. Don't you want to…"

"It's late, very late, and we have a long train trip back to Dublin in the morning. I'm going to bed." He stormed out of the room without saying goodnight to his hosts or anyone else.

As he watched de Valera leave, Mulcahy spoke into the telephone, "I'll see you back in Dublin, George. Thanks for calling. What? No, I'll explain when I see you. Good night, or rather, good morning." He hung up the phone, looked around the room, shrugged his shoulders, and said, "Well, I'm completely gobsmacked. Was that not just blazing strange?"

5 A.M., 6 DECEMBER 1921, LONDON

WHEN MICHAEL FINALLY RETURNED TO CADOGAN GARDENS WITH PAT, Liam, and Tom at five in the morning, they found Peggy Mack waiting in the drawing room. Mary Conlon had already phoned her with the news from Hans Place, where Michael had spent the last couple of hours after leaving Downing Street. When he came in the door, she got up from her chair and on impulse rushed over and gave him a kiss and a hug. "Congratulations, Mick. The news is just grand, just grand!" She immediately blushed and corrected herself, "Oh, dear, I'm sorry, Mr. Collins, I should say."

While the others watched with delight, Michael laughed, held her hands, and exclaimed, "No, Peggy, I should say I would hope everyone could feel the same, but I'm afraid there'll be too many who won't." His brow darkened slightly, and he said, "Even some of our friends over in Hans Place—oh, that reminds me, May Duggan sends her love. She and Eamonn are taking an early train to bring the Treaty back to Dublin."

"Oh dear, and I didn't get a chance to say goodbye. Such nice people."

"Yes, but some of our friends at the Politicians' House are already voicing their disdain for our achievement."

"Well, with God's help, all will be well."

"Yes, Peg. With God's help, we have brought peace to this land of ours—a peace which will end this old strife of ours."[2]

"That's a lovely thought."

"And true, I hope. Well, excuse me, I'm going to go upstairs and write this all down for Kitty and then try to catch an hour or two of sleep before Mass. Busy days, lads," he said, turning to the others. "Still some things to attend to at Hans Place, and I'm sure the Press boys will want some interviews and photos. In the meantime, Tom, why don't you get back a bit earlier and sort through the situation in Dublin."

"Sure, Mick. How about yourself?"

"I'm guessing maybe we can leave by tomorrow night." Turning back to Peggy, he said, "Why don't you come back with me?"

Peggy was surprised at this sudden suggestion and demurred, "I don't know, Mr. Collins. There's too much to do to tidy things up here."

"Well, don't let it go too long. There are people waiting for you at home."

"Oh…"

. . .

4 p.m., 6 December 1921, London

"May I remind you, Prime Minister, that Mr. Griffith and Mr. Duffy are due here soon to discuss the release of internees?"

"Yes, thank you, T.J."

"Oh, perhaps that's them now. Some Press photographers will also be arriving soon to take photos of the signed Treaty for tomorrow's papers." Jones left to greet the Irish arrivals.

Lloyd George asked, "Frances, will you tend to that for us?"

"Yes, sir." Frances Stevenson unlocked a drawer of her desk and took out the Treaty. "Oh dear!" she exclaimed just as Lloyd George was leaving the room.

"Is there a problem?" he asked, turning back.

"Well, yes. Mr. Duffy and Mr. Duggan have yet to sign it."

"That should be easily resolved. Perhaps Mr. Duggan is also coming, and he and Duffy can sign it then. Come along and bring it with you."

After they all assembled in the Cabinet Room, Lloyd George addressed Arthur and Duffy, "Before we start, gentlemen, we've noticed not everyone has signed our copy of the Treaty. We were hoping Mr. Duggan would have noted this oversight and accompanied you."

Duffy looked at Arthur blankly and said slowly, "Ah, well, the thing is, Mr. Duggan has already set off for Dublin."

"I see. Well, that is a pickle."

"There is another bit of a problem," Arthur explained. "Unfortunately, the final draft is entitled, *Articles of Agreement*, and we had all agreed it should be referred to as a *Treaty between Great Britain and Ireland*."

"Excuse me, sir," Frances said, "there may be solutions to both those problems." Turning to Arthur and Duffy, she addressed them, "Pardon me, gentlemen, but do you have any other papers that might have Mr. Duggan's signature on it?"

Startled, Arthur and Duffy stared at each other a moment in silence, then Arthur said slowly, "I don't think I…"

Duffy's eyes widened, and he interrupted, "Sorry, Arthur, but I may have just the ticket. May I?" He asked, placing his briefcase on the Cabinet table.

"Be my guest," Lloyd George responded, clearly amused.

Duffy rummaged through his briefcase, explaining, "I'm fairly certain I, yes, here it is." Beaming with satisfaction, he pulled out a menu card with the signatures of all the other delegates and handed it over to Frances, "Here you go, Miss Frances." He then explained to the others, "You see, sometimes when we have big dinners at the delegates' house, we print up the evening's menus and sign them for each other as mementoes. This one was from a few weeks ago."

"I see," replied Lloyd George as Arthur's eyes went up to the ceiling. "Charming. May I, Frances?"

"Ay, and there's Eamonn's autograph, clear as day," Duffy said, pleased with himself, helpfully pointing as the Prime Minister inspected the menu.

"*Minced Ulster?*" he asked innocently. "And how did that go down?"

Finally realising his *faux pas*, Duffy blurted, "Ah, sure, but no one touched it."

"How reassuring. So, Frances, I assume you have some cunning plan to extricate us from our predicament?" he asked as he handed the menu over.

"Yes, sir. Our copy of the Treaty, if I may," she asked. Lloyd George handed it back to her, and she compared the two documents and announced, "Perfect! If you'll excuse me."

"Certainly. Thomas, perhaps you could join her?"

Back in her office, Frances opened her desk drawer and reviewed the tools of her trade. "Here we are!" She took a pair of scissors, carefully cut out Duggan's autograph, opened a bottle of white paste, and glued the signature to the Treaty.

"You're right; it's perfect!" Jones exclaimed. "It's even the same size as the other signatures. Now, what about the title?"

"Simple." She turned to her typewriter, whirred a fresh sheet through and quickly typed away, removed the sheet and handed it to him, and he read it out loud, "*Treaty between Great Britain and Ireland. Signed 6th December 1921. At London.*"[3]

"They can stitch that over the top page of their copy. I tell you: they don't get the title of their Treaty right, and then they leave without signing it. How Irish!"

"I believe I've heard you say that before. That dinner menu certainly is exceedingly Irish."

Frances giggled as she started to pass her handiwork to Jones but suddenly withdrew it, holding it to her breast.

Puzzled, Jones asked, "Is there another problem?"

"Just make sure Mr. Duffy signs it before he leaves."

"Ah! Of course!"

7.30 p.m., 6 December 1921, Dublin

LATER THAT DAY, AFTER ARRIVING IN DUBLIN AND VISITING HIS FAMILY in Greystones, de Valera was back at Mansion House for a special ceremony in the Round Room. As Chancellor of the National University, he was to preside over the Dante Commemoration, an academic celebration in honour of the medieval Italian poet on the six hundredth anniversary of his death in 1321.

When he arrived, Piaras Béaslaí, the noted author and a member of the Irish Republican Brotherhood, was there to greet him. He was the Irish language scholar Conor Clune had sought advice from before being arrested along with Dick McKee and Peadar Clancy. Also at Mansion House were Cathal Brugha and Austin Stack, and, incredibly, de Valera asked them, "Any news?"

Stack looked at Brugha and then answered slowly, "Have you not seen the papers? They're all over town. The Treaty was signed last night." He showed him a copy of a newspaper, explaining, "This edition of the *Evening Mail* came out a few hours ago."

De Valera took the paper, skimmed through the lead article, reacting as if it was the first instance he learned of the signing, and flew into a rage. "I have to get ready for the Commemoration," he snapped as he started to put on his Chancellor's robes.

At that moment, Eamonn Duggan, having just arrived from London, came in and handed de Valera an envelope, "Here, Chief. We wanted to get this to you as soon as possible for you to read. It's the actual Treaty."

De Valera took the envelope as Duggan watched expectantly, but he just laid it down on his desk and went back to putting on his ceremonial robes. "What should I read it for?"

Looking perplexed, Duggan tried to explain, "The Treaty? Why read it? Arrangements have been made for it to be published in London and Dublin simultaneously at eight o'clock, and it is near that hour now."

De Valera appeared to be shocked and screamed back. "What? To be published whether I have seen it or not? Whether I approve or not?"

"Oh, well, that's the arrangement," Duggan responded tetchily.

"I don't have time to read it now," he snarled back. He stormed out of the room, muttering as he left, "I'll probably soon be back at teaching."

Nonplussed, Duggan turned to Brugha and said, "Well, that was blazing strange."

Brugha stared back a moment and started to say, "That's what Dick…" but his voice trailed off, and he left to join the Chief in the commemoration.

Béaslaí summed up the situation, "I am sorry to say, Eamonn, it would seem the fact that a Treaty was signed without first being referred to him is the source of his agitation. The nature of the Treaty, affecting the people of Ireland, is of only secondary interest to him. Now, excuse me, I have to attend this glorious celebration."[4]

It Won't Do for Cork

7 DECEMBER 1921, LONDON

"WELCOME, GENTLEMEN," SIR JOHN LAVERY GREETED HIS FAMOUS guests. "We're honoured to have you here before you leave London. Naturally, we're happy for you but sad to see you go."

Michael, Arthur, Barton, and Duffy had come to pay their respects to the Laverys. Arthur spoke for everyone, saying, "Thank you, Sir John, for all you have done for us these past few weeks. You and Lady Lavery have been a great aid and comfort while we've been here."

"Not at all, Arthur. The pleasure has been all ours, has it not, my dear?" John Lavery asked his wife.

"Yes, of course. We're so proud of you all and what you've accomplished here." Hazel then turned a little sad, pouting as she turned to Michael and said, "I wonder when we shall see you again."

"Not before long, I should think," Michael answered. "I'm sure I'll soon be back to lock horns again with your friend, Winston. Signing the Treaty was one thing; getting it to work is another, and what a lot of work that will be!"

"Well, come along, everyone," Hazel said, slipping her arm through Arthur's. "We've arranged for tea upstairs in John's studio." She picked up her little dog and said, "This way, gentlemen."

Soon the Irishmen were in awe, walking around the painting studio, viewing their portraits.

"Is that me?"

"Couldn't be. That fella's too distinguished looking."

"Too bad Duggan left already."

"Oh, look at Dev."

"We all will, soon enough."

"Sir John, you've done a remarkable bit of work here. We will forever be in your debt."

"Yes, this is so flattering for us all."

"Well, my thanks to all of you, gentlemen. It's been an honour and a privilege. Now, Hazel, I think it's time for tea."

After enjoying a pleasant interlude of conversation, tea, and sandwiches, Michael announced, "I'm sorry, but we must get going. I'm sure it's complete chaos at Hans Place."

Hazel's Pekingese struggled to his feet and barked weakly at Michael.

"What's the matter, little fella?"

"I'm afraid he's not doing too well these days, Mick," Sir John explained.

"Oh, I'm sorry to hear that," Michael said as he bent down, picked up the little dog, and stroked his head. "Come on, my friend. Time for me to say goodbye."

When they arrived downstairs, Hazel pleaded, "Oh, please, everyone, before you go, may I ask a favour?"

"Anything," Michael replied as he let the dog down gently on the floor. "What can we do for you?"

She walked over to a bookshelf and returned with a leather-bound journal. "This is just a little scrapbook I keep. Would you mind signing it?"

"Glad to," he answered, took out his pen, and signed and dated on the open page. "There, now, that's that! Come on, Arthur. Bob, Gavan, you, too."

Hazel purred, "Oh, thank you, everyone. I'll treasure this."

John then asked, "May we offer you a ride? It's no bother."

"No, thank you, we have our car outside. Besides, the Press are ensconced outside the house in Hans Place, and it will be mayhem."

"Very well, Michael," Hazel answered. "I'll walk you to the door."

The other men stepped outside first, but Michael lingered momentarily to have a last word and to shake hands with Sir John. When he finally stepped into the foyer to leave, Hazel touched his sleeve, and as

Michael turned back toward her, she stood on her toes and kissed him tenderly on the cheek. "God go with you, dear."

Michael stared into her eyes a moment, cleared his throat, and replied, "Till we meet the next time. Goodbye for now."[1]

The four men in the car left with Pat McCrea at the wheel and took the road past Brompton Oratory, where people were arriving for late afternoon Mass. Michael saw a familiar face at kerbside. "Pull over here, Paddy."

Michael rolled down the window and called out, "Give us the evening news, ye bold little gossoon."

The young newsboy turned around, and as Michael got out and walked over, the boy's face lit up. "Oy, Mick, how ye be? The papers are teaming with news on the Treaty. Fair do's, guv!"

"Well, I'm relieved you approve," he answered wryly.

"Seems like the whole world does, by the look of it. Look, here's a photo of you in *The Times!*"

Michael sighed, "Well, there's nothing to be done for that, is there?" He reached into his pocket and handed the boy a coin.

The lad quickly stayed Michael's hand and said, "That's all right. This one's on the house."

Michael emitted a full-throated yelp and, still laughing, gasped, "What a lark! Thanks for keeping us up on the news of the world, mate."

"What? Heading home?"

"That I am, but I'll surely be back before you know it."

"I'll be lookin' for you, then, Mick. So long."

With one last laugh, Michael spun the boy's cap around his head and returned to the car.

A FEW MINUTES LATER THEY ARRIVED AT HANS PLACE AND RAN through a massive gauntlet of reporters and photographers. They were greeted at the front door by Ned Broy, who had been standing watch.

"Howaya, mate," Michael laughed and said, "Quite the scene out here, eh?"

"Wait until you get inside." He turned his back on the crowd and revealed his gun inside his jacket. "Guard duty is more relaxing than the bedlam in there."

Michael slapped him on the back, saying, "You don't say?"

They all went inside to a bustle of activity. Everyone was preparing to leave for Euston Station, where a special boat train awaited the departing delegation to Holyhead for the ferry home. The cooks packed boxes of kitchen and dining room supplies for return to a catering rental service.[2] At the same time, Liam and Eddie helped Alice and Ellie Lyons with their suitcases, adding them to the mass of luggage accumulating in the parlour. Kathleen MacKenna was packing up the typewriters with help from Emmet Dalton, who asked, "Does it go in like this?"

"No, dear, the other way around." She looked up and saw Michael standing, looking around amid all the commotion.

Michael addressed everyone, "Well, I have to say, it's been great sharing our two houses with you all, but I can't wait to get home." He smiled and looked around at the delegates, secretaries and serving girls filing into the room. "Thank you all for all your hard work these past weeks and months."

Liam Tobin walked over to him and said solemnly, "What's this I hear about Mrs. Conlon and Miss McIntyre staying behind to sort things out? Who will guard them and the two houses?"

Michael agreed, "Good point, Liam." As Eddie walked by carrying a box, Michael collared him and said, "Looks like your bodyguard duties aren't finished yet, son."

Eddie looked embarrassed, "Oh, well, of course. I just thought, well, but whatever you say, Mick. Of course, I'll stay behind, and as Mary says, keep a sharp eye."

"Right," Michael answered. "Just try not to kill anyone. Not while you're ahead of the game."

Everyone laughed except for Peggy McIntyre, who stammered, "Well, I'm glad to stay, yes, of course, but, well, I hate to see everyone go. I mean, it's been such, that is, everyone has been so…" her voice trailed off in a quiver of tears.

Mary Conlon stepped over and put an arm around her as Michael took her hand and said softly, "You've been just grand, Peggy. It wouldn't have been the same without you, May, and Mary. But look, we'll see you in Dublin in a few days, won't we?"

"Yes, I suppose." She took out a hanky, blew her nose, and managed a smile. "Well, you kept your word. I'll be back at work for Monsignor McManus again before Christmas."

"And a blessed Christmas it will be, eh?"

"I think so," she answered softly with a smile and a wink.

"Now then, let's get a move on, everyone. So long, Mary, Peggy."

Outside the door, Michael saw a young officer from one of the Southern Divisions who had been part of the security detail. Michael put down a heavy suitcase and called to him, "Could you throw this in the boot for me?"

"Sure, Mick," he cheerfully answered as he came in and grabbed Michael's bag.

Before he left with it, Michael asked, "So, what do you think of it, the Treaty?"

"It won't do for Cork," the young man answered.

The smile vanished from Michael's face. He gave a guttural growl and shot back, "We'll see about that."[3]

Seeing Michael at the door, a reporter called out, "Mick, can we get some pictures of you and your fellow delegates?"

Michael checked his watch and shouted back, "Sorry, lads. We're on a tight schedule."

"Aw, come on, Mick. It's our last chance. Won't take but a minute."

Michael relented and said, "I suppose we should let them have their damn pictures."

When the team members assembled outside, Michael kidded the Pressmen, "All right, lads, do your worst."

One of the photographers asked, "Mr. Collins, can't you smile a little? Just a little?"

Michael grinned and said, "I'll try."

As reporters are wont to do, they used this opportunity to pepper Michael with questions. "Mick, how did you succeed in eluding capture all that time during the hostilities? What disguise did you wear?"

"My moustache was my disguise," he quipped. Everyone had a laugh, then laughed even harder when Michael rubbed the stubble on his upper lip and added, "I never disguised in my whole life."[4]

Another reporter had a more serious question. "Well, you must be pleased to have concluded the negotiations and be on your way to establishing a new nation. What do you envision for the future of Ireland and her place in the world?"

Michael dropped his flippant attitude and answered in a more serious, formal tone. "In the creation of the Irish Free State, we have laid a foundation on which may be built a new world order. The problem of relations between Britain and Ireland is essentially the same as between Britain and the other Free States. The problem can only be solved by recognising without limitation the complete independence of the several countries, and only on that basis can we all be associated together by ties of cooperation and friendship. Such an association, in effect a league of free nations, would be a novelty as the world is now looking to end forever the internecine strife that had torn it asunder for so many ages."

One reporter asked, "Much like President Wilson's League of Nations?"

"Yes, but with more familial binds than that. Would not America, bound so closely by blood ties both to Britain and to Ireland, be willing to enter such a league? The Irish in Ireland would be united once more with the Irish in America and would share common internationality with the people of the Anglo-Saxon race. Ireland would be a link to join America and Britain. And with America in this league of the free nations, what country would wish to stay outside?"[5]

Writing feverishly in his notepad, the reporter responded, "Well, sir, that's a mighty ambitious proposal. I wish you all the best." He looked over to Arthur, who smiled back weakly and shook his head ever so slightly.

Another reporter asked, "Do you think the Boundary Commission will work?"

"If North-Eastern Ireland decides to join us, then there won't be much to it, but if she does not, it will be a different thing."

"Do you expect any trouble getting the agreement accepted in Dublin?"

"Trouble?" he answered with a grin. "You can get the agreement with or without trouble, but I have got over trouble before."[6]

Mary, Peggy, and the few kitchen staff who would remain behind to clean up gathered outside to wave their last goodbyes. Michael told the journalists, "Now, gentlemen, we really must leave. Thank you."

After they took off, Mary looked at her watch and said, "I thought they'd never leave. Come now, Peggy, we have just enough time to make that show in the West End."

"Oh, dear, I nearly forgot. Let me get my handbag."

PAT MCCREA AND LIAM TOBIN HAD BEEN PATIENTLY WAITING IN A CAR for Michael and Arthur. Once they got in and Pat pulled away, Arthur smiled as he turned and said, "'New World Order,' eh? As the reporter back there said, that's a bit ambitious, is it not?"

Michael laughed and said, "Well, at least I mentioned 'association.' Dev will like reading that, even if it didn't make it into the Treaty."

"Don't count on that assuaging his wrath. We have a hard sell ahead of us back home."

"I know. I've had evidence of that already. After breakfast, I went to Grosvenor's Hotel to see our illustrious ambassador to Great Britain, Art O'Brien. He didn't sound anywhere near as enthusiastic about the Treaty as today's papers. 'Not a cause for us to rejoice,' according to him."[7]

"Dev has his man over here, doesn't he?"

"If Art wants to keep his job, he'll have to change his tune, but I'm not counting on that."

"Here we are, gentlemen," Pat called from the driver's seat as he drove through Euston Arch. "Looks like you have some admirers waiting to greet you."

Michael leaned forward to take a better look. "For mercy's sake!"

The station entrance was filled with a cheering, sign-waving crowd proclaiming joy at the signing of the Treaty and gratitude to the delegates for their achievement.

"Mostly women, too, it seems," Pat asked, "What'll we do, Mick?"

"What *can* we do, Pat? We have to get out." The cars pulled up, and Michael sighed and said, "We have no choice. Come on, Arthur. So long, Paddy. It looks like you're in a bind here, too. Good luck!"

"So long, Mick. Thanks for everything."

Michael chuckled and said, "Thanks, nothing. You can save your farewells for Betsy." As Pat nodded with a grin, Michael continued, "See that you and Joe McGrath get these cars back safely to the rental garage, and you get yer arse to Dublin as quick as you can. I'll need you there, as always."

"Ay, then it's back there you'll find me."

Michael turned back to Arthur and said, "Out we go!"

"Wait a second!" Liam got out first and put his hands up to the crowd in a friendly enough gesture but said firmly, "Now, ladies, if you would just step back a bit." He turned back to the car, "All right, now."

However, they were immediately besieged by the crowd when they got out. Michael looked at the other cars in their entourage and saw the same scene unfolding.

"Come on, Arthur," Michael cried, laughing. "Let's make a run for it to our carriage. We didn't fight the English all these years to die here at their railway station."

"Good point, Mick," he answered. "I'll race you."

They hurried through the Great Hall as best they could, but when they reached the platform entrance, an even greater crowd was waiting for them. Dozens of London Police tried to hold the public back, but as soon as Michael passed through the entrance, they rushed forward and surrounded him. One woman threw her arms around his neck and showered him with kisses before a cordon of policemen lifted him off the ground. They carried him to his carriage while the crowd sang the Sinn Féin anthem, "A Soldier's Song." Michael's hat fell off in all the commotion, and as he leaned backwards to retrieve it to no avail, he saw that Erskine Childers, too, was getting crushed as he pushed his way through the crowd.

A tall, lean figure with a fedora pulled down over his eyes was following near the edge of the crowd at a safe distance. Ahead at the centre of the melee, Michael finally reached their carriage, but his feet never touched the ground, for he was lifted onto the carriage, where he was greeted with a kiss from another woman. The tall man in the fedora walked past with his head bowed, smiling grimly, and boarded the next car. Michael glanced over, grinned, and then gave Arthur a hand with his suitcase.

The station master greeted them and apologised, saying, "I'm sorry you've had such a rough passage."

"Oh, that's all right," Michael answered. "I quite enjoyed it."

"That's kind of you to say so, sir. Porter, help them with their bags. Come, I'll escort you to your compartment."

They followed him down the aisle until they found their reserved compartment and went inside.

"Thanks, mate," Michael said cheerily.

"It's been an honour, sir. Goodbye and good luck to you."

"Thanks again." Still exhilarated, Michael told Arthur, "I never thought I'd thank British police for carting my ass away!" He slid the window down, stuck his head out, and waved to the crowd.

"Speech! Speech!" they cried out, but when Michael started to address them, they broke out into even louder cheering. Michael pulled his head back into the car, laughed, and said, "There must be a couple of thousand of them out there."

"Yes, and as Pat noticed, mostly women. They have their darling, don't they?"

"Arrah, give over with that! You give them a speech. You're the leader of the team. They'll want to hear from you."

"I'll give it a go, then."

Standing beside Michael, Arthur stuck his head out the window and raised his hands for silence, but this only resulted in a fresh outburst of cheering, which continued unabated as the train started to pull out of the terminal. People ran alongside the car, waving, laughing and crying for joy until they reached the end of the platform, where they could barely glimpse Arthur's waving hand and Michael's smiling face.[8]

An Urgent Summons

8 DECEMBER 1921, IRISH SEA TO DUBLIN

THE FERRY WAS WELL OUT TO SEA AS MICHAEL AND LIAM TOBIN SAT IN the lounge discussing the day's events with Andy Cope, who accompanied them on their return trip to Dublin. The tall, mysterious figure Michael had noticed at Euston walked by again and headed out to the deck. Michael said matter-of-factly, "I think I'll take in some sea air before turning in. Care to join me, Andy?"

Cope looked at his watch and replied, "No, thanks, I'm done for the day. Good night, Mick, Liam."

"Good night, Andy. Come along, Liam. Keep me company." He nodded along the deck and said, "We have company."

Liam exclaimed, "Well, if it isn't British Secret Service Agent David Neligan himself!"

Dave sauntered over and replied with a grin, "Good evening, gentlemen. Good to see you both, at long last."

Michael looked over his shoulder and said, "I just want to make sure Andy doesn't see us together. He still doesn't need to know about our special relationship. You nearly ran into him at the Gresham the day before I left, and now you show up again the day I return."

"Makes sense. I finished my assignment when you finished yours."

"I worked that out when I saw you on the platform. So, what the hell were you up to in London?"

"Not much, mostly sightseeing, thanks to my British partner who insisted on dragging me around the city. One night he suggested we..."

Michael interrupted, "Yes, I heard 'feminine companionship' was offered. So, you finally relented?"

"Ah, the cheek of ye. As far as why I was sent there at all, I honestly couldn't say. Baffling."

"See that, Liam? He doesn't deny it."

"Now, see here, Mick," Dave protested. When Michael and Liam just laughed, he joined in but then asked, "So, you faced down Lloyd George and Churchill and concluded the Treaty. Well done."

"It was a tough slog," Michael answered, "but I'm afraid the hardest work lies ahead."

Tobin added, "We'll have to face our die-hards now."

Somewhat confounded, Dave said, "I know about those pig-headed Die-Hards in Parliament, but this is the first time I've heard that British moniker used for Irishmen. That's a sad comment on the state of affairs."

Michael agreed, "Sad, but the pure truth, I'm afraid. Listen, Dave, as I said, don't let Cope see us together, and keep your head down when we get back home. When we set up the Government, there'll be a place for you."[1]

ERSKINE CHILDERS LEFT HIS OVERNIGHT CABIN AND WALKED ONTO THE deck in the brisk morning air, cupping his hands. He noticed Michael and Arthur talking as they leaned against the guardrail near the bow. Michael called as he drew near, "Morning, Erskine. We're about to pull into Dunleary. Sleep all right?"

"Why, yes, thank you. Slight bruise to my ribs, though. I nearly got crushed to death in that crowd back at Euston!"[2]

"Really?" Arthur asked in a tone of slightly exaggerated concern.

Erskine was about to answer, but Michael interrupted, "I'm more concerned about our reception here. We'll be docking soon."

A few minutes later the ferry sidled up to the pier, and Michael took a look along the dock before stepping onto the gangway. "Looks like the Brotherhood showed up, but hardly anyone else, Arthur. This does not bode well. Do the people disapprove? Are they apathetic? What's going on here?"

"Don't think twice about it, Mick," Arthur answered, trying to console him. "I wouldn't get up this early to meet me. Look, there's Tom Cullen and some of your boys."

His spirits rose as they walked down the plank to the pier and were met by rows of I.R.B. men standing at attention, Joe O'Reilly and Christy O'Shea among them. When Michael alighted the dock, the men saluted, and a smiling Tom Cullen, who had been sent home from London a day before, stepped forward to greet them all.[3]

"Welcome home, gentlemen."

Michael stopped short, stood straight and saluted Tom and all the men, then grabbed Tom's hat from his head, tussled his hair and called out as he looked around, "After being up to my neck in British Ministers, it's good to be home amongst true friends. Thanks, lads."

As Childers stepped away and left on his own, all the men broke rank and surrounded Michael and Arthur, cheering them and slapping them on the back in a warm brotherly welcome. After saying their hellos and shaking hands, everyone split into happy, animated groups, talking excitedly about the historic changes unfolding.

"So, Tom," Michael whispered amidst all the chatter, "what *are* our fellows saying about the Treaty?"

Tom laughed and answered, "Can't you tell? What is good enough for you is good enough for them."[4]

Michael answered this by nodding enthusiastically, saying, "Good, good to hear."

"However, there is this," Tom said as he pulled a copy of the *Irish Times* from his pocket.

"Shite. I knew the other shoe would drop. What the hell is it? Dev?"

"You guessed it. Take a look."

"Give me that," Michael muttered, then read out the notice in the paper, "*In view of the nature of the proposed Treaty with Great Britain, President de Valera has sent an urgent summons to the members of the Cabinet in London to report at once so that a full Cabinet decision can be taken. The hour of the meeting is fixed for noon tomorrow, Thursday. A meeting of the Dáil will be summoned later.*"

He handed the paper back to Tom and said, "That didn't take long, did it? Sounds ominous, wouldn't you say?"

Joe answered haltingly, "Er, well, it's worse than that, Mick. The Chief held a Cabinet meeting last night and…"

"Hold on. How could he have a Cabinet meeting while Arthur, Bob and I were in the middle of the Irish Sea? What is he feckin' playing at?"

Tom explained, "It all started when Eamonn Duggan brought him the Treaty, and he wouldn't even look at it. Apparently..."

"Apparently," Michael finished the thought for him, "he took it as a personal slight and even an act of disloyalty that he was not consulted first before we signed."[5]

"Enraged is more like it," Joe said. "So, he called a Cabinet meeting with Austin Stack, Cathal Brugha, and W.T. Cosgrave. He announced that he was going to come out against the Treaty and call for your resignation, as well as Bob's and Arthur's."

"He can't get away with that!" Michael exclaimed.

"No, he can't," Tom replied, "and W.T. saw that he didn't. He stood up to the Chief and said he should at least wait until you, Arthur, Bob, and Erskine returned and had a chance to explain the circumstances around the signing. He also urged him not to make any pronouncement until then, but here's a strange thing, W.T. said he saw a look of peace and satisfaction pass over de Valera's face."[6]

Arthur, who had been listening intently, shook his head, saying, "If he just witnessed Cosgrave crossing him, he would have realised he was now outnumbered in the Cabinet. I wonder if that look meant something far different than peace and satisfaction."

"War and chaos would be the more likely outcome, I'd say," Michael replied. "Is there no good news after all we've been through these past months?"

"Well, as a matter of fact, yes." Tom smiled hopefully and added, "That same article in *The Times* is followed by one proclaiming there is no reason both the Cabinet and the Dáil should not accept the Treaty.[7] And besides, people all over town, all over the country, are celebrating what you've done."

"Just not here," Michael said, still sounding deflated. "Present company excluded."

Christy spoke up cheerfully as he pulled out another newspaper. "But they will in America, according to Harry Boland. He was quoted in yesterday's *New York Times*, which arrived this morning. Harry says the Treaty will be received in America with great joy."[8]

Michael smiled and started to say, "Good old Har..." but then he paused and said, "Wait, let me see that, Christy."

Christy handed the paper over, and Michael skimmed the article and frowned, saying, "Look, he was quoted the day before yesterday, the day we signed the Treaty, and it wasn't published until yesterday, so Harry hadn't even read it. I hate to say it, but Harry doesn't seem to know his own mind these days.[9] Let's see how much 'great joy' awaits us in the Cabinet. We have to be there in a few hours."

No Welcome for Me

8 DECEMBER 1921, DUBLIN

12 P.M., MANSION HOUSE

IN CONTRAST TO THE MODEST WELCOME AT DUNLEARY, A LARGE CROWD had gathered in front of Mansion House to celebrate the arrival of the Irish delegates for the Cabinet meeting announced in the Press by de Valera. When they emerged from their cars, they were greeted with wild cheering and shouts of joy. Michael arrived a few minutes before noon, sporting a new tweed cap pulled down over his eyes as if, even then, he could have escaped recognition. Still, he received the loudest cheers, and reporters shouted their predictable questions.

"Mick, any comment for the papers on the Treaty? How does it feel to bring peace home?"

"New cap, Mick?"

"I lost my proper hat in London."[1]

One woman in the crowd was shouting something out to him, but with all the noise, he could not make out what it was. Smiling broadly, he walked over and reached out to shake her hand, but she grabbed his hand, pulled him in close, and spat out, "My son died having taken an oath to defend Ireland, not your English King, you traitor!"[2]

Michael recoiled and pulled away from her but could still hear her over the cheers, "Coward! Traitor!" Accompanied by the other delegates, he walked briskly past the rest of the crowd and went inside and to the Cabinet drawing room. Once inside, he and the others found de Valera seated at his desk with his head cradled in his hands. He looked up blearily and cried angrily, "Michael, how could you have signed? How could you have agreed to that document without first referring back to me, without sending us a draft?"[3]

"You refused to go yourself. If you wanted the right of approval, you should have been there in person, as we had implored you to do."

De Valera cried piteously, "Only last Saturday, I had Arthur's promise that you would not sign without referring back to me. Otherwise, I *would* have gone to London. I would have held out for the association that would not have forfeited the Republic." His voice rose in anger as he cried out, "But now all is thrown away without effort, without consultation, and without permission."[4]

"Yes, we signed," Michael shouted back, "but with the understanding that it would be recommended to the Dáil for approval."

As the heated discussion emanated from the Cabinet, the reporters in the next room wondered what was happening. De Valera's pressman, Frank Gallagher, spoke loudly to them over the din so they could not hear what was happening. "Now, gentlemen, hold your questions until later. I'm sure a full statement will be forthcoming."[5]

In the drawing room, Cathal Brugha answered Michael in a venomous tone, "That's not what you led the Press to believe. All your demonstrations and celebrations have led the people to take the Treaty as a *fait accompli*."

Robert Barton defended Michael and himself, saying, "We were sent to negotiate the best terms we could get, and we did just that. The issue of referring the Treaty to Dublin never arose."

Even Gavan Duffy agreed, adding, "We had not even thought of it."[6]

De Valera responded sarcastically, "That was not teamwork."[7]

"Ah, but it was," Arthur countered, "and I stand by the Treaty and all that is in it."

"If it weren't for your promise, I would have gone to London and said, 'go to the devil, I will not sign.'"[8]

At this, Barton shouted back at de Valera, "Then, why didn't you? This whole situation is your doing and due to your vacillation. You had your chance to go to London, and you refused. The disaster is that, thanks to you, we were not a fighting delegation."[9]

Arguing like this carried on throughout the day and into the evening. Frank Gallagher, pleading for patience, frequently had to assure the waiting Press that everything was all right.

At one point in the discussions, Austin Stack brought up another matter, asking, "In any case, Mr. Griffith, will you not admit that you signed under duress?"

"No, I refuse to admit to that. I signed freely on the merits of the Treaty."

"What of the others, then?" Stack demanded to know.

Barton answered for the team, saying, "I will not go back on my signature, although I was intimidated by the threat that I would be responsible for war otherwise."

"In what way?" Brugha asked.

"Lloyd George employed an insidious form of duress," Barton replied. "Knowing that Arthur was willing to sign, he demanded that every other delegate should sign, or war would follow immediately. He insisted that those who refused to sign must accept the responsibility for the slaughter to ensue, without having a chance to consult the President, the Cabinet in Dublin, the Dáil, or the people."[10]

Knowing that renewed war would be a complete disaster, Michael explained, "I did not sign the Treaty under duress, Cathal. In a contest between a great Empire and a small nation, this was as far as the small nation could get. Unless the British Empire was destroyed, Ireland could get no more. On that basis only were we intimidated. The relationship between England and Ireland has *always* been one of duress."[11]

Gavan Duffy admitted, "I certainly felt duress."

At this point, Kevin O'Higgins spoke up, "I have no vote on the matter, but I do not like the Treaty, and in my opinion, it should not have been signed, but seeing how it has been signed, it should be supported. It is an absolute necessity for unity, and unity is only possible by coming together on the Treaty."[12]

"That's quite enough," de Valera responded. "It's time we take a Cabinet vote." He turned to the Cabinet secretary, Diarmuid O'Hegarty. "Mr. Secretary, please record the votes. I vote against the Treaty."

As expected, Brugha voiced his vote, "Against."

Stack, "Against."

Griffith and Michael responded, "I vote for approval; I vote for."

Robert Barton, who had criticized aspects of the Treaty, had complained of having to sign under duress, but had vowed not to go back on his signature, said defiantly, "I vote for."

Duffy was a plenipotentiary, but not being a member of Cabinet, had no say here, so with the vote tied at three for each side, all eyes turned to the Minister for Local Government, William Cosgrave. Despite his vote the night before blocking the attempt to remove the absent dissenting Cabinet members, de Valera must have held out hope or even expected that his close friend and supporter would vote against the Treaty, given his objections to the Oath.

O'Hegarty looked over and asked, "Mr. Cosgrave?"

Cosgrave looked at his comrades around the table and answered, "I vote to approve."

Arthur spoke up, "So be it. However, I propose we all refrain from any public announcements for the time being. This is not the final answer. That lies with the Irish people, with the Dáil."

Turning to Michael, Stack made a strange claim, "You have signed and undertaken to recommend the document to the Dáil. Well, recommend it. Your duty stops there. You are not supposed to throw all your influence into the scale."

"Where would I be then?" Michael snapped.

De Valera was seething. "That settles it. If the Dáil accepts the Treaty, I will resign."

"If it rejects," Michael shot back, "I'll be the one to resign."

"As will I," Arthur added.[13]

Soon after, at around nine o'clock, Michael walked by the Pressroom, shaken, upset, and tight-lipped, unable to bear any questions. Arthur came alongside him and said to the weary reporters, "I have signed the Treaty between Ireland and Great Britain. I believe this Treaty will lay the foundation of peace and friendship between the two nations. What I have signed, I will stand by in the belief that the end of the conflict of centuries is at hand."[14]

Then Stack came over and announced that a statement on the day's proceedings would be made in about half an hour. Arthur and Michael stepped outside to find the streets quiet and empty, save for a few cars waiting for the delegates. Michael trudged toward one with Pat McCrea behind the wheel and exclaimed, "Paddy! What did you do, fly over in our new aeroplane?"

"I would've if I could've, but I settled for the morning boat train. I took care of the cars first, of course."

"Good man. Get me out of here, Pat."

Back inside Mansion House, the Press reporters sat around listlessly for over two hours while the occasional sound of a typewriter punctuated the dull silence.

"Damn, we've heard the results; what are we waiting for?"

"It's past eleven already. What is keeping them?"

Finally, the typing ceased, and a few more minutes later, Frank Gallagher came in and handed out the statement, which the reporters poured over.

"Jaysus, Frank, what is de Valera up to?"

One of the journalists seized on one line in particular and read it aloud, "*The terms of this Agreement are in violent conflict with the wishes of the majority of this nation.*"[15]

"Violent conflict? Is that where we're headed?"

———

"THANKS, PAT. IT WAS GOOD OF YOU TO DROP ME OFF HERE."

"Sure, Mick. See ye soon. Good night."

Michael walked up to the door and knocked. A moment later Batt O'Connor opened the door and exclaimed happily, "Mick! So good to see you."

Michael said nothing but just stared back at Batt with an odd expression.

"Come in, come in. What are you waiting for? Ah, Michael, my boy, and you just back from London with the Treaty! This is a day I never thought I would live to see."

Michael stared down at his shoes and mumbled, "I thought perhaps you would have no welcome for me, Batt."

"Don't be daft, man! Get yourself in here. You'll let all the chill air in."

Michael stepped inside, and before he even took his coat off, he looked at Batt and said, "Dev is going to repudiate the Treaty."

"How could he do that? Doesn't he realise he'll tear the country apart?"

"Of course, he does. Not only the country, but the Army, as well. Poor Ireland, back to the back rooms again."[16]

"But, Mick…" Batt stopped short and said, "Come, give me your coat, and we'll discuss this over tea."

Just then a little girl cried out, "Uncle Mick!" Batt's daughter, Eileen, came running over and hugged him, and her mother soon followed and did the same. "Michael, my love. Come in, come in, and rest yourself. You must have been on the move for two days straight. Come, sit, sit. And you, Eileen, get yourself back to bed and let Daddy talk with Uncle Mick. I'll fix some tea."

After kissing Eileen good night, Michael sat down but almost immediately sprang to his feet again and started pacing the room, much as he had done at Batt's house shortly before leaving for the negotiations in London. "It's like I said months ago, Dev had the cards stacked against us. He knew he would never win his terms and instead sent us over, having sowed division among our ranks. It was a battle over there, arguing with the British, our own delegates, and more arguing with Dev at home whenever we came back for discussions with him. Now that we have signed the Treaty, I don't know if I can carry it against his opposition. If the Chief is against me, who would be for me? My own brother Johnny will probably stand against me in Cork."[17]

"Now you're talking complete nonsense. Get a hold on. What did the Cabinet have to say today?" Batt asked.

"Approval of the Treaty barely passed. Cosgrave cast the deciding vote."

"Ah, it passed by only one vote."

"Yes, and I don't know if I can carry it through the Dáil." His anxiety welling up, he ran his fingers through his hair. "There's no second chance with Lloyd George and Churchill. This is it. It's acceptance or war, a war we would most surely lose, and lose badly. Morale in the Army is not what it was. There's been a breakdown in discipline and a shortage of guns and ammunition. And now the British know who all our men are, and where they are."

"As you said before, like rabbits out of their holes."

"Ay, that's it. It would be impossible to carry on along the old lines. I will leave Dublin at once and go down to Cork to fight beside my own people. I'll not be hunted down in Dublin as I have been for the last two years."

"Really?" Batt asked. "If we had to go back to the fight, how long could we stick it out?"

"A fortnight, and it would all be over."

"If you left Dublin, who would there be to lead us?"

"Eoin O'Duffy would make a fine successor."

"Ay, that he would, if it came to it. But listen, Michael, I have never shown you any false praise, but now I *am* going to tell you that you are such a man as we never had before in Ireland, so that we have grown to look to you to do what no one else can do for us. Do not fail us. You have brought back the Treaty. It is a massive achievement. The people want it. They must be given the chance to say what they think of it. Then if they reject it—only they will not reject it—you will have done your part and will have no responsibility for the consequences."

Michael stopped pacing about and looked at Batt. "You're right, Batt. Let the people have their say."

"That's the spirit," Batt replied. "Now, sit yourself down and have a mouthful of tea."

Batt's wife brought in the tea, said good night and left Batt and Michael to talk into the small hours. Finally, Michael got up to go at about three in the morning. "Very well, Batt. I'll see the Treaty through the Dáil when it meets next week. I'll see that the terms are fully discussed and put it clearly to the people, and then let them decide."

As they walked to the front door, Michael continued, saying, "Whatever they say, I will accept their verdict."

"No one can expect any more of you than that, Michael. Good night."

Michael pulled out his pocket watch, grinned and said, "Good morning. Thanks, old friend."[18]

When he stepped out into the chilly air, he found Pat McCrea still waiting for him in his car, fast asleep, but waiting all the same. Michael knocked on the car window, waking Pat, and asked, "So, jarvey, ye on duty?"

We Have Declared For an Irish Republic

10 DECEMBER 1921, DUBLIN

A COUPLE OF DAYS LATER MICHAEL WAS SITTING IMPATIENTLY IN THE dining room of the Gresham Hotel.

"Shall I have the waiter get you anything else while you wait, Mr. Collins?" Mr. Donahue asked as he approached his table.

"No, I'm grand, thanks." Noticing the look of concern on his face, Michael checked his watch and assured Donahue, "I'm sure Eddie will be along any moment."

"Oh, excellent, sir."

While they were talking, Joe O'Reilly walked over and joined them.

"Hello, Mick. Pat is just after picking up Mary and Peggy from Dunleary. Oh, and Eddie, of course. They're all at the car outside."

"Fine. I have the meeting with the Supreme Council of the Brotherhood at Billy's pub. Come along, Joe. I may need your take on things."

"Allow me to be of assistance," Donahue politely insisted.

They all went outside, where Peggy McIntyre stood by the car chatting with Mary Conlon as Pat McCrea and Eddie unloaded luggage onto the pavement.

"Hello, ladies. I see Eddie got you home safely."

"Oh, my, yes. We were in good hands."

"Welcome home, ladies," Donahue said politely. "And you, Eddie. You look none the worse for wear."

Eddie turned and was struck to see the maître d'hôtel outside, in front of the building. "Why, thank you, Mr. Donahue."

Michael smiled at this touching reunion and asked, "Peggy, can we drop you off at home? It's no bother."

"Oh, well, hello, Mr. Collins. No, thank you, I think I'll just get a taxi. It was very kind of you to send Mr. McCrea to fetch us at the ferry."

"Don't even mention it." He looked over at Joe and said, "Well, just don't stand there, Joe. Get her a taxi."

Mr. Donahue intervened, waving the hotel footman over, "We'll see to that, Mr. Collins," he said, smiling broadly. "Great work you've done for Ireland, if I may say so."

"You may. Thank you, Mr. Donahue. I'm meeting with some pretty tough characters in a while. I hope they see things your way."

"Tough or not, I'm sure they will."

He shook hands with Donahue and then tipped the footman after he helped Peggy into her taxi. Michael then leaned down to say through the window, "Thanks again, Peggy. Tell Monsignor McManus I kept my word."

"I'm sure he's well aware of that. In more ways than one, in fact. Goodbye for now."

Pat was now holding the door to his car open. "After you, Mary," Michael said cheerfully, and they all got in and started for Conlon's.

Mary was a bit breathless but said as politely as she could, "I agree with Peggy. Very nice of you to ask Pat to pick us up."

"Excited to be home, Mrs. Conlon?" Pat asked from up front.

"Well, yes, I think I am," she said, blushing slightly.

"Hmm," Michael murmured. "That's nice."

"Oh, Michael, you're a terrible man."

"Oh, am I, then?" Michael asked her with a wry grin, "Did Billy know you were getting back today?"

"No, I thought I'd surprise him."

"Then let's show Billy the terrible man you have me for."

"Oh, I think I know what you mean," she said, laughing.

When they arrived at the pub, Michael said, "I know the people downstairs will be happy to see us. I just hope those waiting upstairs will be, as well."

"Sure they will, Mick," Joe answered.

"Ay, Mick, Joe's right, there," Pat replied. "I'll join you in a while."

Mary slipped her arm through Michael's as he accompanied her into the pub. They walked nearly to the bar when Billy finally saw them, and his voice exploded, "Jaysus, as I live and breathe!"

He swung the bar top over and came around and walked up to them but stopped short with a quizzical expression and stammered, "Er, hello, Mary, Mick."

Mary just looked at him a moment and then said to the amusement of everyone in the pub, "Well? Aren't you glad to see me?"

"Yes, Billy, show her happy you are."

"Go on, Billy! What are you waiting for?"

Mary shook her head and laughed, slipped away from Michael, went up to Billy, and planted a big kiss on his lips. The whole bar erupted, with the patrons pounding the bar and tables with their glasses.

"That's better, Billy."

Billy laughed too, and gave Michael a big hug, lifting him off the ground.

Spontaneous thundering applause followed, with cries of, "Well done, Mick," and "Long live, Ireland." A patron with a strong tenor began singing "A Soldier's Song," and everyone soon joined in. Liam Tobin and Tom Cullen came down the stairs at all the commotion and greeted Michael.

"Are all the lads waiting upstairs?" Michael asked.

"Yes, yes. Come along."

"I'll just be a minute. Mary, Billy, could I have a word?"

"Sure, Mick."

"What can we do for you?"

Michael huddled with the two of them and said, "Well, Christmas is almost here…" He whispered something to them, and they both broke out in broad smiles, nodding and saying, "That would be grand, Mick," and, "Michael, are you sure about this?"

"Ay, and I'm glad you approve. That's settled. Now, I believe I'm expected upstairs."

When Michael approached the landing of the upstairs dining room, Seán MacEoin was there waiting for him. Pretending he was about to pounce on him, Seán cried, "Here's where I get even with you!"

"All right, Seán, let's see what you got!" Michael cried out, but nothing rougher than a hug and a handshake ensued.

Tim Kelly was also there waiting for Michael, grinning from ear to ear. "Hello, Mick. Good to have you back."

"Good to be back, Timmy, and good to see you. You been keeping an eye on the place like I asked?"

"Yes, of course," he said, smiling as he motioned to the kitchen behind him.

Michael looked and saw Maureen and Nelly waiting in a state of excitement, but they just waved to him, as they knew that as President of the Irish Republican Brotherhood, he had to preside over this important meeting.

Michael went into the dining room, where he was greeted by all the members of the Supreme Council, who stood and applauded.

"Great, lads, great. I'm glad you could all make it on short notice," Michael began. "So, you've all read the final Treaty. What say ye?"

Richard Mulcahy spoke up first, "It's not perfect, Mick. It doesn't get us the Republic we fought for, but we all knew that was never in the cards Lloyd George was holding, was it?" Besides being the Chief of Staff for the I.R.A., Mulcahy was also a member of the Dáil, and he added, "You can count on my vote, Mick."

One of the men chimed in, "No one likes having the Oath, but Tim here did a good job of patching together the best one we could come up with."

Tim just looked down bashfully at his shoes.

Someone else added, "The one you settled on suited us fine, so no complaints from us."

Gearoid O'Sullivan spoke up, "We all know the circumstances, the inherent restraints. We all know how hard the delegates worked and that you did the best you could and brought back the best agreement possible. Since you all signed it, most of us think it should be supported. You'll have my vote as well."

"I see," Michael said in answer. "Most of you, you say." He looked at Liam Lynch, whose First Southern Division, the largest in the I.R.A., operated in Cork, Kerry, and part of Limerick. "What say you, Liam? I heard from one of your men back in London that the boys in Cork are against it."

Lynch cleared his throat and said, "I'm sorry, Mick. That's about the size of it. We have declared for an Irish Republic and will not live under any other law.[1] The First Southern Division will issue a state-ment declaring against the Treaty. As Oscar Traynor put it, 'The

Treaty is not what the hungry and ragged men of the Dublin Brigade fought for.'"[2]

"Is it not?" Michael looked around the room and asked, "Any word from Harry Boland? When is he coming back from New York? What does he say?"

Seán MacEoin answered, "Harry says he'll vote against."

"Ah, Harry." Michael looked down, then shook his head and said, "Well, we won't have any coercion. Men will need to vote their conscience. We need to issue a statement declaring as much."

All the men there began discussing how to word such a sensitive proclamation. Sitting in a corner, quietly listening to all the arguments, Tim Kelly took out a pad and pen and started scribbling away. After a few minutes, he rose and said, "Mick, how about this: *The present Treaty between Ireland and Great Britain should be signed; however, members who have to take public action as representatives are given freedom of action in this matter.*"

Everyone there stood silently, nodding for a moment until someone spoke up. "That about sums it up."

"Pretty good, Tim."

"Ay, good work, Tim, but we all know what this means."

Michael certainly knew what it meant, but he looked at Tim and said, "Tim, you never cease to amaze." He then walked over to Lynch, put his hand on his shoulder, and said, "I'm sorry to hear how you stand on the Treaty, Liam. I've always respected you for how you led your men. You were a fierce adversary of the British, and it dismays me to find ourselves on opposite sides of the fence now."

It was easy to see why Michael held Lynch in such high regard. A couple of years younger than Michael, he carried himself with a quiet dignity enhanced by his meticulous appearance and dress. His fine, almost delicate features were accentuated by wire-rimmed glasses that gave him a scholarly look, but he was a strong disciplinarian, highly respected by his troops.[3]

"Yes, sorry, Mick. That's just the way it is."

"I understand. One way or the other, though, it will be decided when the Dáil meets next week."

"And either way, this does not make us worse friends."

"No, it does not. Come on downstairs, and I'll stand you a drink."

"Sure, Mick. I'd like that."

"Just give me a couple of minutes. There are two lovely Irish girls in the kitchen I need to say hello to."

Liam laughed and said, "Well, don't let me keep you. See you downstairs."

As Michael walked over to greet Maureen and Nelly, Liam watched from the head of the stairs and turned to someone to say, "I admire Mick as a soldier and a man. Thank God all parties can agree to differ."[4]

A moment later, Nelly was on tiptoes to embrace Michael. "We missed you so much, Uncle Mick."

"And I missed you. I'm sorry I didn't visit you the times I came back. I had so many meetings to attend, but I'll be home most of the time now." He squeezed Maureen on her arm and said, "And you're looking well. How you keeping?"

"Grand, just grand." With a bashful smile, she added, "I've been well looked after."

With a smile over his shoulder at Tim, he replied, "I'm sure you have."

Maureen blushed and said, "Nelly's right; we've missed you, but don't let us keep you."

"Ay, I have some thirsty friends to keep company. Coming, Commandant MacEoin?"

Seán smiled at Maureen and answered, "If this lovely lady would be kind enough to allow me to escort her, yes."

Maureen smiled, curtsied, and slid her arm through Seán's as he steadied himself on the bannister with one hand, and together they led the way down the stairs and over to the bar where Billy was chatting with a tall man. Billy nodded when he saw Michael approaching, and the man turned around, smiled, and called over, "Well, if it isn't my kid brother, back from hob-knobbing with British aristocracy! And Commandant Seán MacEoin himself!"

Seán bowed slightly, but before they could shake hands, Michael called out, "Johnny!" and rushed over to give his brother a big hug. "How are ye? And how are all the little ones? How's the hand coming along?"

Johnny raised a bandaged hand, "Well, as you see, but it's on the mend. Everyone is doing fine, just fine. And by the look of ye, so are you." He squinted at him and continued, "Sort of."

"Thanks, Johnny," he replied with a grin, rubbing his moustache with his thumb and forefinger, and then added in a low tone of voice, "but as I've told you before, I still feel bad about our losing Woodfield on my account."

"There you go, taking all the credit, as usual. You don't think my own activities with the Cork I.R.A. had anything to do with it? I was quite capable of finding trouble on my own without any help from my younger brother, I'll thank you very much."

Even Liam Lynch agreed as he came over and joined the conversation. "He's right, Mick. Give credit where credit is due."

Johnny continued, "That's right, but I'll give you this: It's great work for Ireland you've done, Mick. Just like Dad used to say you would." He then turned to Lynch and said, a little more reservedly, "Hello, Liam. And how are you?"

"Fine, Johnny, thanks. But I have to be going."

"What about that drink, Liam?" Michael asked.

"Another time, perhaps. I'll leave you to your family reunion. So long for now." Lynch shook hands with everyone and left.

"That was a bit queer, wasn't it, Mick?" Johnny asked.

MacEoin answered for him, "Perhaps, but not surprising." Seán turned to Johnny and explained, "He says he and his men in Cork are all against signing the Treaty."

Johnny responded, "Not *all*, but I thought as much. Never mind, as I said, Mick, you've done well."

"I'm glad you think so, Johnny," Michael answered. "You know, Harry Boland and I managed to get so many of our men elected to the Dáil, men who swore oaths to a Republic, but I'm not sure how many of them will approve of what we've brought back. I wasn't sure *you'd* approve."

"Poppycock. You did the best job any man could have asked of you." Johnny cocked his head to one side and said, "Though, I'm not sure I approve of *everything* you did in London." He tapped his upper lip and said, "Next time you're shaving, don't overlook that thing as well."[5]

Wondering When You Might Ask

11 DECEMBER 1921, GRANARD, LONGFORD

"Edgeworthstown, Edgeworthstown," the conductor announced as he walked down the aisle on the train from Dublin.

Michael looked inquiringly at the gentleman seated across from him and asked solicitously, "Now, you're sure I'll not be putting you out?"

"Not at all, Mr. Collins," he answered, beaming. "With all that running back and forth across the Irish Sea you put up with these last couple of months, it's the least I can do."

Michael smiled and replied, "My thanks, then. But I'll have none of this Mr. Collins business. It's Mick to all my friends."

The man's chest expanded as he stood up and exclaimed, "Well, Mick. Here we are. And you can call me Seamus. My car's just up the road."[1]

They were soon headed to Granard, about a quarter of an hour's drive down the road, and Seamus was anxious to continue the conversation with his illustrious passenger. "It's a sad, shameless thing the Tans did to the Greville Arms. There aren't many places left to stay in this town."

"Ay, the owners are friends of mine. I'm just up for the day, though. As you might know, there's plenty to do back in Dublin."

"Indeed, indeed. Everyone knows all you've done in London, and it's a gobsmacking folly you've come home to. I saved this *Times* commentary from a couple of days ago about it. Take a look. It's just there on the seat."

Michael picked up the paper, skimmed the article, and read the summation out loud, "*Will Ireland now, in an impulse of folly or fanaticism, defy the world and turn her back on her last and greatest opportunity?*[2] Yes, Seamus, gobsmacking it is. I'm glad you showed me this."

"Well, I'm sure the Dáil will back you up. By the end of next week, mark my words."

"I will mark your words, my friend, but it's too soon to take them to the bank yet."

Seamus looked over briefly at Michael, now staring out the window. They continued mainly in silence, occasionally commenting on the scenery but no more on politics. Soon they were in Granard, and as they approached the Greville Arms, Michael commented, "Looks like the rebuilding is coming along. Hmm, slowly. You can let me off here if it suits you, Seamus."

"Well, I have to say, it's been a pleasure. God be with you, Mick."

"And ye, Seamus. *Slán*."

Michael walked past the partially restored hotel, noting the piles of bricks and lumber still waiting to be put to good use, but since it was a Sunday morning, all was quiet there and next door at the general store, also run by the Kiernan sisters. Around the corner on Market Street, Michael was happily surprised to see Kitty emerge from the family-run bakery with a parcel. As she locked the door, Michael strode over and asked, "Any chance for a scone or a kiss?"

Kitty spun around and nearly dropped her things as she cried out, "Michael, good Lord, what a shock to the heart!" She smiled and said, "You can have a bit of both, now that you ask!"

Michael stepped up and kissed her on the cheek, and promptly sneezed.

"Oh, dear! Are you coming down with a cold again?" Kitty rubbed her cheek lightly and then looked at him with concern. "Let's get you inside."

"That's all right. It looks like it could rain. Before it does, why don't we take in a walk?"

"That would be lovely. Since you ask, I have some scones to sustain us until we get back to the flat for a proper meal. Where would you like to go? Along the shops?"

"Ay, but why don't we stroll over to the meadow up by the church? It's so peaceful up that way."

As they walked along the high street up to St. Mary's Church, Kitty chatted away, describing the comings and goings of mutual acquaintances. "But why didn't you let me know you were coming?" Kitty asked.

"I would have, but all the wires are down."

"Oh, I'm such a silly girl, and me just after writing to you that they'd been cut.[3] Nothing coming in or going out."

Michael was alarmed, "I hope there's no sabotage already!"

"Not around here, I should think. Friends have been telling me ninety per cent of the people are in favour of the Treaty. If the Dáil doesn't ratify it, the country will."

"That's my Kit, always looking on the bright side."

Kitty laughed softly, prompting Michael to ask her, "What's the joke?"

"Me, it seems. I wrote all this in a letter to you yesterday, and I feel like I'm repeating myself."

Michael put his arm around her and said, "That's just fine. It's better hearing it in person, anyway, isn't it?"

Kitty squeezed his hand, "Oh, yes, dear. It's a wonderful surprise seeing you." She giggled a little and said, "The moustache is a surprise, too."

"Oh, do you like it? I thought you hadn't noticed."

"Oh, no, it's, er, very handsome." She quickly changed the subject, her smile turning to a frown as she asked, "How long can you stay?"

"I have to get back tonight. More meetings tomorrow, and the debates begin on Wednesday."

Kitty responded cheerfully, "Then we'll just have to make the best of these few hours. It's so nice of you to spend them here with me, especially with you feeling under the weather."

"The weather's not so bad, mild for this time of year, and I don't feel all that bad either, just tired." As they walked up the road to the church, Michael turned to take in the view. "Lovely here. We're a long way from London."

"Yes, we are. Back together, and closer together, too, I hope."

"Ah, sure, that we are. Let's go up the hill to the motte. It's a grand view from there."

They continued up to the Granard Motte, a large, circular mound erected by a twelfth-century Norman knight.

"Very impressive," Michael exclaimed. He looked up to the sky, "If those clouds hold up, we'll be fine." Then stooping down to feel the grass, he yawned and said, "It's dry enough. Shall we sit?"[4]

"Why not? We can have a little bit of a picnic."

They sat together, munching on their scones, admiring the view quietly for a few minutes until Michael stirred. He stroked his moustache and then said tentatively, "Kit, you sometimes sound a bit worried in your letters—worried when you have no need to be. London was a load of worry, but none where you and I are concerned. I still feel the same, and, yes, as you say, we *are* closer together."

"Yes, Michael, we are. London was so special."

"As life will be back home. We should be careful about letting everyone else know our feelings or plans." He looked off into the distance. "I worry about Harry, you know. He knows about us, but any formal announcement will still hit him hard."

"Yes. It's so sweet of you how you care for him, even as he has taken sides."

Michael nodded knowingly, "Yes, he has, but I've seen it coming for some time now."

"We barely spoke of it when we were together in London, but I've often wondered when you might ask me about our plans."

"In that case, Kit, I'm glad I'm the one who brought it up. Otherwise, it would have spoiled it for you if you had to."[5]

She said slowly, "Then, shall we say we'll announce our engagement sometime over the Christmas holidays?"

"All right, that's what we'll do. Look, Kit, for your protection, we need to be discreet. I don't want you to be the target of slanderous newspaper hacks on my account. When we meet in Dublin, it should be in the open, like at the Gresham Hotel, but don't come alone. You should send all your letters to me there and mark them 'Personal.'[6] And don't take stock in any insinuations in the Press about me in London. I met a lot of society folks there who proved to be quite helpful, men and women."

"Like the lovely Lady Lavery?" Kitty asked carefully, not revealing any jealousy.

"Yes, exactly," Michael answered, quickly adding with a laugh, "and her lovely husband, Sir John. I'd like to send you any letters that may come from them for safekeeping. Read them and see for yourself the truth of things. I'll not be keeping anything from you."[7]

Kitty replied in a soft voice, "I know. Thank you, dear."

"Good, I mean, thank *you*." Michael stretched out his legs and said, "Well, that's that. Now, shall we go back to your flat?"

"Oh, Mops will be so surprised to see you," Kitty exclaimed, using the family nickname for her sister Maud.

"Remember, mum's the word on our plans for the time being. Is Larry at home?"

"All right, and yes, he will be so glad to see you. My little brother has become quite the man of the family."

"Good lad, er, good man." Michael yawned and said, "Maybe I can get a little kip before dinner and my trip back to Dublin." He pulled out his pocket watch, "We'll still have plenty of time before I catch the early evening train. I don't want to get back too late." He stood up and offered her his hand. "Shall we?"

"Oh, yes, dear. We shall." Kitty laughed, got up, and they walked back down the hill to town.

A few minutes later they went up the stairs to the Kiernan family's flat. Hearing the door open and shut, Kitty's sister Maud called out, "Is that you, Kit? Wherever have you been? Did you bring the scones?"

"Yes, but I'm afraid we've eaten some already," Kitty called out.

Maud came in from the kitchen, took one look at Michael and gave a hearty laugh, "Well, that's just fine. Come on, Mick. Give us a kiss!"

"With pleasure," he quipped with a wink at Kitty.

"We're just getting the Sunday meal going, so you've timed it well." Maud squinted at Michael and asked, "Now, what do you call that thing under your nose?"

Larry came in and, laughing, asked, "Yes, Mick. Is that supposed to be a disguise?"

Michael laughed right back and exclaimed, "Funny you should ask. Before we left London, a reporter asked me what disguises I wore before the Truce."

"Well, you didn't fool us. Doesn't he look dashing, Kit?"

"Tea anyone?" Kitty asked sunnily.

Larry groaned, "Oooh! There you have it, Mick."

"Well, with or without it, you look done in," Maud replied. "Are you feeling all right?"

Kitty answered for him, "He's just tired. You know what he's been through. Michael, why don't you have that little kip before dinner now? This will be a good time for you to rest up."

Michael looked around the room, "Well, if you don't mind, I think I will."

"Take my room, Mick," Larry said.

Kitty walked him to the bedroom and said, "Now, try and get some sleep. I'll wake you in time for dinner."

He smiled back as she closed the door with a little wave.

About an hour later Kitty went in to check on him, but he was sitting up in bed, reading a book. He looked up sheepishly and explained, "I think I'm too tired to fall asleep. I never get like this."

Leaving the door open, Kitty sat on the edge of the bed and said, "I'm glad we had that talk earlier, Michael."

He folded the book in his lap and replied, "Yes, it puts everything in a new light now, doesn't it? We now know each other's hearts, and when we talk, we'll pretty much know what the other is thinking, and when we write, there will be little about our feelings that we don't already know."

Tears welled up in Kitty's eyes, and, unable to speak, she just nodded slightly.

They sat there in silence until Maud poked her head in and called over, "Come along, you two. Supper time."

After their meal, Michael said, "That was spectacular. I needed that, but I'm afraid I have a train to catch." He reached into his pocket for his watch and exclaimed, "Oh, for mercy's sake. Now I've done it."

Everyone looked at him, wondering. He pulled out his watch chain, but where the watch should have been, there was only a bent clasp. He explained, "I must have dropped my watch somewhere. That clasp has been a bit dickey lately. Damn! Oh, excuse me, I'll check the bed."

"You were sitting on the sofa earlier," Maud said hopefully. "Maybe it fell between the cushions."

After everyone rushed around searching, Michael said, "I must have dropped it on the grass up the hill."

"On the grass, you say?" Maud asked with mock suspicion and a sly smile.

"Never mind, you," Kitty scolded her sister.

"Not to worry, everyone. It isn't my only one and certainly not my favourite. I really should be going."

Larry got up from the table, offering, "Come along, Mick. I'll give you a lift. My car is just outside."

With that, everyone got up and rushed down to the street. After mutual goodbyes, waves, and the roar of the car taking off for the station, Kitty said, "Michael took losing that watch fairly calmly. He's terribly attached to his pens and watches."

"Yes," Maud said. "I wonder what put him in such an agreeable mood."

Kitty laughed and cried, "Mops, you *are* terrible. Let's get back upstairs."

Our Victories Will Be Her Joy

14 DECEMBER 1921, DUBLIN

"*ITE, MISSA EST,*" MONSIGNOR MCMANUS CALLED OUT AT THE END OF morning Mass at St. Mary's Pro.

"*Deo gratias,*" the congregation responded.

As everyone filed down the aisle to leave the church, the monsignor noticed Michael Collins lighting a candle in a side chapel for the Blessed Virgin. Their eyes met, and he went to join Michael.

They shook hands, and the monsignor said, "Sit down, Michael. Let's have a little chat if you have time. I know you have a busy day ahead of you, another momentous one, with the Treaty debates beginning today."

"Ay, I have the time and the need," Michael replied with a wry smile. They sat in the front pew facing each other with their arms extended along the back of the bench. Michael continued, "I don't expect the day to go very smoothly. I could use all the support I can muster."

"You have mine, as you know, and that of Cardinal Logue, as well."

"Do I? Do we?"

"Yes, he presided over a bishopric conference. Though they did not come out and endorse the Treaty, they put together a very positive statement, acknowledging, as they put it, 'the patriotism, ability and honesty of purpose in which the Irish representatives have conducted the struggle for national freedom.' It goes on to exhort the Dáil to consider the wishes of the people, who, as we both know, are over-whelmingly in favour."[1]

"That's very good of the bishops. Of you, thanks." Michael assumed a thoughtful countenance and said, "Why don't you put in for that big promotion and go for bishop? I can just picture you with a mitre and crozier, and bishop would look so much better on your *curriculum vitae*.""Rather than slapping you right here and now," McManus replied calmly, "let me just say they would never have me, for all my sins."

'You? What sins, for example?'

"Indulging a recalcitrant lout like you."

"Hmm, I see. Yes, of course."

"You know, Michael, you should be more careful. I think you've lost a step since you went to London."

"How's that, then?"

"You're not watching your back as carefully as you used to."

Someone behind them cleared his throat.

Michael turned around quickly and laughed out loud, "Christy! Peggy! I didn't see you there."

"As I was saying, Michael," McManus said as he stood up to greet them.

"Good morning, Mr. Collins," Peggy said, beaming a smile. "We hoped we might find you here this morning to wish you well. Good morning, monsignor."

"Good morning, Margaret, Christy," McManus replied with good cheer. Turning back to Michael, he commended him, saying, "Michael, you've kept your word and brought Margaret home before Christmas. And my prayers have been answered. You've brought back peace to this land of ours. However, even as Holy Mother Church is divided on this issue, so is Ireland. We are all true, trusted friends here, but be careful, my son, be more careful than ever. Remember, if Christ Himself could be betrayed by those he loved, all the more reason you should be wary of any Janus-faced turncoats who could wish you harm."

"I understand, though the adversaries I see lining up have been pretty forthright in their opposition."

"Be wary of the ones that aren't; that's all I'm saying. Now, good day to you all," McManus said.

"Monsignor, could you…" Michael started to say.

"You don't have to ask. I still pray for you each day. Good luck later today and in the days to come."

11.30 A.M., 14 DECEMBER 1921, LONDON, OPENING OF PARLIAMENT [2]

"*BOOM!*" SILENCE. "*BOOM!*"

Lloyd George turned in his seat on the front bench and remarked to Churchill, "Either Guy Fawkes lives, or…"

"Or His Majesty has arrived to open Parliament."

The latter was the case. Dreary, foggy weather did nothing to dampen the spirits of the wildly cheering crowds that greeted King George, Queen Mary, and their daughter Princess Mary on their triumphant parade in the royal carriage from Buckingham Palace through Westminster. While their arrival at the Sovereign's Entrance was heralded by a forty-one-gun salute in Hyde Park, a boisterous, friendly banter continued in the House of Commons.

A few minutes later a fanfare of trumpets echoed through the corridors, announcing the entry of Their Majesties into the Royal Gallery, through which they would pass on their way to the House of Lords. F.E. Smith was magnificent in the wig and robes of his office of Lord Chancellor. He and Austen Chamberlain, representing the Conservative majority in the House, accompanied King George, Queen Mary, and young Princess Mary as they walked through the hall past lines of Yeomen of the Guard resplendent in their red and gold Tudor-styled uniforms. A brilliant scene matched by an exuberant atmosphere awaited them in the Lords' Chamber, which was filled to capacity with rows of Peers swathed in scarlet and ermine, Peeresses adorned with sparkling diamond tiaras that gleamed in the diffuse light bathing them and the myriad visiting diplomats and foreign dignitaries arrayed in distinctive, opulent regalia.

Upon arriving in the Chamber, the King took his seat on the Throne with the Queen at his side, but all eyes were on the shy but radiant princess smiling demurely, seated a few steps below. King George then addressed the gathered Lords and Ladies. "My Lords, pray be seated," and the room fell into complete silence. He then gave a slight nod to the Lord Great Chamberlain, who raised his wand of office to signal the Gentleman Usher of the Black Rod to summon the House of Commons. Sir William Pulteney, who had been appointed to this office the previous year, turned and proceeded along the corridors of Parliament to convey his message to the Speaker of Commons, carrying the black mace that gave its name to his title. A voice called out, "Black Rod!" as he walked along, smiling at members of the House who had already gathered in the Commons' Court.

When he approached the open door to the Commons, Churchill leaned forward and to his right to witness the time-worn sight. "Ah, here comes Sir William. I hope he is in good spirits."

"He needs to be." Lloyd George responded, "I love watching this."

Churchill chuckled and said, "Yes, I doubt I shall ever tire of this."

Just before Black Rod reached the door, a voice called out, "Shut the door!" and it was slammed shut in his face.

"Sir William is still new at this. I hope this indignity doesn't bruise his feelings."

This was, in fact, a very solemn occasion, and this opening of Parliament was a particularly auspicious one, with the Irish Treaty having just been signed a week earlier. That did not prevent the M.P.s from enjoying their tradition of taking the ceremony with a great deal of humour. Since the time in 1642 when Charles I stormed into the Commons in an attempt to arrest five purportedly treasonous members, no British monarch had entered a sitting House of Commons. To symbolise the rights of Parliament and its independence from the monarch, the Doorkeeper would slam the door in the face of Black Rod, who would then ceremonially knock on it to gain admittance.

After he banged on the door with the Black Rod three times, a call came, "Open the door!" He entered the Commons with a wry grin and was announced again in a clear voice, "Black Rod!" He bowed slightly to the Speaker of the House and called out, smiling broadly, "The King Commands this Honourable House," then bowing to the front benches on either side, "to attend His Majesty immediately in the House of Lords."

One of the members groaned, "This close to lunchtime? Whatever could he want?"

"Come along, let's get this over with," a friend responded, laughing.

All the members of the House rose and, led by the Speaker, started making their way to the door. Lloyd George gestured to Herbert

Asquith, who was now the Leader of the Loyal Opposition. Asquith had been replaced as Prime Minister by fellow Liberal Lloyd George in a rancorous struggle that left Asquith as leader of the Liberals in opposition to the coalition government of Lloyd George. Usually bitter enemies, they walked together along the corridor to the House of Lords, talking animatedly.

"You know, Herbert, when I rise to speak later today, you'll figure very prominently in my address."

"Oh, dear! I hope you don't go too hard on me, Prime Minister."

"Not to worry," he said with a chuckle as he squeezed his colleague's arm. "You'll love it."

"I can hardly wait."

The members sauntered along, not particularly concerned that His Majesty was waiting patiently and quietly for them, and filed into the House of Lords, standing at the rear of the chamber. Upstairs in the Press Gallery, Sir John Lavery was busily sketching the historic scene in preparation for a painting to memorialise the occasion. When things settled down, the Lord Chancellor walked up the steps to the Throne, knelt, and handed the King his speech. He then stood, bowed his head, and walked backwards down the steps, one at a time, bowed his head again and, continuing to walk backwards, took his place on the King's right.

Then King George began to read his speech in a loud, clear voice and a noticeably happy tone.

"My Lords and Members of the House of Commons, I have summoned you to meet at this unusual time in order that the Articles of Agreement which have been signed by My Ministers and the Irish Delegation may be at once submitted for your approval. No other business will be brought before you in the present Session. It was with heartfelt joy that I learnt of the Agreement reached after negotiations protracted for many months and affecting the welfare not only of Ireland but of the British and Irish races throughout the world. It is my earnest hope that by the Articles of Agreement now submitted to you the strife of centuries may be ended, and that Ireland, as a free partner in the Commonwealth of Nations forming the British Empire, will secure the fulfilment of her national ideals. I pray that the blessing of Almighty God may rest upon your labours."

Then the Lord Chancellor approached the Throne again, and the King handed the speech back to him. When Birkenhead had returned to his place, the King stood, and all rose with him. When the King had left the chamber, Lloyd George and Churchill walked together down the hall back to Commons.

Winston remarked, "It's been said that the Queen told some friends that the day the Treaty was signed was the happiest day of their lives since the King came to the Throne. It certainly seemed so, the way His Majesty delivered his speech."

"Yes, Winston, he was positively beaming. Why on earth can we not expect the same of Mr. de Valera? He seems to have had a vastly different reaction. I believe their debates are about to start this very hour. I think we will have a better time of it in the House than our friend Mick Collins will have in the Dáil."

"We shall see. We shall see."

---

11 A.M., 14 DECEMBER 1921, DUBLIN, DÁIL PUBLIC SESSION [3]

PAT McCREA STOPPED HIS CAR AT THE BARRICADE ACROSS FROM ST. Stephen's Green and rolled down his window to talk to the approaching uniformed military policeman.[4]

"Oh, hello, Paddy." The policeman looked in the back seat and exclaimed, "Well, well, now, Mick, is it yourself, then? Oh, and hello to you, Tom. Sorry about this."

He stood at attention and saluted Michael. Tom Cullen laughed heartily, but Michael just shook his head and said, "For what? Doing your duty?"

"There you are, on with you, quick as you like, Pat," he replied, pulling the barricade back. "Give 'em hell, Mick!"

Pat drove down Earlsfort Terrace to the imposing central building of the University College Dublin and pulled up by the entrance steps.[5] He turned around and said, "Here we are, Mick. Like the man said, go in there and give 'em hell." He paused, tilted his head to one side and remarked, "Now, I can't for the life of me put my finger on it, but you look different this morning."

Michael had slipped into deep thought anticipating the coming debate and answered somewhat absent-mindedly, "If you say so, Pat." When he and Tom emerged from the car, a roar of recognition and applause rose from the large crowd, loosely held in check by the police.

Michael bounded up the steps past the jubilant crowd and thorough a security detail of Volunteers. Tom Cullen followed just behind but paused when he saw Seán MacBride and went over to greet him.

"Howaya, Seán. All's well?"

"Yes, Tom, and thanks for arranging a spot for me with the guards. I'm glad to be here for the debates."[6]

"Come on inside. Mick will be happy to see you."

"Sure, Tom, or rather, I'm not so sure of that."

"Why, whatever for?"

"It's just that, well, never mind. There's Mick," he answered as they went inside. The truth was Seán opposed the Treaty, but, always the gentleman, even at his young age, he wasn't about to spoil the moment by saying anything just then, so he held back and assumed his guard position at the entrance.

Tom made his way over to Michael, who was already surrounded by a group of delegates discussing the day's agenda with him. After a minute, Tom managed to get close enough to tell him, "Seán MacBride is here, Mick."

"Really? Where? Oh, I see him," he replied, waving over at Seán, who smiled and nodded back. "I think we're about to start, Tom. I have to go."

"I'll leave you to it, then, Mick. Good luck."

"Thanks, Tom. Why don't you join Alice and Sinéad? They'll be in the public gallery behind the delegates."[7]

Michael then entered the Council Chamber, from which dividing doors had been rolled back to provide one long, narrow room for the occasion, with one side for the members of the Dáil and the other for the Press. In the middle was a low dais with the Speaker's table and a couple of tables set with chairs on either side. When he stepped onto the floor, loud whispers of "There's Collins! Here comes Mick!" spread among the reporters representing not only the local Press but newspapers and magazines from all over the world. Seated at the back of the hall in the few chairs provided for the public were Alice Lyons and Sinéad Mason, who also noticed Michael's arrival.

"There's Mick," Alice remarked. "It should start soon."

Sinéad surveyed the rows of onlookers around her. "Oh, and there's Tom Cullen," she cried out as she waved at him until he took notice and squeezed through the aisles to join them.

While Alice and Sinéad exchanged hellos with Tom, Michael

walked up to the Speaker of the Dáil to shake hands, "Howaya, Eoin? Where do you want me, then?" This was Eoin MacNeill, the founder of the Irish Volunteers, who was also well known as a highly respected Gaelic scholar and professor at University College Dublin.[8]

"Hello, Mick. You're the first to arrive, as usual," he said with a laugh. "That'll be your table over there on the left, to my right," he replied.

"Come again?" Michael asked with a grin.

"Pardon? Oh, I see," he chuckled and pointed. "Over there will be fine."

Soon Arthur Griffith entered, causing a renewed commotion in the hall. He took a seat next to Michael, squinted at him, smiled, and said, "Thank heavens you rid yourself of that irritating moustache. I already feel like we'll carry the day."[9]

Michael chuckled, "You're not the first to say so. It seemed like the general consensus was Treaty, Yea; moustache, Nay."

Cathal Brugha entered and greeted MacNeill, who gestured for him to take his place at a table to the left of the Speaker's desk. Brugha stared coldly at Michael as he took a seat at the table directly opposite him. Robert Barton arrived, and he and Michael soon fell into deep conversation. Occasionally Michael would spring to his feet to talk to someone or lean over to confer with Arthur or Eamonn Duggan, who soon joined them.

When Erskine Childers slinked into the hall, Alice remarked, "My, Erskine looks pale and wan, does he not?"

"Yes," Sinéad agreed. "And Brugha and Austin Stack looking positively venomous! It certainly looks like the battle lines are already clearly drawn."

"Yes, there's no hiding the fact that the opposing sides are literally lined up against each other."

"Only Éamon de Valera is missing at this point."

Tom got up to look and remarked, "Oh, no! Michael is looking at his watch. That's a sure sign he's annoyed."

Michael snapped his watch cover shut and exclaimed, "We're half an hour late getting started already. Where the hell is Dev? I'll bet even King George doesn't keep Parliament waiting."[10]

When de Valera finally arrived, Sinéad noticed something different. "There he is at last, looking rather casual in that brown suit, wouldn't you say?"

"Doesn't he, now? It's a change from his usual black attire," Alice noted as de Valera took his seat, casting a penetrating stare over at Arthur and Michael.[11]

Sinéad also noticed Michael's changed appearance. "Mick looks so much nicer without that moustache, doesn't he? I'm so glad he shaved it off."

Tom smiled and said, "I'll bet Kitty will appreciate the lack of whiskers the next she and Mick…"

Alice cut him off with a great show of indignation, "Thomas Cullen!"

"See each other. That's all I meant," Tom said defensively before quickly changing the subject back to de Valera. "Dev looks deathly serious, brown suit or not."

"Yes, everyone's all astir," Sinéad noticed. "There seem to be as many observers as there are deputies."

After more unexplained delays, Tom looked at his watch and said, "What is taking so long? This is ridiculous!"

No longer teasing him, Alice agreed, "Yes, it certainly wasn't like this when we saw Lloyd George address the House of Commons, eh, Tom?"

"No, what a contrast. I'm sure some in the Press will take notice."

Finally, the proceedings got underway. The clerk called the roll of the hundred and twenty-two deputies present, and while he did, Pat McCrea tip-toed over to the public gallery, spotted his friends, and walked across the aisle to join them. Everyone just nodded hellos, keeping quiet during the roll call.

After an opening prayer by a priest, the Speaker nodded to de Valera, who rose to address the assembly. He spoke slowly and deliberately in Irish, beginning the day's proceedings:

"*Níl mo chuid Gaedhilge chó maith agus ba mhaith liom í bheith. Is fearr is feidir liom mo smaointe do nochtadh as Beurla, agus dá bhrí sin is dóich liom gurbh fhearra dhom labhairt as Beurla ar fad.*"

Seated among all the Dáil delegates was Piaras Béaslaí, who nodded approvingly, explaining to the deputy seated next to him, "Fair enough. He admits his Irish isn't as good as he'd like, so he'll stick to English."

His friend nodded, "Just as well, for my sake. Sad to say, I do not have the Irish."

However, then de Valera went on to say, "Some of the members do not know Irish, I think, and consequently, what I shall say will be in English."[12]

Béaslaí's companion replied, "Hold on, is that not just a shade off the mark?"

"Very astute observation, my friend," Béaslaí replied.

Michael also knew Irish well enough to notice the discrepancy and mumbled, "Here we go."

After his patently dishonest opening, de Valera went on, "The question we have to decide is one which ought to be decided on its merits, and it would be very unfortunate if extraneous matters such as what I might call an accidental division of opinion of the Cabinet, or the causes which gave rise to it, should cut across these considerations. I think, therefore, it would be wise to give a short narrative of the circumstances under which the plenipotentiaries were appointed."

Unfortunately, what followed was not a short narrative but a long, rambling explanation of the plenipotentiaries' instructions. De Valera then turned sharply to Arthur Griffith and asked, "I do not know if the Chairman of the Delegation or the plenipotentiaries would have any objection—it would not in any way interfere with public interests—if the Cabinet instructions were given. Is there any objection? I do not think there is."

Arthur answered coldly, "No."

Since many members were surprisingly uninformed about the details of the treaty deliberations handled by the Cabinet, they listened intently as de Valera read out the instructions, "Here is the actual text of the instructions I wrote with my own hand at the Cabinet meeting on October seventh.

"One. The Plenipotentiaries have full powers as defined in their credentials.

"Two. It is understood before decisions are finally reached on the main question, that a dispatch notifying the intention to make these decisions will be sent to members of the Cabinet in Dublin, and that a reply will be awaited by the Plenipotentiaries before final decision is made."

Then he raised his hand in emphasis and continued, *"Three. It is also understood that the complete text of the draft treaty about to be signed will be similarly submitted to Dublin, and reply awaited.* Now I want you to pay particular attention to that paragraph in particular. The instructions proceed.

"Four. In case of a break, the text of the final proposals from our side will be similarly submitted.

"*Five. It is understood the Cabinet in Dublin will be kept regularly informed of the progress of the negotiations.*

"That was all done, with the exception of paragraph three."

After a tedious explanation of how paragraph three had not been adhered to, he called for a significant change in the proceedings, a move to a private session. "I am ready to answer any questions about the conduct of the negotiations, and if there are any questions or any matter which you wish to probe, I would be glad to answer it in a private session so that you may understand it thoroughly."

Arthur was incensed at de Valera's claim that the third directive to refer to Dublin had been ignored. He rose and declared firmly, "I wish to say as regards any suggestion that the plenipotentiaries exceeded their instructions, that I, as Chairman of the Delegation, immediately controvert it."

De Valera responded dismissively, "It will settle nothing if one says one thing, and another says the other. Paragraph three of the instructions was not exceeded, but paragraph three was not carried out."

Equally incensed, Michael Collins rose quickly to defend Arthur and his fellow delegates. He assumed a posture familiar to anyone who had ever seen him give a speech at a political rally. With his hands in his pockets, he leaned forward from the waist, his jaw set defiantly slightly upward, and with a simmering yet controlled anger, declared to the riveted delegates, "The original terms that were served on each member of the delegation have not been read out. I am not in favour of a private session. Anything that the Dáil has a right to know, the Irish people, who are our masters, have a right to know." His eyes narrowed as he cried out, "I must protest against what I call an unfair action. If one document had to be read, the original, prior document should have been read first. I must ask the liberty of reading the original document which was served on each member of the delegation of plenipotentiaries."

De Valera asked in a prosecutorial tone, "Is that the one with the original credentials?"

"Yes," Michael answered.

Standing there facing Michael from across the dais, de Valera asked accusatorially, "Was that ever presented? It was given in order to get the British Government to recognise the Irish Republic."

Over in the public gallery, Tom whispered to Alice, "I remember Gavan Duffy brought up those credentials just as everyone was leaving

Hans Place for their first meeting at Downing Street. They were never going to fool the Brits with that ploy."

Alice whispered back, "As Dev was well aware. He foresaw this very moment. Now, shush, and listen."

Over on the dais, de Valera persisted, demanding to know, "Was that document giving the credentials of the accredited representatives from the Irish Government to the British Government presented to, or accepted by, the British delegates? Was that taken by the British delegates or accepted by them?"

Arthur was simmering with anger but answered from his chair quietly and calmly, "We had no instructions to present it."

Insulted by this evasion, de Valera shot back, "I am asking a question."

His anger rising, Michael turned to Eoin MacNeill, "May I ask that I be allowed to speak without interruption?"

De Valera shot a spiteful look at Michael and turned to the Speaker. "I must protest."

The room erupted with deputies shouting out remonstrations in reaction to these heated exchanges.

"Order! We must have order!" MacNeil cried out, repeatedly banging his gavel on the table.

Michael stood his ground and called out above the fray, "I only ask that I be allowed to speak without interruption. I am not going to interrupt any speaker, and that is a small right to ask."

Bowing his head slightly at MacNeill, Michael spoke clearly and resolutely, "The original credentials were presented, and they read, *In virtue of the authority vested in me by Dáil Éireann, I hereby appoint Arthur Griffith, T.D., Minister for Foreign Affairs, Chairman; Michael Collins, T.D., Minister for Finance; Robert C. Barton, T.D., Minister for Economic Affairs; Edmund J. Duggan, T.D.; and George Gavan Duffy, T.D. as envoys plenipotentiaries from the elected Government of the Republic of Ireland to negotiate and conclude on behalf of Ireland, with the representatives of his Britannic Majesty George V, a treaty or treaties of settlement, association and accommodation between Ireland and the community of nations known as the British Commonwealth. In witness hereof I hereunder subscribe my name as President. Signed, Éamon de Valera.*"

Without pausing, Michael explained, "And that was sealed with the official seal of Dáil Éireann and dated the seventh day of October 1921. Then there were five identical credentials. Now those of us who differ, publicly and privately, did not prejudge the issue. We even refrained from speaking to members of the Dáil. I have not said a hard word about anybody."

He was interrupted by cries of "Hear, hear!"

He turned his shoulders from one side to the other, then leaned forward, waving a fist and shouting, "I know I have been called a traitor." In answer to this angry declaration, cries of, "No, no!" filled the hall.

Demonstrating surprise with a considerable measure of scepticism, de Valera asked, "By whom?"

Ignoring de Valera's question, Michael shouted passionately, "If I am a traitor," and was met by more cries of, "No, no!" Speaking even more passionately, he raised his voice over the crowd and went on, "If I am a traitor, let the Irish people decide it or not, and if there are men who act towards me as a traitor, I am prepared to meet them anywhere, anytime, now as in the past."[13]

This emotionally overwrought challenge was answered with gasps throughout the hall, but Michael quickly resumed in a measured, determined tone, "I am in favour of a public session here now. I understand that members of the Dáil may differ as to the advantage to be gained on one side or the other by a private session, but on the essentials, I am for publicity now and all along."

After mild applause, he changed the mood by asking in a conversational tone, "May I just put one point, right?" he said, turning to de Valera. He paused and declared, "Ireland is fully free to accept or reject this document." He paused again and then spoke with increasing intensity, "I can only make plain again that the document is agreed to by the signatories and recommended to the Dáil for acceptance. If the Dáil do not accept it, I as one of the signatories will be relieved of all responsibility for myself, but I am bound to recommend it over my signature. The Dáil is perfectly free to accept or reject; we are only bound to recommend it to the Dáil for acceptance. The Articles of Agreement are put forward on our recommendation."

As Michael took his seat amidst cheers, de Valera rose to counter Michael's argument, further shading the truth. "At earlier meetings of the Dáil, I made our position perfectly clear, that the plenipotentiaries were to have the fullest freedom possible. It would be ridiculous to send them over if we were all the time to interfere with them from Dublin. In fact, one of the reasons I did not want to be a member of the delegation was that the delegation should be provided against hasty action."

Michael was about to reply to this dissembling when, somewhat incongruously, Cathal Brugha stood and declared, "I object to a private session."

Michael smiled over at Brugha upon this rare instance of finding themselves in agreement, and another delegate rose to speak. "On a point of order, there is one important matter I would like to clear up. Was the document referred to presented to and accepted by the Prime Minister as the original credentials of our delegation?"

Michael stood to respond, "I do not wish to create a wrong impression. I did not say accepted; I said presented."

As Michael sat back down, he glanced at Arthur, who sat back in his chair, remembering their credentials never left their pockets. He looked at Michael queryingly as if to say, "Really?" but remained silent and wondered how Lloyd George would react if he were to learn of this statement.

De Valera was already on his feet with another accusation. "This is a most important matter. In the original credentials, in order to give them the fullest powers, they were empowered to negotiate and conclude a Treaty. Evidently, the Minister for Finance wishes to lay stress on the word *conclude*."

Michael stayed seated but answered vehemently, "*No*, sir."

Continuing this new attack, de Valera asked, "What is the point then of raising the original credentials, if the word 'conclude' did not mean that when you had signed, it was ended? I want to know whether the delegation of the British Government accepted these credentials as the basis. The honour of this nation, which is dear to us, is at stake. I say it was never intended that the plenipotentiaries—that the five people sent from this nation—should have power to bind this nation by their signatures irrevocably. I want to know whether the British Government accepted the credentials as the basis on which they accepted you as plenipotentiaries to negotiate a treaty or not."

Arthur spoke to defend his fellow delegates on the issue, calm but resolute, "There will be no wrong impression at all events in the minds of members who have to vote." If Michael had misspoken earlier, Arthur sought to clarify any misunderstanding, saying, "These credentials from President de Valera were carried by us. We were instructed if the British delegates asked for credentials to present them."

Joining the fray, Austen Stack added, "They were not presented."

Arthur nodded at Stack and explained further, "I believe Mr. Lloyd George saw the document. They were not presented or accepted. President de Valera wants to know whether we considered that we had full power to make a treaty to bind the nation without the Dáil being consulted." For the first time raising his voice that morning, Arthur filled the hall with his rejoinder to de Valera's disputation, "Now the British Ministers did not sign the Treaty to bind their nation. They had to go to their Parliament, and we to ours for ratification."

At this salvo, the room erupted into applause. Back in the gallery, Alice shouted over the cheers to Tom, "That's practically word for word what Lloyd George said when we saw him defend the Treaty in Parliament, Tom."

"Yes, yes, I remember! He said something like it would be ridiculous to refer to the whole House of Commons during the daily negotiations, but the finished Treaty would need its consent. Same story here. Arthur just said it all. Everyone can see that."

Sinéad pointed and said, "Look, even Dev is smiling."

It took a few moments for the hall to quiet down. Michael patted Arthur on the back and congratulated him, "Well done, Arthur. That nicely sums up all our weeks of work in London and where we are now."

Arthur was slightly flushed from the excitement but smiled and said, "Thanks, Mick. Thank you. All this talk about our instructions and credentials is a red herring to divert attention from the obvious. Dev didn't go to London with us because he already knew he couldn't bring back a Republic."

Michael nodded in agreement, "We did not exceed our authority, but you could argue we exceeded expectations, sure, not bringing back a Republic, but bringing back a better agreement than anyone expected, Dev included."

What followed was a less impressive exegesis of the merits of going into private session. Deputies bobbed up and down with competing motions and inappropriate, contradictory amendments in an almost comical display of parliamentary inexperience.

Watching from the visitors' gallery, Alice shook her head, wondering, "Whatever are they up to?"

Pat piped up, "Well, it's like I told Mick. The Brits sure know how to build a fine, smooth-running motorcar. From what I gather, how to run a smooth Parliament, too, compared to the bedlam over there."

They all laughed at this, but then Sinéad told them, "Mick's about to speak again. Maybe he can sort this out."

Having acquiesced to the motion to suspend the public debate, Michael announced, "I suggest it is only right to the Press and public that we should give definite times and state the limit of the private session."

At last, de Valera, too, found something to agree on with Michael, saying, "I propose that we take the private session this afternoon and that we go back into public session at eleven o'clock tomorrow morning. This means that we continue the meeting in private this afternoon, and we meet again in public tomorrow for the sole question of ratification."

"Well, that's a rather optimistic schedule, given what's gone on here this morning," Alice said.

Sinéad nodded, adding, "Yes, if they can spend an hour and a day squabbling over credentials for a Treaty that's already been negotiated, how long will it take them to discuss what's actually *in* it?"

A more immediate element of the day's schedule occurred to Pat, who jumped up and looked over to see Michael leaving, "Jaysus! I better get back to the car in case Mick needs me. I wouldn't want to keep him waiting, not on a day like today."

---

1 P.M., 14 DECEMBER 1921, DUBLIN, DÁIL PRIVATE SESSION [14]

"NO, YER ALL RIGHT, PAT. WE'VE NOT THE TIME FOR SO MUCH AS A CUP of coffee, much less a meal. I'll catch you up later."

While Pat followed the Press and visitors who had been asked to leave the hall, Michael noticed Eileen McGrane in an animated discussion with Cathal Brugha. As he was watching them, Sinéad came over and touched him lightly on the shoulder. Roused from his thoughts, he turned and said brightly, "Quite the holy show, wouldn't you say?"

She took him by the arm and said in a low voice, "I'm afraid we've been making some unfortunate comparisons to Parliament. In fairness to our delegates here, though, it is an awesome responsibility they've had thrown at them."

"Yes, and with little or no experience in how to grapple with it. Fighting a war is one thing; forging a peace is another. Still, every man is due his right to voice an opinion."[15]

"I hope that extends to women, as well, Mick," Eileen said with a smile as she joined them.

"Ay, goes without saying, Eileen. It's so good to see you again," Michael exclaimed, shaking her hand.

"And you. Hello, Sinéad."

"Eileen, nice to see you," Sinéad said cheerfully.

Michael let go of Eileen's hand and said softly, "I'm so sorry for all you were put through on my behalf until the Truce. You endured your time in prison with stoicism and true bravery."

"We all had our part to play, so no apologies necessary. It was kind of you to send those parcels to Patricia Hoey and me; it made the time pass a little easier. I didn't get a chance to thank you properly with you away in London most of the time, so thanks, Mick."

Michael shrugged it off, saying, "Arrah, but it was the least I could do. How is Patricia? Have you and she stayed in touch?"

"No, not really. I found that she and I, well, we didn't have all that much in common. I don't think she has found work again yet as a journalist."

"Oh? That's a shame. Well, it must feel strange having the debates here at the College where you've taught classes." He paused and cautiously asked, "So, what did you think of the morning session?"

Eileen looked at Sinéad and then turned to Michael, lowering her eyes, and said, "I'm sorry, Mick. I don't think I can support the Treaty you brought back, not in its present form. It's not the Republic we had hoped for."[16]

"I see," Michael responded. "Well, thank you for telling me. I'm sorry you see it that way, but I've always respected your opinion."

Eileen looked up and replied, "Thanks, Mick. I think I better be going. So long. Goodbye, Sinéad."

Over at the Speaker's chair, Eoin MacNeill checked his watch and saw it was coming on one o'clock. It was time for the session to resume in private, absent the Press and visitors. He banged his gavel and nodded to de Valera, who almost at once registered a complaint, saying, "I have only one thing to say, one thing I feel hurt about, with respect to the delegation, and that is that a Treaty was signed in London, and when I heard of it first, the signatures were already appended to it."

Richard Mulcahy, there as a representative for Dublin, whispered to a delegate seated next to him, "I was there with him at Jim O'Mara's," his finger pointing in the air as if to give the location of the home in Limerick. "He was livid."

De Valera paused at the whispers, cleared his throat, and continued, "As I came in the door of the Mansion House, I was given a signed copy of the document, and it had already been given to the Press in London."

This gave the impression that he had not heard of the Treaty signing until Eamonn Duggan handed him a copy at Mansion House. "Bollocks!" Mulcahy mumbled, none too softly. More than a few heads turned his way.

De Valera continued, "The plenipotentiaries were sent because they were likely to be people whom the British Government would be induced to try and do business with. I knew the men perfectly. It would not be quite the team I would have sent, but they were the best team I could get, and I felt that we could do the work here because we were in constant communication."

At this less than ringing endorsement, Arthur lowered his spectacles and looked down his nose at Michael, who responded, "Jaysus! The best team he could get? That cuts deep. I didn't realise we were merely the second string, did you?"

Arthur shook his head and tried to concentrate on de Valera, who was still speaking.

"Now, back on October twenty-fifth, I wrote that there can be no question of our asking the Irish people to enter an arrangement which would make them subject to the Crown or demand from them allegiance to the British King. If war is the alternative, we can only face it, and I think that the sooner the other side is made to realise that, the better."

Fully remembering how the delegation reacted to this letter, Arthur asked calmly, "Would you mind reading our reply?"

De Valera cleared his throat and read out loud, "*The delegates regard the first paragraph of your letter as tying their hands in discussion and as inconsistent with the powers given them on their appointment and the 'Instructions to Plenipotentiaries from Cabinet' dated 7th October.* I, for one, could not see that.

The delegates sent this letter in protest, signed by every one of them. In reply, I wrote: *There is obviously a misunderstanding. There can be no question of tying the hands of the plenipotentiaries beyond the extent to which they are tied by their original instructions."*

Arthur explained to everyone, "I merely want to get the facts clear in the minds of the members here. I came back on the Saturday to Dublin. I attended a Cabinet meeting. I went back to London that evening. I told the President we brought back what seemed to be the final proposals of the English Cabinet. At the Cabinet meeting before we returned to London, I said we were now up against this question of the Crown and the inclusion in the Empire. I told the President that I would not break on the Crown if the other points we wanted were conceded. We suggested the President himself go to London, but for reasons which I know are perfectly cogent in his mind, he decided not to go. The President took his stand upon these Irish proposals which meant external connection with the Crown."

At this point, Arthur held up some papers he had with him, and while holding his spectacles in place, he read out, "He suggested the following amendment to the Oath of Allegiance: *I do solemnly swear true faith and Allegiance to the Constitution of the Irish Free State, to the Treaty of Association and to recognise the King of Great Britain as head of the Associated States."*

One delegate at the back of the room had a copy of the Treaty on his lap and looked down at it as Arthur read de Valera's suggested oath. He looked up to hear de Valera's response, "I was only showing how to get around the thing that was objectionable, but surely nobody would take a thing like that until it was presented."

Arthur would have none of this and held up the papers higher and responded, "I am reading the official minutes of the Cabinet meeting."

De Valera responded defensively, "I say these minutes were never signed and never read and never adopted."

Michael glanced at Arthur with a look of incredulity.

The delegate at the back said to his seatmate, "Dev's version refers to 'Associated States,' whatever that means, and the one here says the Commonwealth."

"For fuck's sake, are we going to go to war over synonyms? Christ, I had no idea all this nit-picking had been going on."

"Nor did I."[17]

Arthur continued his account, "Now there is the position on the

Saturday. We went back to London, and we met these people on Sunday and fought straight up and down all day. We nearly broke on Sunday night. We did make a break, as a matter of fact, but we went back again on the Monday morning, and we started in. That Monday evening, Lloyd George was sending his final reply to Craig. We fought all day, and he had two letters written to Craig, and they were going off at ten o'clock that night. One letter was informing him that the negotiations were broken off with us, and the other was putting this proposal to him which now is the Treaty. We had the alternative, and we had to face the alternative in making the decision. Then I tried to get them to put it back for a week to get back to the Dáil. I could not get it done. We had to take a decision. We were plenipotentiaries. If we did not take a decision then, if we left the place, the people of Ireland would have very properly come to us and say, 'We entrusted you with powers to make a decision, and you hadn't the courage to do it. You have thrown us back into war without our knowledge.' We did make a decision, and we made the decision when they came to us and said, 'Will you be within or without the Empire?' We said if you give us this and that, we will propose that to the Dáil. Under these circumstances, we have signed that document, and we have come back with it now. When we were sent, I stated to the Cabinet I would strive to bring back a Republic, but I could not bring back the Republic. On this, no member of the Cabinet had the slightest misunderstanding."

Even de Valera nodded in agreement, confirming, "None whatever."

Arthur likewise nodded to de Valera and went on, "We went there to get the best settlement possible consistent with the honour and the interests of Ireland. Once you start negotiations, you are going to give away something, and you are going to get something. President de Valera met Mr. Lloyd George last July, and Mr. Lloyd George made certain proposals to him. These proposals involved the acceptance of the Crown and Empire. President de Valera did not immediately reject them.

"We explored every possibility of a settlement for eight weeks, and in the end, we brought back this Treaty. Now I know what is going to be said about it. If we brought back heaven and earth, we would be blamed. Before I went away, I said: 'Whatever the plenipotentiaries bring back, someone is going to kick them,' and I said, 'If so, I am going to kick back.'

"I want it understood that the difference between us and the members of the Cabinet at home in the end was not the vital difference between the Republic and the Crown. It was a difference of the degree of recognition of the Crown, a difference between the degree of the Oath of Allegiance, and on that principle, that small difference to ask the people of Ireland to go back to war is a thing I will never do. What we got was better. I stand by it on the merits, and I believe the Irish people, if they accept it, will a month hence see the British troops out and our own Army in."

Many of the delegates stood up at this, cheering and applauding. When the room quieted, Michael rose and said, "There is one point about the signing of this. It occurred about half past one o'clock in the morning, and a question was asked direct across the table from Mr. Lloyd George to Mr. Griffith. We had been fighting about the alteration of certain clauses, and he said: 'If we alter those to what you want will you recommend this document?' Mr. Griffith said, 'Yes.' That committed us as well as the signatures. When we were asked for our signatures, I thought it was an advantage to have their signatures, and if we came back with an unsigned document, they would be able to say, 'They have not signed it: they're codding you.'"

Ignoring this argument, de Valera rose and announced, "I want to answer a question. I was asked whether it was a *fait accompli*. I was captaining a team, and I felt that the team should have played with me to the last and that I should have got the last chance which I felt would have put us over, and we might have crossed the bar, in my opinion at the high tide."

At this point, Barton looked over at Michael and turned his head with a quizzical expression.

De Valera confused him further as he continued, "They rushed before the tide got to the top, and they almost foundered the ship. It was not through my fault as captain that this was done. It was a *fail accompli*, but our position can be restored somewhat. I have proposals such as I would have tried to write. They may not suit one or the other, but if you don't reject them, I will do my best."

The Speaker then adjourned the meeting for luncheon. Barton then put his confusion into words. "Mick, I think the Chief is mixing his metaphors. Did he mean he was the captain of a football team or a captain of a ship?"

Michael remarked to Barton and Arthur, "I think it devolved to the latter. A captain who sent his crew out to sea and tried to direct them from dry land!"[18]

3.45 P.M. (LONDON), 14 DECEMBER 1921, LONDON, HOUSE OF LORDS, Carson Speech [19]

EDWARD CARSON, THE MAN TO WHOM F.E. SMITH HAD ONCE PAID allegiance, earning F.E. the pejorative Galloper Smith, had relinquished his position earlier that year as leader of the Unionist party in Northern Ireland and subsequently been elevated to the House of Lords. Among his many other accomplishments, besides ruining Oscar Wilde, Carson succeeded both Winston Churchill and Arthur Balfour as Lord of the Admiralty. More recently, for the sake of creating the new Northern Ireland Parliament, he acquiesced to the partition that gave the South three overwhelmingly Catholic Ulster counties, Monaghan, Cavan, and Donegal. Now, as Lord Carson, he was making his maiden speech to the House of Lords, and the words he used to describe the Treaty and those who had brought it about were no less venomous than the words he had used to eviscerate Wilde.

A few steps below the Throne from which King George had addressed Parliament earlier that day, the formerly galloping F.E., Lord Birkenhead, presided over the House from the comfort of the Woolsack, the Lord Chancellor's red wool-stuffed cushion.

Referring to the preceding speaker, Lord Curzon, Carson said, "The noble Marquess paid a generous and eloquent tribute to Michael Collins, the head of the murder gang, as Sir Hamar Greenwood described him only a few months ago in the House of Commons."

As Conservative Lords called out, "Hear, hear!" Curzon protested, "I never mentioned *him*."

"You mentioned the delegates. Perhaps you did not know he was one of them. I do not know if you were ever there, but he was. He committed many murders with his own hands—the hand that you have now so willingly grasped." To be precise, this was not true, but Carson went on, "There is not a noble Lord in this House who believes for a moment that these Articles of Treaty were passed upon the merits. They were passed with a revolver pointed at your head. You know you passed them because Sinn Féin, with its army in Ireland, has beaten you."

As Birkenhead sat there quietly on the Woolsack with eyes closed, it could've been construed that he was dosing, but he was listening intently to every word while Carson fulminated. "You may talk of a Free State, but from the beginning to the end of this document there is nothing you will find except that England, beaten to her knees by the gun of the assassin, says, 'We are willing to scuttle out of Ireland and to leave to the tender mercies of the assassins everybody who has supported us in the past.' I believe that what has happened in this case will make public life and politics stink in the nostrils of the country for the next twenty years.

"I thought of the last thirty years, during which I was fighting with others whose friendship and comradeship I hope I will lose tonight," causing many of the Lords to laugh, "because I do not value any friendship that is not founded upon confidence and trust. I was in earnest."

As if awoken from slumber, Birkenhead suddenly looked up, but just as quickly resumed his position of repose as Carson continued his rant.

"What a fool I was. I was only a puppet, and so was Ulster, and so was Ireland, in the political game that was to get the Conservative Party into power. And of all the men in my experience that I think are the most loathsome, it is those who will sell their friends for the purpose of conciliating their enemies." This diatribe brought on a chorus of cheers, which intensified after his following statement, "I hope you are proud of your Treaty, a Treaty between different parts of one Kingdom. Was such a thing ever heard of before?

"A Treaty! On the very face of the document itself, it is false. It says, *A Treaty between Great Britain and Ireland*, and before you signed it, you never even asked Ulster. Nor is her signature necessary. It is only to be signed in the House of Commons of Southern Ireland and by this House, and your Lordships. Like everybody else, you have betrayed Ulster. The other evening, I saw with disgust that Mr. Austen Chamberlain, the son of Mr. Joseph Chamberlain, having agreed to put Ulster into these terms, then said he made an appeal to the comradeship of his old friend Sir James Craig to come in and submit to the domination of Sinn Féin. I could not help thinking that it was very like, after having shot a man in the back, going over to him and patting him on the shoulder and saying: 'Old man, die as quickly as you can, and do not make any noise.'"

Here and there laughter broke out at this jibe, but most voiced their disapproval, and he pressed on, "Without one word of warning to Ulster, there is sprung upon them this: 'We have arranged with the Sinn Féiners that there is to be a Parliament for the whole of Ireland, that the six counties are to go in, and if you go in, here is good news for you, because you are not to pay a six shilling Income Tax, but probably only a shilling and a half, and now how happy you ought to be.'"

Birkenhead shifted slightly on the Woolsack at this, and a smile briefly passed over his face as he recalled Lloyd George's characterisation of James Craig's proposal that the North be demoted to Dominion status, thus reducing their income tax from a "six bob tax to a three bob."

"Ulster is not for sale. Her loyalty does not depend upon taxes. Ulster values her heritage as citizens of the United Kingdom, and neither you nor the Press, nor your friends in the South of Ireland, need try to terrorise her by the bogey of her having to pay a higher tax."

Summing up his address, he warned the Lords, "Loyalty is a strange thing. It is something which you cannot get by merely sitting around a table and trying to find a formula for an Oath of Allegiance which means nothing. It is something born and bred in you. But do not try us too high. Do recognise that we have tried to help you, as you have helped us, and do not, when we want to stay with you, do anything to turn us out."

With that, amidst another round of cheers and calls of "Hear, hear!" the debate adjourned until the following afternoon. Without saying a word, Birkenhead rose from the Woolsack and left.

---

4 P.M. (APPROX., LONDON), 14 DECEMBER 1921, LONDON, HOUSE OF Commons [20]

WHILE CARSON WAS RANTING AGAINST THE TREATY, LLOYD GEORGE was making last-minute notes before giving his own speech in Commons. At three o'clock, he slipped into his seat "with every appearance of wishing to escape notice," as an American newspaper reporter put it. Whether this was the case or not, he was met with "cheer after cheer." He leaned over to Churchill and said with great mischief, "I just read the most delicious quote from an Ulster M.P. He called me a card sharper who keeps an extra ace up his sleeve and produces it as the necessity of the game demands. I quite like that."[21]

Winston chuckled and replied, "I would never accuse you of cheating, but then again, I wouldn't want to bet against you."

"I may need that ace up the sleeve yet, Winston."

The Prime Minister stepped up to the dispatch box and, after complimenting the men who spoke before him, proclaimed, "No agreement ever arrived at between two peoples has been received with so enthusiastic and so universal a welcome as the Articles of Agreement which were signed between the people of this country and the representatives of the Irish people on the sixth of this month. They have been received in every quarter in this country with satisfaction and with relief. They have been received throughout the whole of His Majesty's Dominions with acclaim.

"At home, in the great Dominions of the Crown, among our Allies, throughout the whole of the civilised world, this has been received not merely with satisfaction, but with delight and with hope.

"Let me say at once that, in so far as this Agreement has been achieved, it would not have been done without the most perfect collaboration among all the members of the British Delegation. Every one of them worked hard; each of them contributed from his mind and from his resource. The same thing applies to the part played by the representatives of Ireland. They sought peace, and they ensued it.[22] There were some of my right honourable Friends who took greater risks than I did in signing this Treaty. It will be remembered to their honour. There were men on the other side who took risks. The risks they took are only becoming too manifest in the conflict which is raging at this hour in Ireland, and all honour to them. Not a word will I say—and I appeal to every Member in this House not to say a word—to make their task more difficult. They are fighting to make peace between two great races designed by Providence to work together in partnership and in friendship.

"The main operation of this scheme is the raising of Ireland to the status of a Dominion of the British Empire—that of a Free State within the Empire, with a common citizenship, and, by virtue of that membership in the Empire and of that common citizenship, owning allegiance to the King."

One of the members interrupted him, shouting out, "There is no allegiance!"

Lloyd George raised his voice above the resulting jeers, declaring, "And swearing allegiance to the King." He had to pause at all the cross-aisle shouting but ended it by stating, "My honourable Friend can make his observations later on." After a few chuckles from Government backbenchers, he resumed, "In regard to allegiance, I will confine myself to the statement that there has been complete acceptance of allegiance to the British Crown, and acceptance of membership in the Empire and acceptance of common citizenship."

After a round of robust cheers, the House quieted down, and Lloyd George explained the Treaty's elements, touching on disarmament, the navy, the pledge to Ulster and the Boundary Commission. He then got to the remark he had promised Asquith earlier on their way to hear the King speak in Lords.

"My right honourable Friend, the Member for Paisley, and I belong in different ranks to the same profession," he started with a nod to Asquith. "I belong to the lower and working ranks, and consequently the less remunerated." The House roared with laughter, knowing that in his practice as a barrister, Asquith commanded much higher legal fees than the modest earnings the Prime Minister once procured as a solicitor. From across the aisle, Asquith nodded back with a broad smile. While the laughter continued, so did Lloyd George, "He knows what it is to settle an action, and he knows it depends upon your choosing exactly the moment. In 1917 we tried a settlement. Representatives of Sinn Féin would not come to the Convention, and for the rest, one party would not agree to the unity of Ireland, and the other party would not look at anything without it. The result was division. There are those who still think it could have been done a year or two ago. We do not think so."

The ordinarily sedate Austin Chamberlain called out, "Hear, hear!" and, in doing so, nearly dropped his monocle. His chant was echoed around the government benches as Lloyd George went on. "It was only when it came to be realised by everybody that prolonging the agony would only mean more loss, devastation, irritation, and trouble that the moment came when men of reason on both sides said, 'Let us put an end to it.' You could not have done it earlier, but here it is. We have got this document."

More loyal cheers followed, as well as a dissenting voice from the Opposition, "A scrap of paper!"

Ignoring the outburst, he began his summary, "On the British side, we have allegiance to the Crown, partnership in the Empire, security of our shores, non-coercion of Ulster. These are the provisions we have over and over again laid down, and they are here, signed in this document. On the Irish side, there is one supreme condition—that the Irish people as a nation should be free in their own land to work out their own national destinies in their own way. These two nations, I believe, will be reconciled. Ireland, within her own boundaries, will be free to marshal her own resources, direct her own forces—material, moral and spiritual—and guide her own destinies.

"The freedom of Ireland increases the strength of the Empire by ending the conflict which has been carried on for centuries with varying success, but with unvarying discredit, for centuries.

"By this Agreement, we win to our side a nation of deep abiding and even passionate loyalties. What nation ever showed such loyalty to its faith under such conditions? Generations of persecution, proscription, beggary and disdain—she faced them all. She showed loyalty to Kings whom Britain had thrown over. Ireland stood by them and shed her blood to maintain their inheritance—that precious loyalty which she now avows to the Throne, and to the partnership and common citizenship of Empire. It would be taking too hopeful a view of the future to imagine that the last peril of the British Empire has passed. There are still dangers lurking in the mists. Whence will they come? From what quarter? Who knows? But when they do come, I feel glad to know that Ireland will be there by our side, and the old motto that 'England's danger is Ireland's opportunity' will have a new meaning. As in the case of the Dominions in 1914, our peril will be her danger, our fears will be her anxieties, our victories will be her joy."

Amidst thunderous applause and cheering, he backed away from the box and took his seat next to Churchill, who was beaming with pride at his Prime Minister's performance.

4.40 p.m., 14 December 1921, Dublin, Dáil Private Session [23]

. . .

AROUND THE SAME TIME LLOYD GEORGE WAS WINDING UP HIS SPEECH in Parliament, Seán Milroy was given the nod to reopen the private session of the Dáil. Seán, whose artistic talents in postcard design had been integral to de Valera's escape from Lincoln Jail years earlier, obviously had not lost his sense of humour. He addressed his fellow members, "It does seem to me that it is a most extraordinary thing that Ireland should be thrown into the vortex of a great cleavage and on the brink of war for the trifling, small, pettifogging points that have been brought up today."

This observation brought some wry smiles to several faces. Seán went on, "As we came in today, we heard certain members of the public shouting, 'Up the Republic.' Ever since this controversy arose, the impression on the public mind has been that one section of the Cabinet has been standing for the Republic, and the other standing for the Treaty. That is not the issue. I trust that in any future discussions we may have, that the members of the Dáil will rise to the seriousness of their responsibilities and remember that this is not either a class of schoolboys or a debating society, but that it is the Parliament of the Irish nation, where the future of Ireland is going to be decided for generations."

Another member rose in agreement with Seán. "I would like to ask one question. We have been here since eleven this morning, and we have heard a lot of arguments, but I don't know yet what the difference between us is."

Rather than addressing issues about the Treaty itself, a demand for documents relating to the private meetings held in London was made by a woman delegate, Mary MacSwiney, with the underlying insinuation that something underhanded went on during those meetings. Her demand prompted a spirited defence of the private sub-committee meetings not only by Michael Collins, who offered to produce all the documents possible, but also William Cosgrave, who proclaimed, "I felt then that the delegation did not get justice from us. They were in the heat and thick of controversy with a British delegation in close touch with their own Cabinet, while they were twenty-four hours from ours. They could not possibly get back the views of the other members of the Cabinet to be in time for the discussion on the matter before them. I will go further and say I believe the plenipotentiaries have committed the Dáil by reason of their action according to a point of law."

Cathal Brugha asked sarcastically, "English law?"

"No," Cosgrave shot back, "but international law of which nobody here knows the first tittle."

De Valera shook his head and exclaimed, "This is the most painful experience I have ever had in my life. I was compelled to make a public statement with reference to the Treaty because everybody would assume that the plenipotentiaries and the Cabinet would be in agreement if I did not."

At this point, Kevin O'Higgins, who had stood up against de Valera at the Cabinet meeting before the debates began, declared, "We cannot change one comma of the Treaty. We must ratify or reject it."

De Valera shocked everyone with his angry retort, "This Dáil can do other things, but it cannot ratify this Treaty. It can do as the British Parliament is doing. You can pass a resolution if you like recommending it to the Irish people, but you cannot accept it until you refer it to the Irish people." Seán Milroy mumbled to the delegate seated next to him, "Well, then, shite! What are we bothering ourselves with if he now says the Dáil cannot ratify? That captain of the team, or whatever he calls himself, keeps moving the goalposts. Now he wants a vote by the people who voted us in to represent them."

De Valera made the situation worse when he announced, in a somewhat clumsy phraseology, "It is right to say that there will be very little difference in practice between what I may call the proposals received and what you will have under what I propose."

Richard Mulcahy summarised the situation by stating, "We are meeting and speaking to absolutely no purpose."

Mary MacSwiney then declared, "I would like to give you, as one of what you may like to call the die-hards of the Dáil, my opinion from beginning to end about this conference. She went into a long diatribe against the 'air of compromise,' as she put it, and castigated the delegates for folding before an ultimatum from Lloyd George on the last night of negotiations. We know and they know now that they were bluffed. When he said to them at three o'clock, 'You will sign or we will declare war,' they should have said, 'Very well, do your worst.' For God's sake and the sake of the dead, let us keep together."

Michael dismissed this criticism and the conjuring of her dead patriot brother's memory by saying, "In my opinion, no good purpose is served by making speeches in the private session that can be made in the public session. I, as one of the signatories, will state my position tomorrow. It is the least compromising position in all Ireland. I suggest it is only a waste of time making speeches that can be made in public session."

After this acrimonious exchange, another element of humour was introduced into the proceedings. Andrew MacCabe, a delegate from Sligo, rose to give the Dáil the benefit of his opinion. "I have a suggestion to make. It is that you appoint a committee from the rank and file to consider this division in the Cabinet, and see if we could not maintain unanimity. I suggest the rank and file of the House exclude all the members of the Cabinet."

MacCabe paused as the room broke out in laughter but then continued in earnest. "I suggest that the Speaker summon this meeting immediately after tea to evolve some programme, or some modus vivendi or operandi that will save us from the disedifying scene witnessed this morning. I believe if the rank and file get together, they will furnish as much brains in the assembly as there is in the Cabinet." Here he was again interrupted by both laughter and applause. "I believe they will discuss the matters in dispute in a much more decorous fashion than at present. I will move that a private meeting of the rank and file be held after tea, and that the Cabinet and everyone else be excluded."

Michael doubled over in laughter, crying, "Oh, I'm weak!"

Barton asked, "Is Andy serious?"

"I don't know, but he is good for a wheeze."

The Speaker wasn't sure, either, but to be safe, he banged his gavel and declared, "Any motion of that kind is absolutely out of order."

Michael gasped, "Out of order, and great gas!"

Arthur feigned to disagree and replied, perhaps facetiously, "I think it is a very sensible suggestion. I second it."

MacCabe maintained a straight face and did not let on what he really meant, but de Valera, for one, saw no humour in the moment, decrying, "I hold that is quite unconstitutional. I am here as President until you remove me."

"Jaysus, Dev, keep yer shirt on," someone grumbled.

"I spent last night getting proposals together to recover the ground that was lost. If we could modify them to get something that would be purely unanimous as a counter-proposal, I believe we'll win with this thing. If there had been a break, I would have published counter-proposals. The British will not go to war for the difference."

"Nor would we!" someone else called out.

After all this bantering, Arthur rose and stated firmly, "This meeting is summoned here to reject or endorse this Treaty, and there is no third course open. The British Parliament has either to accept or reject it. Everybody here is going to vote one way or the other. We took your responsibility, and you must take ours."

To which Cathal Brugha countered ominously, "And if you reject it, we can do what we like."

Michael said out of the side of his mouth, "And that coming from the man who insisted the Army would accept any outcome from the Dáil."

7.25 P.M., 14 DECEMBER 1921, DUBLIN, DÁIL EVENING PRIVATE SESSION 24

SHORTLY INTO THE EVENING SESSION, A TROUBLING REVELATION WAS delivered by a member from Cork, who declared, "Deputies from Cork City and County were presented with an order from the Headquarters Staff of South that if we didn't vote for the rejection of the Treaty, we were guilty of treason to the Republic. We can presume what the consequences would be. It is most important for the Minister of Defence to consider this and give an answer to us who are threatened to be shot like dogs if we take a certain action here."

De Valera seemed appalled at this accusation and condemned it, saying, "I think it is absolutely wrong for the Army to send any notice to any members of this Dáil. And if I were directly in charge, I would make it my duty that every member of the Headquarters Staff who sent that thing to the paper I would immediately ask for his resignation off the staff and I would do the same with the Southern Division."

Catha Brugha appeared equally outraged. "This is news to me. I didn't hear anything about this till now."

Michael, too, expressed his surprise, "It is news for me also."

Gearoid O'Sullivan, however, had heard of this new threat. "The remark was if Mick Collins goes down to Cork, there are men there to shoot him. And a woman in Dublin said, 'If there is not a man good enough in Cork or in Ireland to shoot Mick Collins, I will do it myself.'"

With so many of the delegates hard-line I.R.B. men hand-picked by Collins and Boland, there was a disproportionate number of extreme Republicans in the Dáil.[25] In war, they supported Collins, but when it came to the Truce and the Treaty, they were particularly critical of any negotiations that promised anything less than a full Republic. In Cork, which had suffered terribly at the hand of Sir Hamar Greenwood during the war, even a native son such as Michael faced considerable backlash and, as now revealed, physical danger for advocating for the Treaty. Arthur looked over at Michael, who was staring straight ahead with his jaw clenched.

Fresh from de Valera's recent tour of Limerick visiting the Army, Richard Mulcahy had his own perspective. "The Army first came into this matter when the President sent for the members of the Headquarters Staff to ask them for certain opinions with regard to the Army strength, and he subsequently asked for their opinions with regard to the Treaty, and then he asked us generally how the Army stood."

Denying any ulterior motives, de Valera explained, "With reference to my meeting with the Headquarters Staff, I want to make it clear I didn't ask them for their political opinions. I brought the chiefs of the staff to find out from them to see how they stood as regards the strength of the Army. I asked would you be for continuing or not. It was only in that particular way that the question of the Treaty or anything like it came in. I didn't discuss the Treaty.

"I must say that the day any portion of the Army does not obey the Government, then there is an end of your fight for freedom. If the Army as a national army does not obey the Government, and until this Dáil is dissolved, any man who does not obey the Government, if there is any scrap of an army left to arrest him, he will be arrested."

This acknowledgement seemed to close the matter for the time being, and Cathal Brugha said he would look into the matter and report back to the Dáil.

A little further into the evening session, as Gavan Duffy sat down after delivering a tortured argument about whether the British Parliament needed to ratify the Treaty, Michael groused, "Christ, Gavan means well, but leave it to him to muddy the waters with his legalistic shite."

Sure enough, more niggling observations by de Valera followed.

"The curious thing I notice about this is that the word Treaty is blocked out in the only signed document I got, and in the Press, the word Treaty is used. I pointed it out to the members of the delegation."

An exasperated Arthur Griffith intoned, "Mr. Childers can explain all that."

Erskine rose and gave an honest, measured response to the situation he had personally addressed before leaving London. "The draft Treaty as signed was not described as a treaty. It was described as articles of agreement, and in that form it was signed by the delegation. On the following day it was observed that the word treaty was not used in connection with this draft, although Lloyd George frequently used the word treaty. A communication was made to Downing St. pointing out the omission and suggesting that there should be added to the words 'Articles of Agreement,' 'Treaty between Great Britain and Ireland.' That was agreed to by the British. These words were inserted, and they appear in the copy before me."

De Valera insisted the opposite, saying, "At the head of my copy, it is blocked out and 'Articles of Agreement' are at the top."

"Bollocks," Arthur whispered to Michael. "I'd like to see that copy."

Losing his patience, Michael stood up and complained, "All this can be discussed at a public session. We are now on our trial because we are not constitutional lawyers. Did anybody suggest I was a constitutional lawyer before I went over there? I saw some of our barristers, and they looked damn poor fry before some of the other fellows. They didn't do as well as some of the fighting men did before them. We noticed on the following day that this document didn't bear the words 'Treaty between Great Britain and Ireland.' We immediately arranged for it to be put in. If we are expected to be constitutional lawyers and to know how all free states in the world came into existence, now is not the time to tell it."

Arthur agreed and said, "If these points are going to be made, we will meet them and beat them in public session. In the copy of the Treaty between Ireland and the British Government, you make that ground of omission an object for attack on us."

De Valera protested, "I beg your pardon; I am not attacking anybody. I am looking after the interests of Ireland. If there is anything wrong in this Treaty and if this Treaty be ratified, I want, at least, to see that we don't be held up as fools. We don't want Lloyd George again to trick us, and we do not want to be a laughing stock."

Fuming at de Valera's apparently fraudulent claim about his copy, Arthur contradicted him, "President de Valera said the word 'Treaty' was blocked out at the top of the page. It is not."

Feigning a complete lack of guile, de Valera said, "I will bring the copy I have. I am not a tactician. I never tried tactics on debate. I don't believe in that one bit. I suggested External Association. I was ready to break if we didn't get it because I felt the distance between the two was so small that the British would not wage war on account of it. You say if it is so small why not take it? But I say that small difference makes all the difference. But presented with the *fait accompli* that we are presented with, and with the danger of a division, my own feeling is that if a plebiscite were held in the country, at a time with the papers against us, that our people would accept that Treaty under duress. I believe they would; however, I am anxious that they should not accept anything less than they can get. It will not mean war. That is my proposal."

Arthur said wearily, "This is exactly the same proposition we put up twice to Lloyd George, and we fought it for two weeks. The fact of it is this: the Treaty is a thing you have to take it as it stands. The fact of this Treaty is we have to accept it or reject it. We have got to take it as it stands."

Michael backed up Arthur, saying, "I, for one, want to have it on record that we have put up this already, and there is no other delegation that would have got a better or a greater treaty than the delegation that went. But let it be understood that no delegation should go back to these people whom we distrust. I know the answer they would get: 'You can go to the devil. You can't speak for anyone, you can't deliver the goods.' In my opinion, they won't treat with any other delegation. Let there be no mistake about the alternatives. We have heard about external and internal association. Association means association with them. I have done my best to secure absolute separation from England. I am standing not for shadows but for substances, and that is why I am not a compromiser.

"Let no man here put me into the position to argue for anything less than full freedom for Ireland. I couldn't say in my heart that I would regard the Irish nation committed to anything less than full freedom. I could not say in my heart that anything would satisfy me personally less than full freedom. But if we go arguing on this, I want to say that we have put up the same thing to the English, and it was not acceptable to them. We were not able to prevail on them to accept it. Don't put us in the position of doing anything else than what we tried to do. If we went to Lloyd George, he would say: 'If I accept this Document No. 2, you will come back after and say, we can't accept this now, I want my Republic.' That would be in reality the position as I see it. The correspondence shows that we have already tried it. And I, as one man, can do no more."

Then, in an odd emotional outburst, Michael said, "I think in fairness to us, the Dáil should ask for our resignations."

Cries of "No, no!" ensued, and the meeting ended for the night.

This Mysterious Power of Ireland

15 DECEMBER 1921, 10 DOWNING STREET, LONDON

"Prime Minister, your speech to the House yesterday should be printed and scattered abroad through Ireland."

"Thank you, T.J. My speech was meant for Ireland rather than for England."

"Yes, sir," Thomas Jones replied.

"Sadly, the House did not tumble to that fact. What troubles me, though, is this comment Michael Collins made to the Dáil yesterday about the damn credentials the Irish delegates, as we suspected at the time, were carrying in their pockets the day they arrived. I saw this problem coming, and for our part, I'm glad we could skirt the issue, but de Valera has made a right stink about it, and now Collins has claimed they were presented but not accepted."

Jones answered, "Had they been presented, we would have had to reject them."

"Yes, as we then suspected and now know, those so-called credentials declared the delegates were representing de Valera's damn republic. It was a trap and not a very clever one at that."

"It may raise questions, though, today in Commons. The Die-Hards will seize on the opportunity to question whether we did, in fact, accept such credentials."

"Yes, Thomas, Mr. Collins may have landed us in a bit of trouble. We have to devise a way to avoid the issue, and if we cannot, cover up for his statement. It may have just been a slip of the tongue, and if we say the credentials were never shown, we'll be seen as contradicting him. I don't want to let him down." Lloyd George thought for a moment and then came up with a suggestion. "Why don't you see F.E. and get his take on the situation?"[1]

---

15 DECEMBER 1921, LONDON, HOUSE OF LORDS

WHEN JONES ARRIVED AT BIRKENHEAD'S CHAMBERS AND EXPLAINED THE reason for his visit, F.E. said, "Yes, I read the details in the morning papers, and I was equally concerned. An unfortunate turn if the matter is raised, and I very much doubt it will, but not irreversible. Why don't we fasten on Griffith's response a little later on in his speech? He said the credentials had neither been presented nor accepted, but he believed they had been shown to the P.M. Perhaps this will give us and our friend Mick some cover."

Relieved already, Jones smiled, "Yes, I think this may just do the job. I'll return to the P.M. straight away. Thank you for your time, sir."

"Excellent, T.J. Hopefully, the P.M. will convince any doubters in Commons as easily as I trust I will trounce those in Lords later this afternoon."[2]

---

15 DECEMBER 1921, LONDON, HOUSE OF COMMONS, ASQUITH SPEECH [3]

AS BIRKENHEAD HAD PREDICTED, THE ISSUE REGARDING THE presentation of the Irish credentials did not make its way into the afternoon debate. When Howard Asquith addressed a crowded House of Commons, he reflected on some of the apprehensions shared by many, including the right granted to the Irish to raise an army and build a navy. However, after voicing these concerns, he asked, "What is there between us? That is, after all, a matter of detail, though a very important one. I must come now to another point. In his speech yesterday, the Prime Minister went back in a reflective and, perhaps, a humorous mood to his and my experience of a great profession—perhaps the greatest of all professions."

Reminded of the Prime Minister's quip from the day before, the House erupted into laughter, and he used the moment to smile over at Lloyd George, who was as amused as any other member. When the laughter abated, Asquith continued, "He said that if you want to come to a settlement between parties to a dispute, you must choose the right moment. He appeared to think that the right moment—and if he does think so, I agree with him—was to try and agree before the case came into Court; and, from the point of view of my branch of that great profession, before the briefs were delivered. The worst moment for settlement is after you have opened the case. That is what the Government have done in this case."

Even this criticism was not taken as cause for rejection of the Treaty, and he wound up his address, saying, "I wish, before I sit down, to give, if I may, a serious and, indeed, a solemn warning to the House. It will be a very great mistake, in my opinion almost a fatal mistake, when this Agreement has been ratified, as I not only hope but confidently believe it will be by both Houses of Parliament here in the course of these few days, to suppose that you have come to an end of your difficulties.

"I speak with a firm belief that the Government have taken the right course, the courageous course, the only course that offers any hope of a real future between these two nations. Whatever the future may have in store, he would be a bold, and as I think, an audacious man who would venture to be a seer. At any rate, we shall have this satisfaction, that if this great international pact is ratified now by both these Houses of the Imperial Parliament, we can start on our future relations—troubled, stained, in many ways discreditable and even disastrous as they have been in the past—with clean hands and a clear conscience."

Lloyd George joined the House by standing and applauding loudly at the end of his old adversary's speech.

---

16 December, Dublin, Gresham Hotel

• • •

"I THOUGHT I'D BRING UP YOUR MORNING COFFEE MYSELF, MICK. HOW are you?"

Michael had already been to Mass around the corner at St. Mary's Pro and was back at his Gresham Hotel office. He was exhausted and in a foul mood, but it dissipated at a chance to tease Eddie, now back at work at the hotel. "Ye miss all the glamour of London, Eddie?"

"It was grand, but I'm happy where I am."

"There's not many as can say that, Eddie. At least somebody around here is of good cheer."

"Clearly, you haven't seen the morning papers with news from London, but in anticipation of that, I've brought them up for you." He put the breakfast tray down on a table, took the roll of papers from under his arm, and handed them to Michael, saying, "The powers that be in London are all coming out for you. Well, most of them. Look. You could start with Asquith."

Michael spread the papers out on his desk and picked one up, and sat down to read out loud, "*We can start on our future relations—troubled, stained, in many ways discreditable and even disastrous as they have been in the past —with clean hands and a clear conscience.*"[4] He smiled up at Eddie, "Not bad, not bad."

Joe O'Reilly entered, saying, "And that coming from the Leader of the Loyal Opposition. Hello, Mick."

"Hello, yourself, Joe. I wish our opposition were as loyal. Let's see what Winston had to say." He looked at his watch and said, "Better yet, let's drop in on Billy and Mary for breakfast. We can go over these papers with them. Thanks, Eddie. See you later."

Michael took a gulp from his cup and put it down, saying, "But first, I've had a wondrous Christmas idea, and now's as good a time as any to act on it." He took some biscuits and cubes of sugar from the table, put them in his pocket, and said, "Come on, Joe."

A few minutes later they entered the alley behind Conlon's Pub when they heard a horse neighing from its stable around the bend.

"Mick, Joe, this is a surprise. Howaya?" Christy called out. He and Crumpet weren't the only ones happy to see Michael, who reached into his pocket for a sugar cube but held it back until Crumpet nodded her head and neighed. Danny Boy barked, ran around in a circle, and as Michael knelt, leapt up into his outstretched arms.

"There's a good lad, now, calm down, calm down, or you don't get yours," Michael said as he reached into his pocket and treated the puppy to a biscuit. He stood up, stroked Crumpet's mane as she nuzzled him, and gave her another sugar cube. "Where are the other puppies?"

"Up in my flat, for now, happy as can be. We've found homes for all of them."

"Fine, fine. Christy, do you have Danny's leash? The time has come. He's going to give someone the best Christmas ever."

"Ah, Mick, that would be grand, but I fear Crumpet will miss him something fierce."

"So will I, but we'll know where to find him. Come along."

They all walked over to Conlons' back door, knocked and went inside. When Michael took off the leash, Danny Boy dashed up the stairs to the kitchen where the Conlons were getting ready for breakfast and immediately went up to Nelly, barking and wagging his tail.

"Oh, he's so cute!" Nelly cried out. "What are you doing here, little fella?"

Michael reached the landing and proclaimed, "I'll warrant he knows exactly what he's doing here, Nelly. It's a little early, but Happy Christmas, sweetheart."

Nelly burst into tears, jumped up and gave Michael the tightest hug she could. Then she let go and turned to Mary with a worried look and asked, "Is it all right, Momma? Can we keep him?"

"I don't see how we can't. It looks like love at first sight for you both. Not to worry, luv. Michael asked us almost as soon as he was born."

"Is this Danny Boy?" she cried. "The puppy who won the prize for Uncle Mick?"

"Ay, the one and same," Michael said, beaming. "Christy's been hiding him with Crumpet in her stable." He knelt, held Danny Boy's face in both hands, and kissed him on the snout, "Now you take good care of Nelly, won't you?"

Two loud barks in answer settled it. "That's that, then. Now, Joe and I have the morning papers to share with everyone—over a little breakfast, if that's all right?"

---

15 December 1921, London, House of Commons, Churchill Speech (the previous day) [5]

. . .

H.A.L. FISHER, THE PRESIDENT OF THE BOARD OF EDUCATION, stopped on his way back to the bench with a word of encouragement for Churchill. "We've all been looking forward to your turn, Winston."

"So have I," he beamed back.

After a couple of Die-Hard members denounced the Treaty by submitting and seconding amendments denouncing the Treaty, an Irish-born member for the Silvertown area of London named Jack Jones, acting entirely out of order, interrupted the proceedings with an emotional outburst.

"I belong to a long-suffering race. I protest against the plenipotentiaries of Ireland being called a murder gang in this House. They were invited to a Conference by this Government. You can throw me out if you like, but I am going to stand up for them."

After the Speaker and several Members thoroughly chastised Jones, a few more hot exchanges followed, and then it was Churchill's turn to speak. As usual, he had a carefully prepared speech but used the prior outburst to improvise a bit of humour. With a nod and a smile at Lloyd George and Austen Chamberlain, he rose from the front bench to address the House.

"I have always been a strong partisan of the liberties of Debate, and certainly I take no exception—save on one small point, which, I am sure, my honourable Friend will realise—to any of the taunts and sallies which he has made in his excellent and sprightly speech. Indeed, I was very much surprised that the honourable Member for Silvertown, who certainly does not bear the reputation of being mealy-mouthed, should have been brought into such a state of extreme agitation by language which, I should have thought, a man of his moral fibre and physical structure could have afforded to sustain with a fair degree of composure."

As laughter rippled through the chamber, some members who had drifted out to the hall during the Die-Hard speeches were summoned back by their friends, "Winston's speaking now. Hurry!"

Acknowledging the returning Members with a pause and a smile, Churchill proceeded. "I should like the House, however, to turn its mind from the amusing excursions and the effusion of the fancy of my honourable Friend to the realities of the Irish situation—grim, grave, and, in many cases, shocking realities—during the last two years. One would think, to hear the Mover and Seconder of this Amendment, that all we have to do is to lay down the conditions which commend themselves to us, to veto anything which is not to our liking, and that there will then be an end to all this tiresome Irish business. During the last two years the condition of Ireland has been worse than at any time during living memory. Whether it was a war that was going on or not is not worth arguing. It is not my purpose to argue it, but, at any rate, a violent and homicidal campaign was being conducted by persons ready to risk their lives and liberties, and for no personal object. And the actions of these persons were very widely supported, or, at any rate, countenanced among the general population of the South of Ireland. It was a war, as it were, or a struggle in a forest, in which the enemy was protected by a forest of other human beings, many of them law-abiding, many of them peaceable and harmless, and some of them actually friendly to the British Government. These conditions involved and led to a demoralising and detestable form of strife."

"I HOPE YOU REALISE HE'S TALKING ABOUT LAW-ABIDING PEOPLE LIKE YOU, Billy," Michael said as he read Churchill's speech along with Billy and Mary Conlon over breakfast the following day.

"Peaceable, for the most part, maybe," Billy answered, "but I don't know about friendly to the British."

WINSTON CONTINUED, "OUR SOLDIERS AND POLICEMEN WERE murdered. Unable to catch the guilty persons, and unable to convict them very often when they were occasionally caught, our soldiers and policemen, infuriated beyond endurance, retaliated. I am not going to blame them now or at any other time for their behaviour in those circumstances, but the Government and the whole country became inevitably involved in the discredit of these violent actions."

Lloyd George whispered to Chamberlain, "Or war with the utmost violence, as he once put it."

Amidst some rumblings from the opposite benches, Churchill admitted, "Nor was the movement of the rebels quelled. On the contrary, it attained larger proportions every week. There was more fighting; there were more casualties; there was fighting on a larger scale."

"No! No!" came cries from those who perhaps thought there had not been enough.

Speaking over them, he said, "There was bloodshed on a larger scale. The gaols are filled with Irish convicts."

"They were, you mean," someone called out.

"They are filled. Four thousand interned persons, against whom there was no evidence, and no means of formulating a charge—"

"Shame! Shame!"

"—were detained in compounds all over the country."

Loud cries and mumblings from the Opposition obliged him to pause. "I hope I may be allowed to have the full liberty of debate, and to pursue my argument without interruption." As the dissenting voices died down, he continued, "Martial law was declared over a large portion of Ireland. Plans were made to declare it over a much larger area. The troops at our disposal were insufficient. Plans were on foot to raise much larger bodies of troops. At a certain stage, with a view to trying to curb the reprisals in which the troops and the police indulged, official reprisals were instituted under Martial Law. Our whole army was tethered to Ireland. Our great interests, to which both honourable Members who have spoken have referred, in India and in Egypt, were sensibly affected by that weakness. So were our interests all over the world, especially in our Dominions and in the United States. They were affected, and prejudicially affected, by the reproach directed against us, and by the loud, insistent outcry raised by the Irish race all over the world. There was, of course, no doubt of the power of Great Britain to crush Irish resistance, if we chose to employ enough men and to employ them long enough. And I, myself, believe that the nation would have been willing, and would still be willing if there was no other way, to make the sacrifices and the exertions necessary, and to face the obloquy which would be inevitable.

"Another way has been found," he asserted, but at more angry mumblings, paused momentarily for effect.

Chamberlain whispered to Lloyd George, "War with the utmost violence, peace with the utmost patience."

Lloyd George nodded as Churchill went on, "We believe that since that way has been found, a new, a completely new situation has been created. Let me ask the House to consider how these negotiations which have reached a conclusion originated. Have the Mover and Seconder of the Amendment considered that? It is quite true, as my right honourable Friend the Prime Minister reminded me when the right honourable Gentleman, the Member for Paisley was speaking," he said with a smile at Asquith, "that we announced in this House last year that we were perfectly ready to negotiate with Sinn Féin. No response was made. How did the negotiations in the present year originate?"

Here he reminded the House of Sir James Craig's part in the Truce and his political kinship to Edward Carson. "They originated on that day when the Prime Minister of Ulster, the brother of the leader of the party in this House, to whose serious speech we listened with so much attention yesterday—those negotiations originated on that day when the Prime Minister of Ulster sought Mr. de Valera in the remotest haunts of the rebels, or what might be called in the secret hiding places of the murder gang, and when he demanded fair speech for his Irish fellow-countryman."

Upon hearing the phrase "murder gang" again, many Members broke out in laughter, taking it as another tease of Jack Jones, who had earlier objected so vociferously to its use in Parliament. Jones just sat there with his arms folded at first and then smiled and nodded to those having a laugh at his expense.

While this was going on, another Member from the Opposition rose and said, "I do not want to interrupt the right honourable Gentleman, but it is hardly fair to say that Sir James Craig sought Mr. de Valera. It is well known that Mr. de Valera asked for an interview with Sir James."

Here Michael paused from reading to comment, "Splitting hairs, that is. Cope suggested it, Lloyd George approved it, and I helped facilitate it. I had Emmet Dalton escort Craig to the talks in Dublin."

"Anything come of it?" Billy asked.

"Besides them meeting for the first and only time ever? No, decidedly not. Emmet said Dev was impossible.[6] Still, it was significant in that they met at all." He shook the paper, saying, "Let's see how Winston answered."

"Winston, is it?" Christy asked.

"Well, come to think of it, at this point, why not?"

"Won't that be nice? 'Oh, Winston, isn't the brandy superb?'"

Michael's head dropped to his chest. Danny Boy ran to him, stood on his hind legs, and licked Michael's hand. As Michael listened, he patted the puppy on his head, then attempted to explain, "But now that we've signed the Treaty…"

"'Oh, pray, continue, Winston.'"

"Cease your babbling, Christy, and I will get on with it."

CHURCHILL TOOK THE INTERRUPTION GOOD-NATUREDLY, "CERTAINLY, I do not desire to take any advantage involved in that point. Sir James Craig undoubtedly responded to that invitation by an act of statesmanship and superb courage, full of hope for the future, and probably destined when the passions of this time are dead to rank among the most famous and fruitful of the episodes of Irish history. That was the beginning of all that evolution of opinion in the Cabinet and in the country which has led us to our present position. What was the second step?

"The Cabinet were confronted with the preparations for the autumn and winter campaign in Ireland. It was obvious that many, many thousands of troops would have to be raised, and that Martial Law must be extended to the whole of the Twenty-Six Counties. There were a good many Ministers who, at that time, with this meeting of Sir James Craig and Mr. de Valera in their minds, were determined that before operations of that gravity were undertaken, and war really begun on an extensive and almost universal scale in Ireland, we should be absolutely sure of where we stood in relation to the Sein Féin leaders—that we should know for what it was that we were going to make these great exertions, that we should be sure it was not merely a question of finance or of Dominion status that stood between us and peace, but that we were confronted with an irreconcilable demand to build up an independent sovereign republic on the flank of this country."

Here Churchill took the opportunity to praise another sometime adversary, Sir Hamar Greenwood. "The meeting between Sir James Craig and Mr. de Valera was reported to the Cabinet by my right honourable Friend the Chief Secretary, and it was so stated in the Press —and may I say that my right honourable Friend has received far less than justice—"

A Liberal M.P. called out, "Hear, hear!"

"—far less than justice from both sides of the House, and from all three of the great parties in the State. I am going to read to the House the report which my right honourable Friend made on seventh May. It is as follows: 'The meeting between Sir James Craig and Mr. de Valera must be regarded as an event of the first political importance. This is the first occasion in modern history on which duly accredited representatives of the North and South of Ireland have met of their own initiative, and without the intervention of British statesmen, to discuss the differences that have so long divided the two sections of the Irish people. Although neither Sir James Craig nor Mr. de Valera appears to have emerged from the interview with his convictions in any degree shaken, the fact of their having entered into direct negotiations has produced a deep impression in the minds of men in all parties and has materially improved the prospects of peace.' In view of the hideous prospect which lay before us in the autumn and winter and of this new hope and new light that began to break through the parley of Irishman with Irishman, Ministers decided to make an effort to secure a clear declaration as to where the Sinn Féin leaders really stood.

"The next step was the speech which Ministers put into the mouth of the King," an unfortunate phrase that drew some gasps from some Members that Churchill answered, undaunted, "that is the correct and constitutional form—at the opening of the Belfast Parliament—a speech for which, of course, as well as for every other utterance of His Majesty, Ministers are solely responsible."

During the slight interruption that followed, Lloyd George leaned to Chamberlain and added quietly, "With a little help from Winston's old friend, General Smuts."

Churchill resumed, "But it is perfectly correct and proper to say that never did the Sovereign accept advice with more sincere gratitude and more heartfelt conviction than did His Majesty on that occasion. That was the next step. That speech undoubtedly and immediately created a new situation. There was on every side made manifest a profound desire for an honourable peace. It is in consequence of that desire that the Government has laboured for the last five months. It is to that that we have addressed ourselves, but within severe and rigid limitations which almost at the last minute seemed to make all prospect of agreement impossible. Sinn Féin Ireland demanded an independent sovereign republic for the whole of Ireland, including Ulster. We insisted upon allegiance to the Crown, membership of the Empire, facilities and securities for the navy, and a complete option for Ulster. Every one of those conditions is embodied in the Treaty."

Members began shouting out, "No, no!"

"What about allegiance?"

"What about the navy?"

Churchill calmly addressed all the shouting, "I am going to refer to these matters. I say every one of these conditions is embodied in the Agreement, and the Government is perfectly prepared to deal at length and in detail with every one of these points. If I have not time to deal with them all, other Ministers will, and every point will be rigorously and rigidly defended."

Another objecting Member challenged him, "The Prime Minister did not deal with allegiance yesterday."

Smiling as if he was glad to have been asked this, he replied, "As a matter of fact, *I* am going to deal with it. I say that our debt to Ulster is great. Not only has Ulster shown unswerving loyalty and allegiance to the British Empire, but she has taken the most important steps to promote peace in Ireland. It is no longer open to anyone to say that Ulster is barring the way to the rest of Ireland, that Ulster is forbidding the rest of Ireland to have the kind of Government they want. That is all past. These great sacrifices of opinion have been made by that small but resolute community at a time of great, distressing, and protracted anxiety to them, and they have been made for the sake of their common interests in the British Empire. Ulster has boldly said to the rest of Ireland: 'Have the Government you choose; we will do our best to make things go right, and as long as you stay within the British Empire, we close no doors on the future.' That, it seems to me, is what Ulster has said, and I repeat that our debt to her is great. It is the view of the Government that the Treaty strictly, fully, and finally pays that debt. The option is absolute. There is no time limit on the action of Ulster. There is on our part a complete obligation for the defence of Ulster whilst she remains in the Imperial Parliament. If Irish unity can be achieved, it can only be because the Government of the Irish Free State will have convinced Ulster of its loyal association with the British Empire, and will have offered Ulster conditions of security and partnership in every way satisfactory to her. Of those conditions Ulster is the sole judge. The worst that can happen to Ulster in the meanwhile is what happens to all of us. That is the worst that can happen to her. They share our fortunes for good or for evil, taking the rough with the smooth, no more and no less."

·   ·   ·

Mary responded to the mention of shared fortunes, saying, "That sounds reasonable enough."

Michael replied, "Yes, reasonable as well as highly unlikely. If I could meet Craig, I might fare better than Dev, but I wouldn't bet on it."

"We do not at all conceal the fact that we hope that someday —surely we are permitted to do so—Ulster will join herself with Southern Ireland, and that the national unity of Ireland within the British Empire will be attained. That is our policy, and I have frequently heard it approved in bygone days by Lord Carson when he was a Member of this House. If, on a satisfactory agreement being made, Ulster, of her own free and in her own time, chooses to join with her Irish fellow-countrymen in the Government of Ireland, we are sure that this would be a great advantage to the general interests of the British Empire as a whole, to the interests of all Ireland, to the special interests of Ulster, and to the particular interests—and this is referred to in the closing lines of the Amendment now before us—of the Unionists and Protestants in the South of Ireland, whose position would be enormously fortified, and who undoubtedly look forward to that day with the keenest hope. This opinion, Mr. Speaker, we feel entitled to proclaim, and we are fully entitled to make sure, as we have done, that our legislation and our policy contain nothing that shall be a barrier to such an ultimate consummation. Further than that, we cannot go. Ulster is absolutely free. She is the sole judge, and the initiative rests entirely with her."

"Hope for a united Ireland, from the lips of Winston Churchill," Mary said in wonderment.

"We've come a long way," Billy replied.

"So has he," Mary said.

"We'll see. I'll reserve judgement," Michael answered.

Amidst a lot of cheering at this summation of the position of Ulster in the Treaty, Lloyd George murmured to Chamberlain, "Unfortunately, Craig seems to have chosen to stand apart."

Chamberlain murmured back, "And sit on a rock."

Churchill continued, "Of course, it is quite easy to find fault with the details of the Treaty. I am not at all complaining that honourable Members who hold strong views, and have always held those views, and who are represented by the supporters of this Amendment, should point to the shortcomings, as they regard them, of what is admittedly a compromise agreement."

He then turned to Colonel Gretton, who had interrupted Asquith's earlier speech, complaining about the weakness of the Oath to the King. "This is not a partisan solution. It is not the triumphant assertion of one extreme view over all others, and, as my honourable and gallant Friend has pointed out, the oath is not the same in this case as in the rest of the British Empire. Complete fiscal autonomy is conceded. It is true that the Irish Free State can raise, within certain limits, a small army of its own. But to all these arguments we can reply, and no doubt replies will be made to them. In our view they promise allegiance to the Crown and membership of the Empire."

Here Churchill countered more shouts of "No, no!" saying, "That is our view. The oath comprises acceptance of the Irish Constitution, which is by Articles 1 and 2 of that Constitution exactly assimilated to the constitution of our Dominions. This oath is far more precise and searching than the ordinary oath which is taken elsewhere." Ignoring more negative cries, he spoke over them, "It mentions specifically membership of the Empire, common citizenship and faithfulness to the Crown, whereas only one of these matters is dealt with in the Dominion oath."

One Member interrupted him again, "Why should they not take the Canadian oath?"

Churchill explained, "The oath they are asked to take is more carefully and precisely drawn than the existing oath, and it was chosen because it was more acceptable to the people whose allegiance we are seeking, and whose incorporation in the British Empire we are earnestly desirous of securing.

"With regard to fiscal autonomy, I cannot conceive how this can be a peril to Great Britain. On the contrary, I think the boot is on the other leg, because never was one country so absolutely dependent in economic matters upon another as Ireland and Great Britain, because we are her sole market and her only source of supply.

"Then there is the question of the army, and I ask how can we talk of Dominion status if you deny the right of raising an armed force for local purposes, which every Dominion enjoys, which we conceded to South Africa within a few years after the closing of a war in which we lost 50,000 men. How can you deny that principle, and talk about giving Dominion status? I think it is better that there should be a moderate armed force maintained there for keeping internal order, and for absorbing into a disciplined or responsible organisation the elements of potential unrest. Certain I am that any force which is raised by Ireland will not be a force beyond the military power of the British Empire to control.

"As for the navy, nothing has been conceded which is essential to the security of this country. The British Government is solely responsible for the safety of these islands and the seas around them. We have secured these small conveniences and facilities in time of peace that the navy is likely to require upon the coast of Ireland, and they are all set out in the Schedule. Scarcely any use will be made of them in time of peace, but in time of war or strained relations with a foreign power, we have an absolute right to the freest possible use of all harbours and inlets of Ireland, to enable us to undertake the control of coastal waters, the defence of these islands, and the sea routes by which our food is brought to this country."

MICHAEL PAUSED TO COMMENT, "CHURCHILL WAS ADAMANT ON THIS ISSUE, but time will tell whether this article will actually be adhered to."

"How so, Michael?" Billy asked.

"Just suppose there was another war with Germany…"

"I'd rather not, thank you," Mary interjected.

"Likewise, but if there were, would we really want all 'the harbours and inlets of Ireland' filled with British battleships? Maybe, maybe not, depending on the circumstances. As I said, time will tell."[7]

"THOSE ARE THE ANSWERS THAT CAN BE MADE TO THE CRITICISMS which have been raised. No doubt similar answers are being made at this moment to similar objections in Dublin from an opposite point of view. Here then is the question which those who take most sincerely the extreme view on either side of the Channel should be asked and should answer. They say the Treaty is not satisfactory. They point to various provisions in which it is unsatisfactory, but are the differences outstanding between what they would wish and the Treaty on their side sufficient to make it imperative to renew the fighting, with all the loss and risk entailed thereby?"

"No, no!" came the cheers, now in support of what Churchill was asking.

"I cannot believe you will find any body of responsible men here or in Ireland, Liberal or Conservative, North or South, soldier or civilian, who would solemnly declare that on the margin of difference remaining between these extreme views and the Treaty it would be justifiable to lay the land of Ireland waste to the scourge of war, or to drag the name of Great Britain through the dirt in every part of the world. For you cannot embark on such a struggle without being prepared to face conditions of public opinion all over the world which undoubtedly would be profoundly detrimental to your interests. You could not do it without being prepared to inflict the most fearful injury on the land and people of Ireland. When we have this Treaty, defective, admittedly, from your point of view, but still a great instrument, I ask: Are the differences between the Treaty and the extreme desire worth the re-embarking on war? You cannot do it. If you tried, you would not get the people to support you."

During the sustained cheering that followed, Lloyd George leaned over again to Chamberlain, saying, "Did you read your friend Arthur Griffith's speech yesterday?"

"Yes, yes!" Chamberlain answered with unusual enthusiasm. "He said much the same to the Dáil."

Michael put the paper down for a moment, "Churchill is practically quoting here from Arthur's speech. Amazing."

Churchill resumed, "On the contrary, they would complain in both countries of their leaders, and they would complain with violence and indignation that they were dragged from their hearths to maltreat each other on pretexts which had been reduced to such manageable dimensions. It is high time that the main body of Irish and British opinion asserted its determination to put a stop to these fanatical quarrels.

"Let me direct the attention of the House to a remarkable

phenomenon. Yesterday, at the other end of the passage, I heard Lord Carson, with sonorous accents and with brilliant and corrosive invective, denouncing Lord Curzon as a turncoat and a traitor. I do not think it necessary to deal with such a charge, because everyone in this House knows that Lord Curzon's whole life has been devoted to the patriotic service of this country, and those of us in this country who have served with him know well that his counsel was always robust and vigorous in the time of the greatest difficulty and danger through which we passed. At the very moment when Lord Carson was denouncing the Secretary for Foreign Affairs as a traitor and a turncoat, Mr. de Valera in Dublin was almost simultaneously denouncing Mr. Collins for a similar offence."

As Michael read the speech aloud, at this point, Billy interrupted him, "Remarkable, isn't it, to see your old nemesis standing up for you in Parliament. Humph!"

"Strange days, Billy. Strange days."

Mary chimed in, "Oh, I don't know. Mr. Churchill should be grateful for the work Michael did over there."

Loud laughter erupted at the comparison of Lord Carson and de Valera, easing the tension in the House and setting up Churchill's following argument. "Both were held up as traitors to their respective countries, and for what? For having supported a treaty of peace which nineteen-twentieths of the people of both countries are determined to carry through. Are we not getting a little tired of all this?"

This question was received with great applause from both sides of the House. "These absolutely sincere, consistent, unswerving gentlemen, faithful in all circumstances to their implacable quarrels, seek to mount their respective national war horses, in person or by proxy, and to drive at full tilt at one another, shattering and splintering down the lists, to the indescribable misery of the common people, and to the utter confusion of our Imperial affairs.`

"My honourable Friend who proposed this Amendment referred to the charge so frequently made that we are humiliated by this Treaty which we have signed and by these negotiations, and referred to it as a Danegeld, while his Second referred to it as a surrender. No doubt

England is conceding more to Ireland in this Treaty than she has as a nation ever been willing to concede before, and no doubt she has done it, not only with a view to the future, but with a sincere desire to end a period of brutal and melancholy violence. I agree with my honourable Friend who proposed the reply to the Gracious Speech that our reputation is such that we can afford to take the step we have taken. If we had shown ourselves a feeble nation, fat and supine, sunk in sloth, our mission exhausted, our strength gone, our energies abated, our credentials impaired, if we had shown this lack of quality in the struggle from which we have emerged, then indeed there would be some explanation and justification for such misgivings in the breasts of many gathered here. But when we have just come out of a world war with our record such as it is, in which our armies have broken the German line, in which our navies have carried on the whole sea business of the Allies, in which our finances have sustained Europe, when we have come out of all these dangers, and have shown that we are capable of taking a leading part, if not the leading part, in the great struggle which has overthrown the largest and most powerful military Empires of which there is a record—when all these facts are considered, surely we can afford to carry on these Irish negotiations according to a clear, cool judgment of what is best in the country's interest, without being deflected or deterred from any particular course of action by a wholly unjustifiable self-accusation of humiliation. But in truth it is not humiliation. It is not as a humiliation that this event is viewed by the world or by the Empire. It is as a great and peculiar manifestation of British genius, at which the friends of England all over the world have rejoiced."

Cheering erupted again and continued as he went on to say, "Every foe of England has been dumbfounded. Every Colonial statesman will feel that if this succeed, his task in his Dominion of bringing people closer and closer into the confederation of the British Empire will be eased and facilitated. There is not a Dominion Parliament throughout the British Empire where this Treaty will not be accepted and endorsed."

"My point exactly," Michael exclaimed as he pounded the table. "I told everyone the Dominions will throw their support with us, for if England harms us, so also does she harm the Dominions."

. . .

CHURCHILL BEGAN TO WIND UP HIS SPEECH BY MUSING ON THE ANCIENT relationship between Britain and Ireland.

"It is a curious reflection to inquire why Ireland should bulk so largely in our lives. How is it that the great English parties are shaken to their foundations, and even shattered, almost every generation, by contact with Irish affairs? Whence did Ireland derive its power to drive Mr. Pitt from office, to drag down Mr. Gladstone in the summit of his career, and to draw us who sit here almost to the verge of civil war, from which we were only rescued by the outbreak of the Great War. Whence does this mysterious power of Ireland come? It is a small, poor, sparsely populated island, lapped about by British sea power, accessible on every side, without iron or coal. How is it that she sways our councils, shakes our parties, and infects us with her bitterness, convulses our passions, and deranges our action? How is it she has forced generation after generation to stop the whole traffic of the British Empire, in order to debate her domestic affairs? Ireland is not a daughter State. She is a parent nation. The Irish are an ancient race."

Jack Jones rose from his bench to cheer loudly at this avowal of admiration of Irish heritage, and many in the House joined him.

"'We, too, are,' said their plenipotentiaries, 'a far-flung nation.' They are intermingled with the whole life of the Empire, and have interests in every part of the Empire wherever the English language is spoken, especially in those new countries with whom we have to look forward to the greatest friendship and countenance, and where the Irish canker has been at work."

"CHURCHILL'S PARAPHRASING ME THERE. I TOLD HIM THAT IRELAND IS A nation, and every Irishman feels this in his heart. I'm not sure I appreciate the word 'canker,' but you can see he appreciates the importance of the Irish in America," Michael mused. *"He knows he made it through the Great War with America's help, and he may need it again someday."*

"HOW MUCH HAVE WE SUFFERED IN ALL THESE GENERATIONS FROM THIS continued hostility? If we can free ourselves from it, if we can to some extent reconcile the spirit of the Irish nation to the British Empire in the same way as Scotland and Wales have been reconciled, then indeed we shall have secured advantages which may well repay the trouble and the uncertainties of the present time.

"I am told that we are not to refer to South Africa, because the cases are not parallel."

Here Winston turned and glanced in the Prime Minister's direction. Lloyd George smiled at this acknowledgement of an earlier criticism he had directed at Winston and leaned forward to hear where he was taking it.

"Of course they are not, but surely it would be very foolish for us to cut ourselves off from the encouragement and inspiration which we may naturally and legitimately derive from studying the most adventurous and most modern instance of trust and conciliation which the annals of the British Empire records! I remember when I was charged with the duty of commending the Transvaal Constitution in this House. I remember many facts which were known to me, and which certainly would have justified the gravest pessimism, and would have caused the deepest anxiety. I remember the intelligence reports which we got of Boer wagons moving about the veldt in the moonlight, leaving their dumps of rifles and ammunition here and there in lonely farms. They were reports which caused the greatest disquietude in all who were responsible for the policy. But we persevered. We grasped the larger hope, and in the end, when our need was greatest, we gained a reward far beyond our hopes. In those days we had far less satisfactory Parliamentary circumstances than now exist. Party fighting was very bitter in those days. I appealed to the Opposition of that time to join with the Government in this matter. I said: 'With all our great majority we can only make this the gift of a party, but you can make it the gift of Britain as a whole.' The appeal was not acceded to."

BILLY CONCLUDED THIS ARGUMENT, "I SUPPOSE, MICK, YOU'LL BE BACK IN London before long discussing another Constitution with this very man."

Michael frowned, saying, "Ay, that I will!"

Danny Boy growled, causing Michael to bend down and pet him, "Yes, I know, but I'll be back."

· · ·

WINSTON'S LAST WORDS WERE AN INVITATION FOR UNITY TO ALL THE Conservative, Liberal, and Labour Members listening there. "Today in this enterprise, which also is full of uncertainty, but full of hope, we can undoubtedly count upon the active and energetic support of all the three great parties in the State, who are resolved to take what steps are necessary to bring, if possible, this Irish peace to its consummation, to carry it out in the spirit and in the letter, and to stand firmly against all efforts to overthrow it, whether they be in Parliament or out."

He then withdrew to his seat on the bench to the sound of loud, enduring cheers. Lloyd George clapped him on the back, and Chamberlain reached over to shake his hand. "That was magnificent, Winston. Unanswerable. I shall write to the King of your speech here today. It will do his heart good."

H.A.L. Fisher came over, now beaming himself, and told Churchill, "Winston, that was one of your finest speeches ever."[8]

The Prime Minister's Chief Whip, Freddie Guest, also came over to congratulate him. "Winston, that was much the best speech I have ever heard you make. Its simplicity of style and fervour of advocacy has won you a genuine reception from all quarters. Splendid, Winston. Splendid."[9]

LATER THAT DAY KING GEORGE STOOD IN THE AFTERNOON LIGHT OF A window at Buckingham Palace, reading the letter from Austen Chamberlain. His hand dropped to his side as he paused to look over the gardens. He smiled to himself and then continued reading the description of Churchill's speech.

"HE SPOKE WITH GREAT FORCE AND POWER AND WITH EQUAL SKILL AND tact. The case of the Agreement could not have been better put. At the same time, he paid tribute to the great services which Ulster had rendered and even to the part which her attitude had had in producing the present Agreement. But it is impossible to summarise the speech. It had a profound effect upon the House."[10]

Cerebral Excitement - Only Prime Minister

16 DECEMBER 1921, DUBLIN

BILLY SMILED AT JOE O'REILLY WHEN MICHAEL FINISHED READING Churchill's speech. "Seems like Christy was right about 'Winston' after all. By all accounts, Michael made quite a friend there, wouldn't you say, Joe?" [1]

Michael laughed but shook his head in answer, "I wouldn't go that far. However, Birkenhead told me Winston would be a great advocate. He'll have to be. The Conservatives have a three-to-one advantage in the House over the Liberals. But friend? I still don't trust him." He turned to Christy and said, "Sorry, Christy, we may have gotten along well enough at times, but he's as wily as Lloyd George." He paused and thought a moment, "If I could consider any of that lot a friend, it'd be Birkenhead. He's due to speak in Lords today. I would've liked to be there for that."

Michael glanced through some other articles covering the speech and then put the newspaper down.

Billy reached over, asking Michael, "May I?"

"Help yourself."

While Billy looked the paper over, Mary asked, "How is Kitty, Michael? Such a fine girl. It was so nice finally meeting her in London. I'm sure she's a comfort to you."

"Ay, she is, but I hope I don't lean on her too much sometimes. I'm just after writing to her what a dreadful strain these Dáil sessions have been."[2]

Billy remarked as he perused the headlines, "Well, now, even Bonar Law has come out for the Treaty." He skimmed down the column and read out loud, "*Let me say at the outset that I am in favour of this Agreement.*" Lowering the paper, he peered over the edge at Michael and asked, "Now, there's a gift, eh?"

"It certainly is. In London, we were repeatedly presented with the spectre of Bonar Law sweeping the Conservatives into power and dashing all hopes for the Treaty. Now we have Dev complaining that the document we signed is labelled 'Agreement,' instead of 'Treaty,' as if what it is called is more important than what's in it."

"Don't judge a book by its cover," Tim Kelly called out as he came up the stairs and joined everyone at the breakfast table.[3]

Everyone laughed at this remark, but Michael nodded approvingly and said, "Aptly put, Tim. You've be reading your George Eliot and one of my favourites, *Mill on the Floss*.[4] Howandever, the document we brought home from London was clearly adjusted to read 'Treaty,' and look here," he said, pointing to one of the newspaper articles, "even Bonar Law and Carson called it a Treaty."

Christy replied, "But, of course, Carson and Craig are not in favour of it."

Mary added, "Nor is Harry Boland, we hear."

Michael sighed, "Harry doesn't know what he thinks until Dev tells him. First, he was in favour before he had read the Treaty, and then he sent a telegram that was read out before the Dáil yesterday, asking his vote to be recorded as against. He's lost his way, our Harry has. Anyway, read further down, toward the end of Law's speech, the bit about the Empire."

Billy skimmed the article and then said, "You mean this? *I think there is a feeling all through the Empire of rejoicing, but there is going to be a reaction from all this. Six months hence I do not think this will be a political asset to my right honourable Friend, but I do hope that it will be otherwise in the distant future, and that by the verdict of posterity it will be a permanent triumph for him.*"

"The way I take that," Michael explained, "in six months' time, for all their efforts, Lloyd George and the rest of them could be kicked out of office. Likewise, in six months' time we could be fighting a civil war, the way things are going in the Dáil."

"I hope neither of those prophecies is fulfilled." Billy looked back at the paper. "Listen to this. Law goes on to say, *A great many of those who are opposed to this Treaty say that when the men who signed it get this power, they mean to have a republic and to upset it all. The facts do not seem to tally with that. It looks really as if the men who signed it intend to carry it out loyally, and is it not worth our while giving them the chance?*"

"That's a generous statement. I didn't notice that. We won't have a republic in six months, but, as I keep telling everyone, we have a stepping stone to one *now*."[5] Michael ran his fingers through his hair, then looked around the table and remarked, "What I find so distressing is, with all the talk about the Oath and whether the word 'Treaty' was on the document or not, such short shrift is being paid to Ulster. Churchill talked more about Ulster than Dev ever did. It was one of the most important elements we fought so hard over, the essential unity of Ireland. Yesterday Dev objected to the right of Ulster to secede from the South, but at the same time said the Ulster question should be eliminated from the fight between Ireland and England. 'Let us not start to fight with Ulster,' he said."

Nelly asked hesitantly, "Excuse me, Uncle Mick, can I ask a question?"

"Of course, you can, dear. I'm sure it will be better than most I've heard this week. What is it?"

"Well, why are some counties in Ulster part of Northern Ireland, and some part of the South? It's not just because some are Protestant and some are Catholic, is it?"

"Not entirely, darling, and that is what we are all working at. People like your father and I think all of Ulster should come and join us in a united Ireland, whether they are Catholic or Protestant, because we all are Irish, after all."

"But when I look at a map, I don't know which is which."

"Three of the counties, Monaghan, Cavan, and Donegal, are part of the province of Ulster, but since most of the people there are Catholic, it was agreed that those three counties would remain with the South. That still leaves a lot of Catholics in the Northern counties of Tyrone and Fermanagh who would like to join us, and many in Armagh and County Down, too, so we're hoping that we can bring most of them in with us, but the boundaries will be difficult to draw."

"But, Uncle Mick, what about the people who want to stay with England? What would they do?"

Before anyone could answer her, Tim cleared his throat and began to recite:

What answer from the North?
  One Law, one Land, one Throne.
  If England drive us forth
  We shall not fall alone!

Everyone remained quiet for a few moments, until Maureen asked, "That's Kipling's poem 'Ulster' is it not?"

Tim explained, "Ay. He was a favourite of the British soldiers I met at Gallipoli. I picked it up from them."

Michael responded, "They would favour him. Personally, I prefer Yeats and Wilde, but old Rudyard's poem shows what we're up against. You can see how complicated it all is, Nelly."

"Yes, I think so," she said softly, but she was still troubled. "Then what about the Catholics in the North who would rather join with the South but are left behind?"

"That's as shrewd a question as I've ever been asked and one that hasn't bothered more minds than it should have. Those Catholics will remain in Northern Ireland, but I am doing my best to protect them, and I have plans to that end," Michael added, somewhat mysteriously. He checked his watch, stood up and stretched, and said, "Come on, Joe. Time to make our way back to today's session, though I suspect that's why Tim has showed up."

"Heh-heh. The car's downstairs."

---

16 DECEMBER 1921, LONDON, HOUSE OF LORDS

AT NOON THAT DAY, BIRKENHEAD TOOK HIS PLACE ON THE WOOLSACK, and just as he had the previous two days, sat there silently with his head bowed, concentrating intensely on the various Lords' speeches, while to all appearances he seemed to be dozing. Up in the Visitors' Gallery, Lady Lavery followed the proceedings, slightly bored, as she was only there to hear her friend F.E. give what would most likely be the ultimate speech of the session before a vote on the Treaty was to be taken.

After a while, F.E. suddenly sat upright with a start, checked his watch, and wordlessly slipped away from the chamber.

"Wherever could he be going at a time like this?" Lady Lavery asked a companion.

Where F.E. was going was to the American Luncheon Club at the Savoy Hotel, where he had a long-standing commitment to speak, and once outside the House of Lords, he hopped into a car he had pre-arranged for the occasion. Rushing into the meeting at the Savoy, he was greeted with much applause and a warm greeting from the American Ambassador, who introduced him by declaring, "The Lord Chancellor's participation in Irish peacemaking proves the maxim that great occasions find great men. His presence here today, on perhaps the most momentous day in his illustrious career, is a most flattering compliment to all of us gathered here."

F.E. thanked his host and the guests and spoke in broad generalities about the friendship and shared values held in common by the Americans and the British. Not until the end of his brief address did he mention the auspicious events of the day.

"Today marks a day that can never be forgotten in the history of the English-speaking peoples. I know of no quarrel, actual or potential, or discernible by the most acute eye, among them. I *knew* of one—the spectre of the old Irish quarrel. I don't know yet whether we have laid that spectre, but if we are successful in this task, we shall have done more to banish the last trench in which misunderstanding might have lurked than our predecessors accomplished in the past two centuries.

"Now, if you'll excuse me, I have another commitment which you are possibly acquainted with. However, I cannot leave you without thanking everyone gathered here for sending me on my way greatly strengthened by your good wishes as I go to face my Philippi."[6]

All the guests burst into laughter but rose to give him another ovation as he shook hands with the Ambassador and swiftly left.

Once outside, his driver opened the door for him and commented, "That did not take long, sir."

"I kept it as short as an American's attention span," he replied as he got in the back of the car. "Now, step on it."

---

16 December 1921, Dublin, Dáil Morning Private Session [7]

. . .

THE MORNING SESSION OPENED JUST BEFORE NOON THAT DAY, AND Cathal Brugha rose to address the issue brought up two days earlier about the Army. "I have been asked as the Minister of Defence what I intend to do as regards rumours that are going around to the effect that certain Deputies of this body from Cork City and County are to be shot if they do not vote against the ratification of the Treaty. I would like everyone to realise that I cannot deal with rumours. As long as I am Minister of Defence, there is going to be discipline in the Army."

Although these genuine threats were disparaged as mere rumours, there was much applause with cries of "Hear, hear!" and the subject ended there.

A while later the proceedings took a nasty, personal turn when Brugha again rose to speak. "Will you give me two or three minutes? I can forgive the five men who have landed us into the present position because I realised before they went there the terrible influence that would be brought to bear upon them. We have got the proof of that."

Gavan Duffy was incensed at this new accusation and demanded, "Where is it?"

Michael, too, was furious. "On a point of order, Mr. Chairman, please, I must insist on this. It is for us to explain our mental condition in London, not for somebody else."

Cries of "Hear, hear!" again filled the hall, but Brugha's voice rose above the din, "Will you kindly listen to me without interruption, and anybody who has any explanation to make can do so at the proper time. I have heard Mr. Lloyd George referred to as the 'wizard from Wales' without properly understanding what was intended by it, but I have got a proof of his wizardry in what has happened within the last fortnight. We have the chairman of the delegation, an honest man as I know him to be, coming along the day before yesterday and telling us that this thing was freedom. I say that Mr. Lloyd George, who is the wizard, has cast a spell over the chairman of our delegation and has put him into such a stupor that he does not know the difference between this document and freedom. It is obvious no offence was intended. We heard the Minister for Finance confess yesterday that he was in a fog."

Michael answered testily, "That is not so."

Beyond that, he held his tongue while Arthur rose to his defence.

"There was, I think, an understanding arrived at that we should avoid personalities as much as possible in this place."

Brugha countered impetuously, "There were statements made about me."

His voice rising in anger, Arthur answered back, "There has been a gross personal attack made here on one man. There have been most offensive statements made about members of this delegation." Directing his wrath at Brugha, he went on, "I say I do not need his forgiveness. I do not ask his forgiveness. I have done nothing that I have not a right to do, and I have done nothing which I believe is inconsistent with the honour and interests of my country. I shall not ask or seek any man's forgiveness for the action which I took. An attempt has been made undoubtedly to represent the Cabinet as standing firm and immovable on the rock of the Irish Republic and to show that we were the people who went to London and let them down. Now the documents are before you. Base your judgement not on what any man says, but on these documents. That is what I ask you to do."

Michael continued this argument, turning to address Eoin MacNeill, "Mr. Speaker, one statement was made that I said I was in a fog. That statement is incorrect. What I did say was that I was constantly being befogged by constitutional and legal arguments on cases and points which I did not understand, which I do not now understand."

MacNeill was dismayed by these personal attacks and fairly lost his temper, banging his gavel and declaring, "I am not going to stand much more of this, and I don't believe the country will stand much more of it. I am an Irish Republican now, and I am going to remain one. So are we all. Isn't that so?" Acknowledging an outburst of applause, he went on, "Yes, and there are no Dominion Home Rulers here, not one, and there is not going to be one, no matter what any person reads out of it. Isn't that unanimous?" Taking the ensuing applause as an affirmation, he said, "Very well then, aren't we wasting our time with a lot of nonsense?"

Now de Valera became angry and cried out, "I must protest the Speaker of the House making a speech which is prejudicial to what is a most important question, because he tried to make it a question of persons."

Fed up, MacNeill rose and said, "I leave the Chair then. Before I leave the Chair, you will carry out the arrangements you have made already with regard to handing back those documents."

With that, he left the room.

---

16 December 1921, London, House of Lords, Birkenhead Speech [8]

Lady Lavery was chatting with her friend when Birkenhead returned to the House of Lords. "Oh, look, his Lordship is back," she said facetiously. "I wonder what the hell he's been up to."

Birkenhead resumed his position on the Woolsack and again assumed his thoughtful pose, listening to more criticisms of the Treaty and his part in it. When at last he rose to speak, a messenger rushed over to the Commons, bowing low along the front bench as he approached Lloyd George and whispered in his ear as some Member was droning on about the faults of the Treaty.

"Thank you," The Prime Minister replied and leaned over to Churchill. "The Lord Chancellor is about to speak, Winston. Shall we?"

"Yes, *please*. I feel myself succumbing to ennui with this anaemic harangue, and F.E. would be the perfect antidote. Besides, we have time before our division. Coming Austen?"

They hurried along the hall to the House of Lords, followed by a stream of other House Members to hear F.E. bring the proceedings to a climactic ending. Rather than resuming the robust, jocular tone he had just employed at the luncheon he had just addressed, he now stood before the House and began with a blank expression on his face and a quiet tone in his voice to deliver an apology to the House that was also an underhanded slight to one Lord in particular.

"My Lords, my first task should be to apologise to your Lordships for having absented myself for more than an hour in the middle of the day from my place upon the Woolsack. I had understood it was the proposal of your Lordships to adjourn for the luncheon interval, and I, therefore, thought myself at liberty to keep an old-standing engagement. My apologies are particularly due to the noble and learned Lord, Lord Sumner, whose speech, for the reason indicated, I was so unfortunate as to miss."

A careful listener would not have missed the sarcasm, particularly his newly arriving friends from Commons, whom he acknowledged with the slightest glimmer of a smile. He quickly followed with an understatement. "This debate has been a very remarkable one. It has continued now for three days. It has ranged over the widest possible variety of subjects, and it has been contributed to by almost every section of opinion in this House.

"The noble Lord, Lord Carson, on whose speech it will be necessary for me to say more hereafter, told us that we dare not consult the country upon these proposals. Is he quite sure that we dare not? It is sometimes unwise to utter these taunts too confidently, and the development of circumstances can easily put into a position of absurdity those who make them with so much assurance.

"I say plainly there is much in that instrument which I would have arranged differently had I the power. There is much in that instrument which would have assumed an entirely different form of expression if my colleagues and I had been able to impress our views upon those with whom we negotiated.

"But what do your Lordships imagine that we were doing for three months? Strange as it may seem, we were negotiating."

Churchill and Lloyd George smiled slightly at this revelation, nodding as F.E. added, "When you negotiate, you exchange opinions, you balance suggestions, you consider what is vital to the one party, and you weigh it against that which seems to be vital to the other. It is by this process, the only possible process, that one discovers in the end whether that which emerges after all these processes is, upon balance and upon the whole, is the best that is attainable in the existing and evident difficulties, and that which we should recommend, as we do today, not without heart searching, not without anxiety, to Parliament.

"The noble Marquess, Lord Londonderry, in a speech which he made yesterday, and to which I listened with deep attention, spoke of utterances which I have made in the old days of this controversy. I listened to them with a very considerable degree of composure. It is unquestionably true that some of those quotations, which his industry had unearthed, were expressed in a livelier fashion than I should, in my present condition, unless I am in a condition of cerebral excitement, repeat." This self-effacement was met with ripples of laughter. "It may be that they owe something to the atmosphere in which they were uttered, but I say here perfectly plainly that I recede not by one iota from the position which I assumed throughout the whole of those old bitter controversies. I do not recall one act that I would undo here and now if I could, and I only recall one or two incautious expressions which I would have put in another way if I had recollected that when I was Lord Chancellor they would be quoted against me in this House."

When another wave of laughter subsided, Birkenhead resumed, still calm and expressionless. "We had another contribution to our discussion, one which was made by the noble and learned Lord, Lord Carson. I shall be forgiven for saying that it was a very remarkable performance. The noble and learned Lord has publicly repelled and proscribed me from a friendship which had many memories for me, and which I deeply value. The noble and learned Lord can do that— no one can prevent him—but he cannot deprive me of memories indissolubly bound up in the past, when we ran common risks, and in speech and act I matched and was glad to match the risks that he ran."

Then referring to another Marquess, Lord Salisbury, who had also spoken earlier in the debate, he said, "The noble Marquess says that we are prevented by circumstances from carrying out our pledges. In the jaundiced view of the noble Marquess, we are weak puppets, kicked about from one crisis to another, with instability of purpose and insecurity of conscience. We are not, indeed, supermen, Napoleons; we do not belong to the class to which the noble Marquess in that respect belongs. It is perfectly true that we have changed our minds more than once in the last three years, and, for all I know, we may, on these and other matters, change our minds again."

This frank admission was met with more cheers and laughter.

"We, at any rate, realise this—we who have handled the burden and responsibility of the last three years—that we live in a changed world. Our difficulties lie in attempting to convince the mediaevalists among us that the world has really undergone some very considerable modification in the last few years. The noble Marquess, Lord Salisbury, says that he, too, is a Home Ruler now, and shares our turpitude to that extent, but he does not indicate what particular form of Home Rule he intends to honour with his support, or what particular body of people he thinks he will succeed in persuading of the merits of his scheme. As for the speech of the noble and learned Lord Carson, as a constructive effort of statecraft, it would have been immature upon the lips of a hysterical schoolgirl."

This derisive taunt brought the house down. While the assembled

Lords were convulsed in laughter, the division bells rang out, summoning the M.P.s back to the House.[9]

"Oh, damn," Lloyd George exclaimed, "just when this was getting really good."

Birkenhead paused before continuing, but remained expressionless, only glancing slightly at Lloyd George and Churchill as he patiently waited for them and the other Members to leave. Upstairs in the gallery, Lady Lavery whispered to her friend, "This is it. They're returning for their vote on the Treaty in the House of Commons."

Then, as if nothing had happened, Birkenhead said, "Now I am asked by the representatives from Ulster: 'Is it because you have not the courage and the heart to go on with this quarrel that you are surrendering?' I confess that I am not much impressed by this representation. Three years only have passed since we drove the mightiest military power in the world in flight from before our trenches, at a moment when our Armies were stiffening the Italian Army, sweeping the Turk from Palestine, and storming the Bulgarian heights. This country raised more millions in soldiers than there are men, women and children of all ages in Ireland. Are we then to be told that we cannot accept this Agreement because we are making ourselves parties to national change and national humiliation? Is it not the truth that those who are great can afford to do great things in a great way?

"I observed, while I was making these remarks, the noble and learned Lord, Lord Carson, making common cause with the noble and learned Lord Salisbury who sits in front of him, and perhaps it interested me to see these two noble and learned Lords, who take such divergent views, making common cause."

Carson challenged him, calling out, "So are you and the Sinn Féiners."

Birkenhead silenced him with a caustic suggestion. "Would the noble and learned Lord desire me to give way to him? It is customary in this House for only one speaker to address the House at a time." With a brief shake of his head feigning umbrage, he said, "To continue, one noble and learned Lord alleges that we are treacherous scoundrels for entering into negotiations at all, and the other is of the opinion that we are incorrigible fools for not having undertaken them two years ago.

"I am asked whether I hold out any confident hope to your Lordships that this arrangement will succeed, and I wish upon that matter to speak very cautiously. The Irish people are a very strange, wayward, incalculable people. Nobody can ever say confidently whether they will do this or whether they will do the other thing in an unexpected contingency, but of this I am sure, that for the first time, with due and, as I think, adequate protection of the legitimate interests of Ulster, we have given a population which is overwhelmingly homogeneous an opportunity of taking its place side by side with the other communities which compose the British Empire. Now, that is an immense moment in history."

WHILE BIRKENHEAD WAS SPEAKING, THINGS WERE MOVING QUICKLY across the hall in the House of Commons. The voting proceeded as Members walked through one of the two division lobbies on either side of the House and gave their names to the division clerks at the end of the respective lobbies to record their votes. After the tallies were complete, the Members returned to their seats, and the teller called out the result, repeated by the Speaker.

"The Ayes to the right, 401. The Noes to the left, 58. The Ayes have it."

With that, the House approved the Truce.

"Congratulations, Prime Minister," Winston beamed.

"Shall we, Winston?" Lloyd George asked.

"Certainly. We may have time yet to hear the end of F.E.'s speech."

The same procedure as earlier followed, only this time F.E. did not pause but smiled ever so slightly at Winston, who, as he returned, signalled success in Commons with a thumbs up.

"They are, as was said by Mr. Churchill yesterday in another place," he continued, "an ancient people, they are a people who are as entitled as anybody else to have all the respect that can be paid to that part of the country which is homogeneous, and which takes a pride in its nationhood and in its history." Churchill was delighted at this reference to his own speech, which he acknowledged with a nod and a grin.

"We believe that there is a chance that this settlement which we propose will satisfy that sentiment in the minds of the overwhelming majority of the citizens of Southern Ireland. If it does, what will happen if it does, we shall see year by year the disappearance of those animosities which have poisoned our national life and weakened our national effort for several hundreds of years. Now, let me say here and now, at the expense of incurring the censures of the noble and learned Lord and others, that I have formed a clear view as to the intentions and dispositions of the men with whom for so long we negotiated. I ask nobody else to accept that view from me; one must form these impressions for oneself; one may be right or one may be wrong. But when we are told that we ought not to have gone into a Conference at all, one very remarkable circumstance emerges. Who set us the example of discussion with these men? It was the insight and the statesmanship of Sir James Craig which first realised that no lasting peace could come about in Ireland unless there was discussion between himself and the representatives of Southern Ireland, and he went, long before we had our Conference, and had a conversation with Mr. de Valera in Dublin."

Here Lord Londonderry rose to make the same point made the day earlier during Churchill's speech, "I think I ought to draw attention to this, that the invitation came from Mr. de Valera, and not from Sir James Craig, as the noble and learned Lord seems to imply."

Birkenhead, apparently ignorant of the same correction made the previous day in Commons, answered, "To be perfectly honest, I thought it did come from Sir James Craig, but it was equally creditable to have lain in either case. He realised that this old, bloody, unhappy quarrel cannot be carried on indefinitely, that some time or other there must come peace. And of those who criticise us most bitterly today I would ask this plain question—Is your alternative any other than this, that we shall now resume the war, that we shall take and break this people, as we can with our military strength take and break them? And, when we have done that, how shall we be any better off? Shall we be any nearer a settlement than when Lord Salisbury, if he becomes Prime Minister tomorrow, has raised the Army, has carried fire and sword into every village in Ireland, and has finally brought back a new laurel to add to the military standards of the great war? When all that has been achieved shall we be any nearer an Irish settlement? There is no one listening to me now who does not know that at the conclusion of that war, with memories a thousand times more bitterly inflamed, you would then—Lord Salisbury would have to do then, what we have done now—have to enter into negotiations with these people, to define the conditions under which they and we will live our lives in these islands.

"Let us give this vote, not indeed in a spirit of light and easy optimism, but nevertheless let us be bold to give it in a spirit of high hope. I am, indeed, expectant that, in one form or another, the sanction of the people of Ireland will be given to this proposal by an overwhelming majority, and that they, too, will share in the sentiments of the civilised world which the noble and learned Lord thought proper in this connection to disparage and to decry.

"It is not only in the Dominions. In every country in the world in which these old islands of ours have got friends this settlement has been hailed with acclamation and with enthusiasm. And I would invite your Lordships to vote tonight with a deep sense of responsibility—not confidently, but still hoping that we shall see in the future an Ireland which will at last, after centuries, be reconciled with this country, an Ireland to which both the contrasted systems will make each its own splendid and individual contributions, and an Ireland which will sit when the Dominions meet at 10 Downing Street to decide, according to the evolutionary organisation of the British Empire, the supreme issues of policy which affect the fortunes of that Empire, and the Prime Minister of Ireland, an equal by the side of equals, will lift up his voice to support and give expression to the historic destinies and the rightful influence of that unhappy country."

There was an outburst of cheering at the conclusion of the speech. One Lord who had risen to criticise the Treaty the day before shook his head and said to a like-minded friend, "That was the most wonderful speech I have ever heard."

"Yes, very impressive. Look around; its effect is obvious. We will lose this vote."

As required, Churchill and the other visitors left the Chamber before the vote was taken, and outside in the hall, he was met by his friend, H.A.L. Fisher. "The Lord Chancellor quite outdid himself today, wouldn't you say, Winston? And right on the heels of your speech yesterday."

"He was, as always, magnificent!"

"A fine piece of insolent invective," Fisher replied. "Cogent in argument, rich in feeling, powerful in pleading. I hope our friends in Dublin are equally persuasive."[10]

Churchill's brow darkened at the mention of the debate in the Dáil. "Yes, I worry about the pace of the proceedings there. It does not bode well, nor do these reports of continued killings of British soldiers in Ireland."

Just then, Lady Lavery came up to him and grabbed his arm, "Winston, dear, wasn't F.E. superb?"

Winston brightened up at the pleasant interruption. "Oh, Hazel, my dear. Yes, he was in top form today, wasn't he? I'm glad you were able to hear him speak."

Fisher smiled at Hazel, "Lady Lavery, always lovely to see you, but if you will excuse me." He left to say hello to some other friends.

Winston turned back to Lady Lavery, took her gently by the arm, and asked, "Hazel, if I may have a word."

Intrigued, she walked with him a few steps away from the crowd. "What is it, Winston?"

"I have had some troubling reports of continued attacks on R.I.C. and British officers across Ireland, in the North as well as the South, and this will only serve to make the situation here untenable. Hazel, you and Sir John certainly are on amicable terms with Michael Collins, and I was hoping you might send him word on the matter and try to impress upon him the importance of putting a stop to these murderous adventures."

"Of course, Winston. I'll write to him today."

"That's very good of you."

"No, thank you for entrusting me with such an important task. You know how desirous John and I are of peace in Ireland for all."

"Yes, of course. That's why I venture to impose on you."

Austen Chamberlain came along, and after greetings were exchanged all around, he asked, "Excuse me, Winston, but I was wondering if I could steal Lady Lavery away from you."

"By all means. Good day, Hazel, and thank you."

"Good day, Winston, and thank you!"

Chamberlain turned back, "Now, Hazel, why don't you join my wife and me for lunch?"

"Oh, I'd love to."

"Splendid! And there is so much to talk about today, now, isn't there?" As they walked away, he said, "Now that the Treaty has passed Commons and seems about to do the same in Lords, we can turn our attention to Dublin. You know, Arthur and I have such high hopes, well, I should say, expectations from our friend Michael. He is a fine young man. Extraordinary fellow, with so much wit and enthusiasm. If you write to him, please send my regards."[11]

---

16 December 1921, Dublin, Dáil Afternoon and Evening Sessions
12

LATER THAT DAY MICHAEL LISTENED ATTENTIVELY TO A SPEECH BEING given by the Dáil delegate from Leitrim, James Dolan.

"Now, there is great talk here about the Oath that has been inserted in this Treaty and which the members of the Government of the Free State are asked to take. I will read the Oath in order to refresh the memory of everybody. *I do solemnly swear true faith and allegiance to the Constitution of the Irish Free State as by law established and that I will be faithful to H.M. King George V, his heirs and successors by law, in virtue of the common citizenship of Ireland with Great Britain and her adherence to and membership of the group of nations forming the British Commonwealth of Nations.* To my mind, that Oath is no different in substance to the oath suggested by our President when giving his last recommendation to these men going to the council chamber to tussle with the delegates of the British Empire. We are told that the difference was very little, merely a shadow, but that he was prepared to make or break on that shadow. I put it to you, the representatives of the people of this country, are you prepared, as the Minister of Defence has said we will have to do, are you prepared to ask the men and women of Ireland to stand up and fight for what? For a shadow? For a quibble of words, I say, not for a principle."[13]

Michael leaned over to Arthur to say, "Nice turn of a phrase, that. A quibble of words. I couldn't agree more."

Arthur agreed, but not everyone saw it that way. Kathleen O'Callaghan, a delegate from Limerick, raised a very logical quibble. "I understand that the Oath of Allegiance to the Free State was the oath in honour of the Free State and was an oath of fidelity in virtue of common citizenship to the head of the Government. I find that Mr. Lloyd George, in his speech on Wednesday, says that under the Treaty, he has secured an Oath of Allegiance to the British King and the British Empire. Mr. Churchill says the same. How are we to interpret this article?"

One delegate suggested, "Refer it to a constitutional lawyer as to our position under the Treaty and the application of the Oath. It is a reasonable suggestion. We are not lawyers."

Michael spoke up in answer, "I think Mr. Duggan took a legal opinion from a lawyer on it. He could give the opinion."

Eamonn rose in response. "I did. It was my own opinion also. Members of Parliament are required to swear an Oath of Allegiance to the Constitution of the Irish Free State. This is the one thing absolutely clear about the Oath. They then say they will be faithful to the King and his successors, not absolutely and unconditionally, but by virtue of the common citizenship of Ireland with Great Britain and her adherence to the group of nations forming the British Commonwealth. That is the legal interpretation of one of the lawyers working with the delegation."

Unfortunately, that did not end it, and the arguing went back and forth between Griffith and Austin Stack until Michael could not take any more. He rose to complain, "I have not heard a single word this afternoon that might not be said more profitably at a public session."

This observation didn't help push the meeting any closer to an end of private debate, but soon they all took a short break.

Eamonn Duggan joined Michael for a cup of tea and whispered to him, "You know, Michael, there is another matter we ought to discuss in private session. These reported attacks on the R.I.C. are not going to look very good."[14]

Michael nodded in agreement, "No, I suppose you're right, Eamonn. You had better bring them up."

Duggan did so when the session resumed, saying, "I think this is a matter that is urgent. Within the past three days there have been six members of the British Crown forces shot in different parts of the country. Two of these were killed: a British officer was shot at Ballybunion; on the 14th an R.I.C. sergeant was shot dead and a constable wounded near Kilmallock. That thing is spreading and reprisals will ensue."

Not much, if anything, was made of this development, but as Michael feared, more tedious procedural discussions ensued over whether the Dáil should remain in private session or finally move to a public session. At one point he finally cried out, "Let us talk about this thing in public for the next ten years if we like, but let us talk in public."

Even that plea did not help, and a while later de Valera again brought the discussion back to his pet disagreement. "I would not take that Oath if I could help it. We talk of all this in private session. It is obvious that that is not something to go outside."

Then he took a remarkable turn with a new argument. "There is only one thing, and I hope you will not consider it a personal matter though it might seem so. I hold in myself two offices. In my own person I combine two offices. One is President of this assembly, and by courtesy—I don't know whether it is legal—I am also President of the Republic. Now it is obvious that if the Treaty is ratified and if Mr. Griffith is allowed to govern, he could not very well be called President of the Republic, but only Prime Minister. Certainly not with a Treaty requiring allegiance to the King. I know that most of you will vote for the ratification of the Treaty."

Michael was astonished at this admission, but before he could take any comfort in it, de Valera rambled on somewhat disconsolately about his reputation as President and the ensuing spectre of renewed war. Then after a brief discussion about the agenda for the next day, the day's meeting finally came to a close.

"It's nearly nine o'clock," Arthur remarked. "Another late dinner tonight, eh, Mick?"

Michael smiled as he answered, "Yes, Mr. Prime Minister. Care to join me at the Gresham for a late supper?"

Arthur laughed and said, "No, I'll never get to sleep if I eat again now. And please, don't call me that. Dev is the one with an overriding interest in titles, not I. Anyway, aren't you just jumping the gun a little?"

"Not at all. Didn't you hear Dev? Most of the delegates are going to vote for the Treaty. I wish I could be so assured of the result. The longer this drags on, the less our chances are of winning, I'm afraid."

"Yes, the initial euphoria seems to have dissipated through these endless squabbles." Then Arthur paused and said in exasperation, "Ridiculous!"

"I wonder how the votes in Parliament went today."

Michael turned to see Joe O'Reilly rushing over. "Something tells me Joe knows the answer to that, right Joe?"

"If you mean the news from London, yes, we just got a telegram with the results. G'evening, Arthur." For once, Michael didn't berate him for not coming right to the point, as he could see Joe was bursting to tell him.

"The House voted overwhelmingly in favour, and the Lords by a large margin."

Well-pleased, Michael slapped his thigh and exclaimed, "Well, that is grand. So, Winston came through as promised. However," he added mordantly, "now that they have finished their quibbling in Parliament, it would seem we are just getting started with it here."

"That reminds me, Michael, when Cathal said you had confessed to having been in a fog, I could barely contain my temper. The temerity, twisting your words like that."

"Yes, and, by the way, wasn't that a dramatic exit by Eoin earlier in the day? It looks like his temper got the better of him."

"And for drama, what about the Chief admitting most will vote for the Treaty?"

"I'm starting to worry about that," Michael replied. "I'd say Limerick, for example, could go either way. Kathleen O'Callaghan had a reasonable enough question about the Oath, but there's no doubting which way *she's* leaning."

ONE HUNDRED THIRTEEN

Talk the Teeth Out Of a Saw

SATURDAY, 17 DECEMBER 1921, DUBLIN

Dáil Private Session [1]

THE SATURDAY MORNING SESSION STARTED WITH EOIN MACNEILL retaking the Speaker's Chair after having left it so abruptly the day before. He was about to make a statement, but Cathal Brugha immediately rose to register a protest.

"Sir, before we begin the work of the day, I wish to make a statement. Just when we were concluding the proceedings yesterday before the interval, you made what I cannot describe any other way than as a partisan harangue. I wish now to get an undertaking from you that this will not be repeated; otherwise, I will object to your occupying that Chair during the proceedings here today or on Monday."

Although the preceding day's proceedings had reached a very rancorous level before he had interjected himself into the debate, MacNeill probably felt partially responsible for worsening the situation and had already prepared some remarks. He addressed the assembly in a clear, loud voice.

"It was my intention before the Minister for Defence rose to speak and before I would call on anyone to speak, to make a statement with regard to the statement which I made here from the Chair yesterday. Several of the most respected members of this assembly have also said to me that the statement I made from the Chair was a partisan statement. I can say plainly when the representation was made to me that the concluding portion of my statement could be held as bringing in a matter of argument on one particular side with regard to the course of the discussion which took place, I admit that, and I apologise to the Dáil for it. In making that apology, I hope you will all recognise it was not my interest to make a partisan statement. If what I have said has not satisfied the members of the Dáil, first of all, my regret for having said anything which could possibly bear the imputation of partiality, and secondly, my sincere desire to conduct the affairs of this assembly with impartiality. If anything can be suggested that remains for me to say in order to satisfy you on that point, I will say it."

The sheer honesty of this apology touched everyone and was greeted with a great round of applause that continued as Brugha responded graciously, "I am fully satisfied on the matter."

Then one of the members directed a question at Brugha. "One question I have is how long in the opinion of those responsible for defences would our Army hold against the British Army in the case of warfare being waged upon us?"

Brugha hedged his answer somewhat, saying, "At a moment's notice, I would not take it on myself to answer that question definitely. I may, if you think it necessary for me to do so, later on give a more definite reply but just now, what I do say is this. We are in a very much better position militarily than we were when the Truce started."

Michael, who knew the true relative strength of the Army, muttered, "Does he really believe that? He more than anyone should know better."

When Seán MacEoin had a chance to speak, he returned to Brugha's statement. "We are told by the Minister of Defence that the Army is in a much stronger position, infinitely stronger now than it was before the Truce. It may be stronger in some points. In point of members, it is a bit stronger; in training, it is a bit stronger, and there were two members of Purchases who were not idle during the Truce."

Arthur turned to Michael and whispered, asking as much as confirming, "One of them being Seán MacBride?"

Michael gave him a slight nod.

Then MacEoin delivered the news that disproved Brugha's contentions about army strength. "I know perfectly well I have charge of four thousand men. I do not here hesitate to say that number. But of that four thousand, I have a rifle for every fifty."

Many members gasped at this acknowledgement and MacEoin's following statement. "Furthermore, the British know now every officer and man from one end of Ireland to the other."

A COUPLE OF HOURS LATER WHEN THEY BROKE FOR LUNCH, MICHAEL found Batt O'Connor waiting for him in the lobby. "Fancy a bite, Michael?"

"I could use some sustenance, and not just food. Let's go."

They walked to a restaurant on Leeson Street Lower, but Batt asked, "Would you prefer a quick pub lunch?"

"No, Batt. I need a proper meal. This will do nicely."

After they ordered, Batt asked, "So, Michael, where do we stand?"

"Hard to say. Dev is still holding out for his External Association, a classic work of political sophistry if ever there was one."

"Which Lloyd George slapped down the second he heard it, if I remember correctly from what you told me."

Michael smiled sardonically, "Yes, he did, and the second, third, and fourth time he heard it. But that has no effect on Dev. He wants us to submit his proposals to the British still again, ignoring the fact they've already debated the Treaty and approved it."

"Still hanging on to his 'Document No. 2,' is he?" Batt asked.

"That he is."

"Hmm. Dev had two or three versions of the Oath before your last trip back to London, but I noticed there doesn't seem to be one in his Document No. 2."

"See, Batt, I always knew you to benefit from a sharp eye."

"Thanks, but I wouldn't be much of a builder without one."

"True, but God only knows how an agreement lacking an Oath would ever get through an English Parliament."

"Well, Michael, we always found Dev difficult to fathom."

"And simply difficult." Batt laughed as Michael added, "Try fathoming this: he said that if we had brought the Treaty back before signing, it would be subject to Cabinet policy, but—I swear these are his own words—there is no question of majority rule in the Cabinet, none whatever."[2]

"Imagine him saying that! Lord protect us." Batt thought for a second and said, "You know, Michael, your opponents are canvassing extensively in the country and pressure is even being brought to bear on the Army."

"I know, Batt. In fact, this was brought up during the debate. I won't have any of it, and I won't allow any of my supporters to approach the Army to try and influence the Dáil. I'll defend the Treaty there and explain its provisions and my reasons for accepting it. After that, the people can take it or leave it."

"But once the Dáil decides, surely Dev would accept their final say."

"Would he?"

"Do you have any sense where the votes are?"

"It seems evenly divided. I can't tell which way it will go." Michael looked up to the waiter who had just arrived with plates of food. "Let's enjoy this."

After their lunch Batt said, "Well, thanks for enlightening me on the situation again, Michael. Do you see an end to these debates?"

"Sure, but tonight's will be the last private session. Almost everyone has had his say by now. The public debates resume on Monday."

"That at least is something. Would you like to meet for a nightcap later this evening?"

"Sorry, at the rate we're going, the pubs will be long closed by the time we're done."

"Good luck, then, and get some rest on Sunday."[3]

―――――――

DURING THE NEXT SESSION BREAK, MICHAEL WENT TO THE LOBBY TO find Joe O'Reilly waiting for him. "Howaya, Mick. I've brought you some mail."

"Thanks, Joe. Anything look interesting?"

"Yes, actually. A couple of letters postmarked London, one from Lady Lavery and one from Edward Marsh. Who would that be, Mick?"

"Eddie is Churchill's secretary. Nice enough fella. Come, have a cuppa with me. I need a lift."

In need of a lift himself, Arthur Griffith stopped by and asked, "You seem to have found something to raise your spirits, Mick. What is it?"

"News from Hazel and Eddie Marsh. Let's go over these letters together, shall we?"

They helped themselves to some tea and biscuits that had been laid out and settled down in some chairs.

Joe asked cautiously, "Would you prefer to have some privacy?"

"What? No, relax," Michael assured him. "First, let's see what news from London Hazel sends." He read and summarised, "She writes that she went to hear Winston's speech, that it was very long but excellent, well received, excepting of course by the Tories."

Joe smiled broadly and said, "Except that didn't prevent most of the buggers from voting for the Treaty."

"True enough."

"Yes," Arthur agreed. "I read it, and it was impressive, as was the tally in favour of the Treaty."

Michael read further, chuckled, and explained to Joe, "I became quite friendly with the Prime Minister's Secretary, a funny chap named Philip Sassoon—a bit of an eccentric, but a good sort all the same, and he has a wide sphere of influence, as does Hazel. Let's see, besides mentioning that she had lunch with Lady Fitzalan, the Viceroy's wife, she says that she discussed a matter concerning the Unionist Lord Londonderry. If you'll remember, he had had some hard words for Birkenhead during the debate on the Treaty, but Philip and Hazel think his close relationship with Sir James Craig could be put to some advantage."

"Provided Lloyd George would go along with it," Arthur said.

"Oh, they're all great friends. Hazel says that *thanks to his oriental blood Philip delights in a secret, and he undoubtedly has a certain influence over his illustrious Master,* by whom I assume she means the P.M."

Joe asked, "Sassoon, oriental blood? Is she serious?"

Michael chuckled and said, "Actually, yes. His great-grandfather was the leader of the Baghdadi Jews in Iraq, with significant business concerns there and later in India and China, including the opium trade. Not only that, his mother was from the Rothschild banking family, making him one of the richest men in England." Michael recited more from the letter, "Hazel says of Philip, *He is a clever creature, with imagination and warm towards you—you must get him that dog.* When we were in London, she suggested that I might surprise him with an Irish Blue, but I think she was secretly hoping I'd bring her one. The poor old dog she has is literally on his last legs. Well, that settles it. Next trip over, she'll get her puppy."[4]

Arthur smiled and asked, "More canine diplomacy, eh, Mick?"

"Whatever it takes." Michael flipped over to the envelope from Eddie Marsh, but found inside no letter but another envelope. "That's odd. This one's from Hazel, too. She may have thought it was a safer way of sending it."

As Michael read through it, his brow darkened. Joe asked, "Something wrong?"

Reading through the letter, he murmured, "Hmm. Churchill says…" When he reached the end, he smiled and said with surprise, "Well, what do you know? After all that good news, there's some not so good, and some just nice to hear."

"How so?" Arthur asked.

"The bad news is, Churchill sends his concern over those shootings of the R.I.C. men."

"We shouldn't be surprised," Arthur replied. "It's just as we feared, and just as Duggan warned during yesterday's debate."

"Yes," Michael agreed, skimming further through the letter. "We'll have to deal with that. But here's something you'll appreciate. Hazel also says she had lunch with Austen Chamberlain and his wife, who apparently, well, let me just read it to you. *I lunched with the Austen Chamberlains today and sat next to him.* Here's the amusing bit, well, more charming than funny. *We talked about you, and he spoke most warmly and kindly of both you and Mr. Griffiths.* Well, Arthur, maybe spelling isn't her strong point, but…"

"But she's charming all the same, as is her husband, Sir John."

"Yes, isn't he? He did a nice job of your portrait, didn't he?"

"I must say, I was very flattered to be asked to sit for him. And it was a very flattering painting. I enjoyed their company."

"Well, I'm sure we'll see them again soon." He glanced down at the letter and read again from it, "*I feel you have a true friend in him.*[5] Isn't that something? At first, Chamberlain seemed like such a dry shite, so stiff and formal."

"Yes, and then showed a very kind, considerate side. Well, it's nice of Lady Lavery to pass that along."

Michael looked at his watch and said, "Seven-fifteen. Time to get back to it." Turning to Joe, he said, "No need to wait for me, Joe. I'll catch you up tomorrow or Monday."

ONCE EVERYONE HAD ASSEMBLED, EOIN MACNEILL CALLED ON MARY MacSwiney, whose constituency was Michael's own County Cork. After an interminable day of mind-numbing speechifying, her opening statement did not endear her to Michael.

"At the outset, I should like to say that I must ask from the members of the Dáil for forgiveness if I speak too long."

Michael sighed, "Oh, Sweet Jaysus, have mercy. That woman can talk the teeth out of a saw."

"I stand here tonight in the name of the dead to ask the men of this assembly, and I know I need not ask the women, every one of you to face your consciences tonight to ask yourselves if you are going to disunite this country, to create a split where we had been most perfectly united to all appearances at all events, whether we are going on Monday, before the world, a watching waiting, anxious world, to act together by a large majority so that there need be no questioning if or whether we are going to split this assembly into two halves and drive the country back again for a generation."

Michael muttered, "Where have I heard this before?" He took out his pen and began writing on the sheet of paper before him. He appeared to be taking notes on her speech, as he would occasionally look up at MacSwiney and then go back to his writing. Slightly distracted, Arthur observed him with amusement.

When hours later the last private session finally ended at well past 11 p.m., Michael got up, stretched, and, seeing Seán MacEoin, went over and exclaimed, "I'll tell you, Seán, I'm worn out."

"I am, too, and I have a long drive ahead of me, to boot," Seán yawned and replied.

"I wanted to ask you about that. Are you going to Longford tonight, then? I was so bored; I wrote a letter to Kitty while our Miss MacSwiney was droning on. As soon as she went on 'in the name of the dead,' I could only think of those who *will* die if we don't end this strife." Michael paused and said, "Sorry, about this letter…"

"Would you like me to drop it off with Kitty in Granard?"

"Handsome is as handsome does. Thanks, Seán. I'd love to take a ride with you, but just can't. Please tell Kit I'm sorry I couldn't join you."[6]

"Will do, Mick. Good night."

Michael stepped outside and found Christy and Tim Kelly waiting for him.

Christy stretched and yawned, saying, "Faith, it's almost midnight. We were about to go in to see if the whole Dáil hadn't fallen asleep."

Michael agreed, "You're not far off. Mary MacSwiney had everyone kipping for at least an hour." Michael looked over and saw Pat McCrea dozing at the wheel. "As a matter of fact…" He nodded to Christy and Tim, walked softly to the car, gently opened the door, reached in, and blew the horn.

Pat nearly hit the roof but covered his embarrassment by checking his watch and joking, "11.30, done already?"

Michael laughed and said, "That's right, Pat. Another early night. Come on, Christy, Tim."

They all got in and took off. Pat asked, "Anywhere special, Mick, or straight to the Gresham?"

"The Gresham it is, and you might have to carry me up; I'm so knackered."

Christy asked, "So, a long-winded speech from one of the ladies?"

"Yes, from most of the women delegates, very long speeches, very much against, and very much like Arthur's favourite, Erskine Childers."

"Ah," Tim surmised, "the Women and Childers party."[7]

Tired as he was, Michael couldn't help bursting out laughing and was still wiping the tears away when they reached the hotel. "Ah, thanks, lads. I needed that after the week I've had. Must get my rest for Monday. The public session resumes then, at long last."

ONE HUNDRED FOURTEEN

That's the Stuff!

MONDAY, 19 DECEMBER 1921, DUBLIN

DÁIL PUBLIC SESSION RESUMES [1]

AS HAD BECOME THE NORM SINCE THE TREATY DEBATES FIRST BEGAN, A cheering crowd outside University College greeted delegates from both sides as they showed up for the resumption of the public sessions. Michael, followed discreetly by Joe O'Reilly and Tom Cullen, rushed up the steps with a quick wave of his hat and went inside. Catha Brugha, who, as usual, cycled to the College, was one of the last to arrive that day. He pulled up amidst cheers, left his bicycle off to the side, and hurried up the steps.

When Michael took his seat at the table and slammed his briefcase down on the table, some members of the Press took notice. "Our Mr. Collins isn't looking his usual jovial self this morning, is he, Mr. Dowd?" Robert Harding, the chief reporter of the *Freeman's Journal,* asked his colleague from the *New York Times.*

"No smiles today, Robert. I'd say he's ginning himself up for his speech later."

"I think you're right there, Matthew. Let's listen."[2]

Speaker MacNeill banged his gavel and started the day off with a mostly unwelcome announcement regarding de Valera's Document No. 2. "The President informs the House that the document presented to the Dáil at the Private Session is now withdrawn and must be regarded as confidential until he brings his own proposal forward formally."

Although he suspected such a move on de Valera's part, Arthur Griffith, inwardly seething, rose in polite protest and addressed the Speaker. "Am I to understand, sir, that that document we discussed at the Private Session is to be withheld from the Irish people?"

De Valera answered "No," but by the end of a tortured explanation, it was clear he meant the opposite. "But I don't want to have the debate on the Treaty interfered with by a discussion on a secondary document put forward in Private Session. That document will be put forward in its proper place."

Still, Arthur insisted, "I want to know, is the document we discussed as an alternative to be withheld from the Irish people, or is it to be published in the Press for the people to see?"

MacNeill wanted to move on with the actual debate and said, "We cannot have a discussion on this at this point. We must now proceed with the orders of the day."

Undaunted but growing increasingly angry, Arthur kept demanding, "Are my hands to be tied by this document being withheld after we were discussing it for two days?"

In support of Arthur, Michael rose to say, "I cannot consent, if I am in a minority of one, in withholding from the Irish people my knowledge of what the alternative is. We have to deal with this matter in the full light of our own responsibility to our people, and I cannot refrain from telling the Irish people what certain alternatives are."

De Valera had a further answer, which to his mind, made perfect sense. "It is not proposed to withhold either that document or any documents from the Irish people, if this House wishes it, in its proper place, but I hold it is running across the course of the debate to introduce now for the public a document which has been discussed in Private Session. It means that the Private Session might as well not have been held."

Tom Cullen, now in the visitors' gallery with Joe O'Reilly, whispered to him, "Isn't that just what Mick and Arthur were arguing last week? No Private Sessions! Typical de Valera twisted logic."

"Yes, why bring up something now that only dominated two days of debate?"

MacNeill plodded on, stating, "I wish the members to understand that this is not a matter of the Chair's ruling that this document is confidential. It is simply a matter of a request made by the President and communicated by me to the Dáil, through the ordinary courtesy of procedure, as the President's desire. I do not make any ruling on it, but any discussion on it is out of order. We must proceed now with the orders of the day."

Arthur showed signs of nerves during this dispute but had one final statement on the matter. "It is not a question of courtesy; it is not a question of the rules of procedure; it is a question of the lives and fortunes of the people of Ireland. While so far as I can respect President de Valera's wish, I am not going to hide from the Irish people what the alternative is that is proposed."

Amidst cries of "Hear, hear!" Arthur summoned his self-command, put this exchange behind him and pressed on to the most important order of the day in quiet, even tones.[3] "I move the motion standing in my name—That Dáil Éireann approves of the Treaty between Great Britain and Ireland, signed in London on December sixth, 1921."

Applause and cheers spread through much of the room, though many delegates, anti-Treaty or those still undecided, remained quiet.

"Nearly three months ago Dáil Éireann appointed plenipotentiaries to go to London to treat with the British Government and to make a bargain with them. We have made a bargain. We have brought it back. We were to go there to reconcile our aspirations with the association of the community of nations known as the British Empire. That task which was given to us was as hard as was ever placed on the shoulders of men. We faced that task. We knew that whatever happened, we would have our critics, and we made up our minds to do whatever was right and disregard whatever criticism might occur. We could have shirked the responsibility. We did not seek to act as the plenipotentiaries —other men were asked and other men refused. We went. The responsibility is on our shoulders. We took the responsibility in London, and we take the responsibility in Dublin. I signed that Treaty, not as the ideal thing, but fully believing, as I believe now, it is a treaty honourable to Ireland, and safeguards the vital interests of Ireland."

This was building up to be the greatest speech of his career, and the assembled Dáil members had to have been impressed as he stood before them, his hands pressed to his sides, calmly, earnestly defending his advocacy of the Treaty.

"And now by that Treaty I am going to stand, and every man with a scrap of honour who signed it is going to stand. It is for the Irish people —who are our masters," and at this point, he was again interrupted with strong shouts of "Hear, hear!" He continued, "Who are our masters, not our servants as some think—it is for the Irish people to say whether it is good enough. I hold that it is, and I hold that the Irish people—that ninety-five per cent of them believe it to be good enough. We are here, not as the dictators of the Irish People, but as the representatives of the Irish people, and if we misrepresent the Irish people, then the moral authority of Dáil Éireann, the strength behind it, and the fact that Dáil Éireann spoke the voice of the Irish people is gone, and gone forever. Now, the President—and I am in a difficult position —does not wish a certain document referred to read. But I must refer to the substance of it. An effort has been made to represent that certain men stood uncompromisingly on the rock of the Republic—the Republic, and nothing but the Republic."

Then Arthur made one of the most memorable statements in all the debates. Still looking straight ahead, he calmly observed, "It has been stated also here that the man who won the war—Michael Collins —compromised Ireland's rights."

If Michael was embarrassed by the remarkable compliment inherent in this statement, he showed no emotion. He only looked down at some papers as Arthur continued, "In the letters that preceded the negotiations, not once was a demand made for recognition of the Irish Republic. If it had been made, we knew it would have been refused. We went there to see how to reconcile the two positions, and I hold we have done it. The President does not wish this document to be read. What am I to do? What am I to say? Am I to keep my mouth shut and let the Irish people think about this uncompromising rock?"

De Valera stood up and said, "I will make my position in my speech quite clear."

Ignoring this interruption, Arthur continued as de Valera sat back down, "What we have to say is this, that the difference in this Cabinet and in this House is between half-recognising the British King and the British Empire, and between marching in, as one of the speakers said, with our heads up. The gentlemen on the other side are prepared to recognise the King of England as head of the British Commonwealth. They are prepared to go half in the Empire and half out. They are prepared to go into the Empire for war and peace and treaties, and to keep out for other matters, and that is what the Irish people have got to know is the difference. Does all this quibble of words—because it is merely a quibble of words—mean that Ireland is asked to throw away this Treaty and go back to war? So far as my power or voice extends, not one young Irishman's life shall be lost on that quibble. We owe responsibility to the Irish people. I feel my responsibility to the Irish people, and the Irish people must know, and know in every detail, the difference that exists between us, and the Irish people must be our judges. When the plenipotentiaries came back, they were sought to be put in the dock. Well, if I am going to be tried, I am going to be tried by the people of Ireland." "Hear, hear!"

"Now this Treaty has been attacked. It has been examined with a microscope to find its defects, and this little thing and that little thing has been pointed out, and the people are told—one of the gentlemen said it here—that it was less even than the proposals of July. It is the first Treaty since the reign of Henry II between the representatives of the Irish Government and the representatives of the English Government signed on equal footing. It is the first Treaty that admits the equality of Ireland. It is a Treaty of equality, and because of that, I am standing by it. We have come back from London with that Treaty— *Saorstát na hÉireann* recognised—the Free State of Ireland. We have brought back the flag. After seven hundred years, we have brought back the evacuation of Ireland by British troops and the formation of an Irish army." This declaration elicited applause throughout the hall.

"We have brought back to Ireland her full rights and powers of fiscal control. We have brought back to Ireland equality with England, equality with all nations which form that Commonwealth, and an equal voice in the direction of foreign affairs in peace and war. Well, we are told that that Treaty is a derogation from our status, that it is a Treaty not to be accepted, that it is a poor thing, and that the Irish people ought to go back and fight for something more, and that something more is what I describe as a quibble of words. Now, I shall have an opportunity later on of replying to the very formidably arranged criticism that is going to be levelled at the Treaty to show its defects. At all events, the Irish people are a people of great common sense. They know that a Treaty that gives them their flag and their Free State and their Army is not a sham Treaty, and the sophists and the men of words will not mislead them, I tell you.

"Various different methods of attack on this Treaty have been made. One of them was the British did not mean to keep it. Well, they have ratified it, and it can come into operation inside a fortnight. We think they do mean to keep it if we keep it. They are pledged now before the world, pledged by their signature, and if they depart from it, they will be disgraced, and we will be stronger in the world's eyes than we are today. During the last few years a war was waged on the Irish people, and the Irish people defended themselves, and for a portion of that time, when President de Valera was in America, I had at least the responsibility on my shoulders of standing for all that was done in that defence, and I stood for it." Pausing a moment to acknowledge more applause, he went on, "I would stand for it again under similar conditions. Ireland was fighting then against an enemy that was striking at her life, and was denying her liberty, but in any contest that would follow the rejection of this offer, Ireland would be fighting with the sympathy of the world against her, and with all the Dominions—all the nations that comprise the British Commonwealth—against her.

"The position would be such that I believe no conscientious Irishman could take the responsibility for a single Irishman's life in that futile war. Now, many criticisms, I know, will be levelled against this Treaty. One, in particular, one that is in many instances quite honest, is the question of the Oath. I ask the members to see what the Oath is, to read it, not to misunderstand or misrepresent it. It is an Oath of Allegiance to the Constitution of the Free State of Ireland and of faithfulness to King George V in his capacity as head and in virtue of the common citizenship of Ireland with Great Britain and the other nations comprising the British Commonwealth. That is an oath, I say, that any Irishman could take with honour. He pledges his allegiance to his country and to be faithful to this Treaty, and faithfulness after to the head of the British Commonwealth of Nations. If his country were unjustly used by any of the nations of that Commonwealth, or its head, then his allegiance is to his own country, and his allegiance bids him to resist."

This critical distinction was met with loud approval.

"We took an oath to the Irish Republic, but, as President de Valera himself said, he understood that oath to bind him to do the best he could for Ireland. So do we. We have done the best we could for Ireland. If the Irish people say, 'We have got everything else but the name Republic, and we will fight for it,' I would say to them that they are fools, but I will follow in the ranks. I will take no responsibility.

"This is what we have brought back, peace with England, alliance with England, confederation with England, an Ireland developing her own life, carving out her own way of existence, and rebuilding the Gaelic civilisation. I ask then this Dáil to pass this resolution, and I ask the people of Ireland, and the Irish people everywhere, to ratify this Treaty, to end this bitter conflict of centuries, to end it forever, to take away that poison that has been rankling in the two countries and ruining the relationship of good neighbours. Let us stand as free partners, equal with England, and make after seven hundred years the greatest revolution that has ever been made in the history of the world —a revolution of seeing the two countries standing not apart as enemies, but standing together as equals and as friends. I ask you, therefore, to pass this resolution."

Michael jumped to his feet to join in the standing ovation bestowed upon Arthur. As the applause started to fade, Michael nodded to Seán MacEoin, who paid his respects to Eoin MacNeil as Chairman and Speaker of the Dáil by addressing him by his official title in Irish, "*A Chinn Chomhairle*. I rise to second the motion to approve this Treaty, as proposed by the Deputy for West Cavan and Chairman of the Irish Delegation in London. In doing so, I take this course because I know I am doing it in the interests of my country, which I love. To me, symbols, recognitions, shadows, have very little meaning. What I want, what the people of Ireland want, is not shadows but substances, and I hold that this Treaty between the two nations gives us not shadows but real substances, and for that reason, I am ready to support it."

If MacEoin had been pre-chosen to second Arthur's motion, it was a shrewd choice to have selected one of the most respected military men in the country, the same man Michael had pressured both the British and de Valera to have freed from prison as a prerequisite for accepting the Truce. For these reasons, his words had a palatable impact on the Dáil. "It may seem rather peculiar that one like me who is regarded as an extremist should take this step. Yes, to the world and to Ireland, I say I am an extremist, but it means that I have an extreme love of my country. It was love of my country that made me and every other Irishman take up arms to defend her. It was love of my country that made me ready, and every other Irishman ready, to die for her if necessary. This Treaty brings the freedom that is necessary; it brings the freedom that we all were ready to die for, that is, that Ireland be allowed to develop her own life in her own way, without any interference from any other Government, whether English or otherwise."

As he sat down after this brief speech, he was met with wild applause from around the room.

In a desire to quickly counter this wave of affirmation, de Valera barely acknowledged the Speaker and rose to speak. He stood silently, waiting for the applause for MacEoin to abate.

The *Freeman's* reporter, Robert Harding, muttered, "He looks a little tired, doesn't he?"[4]

"Tired and angry," Matthew Dowd answered.

De Valera glanced around from one end of the house to the other, challenging pockets of applause with a hostile glare until the room finally settled into an uncomfortable silence.[5] After a long pause, he finally addressed the hall, "I think it would scarcely be in accordance with Standing Orders of the Dáil if I were to move directly the rejection of this Treaty. I daresay, however, it will be sufficient that I should appeal to this House not to approve of the Treaty. When the proposal for negotiation came from the British Government asking that we should try by negotiation to reconcile Irish national aspirations with the association of nations forming the British Empire, there was no one here as strong as I was to make sure that every human attempt should be made to find whether such reconciliation was possible. I am against this Treaty because it does not reconcile Irish national aspirations with association with the British Government. I am against this Treaty, not because I am a man of war, but a man of peace."

Some people scoffed at this, but he continued in a bitter tone, "I am against this Treaty because it will not end the centuries of conflict between the two nations of Great Britain and Ireland. We have brought back a thing which will not even reconcile our own people, much less reconcile Britain and Ireland. That document makes British authority our masters in Ireland."

Then, pointing a finger at Michael and Arthur, de Valera claimed defiantly, "These men are subverting the Republic.[6] It would be a surrender which was never heard of in Ireland since the days of Henry II."

Then he continued in an impassioned torrent of words, "I say it is quite within the competence of the Irish people if they wished to enter into an association with other peoples, to enter into the British Empire. It is within their competence if they want to choose the British monarch as their King, but does this assembly think the Irish people have changed so much within the past year or two that they now want to get into the British Empire after seven centuries of fighting? Have they so changed that they now want to choose the person of the British monarch, whose forces they have been fighting against, and who have been associated with all the barbarities of the past couple of years? Have they changed so much that they want to choose the King as their monarch? It is not King George as a monarch they choose; it is Lloyd George, because it is not the personal monarch they are choosing; it is British power and authority as sovereign authority in this country. The sad part of it, as I was saying, is that a grand peace could at this moment be made. I say, for instance, if approved by the Irish people, and if Mr. Griffith, or whoever might be in his place, thought it wise to ask King George over to open Parliament, he would see black flags in the streets of Dublin. Do you think that that would make for harmony between the two peoples? What would the people of Great Britain say when they saw the King accepted by the Irish people greeted in Dublin with black flags? If a Treaty was entered into, if it was a right Treaty, he could have been brought here."

Provoked by this ludicrous speculation, supporters of the Treaty called out, "No, no."

"Yes, he could," he insisted.

"No, no."

"Why not?" he cried out angrily. "I am once more asking you to reject the Treaty for two main reasons, that, as every *Teachta* knows, it is absolutely inconsistent with our position. It gives away Irish independence. It brings us into the British Empire. It acknowledges the head of the British Empire, not merely as the head of an association, but as the direct monarch of Ireland, as the source of executive authority in Ireland." His voice rose in a threatening tone, "The Ministers of Ireland will be His Majesty's Ministers; the Army that Commandant MacEoin spoke of will be His Majesty's Army."

"No, no!"

His temper rising, he answered, "You may sneer at words, but I say words mean something, and I say in a Treaty words do mean something, else why should they be put down? They have meanings, and they have facts, great realities that you cannot close your eyes to. This Treaty means that the Ministers of the Irish Free State will be His Majesty's Ministers..."

More cries of "No, no!"

"...and the Irish Forces will be His Majesty's Forces."

With this final insult to the Army, delegates rose, shouting ever louder, "No, no! Take that back!"

"Well, time will tell, and I hope this Treaty won't have a chance, and that you will throw it out. If you accept it, time will tell…"

His supporters interrupted him with cheers here, but Tom Cullen said to Joe O'Reilly, "Sure, but you're right there, Chief. Time *will* tell."

Raising his voice over all the cheers and protests, de Valera cried out emotionally, "It cannot be one way in this assembly and another way in the British House of Commons. If there are differences of interpretation, we know who will get the best of them. I hold, and I don't mind my words being on record, that the chief executive authority in Ireland is the British Monarch—the British authority. It is in virtue of that authority the Irish Ministers will function." Speaking ever more feverishly, he railed on, "It is to the Commander-in-Chief of the Irish Army, who will be the English Monarch, they will swear allegiance, these soldiers of Ireland."

He paused for a breath, looked anxiously around the room, blinked, and exclaimed, "Parnell said, 'I have no right to say that any man can set boundaries to the march of a nation.' As far as you can, if you take this Treaty, you are…"

Rival cries of "No!" and "Yes!" vied to drown each other out.

"You are presuming to set bounds to the onward march of a nation."

An outburst of applause, mixed with more cries of "No" and "Yes," washed over him as he sat down, pale as a sheet, thoroughly exhausted from his efforts.[7]

Michael remarked to Arthur, "Now, wasn't that quite the holy show?"

"Appalling, as should be this," Arthur answered with a nod in the direction of Austin Stack, who had just risen to speak. Many considered him both haughty and boring, and he did not disappoint with the tone of his delivery.

"It happens to be my privilege to rise immediately after the President to support his motion that this House do not approve of the document which has been presented to them."

Arthur leaned over to Michael and asked, whispering, "You named a lovely terrier, a cherished pet, after this dull, pompous, unutterably futile windbag?"[8]

Stack went on to say, "Now this question of the oath has an

extraordinary significance for me, for, so far as I can trace, no member of my family has ever taken an oath of allegiance to England's King."

Michael listened for a while and finally answered Arthur, "I know. He used to be such a mate." He thought for a second, "Dev, too."

During a long lunch break, de Valera attended a previously arranged ceremony that officially inducted him as chancellor of the National University. When the Dáil reconvened just before four o'clock, there was a heightened sense of expectation in the hall since Michael was scheduled to speak next. The room was full beyond capacity, and in the visitors' area in the rear of the hall, clergy, students, and telegram messengers were packed in together with journalists from England and Ireland and as far away as New York and Tokyo. After de Valera's return, Michael rose, stood at the small table in front of his seat, placed his briefcase down, opened it, pulled out some typewritten papers, and arranged them in a neat pile before him. Deep in concentration, gone was the usual easy smile, now replaced with a grim expression. He glanced over at Eoin MacNeill but waited a few moments until the buzz of talking in the room subsided. He then began, speaking softly.

"*A Chinn Chomhairle*. Much has been said in Private Session about the action of the plenipotentiaries in signing at all or in signing without first putting their document before the Cabinet. I want to state as clearly as I can, and as briefly as I can—I cannot promise you to be very brief—what the exact position was. It has been fully explained how the Delegation returned from London on that momentous Saturday to meet the Cabinet at home. We came back with a document from the British Delegation which we presented to the Cabinet. We went away with certain impressions in our minds, and we faithfully did our best to transmit these impressions to paper in the memorandum we handed in to the British Delegation. So we went away from home with the original document which none of us would sign, but later another document arose which we thought we could sign. There was no opportunity of referring it to our people at home."

He raised his voice slightly and said, "If my signature has been given in error, I stand by it whether it has or not, and I am not going to take refuge behind any kind of subterfuge."

He raised his voice a little further and proudly declared, with a tinge of anger, "I stand up over that signature, and I give the same decision at this moment in this assembly."

In acknowledgement of the authenticity of this simple declaration, the room erupted in applause. Knowing he now held the room, Michael relaxed slightly and said sarcastically, "It has also been suggested that the delegation broke down before the first bit of English bluff. I would remind the Deputy who used that expression that England put up quite a good bluff for the last five years here, and I did not break down before that bluff."

Amidst renewed applause, a voice called out, "That's the stuff!" and cheers turned to laughter.[9] As the reporter from the *Irish Times* started to scribble on his notepad, he nudged a fellow journalist, "Look. Even de Valera can't help but laugh."

Michael glanced down at his neat pile of papers and turned a couple of sheets over but continued without referring to them. "The results of our labour are before the Dáil. Reject or accept. The President has suggested that a greater result could have been obtained by more skilful handling. Perhaps so," he said, looking from side to side, before continuing with an ironic smile, "Surely the Dáil knew our limitations when they selected us, and our abilities could not have been expected to increase because we were chosen as plenipotentiaries by the Dáil. The delegates have been blamed for various things. It is scarcely too much to say that they have been blamed for not returning with recognition of the Irish Republic. They are blamed, at any rate, for not having done much better."

There was some muttering at this mention of blame, but he went on to another subject. "This question of association was bandied around as far back as August tenth and went on until the final communication. The communication of September twenty-ninth from Lloyd George made it clear that they were going into a conference not on the recognition of the Irish Republic, and I say if we all stood on the recognition of the Irish Republic as a prelude to any conference, we could very easily have said so, and there would be no conference."[10]

Here he raised his voice again to emphasise a point he had made many times before, "What I want to make clear is that it was the acceptance of the invitation that formed the compromise. I was sent there to form that adaptation, to bear the brunt of it. Now, as one of the signatories of the document, I naturally recommend its acceptance. I do not recommend it for more than it is. Equally, I do not recommend it for less than it is."

Then chin leading, he leaned forward, striking the back of his right hand into the palm of the left, and said firmly, "In my opinion, it gives us freedom, not the ultimate freedom that all nations desire and develop to, but the freedom to achieve it."

When the applause that followed subsided, he stood erect, brushed a lock of hair back and said, "Rightly or wrongly, when you make a bargain you cannot alter it, you cannot go back and get sorry for it and say, 'I ought to have made a better bargain.' Business cannot be done on those bases. I must make reference to the signing of the Treaty. This Treaty was not signed under personal intimidation. If personal intimidation had been attempted, no member of the Delegation would have signed it. At a fateful moment, I was called upon to make a decision, and if I were called upon at the present moment for a decision on the same question, my decision would be the same. Let there be no mistake and no misunderstanding about that. I have used the word 'intimidation.'"

He then said derisively, "The whole attitude of Britain towards Ireland in the past was an attitude of intimidation, and we, as negotiators, were not in the position of conquerors dictating terms of peace to a vanquished foe. We had not beaten the enemy out of our country by force of arms."

Many people nodded in agreement, respecting this frank admission as he continued, "To return to the Treaty, hardly anyone, even those who support it, really understands it, and it is necessary to explain it and the immense powers and liberties it secures. This is my justification for having signed it and for recommending it to the nation. Should the Dáil reject it, I am, as I said, no longer responsible. But I am responsible for making the nation fully understand what it gains by accepting it and what is involved in its rejection."

Once again, since most delegates were not privy to all the arguments made in Cabinet debates nor the correspondence between the Cabinet and the plenipotentiaries, this was a welcome, plain-spoken statement. "So long as I have made that clear, I am perfectly happy and satisfied. Now we must look facts in the face. For our continued national and spiritual existence, two things are necessary—security and freedom. If the Treaty gives us these or helps us to get at these, then I maintain that it satisfies our national aspirations. The history of this nation has not been, as is so often said, the history of a military struggle of seven hundred and fifty years—it has been much more a history of peaceful penetration of seven hundred and fifty years. It has been a story of a struggle against the cancer that was eating up our lives, economic penetration, that we discovered that political freedom was necessary in order that that should be stopped. Now it was not by any form of communication except through their military strength that the English held this country. That is simply a plain fact which, I think, nobody will deny. It wasn't by any form of government; it wasn't by their judiciary or anything of that kind. These people could not operate except for the military strength that was always there. Now, starting from that, I maintain that the disappearance of that military strength gives us the chief proof that our national liberties are established."

Through shouts of "Hear! Hear!" Michael looked down at the papers he had mostly ignored thus far and shuffled through them to catch up with the present point in his speech. "I have said that I am not a constitutional lawyer. I am going to give a constitutional opinion in what I am going to read, and I will back that constitutional opinion against the opinion of any Deputy, lawyer or otherwise, in this Dáil."

At this point, he quoted the first article of the Treaty from his papers, "The status as defined is the same constitutional status *in the community of nations known as the British Empire*, as Canada, Australia, New Zealand, South Africa." Still holding the papers, he spoke freely, "And here let me say that in my judgment it is not a definition of any status that would secure us that status; it is the power to hold and to make secure and to increase what we have gained. Any attempt to interfere with us would be even more difficult in consequence of the reference to the constitutional status of Canada and South Africa. They are, in effect, introduced as guarantors of our freedom, which makes us stronger than if we stood alone."

As he spoke in defence of his integrity, he waved a fist and passionately declared, "As I have said already, as a plain Irishman, I believe in my own interpretation against the interpretation of any Englishman. Lloyd George and Churchill have been quoted here against us." With a dismissive tone, he explained, "I say the quotation of those people is what marks the slave mind. There are people in this assembly who will take their words before they will take my words. That is the slave mind. We have got rid of the word 'Empire.' For the first time in an official document, the former Empire is styled 'The Community of Nations known as the British Empire.' Common citizenship has been mentioned. Common citizenship is the substitution for the subjection of Ireland. It is an admission by them that they no longer can dominate Ireland."

Heads nodded in agreement as the logic of Michael's clear, concise arguments made the intended impression. Michael then managed to bring up Document No. 2 without arguing against its being withheld. "Now I was going to present an argument based on a comparison of the Treaty with the second document, and part of the argument was to read the clauses of the second document. In deference to what the President has said, I shall not at this stage make use of that argument. I don't want to take anything that would look like an unfair advantage. I am not standing for this thing to get advantage over anybody, and whatever else the President will say about me, I think he will admit that."

This polite reference to de Valera prompted him to admit just that. "I never said anything but the highest."

Pleasantly surprised, Michael's tone softened as he turned to his following argument. "Now I have explained something as to what the Treaty is. I also want to explain to you as one of the signatories what I consider rejection of it means. It has been said that the alternative document does not mean war. Perhaps it does, perhaps it does not. I say that rejection of the Treaty is a declaration of war until you have beaten the British Empire, apart from any alternative document."

However, emotion returned to his voice as he warned in a stern tone, "Rejection of the Treaty means your national policy is war. If you do this, if you go on that as a national policy, I, for one, am satisfied. But if war is national policy, I want you to understand what it means. I, as an individual, do not now, no more than ever, shirk war. The Treaty was signed by me, not because they held up the alternative of imme-diate war. I signed it because I would not be one of those to commit the Irish people to war without the Irish people committing themselves to war."

After more cheers, Michael led up to a thinly veiled swipe at Erskine Childers. "Deputies have talked of principle. At different times I have known different Deputies to hold different principles. I am not impeaching anybody, but I do want to talk straight." Then, his voice filled with pride, he declared, "I am the representative of an Irish stock.

I am the representative equally with any other member of the same stock of people who have suffered through the terror in the past."

Arthur immediately knew who Michael was comparing himself to and silently appreciated the contrast with non-Irish poseurs. However, he could also have been referring to de Valera, who shifted uncomfortably in his seat.

"Our grandfathers have suffered from war, and our fathers or some of our ancestors have died of famine. I don't want a lecture from anybody as to what my principles are to be now. I am just a representative of plain Irish stock whose principles have been burned into them, and we don't want any assurance to the people of this country that we are going to betray them. I can state for you a principle which everybody will understand, the principle of government by the consent of the governed. These words have been used by nearly every Deputy at some time or another."

Then, palms down on the table and lowering his shoulders, he twisted around to survey the room from side to side and asked, "Are the Deputies going to be afraid of these words now, supposing the formula happens to go against them?"

Unable to avoid the implications of this question, it seemed like all the room responded, de Valera including, "No, no!"

"We have stated we would not coerce the North-East. We have stated it officially in our correspondence. I stated it publicly in Armagh, and nobody has found fault with it. What did we mean? Did we mean we were going to coerce them, or we were not going to coerce them? What was the use of talking big phrases about not agreeing to the partition of our country? Surely we recognise that the North-East corner does exist, and surely our intention was that we should take such steps as would sooner or later lead to mutual understanding. The Treaty has made an effort to deal with it and has made an effort, in my opinion, to deal with it on lines that will lead very rapidly to goodwill, and the entry of the North-East under the Irish Parliament."

While Brugha and de Valera remained stonily silent, seemingly trying to ignore the applause that broke out again, Michael continued the argument. "I don't say it is an ideal arrangement, but if our policy is, as has been stated, a policy of non-coercion, then let somebody else get a better way out of it. Now, summing up, and nobody can say that I haven't talked plainly, I say that this Treaty gives us not recognition of the Irish Republic, but it gives us more recognition on the part of

Great Britain and the associated States than we have got from any other nation."

Then, his voice clear but tinged with a welling emotion, he told the delegates, "As this may be the last opportunity I shall ever have of speaking publicly to the Dáil, I want to say that there was never an Irishman placed in such a position as I was by reason of these negotiations. I had got a certain name, whether I deserved it or not."

Delegates called out from around the hall, "You did! You did well!" He held up his hands to silence their cries, "And I knew when I was going over there that I was being placed in a position that I could not reconcile, and that I could not in the public mind be reconciled with what they thought I stood for, no matter what we brought back."

Next he quoted back the points raised by women delegates such as Mary MacSwiney, saying, "Deputies have spoken about whether dead men would approve of it, and they have spoken of whether children yet unborn will approve of it, but few of them have spoken as to whether the living approve of it. In my own small way, I tried to have before my mind what the whole lot of them would think of it. And the proper way for us to look at it is in that way." Then he summed up this rebuttal defiantly, "There is no man here who has more regard for the dead men than I have."

"Hear! Hear!"

"I don't think it is fair to be quoting them against us. I think the decision ought to be a clear decision on the documents as they are before us—on the Treaty as it is before us. On that we shall be judged, as to whether we have done the right thing in our own conscience or not."

Then placing his hands on his hips, he bent forward and called out, "Don't let us put the responsibility, the individual responsibility, upon anybody else." Then sweeping a pointed finger across the hall, he concluded, "Let us take that responsibility ourselves and let us in God's name abide by the decision."

With that, Michael sat down to thunderous applause and an approving smile from Arthur, who complimented him, "You know, Mick, listening to this fine speech, I was reminded how far we've come from the days when Parnell and Gladstone were advocating for Home Rule, and I was opining about dual monarchy. What we have on offer now is more than I ever dreamed of."[11]

"And whatever we got, we got under your leadership," Michael reminded him.

At the back of the room, Robert Harding remarked, "Clearly, that was the best speech we've heard here. What do you say, Matt?"

"Yes, it certainly was," his friend from the *New York Times* replied. "That fellow is beyond question the outstanding figure in the Dáil," He then wrote in his notebook, "His youth, his confidence, his resonant voice, his sheer robustness worked wonders."[12]

One dignitary who monitored Michael's speech was his political mentor, Tim Healy. He remarked to an associate, "That was worthy of a lawyer as well as a politician. It was big enough for a trained statesman. I was surprised by its precision and detail and rhetoric."[13]

Waiting until the applause abated, Erskine Childers rose to speak, acknowledging the power of Michael's speech. "I think everybody will agree that we have listened to a most able and eloquent speech. I most heartily agree to it, though I am in profound disagreement with the conclusions of the speaker. He has said many things which I admire and respect; he has said others that I profoundly regret. All of us agree, I think, that we have listened to a manly, eloquent, and worthy speech from the Minister for Finance."

CHILDERS' SPEECH STARTED WELL AND WAS MET WITH CHEERS OF "Hear, hear!" but quickly devolved into a dry, lifeless, and seemingly endless dissection of the Treaty, line by line, that took all the air from the room.

A short while later, near the end of a long day, a remarkable turn of events occurred. Robert Barton, who had said earlier in the debates that if the Treaty had first been brought back to Dublin for consideration, he would not have signed, finally had his chance to speak. Given some of the discussion of intimidation applied by the British to induce him to sign, his opening remark had a profound impact on the proceedings.

"I am going to make plain to you the circumstances under which I find myself in honour bound to recommend the acceptance of the Treaty."

This simple, dramatic turn secured for him everyone's full attention.

"In making that statement, I have one object only in view, and that is to enable you to become intimately acquainted with the circumstances leading up to the signing of the Treaty and the responsibility forced on me had I refused to sign. I do not seek to shield myself from the charge of having broken my oath of allegiance to the Republic—my signature is proof of that fact."

"Hear, hear."

"That oath was, and still is to me, the most sacred bond on earth. I broke my oath because I judged that violation to be the lesser of alternative outrages forced upon me, and between which I was compelled to choose."

As people absorbed these solemn words, the room went hushed as he calmly explained how a man like he, who had been opposed to the Treaty at that stage, could be persuaded by the sweep of events to change course. Enthralled, they followed his every word and learned of the very personal dilemma faced by all the plenipotentiaries.

"On Sunday, December fourth, the Conference had precipitately and definitely broken down. An intermediary effected contact next day, and on Monday at 3 p.m., Arthur Griffith, Michael Collins, and myself met the English representatives. In the struggle that ensued, Arthur Griffith sought repeatedly to have the decision between war and peace on the terms of the Treaty referred back to this assembly. This proposal Mr. Lloyd George flatly refused. He claimed that we were plenipotentiaries and that we must either accept or reject. Speaking for himself and his colleagues, the English Prime Minister with all the solemnity and the power of conviction that he alone, of all men I met, can impart by word and gesture —the vehicles by which the mind of one man oppresses and impresses the mind of another—declared that the signature and recommendation of every member of our delegation was necessary or war would follow immediately. He gave us until 10 o'clock to make up our minds, and it was then about eight-thirty. We returned to our house to decide upon our answer. The issue before us was whether we should stand behind our proposals for External Association, face war and maintain the Republic, or whether we should accept inclusion in the British Empire and take peace."

He explained, very quietly and simply, "Arthur Griffith, Michael Collins, and Eamonn Duggan were for acceptance and peace. Gavan Duffy and myself were for refusal—war or no war. An answer that was not unanimous committed you to immediate war, and the responsibility for that was to rest directly upon those two delegates who refused to sign. For myself, I preferred war. I told my colleagues so, but for the nation, without consultation, I dared not accept that responsibility. The alternative which I sought to avoid seemed to me a lesser outrage than the violation of what is my faith. So that, I myself, and of my own choice, must commit my nation to immediate war, without you, Mr. President, or the Members of the Dáil, or the nation having an opportunity to examine the terms upon which war could be avoided. I signed, and now I have fulfilled my undertaking, I recommend to you the Treaty I signed in London."

"Well, that took guts," Matthew Dowd remarked at the back of the hall. The members of the Dáil agreed and gave him a great round of applause.[14]

When the proceedings finally ended about half an hour later, Michael acknowledged Barton's speech with a rare compliment.

"Well done, Bob."

"Thank you, Mick. What can I say?" Barton replied sadly.

"You spoke the truth, your personal truth. No one can ask any more of a man than that." Then he noticed one of the female delegates approaching and excused himself, saying, "Thanks again, Bob. Have a good night."

He approached Kathleen Clarke, the widow of Tom Clarke, one of the leaders of the Easter Rising executed by the British, and gave her a tired smile. "I hope you took no offence from my speech, Kathleen."

"Oh, no, Mick," she said with a hint of apprehension. "I have to tell you, though, I intend to vote against the Treaty. I think Tom would have wanted it so."

"I wouldn't want you to vote for it, Kathleen," he said as he touched her hand. "All I ask is if it is passed, you give us the chance to make it work."[15]

Some reporters saw them talking and rushed over to ask, "Mr. Collins, what are your chances of getting the Treaty approved now?"

As Kathleen stepped away with a smile for Michael, Joe O'Reilly came forward to rescue Michael from the crush of reporters and said, "Good night, gentlemen." He and Tom Cullen then whisked him outside to his waiting car.

Driving him back to the Gresham Hotel, Pat McCrea asked cheerfully, "How'd it go, then?"

Tom tried to take a positive view, "It was a good day, eh, Mick?"

Joe agreed, saying, "Dev looked desperate, but your speech and Arthur's were brilliant."

Michael, exhausted and beaten down, surprised them when he replied, "It was the worst day I ever spent in my life. The Treaty will almost certainly be beaten."[16] He stared out the window and mumbled, "How much longer can this go on?"

ONE HUNDRED FIFTEEN

Seeing is Believing

WEDNESDAY, 21 DECEMBER 1921, WHITEHALL, LONDON

AT THE BEHEST OF LLOYD GEORGE, CHURCHILL HEADED UP THE Provisional Government of Ireland Committee, which would oversee the transfer of power in Ireland from London to Dublin, provided the Dáil approved the Treaty. There was a sense of urgency among the members, which, besides Churchill, included Hamar Greenwood, Worthington-Evans, Gordon Hewart, and Lord FitzAlan.[1]

Greenwood expressed this urgency by informing the other committee members, "I have received word from Macready that he fears that British troops will soon be attacked in an effort to provoke retaliation. He says he is more than ever convinced that unless troops are withdrawn from Southern Ireland with the utmost despatch, they will find themselves in a very difficult and unpleasant situation."[2]

"Yes, General," Winston responded, "for that very reason, I suggest that as soon as possible, troops be withdrawn from all outlying places and concentrated in and around Dublin."

Then addressing the full committee, he laid out the scope of their work. "Assuming the Dáil will ratify the Treaty, the Prime Minister has asked us to arrange the details of setting up the Provisional Government in Dublin. This government would be immediately responsible for the whole internal peace and order of Southern Ireland and would take executive control of the country. We do not wish to continue responsibility one day longer than is absolutely necessary."

"When would that be?" he was asked.

"I hope that the Southern Irish would agree to the definite assumption of power on this coming January first, following which all British military forces would be withdrawn as quickly as convenient. At the same time, both the Royal Ulster Constabulary and the Auxiliaries would be disbanded at Britain's expense, advantage being taken of the decision provisionally arrived at to raise a gendarmerie for Palestine. I envisage a swift transfer of power from Westminster to Dublin, the establishment of Free State Courts at the earliest moment, the uses of all taxes hitherto raised in Southern Ireland for Irish internal administration, and the full responsibility for education and agriculture placed on the shoulders of a Free State Minister.

"I insist there must be no hanging on to British military or civil control. On the contrary, ostentatious preparations to quit should be made everywhere. Seeing is believing. Let the people of Southern Ireland see with their own eyes what they have achieved, and embrace it."[3]

Clonakilty Wrastler

FRIDAY, 23 DECEMBER 1921, CORK

THREE MORE DAYS OF DEBATES FOLLOWED THE STIRRING SPEECHES delivered by Arthur and Michael, allowing the members who had not yet spoken to voice their opinions on the Treaty, but still, there were many speeches to be heard. A proposal by Michael that the proceedings should take a break for Christmas was accepted, and the debates adjourned until the new year.

The following day, Friday, after a three-hour afternoon ride on the train from Dublin to Cork, Michael was understandably tired from the journey, especially after the gruelling debates, but had a pleasant surprise waiting for him when he arrived at the station.[1]

"Uncle Michael!"

Michael turned around as his sixteen-tear old nephew ran up to him.

"Happy Christmas, Uncle Mick."

"Jaysus, Master Seán Powell, you look to be a foot taller than when I saw you last summer! What're they feeding you down here?"

"Plenty of milk and as much sunshine as the Good Lord allows Ireland, Mom says. She's getting exasperated with me. I need longer trousers every six months."

Michael laughed and said, "And plenty of exercise, too, I'll warrant. Let's walk home; I need to stretch my legs. How is Mary?"

As they set off walking, Seán said, "She's fine; everyone's fine.

We're so excited about the Treaty. I wish I could've been there with you for the debates. How do you think it will go? Tell me all about it."

Michael was pleased with his nephew's interest and explained the flow of the debates as best as he could, and soon realised Seán had developed a keen intellect and interest in current events and was fast growing into adulthood.

As they approached home, Seán exclaimed, "I just don't understand how some of the people in Cork, like your friend Liam Lynch, can't support the Treaty. I wish there were something I could do to help, Uncle Mick."

Michael put his hand on Seán's shoulder and told him, "Seán, you're outgrowing this 'Uncle' business. It's time you called me Mick. Someday, I'll think of a way for you to do your part, and that's a promise."

Thrilled to his core, Seán exclaimed, "Thanks, er, Mick," he said excitedly but bashfully. "I promise I won't let you down!"

When they got to the door, Mary opened it, and Seán blurted out, "Mom, Mick's going to let me help win people over to the Treaty!"

"Mick, is it, then?"

"It's fine, Mare. Seán and I have had an interesting conversation about politics." He gave her a kiss and went inside. "Happy Christmas. Hello, kids!"

As Mary's children ran up to him for hugs, she responded by saying, "That's grand, Michael. Now, when are you and Kitty going to get married?"

"Jaypers, Mary, would it be all right if I took my coat off first?"

CHRISTMAS EVE, 24 DECEMBER 1921, CLONAKILTY

THE NEXT DAY MICHAEL TOOK A TRAIN FROM CORK'S ALBERT QUAY through the west of the county, changing at Clonakilty Junction for the two-car train that finally took him to the branch terminal in Clonakilty. As he stepped onto the stone platform, he was heartened to see his older brother Johnny waiting for him.

"Happy Christmas, little brother."

"Ay, and the same to you, Johnny."

"Knackered?"

"Not so much that I'd turn down a drink if one's offered."

"No bags with you, then? Well, we can always fix you up with a drink, but I thought you'd sworn it off."

"For Christ's sake, Johnny, it's Christmas, not Lent!" Michael replied, beaming as he walked with him through the small, rural station. "I could murder a jar of Wrastler at the Four Alls."

Johnny said cautiously as he held the station door open, "It's a bit early. Would you not rather wait till after supper?"

"No time like the present." Michael squinted at him and said, "You don't seem so thirsty yourself, though."

They exited the station, and Johnny nodded to his car and said, "Get in. I'll explain. You might say there's been a bit of a shift in the prevailing winds."

"Prevailing winds? You mean a man can't go for a drink in his own home town?"

"No, but sure, we'll go there. However, let's just say we'll avoid an animated discussion of the Treaty this close to Christmas, shall we?"

As they pulled away from the station, Michael sighed, "Very well."

He looked as Johnny struggled to turn the wheel of the car. "How's the hand?"

"Least said, soonest mended."

"Really? If we saw an animal on the farm that lame, we'd have considered putting it out of its misery."

"All right, to tell God's truth, it's healed enough to drive, just, but not enough to chop a load of wood."

"Then Christmas, or not, let's get you to the local quack for a check-up."

"No need for that. I've made some enquiries, and I'll see a specialist in Dublin in January."

"All right, then." Michael looked out the window as the familiar sights of neighbouring homes and farms passed by. "So, where are you staying these days? Where am *I* staying? No, first, how are the kids?"

"Kids are kids, simply fine, adjusting well. As you know, all eight children are spread out and keep moving around between friends and family, but they love it, like they're on a nonstop holiday. Lately, I've been staying with our cousin Annie at her place next to Woodfield, and we'll have all the kids together there tomorrow for Christmas dinner. You'll be staying with me at Annie's while you're here, but tonight, we'll have Christmas Eve dinner with Margaret and Patrick in Rathbarry. Everyone's been great, but you can imagine how I feel, though, after all the years at Woodfield, to be a guest in the homes of others."[2]

"Friends and family with big hearts, so not to fret, I'm sure. Still, we'll put our heads together and work something out. We need to get you and all the children under one roof again."

"All the same, that's why I'd like another opinion from a doctor on this hand. If there were any hope of its healing, I'd have a go at rebuilding the farm. Speaking of, do you want to stop for a look?"

"Maybe tomorrow we could go for a walk there from Annie's, but not tonight, Johnny. I'm trying to keep my spirits up. Besides, I've seen it. Hardly anything left of it."

"Just the original stone homestead where you were born before it was turned into a stable."

"Yes, after Mom built the farmhouse. It would break her heart to see it all now. So, you think you have it in you for another go at the farm?"

"I'm still young and strong enough, but I'm not nursing any unrealistic hopes. If I can't turn the farm around, I might look around Dublin to see what work is to be had there. Nancy O'Brien has been in touch, by the way, and she also thinks such a move might be something to consider."[3]

Michael kept his own counsel on this admission and said cheerfully, "Does she, then? Well, you know best—you always were the one with the clearest head on his shoulders. I've always admired you for that, Johnny."

"There's nothing wrong with your noggin. How did the last couple of days go with the debates? I've been following in the papers, of course, but what has it been like?"

"More of the same, much more. Last round, Eamonn Duggan got up and fought it out toe to toe with Dev. I didn't realise he had it in him. Very lawyerly, of course, logical and persuasive, but combative, too."

"As was W.T. Cosgrave," Johnny replied. "He admitted he lacked the mind of a constitutional lawyer but quoted back to de Valera his own assertion that if you are prepared to make a bargain, you should be prepared to stick to it."

"Even Dev had to agree with that. Duggan really turned the tables around on my old friend Brugha. He said except for war, Cathal isn't worth a damn, but held him to be a great man for war who, when the spark of life was practically gone out of him, was as full of fight as when he was going into it. It was a very moving tribute and a well-deserved one, I'll admit."[4]

Johnny nodded, "I read that Duggan ended by saying, 'I now formally approve, recommend, and support the Treaty.' I wish I had been there. I would've been bursting with pride to hear your speech. It's one thing to read the accounts in the papers, another thing entirely to be there, feel the atmosphere in the room, sense the effect on everyone there. Your speech was unanswerable, Michael."

"Ah, well." He cleared his throat and asked, "So, what *are* the local lads saying? We know how strongly Liam Lynch feels about our work in London."

"The Hales family is a case in point. I see or hear of them from time to time, and with their brother Tom still in Dartmoor Prison, Donal, Bob, and Bill have been very vocal about condemning you and the Treaty, though their sister Madge is still with you. Now, Tom is the man who underwent torture rather than breathe a word about you or me to that degenerate Major Percival when he was on his way to burn down our farm, but when Tom is finally released, don't count on his backing. Mind you, this past March, their family home was destroyed in the same fashion as ours. Still, it gives you pause when you remember all the times we gave Tom shelter at Woodfield when he was on the run, but then again, what else can you expect in a staunchly Republican county like Cork?"[5]

"Then there's the other brother, Seán, who's in favour. In the first Private Session, he said Ireland's destiny is to be a Republic and whoever gets the closest and soonest to that is the man."[6]

"That's not all. Word has it he's been going around saying something like, 'I agree with Mick. He says the British broke the Treaty of Limerick, and we'll break this Treaty, too, when it suits us, when we have our own army.' What is *that* supposed to mean?"[7]

Michael laughed and said, "Just consider the source. Seán always was a character, going back to our days together at Frongoch. Remember when Percival burned Woodfield and other farms, Seán showed up at Lord Bandon's home to give him a taste of his own medicine, only to surprise the dirty old man in bed with a fetching young wench most decidedly not his wife."

Johnny smiled, remembering one of the few amusing stories from that time. "Yes, he sprinkled the bed with petrol and informed him, 'You burned my castle last week…'"

"Now I'll burn yours," they said in unison.[8] They shared a laugh, and Michael continued, "These Cork lads fancy themselves more Republican than me, but lest they forget, I took an oath to the Republic, too. I am not for breaking the Treaty; I just may have different plans for implementing it, especially when it comes to protecting the Catholics in Ulster. I can't forsake them."

"Nor your word to Lloyd George and Churchill." He shot Michael a stern look but then softened and said, "Sad case, Tom and Seán Hales. Brother versus brother. It sounds like a tale from the American Civil War."

Michael replied warily, "That's my greatest fear, that we'll have our own civil war. The votes in the Dáil are that close."

"But not in the country, some folks in Cork notwithstanding. The Church, business, big farmers, the Press, and most senior defence officers are all with you."[9] You mentioned our friend, W.T. Cosgrave, who, as the Minister for Local Government, has been busy doing just that, ministering to the local governments. He's pressed upwards of twenty City Councils to pass resolutions declaring their support of the Treaty."[10]

Michael laughed a little and said, "Yes, Even Dev's local council, Clare, has come out in favour."[11]

"There, you see? Now, that's enough politics for now," Johnny said as they pulled up to the Four Alls Pub, just across the road from the home of their cousin Michael O'Brien. "Let's just go have a friendly drink."

"I've never had an unfriendly one. Come on; my throat is parched. I wonder if Cousin Michael is there."

"No, he'll be with Aunt Peg at Margaret's by now."

Johnny went into the pub first, and the proprietor, Jerry Collins, called to him, "Ah, there he is. Howaya, Johnny? Say, who's that Big Fella you've got with you? Jaysus, Mick, get yourself in here! Ah, but look at you, now!"

He leaned across the bar and shook Michael's hand with both of his, and called out, "Look who we have with us, now, will you? Him back from merry old, after havin' a go at Lloyd George and Churchill."

The pub was crowded with regulars, and they descended on the local boy back in their midst. "Happy Christmas, Mick. Well done, Mick."

"Happy Christmas, fellas, and thanks, Jerry, but I'll die of thirst if you don't pull me one of your finest soon."

"Clonakilty Wrastler, it is. Coming right up."[12]

"Jaysus, *Mr. Collins*, you've a house full of sinners so early in the day," Michael teased.

"Well, *Mr. Collins*, it *is* a Saturday, and knowing we'll be closed on Christmas, they're getting a head start, aren't you, lads?" Michael and Jerry shared the same last name but no bloodlines they were aware of, so they also shared this long-standing joke about their surnames.[13]

One of the regulars answered, "I'll give you that, Jerry, but Mick, bless you for bringing peace to Ireland."

Michael took his mug and waved it around the room.

Someone began to sing, "*A Nation once again, a Nation once again*," and the small crowd sang along, banging the bar with their fists as they celebrated the old rebel song. After a couple of verses, everyone applauded except for a sullen trio of men at a small table across from the bar. Michael noticed their reticence and walked over and joked, "Christmas spirit hasn't hit you yet?"

They remained silent, looking into their glasses as the room went quiet.

"Come on, Mick," Johnny beckoned to him. "You haven't finished your drink."

"Sure, Johnny, in a minute."

One of the men seated at the table said uncomfortably, "The thing is, Mick, that damn oath you brought back spoils the yuletide joy somewhat, does it not?"

Low murmurs passed around the room. Emboldened by his friend's comment, one of the men said, "And you didn't bring back a Republic, now, did you?"

"Or a united Ireland, either, Mick," the last of the three men chimed in.

Michael stared at them a moment, then smiled and said, "We've waited seven hundred years to get the Brits out of Ireland, and now it'll be just a matter of weeks before you see them leaving Cork. Isn't that the first and most crucial step on the path to freedom?"

The men shrugged and nodded.

"Mark my words. We'll not die waiting for the other things we've fought for, will we?"

They thought silently but didn't answer.

Michael answered for them, "No, my friends, not if we stand together. Now, Jerry, another round for our friends here."

In appreciation for his words as well as his generosity, one of the men at the table stood up to recite a stanza from a famous poem that had been adopted by the Republican cause, knowing full well it to be Michael's favourite:

Oh, the fighting races don't die out,
If they seldom die in bed
For love is first in their hearts, no doubt,

Michael proudly joined in,

Said Burke; then Kelly said
When Michael, the Irish Archangel, stands,
The angel with the sword

And here, everyone in the pub enthusiastically joined in, with Michael in the lead.

And the battle-dead from a hundred lands
Are ranged in one big horde,
Our line, that for Gabriel's trumpet waits,
Will stretch three deep that day,
From Jehoshaphat to the Golden Gates—
Kelly and Burke and Shea.

At this point, Michael waved his arms and raised his voice over everyone else's in the room to conclude with a slight change in honour of his home town neighbours:

Then here's to the Pike and Sam's Cross and the like
Said Kelly and Burke and Shea![14]

Everyone fell to applauding and slapping each other on the back.

One of the men at the table called out, "Jerry, a round for Mick and Johnny."

When Michael walked over to shake hands, the man stood and told him, "Thanks for the drinks, Mick. I can't say we share in all your optimism, but everyone knows you've put a good heart to the task handed you. Happy Christmas to you and the family."

"Likewise, and thanks to you."

Michael and Johnny finished their second round and began to say their goodbyes, pausing at the table before they went out the door.

"Thanks again. Good seeing you, boys," Michael said, smiling. However, when they got outside, he commented, "That was great *craic*, but I see what you mean by the prevailing winds. Things down here are far from settled."

A SHORT WHILE LATER THEY ARRIVED AT THEIR SISTER MARGARET'S home. As they approached the front door, Johnny asked, "One more thing, which, knowing you, you might not want to discuss in front of all the family. How's Kitty? Any imminent news to report on that front?"

Michael laughed, saying, "You *do* know me well, O wise elder brother, as does our sister, Mary, who hit me with a barrage of questions last night on the very subject. I can report we're as good as engaged."

"Oh, how romantic. Good as engaged? What devotion, such affection beating away in that breast and tripping off the tongue!"

Michael stopped on the path up to the front door. "As a matter of fact, I'll be going down to Longford for New Year's, and I think we'll most likely talk about setting a date for the announcement, but privately, and only for the family and the closest of friends to know. Maybe when you come to Dublin we could arrange for you to meet her."

"That would be grand. I take back all the kidding, then. This is all terrific news, Mick. But shouldn't we tell the ladies?"

"Arrah, hold yer whist," he hissed, then said gravely, "with all this division in the country, I don't want Kitty to be a target. Seriously, now, don't say anything when we go inside. When the time is right, we'll make the announcement."

"Understood. Good man," he answered, patting Michael on the back.

No sooner had they gone inside when their sister Margaret showered Michael with kisses, crying out, "Oh, Lord bless us. Happy Christmas, Michael."

Margaret's husband, Patrick, joined in the welcome, "Yes, Happy Christmas, Michael. How is the lovely Miss Kiernan we've all been hearing about?"

"Yes, Michael, when are you and Kitty going to get married? Whatever are you waiting for?"

Johnny intervened, "Now, leave the lad be. In his own time, in his own time. Besides, he and Miss Kiernan," he said with a wink to his brother, who laughed and joined in, "are as good as engaged."

Margaret cried out, "Ah-ha! I knew it! When's the wedding?"

"Johnny, maybe we ought to go rouse up the local doc right away. You're looking a bit peaked."

CHRISTMAS MORNING, 25 DECEMBER 1921, NEAR WOODFIELD

ON CHRISTMAS MORNING, MICHAEL WAS UP BEFORE SUNRISE AND WENT into his cousin Annie's kitchen to find his brother already having some coffee.

"Aren't we the early birds?" Michael asked.

"I may not have cows to tend, but I still keep farmer's hours," Johnny said as he looked out the window to see the dark morning sky broken by a sliver of golden light along the horizon.

Michael replied, "I suppose that's why I keep the morning hours I do, having grown up on a farm. I tend to stay up late working, but I'm still up at the crack of dawn." He helped himself to a draught of coffee from Johnny's mug and said, "Come on, let's go up to Carraig a Radhairc to see the sunrise."

They walked past the family farm, and Michael answered the question before it was asked, saying softly, "Not just now, Johnny. Maybe afterwards on the way back after Mass."

A while later they were climbing up the Rock of the View as birds noisily heralded the break of day. As they made their way up the hill,

Johnny said breathlessly, "We haven't done this since we were kids in school."

"Ye all right?" Michael asked.

"Ay, I'll be fine. It's just…" his voice trailed off, and they continued their hike in silence.

When they reached the summit, Michael commented, "This is a sight better than last Christmas."

"What did you get yourself up to then?"

"I celebrated Christmas Eve at the Gresham Hotel with some mates. Come to think of it, Rory O'Connor was with us." He shook his head, "How things change."

"Another anti-Treaty friend. Sad."

"Anyway, I nearly got arrested by a group of Auxis but fibbed my way out of it and ended up having drinks with them instead."

"Sounds just like you. And a few months later you were negotiating the Treaty with the Prime Minister."

"Yes, and even having drinks at Winston's home." He paused and looked around. Swiftly shifting morning clouds revealed the rising sun moving across the hills below them as herds of cows with clanging cowbells made their way to pastures woven between the surrounding villages of South and West Cork. Soon a bank of clouds rose just above the height of the sun, and a silvery gloss shone on the waters of the Celtic Sea.

"Shall we go to Mass now?" Johnny asked.

"Ay, but I feel like I've just done." He took in a deep breath of the morning air infused with a hint of the sea and said softly, "I've seen more of my old country this morning than I've ever seen in my whole life."[15]

Prudence and Audacity

LLOYD GEORGE LOOKED OUT HIS WINDOW ON THE TRAIN TO Folkestone to see the swiftly passing views of Kent Downs. "Lovely. Beautiful part of England here." He smiled, turned, and asked, "How is your tome on the Great War going?"

Winston opened his briefcase, pulled out a manuscript, smiled and said, "It's coming along, but you can see for yourself."

Lloyd George was pleased with the offer. "Really? May I?" he eagerly answered as Winston passed it over.

He skimmed through the opening pages and alighted on a page that brought a smile to his face. He read aloud, "*Since I had crossed the Floor of the House in 1904 on the Free Trade issue, I had worked in close political association with Mr. Lloyd George. He was the first to welcome me.*"[1]

"Yes, you were," Winston affirmed.

Lloyd George nodded, flipped through some pages deeper into the manuscript, and read quietly for a minute or so. "You present a clear depiction of the choices Germany's faced at the outset of the war in 1914. Whom to attack first, France or Russia? I appreciate that you recognised I felt the Germans would be so unwise to ignore the fatal implications of one choice over the other and how we might respond. You might also want to mention the British Cabinet's musings on that impending decision."

"Excellent idea, thank you."

"Wonderful opening, though. *Prudence and audacity may be alternated, but not be mixed. Having gone to war it is vain to shrink from facing the hazards inseparable from it.* Excellent, Winston, excellent."[2]

"I'm so pleased you approve. I'd appreciate any comments or critiques you may offer as the book progresses."

"Glad to, Winston. Your program of audacity seems to have reaped its benefits in Ireland, despite all the criticism it engendered, but we can't be accused of shrinking from the hazards we faced. I think we all adhered to a policy of prudence in its aftermath and have a Treaty to show for it, don't we?"

"We do. A Treaty we may expect with some confidence to meet with approval soon in Ireland. Our committee on Provisional Government is making great progress. We have ever-developing, detailed plans for the transfer of power across the South of Ireland."

"*Da*, good. The sooner, the better."

"I agree, Prime Minister. Wholeheartedly. I'm looking forward to implementing these plans as soon as feasible."

"It's been quite a struggle. For now, I'm looking forward to our working holiday in Cannes."

"As am I."

Dark Horses

1 JANUARY 1922, GRANARD, LONGFORD

AFTER MASS AT ST. MARY'S CHURCH, MICHAEL AND KITTY STEPPED out into the chilly New Year's morning air, accompanied by Kitty's sister, Maud, and her beau, Gearoid O'Sullivan.[1]

"There's something about going to High Mass when the first Sunday of the year falls on the first day of the year," Kitty remarked as they all proceeded down the hill back into town.

Maud agreed, "Yes, providential, you might say. I think it bodes well for the New Year."

"Yes, Happy New Year, Kitty, Mick," Gearoid replied happily.

For once, Michael responded cheerily to a standard social norm, "Yes, Happy New Year, George, certainly an auspicious one at that, it is."

Maud asked, "You mean it bodes well for the looming decision on the Treaty?"

"Well, yes, there's that, too," he answered. "Go ahead, Kit, you tell them."

Kitty, flushed with joy, announced their news, "Michael and I are engaged, really engaged, at last."

"That's right. We'll be announcing it soon to those closest to us." Then Michael explained, "We should still be careful about the rest of the world knowing, so keep it under your hat and bonnet, but you two are the first to know."

Maud was overjoyed, "Oh, Kitty, dear, that's wonderful. Bless you both, and you can do the same for us."

"What's that?" Kitty asked.

Gearoid nodded, "I suppose this weekend Maud and I were having the same conversation as you. We're not going to make an announcement for a while, though."

"Well, aren't you the dark horse?" Michael replied, slapping Gearoid on the back.

"It's not like you've bolted out of the gate yourself, Mick," Gearoid responded.

Michael laughed, "Ay, true. Still, I say, well done, George. Here, Maud, give us a kiss."

Kitty added to the festive mood, "Let's all tell Larry as soon as we get in the door. Oh, this will be such a festive New Year's dinner."

"That'll set him back on his heels," Michael replied. "I can't wait to see his face."

As they went inside the Kiernan home, Michael said softly, "I'll have to pick the right time to tell Harry."

"Yes, I know," Kitty responded. "I'll need to do the same."

ONE HUNDRED NINETEEN

The Lady Who Is Betrothed to Me

3 JANUARY 1922, DUBLIN

DÁIL DEBATES RESUME [1]

MICHAEL STRODE INTO THE UNIVERSITY HALL WITH HIS USUAL vigour but a grim look of determination to face the resuming debates. The tense atmosphere that pervaded the Dáil proceedings at the break for Christmas resumed unabated, now increased in intensity as the impending vote on the Treaty loomed nearer. However, when Michael took his seat beside Arthur, he took a moment to share his good news.

Dispensing with any wishes for the new year, he got straight to the point, "You'll be pleased to hear that on New Year's Day, Kitty and I decided to make our engagement official, that is, at least to family and friends like you, Arthur. We're not naming any possible dates yet, but I'm determined to keep Kitty's name out of the papers."

"Wise decision." He leaned back and smiled, "Splendid, Mick. I don't know which took longer or was more difficult to negotiate, this Treaty or your betrothal, but I am glad for you. My heartfelt best to you and Kitty."

"Ha! Thanks, Arthur."

The proceedings got underway once again. Piaras Béaslaí gave a moving and even poetic speech in support of the Treaty, saying near the end, "We, the members of Dáil Éireann, must realise that the nation was not made for Dáil Éireann, but Dáil Éireann was made for the nation. I will go further and remind the Republican doctrinaires that if there was an Irish Republic in the past three years, it consisted, not in an abstraction or a legal formula, but in the people of Ireland. I implore you to consider this point—that if you reject this Treaty, the people of Ireland, the poor nation that is trying to be born, will never get a chance of considering it. If you reject the Treaty, even by a majority of one, the British are no longer bound by it, and your country with whose future you are gambling so unfairly, so recklessly, in the name of political formulas which you call your principles, will not be able to say yes or no to it. But the country will let you know what it thinks of you, and what is left of our Gaelic nation in future generations will curse your failure to rise to a great opportunity."

When he finished speaking, Countess Markievicz motioned to be recognised. Michael took this as his cue to leave and whispered to Arthur, "I have some things to attend to, none of which includes enduring another hour of *her*."

It was just as well that he did not remain, for the Countess made some shocking comments about Michael that stunned the delegates. After a break for lunch, Michael returned to the hall to find Joe O'Reilly waiting for him in the foyer.

"Before things get underway, there is something you need to know, Mick."

"Christ, I was only gone for a couple of hours. What is it?"

"Countess Markievicz relayed some deplorable rumours about you. I'm afraid Kitty will be quite shaken when she hears of them."

"What the hell did the old sow say? No, don't tell me. I'll go see the official record."

Michael went over to the clerk, Diarmuid O'Hegarty. "Let me see it, Diarmuid, you know what I mean."

Diarmuid replied, "Yes, I believe I do, and you're not going to like it. You won't be able to make sense of my notes, though," he said as he flipped through pages and pages of shorthand. "Here it is, Mick," he said and then read aloud from his notes. "*I also heard that there is a suggestion that Princess Mary's wedding is to be broken off, and that the Princess Mary is to be married to Michael Collins, who will be appointed first Governor of our Free State of Ireland. All these are mere nonsense.*"

Michael nearly dropped the minutes and, angry and exasperated, spat out, "If it's fuckin' nonsense, then why repeat such slander?"

Michael, clearly upset, clenched his jaw and ran his fingers through his hair as he walked away.

Joe came over to console him, "I'm sorry you had to hear of this, Mick. It's pretty despicable."

Michael stopped and said, "That woman, Countess Markievicz, has turned Yeats' paean to her on its head." He recited the lines that had come to mind:

> *That woman's days were spent*
> > *In ignorant good-will,*
> > *Her nights in argument*
> > *Until her voice grew shrill.*

Joe recognised the lines. "Ay, from 'Easter, 1916.'"
Michael continued,

> *What voice more sweet than hers*
> > *When, young and beautiful*
> > *She rode to harriers?*

"To behold and hear her now, Mick, she makes it seem such a long time ago."

"Her voice has grown shrill, all right. *That woman* has a tongue that could clip a hedge."

Joe couldn't help but laugh, causing Michael's initial wave of anger to dissipate somewhat, but still, he exclaimed, "Seriously, Joe, this is just the kind of attack I was hoping to avoid, for Kitty's sake. I literally cannot let this go sitting down."

A few moments later Eoin MacNeill took the Speaker's chair. Michael rose immediately but before speaking, stared off into the distance for a few moments, gathering his thoughts, then dropped his jaw to his chest. He then raised his head and turned to the Speaker with a polite enough request but delivered in a sharp tone that only thinly masked his simmering rage, "I crave just a couple of minutes to make a personal explanation."

Having heard the Countess's earlier remarks, the delegates felt the intensity of the moment, and the room fell silent. He continued crisply, "When the Deputy for a Division of Dublin was speaking today, I was not present. She made reference to my name and to the name of a lady belonging to a foreign nation that I cannot allow to pass without making this reference to. Some time in our history as a nation, a girl went through Ireland and was not insulted by the people of Ireland. I do not come from the class that the Deputy for the Dublin Division comes from. I come from the plain people of Ireland. The lady whose name was mentioned is, I understand, betrothed to some man. I know nothing of her personally, I know nothing of her in any way whatever, but the statement may cause her pain and may cause pain to the lady who is betrothed to me."

Here he was interrupted with cries of "Hear, hear!" which he acknowledged with a brief pause. "I just stand in that plain way, and I will *not* allow without challenge any Deputy in the assembly of my nation to insult any lady either of this nation or of any other nation."

With that, he sat down in his chair and folded his arms, staring again out across the room, which erupted in applause.

"Eloquent, Mick, as well as chivalrous," Arthur said in praise. "It is regrettable that Kitty will have to hear of this."

"I have a letter to her half-written in my head already."

Men of Their Word

3 JANUARY 1922, CANNES

THE WAITER AT CIRO'S ITALIAN RESTAURANT ON PLACE DU CASINO IN Monte Carlo brought a bottle of brandy over to a party of six and presented it to Winston Churchill, who nodded approvingly.[1]

"Blanche, allow me," Winston insisted, taking control of the bottle.

"Thank you, Winston," Lady Blanche, Clementine's mother, replied, downing her drink as soon as it was placed before her. "Pity Clemmie isn't here to enjoy the evening with us."

If there was a hint of sarcasm in this observation owing to Clementine's strained relationship with her mother, whose voracious appetite for men and drink Clementine openly disapproved of, Winston was not only tolerant but also very fond of Blanche and ignored any suspected aspersions. "She sends her love and will be here soon, though, alas, I will not. Work calls."

"Work in Whitehall, or on your canvasses?" Sir Philip Sassoon asked.

"Yes, Winston," Adele Capell, the Countess of Essex, said. "Consuelo and I were saying earlier how much you have improved."

"Thank you, Adele. It's inspiring being here, away from the affairs of state. The view of Cap d'Ail from Lou Mas is spectacular. It's good of you to put me up there."

Consuelo, the Duchess of Marlborough, was a cousin by marriage to Winston. She added, "Adele is right, Winston. She and I both have been painted by John Singer Sargeant, but we do admire your work. Your new painting of Eze is so lovely."

"Yes, Winston," Consuelo's husband, Jacques, agreed. "It should hang in a salon."

"Well then, you shall have it." Turning to Adele, he said, "I shall try to come up with something commensurate with my gratitude to you, as well, before I leave for my other job."

"And how is that going, Winston?" Consuelo asked. "Do you think the Irish will adhere to the Treaty you worked so hard to bring about?"

Adele answered for him. "You might ask the Prince of Wales. I walked out on my veranda yesterday to find Winston writing him a letter about it."

"Really, Winston? Would you mind telling us what you had to say?"

"Not at all. I wrote to Prince Edward that Arthur Griffith and Michael Collins are men of their word. That final, fateful night when we were waiting for the Irishmen to return to Downing Street, we were wondering if they had the moral courage to sign, and they proved they did. When the Treaty was signed after that dramatic struggle, we shook hands on it and pledged ourselves to put it through on both sides without regard to personal or political fortunes. They are certainly doing their part, and we will not fail in ours."[2]

"Excellent, Winston," Adele responded. "Apparently, there has been much talk of political fortunes, with the newspapers all boiling over with the question of a General Election being called."

"The Tory Press certainly will have none of it," Churchill replied.

Sassoon agreed, "Nor will Chamberlain. He exclaimed: 'Our work is not done. It is not safe to leave the Irish question halfway through.'"[3]

"I agree with Austen," Winston said. "There is still much to do."

Lady Blanche finished another drink and replied, "And I agree with Winston. Much to do. Let's go to the casino. I feel lucky."

"This is my party," Winston declared as he summoned the waiter, spluttering in his best French, *"l'addition, s'il vous plaît."*

ONE HUNDRED TWENTY-ONE

Choose My Own Procedure

WEDNESDAY, 4 JANUARY 1922, DUBLIN

Dáil Éireann Public Session [1]

As Michael was about to enter the hall for the afternoon session of the debates, he was pleased to see a familiar face. Dr. Farnan walked over and shook his hand. "Mick, I understand congratulations are in order, though I must say, I deplore the way in which the news reached me."

"I know, Doc. Everything has taken a nasty personal turn, but thanks all the same."

"It seems there's no room for compromise these days. It pains me to see you and Dev going at each other. I told him over Christmas that his Document Number 2 wouldn't be understood by the country. It's too nuanced a distinction, if at all, from the Treaty. He was adamant, though."[2]

"You mean damn stubborn," Michael replied. "Last night I asked that we submerge personal opinions for the sake of the common good of the country, not to abandon our principles, but to work together to restore unity in the Dáil and the country."[3]

"I wasn't here yesterday, but I hear you put forward a new proposal."

"Yes, I suggested Dev and the anti-Treaty faction allow the Treaty to go through and let the Provisional Government come into existence, and if necessary, fight the Provisional Government on the Republican question afterwards. He refused, naturally."[4]

Farnan replied, "He says he's been re-working his alternative. His idea of compromise is for everyone to accept his new proposal."

"Which has been dubbed 'Document Number 3.' Dev said this morning he will introduce it tomorrow as an amendment, but it's obviously another attempt to avoid a vote on the Treaty signed in London and substitute his own version. To the average Irishman, it will be like choosing between indistinguishable shades of grey."

THE END OF THE EVENING SESSION SAW A FLURRY OF ACTIVITY ON THE debate dais as papers were passed around to the antagonists at the two opposing tables. After reviewing the new document and comparing it to an earlier one, Arthur rose to complain, "A document has been put into our hands this evening that is not Document No. 2."

De Valera countered sarcastically, "You are quibbling. The Minister for Foreign Affairs is quibbling now."

Realizing the introduction of still another new document was a ploy to supplant the actual Treaty, Kevin O'Higgins called it out for what it was, "This document embodies a post-rejection policy, and it should be a matter for the post-rejection Cabinet if the Treaty is rejected."

Valera objected strongly, crying out emotionally, "I am responsible for the proposals, and the House will have to decide on them. I am going to choose my own procedure."

Appalled by this imperious claim, Arthur responded indignantly, "I submit it is not in the competence of the President to choose his own procedure. This is either a constitutional body, or it is not. If it is an autocracy, let you say so, and we will leave it."

Undaunted, de Valera insisted, "In answer to that, I am going to propose an amendment in my own terms. It is for the House to decide whether they will take it or not."

With this assertion of his right to unilaterally change the direction of the proceedings, they ended for the day. Arthur angrily began stuffing his papers into his briefcase, muttering to Michael, "The audacity! He's going to choose his own procedure, is he?"

"Who the blue hell does he think he is?" Michael responded.

Still fuming, Arthur said indignantly, "Exactly. This sounds not so much like *The Rights of Man* as the *droit du seigneur*. Enough of his bollocks!" He picked up his copy of Document No. 2 but rather than put it away, angrily declared, "This has been hidden from the people long enough. I'll show him."

Arthur stormed out of the hall and into the atrium, where he collared Robert Harding from the *Freeman's Journal*. "Here you go, Mr. Harding, have a look at this and let the country know what you think of this so-called amendment."

The journalist started looking over the amendment but paused and looked up, "You know, Arthur, I heard de Valera in there declare that he would choose his own method. So now he assumes the role of dictator, does he?"

Arthur sighed, "I know, but tell me what you think of the latest version of his document."

Harding went on reading and then commented, "This is much worse than the Treaty. This is a criminal attempt to divide the nation. For all his talk about fighting for a Republic, how come the very word does not appear in his document? De Valera doesn't have the instinct of an Irishman in his blood."[5]

Meanwhile, Seán T. O'Kelly, Sinn Féin's representative in Paris who had returned to Dublin to voice his opposition to the Treaty, noticed Joe McGuinness walk by and called over, "Joe, could we have a word?"

"Sure, Seán T. What is it?"

"Would you consider joining us for a conference at my House tonight? Some of the fellows think Mick's new proposal bears a bit more consideration. What do you say?"

Joe looked at his watch and smiled wryly, "Will there be food?"

"Possibly. I daresay there may be drink," Seán T. added quickly.

As Eoin O'Duffy came along, Joe grabbed him by the arm, "Come with us, Eoin. Seán T.'s offering us military men some homespun hospitality to hammer out a compromise based on some of Mick's ideas. Let's get a couple of fellows to join us."

"Count me in."

ONE HUNDRED TWENTY-TWO

Blood-Stained Jewels

THURSDAY, 5 JANUARY 1922, DUBLIN

DÁIL ÉIREANN PUBLIC SESSION [1]

THE NEXT MORNING A GROUP OF DELEGATES GATHERED AROUND Michael and Arthur as they went over the proposal Seán T. O'Kelly helped put together the night before. Michael read it out loud, *"That President de Valera should continue as President of Dáil Éireann. The Provisional Government would be permitted to function by the Dáil and would derive its powers from the Dáil."* He looked up at Seán, saying, "That's what I was saying a couple of days ago." He continued, *"The Army would remain under the control of the Provisional Government, which is responsible to the Dáil, and the same will apply to every other service."*

Arthur then read, *"Only members of the Provisional Government need sign acceptance of the Treaty."* [2] Arthur nodded and said, "This last bit might be a hard sell in London, but…"

Seán T. asked expectantly, "So, Mick, Arthur, what do you think?"

Mick looked over at Arthur and then back to Seán T., "Arthur's right. For Lloyd George's benefit, we'd have to finesse the bit about signing the Treaty, but…"

"Yes," Arthur replied. "This can work. Well done, gentlemen."

A look of relief came over Seán T.'s face, and with a mixture of hope and confidence, he said, "Here comes Dev. Let's put it to him."

Unfortunately, de Valera had a copy of the *Freeman's Journal* tucked under his arm, and that day's editorial did not exactly engender in him any desire to consider another variation on compromise. On the contrary, when Seán T. showed him the agreement just accepted by the opposing side, he flew into a rage, sputtering claims of insubordination, conspiracy, and vendettas. He finished by saying, "Mr. O'Kelly, after you cast your vote, I expect you to return to your posting in Paris at once," and with that stomped off.

After he stormed away, Eoin O'Duffy summed it up, "Apparently, he demurs."

"The problem is," Joe McGuinness surmised, "Dev is determined to show he, not Mick, is the real Irish leader."[3]

Michael clapped Seán T. on the back, "You gave it your best. Let's go inside."

However, Robert Harding's comments about de Valera, particularly the claim he lacked the instinct of an Irishman in his blood, had made their way into the *Freeman's* editorial and caused so much controversy that the morning session was suspended so delegates could decide how to deal with it. When the delegates reconvened, Richard Mulcahy introduced a measure to exclude anyone from the *Freeman's* from the debates until an apology was offered.

Michael had just risen to address the issue when Harry Boland, just back from New York, entered the hall and was given a standing ovation. As the applause abated and Harry sat, Michael smiled at him before saying, "I regard any motion of this kind as being an interference with the liberty of the Press, and I stand as much for the liberty of the Press as I stood and do stand against personalities."

Arthur addressed the assembly in a similar vein. "If you say you condemn the reference to President de Valera in that article, I am heartily with you. I think this is in the worst of bad taste, but I say the Press must be free to say what it pleases."

Even the target of the editorial, de Valera, agreed with Michael and Arthur, saying, "I think any action of ours which would limit the freedom of the Press is a mistake."

Erskine Childers seconded this, declaring, "I endorse what the President has said."

Richard Mulcahy backed down, chastened and a little wiser, and said, "I withdraw my motion dealing with the possible exclusion of any Press representative."

That ended the controversy there, and at the end of the session Michael went up to Harry to welcome him back properly.

"Harry, I know why you're here, but I'm glad to see you anyway."

Harry laughed and asked, "Are you, then? Wait until you hear what I have to say."

"Why not stop by later, and we'll talk things over? I'm staying at the Gresham."

"Till later, Mick."

HARRY ARRIVED THAT EVENING AT THE GRESHAM HOTEL AND WENT UP to Michael's office, where he found him talking with Liam Tobin. They all attempted to get things off on a friendly footing, shaking hands as Michael said, "I meant it earlier, Harry. I am glad to see you." He smiled and added, "I haven't seen you since I sent you off with those two puppies. How are they?"

"Well loved and cared for by some mutual friends in New York." Harry reached into his jacket pocket and said, "By the way, here are the diamond jewels I've been holding as collateral for that loan to the Soviet mission." He handed them to Michael along with some official-looking documentation of the loan.

Michael accepted the jewellery and put it in a drawer, then took out a piece of stationery and wrote a receipt. As he handed it over, he said softly, "Listen, Harry, there's something you should know. Kitty and I have gotten engaged. I wanted you to be among the first to know."

Harry just stood there quietly for a moment.

Michael continued awkwardly, "So, it's good that you are here now before you hear it from anyone else."

"I see." Harry took a deep breath and said coolly, "My congratulations to you both." Perhaps from embarrassment, Harry quickly changed the subject. "I'm also glad to be back so as to cast my vote against the Treaty." Now Michael stood there silently until Harry elaborated, "Of course, one thing has no bearing on the other."

Michael took this in and agreed, saying, "No, of course not." After another awkward pause, he said, "But Harry, doesn't it faze you just a little bit that most of your constituents and fellow Roscommon delegates favour the Treaty?"

Harry Boland felt uneasy with Michael's question but countered, "Most of our supporters in America are against the Treaty, Mick."

"Are you sure about that, Harry? And who is more important anyway, people an ocean away or your very own neighbours?"

"The neighbours I've spoken to are still holding out for the Republic we fought for, not the Dominion you're offering them."

"That's not the case, and you know it, Harry."

"Then what about the Oath to the King?"

"Harry, have you taken the time to actually read the terms of the Treaty? What the hell did you do with all the free time you had on the boat trip back?"

"I read enough to learn you sold us out."

"Take that back, Boland," Michael shouted as he leaned forward menacingly.

"I'll not fight you here, Mr. Collins. I'll do that in the Dáil. Good night!"

Harry turned to leave as Michael went back to his desk, took the jewels from the drawer and threw them at him, shouting, "Out with you, then, and take these with you. They're blood-stained anyway."

Furious at the insulting turn, Harry nevertheless bent down to the floor and picked up the jewels. "Very well, Michael. You always were a bully. I'll see you in the Dáil."[4]

After Harry slammed the door behind him, Liam said to Michael, "Jaysus, Mick, those jewels are supposed to be worth twenty-five thousand quid!"

"Are they? He can do whatever the hell he wants with them. Ireland's pride is worth more."[5]

ONE HUNDRED TWENTY-THREE

Examine My Own Heart

FRIDAY, 6 JANUARY 1922, DUBLIN

Dáil Éireann Public Session [1]

ALTHOUGH THE COMMITTEE THAT SEÁN T. O'KELLY HAD PUT together two nights earlier did produce

a result initially acceptable to both sides, de Valera's reaction to it and a subsequent night of meetings spoiled whatever good might have come of it. Still, the Public Session was prorogued for still another private one to discuss the workings of the Committee that Friday morning.

One of the delegates groaned to another, "So, we're debating whether we should discuss a debate, is that it?"

"Ay, there you have it. And to decide if it was dishonourable to have convened that committee debate in the first place."

"The substance of which is being held back from us. Have I got it right?"

"Right again. That's it in a nutshell."

"The entire morning is wasted."

"Again."

It was all nonsense, and Michael, who hated these Private Sessions, attempted to close the discussion, "If we are not going to have this thing put before us, we ought in ordinary decency go into public session again, and let there be no private committee meetings and then there can be no question of dishonour because everything will be disclosed. Let us have it one way or the other."

The two delegates who had been talking about the debate of a debate joined a chorus of cries of, "Hear, hear!"

Michael closed, saying, "Let us be straight whichever way we have it."

That should have ended the matter, but the squabbling dragged on to no discernible benefit other than to ultimately disregard the Committee's reports. Then it was time for lunch.

WHEN THE PUBLIC SESSION RESUMED THAT AFTERNOON, TOM CULLEN spotted the recently chastised Robert Harding from the *Freeman's Journal* chatting with someone at the back of the room and went over to say hello.

"Howaya, Robert," Tom greeted him with a smile at the other man. "Back for more trouble, are ye?"

"Not if I can help it, Tom. Say hello to my fellow reporter, Matthew Dowd."

Matthew extended his hand, saying, "Pleased to meet you, Tom. Helluva debate, eh?"

Surprised at hearing an American accent, Tom shook his hand, smiling, "Well, now, where do you hail from, mate?"

"New York, the *New York Times*, to be specific."

"Have you been here through all the public sessions?"

"Through every word."

"You poor bastard, but glad to have you here. Oh, de Valera's about to speak."

De Valera began, feeling it necessary to relay his personal history going back to the Easter Rising and earlier, much earlier.

"I was reared in a labourer's cottage here in Ireland. I have not lived solely amongst the intellectuals. The first fifteen years of my life that formed my character were lived amongst the Irish people down in Limerick. Therefore, I know what I am talking about, and whenever I wanted to know what the Irish people wanted, I had only to examine my own heart, and it told me straight off what the Irish people wanted."

Tom whispered, "You getting this down, boys? Instead of all these long, drawn-out debates, we could've asked the Chief to just look into his heart and tell us what to do! Gads, we're such a bunch of galoots!"

Appreciating this line of humour, Harding agreed, "I know. We could've wrapped this all up well before Christmas."

De Valera's supporters, though, were in a state of rapture listening to him. "Now, if you re-elect me…"

"We will! We will!" they cried out.

"Steady for a moment—I will have to have the right to get a Cabinet that thinks with me so that we can be a unified body. If you elect me and you do it by a majority, I will throw out that Treaty."

He was answered with cheers and applause.

"What I do formally is to lay before the House my resignation."

"No! No!"

He put up his hands to quiet them. "As Chief Executive authority, I resign and with it goes the Cabinet. Do not decide on personalities —on my personality. It is not a question of persons. That has nothing whatever to do with it. As I say, it is not a question of persons because where personality is concerned, we are all the best friends. We worked together as one team. Now we are divided fundamentally, although we had kept together until we reached this bridge. My object was that we don't part before we come to this bridge. We are at the bridge. This House has got my Document No. 2. It will be put before the House by the new Cabinet that will be formed if I am elected. We will put forward that document. It will be submitted to the House."

"He can't do that, can he?" Matthew Dowd asked Harding. "Who does he think he is, Napoleon? Cromwell? They're supposed to be voting on the Treaty, not his damn document."

Tom answered for him, "He can try, but wait, Arthur looks ready to wring Dev's neck."

Arthur was having none of this further attempt to circumvent a vote on the Treaty. "I want to make a short statement. I won't go into the speech of the President now. He agreed that I should wind up this debate. Now, I submit that the order of the day is that we are discussing this motion: *That Dáil Éireann approves of this Treaty between Great Britain and Ireland*, and I submit that until that is decided, we can't discuss the President's Document No. 2. We are still on the orders of the day. And if any attempt is made to bring in another issue, it is an unfair attempt to bring in another discussion, and to closure discussion on the motion before the House."

Still, de Valera persisted, "The Government can resign before everything else. There must be an Executive, and you must have somebody to see that the work of the House is carried out."

One of the Dublin delegates countered, "I want to say this: the nation is bigger than any man and bigger even than the Dáil, and we ought to carry out the orders of the day."

Displaying the magnitude of his self-importance, de Valera said, "I decline to take the responsibility for defending the Republic when I have not got the ordinary means of doing it."

Matthew from the *New York Times* mumbled as he scribbled in his notepad, "Narrow, obstinate, obviously vain, hopelessly discredited as a leader."

Michael was as fed up as Arthur, and declared, "The other side may say what they like, and they may put in any motion that they like, but no matter what happens today, it won't be accepted by me. We will have no Tammany Hall methods here. Whether you are for the Treaty or whether you are against it, fight without Tammany Hall methods."

This oblique reference to Harry Boland's dealings in the States was insulting enough, but then he took it a step further, declaring, "A Committee was appointed by the House, and the House was prevented from receiving the report of that Committee—it was prevented by three or four bullies. Are you going to be held up by three or four bullies?"

De Valera blanched at this intemperate remark and asked the Speaker, "Is that a proper thing?"

Eoin MacNeill turned to Michael and replied, "I ask the Minister of Finance to withdraw that term."

Michael was seething with anger, but rather than say anything else untoward, he held his tongue, looking out across the hall, keeping everyone in suspense as to what he could possibly say next to extricate himself from the corner he had painted himself into. Finally, he turned to Eoin, squinted, and said caustically, "I can withdraw the term, but the spoken word cannot be recalled. Is that right, sir?"

A wave of laughter, applause, and some relief swept across the room, after which Michael concluded, saying forcefully, "This motion to suspend the Standing Orders is a motion to draw a red herring across our path here. And it is because of that that I, for one, cannot agree to it." With that, he sat down to renewed applause.

One person who was neither amused nor impressed was Cathal Brugha. "The Minister of Finance has made a statement that the result of a meeting of eight or nine members of this body within the last twenty-four or forty-eight hours was prevented from being brought before us, and that this was the work of some bullies. He was asked to withdraw that. You have seen the way in which he withdrew it. I don't know to whom he referred when he mentioned this word, 'bullies.' Possibly, he may have referred to me as being one of them. In the ordinary way, I would take exception and take offence at such a term being applied to me, but the amount of offence that I would take at it would be measured by the respect or esteem that I had for the character of the person who made the charge. In this particular instance, I take no offence whatever."

Michael sat stoically through this insult and listened passively as Brugha continued. "Now, the Minister for Finance says something about Tammany Hall methods. I know nothing about them. Possibly he does. When the Standing Orders have been suspended, he and his friends can discuss any statements that have been made by the President. That's all I have to say."

Michael responded calmly, "In that case, I am satisfied."

Harry, however, was piqued. "I support the motion for the suspension of the Standing Orders. I presume the remarks of the Honourable member for Cork were intended for me. I am sorry that he has seen fit to make such a suggestion. I will say this: that I don't know anything about Tammany Hall except this, that if he had a little training in Tammany Hall, and reserved some of his bullying for Lloyd George, we would not be in the position we are in today.[2] I maintain that if the orders of the day be suspended, if the President's resignation be accepted and if he goes forward for re-election on a definite policy which he has clearly expressed, that is proper and constitutional."

Arthur was determined to avoid any issue other than the vote on the Treaty. "I want to know why this matter is sprung now instead of letting the standing motion be taken in the ordinary course. If the vote is adverse to us, well and good. If it is adverse to the President, he can do what he suggests to do now. Why we should be stopped in the middle of this discussion and a vote taken on the personality of President de Valera, I don't understand, and I don't think my countrymen will understand it."

De Valera then claimed disingenuously, "I am sick and tired of politics—so sick that no matter what happens, I would go back to private life. I have only seen politics within the last three weeks or a month. It is the first time I have seen them, and I am sick to the heart of them."

This disingenuous complaint did little to tone down the rhetoric. Another delegate, Seamus Robinson, continued the personal attack on Michael. "There are thousands of people who are enthusiastic supporters of the Treaty simply because Michael Collins is its mother—possibly Arthur Griffith would be called its father."

Matthew whispered to Harding, "Griffith and Collins?! I knew they were intimate friends, but that's an unorthodox way of putting it!"

This crack earned him a rebuke from Harding, "Shut up, Yank," and a poke in the ribs from Tom.

Meanwhile, Robinson continued his diatribe. "Now, it is only natural and right that many people should follow almost blindly a great and good man. But suppose you know that such a man was not really such a great man, and that his reputation and great deeds of daring were in existence only on paper and in the imagination of people who read stories about him. It has been said, 'What is good enough for Michael Collins is good enough for me.' Arthur Griffith has called Collins 'the man who won the war.' The Press has called him the Commander-in-Chief of the I.R.A. He has been called 'a great exponent of guerrilla warfare' and the 'elusive Mike,' and we have all read the story of the man riding into battle at Rosscarbery on the white horse. There are stories going around Dublin of fights he had all over the city—the Custom House in particular. Now, I'm forced to think that the reported Michael Collins could not possibly be the same Michael Collins who was so weak as to compromise the Republic."

Kevin O'Higgins addressed the absurdity of this argument. "On a point of order. Are we discussing Michael Collins or the Treaty?"

Another deputy called out, "Or are we impeaching him?"

Michael remained silent, seemingly emotionless, except for a hint of a smile at the mention of the white horse.

Robinson refused to relent. "The weak man who signed certainly exists and just as certainly, therefore, I believe the reported Michael Collins did not ever exist. If Michael Collins who signed the Treaty ever did the wonderful things reported of him, then I'm just another fool. In fact, is there any authoritative record of his having ever fired a shot for Ireland at an enemy of Ireland?"

Shaking his head, Gavan Duffy took a turn trying to stop this tirade. "Is this in order?"

Eoin MacNeill said in a tone of amazement, "I don't want to interrupt, but I think it is as near not discussing the Treaty as possible."

This bit of humour did little to tone down the personal attacks, so on it went in this tedious vein until the closing at 7 p.m. Tom Cullen said to the two reporters, "That was a long day."

"An exhausting one, too," Matthew agreed.

"Long and long-winded," Harding added, "but not without some amusing running commentary."

Tom laughed, saying, "We all needed some comic relief. I have to go now. Say, Matthew, would you like to meet Michael Collins?"

"Oh, yes. In one of my early despatches, I wrote that he's the outstanding figure here, so I would indeed."

As Michael stepped down from the dais a moment later, Tom made the introductions. "Mick, this is Matthew Dowd from the *New York Times*. He's been covering the debates from the outstart."

Michael extended his hand and said, "Ah, sorry to hear that. It looks like you drew the short straw."

"So your friend Tom was saying."

"You missed Christmas at home for this?"

"Not entirely. I spent Christmas with grandparents I had never met before, so it's been more like a homecoming."

"In that case, welcome home to the prodigal son. I don't often get to read your paper, so tell me what you think so far."

"The speeches have been very impressive until today when honestly, I thought de Valera behaved like a hysterical schoolgirl, to borrow a phrase from Lord Birkenhead."[3]

Michael emitted one of his signature yelps and asked with a grin, "I hope you, as a New Yorker, didn't take exception to my accusing Mr. Boland of Tammany Hall methods?"

"Not in the slightest. Harry's well-liked in the States, but he drew fire when he spoke at Madison Square, extolling the crowd to rise up and tear down everything British in America. He seemed to forget that we just came out of a war fighting alongside the Brits, and besides, Americans don't take kindly to being preached to by politicians."

"Ay, that's Harry. Ever ready to put his foot in it."

"Yes," Matthew agreed, "and my paper let him know it. If you'll excuse me, it's getting late, and I have to get to the cable office to get my copy to New York for the morning paper."

Michael laughed and said, "Including the bit about a hysterical schoolgirl? Tom, see that you pick up a copy of that!"

"I'll be sure to, Mick." Tom shook hands with Matthew, saying, "It's been a pleasure. See you, Robert."

Michael was ready to leave as Gearoid O'Sullivan came over with a broad smile. Worn out as he was, Michael cheered up at seeing his friend. "Thanks for your blissfully brief speech today, George. Hearing you declare your support for the Treaty was about the only bright point in the day."

"Oh, I don't know, Mick," Gearoid mused. "Could you tell us the story about the white horse again? That was my favourite bit."

Michael laughed and said, "I can't believe Robinson dug up that old English trope about me galloping into a shoot-out at Rosscarbery on a white horse. I haven't ridden a white horse since I rode 'Gipsy' back in the day in Woodfield when I was just a lad and used her mane as a bridle."[4]

Gearoid said facetiously, "Then tell us again how you confounded the British the day of the Custom House raid."

"You mean the raid I tried to stop?"

"No, don't tell us! Robinson made that one up, too?"

Looking over Gearoid's shoulder, Michael said, "The truth of it is, that day belonged to the likes of Tom Ennis and the redoubtable Joe McGuinness, and here's the man himself."

McGuinness came up to them and said, "G'wan with you. I could throttle Cathal for what he said about you in there."

Michael shook his hand and said, "All I ever did that day was show up to cheer your men on, and I never claimed more than that. Robinson's tall tales notwithstanding, Joe, you played your part well at the Custom House, but I still hold Cathal responsible for that exercise in stupidity."

"Those things Cathal said about you, I'll tell you, it gets my blood going. Then there's Dev. During those committee meetings, we bent over backwards to come up with a compromise to please him, but he just shot it down out of hand."

"I know, Joe," Michael said. "You and Seán T. pulled together some excellent work in short order, but the problem is Dev never has been one to compromise, has he?"

"Well, tomorrow looks to be the big day when things are set right," Gearoid remarked.

"I'll have a thing or two to say," Joe replied.

"How do you think it will go, Mick?"

"It will be close, I'm afraid. So many of our old friends are turning their backs on us."

"Like Harry?" Joe asked.

"Yes, Harry is working like the very devil against us, but I was thinking of the Army. I'm sure you all took notice that two of our best commanders, Liam Lynch and even Oscar Traynor, have issued a statement they cannot support the Treaty. That can only spell trouble down the road."[5]

If My Name Is to Go Down in History

SATURDAY, 7 JANUARY 1922, DUBLIN

Dáil Éireann Public Session and Vote [1]

THE FOLLOWING MORNING, LIAM TOBIN, TOM CULLEN, AND JOE O'Reilly accompanied Michael to University College for what was expected to be the last day of the debates and, more importantly, the day the vote would at last be taken. As they walked through the vestibule, Tom asked who was scheduled to speak first that morning.

"That would be our Harry," Michael told him, "and we can hazard a guess what the general drift will be."

Liam replied, "Sad but true. Then Cathal and Arthur give the closing speeches, don't they?"

"They do, and then, probably after a recess, we vote."

"In that case, we'll catch you up later, Mick, and good luck."

Michael was about to turn away when Alice Lyons and Sinéad Mason approached. "Yes, good luck, Mick," Alice said, having heard the tail end of the conversation.

Sinéad added her good wishes, "Yes, good luck with the vote. We're looking forward to Arthur's speech. How does he seem to you? He's seemed a bit pale lately."

"If so," Michael said with an ironic grin, "I'm sure Cathal will invigorate him. Harry, too. It's grand seeing you, but I must go."

Harry did not fail to live up to expectations. He ardently proclaimed, "I rise to speak against this Treaty because, in my opinion, it denies the sovereignty of the Irish nation, and I stand by the principles I have always held—that the Irish people are by right a free people."

After a lengthy summary of his time in America and impressions of the feelings of the Treaty there, he lightened the mood by pointing out the futility of expecting Americans to come over in large numbers to join the fight. "No one knows better than my friend, Michael, that there were five thousand men in America ready to come to fight in Ireland, and they couldn't come as a foreign legion because it was against American laws."

Michael joined the entire hall in laughter, calling out, "Now you're talking."

"The cablegram that my friend Michael Collins took such exception to was suggested by me to strengthen his hands four days before the Treaty was signed. I would be false to the position I hold in Dáil Éireann if I did not say that the great public opinion of America is on the side of this Treaty. I would be false to my position as a representative of the Government if I didn't fearlessly state that here—that just as it seems the Press of Ireland has adopted a unanimous attitude in favour of this Treaty, so too did the American Press adopt that attitude. However, the people who subscribed the money to enable us to carry on look upon this as a betrayal.

"If I could accept that Treaty as a stepping stone to Irish freedom, I would do it," he explained in deference to Michael's oft-used phrase. "But I know that I would not be doing an expedient thing for Ireland, but doing what, in my opinion, would forever debar Ireland from winning her ultimate freedom. If we reject that Treaty, England will not make war on us. If she does, we will be able to defend ourselves as we have always done."

Harry was followed by his friend Joe McGrath, who had accompanied him the previous summer on the fateful trip to Gairloch, Scotland, to meet with Lloyd George. "I am swallowing a bitter pill in having to vote for this Treaty. As I said before, it is not what I want. I have had to swallow bitter pills before. I want Deputy Harry Boland to tell me now what he meant when he told me he was going back to America on the President's instructions to do an awful thing—to prepare the American people for something short of a Republic."

Ever ready to step in to nitpick, de Valera corrected him, "Short of the isolated Republic." "Something short of a Republic," McGrath firmly repeated. "That was what he was going back for, and now he comes home to talk of sovereign status. Well, consequently, it surprised me to see Harry Boland's telegram stating that he was against the Treaty."

Con Collins, who had good-naturedly endured Michael's dinner mischief at Batt O'Connor's home the day the Truce was signed, gave a short, heartfelt speech imploring the Dáil not to accept anything less than a Republic. He ended by saying, "If it is not yet too late, I would make a last appeal for unity to these people to save their country, and they can only unite on the basis on which I and a number of Deputies in this Dáil stand, and that is the basis of an Irish Republic."

Con's remarks earned him some polite applause, to which Liam remarked, "No one would ever accuse Con of being insincere."

Tom agreed, "No, that was an honest plea."

Joe McGuinness then got a chance to voice his frustration over the failed outcome of the committee meetings in which he had partici-pated. "I have, during the past three weeks, done what I could in a private way to see if, in any way, the two sides could be brought together, if any arrangement could come to preserve the unity of this Dáil. The Committee of which I was a member had almost succeeded in doing that. People who are against this Treaty, for some reason which I cannot understand, refused to allow that document which we had drawn up to come before yesterday's Private Session of the Dáil. Instead of that, a bombshell was thrown in by the resignation of the President. That is the President's own business, but I can say as a member of that Committee that the people on this side literally went on their knees to President de Valera to try and preserve the unity of the country."[2]

De Valera objected to this characterization, "One of the objections I had to that Committee was that they were bringing forward a thing that was impossible. They were trying to put me in the same position as was attempted in America."

McGuinness got in the last word, "To anybody who was present yesterday, it will be clear that what I have said is absolutely true."

DURING THE AFTERNOON SESSION, PERHAPS THE SHORTEST SPEECH OF all the debates was delivered by Seán Hales, coming in at less than half a minute and ending with him saying, "I now state publicly that I am going to vote for this Treaty."

Joe O'Reilly clapped loudly and said to Liam and Tom, "Given his brother Tom's stance on the Treaty, surely that counts for something."

Liam nodded, "Ay, and Tom is a dangerous character not to have on our side."

Next up was Cathal Brugha, who repeated a question raised by Seamus Robinson the day before, "I think it is of great importance that an authoritative statement be made. A: defining the real position Mr. Michael Collins held in the Army, B: telling what fights he has taken an active part in, provided this can be done without injustice to himself or danger to the country, or can it be authoritatively stated that he ever fired a shot at any enemy of Ireland?"

Simmering with rage in his seat, Tom Cullen looked as if he was ready to rush the dais, while once again, one of the delegates asked, "Is that in order?"

Unfazed, Michael replied, "Carry on."

Brugha did, saying, "That is a matter which I approach with great reluctance, and I may tell you I would never have dealt with it, and this question would never have been asked, but for the statement made by the Chairman of the Delegation when he was speaking here. He referred to Mr. Michael Collins as the man who won the war."

Arthur, the Chairman, called out with a touch of sarcasm, "Hear, hear."

"So he did," came another reply.

Brugha replied disdainfully, "And the war is won, and we are talking here. Very well, I will explain to you how that is done."

Michael felt it was finally time to raise an objection, "I would like to rise to a point of order. Are we discussing the Treaty, or are we discussing the Minister of Finance? I think we are discussing the Treaty."

One delegate joined him, "If things are to be said about the Minister of Finance, are we at liberty to say anything we know about other people? I mean, it is becoming personal."

Another added, "I think Cathal Brugha ought to respect the chair."

In self-defence, Brugha admitted, in Irish, "*Táim ní aingeal in aon chor me*," meaning, "I'm no angel."

"*Ní chuirfeadh einne e sin id' leith,*" Michael countered. "No one would accuse you of that."

Still, Brugha was unrelenting. "It is necessary for me to define Michael Collins' position in the Army. To use a word which he has on more than one occasion used, and which he is fond of using, he is merely a subordinate in the Department of Defence. While the war was in progress, I could not praise too highly the work done by the Headquarters Staff. They worked conscientiously and patriotically for Ireland without seeking any notoriety, with one exception. Whether he is responsible or not for the notoriety, I am not going to say."

He was shouted down with cries of "Shame!" and "Get on with the Treaty," all of which he ignored. In the visitor's section, Liam remarked, "Typical Cathal."

"Hasn't the brains of a donkey, but just as stubborn," Tom agreed.

Undeterred by all the outbursts, Brugha kept on, "One member was specially selected by the Press and the people and put into a position which he never held. He was made a romantic figure, a mystical character such as this person certainly is not. The gentleman I refer to is Mr. Michael Collins."

Eamonn Duggan called out, "The Irish people will judge that," followed by another delegate who cried out, "Now we know the reason for the opposition to the Treaty."

Brugha shouted over the ensuing applause, "The Chairman of the Delegation thinks the war is won, so far as he could win it, for England."

"Bravo, Cathal, bravo," Arthur answered, once again, in mockery.

Someone else complained, "I respectfully suggest that the Minister for Defence…"

Another delegate, Dan MacCarthy, the pro-Treaty whip, called out facetiously, "I must protest against the Minister of Defence being interrupted. He is making a good speech for the Treaty."[3]

Impervious to sarcasm, Brugha continued unabated, "I put it up now to the five men, the five members of this Delegation, that they are not to vote at all for this Treaty. They should leave it to the Dáil. They should not vote for it. Finally, I put it up to Mr. Arthur Griffith to fall in with this course, and I tell Mr. Arthur Griffith that when in 1917 he stepped down in favour of Éamon de Valera as President of the Sinn Féin Organisation of which he had been head since its inception—certainly for years—I tell Mr. Griffith that when he did that, he earned the respect of men to whom his name, prior to that, was no more than the name of any other man. However, when he did that, and since that, these men have respect for Arthur Griffith second only to Éamon de Valera. If Arthur Griffith will fall in with this suggestion, I now tell him —and I need not take upon myself to be a prophet to foretell it—I tell him if he does this, his name will live for ever in Ireland."

AFTER A SHORT BREAK FOR TEA ARTHUR DELIVERED THE FINAL SPEECH of the debates, making it clear he would not follow Brugha's advice. "I cannot accept the invitation of the Minister of Defence to dishonour my signature and become immortalised in Irish history. I have signed this Treaty, and the man or nation that dishonours its signature is dishonoured forever. No man who signed that Treaty can dishonour his signature without dishonouring himself and the nation."

The Dáil erupted in applause again, strengthening his resolve, "One other reference will I make to what the Minister of Defence has said. He spoke of Michael Collins; he referred to what I said about Michael Collins—that he was the man who won the war. I said it, and I say it again. He was the man that made the situation. He was the man, and nobody knows better than I do how during a year and a half he worked from six in the morning until two next morning. He was the man whose matchless energy, whose indomitable will carried Ireland through the terrible crisis."

Now every phrase, every word won him shouts of approval and applause, which he only acknowledged by remaining still and silent, breathing heavily, before continuing. "And though I have not now, and never had, an ambition about either political affairs or history, if my name is to go down in history, I want it associated with the name of Michael Collins." In an instant, most in the room were on their feet, cheering him on. Arthur's voice rang out over the tumult, "Michael Collins was the man who fought the Black and Tan terror for twelve months until England was forced to offer terms. That is all I have to say on that subject."

If Arthur had given the greatest speech of his career at the opening of the debates, he was surpassing himself with this one, as once again he reiterated his support for all the salient points in the Treaty. "If the people in this assembly do not understand what is in the document, they are not fit to be representatives of the people of Ireland." Even this singular, brief, caustic statement won applause, as he had clearly captivated the entire room. "Now, the Irish people are going to know, so far as I am concerned, what is the difference. I belong to the Irish people. I have worked for them because they are flesh of my flesh and bone of my bone."

The cheers this brought were as much an affirmation of Arthur as they were recognition of another slight to de Valera's methods. He continued to emphasise the contrast between himself and de Valera, "I have never deceived them, at all events, whatever I have done. I may have misled them or given them bad advice, but I have never concealed from them anything that is vital to their interests. It is vital for them to know what we are up against and not to be misled and not to believe that we, plenipotentiaries, went away with a mandate for the Republic and came back with something else. I have heard in this assembly state-ments about the people of Ireland. The people of Ireland sent us here —we have no right and no authority except what we derive from the people of Ireland—we are here because the people of Ireland elected us, and our only right to speak is to seek what they want."

In the course of the debates, it seemed any mention of the people of Ireland garnered applause, but everyone understood Arthur was getting to the heart of democracy, the soul of a true Republic, and they now hung on every word. "If representative government is going to remain on the earth, then a representative must voice the opinion of his constituents. If his conscience will not let him do that, he has only one way out, and that is to resign and refuse to misrepresent them. But that men who know their constituents want this Treaty should come here and tell us that, by virtue of the vote they derive from these constituents, they are going to vote against this Treaty—as that is the negation of all democratic right, it is the negation of all freedom. You are trying to reject this Treaty without allowing the Irish people to say whether they want it or not—the people whose lives and fortunes are involved."

Growing desperate, de Valera and his supporters shouted out, "No! No!"

Arthur shouted back, "You will kill Dáil Éireann when you do that."

"No! No!" came cries from around the room.

"You will remove from Dáil Éireann every vestige of moral authority, and they will no longer represent the people of Ireland. It will be a junta dictating to the people of Ireland, and the people of Ireland will deal with it. Your constituents told you to vote for this Treaty. The Irish people will not be deceived. They know. They have made their voice heard. Some of you will try to muzzle it, but that voice will be heard, and it will pierce through."

Here Arthur halted, exhausted from the exertion, took a handkerchief from his pocket, and while the room filled with both cheers as well as cries of "No! No!" he wiped his glasses clean. He put his glasses back on and said with renewed resolve, "We had much talk of principles, of honour, and of virtue here. It seemed to me all on one side. We on this side had lost all the effulgence of virtue that emblazoned the faces of the people on the opposite side. Well, I have some principles. The principle that I have stood on all my life is the principle of Ireland for the Irish people."

"Hear, hear!"

"I say now to the people of Ireland that it is their right to see that this Treaty is carried into operation, when they get, for the first time in seven centuries, a chance to live their lives in their own country and take their place amongst the nations of Europe."

Then as Arthur, weak and exhausted, finally sat down, most of the delegates rose to their feet, cheering wildly and applauding. Watching and listening at the back of the room, Alice and Sinéad looked at each other and laughed in relief as they joined in.

"Looks like they've decided already," Alice surmised. "Back at Hans Place, we saw how tough Arthur could be, but I don't think I ever heard him speak in public so passionately."

"Ay, but something's wrong," Sinéad said in a worried tone. "Mick is clapping along with everyone, but all the same, he looks grim enough."

Up at the front of the room, Liam was also concerned. "The way Mick's looking down at Arthur, we better be ready to get them both out of here quickly when this is all over."

Emotions were running high throughout the room, most pointedly with de Valera, who stood and cried out across the din, his voice cracking, "Before you take a vote, I want to enter my last protest—that document will rise in judgment against the men who say there is only a shadow of difference…"

Seán Milroy interrupted to agree with him, at least sardonically, "Yes, that's all."

Some laughs followed, but de Valera insisted, "If everything is in this Treaty that seemed to be covered by it—but it is not—I say that the Irish nation will judge you who have brought this Treaty—if it is approved, they will judge you by comparing what you got for the Irish people out of it with the terms of an explicit document where there is nothing implied but everything on the face of it."

It was evident from de Valera's desperation and twisted, stumbling syntax that his cause was lost. Michael had the final say when he leapt to his feet, vehemently proclaiming, "Let the Irish nation judge us now and for future years."[4]

Eoin MacNeill banged his Speaker's gavel and announced in a steady, clear voice, "We will take a vote now in the usual way by calling the roll. The vote is on the motion by the Minister for Foreign Affairs that Dáil Éireann approves of the Treaty."

The room fell silent as the Clerk began calling on the delegates by alphabetical order of their constituencies. As fate would have it, representing Armagh, Michael's was the first name called.

"*Mícheál O Coileáin.*"

"*Is toil,*" Michael answered, voting "I will it, Yes."

Representing Cavan, Arthur was next. "*Art O Gríobhtha.*"

"*Is toil.*"

Slowly, deliberately, the votes were cast while a tense, strained hush fell over the entire hall. The tension increased when the roll came to Cork, another constituency that Michael represented and could have cast a vote for, but he demurred, saying, "The people on the other side need not have objected. I have already voted."

After ten minutes the roll call was finished, and a couple more minutes passed in agonising silence before MacNeil announced, first in Irish and then in English, "The result of the poll is sixty-four for approval and fifty-seven against. That is a majority of seven in favour of approval of the Treaty."

When the result was announced, a gasp of relief went up from the Treaty supporters. Other than that, the result was met with stunned silence. The delegates, Press, and visitors remained quiet and motionless, as in a state of suspended animation. As word of the result reached the street, the roar of tremendous cheering was heard from outside. At the back of the hall, a young man threw his hat in the air and broke the silence by calling out, "Long live the President of the Republic!" A few delegates around the room attempted to rally themselves by weakly repeating the cheer, but these quickly died out, as did angry outbursts here and there fiercely denouncing the Treaty. Then, as if released from its trance, the rest of the room erupted with ringing cheers while the members of the anti-Treaty faction sat stone-faced, unable to utter a word.

Realising the depth of his defeat, de Valera rose with an ashen face, his hands trembling as he stood at the desk before him. Many of his supporters were in tears as he attempted to remain stoic, announcing, "It will, of course, be my duty to resign my office as Chief Executive. I do not know that I should do it just now."

"No," Michael called out.

While trying to maintain a valiant bearing, de Valera qualified his reaction to the result, "There is one thing I want to say—I want it to go to the country and to the world, and it is this—the Irish people established a Republic. This is simply approval of a certain resolution. The Republic can only be disestablished by the Irish people. Therefore, until such time as the Irish people in regular manner disestablish it, this Republic goes on. Whatever arrangements are made, this is the supreme sovereign body in the nation. This is the body to which the nation looks for its supreme Government, and it must remain that—no matter who is the Executive—it must remain that until the Irish people have disestablished it."

Rather than deliberate the point, Michael was magnanimous in his response as de Valera sat down, "I ask your permission to make a statement. I do not regard the passing of this thing as being any kind of triumph over the other side. I will do my best in the future, as I have done in the past, for the nation. What I have to say now is, whether there is something contentious about the Republic or not, that we should unite on this—that we will all do our best to preserve the public safety."

De Valera appreciated this conciliatory pledge, answering, "Hear, hear."

"That's Mick," Tom remarked to Liam, "the people first."

Michael continued to offer an olive branch of cooperation. "Now, in all countries in times of change—when countries are passing from peace to war or war to peace— they have had their most trying times on an occasion like this. Whether we are right or whether we are wrong in the view of future generations, there is this: that we now are entitled to a chance. All the responsibility will fall upon us of taking over the machinery of government from the enemy. In times of change like that, when countries change from peace to war or war to peace, there are always elements that make for disorder and that make for chaos. That is as true of Ireland as of any other country, for in that respect, all countries are the same. Now, what I suggest is that—I suppose we could regard it like this— that we are a kind of a majority party and that the others are a minority party. That is all I regard it as at present, and upon us, I suppose, will be the responsibility of proving our mark, to borrow a term from our President."

De Valera nodded his head slightly at being referred to in this way and listened as Michael went on, "Well, if we could form some kind of joint Committee to carry on—for carrying through the arrangements one way or another—I think that is what we ought to do. Now, I only want to say this to the people who are against us—and there are good people against us—so far as I am concerned, this is not a question of politics, nor never has been. I make the promise publicly to the Irish nation that I will do my best, and though some people here have said hard things of me—I would not stand things like that said about the other side—I have just as high a regard for some of them, and am prepared to do as much for them, now as always. The President knows how I tried to do my best for him."

Again, de Valera responded, "Hear, hear."

Michael then looked directly at de Valera and told him, announcing to the room, "Well, he has exactly the same position in my heart now as he always had."

The room erupted in applause as delegates rose to their feet to endorse this declaration of profound, unbridled respect.

"Now, there you have a statesman," Liam said, beaming with pride.

Overwhelmed, de Valera dropped his chin down to his chest.

One delegate, however, was considerably less impressed and not at all swayed by the emotion of the moment. Mary MacSwiney rose, and in a vindictive, scolding tone, exclaimed, "I claim my right, before matters go any further, to register my protest, because I, for one, will have neither hand, act, nor part in helping the Irish Free State to carry this nation of ours, this glorious nation that has been betrayed here tonight, into the British Empire—either with or without your hands up. I maintain here now that this is the grossest act of betrayal that Ireland ever endured. The speech we have heard sounded very beautiful—as the late Minister of Finance can do it. He has played up to the gallery in this thing, but I tell you it may sound very beautiful, but it will not do. Make no doubt about it. This is a betrayal, a gross betrayal, and the fact is that it is only a small majority, and that majority is not united. Half of them look for a gun, and the other half are looking for the fleshpots of the Empire. I tell you here there can be no union between the representatives of the Irish Republic and the so-called Free State."

After this overwrought, slanderous outburst, which mainly went ignored, de Valera slowly rose again and in a faltering voice choked with tears, tried to address the room one last time, "I would like my last word here to be this: we have had a glorious record for four years. It has been four years of magnificent discipline in our nation. The world is looking at us now…" Unable to speak any further, broken and defeated, his hands gripping the edges of the little table before him, he braced his long frame and then, exhausted and depleted, sat back down and buried his face in his hands as everyone there expressed their sympathy with a mixture of cheers, applause, and tears.

Amid all this, Cathal Brugha called out, trying to be heard over all the din, "So far as I am concerned, I will see, at any rate, that discipline is kept in the Army."

It was a last, desperate attempt to put a brave face and a positive gloss on the defeat, but it fell pathetically short as the cheering continued.

Packing up his briefcase to leave, Michael looked over to Harry Boland, who returned his gaze with tears streaming down his cheeks. Michael stared back, tears welling in his eyes.

Harry turned away to help de Valera make his way out to the lobby. Some women came up to de Valera, crying as they shook his hand. Out on the street, they were met by a chorus of cheers intermingled with boos, but Harry ushered him into a waiting car, and they drove away. [5]

ONE HUNDRED TWENTY-FIVE

The Other Side Is Killing Me

MONDAY, 9 JANUARY 1922, DUBLIN

Dáil Éireann Public Session [1]

THOUGH THE MONDAY MORNING CAR RIDE BACK TO THE UNIVERSITY hall was tense and sombre, Tom Cullen risked inviting Michael's ire by venturing a question. "Mick, with the Treaty having been approved, what do you think Dev will do next? He's still the President of the Dáil, but do you think he will resign?"

Michael didn't have a clear answer. "He might since he's been dealt a losing hand. Some newspaper called Lloyd George a card sharper, but Dev is just as wily. There's no telling what he'll do next, but rest assured, whatever manoeuvre he pulls, he's not about to retire to private life, as he claimed. Still, whatever he does, we should try to keep him in the fold. I'd rather have him fighting us from within than from out."

"And then, there's Cathal," Liam added.

"Yes, and then there's Cathal, and then there's the Army."

Pat McCrea pulled the car over, "Here you go, Mick."

"You'll soon have your answer, Tom. Let's go."

Although Michael was correct in his estimation of de Valera's cunning, he was nevertheless taken aback at the chosen tactic.

After being recognized by Speaker MacNeill, de Valera started the day's proceedings. "In view of the vote that was taken here on Saturday, which I definitely had to oppose as one that would subvert the Republic and the independence of the country, I could no longer continue in my present office, feeling I did not have the confidence of the House. I, therefore, wish to place my resignation in the hands of the assembly. I resign my office and the responsibilities of it, and the members of the Cabinet all go with my resignation. The first business should be to make arrangements for the business of the Government of the State and for its continuance."

Trying to put the best possible face to this nearly inevitable outcome, Michael rose to say, "In view of that, I suggest that my previous suggestions about forming a Committee on Public Safety be put forward. My belief about the thing is this: that no one here in this assembly or in Ireland wants to be put in the position of opposing President de Valera. We need to stop sulking and get on with the work. We are faced with the problems of taking Ireland over from the English, and they are faced with the problem of handing Ireland over to us, and the difficulties on both sides will be pretty big. It does not matter what happens so long as we are assured that we are taking over Ireland and that the English are going out of Ireland. My suggestion means that we form a Committee on both sides, if necessary, for the preservation of the public peace, and that on our side, we form a Committee to arrange the details and to do all the dirty work—all the difficult work that has to be done, and we will try to do the best we can."

"Hear, hear," the delegates responded.

De Valera then rose to take a vastly different tact. "As far as I am concerned, I think we will have to proceed constitutionally in this matter. I have tendered my resignation, and I cannot, in any way, take divided responsibility."

Realizing that by divided responsibility, he meant divided power, Michael turned and looked over to Tom Cullen, who nodded as if to say, "What will Dev do next? There's my answer."

Then de Valera delivered his surprise. "The majority party say they do not want to oppose my re-election. I was asked the question, what would I do if elected, and I told you what I would do—carry on as before and forget that this Treaty has come. Let those who wish to work it go on. The majority vote at any time can defeat any proposition."

Standing near the entrance, Tom whispered to Liam, "Forget this

Treaty, eh? So now he wants us to vote to re-elect him and let him throw out the Treaty?"

"Apparently so, Tom. He's gambling that his personal prestige is greater than the will of the people to accept the Treaty."

"Look at Mick."

Liam looked over to see Michael shifting about restlessly in his seat. "Yes. You can see how livid he is."

MacNeill banged his gavel on the table and announced, "The motion you are going to vote upon is this: 'That Mr. de Valera be re-elected President of the Irish Republic.'"

Michael stood up to address the assembly. "I am voting against it. I want, at the same time, to register a protest. We have no power here to elect a President of the Republic. The people of Ireland can elect their President. The point is this: I have no power as a representative here to say who can be President of the Irish Republic. I am voting against the resolution."

The succeeding vote was much closer than the one to accept the Treaty, and this time de Valera lost by a much smaller margin.

After the poll was taken, the Dáil Secretary rose to announce, "For the re-election of President de Valera 58, Against 60."

Eoin MacNeill called out, "I declare the resolution lost."

Arthur stood up and called out over the cheers and recriminations, "Before another word is spoken, I want to say, I want the Deputies here to know, and all Ireland to know, that this vote is not to be taken as against President de Valera." This statement drew a wide round of applause. "It is a vote to help the Treaty, and I want to say now that there is scarcely a man I have ever met in my life that I have more love and respect for than President de Valera. I am thoroughly sorry to see him placed in such a position. We want him with us."

The entire room erupted in cheers at this magnanimous paean to an opponent, but its recipient had a less charitable response. De Valera rose to speak amidst cries of "Order" but was interrupted by a member who called out, "Look here, Dev will not speak until I have spoken." Ignoring more cries of "Order," this delegate went on angrily, "I voted, not for personalities, but for my country. Dev has been made a tool of, and I am sorry for it."

De Valera responded defensively, "I want to assure everybody on the other side that it was not a trick. That was my own definite way of doing the right thing for Ireland. I tell you that from my heart. I did it because I felt that it was still the best way to keep that discipline which we had in the past. I did it because, as I said, that I can, in so far as the principal resources of the Republic are concerned—I would conserve them for the Republic. That was the only reason why I allowed my name to go forward. Now, I think the right thing has been done, that the people who are responsible have done the right thing, and therefore I hope that nobody will talk of fratricidal strife. That is all nonsense."

Later, after the meeting finally ended, Arthur said, "Fratricidal strife? And just who could be accused of inciting that?"

Michael replied bitterly, "This is what happens when elections are denied by autocrats. He lost the vote on the Treaty. Then he lost the vote to be President of the Dáil. Nobody was talking of fratricide until he just did. As I told Kitty in a letter yesterday, I'm absolutely fagged out and worn out. The other side is killing me—God help me."[2]

"What else can go wrong? God help us all."

"Amen. Excuse me, Arthur, I need to have a word with MacNeill."

Michael went over to confer with the Speaker, who informed him, "I understand, Mick. Submit it as a motion, and we will take it up in tomorrow's session."

ONE HUNDRED TWENTY-SIX

Deserters All!

TUESDAY, 10 JANUARY 1922, DUBLIN

Dáil Éireann Public Session [1]

EARLY INTO THE NEXT DAY'S SESSION, MICHAEL ASKED THAT HIS NEW motion be moved to the agenda. Speaker MacNeill assented, declaring, "Item number three on the Agenda is a motion by Mr. Michael Collins, 'That Mr. Arthur Griffith be appointed President of Dáil Éireann.' I take it that the first thing that it is necessary for us to do is to make arrangements for the administration of the country."

Despite the obvious need to proceed, de Valera questioned the move. "Is the motion in order?"

MacNeill responded, "I think there is no question that the motion is in order. The administration of the country is the first of all concerns."

Michael rose in support of his own motion, echoing de Valera's previous maritime analogy. "The reason that I do this is that the Irish nation at the present moment is a ship without a captain, and a ship, we all know, cannot get on without a captain. I want to move this motion so that we may have some captain for the ship."

Eoin O'Duffy then spoke up, "I rise to second the motion moved by Mr. Collins. I have only one or two words to say. In the first place, our President thought it well to place his resignation in our hands. Now that the Dáil has approved the Treaty, it is but right that the majority should choose their captain, and we have chosen Mr. Griffith. It is not at all necessary for me to emphasize the claims that Mr. Griffith has in the presence of this assembly. The members of this House know him as well as I do. All I want to do is to say with Mr. Collins: now that the Treaty is approved, we should get on with the work."

Even still, before letting the motion to elect a new president go forward, de Valera addressed the room, "It is absolutely necessary for us to have a definite answer to this question: Will the President of Dáil Éireann about to be elected function hitherto as the Chief Executive Officer of the Irish Republic?"

Arthur rose to explain, "The President is, I understand, President of Dáil Éireann, according to the Constitution. The Dáil will remain in existence until such time—and I will see that it is kept in existence until such time—as we can have an election, when this question will be put to the people. The Republic of Ireland remains in being until the Free State comes into operation. President de Valera yesterday threw this body into confusion by resigning and leaving no government in existence. Public order and security have to be maintained. If I am elected, I will occupy whatever position President de Valera occupied."

Finding nothing in this to criticize, de Valera gave his affirmation, "Hear, hear."

Arthur, however, qualified his statement, "Now, that is right. However, in that position, he was *not* the President of the Republic, but the President of Dáil Éireann according to the Constitution."

This statement upset all the anti-Treaty faction, who cried out, "No! no!"

De Valera contradicted Arthur, "The President is President of Dáil Éireann, which is written down as the Government of the Republic of Ireland. So, I was President of the Republic of Ireland."

Annoyed with these niddling qualifications, Arthur said exasperated, "I do not mind a single rap about words. I say whatever position —if you like to put it that way—that the President resigned from yesterday, I will, if I am elected, occupy the same position until the Irish people have an opportunity of deciding for themselves."

De Valera relented, saying, "That is a fair answer."

Arthur's answer seemed to assuage de Valera's opposition for the moment. However, Cathal Brugha, even at this late stage, still again brought up his favourite complaint, "Mr. Griffith agreed that the delegates would not sign any Treaty until it had first been submitted to the

Cabinet here. Mr. Griffith has broken that, and consequently, no matter what undertaking he gives now, I object to his being elected as President of the Dáil."

De Valera's ire was once again piqued, and he repeated his question, apparently searching for, even hoping for, a suspect answer. "My question then is: Whether Mr. Griffith, who will occupy the same position as I have occupied, and which I interpreted as binding on me by oath, will not use his office to subvert the established Republic?"

Growing more irritated, Arthur answered, "President de Valera has asked me will I use my office to subvert the Irish Republic. I think I have already answered the question, but I will answer it again. I said if I am elected to this position, I will keep the Republic in being until such time as the establishment of the Free State is put to the people, to decide for or against."

This response seemed to be the one for which he had been foraging, for de Valera had famously said the people could not be trusted to make such a decision. He got up, declaring triumphantly, "As a protest against the election of the Chairman of the Delegation as President of the Irish Republic, who is bound by the Treaty conditions to subvert the Republic, and who, in the interim period, instead of using the office as it should be used—to support the Republic—I, while this vote is being taken, as one, am going to leave the House."

With that, he stormed out of the hall, followed by the entire body of his supporters.

Michael shouted after them, swinging his fist in the air, "Deserters all! We will now call on the Irish people to rally to us. Deserters all!"

One of the withdrawing delegates shouted back, "Up the Republic!"

Now with no semblance of control of his temper, Michael continued his rant, "Deserters all to the Irish nation in her hour of trial. We will stand by her."

Madame Markievicz, consistent in her disdain for Michael, shot back, "Oath breakers and cowards."

"Foreigners—Americans—English!" Michael yelled as all the anti-Treaty delegates left the hall.

Watching them file out, MacNeill spoke up, "I am waiting until all those who wish to leave the House have left. The motion is now put—that Mr. Griffith be appointed President of Dáil Éireann."

All the remaining delegates shouted in unison, "*Aye*," "*Is toil*," or

"*Yes,*" and so, by acclamation unanimously elected Arthur Griffith to be President of the Dáil.

Arthur rose to accept, "*A Chinn Chomhairle.* I repeat now what I said before when asked the question. As Premier, I suppose I may say the Dáil and the Republic exist until such time as the Free State Government is set up. When that Free State Government is set up, I intend that the Irish people shall have the fullest power of expression at that election. When the Dáil—the sovereign body in Ireland—passed that vote of approval of the Treaty, it was our business, and our duty to the Dáil, to see it carried through, and I regret, myself, that President de Valera resigned. When he resigned and automatically brought all his Ministers with him, Ireland was left without any Government. Therefore, someone had to be proposed to take his place in accordance with the Constitution. Now, in accordance with the Constitution, the Premier proposes his Ministers and the Dáil ratifies them. Now, I propose the six Cabinet Ministers for the Dáil: 1, Finance Minister, Mr. Michael Collins; 2, Foreign Affairs, Mr. Gavan Duffy; 3, Home Affairs, Mr. Eamonn Duggan; 4, Local Government, Alderman William Cosgrave; 5, Economic Affairs, Mr. Kevin O'Higgins; and 6, Defence, Mr. Richard Mulcahy."

Another chorus of "Agreed!" carried the motion, and the meeting adjourned.

The optimism and unanimity within the chamber did not extend to the steps outside. There de Valera was meeting with members of the Press. Tom Cullen walked over and lingered at the crowd's edge to listen in. He heard the intrepid *Freeman's Journal* reporter Harding asking, "In the event of a General Election and the people declaring for the Free State, what will be your attitude?"

In essence, ignoring the validity of the proceedings he had just stormed out of, he replied, "When the Irish people have had the opportunity to determine their own governments, institutions and their relations with other peoples, I will be satisfied."

"What would you consider to be such an opportunity?"

"When the British troops leave Ireland and put aside the threat of war or invasion. I claim that there is no question of right between England and Ireland whatever. We have a perfect right to resist by every means in our power."

"Even by war?" Harding asked.

"By every means in our power to resist authority imposed on this country from outside."

Harding, hoping to pin de Valera down on where his loyalties would lie under these new circumstances, asked, "In the event of the Free State being set up, did such resistance imply resistance to that government?"

De Valera equivocated, replying, "Any government that derives its authority from the Irish people would naturally have my respect and obedience."

Still trying to press him on the issue of loyalty, Harding pushed further, "Would you sit in the Free State Parliament when constituted?"

Here de Valera finally showed his hand, saying, "I would never take an Oath such as is in that Treaty. You can be sure of that. Of course, I only speak for myself, and others can determine their own line of action."

Tom shook his head and walked back inside to report to Michael, repeating to himself, "War by every means in our power. Oh, Christ! Mick will have a fit!"[2]

Take Over or Get Out

12 JANUARY 1922, COLONIAL OFFICE, LONDON

WINSTON CHURCHILL WAS PREPARING FOR A MEETING OF HIS CABINET Committee on the Irish Provisional Government but beforehand had an unexpected visitor in his Colonial Office chambers.

"Now see, here, Winston, permitting these Republican ruffians to run about Ireland assaulting our men willy-nilly just won't do. No, it just won't do," Sir Henry Wilson repeated.

"No, quite right, Sir Henry," Churchill answered patiently. "I quite agree."

"Well, damn it, we will not stand for it. We must take over the damn place or get the hell out. Just yesterday, some I.R.A. fanatic threw a bomb at a streetcar in Belfast, but thankfully a quick-thinking motorman slammed on the brakes and adverted disaster by a foot."

"Yes, I read about that." Churchill tried to remain calm, "On the other hand, I also read that another bomb injured six Catholic children there, and in retaliation, a Protestant man was shot dead at his front door as he bid his wife goodbye."[1]

Wilson thundered, "The whole damn country is going to hell. Bank robberies, train robberies, even the theft of R.I.C. rifles!"[2]

"Yes, unfortunately, some members of barracks were complicit."

"What? Damn it, Winston, this just won't do."

"Absolutely, Sir Henry, but we anticipate taking that first step to extricate ourselves this Monday when the Provisional Government is due to take over Dublin Castle. Some companies of Auxiliary Police have already left, and many of them will be redeployed to Palestine. As soon as the new government is in place, I will be giving the order to withdraw our troops."

"What, all of them?" Sir Henry demanded.

"No, not all at once. We anticipate peace once Collins takes over, but if necessary, we'll help bolster his position with our own troops."[3]

Sir Henry was incredulous, "British Army men fighting alongside that, that *man*?"

Churchill was losing his patience, "*That man* is the Chairman of the Provisional Government. The troops are not to intervene in disturbances without direct orders from the Viceroy. Lord FitzAlan may not control the country, but he will still control our men while he and they are still there. I am confident you trust his judgment."

"The Viceroy, you say? Well, then…"

"Now, come along, Sir Henry," Winston said as he rose from his chair. "Everything I have just told you will be discussed at my Cabinet Committee, who meet here in a short while, and I can assure you they are all as concerned as you about our getting our men out and getting it done right. As soon as Collins takes over, I expect he and his ministers will come to London to implement all the provisions of the agreement."[4]

"Humph! Very well, Winston. Good day to you."

ONE HUNDRED TWENTY-EIGHT

You Can Have the Seven Minutes

16 JANUARY 1922, DUBLIN

LORD FITZALAN WAS THE FIRST CATHOLIC SINCE 1685, DURING THE reign of King James II, to be appointed Viceroy, Lord Lieutenant of Ireland. He had held this position less than nine months, and that afternoon he was about to hand over Dublin Castle and initiate the transfer of all administrative powers to Michael Collins and the Provisional Government.[1] As he stood by the fireplace in the Council Room, he smoothed down his long moustache, took out his pocket watch, and commented, "I say, we managed to arrive on time, but our Irish friends seem to be running a bit late."

The Joint Under-Secretary for Ireland, Sir John Anderson, walked over to a window and peered at the rows of R.I.C. and Dublin Metropolitan Police officers in the Upper Castle Yard. He looked over to Andy Cope as he entered the room and asked, "What could be keeping them, Andy?"

"We've just received word. They're on their way from Mansion House. They had several constitutional matters to clear up before coming over."

"I daresay they did," remarked Sir James MacMahon, who shared with Anderson the title of Under-Secretary.

Then waves of loud cheers were heard, and Anderson added, "Ah! Here they are."

Michael Collins and Eoin MacNeill were the first to arrive at the

Castle, and when they alighted their taxi, the crowds at the Castle gate exploded with cheers of joy. They pushed their way through the crowd and passed into the Castle Yard, where the assembled police, army officers, and a multitude of reporters and Press photographers warmly greeted them. The other arriving Cabinet members caught up with them, as did Emmet Dalton in his position as Chief Liaison Officer, and they all crossed the yard together.

"Jaysus, Mick," Eoin exclaimed, "who would've expected this? Look, they even rolled out a red carpet at the entrance."

Noting that even Auxis were cheering and waving from rooms that looked out onto the yard, Emmet remarked, "Blood red. Those Auxis are waving from rooms where not so long ago they tortured many an I.R.A. prisoner."

"Ay," Michael said, pulling close to Emmet so he could be heard over the cheers. "Men like Dick McKee and Peadar Clancy."

As they passed rows of saluting policemen, Michael's mood lightened as he noticed a familiar, smiling face. "Well, I'll be damned. Look who's here."

Emmet exclaimed, "If it isn't Dave Neligan! And that's his commanding officer in the Secret Service, Major Poges. Don't they look smart, standing at attention?"

Michael laughed and said, "I don't know about the major, who never had a clue, but our spy in the Castle, right up to his last day on the job, certainly looks smart. Good old Dave."[2]

As they entered the building and walked up the stairs, Michael checked his watch and noted, "Well, we got here a little later than planned."

"You took the morning train from Longford, didn't you?"

"A man has got to get his priorities straight, eh?"

"Goes without saying, well done. Say, there's the Auxi commander, Caine."

Michael stopped, looked over and smiled as Caine stood at attention, saluting.

"There's one tough bastard I won't be sorry to see the back of," Michael commented, "but he's probably glad to see the last of me." Michael gave him a little wave that was met with a tight smile.

When they entered the Privy Council Room, Michael walked directly over to the Viceroy, who was standing at the head of the table with the fireplace behind him. Lord FitzAlan greeted him by dryly noting, "You're seven minutes late, Mr. Collins."

Michael smiled slyly and quipped, "We've been waiting seven hundred years; you can have the seven minutes."

FitzAlan shook his head but replied good-naturedly, "I believe you've brought some papers with you, if I'm not mistaken."

"Yes, sir, indeed we have." He looked around and saw MacMahon, who took a step forward and said, "We're glad to see you, Mr. Collins."

"Ye are like hell, boy," Michael shot back with a broad grin.[3]

"Really, Mr. Collins, I'm always happy to see a fellow admirer of the Irish Blue."

Everyone was puzzled at this riposte, and Michael's response did nothing to enlighten them, "Ay, well, every dog has his day."

Sir John Anderson greeted Michael by remembering their last encounter, "Welcome, Mr. Collins. A lot of water under the bridge, literally, since we last met on the ferry at the onset of the Treaty negotiations."

"Yes, and here we are now."

"Yes, indeed, here we are." Sir John regarded Emmet with a look of recognition. "I believe we have met, young man. Yes, that same night, wasn't it?"

Andy Cope stepped in to explain, "Yes, Sir John. You remember Emmet Dalton, the military liaison. We will all be seeing a lot of each other in the coming days."[4]

"I look forward to it," Sir John answered.

"Is Mr. Griffith not joining us today, Mr. Collins?" Lord FitzAlan asked.

"I'm afraid not. He still has much to do at Mansion House."

"Yes, we thought as much. Now about those papers..."

William Cosgrave handed the signed copy of the Treaty to Michael, and he, in turn, gave it to Lord FitzAlan.

"Thank you, Mr. Collins." He flipped through the document to the signatory page and said, "Yes, everything seems to be in order. Perhaps we should discuss some of the practical details now."

"If I may," Michael said, "allow me to introduce the members of *Rialtas Sealadach*, that is, the Provisional Government."

"Yes, yes, of course."

Two days earlier, to fulfil the terms of the Treaty, a new Provisional

Government Cabinet had been chosen at a Mansion House meeting, and it was this Cabinet, which nearly mirrored that of the Dáil, that was authorised to take over administration from the British.[5] Michael proceeded, "As you know, I will be serving as Chairman but also as Minister of Finance. Mr. Eamonn Duggan, whom I believe you already know, is the Minister of Home Affairs; Mr. Kevin O'Higgins is the Minister for Economic Affairs; Mr. Joseph McGrath, Minister for Labour; Mr. Fionán Lynch, Minister for Education; Mr. Patrick Hogan, Minister for Agriculture; this is Mr. William Cosgrave, the Minister for Local Government; finally, this is Mr. Eoin MacNeill, who served as Chairman of the Dáil during the debates and vote on the Treaty."

The two Dáil ministries of Foreign Affairs and Defence, headed by Gavan Duffy and Richard Mulcahy, respectively, were not included in the Provisional Government since these responsibilities still came under the purview of the British Government.

Andy Cope introduced all the corresponding British ministers as the Viceroy still stood at the end of the table. MacNeill stood at the opposite end of the Table of State, as it was called, and Michael was to the right of the Viceroy, a place usually reserved for the Lord Chancellor of Ireland. Everyone then sat down and began exchanging ideas and proposals, asking and answering questions, and proceeding in a lively, friendly atmosphere of cooperation. Michael constantly jumped from his seat to join one discussion or another, quickly ascertaining the crux of an issue and offering a proposal or rendering a decision before moving on to another topic.

These deliberations continued for about half an hour until the Viceroy quietly rose, walked over to the fireplace, and remarked to Andy, "Mr. Griffith may be their Chairman, but that young man shows every indication of being the real leader. Such an abundance of energy!"

"Yes, sir, I know from experience he uses it well. His pre-eminence was inevitable."

"Yes, the cream does tend to rise to the top." Lord FitzAlan sighed and said, "We shall miss our time here."

MacMahon joined them and asked, "You'll not be staying in Ireland?"

"Once the Free State is established, my work here will be done, and my wife Mary and I shall return to Derbyshire."

When the discussions wound down, the Viceroy cleared his throat and addressed Michael directly, "Congratulations, Mr. Collins, gentlemen. I am happy to inform you that you are all now duly installed as the Provisional Government. Now in conformity with Article 17 of this Treaty, I will immediately communicate with the British Government that the necessary steps might be taken for the transfer to the Provisional Government the powers and machinery requisite for the discharge of all its duties. Now, if I may, I would like to wish you every success in this task that you have undertaken, and let me express my earnest hope that under your auspices, the ideal of a happy, free and prosperous Ireland will be attained."

"Thank you, sir," Michael responded.

"You are most welcome, Mr. Collins."

Michael looked around the room, nodded, and said, "Gentlemen."

As the Irish ministers began filing out, MacMahon walked over to Michael and said in a low voice, "Now that it seems I am taking an early retirement, I hope we will continue to see each other at the Blue Terrier Club's shows."

"Arrah, Danny Boy and his charming new owner and I will look forward to it," he said, tossing his head back with a laugh.

"I shall miss working with your cousin Nancy. Give her my regards," MacMahon said with a wink, which gave Michael pause, wondering precisely when MacMahon had become aware that his secretary Nancy O'Brien was related to Michael.

Michael smiled and left, walking quickly back across the yard, followed by the newly invested Irish ministers. When they all emerged on the street, he instinctively kept his head down to avoid the cameras but caught a glimpse of another old friend in the vast crowd waiting there.

"Batt! Come with us!"

Michael pushed Batt O'Connor into one of the waiting taxis along with O'Higgins and Duggan, and the four of them headed back to Mansion House. When they arrived, Michael rushed into the office and announced, "Arthur! The Castle has fallen."[6]

End of Volume Two: Treaty

The Oath of Allegiance

Article 4 of the Articles of Agreement:

"I... do solemnly swear true faith and allegiance to the constitution of the Irish Free
State as by law established and that I will be faithful to H.M. King George V, his
heirs and successors by law, in virtue of the common citizenship of Ireland with
Great Britain and her adherence to and membership of the group of nations
forming the British Commonwealth of Nations."

Dail Cabinet meeting, 25 November 1921, Proposed Oath:

"Ireland should recognise the British Crown for the purposes of the Association, as
symbol and accepted head of the combination of Associated States." (Pakenham, p.
245; Macardle, p. 572.)

Irish Republican Brotherhood's Proposed Oath, 3 December 1921:

"I do solemnly swear to bear true faith and allegiance to the Constitution of the Irish
Free State as by law established, and that I will be faithful to His Majesty King
George in acknowledgement of the Association of Ireland in a common citizenship
with Great Britain and the group of nations known as the British Commonwealth."
(Dwyer/Warrant, p. 190.)

De Valera's Oath Proposed at Cabinet Meeting on 3 December 1921

"I... do solemnly swear true faith and allegiance to the constitution of the Irish Free
State, to the Treaty of Association and to recognise the King of Great Britain as
Head of the Associated States." (As Erskine Childers recalled de Valera saying,
Coogan/Collins, p. 267; and as Arthur Griffith stated at Treaty Debates, 14
December 1921, quoting what de Valera said at Cabinet meeting.)

"I... do solemnly swear true faith and allegiance to the constitution of the Irish Free
State, to the Treaty of Association and to recognise the King of Great Britain as
Head of the Association." (This version is what de Valera later claimed he said at
the Cabinet meeting, Coogan/Collins, p. 267.)

De Valera's New Version Given at Treaty Debates, 14 December 1921

"I... do solemnly swear true faith and allegiance to the Constitution of the Irish Free
State and to the Community of Nations known as the British Empire and to the
King as the head of the State and Empire."

List of Characters – Style Rules

Titles and abbreviations are written as they were in newspapers and documents of the day. In the records of the Treaty Debates, "treaty" was usually capitalized, so it appears here as "Treaty, anti-Treaty, or pro-Treaty." Likewise, "Truce," "Cabinet," etc. In the Dáil records, *Teachta* is capitalized, but "member" is not capitalized. In Hansard, "Prime Minister" is capitalised, as is Member when referring to a specific person. They are abbreviated P.M. and M.P.

British English spelling is used, but punctuation is in American English style unless quoting from official documents such as Hansard or the Treaty Debates. Quotation marks in American style were standard in British newspapers of the day. Unlike current British custom, in Hansard and the Dáil records and Churchill's own writings, abbreviations of titles were followed by periods, as in, "Mr., Mrs., Dr., I.R.A."

The Intelligence Office

Michael Collins, Director of Intelligence
Liam Tobin, Deputy Director of Intelligence
Tom Cullen, 2nd Deputy Director
Frank Thornton, 3rd Deputy Director
Sinéad Mason, secretary
Alice Lyons, secretary
Charlie Dalton, member
Charlie Byrne, member
Joe Dolan, member
Also, Emmet Dalton, Military Liaison
Also, Joe O'Reilly, assistant to Collins

The Squad (Short List)

Joe Dolan
Paddy Daly
Vinny Byrne
Joe Leonard
Pat (Paddy) McCrea, driver

G Division Detectives:

Dave Neligan, G Division, Dublin Castle
Ned Broy, G Division, Brunswick Street (later Pearse Street)

Dáil Cabinet

de Valera, President of the Dáil
Arthur Griffith, Minister for Home Affairs; founder, Sinn Féin
Michael Collins, Minister of Finance
Cathal Brugha, Minister of Defence

W.T. (Bill) Cosgrave, Minister for Local Government
Kevin O'Higgins, assistant to Cosgrave

Irish Treaty Team (Oct–Dec, 1921)
Arthur Griffith
Michael Collins
Eamonn Duggan
Robert Barton
Gavan Duffy
Erskine Childers, legal advisor
John Chartres, secretary to team
Art O'Brien, Dáil Ambassador to England

Lloyd George's Cabinet/Treaty Team
David Lloyd George (Liberal), Prime Minister
F.E. Smith, Lord Birkenhead (Conservative), Lord Chancellor
Austen Chamberlain (Conserv.), Leader, House of Commons
Winston Churchill (Liberal), Secretary of State for the Colonies (Colonial Secretary)
Sir Laming Worthington-Evans, Secretary of State for War
Sir Hamar Greenwood, Chief Secretary for Ireland
Sir Gordon Hewart, Attorney General
Sir Philip Sassoon, Prime Minister's Parliamentary Secretary.
Thomas Jones, Deputy Secretary to the Cabinet
Frances Stevenson, personal secretary to Lloyd George
Also: General Jan Smuts, Prime Minister of South Africa

British Administration in Ireland
Viscount FitzAlan, Lord Lieutenant of Ireland, Viceroy
Sir Hamar Greenwood, Chief Secretary for Ireland
Sir John Anderson 1920–1922, Under-Secretary for Ireland
James MacMahon, Under-Secretary for Ireland
Alfred (Andy) Cope, Assistant Under-Secretary for Ireland
Also: Sir James Craig, First Prime Minister of Northern Ireland

British Military
Sir Henry Wilson, Chief of the Imperial General Staff
Sir Nevil Macready, Commander-in-Chief of forces in Ireland
Major-General Hugh Tudor, Chief of Police (Police Advisor)

Michael Collins Family, Friends, Associates
Johnny Collins, brother, farmer in Cork
Hannie Collins, sister in London
Mary Collins-Powell, sister, Cork City
Margaret Collins O'Driscoll, sister, Cork
Helena Collins, sister, Sister Mary Celestine
Nancy O'Brien, second cousin

Chrys Kiernan, b. 1890
Larry Kiernan, b. 1891
Kitty Kiernan, b. 1892
Helen Kiernan, b. 1893 (m. Paul McGovern)
Maud (Mops) Kiernan, b. 1894
Harry Boland, T.D., special envoy to the United States
Joe Hyland, driver
Eileen McGrane, friend of Collins, sometimes secretary
Joe McGuinness, member of A.S.U.
Eoin MacNeill, founder of Volunteers, chaired Treaty debates
Batt O'Connor, friend and confidant of Collins

Irish Military

Richard Mulcahy, Chief of Staff
Ginger O'Connell, Deputy Chief of Staff
Gearoid (George) O'Sullivan, Adjutant General, Volunteers
Rory O'Connor, Director of Engineering
Seán Hales, Cork Flying Column Section Commander, TD Cork
Tom Hales, O/C Cork No. 3 Brigade
Pat Harte, QM Cork No. 3 Brigade
Seán O'Hegarty, Commander, Cork No. 1 Brigade
Seán MacEoin, Commander, Longford Brigade
Eoin O'Duffy, North. Brigade liaison, O/C Monaghan Brigade

Winston Churchill Family, Friends, Associates

Winston, b. 30 November 1874
Clementine, b. 1885
Diana, b. 11 July 1909
Randolph, b. 28 May 1911
Sarah, b. 7 October 1914
Marigold (the Duckadilly), b. 15 November 1918
Mary, b. 15 September 1922
Bessie, maid
Detective Sergeant Walter Thompson, Scotland Yard Special Branch, bodyguard
Eddie Marsh, Private Secretary
Miss Jackson, secretary
George "Geordie" Granville Sutherland-Leveson-Gower, 5th Duke of Sutherland
Sir John Lavery, painter
Lady Hazel Lavery, society hostess, painter
Countess Elizabeth "Daisy" Fingall
Lord Londonderry, Charles Stewart Henry Vane-Tempest-Stewart, 7th Marquess of Londonderry
Lady Edith Londonderry, society hostess

22 Hans Place, Politicians' House in London

Arthur Griffith
Eamonn Duggan

Gavan Duffy
Erskine Childers
John Chartres
Mary Conlon
May Duggan
Kathleen MacKenna
Joe McGrath
Various secretaries, cooks, maids

15 Cadogan Gardens, Military House in London

Michael Collins
Liam Tobin
Tom Cullen
Ned Broy
Emmet Dalton
Seán MacBride
Eoin O'Duffy
Ginger O'Connell
Joe Dolan
Pat (Paddy) McCrea
Peggy McIntyre
Alice and Ellie Lyons
Eddie
Various cooks, maids

Conlon's Pub Characters

Tim Kelly
Toby Kelly
Charlie O'Shea
Matty Mullane
Billy Conlon
Mary Conlon
Maureen Conlon
Nelly Conlon
Commander Caine
Sergeant Clarke
Lieutenant Burke

Clergy

Monsignor McManus
Archbishop Clune
Pope Benedict XV

And, of course, Michael's *Best* friends

Convict 224, Mick, and Danny Boy

Glossary

Glossary of Irish & British Names, Words, and Expressions

a chara: my friend

A Chinn Chomhairle: Chairman, Speaker of the Dáil

acting the maggot: acting like a fool

after fixin' tea, I've just made tea

after: Irish indication of past tense (see example, below)

afters: dessert

Ard Fheis: political party convention

Arrah musha: term of endearment or affection

Arrah: indeed, an expression of surprise

arseways: gone wrong

aul boy: old man, father, grandfather

bad dose: severe illness

barman: bartender in American English

be off out of that: go away, you're joking, really?

blather: empty, worthless talk

bob: shilling, twelve pennies

bog trotter: an epithet for the Irish; a country person

boil your cabbage twice: repeat yourself

bold: naughty

bollixing: screw up; bollix, alternative spelling for bollocks

bollocks: testicles; a term to express contempt

bonnet: hood of a car in American English

boon: blessing, good thing

boyo: boy, lad

brass: cheek, impudence

bridewell: the Bridewell, a Dublin jail; any jail in general.

bushed: tired

cacks: trousers

ceilidh: (kay-lee): social gathering w music, singing, etc.

cheek of ya (the), cheeky of you, disapproval at something said or done

china, me old china: Cockney slang, china plate, mate

chukkas: periods of play in polo

close: humid, warm

codding: kidding, fooling

come here till I tell you: as above

come here to me: listen

come out of the fog: come off it

craic: (crack), fun, good time

craythur: creature, but as someone deserving sympathy; also, a drop of that craythur, whiskey.

culchie: someone from the countryside, outside Dublin

cure for sore eyes: same as a sight for sore eyes
cute hoor: sly devil (polite for whore)
Dáil: pronounced dawl, Irish parliament
Danegeld: a land tax levied in medieval England
decent skin: a good person underneath it all
dickey dazzler: extravagantly dressed man
divil: devil
donkey's years: a long time
dosser: lazy layabout, sluggard
dowtcha boy: (Cork) term of approval, "wouldn't doubt you!"
dry shite: boring person with limited verbal skills
Dublin Corporation: Dublin city government, administration
Dunleary: English spelling of Dun Laighoire, also, Kingstown.
eejit: idiot
engage: suppose or bet; also, grant so, wager, warrant.
fagged out: tired
Fáilte: Welcome
fair play: well done
feck, feckin: more polite version than when spelled with a u
fierce: very, fierce angry
fluthered: drunk
Frankie: a deprecating nickname for someone from Belfast.
gack: fool
gaff: house, home
galoot: fool
gammy: damaged, crooked, useless
gas: hilarious, to have some gas with, to have fun with
give it a lash: give it a go
give out: go on a rant
give over: stop it
go away outta (out of) that: you're joking, really?
g'wan: go on; go on, blast you
g'way on: get out, go away
gobshite: idiot (gob: mouth, etc.)
gossoon: child
gowl: idiot, stupid person, vagina
grand: great, fine
grant so: admit, allow
guff: bullshit
gummin': salivating
half a crown: 1/8 £. Churchill's book, £37,500.
hand me down the moon (Cork): extremely tall person
hold yer whist: keep quiet, shut up, wait a minute
holy show: spectacle
hop: play truant from school
how do: hello
howandever: anyway
howaya: how are you, hello

I will yea: sarcastic response actually meaning, "I will not!"

Irish Mail: fast train between London and Liverpool

jacks: bathroom, toilets

jarvey: horse-drawn cab driver

Jaysus: Irish way to avoid taking the Lord's name in vain

Jebbies: nickname for the Jesuits

K.C.: King's Counsel, a British lawyer of high rank

Kingstown: Dunleary, Dun Laighoire

kip: sleep (British)

la: short for lad (Cork)

langer: penis

langered or langers: drunk or drunken

lash: give it a lash, give it a try

lashin: raining

littler: Collins' name for his penny boys, errand boys.

Lord Chancellor: presides over House of Lords & Judiciary

Lympne: pronounced lim; Port Lympne, Sassoon's home.

mad: very, extremely

mail boat: ferry between Dublin and London, meets Irish Mail

manky: dirty, rotten

massive: wonderful

mentaller: nut case, looney

Mo chuisle mo chroí: pulse of my heart, sweetheart

mo stór: my treasure

muck savage: country idiot

Musha: ah, well, an expression of pity

not the full shilling: not mentally competent

omadhaun (ah-mah-dan): fool, idiot

on the hop: skipping school, playing hooky.

oul fella: old man, father

palaver: flattery, cajolery

Parnell Square, Rutland Square, both names in use at story time

pavement: sidewalk (Amer. Eng.)

plain, pint of: stout, Guinness

plonker: idiot

pogue: kiss

poxy: pox-ridden

provost: Scottish term for mayor

publican: pub owner or manager

purdies: potatoes

put the heart crossways: upset

quare hawk: peculiar person

Queenstown: currently Cobh, a port for crossing the Atlantic

Rialtas Sealadach: Provisional Government

Sackville Street: O'Connell Street, both in use at story time

Saorstát Éireann: The Irish Free State

Saorstát na hÉireann: the Free State of Ireland.

sconce: have a sconce, look, take a look at (Cork)

scuttered: drunk

segotia: me ould segotia, me ould flower, my old friend

Shinner: epithet for member of Sinn Féin

skint: broke, out of money

slag: woman of low morals

Sláinte: good health

Slán: goodbye

slash: piss

sleveen: or Irish *slíbhín*, for sly person

snug: a small private room or booth in a public house

spud: potato, also an epithet for the Irish

stater: Republican pejorative for a supporter of the Free State

stuff in the kisser: punch in the face

sweat: me ould sweat, my old friend

taped: taken one's measure, sized up

tayties: potatoes, also, poppies (both Cork)

tit: fool (Brit. & Irish slang)

titfer: hat; tit for tat, rhymes with hat, British rhyming slang

toe-rag: a contemptible or despicable person.

tool: idiot

torch: a flashlight

tosser: wanker

twisted: drunk

up here: to Dublin from the countryside

wager: bet or suppose

warrant: wager, bet, or suppose, "I'll warrant they did."

wash the pot: confess one's sins

wazzies: wasps (Cork)

weak: I'm weak (Cork)

wet the tea: make some tea

wheeze: a good talk, laugh

wondrous: wonderful or extremely, wondrous sunset, wondrous grieved

yer wan: your (nameless) woman

youse: you plural

Sources:

Coughlan, Gerry, and Martin Hughes, *Irish Language & Culture*, Lonely Planet, 2007.

Foley, Cian, *For Focal Sake, A 32 County Guide to Irish Slang*, UpTheDeise Enterprises, Waterford, 2008.

Joyce, James, *The Dubliners*, e-Book ed., Read Forward LLC, 2013.

Joyce, James, *Ulysses*, e-Book ed., "The Project Gutenberg eBook of Ulysses," 2008, 2013.

Murphy, Colin, and Donal O'Dea, *The Feckin' Book of Everything Irish*, Barnes & Noble, New York, 2006.

Notes

73. Welcome, Mr. Collins

1. de Valera was accompanied by Arthur Griffith, Robert Barton, Austin Stack, and Erskine Childers on his visit to meet Lloyd George the previous July.
2. "tremendous responsibility… follow your suggestions." Lloyd George's opening statement and Griffith's short reply are from Jones, pp. 119-121; Pakenham, p. 145.
3. "England would attain political dominance of Ireland plus military powers," Jones, p. 120.
4. "our people might starve," Pakenham, p. 145.
5. "This is a most amazing statement…wish it over Canada; You ought not to put us… break a treaty with you in order to defend ourselves," Jones, p. 120.
6. Broken treaties of the past are brought up by a member of the Irish delegation, Pakenham, p. 146. Childers is named here only as a possible speaker.
7. "You have never… oligarchies ruling this country," Pakenham, p. 146.
8. "That is not conceded," Pakenham, p. 146. Churchill's arguing the similarity with South Africa and Barton's response, Pakenham, p. 146; Jones, p. 120.
9. "A tariff war never… I want it in the treaty." This entire discussion is from Jones, pp. 120-121.
10. "English…had met and out-manoeuvred or intimidated their opponents in hundreds of struggles similar…" Coogan/Collins, p. 240.
11. This re-draft is described in Pakenham, p. 147; Jones, p. 121.
12. "the Irish representatives to Parliament voted in favour of the war; were not truly representative of the Irish people; What we want… between the two countries, not a Jew bargain… without prejudice; partner… a business firm," Jones, p. 121.
13. "We cannot enter… neutral; Bonar Law… out of the British Empire; All that means… the Dominions which did so; What would… happen in… South Africa; you are asking more… in this naval business; No, I think not," Jones, p. 122.
14. "This Truce is not a treaty… We are most anxious to do our best in the matter of treatment," Jones, p. 123.
15. Duggan & Barton negotiated terms of Truce with Macready, Coogan/Collins, p. 216.
16. The Committee on the Observance of the Truce consisted of Collins, Duggan, and Barton for the Irish, and General Macready, Sir Laming Worthington-Evans (Secretary of State for War) and Sir Hamar Greenwood (Chief Secretary for Ireland) for the British.
17. "don't know quite whether he would be a crafty enemy in friendship… don't trust him." Michael's own assessment of Churchill, Taylor, p. 155.
18. "the impression that the English are anxious for peace." Griffith wrote words to this effect in a letter to de Valera, Pakenham, p. 150.
19. Osborne informs us that Michael pronounced eggs as "oiges," Osborne, p. 29.

74. Inventions o' the Divil

1. Michael mentions one of the ties in a letter to Kitty: "You asked me if I really wore the tie? Look at the photograph and the distinctive stripe," Ó Broin, p. 35.
2. "four young typists as good-looking as most Dublin girls," Pakenham, p. 120.
3. "I never said…the devil," Ó Broin, p. 26
4. Macready admitted to having a very favourable impression of Collins in this and their many subsequent meetings in implementing the Treaty the following year, Macready, pp. 602-603. It seems that Macready did not meet Emmet Dalton until after everyone's return to Dublin. Dalton's position as Chief Liaison Officer was made official on 1 December 1921.
5. "Parliamentary criticism… drill in open defiance of the Truce … photographers… in attendance," Pakenham, pp. 150-151.
6. "English forces have commandeered; Liaison Officer; troops…billets for the winter; Throwing elected representatives; accommodations; General Macready… Truce Committee," Pakenham, p. 151.
7. "freedom of trade… American banks," O'Connor, Frank, pp. 161, 169.
8. "by Monday… initiative will pass to the British… on ground of their own choosing," Pakenham, p. 153.
9. Dalton's aeroplane escape plan, Coogan/Collins, p. 234; Boyne, 42, 56-57; Dalton, BMH, W.S. 641; *Emmet Dalton Remembers*, rte.ie/archives, YouTube.

75. A Show of Force

1. Meeting opening recommendations, proposals; Jones, p. 127.
2. "This is… *non possumus*," Jones, p. 127.
3. Birkenhead "aloof and reserved," Dutton, p. 165.
4. "Excuse me… leading up to," Pakenham, p. 155.
5. "What does the British Government propose?" This and the remaining dialogue from this meeting is either directly quoted or adapted from Jones, pp. 128-132.
6. Lloyd George's dialogue with Griffith paraphrased from Jones, p. 128.
7. "Catholics and Protestants… bogey of the Pope and the Battle of the Boyne," Jones, p. 129.
8. The story of the rifle is from *The Times*, 15 October 1921, and is mentioned in Dwyer/Warrant, p. 100; O'Connor, Frank, p. 166. "Non-rusting" or "rustless steel" soon after became known as stainless steel.

76. Mo Chuisle Mo Chroí

1. On this day, Michael wrote a letter to Kitty, saying, "Only one who remembered it was my sister, the nun." The actual text of his sister's letter is imagined here. Michael told Kitty about lighting candles for her at two Masses, and being photographed wearing one of her ties again, Ó Broin, p. 39.
2. "if you went missing… no business of my own?" Broy, BMH, W.S. 1280, pp. 146-147; Forester, p. 223. Michael was always accompanied by a bodyguard while in London, MacBride, p. 44.
3. Harrods, "many fine Irishmen worked here when I lived in London," Broy, BMH, W.S. 1280, p. 147.
4. The population of the two houses is described in Coogan/Collins, p. 234. Politicians' vs Military House, MacBride, p. 45.

5. Dave Neligan wrote that though he was sent to London to follow Collins, once there "day followed day without any further instructions reaching me." Neligan, p. 151. He also mentions, "Nearly every night I used to meet Liam Tobin or Dolan for a chat." Michael was shadowed by British agents at this Mass, but Dave's inclusion in this scene is fictional.

6. "[When Collins was] in London for the ordeal of the Treaty negotiations, he made time to visit him in Pentonville Prison," Coogan/Collins, p. 147. No date is given for this visit. "He (Pat Harte) initially refused food, was fed artificially, and then began to complain that people could read his thoughts," Hart/IRA Enemies, p. 196.

77. The Case of the Poison Letter

1. Poison letter, true story. "All letters received by a good secretary.. justify to the Dáil... analyst to be added to the Delegation," Broy, BMH, W.S. 1280, pp. 147-148.

2. "document issued by one of your officers...my authority less and less within the Conservative Party; if we are to reach a settlement, we cannot leave this in doubt." This document discussion and what follows is from Jones, pp. 132-137. This section's dialogue is directly quoted or adapted from these pages. Dave Neligan as the source of the document is for dramatic effect only.

3. "For the moment... without *my* knowledge," Pakenham, p. 160.

4. "I hope your man was a Catholic, as I don't wish to be accused of conversion as well as subversion!" Osborne, p. 57; not recorded by Tom Jones.

5. "This is going to wreck settlement," Jones, p. 137

6. "tired scholar," Pakenham, p. 131; "that unusual figure, a silent Irishman," Churchill/Aftermath, p. 320; Pakenham, p. 131.

7. "He certainly is a handsome young Irishman. None could mistake his nationality," Pakenham, p. 132; Owen, p. 581.

8. "That swine. A little man neglected... handle big things." This is a quote (minus the "arse") from later, 9 December, Jones, p. 186.

78. The Point Is

1. The Naval Committee was proposed at the Second Session, on 11 October, Jones, pp. 122-123. At the end of the Third Session, 13 October, it was noted, "Fixed Naval Committee 12.30 Monday," Jones, p. 127. However, Jones records, "18 October Committee on naval and air defence at the Colonial Office, October 18th, 1921, 11.0 a.m.," Jones p. 137.

2. Letter from Kitty asking for Emmett, Ó Broin, p. 42.

3. Description of Childers taken in part from Coogan/Collins, pp. 30, 238.

4. Dalton's role at Ginchy in the Battle of the Somme, his "Ginchy" nickname, being awarded the Military Cross by King George V, Boyne, pp. 18-21.

5. "fought for Ireland with the British and fought for Ireland against them," Cottrell, p. 61.

6. As stated here, this memorandum was presented on 18 October, but the meeting continued into the next day, as per Jones, pp. 137-138. For narrative purposes, it is compressed into a single meeting.

7. "this able memorandum... mortal blow," Jones, p. 137.

8. "Ireland, an island... naval defence... existence as a nation," Jones, p. 137.

9. "Now, gentlemen, I mean to demonstrate ... how many times have we wished she

were not!" Coogan/Collins, p. 244.

10. "Have you any answer to these points... For Christ's sake, come to the point," Ryan/Shot, p. 12; Boyne pp. 59-60.

11. "When Winston first asked me ... you spend in discovering his virtues," Hassal, p. 120.

12. "same advantages of education as his elder colleague... [remarkable] elemental qualities and [a] mother wit...stood far nearer to the terrible incidents of [this] conflict... His prestige and influence... far greater," all from Churchill's description of Collins in Churchill/Aftermath, p. 320.

79. An Act of Impertinence

1. de Valera's telegram to the Pope, Coogan/Dev, p. 258.
2. "wreck the Irish Conference" quote, *The Times*, 21 October 1921.
3. Lily Brennan was one of the secretaries to the delegation. Coogan/Collins, p. 234.
4. Griffith had requested Darrell Figgis to be sent over to help in London, but instead, de Valera suggested sending Austin Stack and asked to have Diarmuid O'Hegarty sent back to Dublin. Coogan/Collins, p. 244-245; Coogan/Dev, p. 260.
5. Austin Stack description from Coogan/Collins, p. 205.
6. "Founding members of the Dublin Blue Terrier Club," Fitzpatrick, p. 398, footnote 81; James Comiskey, "An Irishman's Diary," *Irish Times*, 12 November 1996; "Blue Terrier Club," *Dublin Daily Telegraph*, 19 October 1920; Irish Kennel Club website, http://www.ikc.ie/about-us/history/. "Convict 224" did not win that day, as sometimes reported.
7. "I wonder, Mr. Collins... business?" Quoted from Pakenham, p. 167, but changed from Griffith to Collins, to agree with Thomas Jones' account of the meeting, Jones, p. 138.
8. Sligo matter from Jones, p. 138.
9. "I am sorry... arming your forces," Jones, p. 138.
10. The gun-running incidents in Hamburg and Cardiff are related in Coogan/Collins, pp. 246-247; Jones pp. 138 & 131. Bomb-making conspiracy, Pakenham, p. 167; Bomb-making in Neath, *Freeman's Journal*, 22 October 1921.
11. "The next matter... task almost impossible," Pakenham, p. 168.
12. "for creating a serious uprising of feeling in Parliament, but [the] telegram is the gravest incident," Coogan/Dev, p. 258.
13. "First with regard... done before the Truce," Pakenham, p. 169.
14. "In what way?... Because our people took less precautions!" Coogan/Collins, p. 246; Coogan/Dev, p. 258.
15. "[German] submarines... Unfortunately, there was no truth in that," Coogan/Collins, p. 246.
16. "With regard to... Ireland and Great Britain," Pakenham, p. 169.
17. "So far, we have begun... getting over the main difficulty," Pakenham, p. 169.
18. "This situation cannot be prolonged... with regard to naval defence," condensed and paraphrased from Jones, p. 139.
19. "I think it safeguards your security; as Chairman; The document in question is of marked ability... I should offer no objection; Mr. Churchill, do you not agree... than your proposals; I do not accept that;" Jones, pp. 139-140.
20. "Dominion status is not our claim... risks for forty million people," paraphrased in part from Jones, p. 140.
21. "I understand Mr. Griffith... attack by sea; With regard to Mr. Griffith's claim... concession from the Irish side," Jones, pp. 140-141.

22. "playing bridge…to pass the time," MacBride, p.45.
23. Brugha's part in the Cardiff affair, MacBride's role in Hamburg, Coogan/Collins, pp. 246-247, pp. 47-48.
24. "I don't know… instructed… or confused. The latter, I would say," Coogan/Dev, p. 256.
25. Dalton wrote to C/S, Chief of Staff, on 21 October 1921 about the purchase of the aeroplane, Dalton, BMH W.S. 641

80. Unrequited Love

1. Michael's trip to Dublin to try and convince de Valera to London, Coogan/Dev, p. 259. All the dialogue in this chapter is imagined.
2. "…is like trying to pick up mercury… use a spoon?" Pakenham, p. 84, footnote. This is a famous quotation about Lloyd George and his dealings with de Valera, but it is doubtful whether Michael would have repeated it to de Valera. Pakenham did not reveal his source for this quote, so Andy Cope is only offered here as a possibility.
3. McCrea as a member of the Squad, Coogan/Collins, p. 116.
4. Kitty's night out dancing from two letters to Michael, Ó Broin, pp. 48-49.
5. "[meet] any nice girls [or] kissed anybody," Ó Broin, p. 41.
6. "is it you? Are you trying to get out of it? Because I don't want to get out of it." Words to this effect in a letter from Michael to Kitty on 20 October, Ó Broin, p. 45.
7. Michael wrote to Dr. Farnan on Kitty's behalf on 23 October, Ó Broin, p. 50.
8. The next day on the boat back to Holyhead, Michael wrote to Kitty, saying, "you are just about back to the Gresham," where she had stayed that weekend, Ó Broin, p. 50. Kitty wrote back to Michael about getting back to the Gresham, Pat McCrea, and Tom Cullen looking after her, Ó Broin, pp. 50, 53.

81. Some Idea of a President

1. Kitty mentions the trip to Greystones and that Pat drove her back to the Gresham and Tom looked after her in a letter received 26 October, Ó Broin, p. 53.
2. "Joe Dolan or [Liam Tobin] have been meeting [Neligan] most nights," Neligan, p. 151.
3. Dave Neligan's mission in London, Neligan, p. 151.
4. This interesting detail about the "lie-in" amenity allowed by the mail train service is from a footnote to the letter Michael wrote to Kitty upon arrival that morning at Euston, Ó Broin, p. 52.
5. "We must have scapegoats," Coogan/Dev, pp. 257.
6. Substitution of "free" for "neutral," Pakenham, p. 174.
7. "If Duffy spent less time admiring his voice, we'd do better," Taylor, p. 152.
8. "bombastic… ex-officer jingo," more of Michael's opinion of Churchill from Taylor, p. 155.
9. It wasn't known until the publication of Thomas Jones' *Whitehall Diary* that the suggestion for the first sub-conference came not from the British, who welcomed the idea, but from the Irish, Jones, p. 141; Coogan/Collins, p. 243. Duggan's and Cope's roles, Pakenham, p. 176. Keith Middlemas, the editor of Jones' *Whitehall Diary*, informs us that "Cope, at the request of Griffith and Collins, had arranged a private meeting with Lloyd George and Chamberlain before the afternoon session. This proposal was welcomed by the Prime Minister, who wanted to reduce

the size of the negotiating bodies and also to exclude Childers, believed by all the British to be the most extreme," Jones, p. 141.

10. "The Irish counter-proposals had been received at 3.20 and a hurried and interrupted meeting had been held in the House of Commons to consider the document," Jones, pp. 141-142. Jones does not specify who was present.

11. If Irish national aspirations... an ancient and spirited Nation; On the one hand... known as the British Commonwealth of Nations; On the other... authority over Ireland and Irish affairs, Pakenham, p. 174.

12. "could not fail to give offence; haughty, didactic," Jones' description of the document, not "unsatisfactory... not a sufficient cause for coercion." Churchill loosely quoted in Jones, p. 141.

13. "delegates overshadowed by the two leaders... Duggan a sober, resolute man." Pakenham, p. 132; Churchill/Aftermath, p. 320.

14. Prince of Wales visit, from *New York Times*, and *The Times*, 25 October 1921.

15. Almost all the dialogue in this section is either directly quoted or adapted from quotes from this meeting found in Jones, pp. 142-145; Pakenham, pp. 178-179.

16. "common citizenship...incompatible with neutrality in any form," paraphrased from Coogan/Dev, pp. 271. Not actually spoken by Birkenhead at this meeting.

17. "The curse of Cromwell lies upon us all still," Churchill/HESP, *The New World*, p. 292. Quoted here only for effect.

18. Michael's efforts at bed alteration, Broy, BMH, W.S. 1280, pp. 145-146.

82. If War is the Alternative

1. From letters exchanged by Michael and Kitty, Ó Broin, pp. 50, 53. They probably went for a drive the previous Sunday with Pat McCrea driving and Tom Cullen going along to the seaside spot of Greystones and later dropped Michael off at Dunleary. Tom and Pat then escorted Kitty to the Gresham Hotel. Kitty likely arrived in London on this date, 26 October, most likely in the morning, after an overnight crossing.

2. Ó Broin, p. 63, speculates that Kitty might have stayed at the Cadogan Hotel on Sloane Square. Kitty wrote in Letter 42B, "in 123 where I lived (and you) Cadogan." Perhaps this meant Room 123 in the Cadogan Hotel or 123 Cadogan Gardens, a different building near where Michael was staying.

3. Seán MacBride describes this Hamburg gun-running adventure in MacBride, pp. 47-48.

4. "What is this reference... made to recognise it, the better; to put [me] in the wrong; to do [their] dirty work for them," Pakenham, pp. 182-183; Coogan/Collins, p. 247. "The responsibility, if this interference breaks... fullest freedom of discussion; Obviously, any form of... the head of the association; [We] would very much like the President... sent an urgent message," Pakenham, pp. 182-183.

5. This analysis of Michael's refusal to sign the letter, Duffy's and Barton's reasons for at first not signing, and Griffith's argument convincing everyone to sign, Coogan/Collins, p. 247.

83. A Letter of Assurances

1. "This is terrible... horseplay... sent back to Dublin immediately," Broy, BMH, W.S. 1280, pp. 148-149.

2. "very much in love with Kitty," Ó Broin, p. 54.

3. "I haven't seen her since she left home twenty years ago," Ó Broin, p. 143.
4. "There can be no question... plenipotentiaries... Cabinet decision," Coogan/Collins p.248; Coogan/Dev, p. 261; Pakenham, p. 183.
5. Lavery family from Galway, Coogan/Collins, p. 288.
6. How Hannie came to have these letters and the portrait sittings, McCoole, pp. 74-75.
7. Description of 2 Whitehall Gardens from *British History Online*, http://www.british-history.ac.uk/report.aspx?compid=67790. The Whitehall headquarters of the Foreign, India, Home and Colonial Offices later became the Foreign and Commonwealth Office.
8. Duggan's mission to Whitehall Gardens, Jones, p. 150.

84. A Good Price

1. Lloyd George and Birkenhead had dinner at Churchill's house that evening, and were met there at 10 p.m. by Collins and Griffith, Jones p. 151. Clementine's presence there and what was discussed is all conjecture, with the exception of a quote of Churchill's.
2. "worms," Jones, p. 151
3. Thompson's previous service with Lloyd George, Thompson p. 3.
4. This phone call and the feelings of mistrust for Churchill and Birkenhead, Jones, p. 151; Manchester, pp. 723-724.
5. "Secret Service" agents, Hittle, pp. 17, 24, 26-27.
6. "smite the Die-Hards ... essential unity... Northern Parliament subordinate to... Dublin... a plan for a new boundary," Pakenham, p. 194-5
7. Quotes from Tom Jones' letter and analysis of its part at this critical stage from Coogan/Dev, p. 262; Pakenham, pp. 194-5. The exact moment when the letter of assurances written by Jones was handed to Griffith has not been recorded, but since Jones had already discussed such a letter earlier with Duggan, it conceivably could have been mentioned at this meeting with Lloyd George.
8. "your loss. I am very sorry," there is no record of Michael saying anything like this.
9. "Ireland *is* a nation... we'll find room for the King," paraphrased from Forester 229-30. Collins spoke these words on 28 October to C.P. Scott of the *Manchester Guardian*, whom Lloyd George had spoken to earlier that day.
10. "that is a slogan...inspiration," Manchester, p. 452.
11. "the reverence which I feel for my father's memory... pelted with rotten fish," Manchester, p. 454.
12. "Wait a minute... How would you like that?" Manchester, p. 723. Coogan cites various sources that imply there never was any reward. In a letter to Sir John Anderson, Macready had proposed a £10,000 reward, but it never got approved, Coogan/Collins, pp. 209-210.
13. "Prices have gone up..." Lavery, 224. Quoted by John Lavery, but not found anywhere else. A similar quote, "Ah, yes, sir, but you are not allowing for inflation, I fear," Osborne, p. 57.
14. "surely it would be a discredit... did not manage to agree," Michael to C.P. Scott, Coogan/Collins, p. 256; Forester, p. 230.
15. "man of simple tastes... best of everything," Manchester, p. 26.

85. To Negotiate With Murderers

1. Tom Jones described the scene mentioning there were "some intimates of the Irish delegation for whom we had got tickets," Jones, p. 152. May Duggan was there, as evidenced by a Members' Gallery ticket in her name, *National Library of Ireland, Eamonn Duggan Papers, 1913-1968, Duggan, Eamonn.*
2. "not one of the members of the Irish… assume innocence until conviction," Jones, p. 152.
3. This and the following quotes from Lloyd George's speech, as well as the accusation by one of the Members that Michael Collins was a murderer, *The Times,* 1 November 1921, pp. 11 & 14-15.
4. According to Collins as quoted in Pakenham, p. 46, the Irish forces never numbered more than 3000. Seán MacEoin estimated 4000 men, Coogan/Collins, p. 257.
5. The exact date of Kitty's return to Dublin is not clear, but she seems to have stayed into this week. It is assumed here that with the schedule Collins was about to face, she would have left early in the week. In an undated letter, Michael wrote to Kitty, "About this time I hope Gearoid will be taking you away from Dunleary," Ó Broin, p. 57
6. "Don't be vexed with me… differently if you wish," Ó Broin, p. 53. Kitty wrote this in a letter to Michael on 26 October.
7. "You know how difficult my task here is… I visit my nastiness on my best friends," Ó Broin, p. 57.

86. All the Ends Thou Aim'st At

1. As depicted in *Volume One: Truce,* Macready probably knew Ned Broy personally. The two men could have seen each other in London during the Treaty talks, but this encounter is imagined.
2. *Cromwell's Letters and Speeches:* Volumes of Cromwell's writings can be found in the Cabinet Room's bookshelf, as seen in Simon Schama's Tour of Downing Street with Tony Blair, available on YouTube. Blair pointed out to Schama that during the negotiations over Northern Ireland, Jerry Adams was surprised to find these volumes in the glass-enclosed bookcase, much the same as we imagine Michael Collins could have done here.
3. "the Prime Minister would rather resign than start a war of reconquest." Jones had a private conversation with Collins at this time, during which Collins said "he felt disappointed and rather flat after the morning meeting," Jones, p. 152.
4. "Cromwell, I charge thee, fling away ambition. By that sin fell the angels," from an essay written by Collins while taking classes at King's College, Dolan and Murphy, 44-45.
5. Thomas Cromwell was an advisor to Cardinal Wolsey and later the chief minister to Henry VIII. He was the great-great grand-uncle of Oliver Cromwell.
6. Jones' note at the head of letter, Coogan/Collins, p. 255.
7. O'Higgins and his bride were in London around this time for their honeymoon and were feted with a dinner at Hans Place and theatre tickets, courtesy of Michael. At the dinner party, "it became painfully obvious that the gaiety was forced and a basic gloom" pervaded, De Vere White, pp. 59-60.
8. "free partnership of Ireland with the British Commonwealth, the formula to be arrived at later; recognition of the Crown, the formula to be arrived at a later stage," Pakenham, p. 196.

9. "further than either we or the Cabinet at home [have been] prepared to go," Coogan/Collins, p. 253
10. Griffith's intention "to shield Collins from attacks," Pakenham, p. 195. The argument that evening over the letter of assurances, Pakenham, pp. 195-196. The discussion continued the next morning.

87. British Pharmacopoeia

1. "a recognition of the Crown as head of the proposed Association of Free States," Pakenham, p. 197.
2. Visit to Birkenhead at House of Lords, Pakenham, p. 198; Coogan/Collins, p. 254.
3. "On no account… in form or fact," Coogan/Collins, p. 253.
4. "could charm a bird off a bough," Owen, p. 378.
5. "General Dyer, prohibition against… frightfulness… the inflicting of great slaughter… not a remedy known to the British pharmacopoeia; British way of doing business… basis of physical force alone… fatal to the British Empire… base ourselves only upon it," Gilbert/Stricken, pp. 401-407.
6. This scene is based on Pakenham, pp. 198-200; Jones, pp. 153-154; Coogan/Dev, p. 263; Coogan/Collins, pp. 254-255. The discussion of "with" vs "within" the Commonwealth, and the omission of the article "a" in the British draft of the letter, Pakenham, pp. 198-199.

88. Not Budge One Inch

1. "Craig will not budge one inch! …There is too much anti-Irish feeling in this country." This and further dialogue, Jones, pp. 154-5; Coogan/Dev, p. 263; Pakenham, p. 204.
2. This version of the Boundary Commission was Lloyd George's idea, as discussed with Jones the day before, but Jones suggested it as his own, Jones, pp. 155-156.
3. Sir James Craig had proposed a Boundary Commission in December 1919, Coogan/Collins, pp. 334-335.

89. Once a Bookkeeper

1. Scene based on Jones, pp. 155-157; Pakenham, pp. 204-206; Coogan/Dev, pp. 263-264; Coogan/Collins, p. 258. Collins arrived at 5.30 a.m. from Dublin crossing, Ó Broin, p. 58.
2. Lloyd George told Jones about these discussions, including that with the King, later that same day, before this meeting took place, Jones, pp. 155-156.
3. "Suppose the Twenty-Six … strike you?" adapted from Pakenham, p. 204; Coogan/Collins, p. 258.
4. "shone brilliantly… glimmering silver," letter written that morning to Kitty, Ó Broin, p. 58.
5. Coogan described this written record of the discussion between Collins and Griffith as a "political balance sheet," Coogan/Collins, p. 256.
6. "How far can we trust the signatures of the British delegation… whatever our position and authority," undated document, Coogan/Collins, pp. 256-257.
7. Still no engagement announcement as of 10 November, Ó Broin, p. 61.

90. Nine Points of Roguery

1. As stated earlier, Michael was always accompanied by a bodyguard while in London, MacBride, p. 44.
2. Weather report courtesy of a letter to Kitty, Ó Broin, p. 60.
3. Letter from de Valera quoted from Pakenham, p. 206. The letter appears to have been written on 9 November, but it is not specified whether it was received the same day or, perhaps more likely, the following day, 10 November. MacBride "travelled on the night mail at least twice a week, backwards and forwards," MacBride, p. 44.
4. Michael had to return to Dublin that Friday night, 11 November, Ó Broin, p. 63.
5. This party, or one very much like it, was held on 10 November, and critical word of it from the "snarly gob" O'Hegarty did find its way back to the disapproving Liam Lynch, Coogan/Collins p. 287; MacBride, pp. 44-46.

91. Not Queer Your Pitch

1. A private talk in Miss Stevenson's office, Jones, p. 163.
2. "Most men sink into insignificance when they quit office. Very insignificant men acquire weight when they obtain it." Churchill's dialogue here is from a letter he wrote to Lloyd George on 9 November 1921, *Winston S. Churchill*, by Martin Gilbert, Volume 4. *The Stricken World, 1916-22*, Companion volume, Part 3, April 1921-Nov. 1922, pp. 1666-16667; Gilbert/Stricken, p. 674; Churchill/Aftermath, pp. 318-319.
3. "South the status of an Irish State... Ulster could have no grievance if she preferred to stand out," Jones, p. 164.
4. "...Griffith. The actual fruits of our deliberations with Sir James Craig," Jones, p. 164.
5. "lesser evil," Coogan/Dev, p. 264. Griffith learned of Craig's refusal earlier that morning. "Having to forgo representation at Westminster," adapted from Pakenham, p.210.
6. "the cloven hoof of Ulster's sordidness," words spoken by Griffith to Jones earlier that same morning at Hans Place, Jones, p. 163.
7. "weighing a six bob tax as against three bob," Jones, p. 163; "were simply astounded by this proposal; Even Bonar Law is said to be a bit knocked out by it," Pakenham, p. 214. Most of the dialogue which follows is from Pakenham, pp. 214-215.
8. "your proposal, not ours," Pakenham, p. 215.

92. What Memo Is This

1. Jones showed the memo to Griffith that evening at 7 p.m., Jones, p. 164; Pakenham, p. 218. The place of their meeting is not mentioned.
2. "If Ulster did not see her way... wishes of the population," Pakenham, p. 218.

93. Roast Beef in Old England

1. "About 1.0 [p.m.] Hill took two copies of the document and handed them to Erskine Childers," Jones, p. 166.
2. "overcome Arthur Griffith's objections," Lavery, p. 223. Lavery did portraits of de Valera and Griffith in July, and Duffy, Barton, and Duggan in October. In November, Collins was the last to sit for his portrait, as per McCoole, captions to painting reproductions.
3. "were the type of men... even with their lives," Campbell/FE, p. 568.
4. "only required the impetus... anything known previously between the two peoples," Campbell/FE, p. 569.
5. "there's a gun in the pocket," McCoole, p.75. Collins met the Laverys for the first time on this date, showing up unannounced, McCoole, p. 74. Birkenhead was a good friend of the Laverys, as was Churchill, but Birkenhead was not there that day, though Collins frequently met him there on subsequent visits.
6. "walls...gold... crepe-like cloth... mantel... butterfly specimens," McCoole, p. 50.
7. "Salvidging Ulster," *Morning Post* quote from the day after the conference, Campbell/FE, p. 568.
8. Story of Michael's father and the shopkeeper, Forester, p. 8.
9. Jones sent the first draft of the Treaty to Childers at about 1 p.m., Jones, p. 166.
10. No date is given for this incident with Hazel's dog, but it is drawn from Fingall, p. 403; McCoole, p. 76.
11. Collins wrote to Kitty that day about Sir John Lavery and the *Tatler*, Ó Broin, p. 68.
12. Description of the studio, McCoole, pp. 50-51; Michael's portrait sitting, Lavery, p. 224.
13. "The Roast Beef of Old England" was written by Henry Fielding for his play *The Grub Street Opera*, from 1731. It was very popular throughout the 18th and 19th centuries, and shared a tune with a folksong that modern audiences will recognise, "Hard Times of Old England," by members of the English folksong revival such as Steeleye Span.
14. All the items listed in italics are from a menu for a dinner held on 16 November 1922, probably at Hans Place. *National Library of Ireland, Eamonn Duggan Papers, 1913-1968, Duggan, Eamonn.* "Menu Card for a Dinner Given by the Irish Republican Delegation in London."

94. Are They In or Are They Out

1. "Hope you had a nice crossing," letter from Kitty to Michael, probably dated 22 November. Ó Broin, pp. 70-71.
2. "More and more responsibility rests with me, and what responsibility it is." Coogan/Collins, p. 262.
3. The fact that Hazel always called Collins Michael, and never Mick, is from McCoole, p. 77, footnote.
4. Wickham circular explained in Coogan/Collins, pp. 261-262.
5. Barton-Childers authorship and debate over draft, Pakenham, pp. 232-234; Coogan/Collins, p. 262.
6. "following proposals... accepted head of the Association," Jones, pp. 169-170.
7. "Ireland's full claim is for a Republic... concessions from this position." Pakenham, pp. 233-234. Childers did not voice these remarks at this meeting but

instead, put them in a memorandum to the Irish delegation. Griffith's response was to this written memo.

8. "While the rest of us... to prevent one... put it in writing," paraphrased from Pakenham, p. 234.

9. These remarks and all the dialogue in this section are adapted from Jones, pp. 170-171.

10. Tudor and Greenwood regarding the Wickham circular; "Pity Henry Wilson has not gone for a voyage around the world" (this last not spoken to Lloyd George); Jones, p. 169.

11. Cope's visit to Collins and Griffith, discussion of *with* vs *within* the Commonwealth, the word *associated*, a blank cheque, let down by British statesmen, Jones, pp. 171-172.

12. In a letter to Kitty, Collins wrote that on 22 November, "I went to the Court Theatre to meet my sister and the Duggans coming out... They were at *Heartbreak House* by Bernard Shaw... I saw a bit of the end of it," Ó Broin, p. 73. Jones mentions that Cope went to find Duggan "at one of the theatres" that same evening in Jones, p. 172. The dialogue here is a retelling of discussions Collins and Griffith had earlier in the day, from Jones, pp. 170-172.

13. "give categorical assurances on fundamentals like allegiance and the navy," Jones, p. 172.

95. L'Armée Nouveau

1. Bungled arms raid, Coogan/Collins, p. 249; Forester, 242-243; de Valera's scheme for a "New Army," Coogan/Collins, pp. 250-251; Coogan/Dev, pp. 267-269. Michael's reference to Napoleon, Coogan/Collins, p. 250; Coogan/Dev, p. 268

96. Curse All Secret Societies

1. Meeting with Birkenhead, Jones, pp. 171-174; Coogan/Collins, pp. 262-263; Pakenham, pp. 237-245.

2. Michael was at the Wicklow Hotel after arriving in Dublin the morning of 25 November, Ó Broin, pp. 74-75. Michael wrote to Mulcahy suggesting a meeting with the I.R.B. and the G.H.Q. for that morning (Coogan/Collins, p. 250), but the place and attendees are an invention here. The Wicklow Hotel was on the site of Mary's Bar as of this writing.

3. Jones mentions Craig's withdrawal of Wickham's circular in the papers that day, 25 November, Jones, p. 173.

4. "Could count on you to treat all this in your usual fashion," paraphrases Michael's letter, Coogan/Collins, p. 250.

5. "That Ireland should recognise...head of the combination of Associated States," Pakenham, p. 245; Macardle, p. 572.

6. Griffith's first visit back, Pakenham, p. 245.

7. It can be deduced from Michael's letter to Kitty a few days later (Ó Broin, p. 76) that Pat McCrea drove Collins to Granard that Sunday.

8. "retain Eoin O'Duffy, Austin Stack... Deputy Chief on the Staff," Coogan/Collins, pp. 232, 244, 251.

9. "band of brothers... Ye may mutiny if ye like... another army," Coogan/Collins, pp. 250-251.

10. "Curse [all] secret societies," Coogan/Dev, p. 289.

97. No Harm Done

1. New Road flat, Ó Broin, p. 11. Michael's letters do not mention specifically when he arrived in Granard that weekend or when he returned to Dublin, but do mention that he was with Kitty there Sunday night ("I was not in just the proper form on Sunday night."). On 28 November, Michael wrote, "We got back safely," possibly referring to himself and Pat McCrea. He then told the story of Pat's arrest, saying, "Curious thing happened today [this could be Sunday or Monday] —just after Pat McCrea left us, he was run in for furious driving." "Us" may refer to Michael and one of his men in Dublin, rather than Kitty. Michael was definitely back in London on 29 November, where he visited his sister Hannie, Ó Broin, pp. 76-77. "The hotel was rebuilt out of compensation money, but it was well into 1922 before it could be lived in again... While the rebuilding was going on, the family lived in Omard House before taking a large flat over a shop in the New Road, just at the back gate of the hotel," Ó Broin, p. 11.
2. "It's better to wear out than rust out," Ó Broin, p. 76.
3. "I am not demonstrative... And that's that," quoted and paraphrased from Ó Broin, p. 77.
4. "I'd never forgive myself ... but it *is* there," Ó Broin, p. 77.
5. Michael wrote to Kitty about this incident in his letter dated 28 November 1921, Ó Broin, p. 76. The presence of Emmet Dalton here is fictional, but plausible.

98. As Stubble In Our Hands

1. "Michael Collins Owns a Dog," *Freeman's Journal*, 28 November 1921.
2. "Tim Healy was going to join them but apparently had a change of mind," Jones, p. 176.
3. "The Lord made them as stubble in our hands," this scene is set in Jones, pp. 176-177.
4. "This means war," Jones, p. 176.
5. "Dominion status based on the Canadian model," etc.; "that in Ireland the Crown would not function. He said we Irish require a symbolism acceptable to us," Coogan/Collins, p. 263.
6. "This document is impossible. Any British Government...smashed to atoms; no authority... purely Irish affairs; The Crown in the Dominions is merely a symbol, but in Ireland it would be a reality; insert in the Treaty... any other Dominion," Pakenham, p. 249; Coogan/Dev, pp. 270-271; Coogan/Collins, p. 264.
7. F.E.: "Irish Free State," and "the same national status as the Dominion of Canada and be known as the Irish Free State." These two quotes are from a British Cabinet meeting the next day, Jones, p. 177.
8. "difficulty... the Oath of Allegiance... try to modify it if that would help," from a Griffith letter to de Valera, Pakenham, p. 250.
9. "Gwell... Better," Jones, p. 177.

99. The Land Fit for Heroes

1. Dave Neligan noted the ex-officers on the streets of London in Neligan, p. 151-152.
2. Jones mentions "lunch with P.M. for 30 November Wednesday... film of Winston Churchill's latest novel," Jones, p. 178. *The Inside of the Cup* was a 1921 film based

on a novel by the popular American author. The Wikipedia entry for "Winston Churchill (novelist)" describes career and personal similarities between the two men..

3. "that the coastal defence of Ireland is to be undertaken exclusively by His Majesty's Imperial forces... until an arrangement has been made... Irish Free State undertakes her own coastal defence; conference ten years... later," Pakenham, p. 253. All spoken dialogue is fictional.

4. Michael and Childers met with Sir Robert Horne, Chancellor of the Exchequer, in the morning meeting, and at a later meeting, Michael met alone with Horne, Lloyd George, and R.G. Hawtrey of the Treasury, Pakenham, p. 253.

5. Meeting with Birkenhead, Jones, pp. 171-174; Coogan/Collins, pp. 262-263; Pakenham, pp. 237-245.

6. This shouting argument based loosely on the description of the meeting at Hans Place in Coogan/Collins, p. 265; Pakenham, pp. 252-254. Dialogue is based on Childers' diary, not actually spoken.

100. To Go For a Drink Is One Thing

1. Since Tom Cullen is mentioned earlier (October 22-24, in Ó Broin, p. 55) as accompanying Collins back to London, it is imagined here that he made subsequent trips with Collins.

2. "To go for a drink is one thing. To be driven to it is another!" Coogan/Collins, p. 242.

3. "glass of wine... *and there's the trouble*," Ó Broin, p. 79.

4. The description and analysis of Griffith's late visit to de Valera, Coogan/Dev, p. 271.

5. The mailboat collision, Coogan/Collins, p. 266.

101. You Can Get Another Five To Go Over

1. Seán O'Muirthle was the person who contacted and returned with the Treaty appraisal, Coogan/Collins, p. 266.

2. All the arguments made and dialogue adapted from Coogan/Collins, pp. 266-9; Coogan/Dev, pp. 273-277; Pakenham, pp. 255-263.

3. "neither this nor that," Pakenham, p. 283.

4. "selected their men," Coogan/Dev, p. 273; Coogan/Collins, p. 266.

5. "If you are not satisfied with us, you can get another five to go over... full knowledge and consent," Coogan/Collins, p. 266.

6. The I.R.B. Oath: "I do solemnly swear to bear true faith and allegiance to the Constitution of the Irish Free State... the British Commonwealth," Dwyer/Warrant, p. 190.

7. Michael's consultation with the I.R.B. and their suggestions on the oath, Ulster, and defence, Coogan/Collins, p. 273. Charlie is inserted here for narrative effect.

8. There is no mention of Pat McCrea going to London, so this is just an invention. In the author'smind, Paddy is too good a character not to have been invited to accompany the delegation.

9. Michael's stand on the Oath, Coogan/Collins, p. 268.

10. "I do not like this document, but I do not think it dishonourable. It practically gives us a Republic... The first allegiance is to Ireland...will not fight on the question of allegiance alone," Coogan/Collins, p. 267; Pakenham, p. 259.

11. Earlier that day Griffith said, "I'll *not* sign the document, but I'll bring it back and

submit it to the Dáil and, if necessary, to the people." Later in the day he is quoted as having said, "that he would not take the responsibility for breaking off the treaty over the Crown... the Dáil is the body to decide for or against war," Coogan/Collins, pp. 267-268.

12. Gavan Duffy, "I am against acceptance. I believe... propose amendments to the British;" Robert Barton, "This Treaty does not give even Dominion... the question of allegiance... I am against acceptance;" Erskine Childers, "The proposed Treaty would give no national status and renders neutrality impossible;" Cathal Brugha, "I am in general agreement with the President. I am opposed to acceptance;" Austin Stack, "Opposed;" de Valera, "differences can be reconciled... to withdraw those demands;" all these quotes are adapted from Macardle, p. 578.

13. "scrapping the Oath... Yes"; Coogan/Dev, pp. 274-275.

14. "Yes or no; instructed;" Coogan/Dev, p. 277.

15. "Mick is so kind, he thinks of everyone." Mick had once sent a messenger enquiring about the health of a sick relative of Brugha, O'Connor, Frank, p. 54. O'Connor did not mention the time and place of this gesture, but it possibly was for Brugha's wife, Caitlín Kingston.

102. Back From This Precipice

1. Michael's description of London Sundays from letter written that day to Kitty, Ó Broin, p. 84.

2. "Then London came I should not have come. It gave rise to such talk... we were ever to part... want you to end it... We will, won't we, be real lovers? Say we will," Ó Broin, pp. 80-81. Letter written on 1 December, received by Michael, 4 December.

3. The rest of this chapter is primarily based on an accounting of the day's events in Pakenham, pp. 264-70.

4. "Healy... aghast at the prospect of war... strongly in favour of the terms on offer... [meeting] Lloyd George," Coogan/Collins, p. 269.

5. Healy: "Collins is the only sensible man amongst us," Coogan/Collins, p. 269.

6. All of the dialogue in this section, from the apology by Lloyd George to Chamberlain declaring, "That ends it!" is from Pakenham, pp. 267-270.

7. According to Coogan, tongue-in-cheek, "The journey back to Hans Place was enlivened for Gavan Duffy by Griffith's informing him of matters concerning his ancestry he had not previously been aware of," Coogan/Collins, p. 270. No actual quotes are recorded, but perhaps they ran something similar to what is stated here, or as stated in Pakenham, p. 270: "He turned on Gavan Duffy... and he rent him."

8. There is no record of such a discussion between Lloyd George and Thomas Jones, but Jones hardly would have acted without the P.M.'s knowledge and blessing. Pakenham thought that the proposed meeting came at the suggestion of the British, Pakenham, pp. 273-274; Coogan points out that the Jones diaries later revealed that "it was Griffith who asked Jones to arrange the meeting," Jones, p. 180; Coogan/Collins, p. 271. This sub-chapter suggests a little help from the always cunning Lloyd George.

9. "I like my Raleigh bicycle," the brand that he owned, Osborne, p. 23.

10. "I could leave you clean-shaven." In fact, Lavery did just that, and the result was a close-up rendering without Michael's moustache.

11. According to John Lavery's autobiography, *The Life of a Painter*, written nearly twenty years later, Michael visited the Laverys this night, 4 December, Lavery, p. 223. Also, McCoole, p. 80. Maybe this visit did occur, maybe not, but if it did,

perhaps it went as described here. Hazel reportedly convinced Michael "to take what you can get," McCoole, p. 81. However, Hazel could not have driven him that night to see Lloyd George, as John Lavery wrote (and quoted in Ryan/Shot, p. 13), because Thomas Jones visited Griffith that night to get his help in convincing Collins to resume deliberations. If she drove him at all, as Clementine Churchill asserted in a private letter, Hazel could have driven him to Downing Street the next morning, when we know he met Lloyd George, but even this is doubtful. See the footnote below, "According to Clementine Churchill."

12. Pakenham wrote, "Jones saw Griffith at 10. p.m. and begged him to persuade Collins to see Lloyd George alone," Pakenham, p. 273. According to *Whitehall Diaries*, "*4 December Sunday*... Late at night. T.J. sees Arthur Griffith and *struggles to get Michael Collins to see L.G.*," Jones, p. 180 [author's italics]. But in a memo to L.G. composed at 1.30 a.m., Jones wrote, "He [A.G.] and Collins trust you... Would you [L.G.] see Collins and have a heart to heart talk with him? I [Jones] said yes— 9.15 a.m.," ibid., now informing the P.M. that the request for the meeting came from Griffith. Jones wrote, "A.G. went over at 1.0 [a.m.] to hunt out Collins to fix this up," Jones, p. 181. Griffith would then have had to have gone to Cadogan Gardens after Jones left Hans Place, something which Jones did not personally witness, but perhaps it is more likely Griffith telephoned Collins. Jones' memo is the source for all the dialogue from this late-night mission. Pakenham quotes a memo written by Collins, "As I had not made up my mind until after speaking with Mr. Griffith this morning, I did not see Lloyd George until 9.30," Pakenham, pp. 273-274.

103. Moral Courage So Rare

1. According to Clementine Churchill, "it was widely known that Hazel, dressed in her favourite opera cloak, brought Collins to Downing Street," McCoole, p. 81. This is not corroborated in the press of that day, which had been assiduously recording all comings and goings to and from No. 10. John and Hazel Lavery were both sincere in their desire to facilitate peace, but they both had a tendency toward exaggeration driven by faulty memories.

2. "North... forced economically... as agreeable to a reply rejecting as accepting... we would save... [by] the Boundary Commission... put to [Craig]," Pakenham, p. 274.

3. "put his arm around [his] shoulder... You're a capable man... help us," Mackay, 222.

4. A meeting with T.E. Lawrence probably took place sometime that week, most likely that day. One account reads, "On 3 December 1920 Lawrence had met Michael Collins in London," Knightley and Simpson, p. 194. The year should have been stated as 1921, and on the 3rd Michael was in Dublin. On the 4th he apparently did not go to Whitehall, so we assume this meeting with Lawrence took place on the 5th. This meeting is discussed in Coogan/Collins, p. 395.

5. "just released," Ó Broin, p. 84.

6. "two months of futilities and rigmarole," Pakenham, p. 286, Churchill/Aftermath, p. 320.

7. "division of opinion... within the Irish Cabinet... rejected [in Dublin]... counter-proposals [regarding] Ulster," Coogan/Collins, p. 272; CAB 23/27/16.

8. "Ulster proposals given to you... Mr. Griffith agreed with his undertaking not to let us down," Pakenham, p. 287.

9. According to Pakenham, Cope "had inevitably spent Saturday in Dublin," and could have informed the British what he learned of divisions in the Dublin Cabi-

net, Pakenham, p.270.

10. Birkenhead's work on the oath, Campbell/FE, 571; Pakenham, pp., 289-90.

11. "If Ireland were permitted any Navy... from every angle," Pakenham, p. 291. In the ensuing debates in Parliament, this alarmist concern over submarines turned out to be less hyperbole than prescience.

12. Pakenham wrote that "*A phrase was inserted* that the exclusive undertaking of Irish coastal defence by His Majesty's Forces was not to prevent the construction or maintenance of such vessels as are necessary for the protection of the Revenue and the Fisheries," Pakenham, p. 291. He does not specify who proposed this qualifying phrase.

13. The story of "that damn paper," Griffith's pledge, is from Pakenham, pp. 292-293.

14. "Why... did they bring that pipsqueak...Under-Secretary. Perhaps they had failed to cure him of his protectionist theories and brought him along to be faithfully dealt with by you. Not unlikely," adapted from an earlier assessment of Barton in Jones, p. 173. Framed text from the Book of Job, Jones, p. xiii.

15. "five years... *with a view to the undertaking of a* share *in her own coastal defence*... Birkenhead, superbly nonchalant as ever in his exposition of constitutional niceties, explained, 'If the docks were handed over... Crown could not demand payment from the Crown,'" Parkenham, p. 293.

16. "What is this letter? I don't know what the hell it is; Do you mean to tell me, Mr. Collins"; Pakenham, pp. 293-294; Dwyer/Warrant, 208.

17. Letter of Assurances, Pakenham, pp. 218, 294.

18. "proponent of free trade... I am prepared to agree... freedom on both sides to impose any tariffs either country liked," adapted from Pakenham, p. 296; Gilbert/Stricken, pp. 675-676.

19. "concession... affix your signatures to the other Articles of Agreement," paraphrase of Pakenham, p. 296.

20. "the Irishmen gulped down the ultimatum phlegmatically. When Arthur finally began to speak, Winston noticed the softness in his voice and modesty of manner that Winston would later record for prosperity," Churchill/Aftermath, p. 321.

21. "past six in the evening," time approximate, Jones, p. 182

22. "I will give the answer... Do I understand... Yes, that is so, Prime Minister," Churchill/Aftermath, p. 321

23. "destroyer to Belfast... ten p.m. tonight," much debated if this occurred, actually true. Geoffrey Shakespeare was sent to Craig by special train and destroyer, Jones, pp. 182 & 184; Pakenham, p. 298; Coogan/Collins, p. 274; Owen, p. 587; Dwyer, pp. 210, 212-214.

24. "Copy of *St. James Park* given by Mr. Chamberlain to A.G.," Jones, p. 182.

25. "A braver man than Arthur Griffith I have never met," Jones, p. 183.

26. Churchill on MC: Churchill/Aftermath, p. 321; O'Connor, Frank, p. 169.

27. F.E. Birmingham speech, Pakenham, p.300.

28. "If we have no answer by ten p.m., we shall leave them in no doubt as to what we are doing," Jones, p. 182.

29. "Lloyd George was of course bluffing for Barton's benefit," Coogan/Collins, p. 274.

30. Ultimatum regarding the destroyer, Lloyd George's bluff, analysis in Dwyer/Warrant, pp. 210-214.

31. Years later Dalton stated that this aircraft was kept on constant alert during the Treaty negotiations, but did not mention this night in particular, *Emmet Dalton Remembers*, rte.ie/archives, YouTube. Dwyer writes that evening "Collins arrived shortly afterwards at Hans Place with Tobin, Dolan, and Charlie Russell," Dwyer, p. 211.

32. This plea from Griffith is added for dramatic effect.

33. Kathleen MacKenna's mission, the scene outside Hans Place, quoted from her memoirs, Coogan/Collins, p. 275.
34. "Mackintosh... dangled... attaché case... paced... dining room... sherry... Eddie... upstairs... dining room chair... fell deeply asleep... Poor Big Fellow!" Kathleen MacKenna's reminiscences from Coogan/Collins, p. 275.
35. "conscience... oath... Ulster... refer back to the Dáil," Dwyer/Warrant, p. 207.
36. "how few men we have... active Volunteers... send them out to be slaughtered... Barton, you will be hanged from a lamppost in Dublin if... new war in Ireland... when I saw the hangman... lads there," Coogan/Collins, p. 274.
37. "Well, I suppose I must sign," Coogan/Collins, p. 275.
38. "if anyone besides Mr. Griffith... solitary signature express," Churchill/Aftermath, p. 321.
39. "it is curious... moral courage so rare," *Mark Twain in Eruption*, edited by Bernard DeVoto, Harper and Brothers, New York, 1940, p. 69. Excerpts from this early posthumous autobiography were published during Twain's lifetime.
40. "provided he has as much moral courage as he has physical courage. But moral courage is a much higher quality than physical courage, and it is a quality that brave men often lack," Coogan/Collins, p. 276.
41. "Mr. Griffith, Mr. Collins, and Mr. Barton have arrived;" for the British: Lloyd George, Churchill, Birkenhead, Chamberlain; "All seven who were present signed... and the other Delegates signed later;" Pakenham, pp. 307-308; Dwyer/Warrant, pp. 220-221. "superficially calm and quiet... Prime Minister, the Delegation is willing to sign... convenient if I mentioned at once," Churchill/Aftermath, p. 321.
42. "become allies and associates in a common cause—the cause of the Irish Treaty and of peace between two races and two islands," Churchill/Aftermath, p. 322. Not spoken here, but written later.
43. "Treaty [was] worth [that] thousand pounds," F.E.'s drinking bet, Campbell/FE, p. 601. This drink may actually have taken place after the Irish delegates left.
44. "distraught [Erskine] Childers" presence there, Pakenham, pp. 310-311; Dwyer/Warrant pp. 220-221.
45. In his memoirs published in 1924, Macready wrote about this encounter with Collins at 10 Downing Street after the signing of the Treaty, but he may have misremembered the actual date and details, and this conversation is not related anywhere else, Macready, p. 612.
46. "very tired, grave, 'Mick, do you have anything to say?' 'Not a word... I don't know,'" *Westminster Gazette*, 6 December 1921.

104. Peace to This Land of Ours

1. Richard Mulcahy at Limerick home of James O'Mara, Coogan/Dev, pp. 118, 158-159, 280-282.
2. "Finished up at 2.15 this morning. To bed about 5, and up to go to Mass," Ó Broin, p. 85. No mention of Pat, Liam, and Tom, but possible. It is assumed here that upon leaving Downing Street, everyone retired to Hans Place, accounting for the time between 2.15 and 5.00 a.m. Michael possibly went by himself to the Laverys' home, as stated in Ryan/Shot, p. 13, "After signing... Collins went back to the Laverys." However, if John Lavery is the source of this anecdote, he does not mention this after-signing visit in his autobiography, which was written twenty years later and is a dubious source for specific dates. "A peace which will end this old strife of ours," is a famous quote from the same letter from Michael to Kitty, Ó Broin, p. 85.

3. Griffith and Duffy visit to P.M., Jones, p. 185. Treaty title and dinner menu signature from Dwyer/Warrant, pp. 222-223.
4. Dante Commemoration, *Evening Mail*, de Valera's refusal to look at the Treaty, "Apparently... secondary interest to him," Coogan/Dev, p. 283.

105. It Won't Do for Cork

1. This farewell visit was noted in *Freeman's Journal*, 8 December 1921. Also, McCoole, p. 82: "The next day [7 December] Collins again visited Cromwell Place, signing and dating Hazel's scrapbook. He left for Ireland that night."
2. Various documents related to delegation expenses, including a catering bill, were part of an online exhibition of the National Archives.
3. "It won't do for Cork," O'Connor, Frank, p. 171.
4. "elude capture during the hostilities... My moustache was my disguise... I never disguised in my whole life," *Daily Herald*, 8 December 1921.
5. "In the creation of the Irish Free State... what country would wish to stay outside; Association of Free States;" *The Times*, 8 December 1921, Associated Press correspondent; Dwyer/Warrant, p. 222.
6. "Mr. Collins, can't you smile... Boundary Commission... North-eastern... a different thing... get [it] with or without... I have got over trouble before," *New York Times*, 8 December 1921.
7. "Grosvenor's Hotel... Art O'Brien," from receipt in National Archives, as above. Visit to O'Brien, *Irish Times*, 8 December 1921.
8. The scene at Euston Station described, "Mr. Collins Kissed," *Irish Times*, 8 December 1921; Coogan/Collins, p. 296; Dwyer/ Warrant, p. 226.

106. An Urgent Summons

1. This rendezvous and conversation with Dave, Neligan, p.152.
2. Childers "nearly crushed to death," Dwyer/ Warrant, p. 226.
3. I.R.B. reception, Dwyer/Warrant, 226; Coogan/Collins, p. 296. No mention is made of O'Reilly being there, but it is difficult to imagine him not showing up. At the start of the talks in London, Michael confided in a letter to Joe that "the trap is sprung," Coogan/Collins, pp. 229, 242; *Volume One: Truce*. Little is written about Joe's involvement in this period, but a famous photograph of Michael leaving the Debates at Earlsfort Terrace shows Joe close behind. For this reason, he is imagined to have been in closer contact with Michael than historical sources relate.
4. "What is good enough for you is good enough for them," Coogan/Collins, p. 296; Liam, p. 366.
5. "act of disloyalty," de Valera said as much in a letter at the time, Coogan/Dev, p. 284.
6. "saw a look of peace and satisfaction pass over de Valera's face, as if the objection allowed him to hold his hand until the whole Cabinet could meet," paraphrased from Dwyer/Warrant, p. 224.
7. *Irish Times*, 8 December 1921: "In view of the nature of the proposed Treaty with Great Britain, President de Valera has sent an urgent summons to the members of the Cabinet in London to report at once so that a full Cabinet decision can be taken. The hour of the meeting is fixed for noon tomorrow, Thursday. A meeting of the Dáil will be summoned later... Presuming that the Cabinet of Dáil Eireann will at its meeting to-day approve the terms—and there is no reason at the moment to suppose that it will do otherwise—the next step will be to secure the

approval of Dáil Eireann, which it is also assumed will be forthcoming." Coogan/Dev., pp. 284-285; Macardle, pp. 594-595.

8. "will be received in America with great joy," *New York Times*, 7 December 1921.

9. Harry Boland's changing stance on the Treaty is described in Fitzpatrick, pp. 255-259.

107. No Welcome for Me

1. Michael's arrival a few minutes before noon in tweed cap, *Irish Times*, 9 December 1921.

2. A similar encounter with women in the streets, O'Connor, Frank, pp.172-173, and mentioned in Coogan/Collins, p. 298.

3. "Head in hands, reproaching M.C. for signing," Childers quoted in Coogan/Collins, p. 296.

4. Saturday promise to not sign, Dwyer/Warrant p. 226; Coogan/Dev, p. 285.

5. Gallagher's handling the Press, Dwyer/Warrant, p. 226.

6. "referring the Treaty to Dublin... had not even thought of it," Dwyer/Warrant, p. 226.

7. "[It] was not teamwork," Hart, p. 325.

8. "I would have gone to London and said 'go to the devil, I will not sign,'" Dwyer/Warrant p. 226.

9. "whole situation [is of your doing, and is due to your] vacillation... chance to go to London... we were not a fighting delegation," Coogan/Collins, p. 296; Coogan/Dev, p. 285; Dwyer/Warrant, p. 227.

10. "insidious... duress... Knowing already from Mr. Griffith... accept the responsibility for the slaughter... consult the President, the cabinet in Dublin, the Dáil, or the people," Dwyer/Warrant, p. 227.

11. "I did not sign the Treaty under duress... contest between a great Empire and a small nation... one of duress," Coogan/Collins, p. 296; Michael Collins, *The Path to Freedom*, p. 26; Dwyer/Warrant, p. 227; Hart, p. 326.

12. O'Higgins: "I have no vote on the matter... unity," paraphrased from Dwyer/Warrant, p. 228; Coogan/Dev, p. 285; Coogan/Collins, p. 296.

13. "You have signed... not supposed to throw all your influence... Where would I be then?"; promises to resign; Dwyer/Warrant, p. 228.

14. "I have signed the treaty... the end of the conflict of centuries is at hand," *New York Times*, 9 December 1921.

15. "The terms of this Agreement are in violent conflict with the wishes of the majority of this nation," *Freeman's Journal*, 9 December 1921.

16. "Poor Ireland, back to the back rooms again," Mackay, p. 229.

17. "If the Chief is against me, who would be for me? My own brother Johnny will probably stand against me in Cork," Mackay, p. 229.

18. "This is a day I never would live to see; I thought perhaps you would have no welcome for me; I will accept their verdict." All dialogue in this section nearly exactly quoted from O'Connor, Batt, pp. 180-182; Coogan/Collins, pp. 297-298.

108. We Have Declared For an Irish Republic

1. "We have declared for an Irish Republic and will not live under any other law," Coogan/Collins, p. 320, no date given.

2. "not what the... Dublin Brigade fought for," Coogan/Collins, p. 320, from a letter.

3. Liam Lynch description, "meticulous appearance and dress… a strong disciplinarian," partly from Murray/Lynch/Part I.
4. Discussion at the I.R.B. meeting and its communique from Dwyer/Warrant, pp. 230-231; Dwyer does not mention the presence of Seán MacEoin. Also, http://www.irishhistory1919-1923chronology.ie/december_1921.htm; Hopkinson p. 42; Curran, p. 145; Murray/Lynch/Part I. Hopkinson states this meeting took place on 11 December, but that Sunday Collins was in Granard visiting Kitty.
5. "Next time you're shaving, don't overlook that thing as well," Mackay, p. 229. See also footnote below for "*11 a.m., 14 December 1921, Dublin, Dáil Public Session,*" regarding when Michael shaved the questionable moustache.

109. Wondering When You Might Ask

1. Michael visited Kitty in Granard the Sunday (11 December 1921) before the Treaty debates began (Ó Broin, pp. 87, 91-93), but there is no mention of how he got there and back. Kitty wrote to Michael the day before, Saturday the 10th, saying she received his letters in the first post, but makes no mention of an impending trip to Granard. She writes, "I was wondering if perhaps you sent a wire today, as the wires are cut here. None going or coming," Ó Broin, p. 87. Without an exchange of letters to make arrangements or a wire or telephone call for this visit, perhaps Michael arrived unexpectedly, as is imagined here. Michael's next visit was on 30 December by train from Dublin to the station in Edgeworthstown, and from there by car to Granard (Ó Broin, p. 100), so maybe he also travelled by train on 11 December. Kitty wrote on 14 December 1921, "how awful you were looking… you were so tired and longed to sleep," and "Hope your cold has gone," Ó Broin, pp. 92-93.
2. "Will Ireland now… turn her back, etc.," *Irish Times*, 9 December 1921.
3. "all the wires are down," Ó Broin, p. 87.
4. Ó Broin, p. 92, "It (Michael's watch) must have dropped on the grass," Ó Broin, p. 97. Letter from Michael to Kitty, 17 December 1921: "I did enjoy that walk ever so much… It is delightful being out with you—it is so much healthier than remaining indoors." These two letters are the basis for this imagined scene up to the Granard Motte, which was not mentioned at all in their letters.
5. "I've been wondering for some time… about our plans… It would have spoiled it for you," paraphrased from Ó Broin, p. 97. The exact nature of "when I would ask you" is not stated explicitly in this letter dated 17 December 1921, but it's a fair guess that it was about either a formal proposal or a formal announcement of their engagement, which probably was discussed during Kitty's trip to visit Michael in London.
6. "send all your letters to me there, and mark them 'Personal,'" Ó Broin, p. 94, letter from Michael to Kitty, 14 December 1921.
7. "I'd like to send you any letters that may come from them for safekeeping." Leon Ó Broin writes in Ó Broin, p. 88, "in order to protect his name and to assure Kitty that there was nothing in the stories that she might be hearing about Lady Lavery's association with him, he sent these letters to Granard. It should be noted later that for a similar reason, he advised Kitty when coming to see him in the Gresham Hotel in Dublin, not to come alone."

110. Our Victories Will Be Her Joy

1. "the patriotism, ability and honesty… for national freedom, the wishes of the people," *New York Times*, 14 December 1921.
2. *11.30 a.m., 14 December 1921, London, Opening of Parliament*; All the material in this section was drawn from articles in the *New York Times*, 15 December 1921; *Irish Times*, 15 December 1921; and *The Times*, 15 December 1921. The King's Speech was quoted from Hansard, Commons Sitting of 14 December 1921, King's Speech, Irish Free State.
3. *11.00 a.m., 14 December 1921, Dublin, Dáil Public Session.* Text of speeches quoted and adapted from the Houses of the Oireachtas website, Dáil Éireann debate-Wednesday, 14 December 1921.
4. "Uniformed military police were stationed at either end of the street [Earlsford Terrace] to assist the men of the Irish Republican Army in enforcing an order prohibiting vehicular traffic," *New York Times*, "English Used," 15 December 1921. If the street was closed to vehicles, that probably would not have applied to the cars carrying the Dáil members, who otherwise would have had to walk a few streets and through crowds.
5. "the Dáil debate on the Treaty began, in University College, Earlsfort Terrace, because the Mansion House was occupied by a Christmas Fair," Coogan/Collins, p. 298.
6. Seán MacBride stood guard within the debates, and though he opposed the Treaty, remained friendly with Cullen and Tobin throughout the debates and even the Civil War, MacBride, p. 59.
7. "Thanks, Tom. Why don't you join Alice and Sinead?" There was no official or written mention of Tom, Alice, and Sinead being at this meeting of the Dáil, but some friends and associates of Michael would have to have been there. Dwyer mentions Michael as the first minister to arrive, Dwyer/Warrant, p. 233.
8. "Eoin MacNeill, a Gaelic scholar and professor at University College Dublin who eight years earlier had formed the Irish Volunteers," Coogan/Collins, p. 29.
9. Contrary to legend, Michael did not shave his moustache on Christmas Day at the bidding of his brother Johnny, but eleven days earlier. Collins "was, as usual, smiling and good-humoured, and, with his mustache shaved off in the last 24 hours, he looked more boyish than ever," *Freeman's Journal*, 15 December 1921.
10. "The meeting was scheduled to begin in the National University buildings in Earlsford Terrace at 11 o'clock. It was nearly half an hour behind time," *Irish Times*, 15 December 1921. Note: The descriptions of the scene in the Council Room were compiled from the *New York Times*; the *Irish Times*; *The Times*; all from 15 December 1921; Dwyer/Warrant, pp. 233-234; O'Connor, Frank, p.175. A photograph of the meeting of the Dáil meeting that appears in the *Irish Times* was also used to describe the scene: https://www.irishtimes.com/culture/books/time-is-ripe-to-reappraise-eirexit-and-treaty-of-1921-1.3660376.
11. "In the council room of University College half an hour before the appointed time, a few members of the Dáil began strolling to their places in the large adjoining room communicating by unfolded doors. Reporters from all the world were already gathered; scarcely less numerous than the members of the Dáil itself," *New York Times*, 15 December 1921.
12. "Some of the members do not know Irish, I think, and consequently what I shall say will be in English," Coogan/Dev, p. 288; Coogan/Collins, p. 298.
13. "If I am a traitor, let the Irish people decide it or not," Coogan/Collins, p. 299; Dáil Éireann debate.

14. *1 p.m., 14 December 1921, Dublin, Dáil Private Session.* Text of speeches quoted and adapted from the Houses of the Oireachtas website, Dáil Éireann debate-Wednesday, 14 December 1921.

15. Knirck, p.112, quoting Curran, p. 147, states, "The Dáil was ill-prepared for the responsibility thrust on it by the Cabinet's split over the Treaty."

16. This is a fictional meeting of Michael and Eileen, who chose the Anti-Treaty side, Eileen McGrane, BMH, W.S. 1752.

17. Knirck, p.113, states, "Ordinary Dáil deputies had no idea of the intricacies and interactions between the cabinet and plenipotentiaries during the Treaty negotiations, had not been briefed on the emerging details of external association, and were not kept up to date with the shifting substance of the British offers."

18. "A captain who sent his crew out to sea and tried to direct them from dry land," Coogan/Collins, p. 299; Dwyer, Warrant, p. 239.

19. *3.45 p.m. (London), 14 December 1921, London, House of Lords, Carson Speech.* Text of speeches quoted and adapted from Hansard, 14 December 1921, Lords Sitting, Address in Reply to His Majesty's Most Gracious Speech.

20. *4.00 p.m. (Approx., London), 14 December 1921, London, House of Commons.* Text of speeches quoted and adapted from Hansard, 14 December 1921, Commons Sitting.

21. "slipped into his seat… with every appearance of wishing to escape notice…. cheer after cheer," and "a card sharper who keeps an extra ace up his sleeve and produces it as the necessity of the game demands," *New York Times*, 15 December 1921.

22. "They sought peace, and they ensued it." Lloyd George praises the Irish delegates, using an archaic British transitive verb, "to ensue," meaning to pursue. The popular English poet Rupert Brooke wrote, "I wander, seeking peace, and ensuing it."

23. *4.40 p.m., 14 December 1921, Dublin, Dáil Private Session.* Text of speeches quoted and adapted from the Houses of the Oireachtas website, Dáil Éireann debate Private Session- Wednesday, 14 Dec 1921.

24. *7.25 p.m., 14 December 1921, Dublin, Dáil Evening Private Session.* Text of speeches quoted and adapted from the Houses of the Oireachtas website, Dáil Éireann debate- Wednesday, 14 Dec 1921.

25. As mentioned earlier, Collins and Boland had put up a disproportionate number of extreme Republicans for the Dáil, Knirck, p. 83.

111. This Mysterious Power of Ireland

1. "your speech to the House yesterday… House did not tumble to that fact…" issue of credentials, visit to Birkenhead, Jones, pp. 188-189.

2. *15 December 1921, London.* This section is based on Thomas Jones, 188-189. Jones had a discussion at Downing Street with the P.M. at 11.30 a.m. about Collins' speech during the Dáil Public Session the day before, the 14th. From there Jones went to visit Birkenhead at Lords. (The date was incorrectly recorded in *Whitehall Diaries* as "14 December Thursday." The correct date is 15 December Thursday.)

3. *15 December 1921, London, House of Commons, Asquith Speech.* Text of speeches quoted and adapted from Hansard, 15 December 1921, Commons Sitting, Irish Free State.

4. *16 December, Dublin* (Reading of newspapers about 15 December speech by Churchill) "We can start on our future relations—troubled, stained, in many ways discreditable and even disastrous as they have been in the past—with clean hands

and a clear conscience." Text of speeches quoted and adapted from Hansard, 15 December 1921, Commons Sitting, Irish Free State.

5. *15 December 1921, London, House of Commons, Churchill Speech*. Text of speeches quoted and adapted from Hansard, 15 December 1921, Commons Sitting, Irish Free State.
6. Craig-de Valera meeting, "[de Valera] was impossible," described in Coogan/Collins, p. 211.
7. To the great consternation of Churchill, when the time came in the next world war for Irish ports to be made available to the British Navy, access was denied by the then President of Ireland, Éamon de Valera.
8. "finest speeches," paraphrased from what Fisher wrote in his diary, Gilbert/Stricken, p. 681.
9. "much the best speech I have ever heard you make. [Its] simplicity of style and fervour of advocacy [has] won a genuine reception from all quarters. Splendid," From a letter written by Guest to Churchill, Gilbert/Stricken, p. 681.
10. "He spoke with great force and power and... profound effect upon the House," Chamberlain's letter to the King, Gilbert/Stricken, p. 681.

112. Cerebral Excitement - Only Prime Minister

1. *16 December 1921, Dublin*. Text of speeches quoted and adapted from Hansard, 15 December 1921, Commons Sitting, Irish Free State.
2. "dreadful strain," Ó Broin, p. 95.
3. The saying, "Don't judge a book by its cover," appeared in George Eliot's 1860 novel, *The Mill on the Floss*, which was one of Michael's favourite books, Coogan/Collins, p. 9.
4. The line "Don't judge a book by its cover," appeared in George Eliot's 1860 novel, *Mill on the Floss*, which was an early favourite work, Coogan/Collins, p. 9.
5. The phrase, "stepping stone," appears later in the Treaty debates. Hart claims that this was "an old phrase of Griffith's," Hart/Mick, p. 329. Coogan emphatically attributes it to Collins in his "balance sheet" discussion with Griffith in London. Coogan/Collins, p. 257.
6. *16 December 1921, London, House of Lords*. Birkenhead's visit to the American Luncheon Club, Campbell/FE, pp. 577-578; *New York Times*, 17 December 1921. The American ambassador who introduced him was George Harvey.
7. *16 December 1921, Dublin, Dáil Morning Private Session*. Text of speeches quoted and adapted from the Houses of the Oireachtas website, Dáil Éireann debate- Friday, 16 Dec 1921.
8. *16 December 1921, London, Lords, Birkenhead Speech*. Text of speeches quoted and adapted from Hansard, 16 December 1921, Lords Sitting, Address in Reply to His Majesty's Gracious Speech.
9. "Even Premier Lloyd George, accompanied by Winston Churchill, went over to listen for a time," division bells, *New York Times*, 12 December 1921.
10. "the most wonderful speech I have ever heard; A fine piece of insolent invective... Cogent in argument, rich in feeling, powerful in pleading," Campbell/FE, p. 581.
11. Churchill asks Lady Lavery to write to Collins about shootings; lunch with Chamberlain who speaks "warmly and kindly of [Collins and] Griffith," Ó Broin, p. 90.
12. *16 December 1921, Dublin, Dáil Afternoon and Evening Sessions*. Text of speeches quoted and adapted from the Houses of the Oireachtas website, Dáil Éireann debate- Friday, 16 Dec 1921.
13. "For a quibble of words," see the Appendix, The Oath of Allegiance.

14. Shootings of R.I.C. reported in *Freeman's Journal*, 15 December 1921; *Nottingham Journal*, 16 December 1921.

113. Talk the Teeth Out Of a Saw

1. *Saturday, 17 December 1921, Dublin, Dáil Private Session.* Text of speeches quoted and adapted from the Houses of the Oireachtas website, Dáil Éireann debate- Saturday, 17 Dec 1921.
2. "no question of majority rule," Dáil Éireann debate Private Session- Saturday, 17 Dec 1921.
3. Batt O'Connor "kept in touch with [Michael] through the debates; opponents are canvassing … the people can take it or leave it." O'Connor, Batt, p. 182.
4. This undated letter from Lady Lavery is from Ó Broin, p. 89. Hazel wrote, "Yesterday I went to hear W. speak." Churchill's speech was given on 15 December, so the date of the letter is 16 December 1921, and the letter probably would have been delivered the next day. The nature of any communication made at this time with Lord Londonderry is mere speculation, but through Hazel's social connections, Collins did meet with him later, as we shall see. Hazel wrote that she "had a talk with Philip." From the mention of "his oriental blood," we can surmise she was referring to Philip Sassoon and his "influence over his illustrious Master," meaning the P.M. Hazel also recommends Michael, "you must get him that dog." However, there is no further mention of Sassoon receiving a dog from Michael, not in the letters of Ó Broin nor the biography of Sassoon by Peter Stansky.
5. "I feel you have a true friend in him." This second undated letter is quoted from Ó Broin, p. 90. The Lord Chancellor's speech referred to was given on 16 December, so this letter, like the previous one, would have arrived the next day, the 17th.
6. This letter written during the debate is quoted from Ó Broin, pp. 97-98.
7. "Women and Childers party," Coogan/Dev, p. 292; Coogan/Collins, p. 300.

114. That's the Stuff!

1. *Monday, 19 December 1921, Dublin, Dáil Public Session Resumes.* Text of speeches quoted and adapted from the Houses of the Oireachtas website, Dáil Éireann debate- Monday, 19 Dec 1921. Descriptions of the debate that day drawn from Coogan/Collins, pp. 300-301; Dwyer/Warrant, pp.244-249; Mackay 231-233; *New York Times*, 20 December 1921; the *Irish Times*, 20 December 1921; *The Times*, 20 December 1921; *Freeman's Journal*, 20 December 1921.
2. Collins' demeanour from the *Freeman's Journal*, 20 December 1921. The Robert Harding character is based on the *Freeman's Journal* leader writer, or senior journalist, James Winder Good. The Abbey Theatre in Dublin produced a political play about Ulster that he wrote using the pseudonym, Robert Harding, according to the Wikipedia entry for James Winder Good. Since reporters' names were not published along with their articles, this pseudonym is used to credit authorship to whatever *Freeman's Journal* articles are quoted here. Matthew Dowd is also a fictional name ascribed to the *New York Times* reporter covering the debates.
3. Griffith, "signs of nervousness, quiet, even tones," *New York Times*, 20 December 1921.
4. "he looked a little tired," *Freeman's Journal*, 20 December 1921; Hart, p. 332.
5. *New York Times*, 20 December 1921: "Then came de Valera. He stood erect for a few moments, glancing around, challenging at every part of the house. No hesitation, no amiability; extremism, hostility."

6. "pointing a finger at Michael and Arthur, de Valera... 'These men are subverting the Republic,'" *New York Times*, 20 December 1921, accurately paraphrased.
7. "finished pale as a sheet, and thoroughly exhausted from his efforts," Hart, p. 332, quoting from *New York Times*, 20 December 1921.
8. "dull, pompous, unutterably futile," description of Austin Stack by Frank O'Connor in O'Connor, Frank, pp. 175-176.
9. "That's the stuff!" Dwyer/Warrant, p. 247.
10. "On 29 September the invitation was sent for the Irish leaders to come to London on 11 October. This was accepted by de Valera on 30 September," Jones, p. 117. As Churchill put it, "Come or don't come." Andy Cope met Collins at the Gresham Hotel on the 30th. See *Volume One: Truce*, chapters 68 & 69.
11. "Home Rule and dual monarchy," from a comment by Coogan in Coogan/Dev, pp. 295-296.
12. "beyond question the outstanding figure in the Dáil. His youth, his confidence, his resonant voice, his sheer robustness worked wonders," *New York Times*, 20 December 1921.
13. "worthy of a lawyer... rhetoric," quoting Tim Healy, Coogan/Collins, p. 301; Dwyer/Warrant p. 248. Healy was not actually there, having left for London a few days earlier.
14. Description of Barton's speech based on reporting in the *Irish Times*, 20 December 1921.
15. This conversation between Kathleen Clarke and Collins adapted from Dwyer/Warrant, p. 249.
16. "it was the worst day I ever spent in my life. The Treaty will almost certainly be beaten," Coogan/Collins, p. 301. Letter written to Kitty that night, not included in Ó Broin, but quoted by Forester, p. 271.

115. Seeing is Believing

1. *Wednesday, 21 December 1921, Whitehall, London.* Committee members listed in Jones, p. 191.
2. Macready afraid of attacks on British troops, from a letter written 31 December 1921, Hopkinson, p. 53.
3. "This government would be immediately... ostentatious preparations to quit should be made everywhere." This entire dialogue is based on a memorandum circulated by Churchill at this time in advance of the meeting of the Cabinet Committee and served as the basis for discussion at that meeting, Gilbert/Stricken, pp. 681-682; Aftermath, pp. 329-332.

116. Clonakilty Wrastler

1. *Cork, Friday, 23 December 1921:* This date is given based on a letter Collins wrote to Kitty that day, saying, "I may have to go to Cork by the night train tonight." He was on his way to see his brother Johnny (Seán) in Clonakilty, but if he arrived in Cork that night, it was too late to take the connecting train to Clonakilty until the next day, Christmas Eve.
2. According to Clonakilty birth records, Michael's sister Margaret and her husband Patrick O'Driscoll were living in Rathbarry in November 1919 when their daughter Finola was born. They may have still been living there when Michael stayed with Johnny at their cousin Annie's home near Woodfield, about three

miles north of Rathbarry. If so, Michael and Johnny surely would have visited with their sister that Christmas, possibly as imagined.

3. Medical condition for Johnny, question of reuniting family, Coogan/Collins, p. 297. Whether Nancy O'Brien had been in touch is just speculation here. In September, 1922, Johnny and Nancy were married, "and raised a second family at Donnybrook and later Booterstown on the outskirts of Dublin," Mackay, p. 299.

4. "except for war... as full of fight as when be was going into it," from the Houses of the Oireachtas website, Dáil Éireann debate - Wednesday, 21 Dec 1921.

5. Hales family and the sides they took, Hart/Enemies, pp. 196-198.

6. Duggan, Cosgrave, and Hales speeches from Houses of the Oireachtas website, Dáil Éireann debate- Wednesday, 21 Dec 1921.

7. Seán Hales: "I agree with Mick... when we have our own army," Coogan/Collins, p. 339.

8. Lord Bandon's dalliance and quote of Seán Hales: "You burned my castle last week... Now I'll burn yours," Coogan/Collins, p. 178.

9. "Church, business, big farmers, the Press, and most senior Army officers," Coogan/Dev, p. 295.

10. Cosgrave and County Councils resolutions, Coogan/Collins, p. 301.

11. de Valera's local council, Clare, supports Treaty, *New York Times*, 23 December 1921.

12. Michael was not fond of stout, but "Clonakilty Wrestler" porter was his drink of choice when home, Coogan/Collins, p. 408; Osborne, p. 48.

13. The oft-repeated misconception that Jerry and Michael Collins were cousins was cleared up for the author with help from the Michael Collins Museum in Clonakilty, and by the present proprietor of the Four Alls Bar in Sam's Cross. If you don't believe me, you can ask at the pub yourself, but you have to promise to buy a round.

14. Michael's Christmas visit to Clonakilty and the Four Alls is cited in Forester, p. 272.

15. "I've seen more of my old country this morning than I've ever seen in my whole life," Forester, p. 272; Mackay, p. 235. Without citing her source, Forester says this walk occurred Christmas morning. The Michael Collins Centre printed a transcript of an interview Johnny Collins gave in 1963 at the age of 85 to his grandson. Johnny said he and Michael went up to Carraig a Radhairc that Christmas afternoon after attending three Masses before dinner at their cousin Annie's, with whom Johnny was staying during this period.

117. Prudence and Audacity

1. "Since I had crossed the Floor of the House... the first to welcome me," Churchill/World Vol One, p. 29. After Christmas, Churchill went to Cannes with Lloyd George. On 29 December, Churchill wrote to Clementine, "Ll G. read two of my chapters in the train and was well content with the references to himself. He praised the style and made several pregnant suggestions wh I am embodying," *Winston and Clementine*, pp. 243-244. Which chapters Lloyd George read is not mentioned.

2. "Prudence and audacity... the hazards inseparable from it," Churchill/World Vol One, p. 281.

118. Dark Horses

1. Michael travelled to Granard on 30 December, as stated in Ó Broin, p. 100. Neither Kitty nor Michael had yet informed Harry Boland of their decision. This weekend was the most likely time that they decided to privately announce their engagement, though out of deference to Harry, they probably would not make a public announcement until first telling him. Unfortunately, the privacy of their engagement was spoiled, as we shall see, at the Debates. There is no evidence that Gearoid O'Sullivan was with them that day.

119. The Lady Who Is Betrothed to Me

1. *3 January, Dublin, Dáil Debates* Resume. Text of speeches quoted and adapted from the Houses of the Oireachtas website, Dáil Éireann debate- Tuesday, 3 Jan 1922.

120. Men of Their Word

1. At Ciro's: Lady Blanche, Consuelo, Jacques, Adele, Sassoon; painting of Eze; Lady Blanche was lucky—she won 400 francs at the casino; Soames/Letters, p. 246.
2. Staying with the Countess of Essex and letter to Prince of Wales, "Arthur Griffith and Michael Collins are men of their word… we will not fail in ours," Gilbert/Stricken, pp. 682-683.
3. "newspapers [are all] boiling over with the question of a General Election…Our work is not done… Irish question half-way through," Owen, pp. 592-594.

121. Choose My Own Procedure

1. *Wednesday, 4 January 1922, Dublin, Dáil Eireann Public Session.* Text of speeches quoted and adapted from the Houses of the Oireachtas website, Dáil Éireann Debate–Wednesday, 4 Jan 1922.
2. Dr. Farnan did not meet Collins at this time but was later quoted as telling de Valera that the "alternative document wouldn't be understood by the country," Coogan/Collins, p. 302.
3. "submerge personal opinions… common good of the country, not to abandon any principle, but to work together to restore unity in the Dáil and the country," paraphrased from interview Collins gave to the *Freeman's Journal*, 4 January 1922.
4. "the Treaty to go through… the Republican question afterwards," Dáil Éireann Debate, Tuesday, 3 Jan 1922.
5. "Role of Dictator… This is much worse than the Treaty… the instinct of an Irishman in his blood," *Freeman's Journal*, 5 January 1921; Quoted in Coogan/Collins, pp. 303-304.

122. Blood-Stained Jewels

1. *Thursday, 5 January 1922, Dublin, Dáil Eireann Public* Session. Text of speeches quoted and adapted from the Houses of the Oireachtas website, Dáil Éireann Debate–Thursday, 5 Jan 1922.

2. "That President de Valera should continue… apply to every other service… sign acceptance of the Treaty." Béaslaí, iBook Chapter XIV—The Great Disillusionment, December, 1921—January, 1922.
3. "determined to show… the real Irish leader." Coogan/Collins, p. 304.
4. Altercation with Harry Boland, Fitzpatrick, pp. 264-265.
5. "Ireland's pride is worth more." As it turned out, Michael was right. Years later the jewels turned out to be cheap imitations that were valued by Christie's at only £1600, Fitzpatrick, p. 371, footnote 108.

123. Examine My Own Heart

1. *Friday, 6 January 1922, Dublin, Dáil Éireann Public Session.* Text of speeches quoted and adapted from the Houses of the Oireachtas website, Dáil Éireann Debate—Friday- 6 Jan 1922. Eoin O'Duffy reported to the Dáil that morning: "This is the report of the conferences that we held on Wednesday night, Thursday morning, and last night: 'A meeting informally arranged and consisting of five Deputies from the anti-Treaty side, and four men from the Treaty side was held at the house of Deputy Seán T. O'Kelly on Wednesday night. Those present were, anti-Treaty side: Deputies O'Kelly, Mellowes, Ruttledge, Moylan and O'Connor. Treaty side: Deputies Hogan, McGuinness, Joe McGrath and O'Duffy. Agreement was reached with Deputy Liam Mellowes dissenting.' Now as regards the nature of that agreement, those on the anti-Treaty side do not wish that now disclosed. Is that correct?"
2. Tammany Hall was the powerful political machine of the Democratic party in New York City known for helping the city's poor and immigrant populations, most notably the Irish, rise in American politics from the 1790s to the 1960s. Its name was synonymous with graft and political corruption—thus, the "Tammany Hall" methods referred to here.
3. As noted above, Matthew Dowd is a fictional character, but all his comments are taken from an editorial in the *New York Times*, the next day, 7 January 1922, Dwyer/Warrant pp. 260-261.
4. "I haven't ridden a white horse… used her mane as a bridle," Coogan/Collins, p. 177.
5. "Harry is working like the very devil against us," Ó Broin, p. 102.

124. If My Name Is to Go Down in History

1. *Saturday, 7 January 1922, Dublin, Dáil Éireann Public Session and Vote.* Text of speeches quoted and adapted from the Houses of the Oireachtas website, Dáil Éireann Debate—Saturday- 7 Jan 1922.
2. "went on their knees," cited in Coogan/Collins, p. 303; Coogan/Dev, p. 295.
3. Dan MacCarthy, pro-Treaty Whip & Director of Elections, Knirck, p. 122.
4. "vehemently proclaiming," from "Vehement Reply," *Freeman's Journal*, 9 January 1922, p.7
5. Description of the Vote, *Freeman's Journal*, 9 January 1922 pp. 5-7; *New York Times*, 8 January 1922, pp.1-2; Coogan/Collins, pp. 306-307.

125. The Other Side Is Killing Me

1. *Monday, 9 January 1922, Dublin, Dáil Eireann Public* Session. Text of speeches quoted and adapted from the Houses of the Oireachtas website, Dáil Éireann Debate–Monday- 9 Jan 1922.
2. "I'm absolutely fagged out... the other side is killing me," Ó Broin, p. 102.

126. Deserters All!

1. *Tuesday, 10 January 1922, Dáil Eireann Public* Session. Text of speeches quoted and adapted from the Houses of the Oireachtas website, Dáil Éireann Debate–Tuesday- 10 Jan 1922.
2. "In the event of a general election... others can determine their own line of action," Coogan/Dev, p. 303; *Freeman's Journal*, 12 January 1922. "I would never take an Oath such as is in that Treaty. You can be sure of that," ibid. Until he did, in 1927, describing the Oath as "an empty political formula," Coogan/Dev, p. 404.

127. Take Over or Get Out

1. Bombings in Belfast, *New York Times*, "Two Killed in Belfast," 12 January 1922.
2. Petty crimes, theft of rifles with garrison complicit, no delay in removing troops, Hamar Greenwood report, CAB/24/132-5, 11 January 1922.
3. Gilbert: "On Thursday January 12 Sir Henry Wilson... went over to C.O. before lunch and had a talk with Winston... we would not stand it. We must take over... or come out... begin on Monday... anticipate peace under Collins ... bolster up Collins," Gilbert/Stricken, p. 685.
4. "As soon as Collins takes over... provisions of the agreement," Winston Churchill, "Draft of a Bill" to implement Article 17 of the Treaty, CAB/24/132/10, 12 January 1922.

128. You Can Have the Seven Minutes

1. "Surrender" of Dublin Castle, 16 January 1922: "British Turn over Control of Ireland to Michael Collins," *New York Times*, 17 January 1922; "Death of Ascendancy," *Freeman's Journal*, 17 January 1922; "Dublin Castle Handed Over," *The Times*, 17 January 1922.
2. Dave Neligan and Major Poges were present at the handover of the Castle, Neligan, p. 153.
3. "seven minutes; Ye are like hell, boy"; Coogan/Collins, p. 310. These two quips are legendary, but the rest of the conversation in this chapter is imaginary. Collins had spent the weekend in Longford with Kitty, as evidenced from their letters, e.g., "Hope you got back safely. It was a cold morning and I'm sure the train wasn't warm," Ó Broin, p. 107.
4. Newspaper accounts do not mention Dalton being there that day, but Boyne does, Boyne, p. 81.
5. Provisional Government Cabinet, Coogan/Collins, p. 308.
6. Batt joins the team to Mansion House, "Arthur! The Castle has fallen," O'Connor, Batt, p.188.

Bibliography

Augustin, Andreas, Andrew Williamson, Rupert Tenison, *The Savoy London*, The Most Famous Hotels in the World, 2002.

Béaslaí, Piaras, *Michael Collins and the Making of a New Ireland, Volume II*, e-Book ed., Borodino Books, 2018.

Boyne, Seán, *Emmet Dalton, Somme Soldier, Irish General, Film Pioneer*, Merrion Press, Sallins, Co. Kildare, 2016.

Bromage, Mary C., *Churchill and Ireland*, University of Notre Dame Press, Notre Dame, Indiana, 1964.

Buckland, Patrick, *James Craig, Lord Craigavon*, Gill and Macmillan Ltd, Dublin, 1980.

Bureau of Military History, 1913–21, Witness Statements (BMH, W.S.), Defence Forces Ireland, Military Archives https://militaryarchives.ie/collections/online-collections/bureau-of-military-history-1913-1921/

Alice Barry, BMH, W.S. 723

Ernest Blythe, BMH, W.S. 939

Ned Broy, BMH, W.S. 1280

Charlie Dalton, BMH, W.S. 434

Emmet Dalton, BMH, W.S. 641

Joe Dolan, BMH, W.S. 900

Joe Hyland, BMH, W.S. 644

Eileen McGrane, BMH, W.S. 1752

Seán MacEoin, BMH, W.S. 1716

Pat McCrea, BMH, W.S. 413

Frank Thornton, BMH, W.S. 615

Oscar Traynor, BMH, W.S. 340

Cabinet Minutes (CAB), The National Archives, https://www.nationalarchives.gov.uk

Callwell, Major-General Sir C.E., *Field-Marshall Sir Henry Wilson, His Life and Diaries, Volume II*, Cassell and Company, Ltd., London, 1927.

Campbell, John (Campbell/FE), *F.E. Smith, First Earl of Birkenhead*, Pimlico, London, 1983.

Campbell, John (Campbell/If Love) *If Love Were All…, The Story of Frances Stevenson and David Lloyd George*, Jonathan Cape, London, 2006.

Churchill, The Rt. Hon. Winston S. (Churchill/World Vol One), *The World Crisis—1911-1915 Volume 1*, Charles Scribner's Sons, New York, 1923.

Churchill, The Rt. Hon. Winston S. (Churchill/Aftermath), *The World Crisis—1918-1928, The Aftermath*, Charles Scribner's Sons, New York, 1929.

Churchill, The Rt. Hon. Winston S. (Churchill/HESP), *A History of the English Speaking Peoples*, Dorset Press, New York, 1956-1958.

Churchill, Randolph, *Twenty-One Years*, Houghton Mifflin Co., Boston, The Riverside Press, Cambridge, 1965.

Collins, Michael, *The Path to Freedom, Foreword by Tim Pat Coogan*, Roberts Rinehart Publishers, Boulder, 1996.

Coogan, Tim Pat (Coogan/Dev), *Éamon de Valera, The Man Who Was Ireland*, Harper Collins, New York, 1993.

Coogan, Tim Pat (Coogan/Collins), *The Man Who Made Ireland, The Life and Death of Michael Collins*, Roberts Rinehart Publishers, Niwot, Colorado, 1992.

Coogan, Tim Pat (Coogan/Apostles), *The Twelve Apostles, Michael Collins, The Squad, and Ireland's Fight for Freedom*, Skyhorse Publishing, New York, 2018.

Coombs, David, *Sir Winston Churchill, His Life and Paintings*, by David Coombs with Minnie Churchill, Running Press, Philadelphia, 2003.

Cottrell, Peter, *The Irish Civil War 1922–23 (Essential Histories)*, Osprey Publishing, Oxford, 2009.

Curran, Jack, *The Birth of the Irish Free State, 1921-1923*, University of Alabama Press, Tuscaloosa, 1981.

Dáil Éierann Debates, Houses of the Oireachtas, https://www.oireachtas.ie

Dáil Eireann, The Minutes of Proceedings of the First Parliament of the Republic of Ireland, 1919-1921, Stationery Office, Dublin, 1921.

Daunton, M.J., *Royal Mail: The Post Office since 1840*, Bloomsbury Academic Collections, London, 1985.

De Vere White, Terence, *Kevin O'Higgins*, Methuen & Co., Ltd., London, 1948.

Doherty, Gabriel and Dermot Keogh, *Michael Collins and the Making of the Irish State*, Mercier Press, Douglas Village, Cork, 2006.

Dolan, Anne and William Murphy, *Michael Collins, The Man and the Revolution*, The Collins Press, Cork, 2018.

Dutton, David, *Austen Chamberlain, Gentleman in Politics*, Transaction Books, New Brunswick, 1985

Dwyer, T. Ryle (Dwyer/Man Who), *The Man Who Won the War*, Mercier Press, Cork, 2009.

Dwyer, T. Ryle (Dwyer/Civil War), *Michael Collins and the Civil War*, Mercier Press, Cork, 2012.

Dwyer, T. Ryle (Dwyer/Squad), *The Squad and the Intelligence Operations of Michael Collins*, Mercier Press, Cork, 2005.

Dwyer, T. Ryle (Dwyer/Warrant), *I Signed My Death Warrant, Michael Collins & The Treaty*, Mercier Press, Blackrock, Cork, 2006.

Fingall, Elizabeth, *Seventy Years Young, Memories of Elizabeth, Countess of Fingall, Told to Pamela Hinkson*, Collins, London, 1937.

Fitzpatrick, David, *Harry Boland's Irish Revolution*, Cork University Press, Cork, 2003.

Foley, Michael, *The Bloodied Field, Croke Park. Sunday 21 November 1920*, The O'Brien Press, Ltd., Dublin, 2015.

Forester, Margery, *Michael Collins, The Lost Leader*, Sidgwick & Jackson, London, 1971.

Gilbert, Martin (Gilbert/Churchill), *Churchill, A Life*, Henry Holt, New York, 1991.

Gilbert, Martin (Gilbert/Stricken), *Winston S. Churchill*, Volume 4. *The Stricken World, 1916–22.*

Gillis, Liz, *May 25 Burning of the Custom House 1921*, Kilmainham Tales Teo., Dublin 2017.

Gleeson, James, *Bloody Sunday, How Michael Collins's Agents Assassinated Britain's Secret Service in Dublin on November 21, 1920*, The Lyons Press, Guilford CT, 2004.

Hansard: Commons and Lords Hansard, The Official Report of Debates in Parliament, https://api.parliament.uk/historic-hansard/sittings/1920s

Hart, Peter (Hart/Mick), *Mick, The Real Michael Collins, Viking*, New York, 2005.

Hart, Peter (Hart/IRA Enemies), *The I.R.A. and Its Enemies*, Oxford University Press, Oxford, 1999.

Hart, Peter (Hart/IRA War), *The I.R.A. at War 1916–1923*, Oxford University Press, New York, 2003.

Hassal, Christopher, A *Biography of Edward Marsh*, Harcourt, Brace and Company, New York, 1959.

Hickman, Tom, *Churchill's Bodyguard*, Headline Book Publishing, London, 2005.

Hittle, J.B.E., *Michael Collins and the Anglo-Irish War: Britain's Counterinsurgency Failure*, Potomac Books, Dulles, 2011.

Hopkinson, Michael, *Green Against Green, The Irish Civil War*, Gill & Macmillan, Dublin, 2004.

Jeffery, Keith, *Field Marshall Sir Henry Wilson*, Oxford University Press, New York, 2008.

Jones, Thomas, *Whitehall Diary, Volume III, Ireland 1918–1925*, Oxford University Press, London, 1971.

Kearns, Kevin C., *Dublin Pub Life & Lore, An Oral History*, Roberts Rinehart Publishers, Niwot, CO., 1997.

Knightley, Phillip and Colin Simpson, *The Secret Lives of Lawrence of Arabia*, McGraw-Hill Book Company, New York, 1970

Knirck, Jason K., *Imagining Ireland's Independence, The Debates over the Anglo–Irish Treaty of 1921*, Rowman & Littlefield Publishers, Inc. Plymouth, 2006.

Lavery, Sir John, R.A., *The Life of a Painter*, Little, Brown and Company, Boston, 1940.

Leeson, D.M. (Leeson/Tans), *The Black & Tans, British Police and Auxiliaries in the Irish War of Independence*, Oxford University Press, New York, 2011.

Leeson, David (Leeson/Death), "Death in the Afternoon: The Croke Park Massacre, 21 November 1920," *Canadian Journal of History*, April 2003, pp. 43-67.

Liam, Cathal, *Fear Not the Storm, The Story of Tom Cullen, an Irish Revolutionary*, St. Pádraic Press, Cincinnati, 2011.

Lough, David, *No More Champagne: Churchill and His Money*, Picador, New York, 2015.

Lovell, Mary S., *The Churchills, A Family at the Heart of History—from the Duke of Marlborough to Winston Churchill*, Little, Brown, London, 2011.

Macardle, Dorothy, *The Irish Republic*, Farrar, Straus and Giroux, New York, 1965.

MacBride, Seán, *That Day's Struggle, A Memoir 1904–1951*, Currach Press, Dublin, 2005.

McCoole, Sinéad, *Hazel, A Life of Lady Lavery, 1880–1935*, Lilliput Press, Dublin, 1996.

McCrea, John, with Andrew Macphail, *In Flanders Fields and Other Poems*, G. P. Putnam's Sons, New York and London, 1919.

McDonnell, Kathleen Keyes, *There is a Bridge at Bandon, A personal account of the Irish War of Independence*, Mercier Press, Cork, 1972.

Mackay, James, *Michael Collins, A Life*, Mainstream Publishing Co., Edinburgh, 1997.

Macready, Nevil, *Annals of an Active Life, Volume II*, Hutchinson & Co., London, 1924.

Manchester, William (Manchester), *Winston Spencer Churchill, The Last Lion, Volume 1, Visions of Glory, 1874–1932*, Dell Publishing, New York, 1983.

Manchester, William (Manchester/Vol 2), *Winston Spencer Churchill, The Last Lion, Volume 2, Alone, 1932–1940*, Dell Publishing, New York, 1983.

Millin, Sarah Gertrude, *General Smuts, The Second Volume*, Faber and Faber Limited, London, 1936.

Murray, Daniel, *Éireann Ascendant, An Irish History Blog*, "The Limits of Might: Liam Lynch (Part I)," https://erinascendantwordpress.wordpress.com/ (9 June 2021).

Neligan, Dave, *The Spy in the Castle*, Prendeville Publishing Limited, London, 1999.

Ó Broin, León, *In Great Haste, The Letters of Michael Collins and Kitty Kiernan*, Gill & Macmillan, Dublin, 1996.

O'Connor, Batt, *With Michael Collins in the Fight for Irish Independence*, Peter Davies, Ltd., London, 1929.

O'Connor, Frank, *The Big Fellow, Michael Collins and the Irish Revolution*, Picador USA, New York, 1997.

O'Malley, Ernie (O'Malley/Wound), *On Another Man's Wound, A Personal History of Ireland's War of Independence*, e-Book ed. (Google Play), Roberts Rinehart Publishers, Niwot, CO., 2001.

O'Malley, Ernie (O'Malley), *The Singing Flame*, e-Book ed. (Google Play), Mercier Press, Blackrock, Cork, 2012.

Osborne, Chrissy, *Michael Collins Himself*, Mercier Press, Douglass Village, Cork, 2003.

Owen, Fran, *Tempestuous Journey, Lloyd George His Life and Times*, McGraw-Hill Book Company, New York, 1955.

Pakenham, Frank, *Peace by Ordeal*, Jonathan Cape, London, 1935.

Peters, Walter H., *The Life of Benedict V*, Bruce Publishing Company, Milwaukee, 1959.

Ryan, Meda (Ryan/Shot), *The Day Michael Collins Was Shot*, Poolberg Press Ltd., Dublin, 1989

Ryan, Meda (Ryan/Spied), *Michael Collins and the Women Who Spied for Ireland*, Mercier Press, Dublin, 2006

Ryan, Meda (Ryan/Women), *Michael Collins and the Women in His Life*, Mercier Press, Dublin, 1966

Stansky, Peter, *Sassoon, The Worlds of Philip and Sybil*, Yale University Press, New Haven and London, 2003.

Soames, Mary (Soames/Clementine), *Clementine Churchill, The Biography of a Marriage*, Houghton Mifflin Co., Boston, 1979.

Soames, Mary (Soames/Letters), *Winston & Clementine, The Personal Letters of the Churchills*, Houghton Mifflin Co., Boston, New York, 1998.

Stevenson, Frances, *Lloyd George, A Diary by Frances Stevenson*, Edited by A.J.P. Taylor, Hutchinson & Co. Ltd., London, 1971.

Taylor, Rex, *Michael Collins*, Hutchinson & Co. Ltd., London, 1958.

Thompson, Walter H., *Assignment: Churchill*, Farrar, Straus and Young, New York, 1955.

Towey, Thomas, "The Reaction of the British Government to the 1922 Collins–de Valera Pact," *Irish Historical Studies*, vol. 22, no. 85, Cambridge University Press, 1980.

Wilson, Jeremy, *Lawrence of Arabia, The Authorized Biography of T. E. Lawrence*, Atheneum, Macmillan Publishing Company, New York, 1990.

Yeates, Padraig, *A City in Civil War: Dublin 1921–1924: The Irish Civil War*, e-Book ed. (Google Play), Ireland, Gill Books, Ireland, 2015.

Also By John Deane

If you enjoyed this book, please consider submitting a review to its listing on
Amazon.com

A Tale of Michael Collins and Winston Churchill

Stepping Stone to Freedom

Volume One, Truce describes the events in the Anglo-Irish War, from
Bloody Sunday to the truce that led to the negotiations for a treaty.

Volume Two, Treaty covers the period when Collins was in London
negotiating the terms of the treaty with Lloyd George and Churchill
and closes with the debates and vote on the treaty in the Dáil, the Irish
parliament.

Volume Three, Freedom describes the new Provisional Government in
Dublin, Churchill's eloquent support in Parliament of the Irish
Constitution drafted by Collins, the general election in Ireland and the
ensuing civil war.